One man,

One rifle,

One land

One Man,
One Rifle,
One Land

by

J. Y. Jones

Safari Press Inc.

The trademark Safari Press ® is registered with the U.S. Patent and Trademark Office and in other countries.

Jones, J.Y.

Safari Press Inc.

2001, Long Beach, California

ISBN 1-57157-169-8

Library of Congress Catalog Card Number: 99-066874

10 9 8 7 6 5 4 3 2

Printed in Singapore

Readers wishing to receive the Safari Press catalog, featuring many fine books on big-game hunting, wingshooting, and sporting firearms, should write to Safari Press Inc., P.O. Box 3095, Long Beach, CA 90803, USA. Tel: (714) 894-9080 or visit our Web site at www.safaripress.com.

DEDICATION

This must be the easiest part of writing a book. I have known the person to whom this book is dedicated since 1960, before I started writing. We have been married since 1964. She has remained by my side through good times and bad, through my many years of schooling and training, through the trauma of Vietnam, and through rocky times early in our marriage. She has withstood the brunt of my many absences with little complaint, and she has supported every aspect of my life, including my all-consuming endeavor to complete this book. My wife, Linda Grace Jones, above all others, deserves the honor of this dedication.

Linda was born in Atlanta, Georgia, the same year I was born in the northern Georgia mountains. We met in high school and began dating in college. Something about her appealed to me in a profound way, and as I got to know her it was as though a light had come on in my life. Even today, when I need a word of encouragement or advice, when I need a tender touch, I turn to Linda. She is discerning in many ways, and is seemingly wisest in those areas where I am weakest. She complements me perfectly and is the kind of companion most men only dream of finding.

In my hunting career, I have been away from home for as long as three weeks at a time. Even when I have been at home in body, I have often been absent mentally. I have spent countless hours in front of a computer monitor, rather than with the woman I love.

She has brought me food and drink while I have been engrossed, interjecting her love into the rigors of writing this book.

She has never complained about my passion for hunting. She has known since we first met that my avocation is an integral part of who I am. She has allowed me to pursue my dreams and has even encouraged them. Some couples, in the pursuit of their individual dreams, become hostile toward each other. These are battles I have never faced. I love my wife all the more for her unselfish love, and I reaffirm my commitment to put her ahead of my own interests, as she has done for me.

Such is the nature of a real marriage. Keeping score is not what Linda Grace Jones is all about. She needs me, and I need her beyond measure. If you have such a marriage, you know what I mean. If you are still searching, I hope you find it.

The ideal marriage is one in which each partner devotes all to the other party. In so doing, incredible benefits accrue for the sacrifice. Our marriage has been greatly enriched by this and I continue to marvel at the woman I love. To me she is the visible manifestation of God's enduring and unfailing love: Linda Grace Jones declares to me in resounding terms what life is all about, often without uttering a word. A simple book dedication is a small thing, but in the final analysis words simply fail anyway.

Linda Grace Jones, I love you. I dedicate this book to you with no hesitation and no regrets.

TABLE OF CONTENTS

SECTION THIRTEEN: FAILINGS, FEELINGS, PHILOSOPHIES, AND THE FUTURE

FOREWORD

When browsing a bookstore, most of us scan a book's table of contents before taking it to the cashier. If ordering by mail, we've seen the publisher's synopsis, or perhaps we've read a review. Whatever sparked the purchasing decision, almost invariably a reader will have some idea of a book's contents before plunking down hard-earned cash for a bit of paper and dried ink. So by the time you read these words I must assume that you have some passing familiarity with the chapters that follow—and if you're like me, you've probably thumbed forward and looked at many of the photos. What I'm not sure will be apparent is the magnitude of accomplishment this book represents.

No one, I repeat no one, has ever achieved the scope, span, or breadth of experience in North American hunting that J. Y. Jones has attained. Experience alone, of course, does not make a good book. As a successful eye doctor, Jones has had the resources to pursue his passion. But financial capability to pursue far horizons also does not make a good book. J. Y. Jones brings not only his extensive experience but also a keen and inquiring mind, the insight one might expect from a medical professional, and above all his passion and drive. Together, these render this volume the most comprehensive work ever published on the subject of hunting North American big game.

This is not the first book ever written on the subject . . . and I suspect it will not be the last. But there has never been another book that so completely explores the diverse world of North American big-game hunting. Its existence, of course, is due largely to the determination of the author. But there is also an evolutionary process in evidence.

From the time of the first explorers through the nineteenth century, our knowledge of North American big game grew quite slowly, although there were some quantum leaps along the way. It was probably Henry Kelsey, representing the Hudson's Bay Company in the late seventeenth century, who first described the humpbacked bear we know as the grizzly. His journal from 1691 contains the entry, "Bigger than any white Bear & is Neither White nor Black But silver hair'd like our English Rabbit." Throughout the eighteenth century, fur trappers and other early wanderers brought back rumors and tall tales of the game inhabiting the far reaches of our continent, but it was the diary of Meriwether Lewis, scrupulously kept on their historic 1804-1806 expedition, that brought back the first genuine knowledge of our western species.

By the end of the nineteenth century, the major varieties of North American big game had been, more or less, scientifically identified. There were mistakes, such as the categorizing of the grizzly bear and Alaskan grizzly into two separate species, and the categorizing of the Elliott Coues whitetail into its own species rather than as a whitetail subspecies. To this day we continue to sort through the lumping and splitting of subspecies, but by 1887, the year Theodore Roosevelt and his friends formed the Boone and Crockett Club, all the major varieties of North American wildlife were documented. But trophy hunting, as we know it today, was not known.

After the turn of the century, following the example of London taxidermist Rowland Ward, the Boone and Crockett Club began gathering data to compile records of North American horns, antlers, and skulls. The first record book was not published until 1932, with a second edition in 1939. In the decade that followed, members of the Boone and Crockett Club went back to work, revising their measuring criteria as well as the categories to be recognized. While those first two record books are of great historical significance, they show little resemblance to *Records of North American Big Game*, now in its eleventh edition. The current Boone and Crockett measuring system, little changed over the past fifty years, was adopted in 1950, with the first record book published in 1952.

The record book itself is not critical to this volume, for J. Y. Jones is not a "record-book hunter." He is what we might call an "experiential" hunter, for his dream has been to experience as much of the North American wilderness as possible. This is not to conclude, however, that he totally ignores the record book, which he seems to view as both a frame of reference and a point of departure.

As I said, this book is not altogether without precedent. Grancel Fitz was perhaps the first person to embark on a quest to hunt at least one each of all varieties of North American big game. A New Yorker and a man of means, Fitz was an avid sportsman and active member of the Boone and Crockett Club. The 1932 compilation of trophy records sparked him to begin his quest, but it was the greatly updated 1952 edition of *Records of North American Big Game* that provided him with a framework that enabled him to complete his quest a quarter-century later. The result is *North American Head Hunting* (Oxford Press, New York, 1957). In those days of pre-jet travel and greatly reduced communications, Fitz's accomplishment remains remarkable, and is hardly denigrated by the fact that he contented himself with the Boone and Crockett interpretation of what constitutes North American big game.

There is another parallel between Fitz and J.Y. Jones. Both used the .30-06 caliber exclusively, Fitz with his Griffin & Howe Springfield, Jones with his now-famous Remington 700 ADL. However, it would be unwise and unfair to draw that parallel too far. Jones's decision to cling to his old .30-06 should not be construed as following in Fitz's footsteps. I am reasonably certain that J.Y. Jones had never heard of Grancel Fitz when he acquired his Remington, although as his quest solidified in his mind he certainly studied the works of great hunters who came before him. Even so, if one were to desire to hunt each and every species of North American big game with a single rifle, the .30-06 just happens to be one of the very few logical choices. There is never anything wrong with sticking with the rifle one knows best, shoots best, and has the most confidence in.

Fitz (who also coined the term "grand slam" to indicate the taking of each type of wild sheep) must be given credit for being the first to successfully hunt all varieties of North American big game. He did indeed use one rifle of like caliber to do it, but beyond these bare facts I would not and am not comparing this present volume to Fitz's 1957 work. As you will see, Jones is a serious researcher with a keen eye for detail. He studies not only the game, but also the diverse habitats he visits. He is not merely a pilgrim whose guides lead him from victory to victory, but a participant and an observer. He learns the flora as well as the fauna, and he knows what the animals eat and why they have evolved in the ways they have.

There is also a tremendous difference in the framework used to define North American big game. In 1957 the fledgling Boone and Crockett trophy system was virtually the only reference available, and Grancel Fitz was content to stand on that. As we know, "B&C" has continued to evolve. Today, B&C recognizes more caribou, more elk, and more deer than in Fitz's day. Of even greater significance, B&C is no longer the only reference available. Safari Club International's extensive record-keeping system recognizes categories that B&C does not. These and other references provide guidelines, but in framing his dream and his quest, J. Y. Jones ultimately and wisely decided that it was *his* dream and *his* quest. He would frame the guidelines for himself.

In so doing, he outlined for himself a herculean task, a journey that would take him to the haunts of virtually all the varieties of big game recognized by any and all of the diverse record books. He would also hunt animals that he considered unique. Jones was not content with the traditional four-sheep "slam." He added the considerably smaller California bighorn. Based on differences in habit, habitat, and hunting technique, he separated the grizzly of the barren tundra from the mountain grizzly. While no one has ever, nor will ever, hunt all of the many whitetail subspecies, Jones distinguishes the northern deer from his familiar southern whitetails, and adds the pretty little Carmen Mountains whitetail to the Coues whitetail. He hunted walrus as soon as a season was opened, and he was a tireless leader in the fight to allow importation of Canada's legally hunted polar bears. And for completeness he includes the alligator—definitely "big" and now classed as "game" in several states. In each chapter J. Y. Jones describes a hunt for what he considers North American big game. Neither you nor I are required to altogether agree; any informed reader might prefer to lump some and split others. But there can be no argument about the comprehensive nature of this book, which I doubt will ever be surpassed.

Several good books have been published on hunting North American big game since the publication of Fitz's work in 1957. It is probably appropriate that I mention that one of them was written by me. Fortunately, the volume is now out of print and is perhaps best forgotten. In 1957 Fitz was limited by existing knowledge. I, along with every single one of the professional writers who have attempted to address this subject, have limited big-game hunting experience. I can research the hunting of desert bighorns and then write about it. But on a gunwriter's income, I have never been able to afford a hunt in Mexico. Thus, I can write about big game in Mexico not as a participant but only as an observer and researcher. When I wrote my book about

North American big-game hunting, I had also not hunted polar bear, walrus, or jaguar.

In my defense, I will say that I have extensive experience across North America and in-depth knowledge in many areas. But after studying this volume, I seriously question why I had the temerity to write a book about North American big game—especially fifteen years ago! I think the answer is that writers must write; it is what we do. Nevertheless, no professional writer has ever been, or will ever be, capable of gathering the experiences that J. Y. Jones has put into this volume. This book was not written for profit. It is not a means to an end. It is, rather, the culmination of a grand quest. It is the pot of gold at the end of the rainbow.

This is the definitive work on hunting big game across our continent. I am in awe of J. Y.'s ability to capture his experiences, knowledge, and passion in its pages. You may begin at the first chapter and follow Jones's grand quest as it unfolds, or you may choose to skip around, reading first about the animals and habitats that most interest you. Either way, this is a book you will enjoy, for the author's genuine love of sport hunting and wildlife is obvious on every page. Perhaps more important, this is a book you will return to again and again, especially when planning a hunt of a big-game animal in a locale that is new to you. That is how I plan to use my copy!

Craig Boddington
Paso Robles, California
August 1999

ACKNOWLEDGMENTS

Numerous individuals have contributed substantially to this book, and it is impossible to list all of them. However, I wish to thank as many of them as possible.

Most of the guides and outfitters are listed by name but they still deserve my wholehearted thanks for going the extra mile to make my hunts successful, even when no animal was taken. Some of them had to go many more than one extra mile, and their tireless efforts have finally come to fruition in this book. If, by some oversight, any are omitted or have their names misspelled, I beg forgiveness.

My late friend, gunsmith Dick Green, did all my handloads and most of my rifle repairs and modifications. He deserves my utmost gratitude. For remuneration, he would only allow me to cover his costs.

My indispensable chapter reviewers deserve more than mere thanks. Because of their careful analysis of the information sections, this book must be counted authoritative. Each reviewer is an authority on the subject. In most cases the species chapter reviewers (chapters 4–45) reviewed only the biological portion and not the actual hunting stories. The remaining chapters are not divided into sections, so the entire chapter was reviewed. None of the reviewers had opportunity to correct the final text, so any errors are solely my own. Some of my biological reviewers are "lumpers" and others are "splitters," so in a few cases there might be outright disagreement among them over the true scientific classification of a particular animal. I have made the final decisions regarding which animals should be included or omitted, according to criteria elaborated in the introduction.

I also want to thank Ludo Wurfbain, Jacque Neufeld, and B. J. Lambert of Safari Press for their interest and excellent help with this project. They put up with my idiosyncrasies and impatience almost without complaint, and I appreciate them more than I can express. Thanks also to Martin Hanft for his much-needed editing input.

My wife, Linda, to whom this book is dedicated, deserves the most recognition of all. Her contributions are further elaborated in the dedication, but to fail to acknowledge her here in brief would be an oversight. The rest of my family has also suffered deprivation because of the insatiable demands of this book. They have all been patient, understanding, and loving in allowing me to pursue my quest. I deeply appreciate them.

Most of all, I thank God for His divine grace in allowing me to accomplish this work. Without the means and the passions with which I have been endowed, without an established tradition of hunting by human beings, and without the beautiful creation and its wonderful creatures, there would be no book. All of these factors are beyond my control, and I fully recognize them to flow only from the manifold grace of God.

INTRODUCTION

It has been quite a few years since I began exploring the possibility of putting together a book about taking all forty-one of the native North American big-game animals with the same rifle. The story of how the quest came to be is covered in the first chapter, but some explanation is in order regarding how I settled on that specific number of animals and the arrangement of the book.

Any activity must be guided by a set of rules to achieve any semblance of order, so three parameters were established for inclusion of an animal in this work. I decided to include animals that (1) are legally huntable by the sport hunter in natural habitat, (2) have a weight of at least one hundred pounds for an average trophy male of the species, and (3) range into the United States and Canada. Mexico is a part of North America, but where the dividing line should be drawn in that country (or south of it) is still open to some question. Four animals in this book (including the jaguar, an exception in several regards) came from Mexico, but all range, or have historically ranged, into the United States.

This last condition was necessary to limit the tropical subspecies of white-tailed deer—about a dozen or so in Mexico—as well as the tropical brockets and peccaries. Most of these seldom reach one hundred pounds in weight, so they would not be included on that basis. The Carmen Mountains white-tailed deer has been included as an afterthought because it ranges into Texas as well as Mexico and is a recognized subspecies distinct from the Coues deer and the common white-tailed deer of the Texas and Mexico lowlands. The white-tailed deer that is widespread across the United States and Canada is undoubtedly the same animal wherever it occurs, but for the purposes of this book it was decided to split them into northern and southern subspecies. This split is based more on habitat, survival strategies, and differences in hunting techniques than on any true taxonomic variation. Nonetheless, there are currently distinct scientific

designations although the different anatomic features are negligible, so this accounting ultimately may be revised.

Since they are not recognized by any major records-keeping organization, the mule deer of Southern California are not included as distinct subspecies, nor are any of the several questionably discrete subspecies of Baja Peninsula and island desert mule deer. Most of these deer appear to fit into the general category of desert mule deer and several of them occur only in Mexico. The Manitoba elk is not included because it is available only to residents of the Canadian provinces where it occurs. No endangered species, as reflected by their CITES (Convention on International Trade in Endangered Species) status, were included.

I have included all animals that meet these simple criteria, and are either recognized by big-game records-keeping organizations (principally Safari Club International and the Boone and Crockett Club) and/or have different scientific names to designate a biologically recognized species or subspecies. A total of forty-one different species and subspecies has been harvested with my Remington 700 .30-06, but there is a total of forty-two species chapters because of the exceptional case of the jaguar.

The jaguar deserves to be included for two reasons. It meets all of the three major criteria above if one includes a darting sport hunt. Obviously, it would be difficult and perhaps irreversible to retool my precious old .30-06 to shoot darts, so I have simply written a story about a conventional scientific study dart hunt. I hope that someday I will be able to bring the old rifle out of retirement for a real hunt for one of the awesome big cats. This could happen if they are downlisted by CITES and harvest quotas are established in countries with sustainable populations, an eventuality that is almost certain to occur when the strict preservationist mentality that is threatening the very existence of our world's wildlife is finally vanquished. As biologist Dr. Mitchell Taylor has stated, a species that cannot sustain a harvest is a species headed for extinction. I pray that the jaguar can be saved through a quality sport-hunting program, which in many areas is its only hope.

All species chapters (chapters 4–45) are arranged so that the first section of each chapter is informational. This part includes biological information, habitat, management data, hunting techniques, expected weather, special equipment needed, and anything else that may be useful. This section has been reviewed by a competent and recognized authority on that particular animal, usually (but not always) an active species biologist working for the government of the state or province in which the hunt occurred. Where appropriate, redundant information has been diminished, or omitted altogether from subsequent chapters involving similar subspecies, and the informational section concentrates on the distinctive characteristics of the subject of that particular chapter. For example, the information section on barren ground caribou is quite comprehensive, but subsequent caribou chapters concentrate on the unique features of the subspecies, including biology and hunting information.

The second part of each species chapter features a story about one of my hunts for that animal. The involved hunt may be the only time I ever hunted a species or subspecies, but it is frequently a repeat hunt for an animal previously hunted without success, or a hunt for a larger specimen than I had previously taken. The pronghorn antelope hunt in chapter 4 was my first successful hunt with the subject rifle, but since no pictures were taken on that excursion, the featured photo is another animal from a 1987 hunt.

The order of the species chapters bears little resemblance to the order in which the animals were harvested, except for the pronghorn, which was the first animal I took with the rifle, and the Carmen Mountains whitetail, which was the last. All other chapters are grouped with similar animal species and subspecies, without regard to the date of the hunt.

None of the animals taken came from anything other than fair-chase hunts. All the animals available in a wilderness setting were hunted there whenever possible, the major exceptions being the white-tailed deer, mule deer, tule elk, and pronghorn, all of which came from free-ranging ranch or farmland populations. No animal taken was confined in any way by a fence, with the singular exception of the plains bison, which roams over seventy-one thousand acres of Custer State Park in South Dakota and meets even the stringent Boone and Crockett criteria as a free-ranging animal. All hunts were conducted to harvest a representative specimen, with little or no consideration of record book trophy status. This is not to say that a great deal of selectivity was not exercised in most cases. The majority of the animals meet minimum standards for Safari Club International's record book, and some of them qualify for Boone and Crockett.

The real pleasure in doing this book has been the actual hunts. Writing was simply a way of prolonging my enjoyment of the hunt and sharing both the happy times and the hardships. It is a way of recounting resounding victories and painful disappointments, reminiscing about blue skies on top of the world and the merciless onslaught of violent weather, and relating fickle decisions by prey that led to my defeat and unexpected turns that led to unlikely success. The work has been laborious, but it is my fervent hope that the result will be worthwhile and the reading of the book will be pure pleasure.

CHAPTER REVIEWERS

Chapter 1	Dr. Reece Lester	Dublin, GA
Chapter 2	Mr. John Lacy	Houston, TX
Chapter 3	Mr. Ron Kea	Dublin, GA
Chapter 4	Mr. Reg Rothwell	Cheyenne, WY
Chapter 5	Dr. John Elliott	Fort St. John, BC
Chapter 6	Mr. Ron Walker	Custer, SD
Chapter 7	Dr. Cormack Gates	Calgary, AB
Chapter 8	Dr. Anne Gunn	Yellowknife, NT
Chapter 9	Dr. Anne Gunn	Yellowknife, NT
Chapter 10	Mr. Ken Whitten	Fairbanks, AK
Chapter 11	Dr. John Elliott	Fort St. John, BC
Chapter 12	Mr. Mike Frisina	Butte, MT
Chapter 13	Mr. Raymond Lee	Phoenix, AZ
Chapter 14	Dr. John Elliott	Fort St. John, BC
Chapter 15	Mr. Rick Ward	Whitehorse, YT
Chapter 16	Dr. Shane Mahoney	St. Johns, NF
Chapter 17	Dr. John Elliott	Fort St. John, BC
Chapter 18	Dr. James Peek	Viola, ID
Chapter 19	Dr. Mike Gratson	Lewiston, ID
Chapter 20	Dr. Thomas Keegan	Salem, OR
Chapter 21	Dr. Vernon Bleich	Bishop, CA
Chapter 22	Mr. Pat Valkenburg	Fairbanks, AK
Chapter 23	Mr. Rick Farnell	Whitehorse, YT
Chapter 24	Dr. Anne Gunn	Yellowknife, NT
Chapter 25	Dr. Serge Couturier	Quebec City, QB
Chapter 26	Dr. Shane Mahoney	St. Johns, NF
Chapter 27	Dr. Anne Gunn	Yellowknife, NT
Chapter 28	Mr. John Beecham	Boise, ID
Chapter 29	Dr. James Teer	Sinton, TX
Chapter 30	Dr. John Elliott	Fort St. John, BC
Chapter 31	Mr. Dick Sellers	King Salmon, AK
Chapter 32	Dr. Francois Messier	Saskatoon, SK
Chapter 33	Mr. Alan Baer	Whitehorse, YT
Chapter 34	Dr. Mitchell Taylor	Iqaluit, NT
Chapter 35	Mr. Bob Hayes	Haines Junction, YT
Chapter 36	Dr. Rob Stewart	Winnipeg, MB
Chapter 37	Mr. Dennis David	Gainesville, FL

The Man.

ONE MAN

Through many dangers, toils, and snares,
I have already come;
'Tis grace has brought me safe thus far,
And grace will lead me home.

—John Newton (1725–1807), *Olney Hymns*

It has always been my destiny to be a hunter. Some would say it is a genetic quirk, a burning passion molded by chance, but I've never thought of it that way. I prefer to believe that my hunting instinct is a divinely created obsession with the capacity to control, tempt, and corrupt me; conversely, it also refines, purifies, and dignifies me.

As hundreds of thousands of Allied troops poured into Europe following D-day, 6 June 1944, I was safely housed in my mother's womb. She was a war widow, enduring the indefinite separation that was the order of the day for women married to fighting men. My father, a young career soldier, was anything but safe. By God's grace, however, he survived the ravages of war, and on 17 September 1944 he received the welcome word that he was the father of a newborn son—me.

Somehow, Dad knew I would be a hunter. In the northern Georgia mountains, nearly everyone hunted. It was a matter of survival as much as anything else, although the winds of change would soon blow in postwar prosperity. Dad took the first opportunity to "liberate" for his newborn son a German .22-caliber Anschutz rifle. The military authorities in Germany actually encouraged such confiscations as a means of disarming as many Germans as possible, or so Dad always said.

Thus I've owned a hunting rifle for virtually my entire life. I grew up wanting to take that rifle hunting, and from the start I had plenty of tutors. My father was one, although he remained in the army long after the war ended, traveling to Europe, Central America, and the Far East, and was often away. But an assortment of uncles, cousins, and friends all stood by to take me hunting anytime game was in season, and that diverse crew of characters molded my life.

When I was a boy in the mountains of Georgia, all we had to hunt was small game. At that time, raccoon was the largest game animal around, as all the deer and turkeys had long been hunted out. In fact, my grandfather, born in 1885, lived his entire life in our mountains without ever laying eyes on either a deer or a turkey in the wild—an astounding fact in view of our game-rich landscape today.

As a youth, I aspired to being absolutely trustworthy—a necessary trait if I wanted to carry that esteemed .22 into the fields unencumbered by adult supervision. That aspiration contributed significantly to my development. It encouraged me to hold myself to a much higher standard than most of my peers, and I soon established a reputation for dependability. My desire to pick up my rifle whenever the whim struck, which it did often, was strong motivation.

I learned the importance of reliability early. When I was four, Grandmother Anderson suddenly took sick. We had no vehicles at the mountain farmhouse, and the telephone hadn't yet made it to our part of the backwoods. My aunt was only three miles away, but for us she might as well have been in Atlanta. With both my baby sister and grandmother to care for, my mother could only wait it out and hope—or send me. In desperation, she pinned a note to my collar with a safety pin and pointed me down the narrow mountain road. She gave me a lecture I still remember.

Knowing that distractions tempted me, she stressed that I was not to stop for anything. The chance of my encountering people along the way was slim, so her main concern was that I would wander off into the woods after a rabbit or squirrel, leaving her with two problems instead of one. Well, I did stop to pick some huckleberries, and I climbed a roadside bank to inspect the bones of a dead opossum, but otherwise I pretty much stuck to the plan. I even remembered where to make my turn, down a shady side road. Unfortunately, I forgot to tell my aunt why I was there—a small oversight—but she of course realized that

I wouldn't have come alone but in a dire emergency. She also noticed the note prominently attached to my collar. I'll never forget the exciting ride home aboard my uncle's horse, stretched out at full gallop, or the look of heartfelt relief in my mother's eyes and the warm hug she gave me when we arrived. "Ma" Anderson died soon thereafter, but the episode forever impressed upon me the importance of absolute reliability.

From a very early age I associated that little single-shot rifle with the idea of dependability. Dad, when he was home, would dig it out of the closet, and I would hold it proudly, running my fingers over the beautiful German steel and polished wood. We lived in my grandfather's house on the mountain near Fairmount, Georgia, and there were few precious things in that house. Owning a beautiful firearm was very special for a lad like me.

My interest in wildlife goes back to my earliest recollections. Every Saturday, "Pa" Anderson would hitch his white horse, Tony, to the wagon, and we would head to town, an hour or so down the winding mountain road. On one such excursion we came across a dead opossum in the road, probably killed by one of the automobiles that sometimes passed that way. I believe it was the first opossum I had ever seen, and I wanted to linger and examine it. Pa finally took it by the tail and cast it onto the red-clay bank alongside the road, a spot I took pains to mark accurately. For the next few months, whenever we passed that spot my patient grandfather had to halt the wagon, help me down, and wait while I scampered up the bank to check on its level of decomposition.

Sometimes my rifle would go hunting without me. That was especially true in the early years, when I was too young to know the difference. As I became older, however, any relative who borrowed my rifle to harvest the day's meal felt an insistent presence at his heels. I am sure I was more of a hindrance than a help, and it irked me that my grown relatives would not let me pull the trigger for the paltry reason that I was too young. I vividly remember walking close behind an uncle one day and seeing a rabbit sitting on the edge of the farm road. I begged to make the shot, but, because the rabbit was relatively critical to the meal, my uncle refused. He missed, and down deep in my childish heart I was certain that I would have brought that rabbit home.

Being trustworthy is essentially what hunting is all about. It's about holding rigidly to a code of honor that trusts us to manage wildlife for the good of both mankind and the animals. It's about making the right decision in the field when no one will ever know what moral judgment you made. Sometimes it means staying within the law even when that law doesn't make sense. And often the correct decision has nothing to do with law—such as deciding not to harvest a legal animal, for any number of valid reasons. The trustworthy hunter is discerning in the field. Hunting can bring out the best or the worst in a person. I've seen it go both ways, sometimes in the same individual.

One of my worst mistakes in judgment is indelibly etched in my mind. My other grandfather, "Papa Jones," was a grocer. One day he stepped through the front door of his rural store just in time to see a splendid bluebird fall from the power line, the victim of a well-placed BB from my Daisy lever-action. Disappointment and anger filled his Scotch-Irish countenance, and it was immediately apparent to me that a good shot alone would not merit approval. The BB gun disappeared for a while, and I learned the lasting lesson that one must carefully evaluate the moral implications of the kill before pulling the trigger.

At about the same time, a neighbor down the road from my grandfather's store planted the first seeds of big-game hunting in my head. He was a likable young man named Lloyd Thompson, and he had developed a passion for hunting Georgia deer, which were just then returning to the state as a result of a reintroduction program. On Lloyd's living room wall I saw my first hunting trophy, a neck mount of a nice eight-point buck. How my young hunter's blood surged! I keenly wanted to make one of those awesome creatures mine. At the time it seemed an impossible dream, but years later I saw live wild deer for the first time when a doe and two fawns crossed the road in front of our school bus, causing quite a commotion. With such obviously increasing abundance, perhaps someday I could go deer hunting.

Finally, when I reached age eleven, my parents deemed me reliable enough to hunt alone with my little .22 rifle. Unfortunately, by then we had moved to a location where small-game hunting was poor, but that didn't stop me from trying. While more studious boys were doing homework and more athletic ones were practicing ball, I was changing into clothes I could wear while wading in the briar patch. More often than not I came home empty-handed, but I always came home safely. Occasionally I brought back real game.

One day I arrived home proudly carrying a beautiful cock pheasant, downed by a single shot. It was hunting season, to be sure, but there was one small problem. There are no pheasants in Georgia—at least, not in the wild. A little checking revealed that a nearby farmer had allowed some to escape. I dutifully apologized for shooting the bird, although I felt no remorse; the creature was fair game on my hunting grounds. Nonetheless, I turned the carcass over to the rightful owner, postponing the pleasure of fresh pheasant for several decades.

Soon after that incident, we moved back to the beloved mountains of northern Georgia. An interesting character lived across the road from us, a part-time preacher and full-time pack rat named Mr. Hickey. He had a vast accumulation of junk, and I spent hours going through it. He and his wife were the first full-fledged hypochondriacs I ever met, and in addition to everything else they had a virtually complete pharmacy in their hall cabinet. I don't know whether they actually took any of the medicines, but they sure had plenty of them. Mr. Hickey would answer almost any salutation with, "Don't ask me how I am; just ask me where I hurt." Both Mr. Hickey and Her (I never knew her real name, since Mr. Hickey always referred to his wife as Her) appeared eminently healthy to me. My mom always used to say, "They'll have to knock them both in the head on Judgment Day," a prospect I always found somewhat disturbing.

What really captured my attention was Mr. Hickey's single-shot .410 shotgun. When I made my daily pilgrimage across the dirt road, I always insisted he get it out and let me look at it. It was a break-open with a single hammer that you had to cock for each shot, and the little cartridge ejection mechanism would literally fling the spent shell over your shoulder when you opened the gun. Not that we ever actually shot it, shells being so expensive.

I developed a lust for that little shotgun. Our family owned a power lawn mower by that time, and Dad gave me permission to go into business mowing grass in the town down the hill—the hamlet of Ball Ground, Georgia. My main motivation was that Mr. Hickey had priced the shotgun at an astronomical $20, and to get that kind of money I had no choice but to work. I bought the shotgun before the end of the summer.

That little gun opened up the world of wingshooting for me, another real love. It may seem strange to bring this up in a book about big-game hunting, but I've discovered that most big-game hunters share this same passion. I still keep bird dogs, and for me, walking up behind a brace of fine dogs locked in on wild quail remains one of the greatest thrills in hunting.

My chief mentor in those days was Henry McCard, an irreverent, elderly squirrel hunter who lived a quarter-mile down the dirt road that ran past my house. Mr. McCard and I would sit for hours in the warm, sticky Georgia evening, rocking on his front porch and discussing great squirrel hunts, noteworthy squirrel dogs he had owned, why he disdained rabbit and bird hunting, and an infinite variety of other topics. During squirrel season, we hunted the bushy-tailed varmints with a vengeance, taking his experienced dogs, Bruno and Spot, to tree them. Mr. McCard was a rifleman, so when we hunted together I left my shotgun at home and reverted to my .22. It would have been unthinkable to take the scattergun squirrel hunting because Mr. McCard had drilled into me the virtue of putting only one small hole in your quarry. The .410 had a way of making more than that, and I knew better than to show up with it. What's more, the cartridge ejector had broken the first season I used it.

Mr. McCard had one outstanding trait: He knew squirrel hunting, possibly better than anyone who ever lived. Taking squirrels where hunting pressure is heavy is a challenge akin to hunting big game. The bushy-tails become alert and difficult to take. I learned more about my avocation during those few years than many people learn in a lifetime. I have only recently begun to appreciate how much of my early learning I apply to the pursuit of North American big game.

One of my unpleasant educational experiences involved Mr. McCard's son, who was an avid hunter but, unfortunately, also a heavy drinker. My mom would occasionally, and reluctantly, allow me to hunt with J.T. He introduced me to the joy of bird dogs, another aspect of hunting his father held in contempt—for reasons I never understood. I loved J.T. and I loved watching those dogs, so I didn't care much about his choice of beverage.

On one of our outings, J.T. slipped on a muddy bank as we returned to the car. His 12-gauge discharged and blew away a sizable portion of the upper chest wall on his right side, including the complex of nerves under the arm. I had never seen so much blood. I had to get help, and fast. The car was there, but at age fourteen I had no idea how to operate it. I stuffed some cloth into the wound and then ran to a house a mile away. By some miracle J. T. survived, but the incident left an indelible impression on me. I never apologize for being adamant about gun safety, and I won't hear of mixing alcohol with shooting. That incident also was the beginning of my understanding of the grace of God. It could just as easily have been my head that caught that load of shot, since I had been walking directly in front of my friend.

The tragedy didn't dampen my enthusiasm for hunting in the least, although it made me a great deal more cautious, especially about my choice of hunting companions. My enthusiasm heightened that Christmas with the gift of a brand-new Stevens 12-gauge double-barrel shotgun. Purchased by my parents from Sears, Roebuck and Co., the beautiful firearm greatly improved my ability to bring home game. I had long since outgrown the .410, and its broken ejector now required help from a pocketknife, making reloading tedious.

My dear father had ridden the coattails of the U.S. Army out of the poverty of the northern Georgia mountains. Dad always mistrusted the economic future in that region, and he wanted to move the family away. I had begun high school, and Dad was concerned that I might marry locally and settle into hunting squirrels for a living. We moved only sixty miles away, to a suburb of Atlanta, but the difference was enormous. My father's wisdom became quickly apparent after the move.

Stone Mountain, Georgia, was our new home, where I finished high school, complete with high school football and all the other activities that go with a bustling suburb. I met my future wife on my first day at South Gwinnett High School, although it was several years before I realized that she was the one. My hunting abated only slightly, although opportunities were harder to find in this urbanized world. I scouted diligently, and not far from my house I found a grove of oak woods with an almost unhunted population of gray squirrels. There were rabbits and quail, as well, on an undeveloped tract of land beside our home.

After the early carefree years, it was off to college and later to medical school, the rigors of which deprived me of my beloved avocation almost as much as my year in Vietnam. I viewed the forfeiture as a price I had to pay, however. *Someday I will have time to hunt*, I told myself.

I did manage to hunt occasionally while attending medical school. There was a group of enthusiastic hunters in my class, and we occasionally fled the academic studies, patient care, and medical

research to pursue doves, ducks, quail, and squirrels. Steve Jordan, a friend of mine from Statesboro, Georgia, was a member of a deer hunting club, and he became my very first big-game guide. At this particular club, the deer hunting involved pursuit by dogs, and all shooting was with shotgun and buckshot. I killed my first deer with my Sears shotgun. It was the only time I ever shot deer, or any other big game, with a scattergun.

I did not hunt much while I was doing my ophthalmology residency, but incredible opportunities ultimately came my way. I had been an army flight surgeon in Vietnam, and I had never considered a career in ophthalmology. But while attending the army's flight surgeon school in Fort Rucker, Alabama, I gradually realized that this wouldn't be a bad field in which to specialize. As a returning veteran who had served in the war zone (where I had received, rather undeservedly, a Bronze Star), I had a good chance at a residency. I decided to apply for the army's training program in ophthalmology.

The program took me in, and after I'd spent two years at Walter Reed Army Medical Center in Washington, D.C., the colonel offered his upcoming senior residents an unbelievable option. One of us could elect to do his last year of training at Madigan Army Medical Center in Washington State. Would any of us be interested? I contained myself long enough for the other three to decline before I nearly hugged the old man's neck. There was hunting in Washington State!

By this time I was married, and my wife and I had two lovely daughters. We packed them and all our belongings into a station wagon and set out. At Madigan we received a nice house on the base, very close to my work. I rode my bike to the clinic every day, which I much preferred over fighting red lights in D.C. I got to keep that assignment for my final year in the army, after I finished training.

My next-door neighbor on the army base, a pediatric resident named Bill Butler, was a native of Washington State. Our conversations were invariably about hunting. Bill had a prize Brittany spaniel named Sparky, and before I knew it I was enjoying my first real pheasant hunt. The big, colorful birds couldn't fly as fast as our Georgia quail, but it was still a challenge to hunt them—they tend to run away from hunters. When the feathered critters do get airborne, it takes a good shot to knock them down cleanly.

While we hunted, Bill and I talked about many other things, as hunters are prone to do, and often the talk was about other kinds of hunting. Bill was an enthusiastic big-game hunter, and he had killed a trophy elk with his bow on the Olympic Peninsula the previous season. He wasn't a purist bow hunter, for he also enjoyed hunting big game with his .30-06, using handloads he assembled himself. Besides elk, he sought the local black-tailed deer, and he had drawn a goat tag in the northern Cascades a few years earlier. We spent many hours talking about his adventures, and I longed to enjoy similar ones.

In the fall of 1974, Bill invited me to go elk hunting with him. Bill was a native of the Tacoma area, so I figured that he knew what he was doing. He did—except for inviting a complete greenhorn on an elk hunt.

All I owned in those days were my shotguns and German .22, so Bill lent me his extra rifle, a nondescript old military bolt-action .30-06 that certainly looked as though it had been through a war. As we prepared to embark on my initial foray into the wilds in pursuit of elk near Eatonville, Washington, Bill handed me a pocketful of his precious handloads, so valuable to him that I believe he knew each cartridge by name. He showed me how to insert them into the magazine and how to work the safety and the bolt. With that as my introduction to elk hunting, out I set.

Most folks as ill prepared as I probably get a big bull elk their first time out. Life seems to work that way sometimes. But that wasn't my experience. I did see a spike bull, but he saw me first and ran off like a rabbit before I could even raise my rifle. To make matters worse, I soon found myself completely lost, with darkness falling. I fired off a few rounds in an attempt to get Bill to come to my rescue. By the time he did, I had lost several of his cherished matched brass casings, which in my agitation I had failed to retrieve in the darkness. I'm still not sure if he's ever forgiven me.

After my introduction to big-game hunting, at Bill's urging I put in for a Washington State mountain goat tag. It was then that my beginner's luck showed up, and I drew one. Now I desperately needed a rifle of my own.

My first hunting rifle was a used .300 Savage lever-action that I bought from another soldier. It was a beautiful old piece—with the emphasis on *old*—but neither the rifle nor the scope was capable of any kind of accuracy. I almost despaired of hunting big game because of the frustration of dealing with such worn-out equipment.

Help came from a retired army colonel who visited the eye clinic from time to time. Colonel Welcher owned a gun shop, and he confirmed my worst fears when he examined my rifle. The fifty dollars I had spent on the old piece was all it was worth. The bore was completely worn out, and the scope, a cheap model, was beyond repair.

The colonel was a military man of the old school, and he highly recommended that I get a bolt-action rifle for hunting because of the dependability of the mechanism. He helped me select a Remington Model 700 ADL .30-06 from his ample stock. We tried several, but one in particular seemed to his educated eye to fit me perfectly. He patiently went through his stock of scopes, looking for the right combination of dependability, quality, and price. We settled on a Redfield Widefield in 2X7 variable power, and the colonel mounted it on the rifle with Weaver mounts.

The whole setup cost me about $100 plus my trade. I could afford that, even on a soldier's salary. The colonel even offered to help me sight in my new gun, and under his professional tutelage my shot groups soon had shrunk considerably.

I had always heard that the .30-06 would take any North American animal. Many years later, when I had taken eight or ten species with my new rifle, I decided I would try to take them all with the same gun. I have now done so, with the exception of the jaguar, which is protected. I did take a jaguar on a darting expedition in Mexico, just to get the feel of a hunt for the other great cat of North America. The old .30-06 is exceptionally versatile when it comes to loads, but my late friend Dick Green, who did all my handloads for me, couldn't assemble darts for it. Consequently, I used the apparatus provided for me on that hunt.

I continue to use my now-old rifle and scope to hunt, but it is semiretired; I've become pretty particular about not subjecting it to harsh conditions. I try to use a smaller caliber for hunting deer and hogs locally, so I won't develop a recoil flinch. That happened once, but I was able to work my way out of it by practicing with a certain .22 rifle.

My collection of North American big-game animals began before Linda and I left Washington State for Georgia to open our practice. I took a pronghorn antelope in Wyoming on the Clyde Ranch near Upton. I also harvested my first mule deer before I left the army. As for that mountain goat tag I drew—I never did get that goat.

The rifle: A Remington Model 700 ADL chambered in .30-06.

ONE RIFLE

*Novelty is exciting, I suppose, but it isn't anywhere near as rewarding
as advertised. I'd rather know from the past what to expect. . . .
I'll take proven friends and old rifles. They're built to last.*

—G. Sitton, *Petersen's Hunting*, January 1996

My rifle, the Remington Model 700 chambered in .30-06 that Colonel Welcher helped me select, was not built to be anything special. Remington produced it as a plain Jane hunting rifle, one that would be both dependable and inexpensive. I'm glad to have one, and I feel some pride in knowing that I own a piece of tried-and-true Americana.

Only as I began closing in on completing my quest for all the North American big-game animals, however, did I truly start to appreciate the wisdom and experience that old Colonel Welcher displayed in helping me to select the Remington Model 700 ADL. It was the perfect gun for me.

The Remington 700 ADL has an interesting history. It came about as the result of improvements to the design of its predecessors, the bolt-action 721 and 722 models, made by Mike Walker, a longtime Remington employee. Since 1962, Remington has produced more than three million of the Model 700 series in two versions, the ADL and the fancier BDL. Both come chambered in .30-06, the largest caliber offered in the ADL series. The Model 700 remains the most popular production bolt-action centerfire rifle in history. When it first came out, it retailed for a mere $114.95.

In 1921, Remington offered the Model 30, which was based on the 1917 design for the World War I Model 1917 Enfield. The 720, a later version, was the ultimate refinement of that Enfield design. It was a beautiful firearm, but unfortunately it became a financial loser for Remington. When World War II broke out the need for further development became obvious, and Remington set out to produce a rifle that was lightweight, fast in action, and competitively priced. The civilian version became the relatively successful Remington models 721 and 722.

The 721 and 722 were crafted with a cylindrical receiver, still the most notable design feature of the Model 700. To construct it, Remington machines a 64-ounce piece of chrome-molybdenum annealed steel down to a 15-ounce jewel, the real difference between the Remington 700 and the competition. They then tap the receiver with ten holes (four for scope mounts, two for receiver sights, three for action guard screws, and one for a gas port). My rifle has all ten, although in 1982 Remington discontinued the two receiver sight holes. The gas port is nonfunctional, since no gas reaches that portion of the receiver.

Remington had been plagued by problems with the extractor mechanism in the 720 and earlier models. The 721 and 722, as well as the Model 700, all have Mike Walker's enclosed breech system, which made possible the revolutionary modern extractor found today on all Remington centerfire rifles. The extractor is inside the bolt face, and owners of the Remington 700 seldom have to think about it. My own 700 has extracted thousands of spent cartridges under all weather conditions without the slightest hint of trouble.

Another change incorporated into the 721/722 series, and later the Model 700, is the single-piece sear safety cam, made of powdered metal that is sintered (welded by heating but not melted) and then hard plated. It was another modification that contributed immensely to the overall reliability of the weapon.

The bolt of the Model 700 is among the strongest and most reliable in the industry. Remington centerfire rifle bolts are machined from one piece of steel, with the handle added later. Despite the two-piece construction, bolt handle failure is extremely rare, even on the older models 721 and 722. In designing the 700 series, Remington at first changed the bolt handle knob from round and smooth to oval and checkered, also changing the angle of the handle from a right angle to one that is radically swept back. Unfortunately, that swept-back handle caused many skinned knuckles from recoil, so in 1974 (the year my rifle was manufactured) it was moved forward a quarter of an inch. That cured the problem. In 1983 a Model 700 with a smooth bolt-handle knob was available for shooters who wanted an old-time look to their weapon. That option has since been discontinued.

The trigger assembly of the old 721 and 722 models is said to be perhaps the best ever constructed on a mass-production rifle. The 700 series still uses that same assembly, and it continues to function superbly. The trigger guard is aluminum, but a steel guard is available on the Remington 700 Custom series. There is a two-position safety operated by a mechanism that cams off the sear from the trigger connector. It functions smoothly and quietly, and is much safer than systems that simply block the trigger pull.

My rifle has a safety that prevents working the bolt while it is in the safe position. In 1982, presumably for liability reasons, Remington altered the design so that the bolt operates when the safety is engaged. Thus it is not necessary to chamber a round with the safety off in order to unload the rifle. In the BDL series you can empty the magazine by opening the magazine door, located underneath. In the ADL there is no underside door, so that's not possible. The new design sounds safer, for obvious reasons. My gunsmith, the late Dick Green, once offered to modernize this aspect of my Model 700, but somehow I never took him up on it.

I own another Remington 700, a custom rifle in .270, and have done a fair amount of hunting with it. It has the feature that allows one to work the bolt while the safety is on. While hunting with the weapon, I have several times been horrified to find the action accidentally open, the interior of the magazine exposed to the elements, and the bolt floating in the breeze where it might easily be lost if something bumped the bolt release. The position of the bolt handle on a right-hand rifle, when slung over the right shoulder, is such that in heavy cover it is continually brushed by branches and weeds. Eventually losing a bolt seems almost inevitable if one hunts in thick brush with this modern improvement.

Naturally, I strongly prefer the old setup. I'm just extra careful when removing cartridges from the rifle. Unloading is accomplished most expeditiously by running hot rounds through the chamber with the safety off. It is possible to remove the rounds without actually chambering them completely, by partly feeding each cartridge until it falls loose. Alternatively, with some force you can engage the extractor without actually chambering the round. Those maneuvers take a little practice but are probably safest.

While on the subject of triggers and safeties, a word about the trigger-pull adjustment: Remington recommends that the poundage required to trip the trigger be left at the factory setting, which is about twelve pounds. They are certainly the authorities, but I must confess that I improved my accuracy considerably by ignoring their recommendation. A savvy guide on one of my early hunts pointed out that my trigger pull was too hard, so I had Dick Green loosen it to two and a half pounds. The result was a big improvement in my accuracy. This was an "unauthorized" adjustment, and I don't necessarily recommend it. I have shot numerous wild hogs with an unaltered .243 Remington. Nevertheless, I find that I am able to shoot straighter with my "customized" .30-06.

The follower in the magazine of the Model 700 was made from stamped metal until 1974, when Remington switched to stainless steel. In my rifle the spring and follower at first were the cause of some minor grief, because the cartridges must be chambered exactly in order to feed smoothly. Early in my career a few cartridges got stuck in the rifle, but now that I know how to position them properly that seldom happens. Perhaps the magazine design in later models is more forgiving.

The barrel, originally twenty-two inches long, is a marvel of modern engineering. It is made of a proprietary steel alloy that is resistant to magnetizing. The rifling is hammer-forged by machinery that produces barrels at the astounding rate of one barrel per minute. The twist is right-handed, one turn per ten inches.

Accuracy is one of the most important factors to consider when buying a rifle. The Remington models 721 and 722 had a reputation for accuracy, but those guns still needed some overall improvements. Accuracy, however, was never the issue. The 722, particularly, developed an impeccable reputation as a "tack driver." The .222 varmint round, developed for the basic 722 frame, is the epitome of accuracy, and its reputation led to many highly accurate offspring rounds, such as the .222 Remington Magnum, the .17 Remington, and the .223 Remington. The Model 700 continued that tradition. One variation of the Model 700, in fact, was a highly accurate sniper rifle used extensively during the Vietnam War.

The accuracy of these guns is perhaps attributable to the bedding surface, the strength, and, to some degree, the rigidity of Mike Walker's famous receiver. Rigidity, however, is not a simple matter, as the Model 700 receiver is the *least* rigid at midsection among modern centerfire rifles. That is more than offset, however, by the stock design, which directs recoil through the center of the receiver. Thus the seeming lack of rigidity is neutralized, as far as accuracy is concerned.

Production of the receiver for the Remington Model 700 is identical to that of the ADL and BDL models. In all the models, the components are assembled by hand. A major step is the mating of a compatible bolt and receiver. After final assembly, the rifle is "proof fired" with a 50 percent overload cartridge. After that test Remington stamps the barrel with the proof mark REP, and the weapon goes on to "test firing," where it must meet accuracy standards for a three-shot group. The receiver then receives its serial number, the last four digits of which are etched onto the bolt, effectively marrying the two for life.

My rifle, a Model 700 ADL with the serial number 6722019, is proof stamped REP on the right side of the barrel near the receiver. The opposite side of the barrel is stamped 9 LY R, a code signifying that in February 1974 the rifle was assembled and then inspected by inspector 9 and that the final assembly was done by assembler R.

My rifle was the beneficiary of several important changes instituted by Remington in 1974. An antibind modification that year improved the smoothness of the action, and mine has always been flawless. In addition to the changes to the magazine follower and the bolt handle in 1974, a new rear sight with graduated settings was installed. From Remington's standpoint, the most important change in 1974 was that sales of the Model 700 broke 100,000, beginning a mind-boggling run of seven years of equally staggering sales.

My Model 700 .30-06 has undergone two additional elective modifications. In 1978, I had a recoil pad installed, since the stoked-up handloads I was using were pounding my shoulder. And in 1979 I had Dick Green "float the barrel" and bed it in glass so that no pressure points exist between the barrel and the stock, theoretically improving accuracy in adverse weather. The rifle is manufactured with a single controlled pressure point, and a wet stock can swell enough to apply sufficient tension to affect the accuracy. I like that modification a lot, not only for the sake of accuracy but also because it makes it easy to remove dirt and moisture from between the stock and barrel, using a cloth lightly moistened with oil, after a wet day in the field. And I can do it without removing the stock from the rifle.

My rifle is topped with a Redfield 2X7 Widefield, an inexpensive scope that has never fogged or otherwise malfunctioned despite being exposed to some of the worst conditions imaginable. Moreover, it has never required sighting in after a journey, airline handling notwithstanding. That may be due more to the sturdy Weaver mounts than to the scope, which is now almost an antique, being of three-piece construction rather than the more modern and reliable one-piece design. Prior to my muskox and polar bear hunts in 1993, I removed the scope and returned it to Redfield for refurbishing to avoid any malfunctions at minus 40 degrees. Being quite partial to my old scope, I declined Redfield's offer to replace it with a more modern one for about the same amount of money that I had originally paid for the rifle, scope, and mounts combined. The old scope continues to perform perfectly.

The accuracy of my combination has not been just good; it's been unbelievable. My friend Ed Hall, who produced some of the first handloads I ever used in the rifle, said, after an afternoon of bursting six-inch melons at 300 yards: "A sporting firearm isn't supposed to be that accurate." I have occasionally missed with the rifle, but the misses have almost never been the gun's fault. The rifle has a balance and fit that seem tailor-made for me.

When I pull the recoil pad into my shoulder and lay my cheek against the weathered Monte Carlo stock, I feel completely one with it.

My part-time gunsmith and full-time friend, Dick Green, custom handloaded every bullet that I used to take the forty-one species and subspecies of big game detailed in this book. He used either Remington or Winchester brass, tailoring the powder and primer to the size of the Nosler partition bullet. When Dick died unexpectedly in 1998, I needed only three animals to complete my quest and had only twenty-two handloads left. I tried not to waste any of them, and after the final hunt I still had fifteen of Dick's handloads in my possession.

I started out using four bullet weights, but in recent years I have settled on two—the 165-grain for deer-size game and the 200-grain for bear and the large ungulates, such as bison and moose. In all those years of shooting Dick's handloads, only one cartridge failed to fire, and I think that one had a bad primer.

In 1996, with a lot of important hunting coming up, I suddenly discovered that my priceless rifle had completely lost its ability to pattern as it used to. The change came on rapidly, and Dick Green tried everything, all to no avail. The gun wasn't merely grouping poorly; it was grouping terribly. I ordered a new scope from Redfield, thinking that perhaps my old three-piece had bitten the dust. That didn't help, and I put the new one back in its box.

In desperation I contacted Charles Henry, another highly regarded local gunsmith, and he at last discovered a subtle dilation beneath the front sight screw that was causing the bullet to rattle around immediately before exiting the barrel. No wonder it didn't pattern anymore. I was left with the choice of putting on a new barrel or bobbing a couple of inches off the old one and recrowning it. I chose the latter so that I could complete my goal with the same barrel. The rifle immediately went back to inch-and-a-half groups at 100 yards. My hat is off to Charles, who saved me from quitting my quest just short of the goal. Perhaps the rifle has lost a few feet of muzzle velocity, but I can't tell the difference.

My attachment to my .30-06 is such that I have lived in constant fear that the airlines would lose it, or that some scoundrel would steal it from my car. It has endured the harshest of weather and years of hard use, but at every opportunity I treat it like a baby. I have always packed cleaning materials, even for backpack hunts (when cleaning materials consisted of only an oily rag in a plastic bag). I handle it with great care, and I have never dropped or stepped on it. I abhor the thought of handling any weapon by the barrel, and I cringe when I see others doing so. I take great care to touch only the wood. But despite all my precautions, I made the mistake of leaving the rifle too long in my damp saddle scabbard after a miserably wet hunt in 1986. The barrel pitted, an unwelcome memento of that adventure. The pitting has not worsened, however, and I regularly apply oil for added protection.

I have gazed at every kind of North American big-game animal through the same Redfield scope, and I have sent one of Dick Green's custom handloads rifling down the barrel for a killing shot. Most have been clean, one-shot kills, or else required only an assurance shot. I have wounded and lost only one animal, a pronghorn antelope in 1980. My shots have sometimes missed, but almost all have been clean misses.

I hunt sparingly with the rifle these days, since I want to pass it on to a grandson who shares my passion for hunting. In it the boy will have more than memories of grandfatherly advice about hunting. He will also have a one-of-a-kind rifle that has done it all in North America, by the grace of God.

Packing out the kill, and as always, packing the rifle.

Whether in the desert or in the Arctic, the rifle always accompanies the hunter.

ONE LAND

This globe, the Earth which we inhabit, is, in its natural state . . .
universally, wherever the Waters do not prevail, covered with Woods. . . .
Except where the Land is worn to the Bone, and nothing remains
of the Surface but bare Rocks, every Soil, even the poorest,
hath its peculiar Cloathing of Trees or Shrubs.

—Thomas Pownall (1722–1805), *A Topographical Description of Such Parts of*
North America as Are Contained in the (Annexed) Map, 1776

My hunting aspirations have always been confined to my homeland, and seldom have tales of hunting faraway places stirred my blood. I don't envy those who search the African bush, climb the Asian steppes, or gaze down upon game from some Himalayan height. They are my fellow hunters, and I salute them. Nor do I rule out the possibility that I might someday develop a yearning to join them. But for now, my dreams are eminently fulfilled hunting my home continent.

Overall, North America is the most challenging place to hunt in the world. That is not only my opinion, but also the opinion of most others who have hunted both in North America and elsewhere. Here we have at least forty distinct species and subspecies that qualify as big game. Only Africa has more. Here we have an endless variety of terrain and habitat such as no other continent can boast, except perhaps gigantic Asia. For hunting diversity, North America is unmatched. It is axiomatic that one can spend a lifetime hunting here and never see all the faces and moods of this great land.

North America is blessed with a stunning variety of climates and terrains, far more than its size would suggest (it makes up only 16.3 percent the world's total land): Here we have the world's largest island (Greenland), whose topography has barely changed since the Ice Age. Subtropical and tropical jungles in southern Florida and the Yucatan are home to reptilian giants reminiscent of ages past. A mighty spine of mountains stretches from the Yukon River to the Andes, and to its east spreads the world's largest unbroken plain, reaching from the Canadian Arctic to the Mexican coast. Within that expanse are found the world's largest gorge (the Grand Canyon, in Arizona); the world's deepest gorge (Hell's Canyon, in Idaho); the world's fastest winds (on Mount Washington, in New Hampshire); the world's highest tides (in the Bay of Fundy, in Nova Scotia); and the world's biggest meteor crater (in northeastern Canada).

I was born and raised in North America, and from my childhood I remember my corner of it as a gentle place of soft summers and mild winters, where one could count on the rhythmic and forgiving pulse of nature. In Georgia, my home, that is as true now as it was in the 1940s. The wet of winter gives way to the flowers of spring as regularly as clockwork. The pine pollen starts flying in February, and soon the dogwoods bloom and tiny new-growth crosses appear in the tops of the pine trees—just in time for Easter. In June the spring flowers wither under the scorching summer heat, and a whole new crop of blossoms takes their place. Fireflies light up the evenings of early summer, lending their eerie and pulsating glow to every shadowy woodlot. Some July days edge above 100 degrees Fahrenheit, with the humidity not far behind. Noisy cicadas, "July flies," resonate rhythmically in the tall pines, their clamor at times enough to make sleep impossible. Occasionally a cool hint of September intervenes, and by the beginning of that magical month one can look forward to cooler mornings and perceptibly less haze.

September in Georgia heralds the traditional onset of hunting season, although in recent years squirrel season has been moved back to August. Dove season opens on the first Saturday of September and has been a special time of fun and fellowship for most of my years—a time for socializing and shooting, followed as often as not by a fine barbecue. Bow season for our local white-tailed deer also starts in September. I took a significant number of my North American trophies in September—ten each for the months of September and October, accounting for almost half of my total species and subspecies. Add to all of that the moderation of the weather, and it is no wonder that I am enthralled by the fall.

Over all, my big-game excursions have taken me to some fifteen states of the United States, to six Canadian provinces, and to four states of Mexico. Canada's vast Northwest Territories provided me with the greatest number of trophies from any single principality: eight distinct species or subspecies. Among all the states and territories of North America, the Canadian province of British Columbia has the largest variety of native big game, including four kinds of deer, two elk, two bear, four sheep, two moose, plains bison, mountain goat, mountain caribou, wolf, and cougar. Five animals of my North American collection came from British Columbia.

The diversity of habitats across the North American continent is enormous. In the high Arctic, the land at first appears scoured of vegetation by the winds and cold. When one looks more closely, however, there is a profuse growth of low vegetation, consisting of grasses and sedges, flowers and willows. The bountiful tundra grows 1,700 types of plants and 900 types of flowers. This amazing profusion sustains caribou and muskox and, indirectly, the predators that share their domain. The secret of the Arctic lies in the continuous daylight of its summer, stimulating sufficient plant growth to last the rest of the year. The region is actually a frozen desert where the sparse annual precipitation is adequate only because it is locked in surface ice and in subsurface permafrost. When in summer that ice partially melts, the moisture supports plant growth.

Included in the Arctic habitat are the sea ice and the waters underneath. Polar bear and Arctic fox eat seal, the fox being a scavenger that follows the polar bear and consumes its leavings. There is more sea ice in the Arctic than there is land, so that forbidding and continually shifting expanse is an important part of the northern ecosystem, despite its being as sterile in appearance as a hospital operating room. Having traveled the sea ice for hundreds of miles on hunts for five species, I am well aware of those icy life-giving yet deadly waters just a few feet beneath the sled runners.

South of the Arctic region, and intruding into it in some places, is the taiga, a region of stunted evergreens and willows, endless lakes, and icy streams. In the Mackenzie Delta on the Arctic coast, dwarf trees extend all the way to the very brink of the ocean, the northernmost trees in the world. Arctic mountain chains such as the Brooks Range of Alaska have timberlines so low that only the lowest valleys have shrubs more than knee high, but on the southern edge patches of evergreens are visible. The same is true of the Mackenzie Mountains on their northern extreme. Dall sheep are there, along with the most northerly moose on the continent. The mountains at the Arctic extremes of North America are mostly a gently rolling lot, with few areas of truly precipitous terrain.

The taiga is a dense evergreen forest of fir, spruce, pine, and cedar, with stands of birch mingled in here and there. Into this land of feast and famine the caribou of the mainland migrate to pass the harsh winter, and the wolves inevitably follow. Do not look for caribou here beyond springtime, however. Their wanderings take them back to the calving grounds far to the north. Starvation may be the end for the wolf that fails to follow—and, of old, the same was true for man.

Farther south is the rugged high country. Heavily timbered valleys characterize the middle and southern mountains of Alaska and Canada, and jagged escarpments are the norm. More southerly species of sheep appear there, the Stone and the various types of bighorn. Caribou disappear, except for endangered and rare bands of the woodland variety, at the Canadian border. In the eastern part of North America, the mountains slope more gently and are heavily timbered across their rounded tops. Vertical terrain there is the exception rather than the rule.

Mountains remain as scattered oases in the desert Southwest, where trees grow only on the mountaintops and only the high country yields flowing water. Some mountains are dry, but from others crystal rivers cascade from great heights, as often as not to vanish into the surrounding desert. The desert bighorn sheep and the mule deer, as well as the diminutive Coues and Carmen Mountains deer, inhabit these parts. The valley floors of the great Arizona-Sonora, the Chihuahuan, and the Mojave Deserts may seem barren, but even those dry places teem with life.

On the great plains that stretch from the Arctic to eastern Mexico, the pronghorn still abounds. The native bison is mostly absent, but the white-tailed deer thrives in the lowlands along rivers and streams. The grasses and sedges that nourished vast herds of bison in centuries past have today been replaced by equally endless fields of corn and other grain. Still, along riparian corridors, in brushy draws, and on the low hills unsuitable for planting, big game is mostly abundant and well managed.

The eastern parts of Canada and the United States are similar in many respects, with hardwood and coniferous forests covering all the nonarable land like a vast living blanket, even to the mountaintops. Man's pervasive agriculture has taken over the flattest and most useful land, relegating much of the wildlife to the mountains. The Appalachian chain of mountains begins at Quebec's Notre Dame Mountains and extends southward as the Catskills of New York, the Green Mountains of Vermont, and the White Mountains of New Hampshire. It terminates in Georgia and Alabama, having spanned virtually the entire East Coast, forming the boundary between watersheds that drain into the Atlantic Ocean on one side and the Gulf of Mexico on the other. Along its path are myriad streams, lakes, and a nearly unbroken blanket of hardwood forest. North Carolina's Mount Mitchell is the highest point east of the Mississippi, at 6,684 feet. Over the entire length of the chain threads the longest footpath in the United States, the Appalachian Trail, extending 2,000 miles from Mount Katahdin, Maine, to Springer Mountain, Georgia.

The Rocky Mountains form the largest outcropping of high terrain in North America, the northern portion of the chain being made up of the Brooks, Selwyn, and Mackenzie ranges. To the south of those ranges are the mountains of western Alberta, eastern British Columbia, and Montana, where some of the world's most beautiful scenery and best big-game hunting can be found. The world's first national park, Yellowstone, is a central jewel of the Rocky Mountain chain, although today it struggles with problems that Teddy Roosevelt never envisioned. Just to the north of the park, the Absaroka Range comprises some of the least spoiled wilderness in the Lower Forty-eight, encompassing the continent's longest chain of peaks over 10,000 feet. It is there that on three occasions I have pursued bighorn sheep while backpacking, one of the most challenging ways to hunt. The coastal ranges of the West, which begin in Alaska and extend almost to the southern tip of Baja California, also offer great big-game habitat and breathtaking vistas. In addition they boast the only true volcanoes in North America south of Alaska and north of central Mexico. This range of mountains features the highest peak in the Lower Forty-eight, Mount Whitney in California. That monarch of the Sierra Nevada, on the border of

California and Nevada, rises to 14,495 feet. It looks down on Death Valley, at 282 feet below sea level the lowest point on the continent.

On the slopes of these desert mountains lives the world's oldest inhabitant: a bristlecone pine named the Methusalah Tree, which is believed to be 4,600 years old. Farther west are the world's largest living creatures, the giant sequoia on the western slopes of the Sierra Nevada. The General Sherman Tree is 275 feet high and 103 feet in circumference at its base. Big in North America doesn't refer only to game!

The great southern swamps begin in southern North Carolina and terminate in eastern Texas, finding their most profound expression in the Everglades of southern Florida. This is the largest subtropical wilderness in North America, where fresh water and salt water mix to form brackish estuaries. It mingles charmingly with dense forests of mangroves standing on exposed roots, their woody legs intertwining like the threads of a roughly woven tapestry. In many places saw grass prairies reach to the horizon. Myriad plant and animal species call this complicated flat watershed home, perhaps the premier being the formerly endangered American alligator.

The only truly tropical region that I describe in this book is the coastal plain of Mexico. The Yucatan and its environs have a rich history and are home to many types of creatures. The region captivates and enchants its visitors. The Yucatan was where the Mayan Indians lived, their crumbled cities giving us only a glimpse of the grandeur of their civilization. Their citadels, towers, and temples still dot the landscape, conjuring up visions of ancient battles, dynasties, religious rituals, and royal intrigues. The jaguar, the zenith of this region's food chain, was a powerful symbol in the religion and lore of the Maya.

God created the heavens and the earth by speaking the divine Word, and mortal language fails to convey even a part of His creation. North America defies any attempt to capture it in words. To appreciate what I hope to convey, one must stand breathless and muted on the brink of a cliff peering after a mountain goat. One must spend countless days backpacking for bighorn sheep, or hiking the ice pack while the numbing silence glides by hour after hour. One must wade in black water in search of the alligator, or sit quietly on a deer stand as the sun rises on auriferous wings. Even then it is impossible to say that one truly knows North America.

Pronghorn antelope. (Photo: courtesy of Eric J. Hansen)

PRONGHORN ANTELOPE
(Antilocapra americana)

*The Prong-horn Antelope is an animal of wonderful fleetness,
and so shy and timorous as seldom to repose,
except on ridges which command a view of the surrounding country.
The acuteness of their sight and the exquisite delicacy of their smell,
renders it exceedingly difficult to approach them;
and when once the danger is perceived, the celerity with which the
ground is passed over appears to the spectator to resemble the flight of a bird
rather than the motion of a quadruped.*

—Meriwether Lewis, quoted in
Frank Forester's Field Sports, 1849

When I first saw a pronghorn antelope, the words of Lewis flashed through my mind. The animal seems to glide above the ground, so rapid and level is its motion. To observe a herd of pronghorns is like watching a flock of birds sailing low over the prairie.

The pronghorn is a conservation success story. In the 1920s there were only 13,000 left, the result largely of habitat destruction and overhunting. Those problems have been corrected, however, and the pronghorn is thriving once again. There are now more than a million of them on the plains of the American and Canadian West, with a smattering as well in Mexico. Wyoming has just under 400,000, but at times of peak population that number may rise to over 600,000. Second to Wyoming in pronghorn population is Montana; the Dakotas, Colorado, New Mexico, Texas, Oklahoma, Nebraska, and Kansas all have good populations as well. And every state to the west of those has at least some pronghorns, although they are not native to Washington State, and introduced animals there have not thrived. In Canada they are moderately abundant in the southern parts of Alberta and Saskatchewan, the northern extremes of their range.

Populations can go through radical fluctuations during certain years, usually because of severe winters or summertime drought. There was a long period of cold, wet weather in May and June of 1995, for example, that killed many fawns. Fortunately, the species is adapted to periods of "boom or bust," and when conditions improve the animals recover quickly.

Originally there were five subspecies of pronghorns recognized, but none were highly distinctive. Today, transplants of the most common subspecies (*Antilocapra americana*) have erased the characteristics that formerly distinguished subspecies. Essentially, now there is only one pronghorn.

The pronghorn antelope isn't actually an antelope at all, biologically speaking. Like the Rocky Mountain goat, it is a creature with no close relatives, and it fits rather uncomfortably into most schemes of classification. Scientifically it is in the family of the bovids, although in my mind that appears to be stretching things somewhat.

These fleet animals are well known to most hunters for their attractive light-brown upper bodies with streaks of tan across the white neck, contrasting with the black cheek patches (and sometimes black heads) of mature males. The towering ebony horns have distinctive curved tips and a single prong angling forward, from which the animal derives its name. The does also have horns, although theirs seldom reach three inches in length and rarely have prongs. Does almost always lack the dark head coloration and are generally lighter overall than bucks. The animals lack dewclaws, a characteristic

Pronghorn antelope. Wyoming, October 1987.

shared by no other North American ungulate. Bucks weigh about 100 to 125 pounds when mature, and the average weight for does is 90 pounds. All antelope appear to have a slight midriff bulge, and older bucks have a distinctive and easily recognizable potbelly.

Bucks with horns of fifteen to sixteen inches are excellent trophies, and every year some are taken that exceed those measurements. Horn growth varies with range conditions, and some years are better than others. At first glance one would think that pronghorns keep their headgear year after year, in the manner of mountain goats or bison, but such is not the case. After the October rut (usually in November), the bucks rapidly cast off the dead outer sheath of their horns, which is separated from the inner living, bony core by a layer of velvetlike skin. That inner core nourishes the new horn as it forms, and the curving of the tips and the new prongs are visible within a month or so. During spring and summer the new horns gradually lengthen and harden, with growth complete in August. The horns are flattened below the prongs and cylindrical from the prong to the tip. Mature animals have "ivory tips," a sure signal

the animal is an old buck. Ivory-tipped horns make a fine trophy.

Getting a good-looking antelope mount can be difficult, because it is easy to rub the hairs the wrong way and ruin the trophy. The stiff, air-filled hairs of the winter coat are excellent insulation for the pronghorn, but once bent out of shape they are virtually impossible to straighten. Of five antelope mounts, only one has turned out to my satisfaction, despite the fact that all were done by competent taxidermists. This frustration for the hunter is no disadvantage for the pronghorn, however. The individual hairs consist of a soft, foamlike core surrounded by a hard sheath whose excellent insulation compensates for the rabbitlike thinness of pronghorn skin. The antelope can erect the hairs over their entire body to catch and hold air that keeps them warm.

Being able to endure deep winter is an absolute necessity for any creature of the high plains. Pronghorns have a countercurrent recirculation system for blood vessels to the legs that essentially transfers the heat of outgoing arterial blood to incoming venous blood before it reenters the body core. In addition, the fat in the antelope's legs freezes at a lower temperature than that in the rest of the animal.

The pronghorn is an animal of the open plains. Speaking of the plains bison of the American West, Theodore Roosevelt observed in 1901: *"Now that the buffalo are gone, it [the pronghorn] is the only game really at home on the wide plains. . . . They live by preference where there is little or no cover."* That trait is deeply ingrained and maximizes their speed and keen eyesight as defenses against predators. Their fleetness is legendary; they are the fastest of all North American mammals. Some claim to have clocked the pronghorn at 70 miles per hour, but most biologists believe that figure to be an exaggeration, and that their top speed is around 45 miles per hour. Pronghorns are commonly thought to be second in swiftness among mammals only to the cheetah of Africa, and they can maintain their top speed far longer.

The pronghorn is designed for running, and their heart and lungs are reportedly the largest in proportion to body size of any ungulate. The foreleg bone is the densest bony material in the natural world, rivaling tooth enamel in its hardness, likely a necessary trait for the leg to maintain its integrity at such high speeds. Muscles are concentrated in the hips and shoulders, and there are long tendons that reach down into the skinny lower legs, an arrangement that allows for a faster, more efficient stride. The middle joint of both front and rear legs moves in only one direction, much like a hinge, with no lateral flexibility at all. This highly stable setup greatly reduces the probability of dislocation at high speeds over rough terrain.

Eating habits and metabolism also facilitate the quickness of the animal and its survival during winter. Small stomachs ensure that pronghorns are never encumbered by excessive food. They like to browse on shrubs and forbs, and they ingest grass sparingly, except in springtime when it is tender. To some degree their diet varies with the region they inhabit, but in general the pronghorn likes to dine on various kinds of sagebrush as well as broomweed, green woolly senecio, stickleaf, groundsel, goatweed, javelina bush, Mexican tea, and sacahuiste. During winter pronghorns browse on big sagebrush, black sagebrush, black greasewood, juniper, and cedar, where available. Although the animals compete with cattle for food only in a minor fashion, they directly contend for many of the plants eaten by domestic sheep. The pronghorn is able to eat some plants that are toxic to domestic animals, its liver having the capacity to detoxify them. The quantity of sagebrush consumed by antelope in winter would be deadly to most animals.

Although pronghorns don't compete intensively with cattle for food, they can still suffer ill effects from cattle ranching. On one ranch where I have hunted several times, it had been fashionable in years past to use chemicals to kill

Long shots are the norm when hunting antelope, so a good rest is a necessity.

The work begins after the kill.

the sagebrush so as to allow more room for grass to grow. This unwittingly placed the pronghorn at a great disadvantage, especially in winter, when browsing on sagebrush is very important to the animal's survival. As far as I am aware, that practice has now been discontinued. I still recall the rancher's pointing to the top of a grassy hill behind the ranch house, the spot where a spray plane had crashed, killing the pilot, many years before. Pilots and pronghorns are both better off without such spraying, and the cattle of Wyoming appear to be just as fat and happy as ever. Many aspects of range utilization are only now becoming understood, but it seems clear that intensive overgrazing by domestic stock and some of the practices associated with ranching, such as spraying, fire suppression, and fencing, have damaged the pronghorns' habitat. Also, loss of the natural fire cycle has contributed to pronghorn declines in the past. When overmature sagebrush shrubs are allowed to accumulate, devoid of new growth and the nutrients derived from ash-containing soil, the sagebrush is of little value to the pronghorn.

These speedsters of the plains can go for long periods without water, and in arid regions they reportedly can survive without it for months. If there is water-containing vegetation to supply their needs, they may not drink from water holes even when they are available. They apparently have an extraordinary ability to conserve water, even manufacturing some of it through metabolic processes.

The rut occurs from late July through early October, depending on the area, with northern areas having a later rut. The bachelor herds of summer break up in June or July, and the dominant bucks settle into their home range, which they defend against encroachment. In a few places the animals appear to tend a harem of does, driving away all competitors. In most regions, though, the dominant bucks are territorial, breeding whichever does pass through. The territories can be quite small, seldom exceeding four hundred acres or so, with the largest being on the land of poorest quality. Does wander more or less freely from one buck's territory to another, showing no fidelity to any particular male. A buck encountering a male intruder will display a dominance posture, which includes a "snort-wheeze," laid-back ears, the grinding of its teeth, and a stiff walk toward the opponent.

Does usually breed for the first time at the age of sixteen months. Antelope have the unique ability to implant five or six fetuses, then resorb the appropriate number to allow the doe to survive the prevailing conditions. During a severe winter all of the fetuses may be resorbed, allowing the doe to live to breed when conditions are more favorable. Gestation averages 252 days, and most often twins are born. Each tiny animal weighs only five to seven pounds at birth, and they spend most of their first week hiding, coming out only to nurse two or three times a day. Studies have shown that fawn survival during the first year is less than 50 percent, but that figure improves greatly when there are readily available natural bedding areas—such as silver sagebrush—and plentiful tall grass. Coyotes are a major predator of newborn fawns, and survival increases dramatically where coyote control programs are in force. By the end of a week the youngsters are much more mobile and already beginning to nibble tender vegetation. After a month they are experienced browsers, and after six weeks they gather into herds for safety.

In winter the pronghorn may gather into much larger herds, sometimes numbering into the thousands. Mortality in extreme snow conditions is much higher on grassland than on sagebrush prairie, since the animals are reluctant to dig for food. Migration to better feeding grounds and less challenging snow conditions is a major survival tactic, and fences obstructing their passage have resulted in disastrous winterkill. The pronghorn is not a jumper, and three-foot-high interlocking wire fences stop or greatly impede its travel. When encountering barbed wire, pronghorn will almost invariably go under it or between the wires instead of over the top.

The pronghorn population has been greatly aided in its recovery by the creation and enforcement of game laws that employ a draw system and a scientifically designed harvest quota. In addition, ranchers are discouraged from altering the vegetation to exclude species of plants agreeable to the pronghorn. High fences are still present in pronghorn habitats, but gates have been designed that allow the animals to pass. In addition, coyote-control programs have been instituted in selected areas.

Hunting techniques today are varied. In prehistoric times the native people of North America sometimes built herding chutes that channeled the animals toward waiting hunters. Nobody knows what kind of success rate they achieved trying to hit fleeing antelope with primitive bows and arrows, but likely they had some kind of ingenious setup that tipped the odds in favor of the archer. They knew long before barbed wire invaded the continent that pronghorns don't jump, and that a relatively low fence would be sufficient to move the herd in the desired direction.

The most popular modern hunting approach is the classic spot-and-stalk, in which the hunter selects the desired animal from a distance, usually with the aid of a spotting scope, and then stays out of sight and approaches from downwind. Other methods include waiting at a likely spot in a buck's known vicinity, setting up an ambush at a water hole, or using a decoy. The bow hunter is most likely to use these latter methods, though they work as well for the rifle hunter. Drives are of limited value, especially if the animals are in wide-open terrain where approach is impossible without detection. The hunter waits at a likely escape route while his partner circles the herd and starts it on the move. My experience with drives has been mixed; I usually wind up wondering which way the herd has gone.

The pronghorn is an animal that displays extraordinary curiosity. A handkerchief flapping in the breeze, or some similar unexplained motion, will often bring them within range of a waiting hunter. Never having tried the trick, I cannot vouch for its effectiveness, but I don't doubt the claim.

Most experienced hunters recommend a flat-shooting rifle, a spotting scope, and a good pair of binoculars. Tough double-knee pants are a good protection against the spines and stickers common in antelope country. Likewise, you will greatly appreciate a shirt with elbow pads during the inevitable belly crawl on final stalk. You will find a bipod attachment for your rifle to be extremely useful in the wide expanses of antelope country, where the shots are often of two hundred yards or more. And it can get hot, so take a water bottle in a light daypack.

Hunting pronghorn antelope is a lot of fun. One sees lots of game and gets involved in judging trophy quality, and it's an activity that can be accomplished without extreme physical exertion. There's the classic stalk (or more likely, several of them) and then a very high chance of success. The pungent smell of sagebrush wafts through my memory as I write, stirring visions of endless prairies, rolling hills dotted with antelope, awesome vistas stretching to the purple horizon, and Wyoming sunsets of years gone by. This is an ideal experience for youngsters, one that is likely to turn them into lifelong hunters.

A FIRST TIME FOR EVERYTHING

The year is 1975. I stand outside the ancient ranch house and gaze at the low sagebrush hills that stretch like tundra in all directions. I am on my first hunt for a pronghorn antelope, a creature I have only seen on cross-country journeys. Indeed, I have never killed but one deer in my life, that with a 12-gauge, double-barrel shotgun. I am only thirty-one years old, eager, and ready to leap into this new challenge.

I proudly hold my new hunting rifle—my Remington .30-06 in Model 700 ADL. The bolt works smoothly, the new finish gleams in the Wyoming sunlight, and I already know that the pattern it shoots is a tight, confident group. Topped with my brand-new three-piece 2–7X Redfield scope, it is nothing but pure beauty, a hunting blend that is state-of-the-art for 1975. I still haven't harvested anything with it, but I know I can if the chance comes.

My friend Tom Clyde has told me that these pronghorn critters are fast and spooky, and that the best way to hunt them is to use your head. Tom has been hunting pronghorn all his life, so undoubtedly he knows. He's mentioned leading them when you shoot if they're on the run. I'm used to doing that for doves, but using a big-game rifle to lead an animal seems odd. I haven't the prudence or the experience to imagine how to go about it. If I get close enough to the right one, though, I plan to throw some lead.

I'm dead tired after the twenty-four-hour drive from Tacoma to Upton, Wyoming, so I don't have much energy left to meditate on it right now. The season opens tomorrow. We will stay here at the ranch with the family and various relatives and friends who have gathered for the opening of the season. It's crowded, and I feel a little out of place—I essentially talked my way into an invitation to come along with Tom. Nobody seems to hold it against me, though, least of all my friend, who is as amiable as ever.

I will bunk with another chum of Tom's in an old camper trailer that sits with wheels long gone in the yard of the ranch. A substantial population of barn mice live in the trailer, and I sweep away some of their droppings before spreading my sleeping bag. But indeed I came here expecting no special treatment, and the old bed is actually quite comfortable. We will eat in the main house, where Tom's aging mother will do our cooking, a task she savors, I'm told.

Before retiring, I take a walk around the ranch. There is an old horse-drawn hay rake, along with antiquated farm equipment and the debris of more than a century of subsistence ranching. The corral is a foot deep in manure. Tom's father is busy tending a sick cow, and cattle dot the hills in the distance. Out there too are occasional white spots—pronghorn.

The ground is littered in places with misplaced tools, a tin can here, a bit of wire there. In these objects I can feel the Clyde family's dogged determination to eke out a living from this ranch. When one is ranching to survive, aesthetics take a back seat. We clutter the land no less in my home state of Georgia, but there the bacteria and a hot, humid climate combine to erase the evidence. Here, things set down remain for centuries. Despite them, I still see the pristine as I walk: the ubiquitous sagebrush, the spiny cacti, and other less familiar plants that share this ranch with the Clydes.

My old friend the rattlesnake and his impersonator, the deceitful puff adder, also share this land. This look-alike, which mimics every mannerism of the rattler except its bite, is present in appreciable numbers. Although harmless, it is in fact more aggressive than the rattler; its very survival depends on a brash show of bravado that it is unable to back up. Simply knowing that the creature they mimic is also here makes one vigilant when crawling among the rocks.

Ma Clyde, mother of five sons and a daughter, is as rough as the range she and her husband have supervised for six decades. She suffers from a variety of ailments, but none prevent her from rustling up a good spread of grub. There is plentiful beef right from the ranch, served with all the

Covered with sagebrush, this antelope country is big and open.

necessary trimmings. Like cowhands, we all dig in around the big kitchen table, one guest getting up politely to make way for the next. I hang back, feeling the ugly stepchild on this begged hunt, but Ma is not having any of it. She brusquely moves a relative out of the way, a firm hand on the scruff of his neck, to make room for me at the table.

Sleep in the trailer is good, considering. An insistent knock on the door announces the approach of morning. It's Tom, summoning us to breakfast. The light of the coming dawn tints the eastern horizon as eggs and beef tenderloin sizzle on the stove in Ma's kitchen.

Breakfast done in fine fashion, we load into well-used pickups. I have never hunted with higher expectations, though indeed I hardly know what to expect. My knowledge of big-game hunting is about that of the average stroller through Central Park, although I have hunted small game for years. As we depart the ranch for the open fields of antelope country, several herds of the fleet creatures are visible in the distance. The plan is to drop off hunters at regular intervals to intercept the herds when they start moving. The Clyde boys know generally where the animals are prone to cross the patchwork of fences, so there is underlying order to the apparently haphazard deposition of hunters.

My assignment is to walk down a fence row and position myself for a possible shot. The sagebrush lofts its pungent scent as I step through.

There is abundant nutritious grass here as well, the heads thick and bowed low in the gentle breeze as if in prayer. The sun is rising well above the low hills to the east, and I remove my jacket before I have walked very far. I settle into a niche behind a large fence post to wait.

The breaks go to others this morning. A sizable herd passes within a quarter-mile, far outside the range of my rifle. Tan and white bodies streak across the sagebrush flats at the report of another hunter's weapon. I have seen animals run before, but not like this. I stand and reveal my position, staring in open-mouthed admiration as the speeding assemblage flows past, the smooth gait of the antelope giving the impression that wheels, not legs, are responsible for the fluid movement.

Shortly a pickup arrives to retrieve and reposition us. Two hunters have connected, neither taking a truly trophy animal. Tom's father, however, has taken a mule deer with massive horns that rise well above the sides of the pickup bed, a monster of an animal that makes me salivate with envy. But today I have a different tag to fill.

A change in location does me no good. Lunchtime comes and we return to the ranch house, where I inspect the harvested animals and admire the wonderful texture and color of their coats. Antelope hair is more coarse than I had imagined, almost like a pelage composed of bristles rather than hair. Mule deer hide has a much more familiar feel, thicker but otherwise similar to that of the white-tailed deer. I observe the technique for field-dressing and skinning the animals and hanging the meat. My schooling has begun in earnest, and I am an eager student. Before we enter the ranch house for lunch my arms are covered halfway to the elbows with the blood of hard work.

Afternoon comes, and I am now in a charming and remote little valley where antelope trails crisscross and converge like tree branches. I position myself behind a strategic boulder overlooking a crossing so that I can intercept any passing pronghorn. Tom cautions me to be wary of rattlers, and I check carefully before assuming my position.

The promontory is bare except for some low cacti. I prepare my rifle and wait, sighting in on the crossing repeatedly to be certain that I can do so without much movement. In the process I have my first entanglement with the awful prickly pear, garnering an elbow full of the penetrating spines as a warning against future carelessness. I remove the thorns, leaving the detachable tips in my flesh, where they will fester for weeks. One learns quickly that the inattentive pay a price in this harsh country.

The weather can be unpredictable in Wyoming in October. This week it is fairly hot, and there is no cloud cover. The burning sun drives me to seek shade behind the rock, though it is inadequate to protect me fully. Vehicles rumble in the distance, and an occasional gunshot breaks the stillness. Overall, the situation is pleasant enough. I have seen no antelope since lunch, so I find myself lulled into a sense of apathy; my full stomach and the warming sun make me sleepy. If this is antelope hunting, I like it, but I could stand more action. The closest I've been to a live antelope is several hundred yards.

Something is now changing about the character of the prairie, though I can hear no noise and the smells and view are the same. My muscles tighten and I strain my eyes to see, but I am uncertain exactly what is happening. For long moments nothing appears, and there is no sound except for the gentle rustle of the plains wind and the screech of a hawk overhead. I begin to relax once more and tell myself that all is quiet and peaceful. I almost close my eyes, but something compels me to maintain a hazy vigil.

Suddenly there is a movement on the top of the next hill, a telltale motion that is fluid and fleet. Antelope! The creature is not alone, either, for the horizon suddenly is filled with animals, all of them progressing in my direction. It is hard to maintain

Taping the antlers of a nice buck.

my wits—it appears they may run right over me. Squinting, I scan excitedly for a buck, while at the same time trying very hard to remain still. In a cloud of dust that reminds one of a cavalry charge, more than a dozen antelope—all does and fawns—thunder onward, approaching the fence that separates us. Moving at an acute angle they descend the sagebrush ridge to the lowest point in the valley, virtually a stone's throw from me. Fascinated but disappointed, I nervously finger the safety of my rifle.

One more animal is coming, and I see the upthrust of black horns towering skyward. It is a buck trailing in the beclouded path, materializing like a ghost out of the haze. This is a very good buck, one that more than meets my humble expectations. I fix my eyes on the animal as I crouch with my finger on the safety, and when I am certain of what I'm viewing, I flip it forward.

With my peripheral vision, I observe the does and fawns negotiating the barbed wire, each nimbly slipping under like a rabbit escaping a pen. The buck is last, and I now have him in my scope. It is tempting to shoot before he reaches the fence, but I will wait for him to get up after crossing, when he will be at his closest and moving at his slowest.

The buck is an expert at this game, I can tell. The horns go first, and in one fluid motion he is up on the near side. The agility of the masterful pronghorn is majestic. The buck is up and running before I can shoot, his pace almost as rapid as before he crossed. It's now or never. I place the cross hairs somewhere in the vicinity of the front shoulder and squeeze firmly on the trigger.

The thunder of hoofbeats fades into the distance as I look for my quarry among the fleeing band. Almost as if he were a phantom, a figment of my imagination, the buck has vanished. Bewildered, I look after the receding herd. Where is he? Completely baffled, I take several steps forward.

A small patch of white is visible at the bottom of the gully, and my eyes rivet on it. Could it be? Hope rises as I bolt forward and more of the animal becomes visible. It's a miracle, but he's down—and resoundingly out. There is no movement. The beautiful buck is piled up in the bottom of the gully, unmistakably dead.

The magnitude of my triumph is quickly apparent. The animal's horns are far superior to any of the others taken this morning. I kneel beside the fallen creature and survey the gorgeous coat, the tapering black horns, the fleet feet, and the tireless legs. I roll the buck over to see exactly where the bullet hit, there being no wound on the side I can see.

There it is. The neck has taken the full impact of the bullet, and there is a sizable hole. It doesn't say much for my marksmanship, but it was effective. I shudder to think that had the shot been off that much in some other direction I might have missed entirely—or far worse, I might have wounded the animal and lost him. I'm obviously going to have to work on trigger squeeze. My shotgun technique just won't work with a .30-06.

I hear the sound of an ancient engine as I dig in my pocket for my license. A rusty pickup bounces along the rutted range road, approaching slowly and with considerable noise. Soon I am being congratulated on the best buck of the day and on a terrific shot. I find I'm not able to swallow my pride and tell them that the shot was actually a miss. The cape is nearly ruined, a tragedy of the first order as far as I'm concerned, but somehow I just can't mention it. We skin out the animal for a shoulder mount. This will be my first mounted animal.

Nobody is the wiser. I got him, anyway. There are continuing congratulations over supper in the ranch house on a terrific neck shot at a running antelope. Someday, when things have settled down, I'll tell them the truth. But for today, I'm going to enjoy it. That old .30-06 sure shoots straight, all right. I can do a lot with a gun like that—if I can learn to put the bullet where I'm aiming, that is.

Rocky Mountain goat. (Photo: courtesy of Eric J. Hansen)

ROCKY MOUNTAIN GOAT

(Oreamnos americanus)

While among the herbless crags and awful precipices of those
dread mountain solitudes which it inhabits, and among which
it bounds fearless and sublime, where man can only creep and cling,
it is out of the nature of things that it can be captured easily.
It is not easy to see it, in the first place; and when seen,
to outclimb and circumvent it, must require that the
hunter should be every inch a man.

—Henry William Herbert, *Frank Forester's Field Sports*, 1849

There is only one animal I have ever hunted that, on completion of a successful quest, I swore I'd never hunt again. That animal is the mountain goat, a creature that inhabits such appalling terrain as to seem virtually unapproachable. I have backpacked into mountain goat country on four occasions seeking these intriguing ghosts of the vertical cliffs, three times on my earliest hunts in the back country of Washington State and later on a hunt in British Columbia. On each of those trips I found myself clinging to alders protruding from ground so steep that hand-over-hand was the order of the day. As often as not I would arrive in precarious places from which I thought I'd never return. Since that last expedition I have discovered that there are some mountain goats that reside in less intimidating topography, and with that in mind I have hesitantly entertained the idea of seeking out another one.

The Rocky Mountain goat is, in reality, neither native to the Rocky Mountains nor a true goat. They are more like the Old World chamois than anything else, and scientists believe them to be a type of antelope that adapted to specialized habitat. There are no fossil remains of mountain goats anywhere in the world except North America, though scientists are convinced that their ancestors almost certainly crossed the Bering Land Bridge during the Ice Age.

The mountain goat originally inhabited the steep mountains of only four U.S. states—Alaska, Washington, Idaho, and Montana—and four Canadian provinces and territories—British Columbia, Alberta, the Yukon, and the Mackenzie Mountains in the far western Northwest Territories. Unlike most native North American large mammals, its range has expanded considerably, the result of transplants—most of them planned but at least one of them in part accidental. The range in both Montana and Idaho has grown greatly, and in Alaska the animals have been liberated on several islands, most notably Kodiak, Chichagof, and Baranof. There are also huntable populations in Oregon, Wyoming, Utah, Colorado, and South Dakota. I have seen numerous mountain goats in the Absaroka Range of southern Montana, where the animals were introduced in 1956, on my trips there to hunt bighorn sheep.

A northern limit exists beyond which weather conditions and forage limitations prohibit the animal from surviving. There is terrain north of their historical range in which goats should be able to survive, but they appear not truly adapted for Arctic conditions, despite the thickness and length of their hair. Perhaps the insulating qualities of their coat are insufficient for prolonged subzero weather. The animals love to lie in the sun on a dizzying pinnacle, but in bad weather they seek shelter beneath rocky overhangs and in shallow caves.

There are approximately 100,000 mountain goats in British Columbia, perhaps two-thirds of the world's population. Figures show that about 1,000 are harvested in that province annually. There are perhaps 25,000 in Alaska, more than any other state or province besides British Columbia. The total of all other populations is probably no more than 25,000. Sport hunters harvest about 1 percent of the total population annually, a take that should have little or no effect on populations as a whole. In Colorado, 7 percent of the population is harvested each year, and the population remains stable.

The South Dakota population is the accidentally introduced one, although the animals were intentionally brought into the state initially. Early in the twentieth century, Peter Norbeck, senator from South Dakota, suggested to that state's game department that they consider introducing the creatures into Custer State Park. In 1924, four females and two males were imported from near Banff, Alberta. A number of the goats escaped from their enclosure and took refuge on nearby Harney Peak, where the terrain is apparently adequate for them. This population of mountain goats in the Black Hills has thrived and is now between 300 and 400 animals.

One transplanted population embroiled in controversy is the one on the Olympic Peninsula of Washington, where the animals were introduced in 1925 and again in 1928-29. The introduction seemed an ideal project, considering the proximity of the Cascade Mountains to the east, which are

Rocky Mountain goat. British Columbia, September 1986.

well known for their mountain goat populations. The National Park Service, however, believes the goats to be destroying certain plant species, and they are considering eradicating them as unwanted exotics.

While mountain goats love steep cliffs and are exceptionally adept at negotiating such terrain, they will live on more gentle slopes if rugged, vertical escape areas are nearby. The animals need an environment that offers a good source of food and water as well as nearby cliffs where they can escape predators. The billies are quite solitary except during the rut, while the nannies and kids tend to be more gregarious. During winter a female

with one or more kids usually inhabits a home range from which other goats are excluded. Females are dominant and will drive away any unwelcome billy that invades their territory.

Mountain goats are stocky, and both males and females have a pelage, which is solid white except for occasional dark hairs on the back, rump, and tail. Goats are the only big-game animal of the Lower Forty-eight that are typically solid white. The horns, hoofs, eyelids, nose, and lips, however, are black. The hair consists of two parts, the outer long guard hairs, which may reach eight inches or more and form a distinctive beard, hump, and leg chaps on both males and females, and the underfur, which is a thick, insulating wool that is more effective in dry cold than in rain. The hair sheds annually in the spring, usually starting in late April or early May, and from that time until midsummer goats take on an extremely ragged appearance. The loosening hair seems to be irritating to the animals, and they take considerable pains to rub and scratch it away. In goat country, it is not uncommon to come upon sizable accumulations of hair at rubbing stations such as rocks and trees.

Molting and the need to dislodge ectoparasites such as ticks cause goats to engage in "dusting" during this time of year, and in summer they like to roll in dry wallows and spread dirt over their bodies. After the molt, their coats return to a pristine white. By September, trophies are splendid and smooth, but the whole cycle does not finish until November, when the long guard hairs and thick underfur have matured once more. November trophies are the most spectacular specimens.

A mature male mountain goat may weigh up to 300 pounds, though that seems to be the exception. Female mountain goats average 40 to 60 pounds less than males. An adult animal will stand between 35 and 45 inches at the shoulder. In the wild they may live for fourteen years or more, with females living slightly longer than males.

The horns of any game species are of great interest to the hunter, and the mountain goat is no exception. Both sexes grow impressive black horns, the rudiments of which are present from birth. They may attain more than a foot in length on extraordinary specimens, with the nannies usually achieving the greatest lengths and the billies the most mass.

The horns begin growing soon after birth and continue to do so throughout the animal's life. They consist of an inner core of bony material covered by the dark epidermal sheath. The horns never shed, but they may break or be lost in falls or other accidents. The annual growth rings on the outer part of the horns are useful in determining the age of an individual goat, much like the rings on the horns of mountain sheep. The first ring appears during the animal's second winter, and one forms each subsequent year. Some scientists believe that the rings form in this fashion as a result of softening

of the horn by physiological processes during the rut; others attribute it to the stress of winter.

An experienced hunter can often tell a male from a female by horn configuration, but for the novice it's difficult. Billies typically have much broader bases to their horns, which taper gradually to the point. The nanny achieves most of its horn mass early in life, so the horn is the same thickness along its entire length. The horns of nannies are also more curved than the male's. My guides have always been able to differentiate between billies and nannies, but it hasn't been as obvious to me in most instances.

It is the hoofs, in conjunction with innate agility and leg strength, that allow the mountain goat to reign supreme in its vertical habitat. These remarkable structures are made of keratin, the substance of our own fingernails. They have a flexible cup-shaped underpad that extends slightly peripherally to the main hoof, allowing for excellent traction and mobility on precipitous terrain. The track created by the foot is like that of the mountain sheep, and differentiating the two can be quite difficult. The toes diverge slightly, giving them a V shape, with the point of the V directed to the rear. Unlike sheep, mountain goats often drag their feet and create marks on the ground between tracks, an effect most noticeable in snow. Depending on the size of the goat, the footprints are between one and a half and two and a half inches, sometimes a bit more.

The rut begins in mid-November and ends in early December. Until then billy goats are mostly solitary, though they may join in small bachelor groups that are loose in composition. When the rut begins they join the nannies for the mating ritual, at which time the males may fight for dominance and the attendant breeding rights. Battles can be mortal but are usually benign. When actual combat occurs, goats almost never clash their heads together. Rather, they stand beside one another and inflict damage to each other's flank and hindquarters, where thick skin prevents penetration to the vitals. The rump skin, which was used for centuries as chest armor by Alaskan Indian tribes, is almost an inch thick in places. This form of contention is much to the benefit of the goats, in view of their relatively fragile skull and thin facial skin.

Despite the protective flanks, such fights are hazardous, and most often threat displays and posturing are sufficient to establish dominance. Male goats dig rutting pits and wallow in the aromatic mixture of mud and their own urine, soiling their snowy coats and making them easily distinguishable from the nannies at this time of the year.

Female goats seldom leave their home range to find a mate. Males, however, may travel long distances in search of females. The females usually first breed at age five, although about a third do so a year earlier. Following a gestation period of 180 days, a kid weighing six to seven pounds is born. Most births occur between mid-May and mid-June. Twins are relatively frequent, occurring up to 30 percent of the time, although in some populations the rate is much lower (it is 2 percent in a recent study from Alberta). The wide gulf between these numbers may be more spurious than real, since a twin may succumb early to predation or accidents, or a nanny may appear to have twins when indeed one of the youngsters is that of another goat.

Young goats begin eating vegetation within days of birth, and they can run and climb when only hours old. Survival is about 60 percent for the first year and 52 percent for the first four years. Some young goats die in brutal falls, but most losses are the work of predators such as cougars, wolves, and grizzly bears. Coyotes and bobcats may be important predators in some areas. Golden eagles take some kids during the first few weeks of life. For obvious reasons, nannies select extraordinarily rough terrain for birthing.

Wolverines will occasionally take an adult goat. It is impressive that a 60-pound wolverine can take down a 250-pound goat. In some populations, wolf predation is significant. In one study, scientists documented a population of 75 goats entering the winter period only to find twelve goats and a pack of well-fed wolves in the spring. In that case deep snow limited the mobility of the goats, so that when they left the steep cliffs they were unable to return rapidly enough to escape the predators. This underscores the extreme importance of adequate escape cover for the survival of mountain goats. Most scientists believe that the mountain goat

does well in the coastal mountains of the American West because those areas are not rich in game species, which limits the number of wolves the region can sustain. In the Rocky Mountains there are many more game species and also many more predators, making the mountain goat more vulnerable overall. Mountain goats can thrive in the presence of a healthy wolf population only in areas where escape terrain is close to good sources of food.

The food preferences of mountain goats, like those of most ungulates, vary seasonally. They are largely grazers, and as a rule they move on naturally before overgrazing. They eat mainly grasses and sedges such as tufted hairgrass and sheep fescue, supplemented heavily in the summer with various forbs and leafy shrubs. Mountain goats are the only North American big-game animal other than caribou that can digest lichens, though thinhorn sheep sometimes eat them too. Neither mountain goats nor thinhorn sheep have a preference for lichens, however. When the snow is not too deep, grasses remain the preferred food, but if there is plentiful accumulation of snow, goats readily switch to browsing shrubs. They also will not hesitate to eat conifers if those are all that is available, as sometimes occurs in winter.

Overall, mountain goats are healthy as a species, infections and infestations not being a prominent management factor. Mountain goats can harbor a variety of intestinal parasites, however, mainly relatively benign roundworms, and they are also susceptible to lungworm. About two-thirds of the mountain goats introduced into South Dakota suffer this latter infestation, probably because those goats range farther south, where a variety of environmental factors favor invasion by parasites.

Like wild sheep, goats are susceptible to contagious ecthyma, which causes sores and scabs around the mouth and elsewhere. Ecthyma most often affects young goats, and in severe cases it can be fatal. It is believed to originate from contact with domestic animals, although it has been reported in Kootenay National Park of British Columbia, where no such exposure exists. Other diseases occasionally reported are "lumpy jaw" and paratuberculosis. A dietary abnormality known

The majestic goat mountain on the Turnagain River.

as white muscle disease also sometimes occurs, thought to result from high levels of sulfur in the diet. The sulfur competes with selenium for absorption in the intestines, and the animals thus become selenium deficient, making them highly susceptible to the consequences of stress.

Some goats die from falls. On my own successful goat hunt we saw a dead goat at the bottom of a chasm. The animal probably died from the fall, though we were unable to get close enough to be sure.

Where terrain is reasonably accessible, mountain goats are quite sensitive to overharvest. There they are conspicuous (despite the opening quotation from Henry William Herbert), and they do not readily flee from hunters the way deer or elk do. Moreover, there is no legal requirement to harvest only males, although I believe that the ethical hunter should make every possible effort to do so. Goats may concentrate at mineral licks, and when hunters find and exploit such areas the impact on the population may be significant.

Hunting techniques are simple, though unavoidably difficult. It is better to try to get above

mountain goats whenever possible—something that is often hopeless. Owen Wister stated rightfully, "These animals watch the valley. There is no use attempting to hunt them from there. Their eyes are watchful and keen, and the chances are that if you are working up from below . . . ten minutes will be enough for him to put a good many hours of climbing between himself and you." They will watch you and frequently move up and away with your approach. Surprisingly often, however, you can stay out of sight enough to get within range, and they will stay put. Perhaps their natural curiosity overcomes their fears (which seem to be few). I have been within easy range of quite a few mountain goats while sheep hunting, and the animals seemed to know that I was no threat.

It is understatement to say that you must be in good physical shape to hunt these creatures. One writer advises that a person be able to run five miles without stopping before attempting the climb for a mountain goat, but I would suggest you be able to run five miles three times a week, and put in thirty minutes of stair climbing as well.

When I was preparing to hunt mountain game, I wore a forty-pound backpack while stair climbing. It may not be necessary to go to that extreme, but you will certainly want to be in good shape.

Do not attempt a mountain goat hunt if acrophobia is a problem. You will almost certainly find yourself only a short step from eternity, and quite often you may be there for some time. I know of no solution to that difficulty, except perhaps to try to find a place with more accessible goats. There are certainly a few of those around, so if steep drop-offs bother you, mention it to your outfitter.

The very best in leather climbing boots, with the very best soles, are essential. Sticking to a slippery rock instead of sliding off can make the difference between life and death in goat country. I like tough, durable Patagonia climbing pants with suspenders for most high-mountain hunting. Camouflage clothing is unnecessary in pursuing mountain goats, so I wear colorful chamois or cotton shirts because they make better pictures. Survival supplies, such as a space-blanket sleeping bag, matches, a candle, and extra chocolate bars, will come in handy in emergencies.

I had not assembled my sheep-hunting pack the last time I hunted mountain goats, but it is ideal for a mountain goat excursion. My old blue pack features a rubber-sleeved metal hook attached to the internal frame for the rifle, and a huge interior cargo space that ensures that I won't have to ascend to my goat twice to get it all off the mountain. Always include a couple of roomy plastic bags in your pack.

The .30-06 is very adequate for mountain goats. I used handloads of 150-grain Nosler Partition bullets, which were effective for long-range shooting. A rifle of .270 caliber is very good and shoots a bit flatter. I'd stay away from anything less than that, because mountain goats are far tougher to kill than mountain sheep and can absorb a lot without going down. Worse, they may escape to inaccessible or extremely dangerous terrain and die beyond the reach of anyone without the climbing skills of Sir Edmund Hillary. You don't want to be rock climbing (or vertical ice skating) without proper equipment, so make certain your goat is in an accessible place and then do your best to anchor it there with a well-placed shot.

All access to the area is by float plane or a very long horseback ride.

I didn't do that on my goat hunt, but maybe I'll get another chance someday.

MASTER OF THE VERTICAL

A vertical cliff stands just to our north, a frightening mountain carved by innumerable bottomless ravines. Rock slides threaten to cascade down the throat of seemingly endless granite chutes. Countless plunging rivulets fall from the face, and a chill courses my spine as I gaze at that awful peak.

My young Indian guide misreads my apprehension as mere concern over finding the right billy. We are sitting on a sandy beach alongside the Turnagain River, leaning back against a driftwood log and peering through a spotting scope. He speaks with only a hint of Dene dialect.

"Don't worry. We'll find what you're looking for."

Kevin Franks is no prophet, but he has a reputation as a pretty good sheep and goat guide. We are ten miles upstream from our main camp, and a hundred miles south of the jumping-off place, Watson Lake, Yukon. We are hunting in the Cassiar Mountains of northern British Columbia for the most underrated trophy in North America—the Rocky Mountain goat.

"I can't understand it. There must have been thirty goats on this mountain just two weeks ago. Took a nine-incher right up there," Kevin says, motioning toward a steep canyon that looks frankly terrifying.

"It's pretty warm for a goat, I guess," I say quietly, awe probably showing in each word as I take in the view. "Maybe they're all lying in the shade."

"Could be. They should be up by now, though." The chill of a superb September morning causes me to shiver and draw my down jacket closer. The sun has just edged over the horizon.

We left camp this morning in a small open johnboat just as day was breaking, and Kevin expertly piloted the craft upriver to our present location, the journey consuming about an hour. Our trip, over crystal-clear river waters, took us through some of the most fantastic wilderness scenery in North America, with towering snowcapped peaks on all sides. Feeder streams pour into the main body at intervals. There are whitewater rapids to negotiate, and the surging current conceals treacherous rocks.

The fall colors are already in full blaze, and as the sun creeps higher the flaming mountainsides are a sight to behold. Reds and golds color the alpine brush, with bright yellow poplars farther down the slope. Deep green dominates the so-called shintangle of willow and dwarf juniper; likewise the pines of the lower slopes. Ice cream cone peaks gleam brilliant white with dark granite shoulders, and all contrasts with the deep cloudless blue of the heavens. This is a great day to be alive!

My attention snaps back from the Creator's handiwork to goat hunting. I was told there is a nice billy up there somewhere, but an hour of diligent glassing fails to reveal his location. I am in no hurry, though, for a variety of reasons: the sandbar is now warming with the rising sun, we are comfortably situated, and it is the first day of my goat hunt. Also, I don't particularly look forward to scaling that imposing face.

Several hours of intensive glassing are unproductive of anything but a few nannies and kids, whose presence proves that goats do, indeed, inhabit this vertical ground. I ask Kevin about climbing a bit for a different perspective.

"No way," he replies. "When we see him, we get him. I don't climb this mountain but once more this year."

I'm silently glad, because the comfort of the present situation is enticing. We can also fish here for Dolly Varden trout for supper if our quarry doesn't show.

As late afternoon approaches, we abandon our quest. Goats are fairly predictable in their location, but this time we are simply unable to locate the one we want. He could be on the backside of the mountain, or he could have simply changed country since Kevin was last here. Heading back downriver, we tangle with the feisty trout that inhabit these waters. A delicious meal is ours for the taking.

Back at the main camp, where outfitter Kirby Funnell deposited me earlier, we reconsider our options. There are several goat hot spots in the area, but all have already been checked this year.

"Tomorrow we try another place," Kevin concludes after our deliberation. "That area isn't the only place to hunt goats. We'll get one."

There is a place he has been itching to try, but it requires a six-hour pack-in from our present camp. It's called Cy Lake, and it is even higher and deeper in the wilderness. Tomorrow we will prepare the pack boxes and the horses and head out. I dread the long ride, because six hours on horseback seems twice as long to me.

The sun is blazing by the time we depart the roaring Turnagain River for our fly camp, and despite the biting insects I strip to my undershirt to keep cool. While the scenery is no less spectacular here, the insects are much more aggressive, the ride is rougher, and the willows grow ever deeper as we travel. In places the swarms of bugs stirred by our passing make life miserable for both man and beast.

The worst, however, is the frequent bogs, where water seeps incessantly from the thawed ground

Glassing for goats.

in search of drainage to a lower elevation. In several places I am forced to hold onto the saddle horn like a dude as my mount founders in the deep muck. One beaver dam we cross is so treacherous that my horse plunges into the deep water and swims to make landfall. My pants are soaked almost to the crotch, but I breathe a sigh of relief that I have been able to stay mounted. My saddle scabbard is almost completely soaked, but my rifle seems otherwise unscathed.

Our six hours have stretched into a bone-tiring eight, and as we set up camp I am near exhaustion. I understand now why cowboys sang songs about reaching the end of the long trail. I will sleep well tonight.

There is a tent frame at Cy Lake, but it is small; we elect to use it only as a kitchen. We will sleep under a "fly tent," a first for me. One long pole angles from the ground up to a nearby tree, serving as the essential backbone. A large piece of canvas goes over the pole and is held in place by ropes stretched tight to four firm stakes, creating a sleeping space that is open on all four sides. Despite the inherent draftiness it is actually quite cozy, since one end is close to the ground.

After supper I witness a panoramic view of the aurora borealis, the enchanting dance of light across the heavens. I am thankful that the long ride is behind us and that I can enjoy such bounty and blessing. Sleep comes easily.

Ominous dark clouds fill the sky the next day as we prepare to depart camp for the nearby goat mountain, some three miles away. The threat of rain soon materializes into a cold, wet reality, and the thick willows slap face and body with soaking moisture that pools between one's derrière and the saddle. Even the best of rain pants leak under those conditions.

A misty haze pervades the lofty site where we plan to hunt, reducing visibility to a few hundred yards. We ride the horses as high as practicable and tether them to a couple of evergreen trees, as protected from the weather as possible. We now must walk in, a couple of miles and a couple of thousand vertical feet, by my estimation. The rocks are crumbled and layered, with that consistency of rotten shale that goats seem to prefer.

The frigid rain is light but relentless, and finding our way to the top of the ridge is quite a task. Despite the obstacles, we eventually reach the top. Visibility continues to decline as a thick fog rolls over us, tantalizing us with occasional clear views of the long hogback. The ragged ceiling lifts at one point to reveal a nearby band of Stone ewes and lambs that peer at us through the fog before retreating over the next ridge. We also spot a crispy-fresh grizzly track, a decent-size bruin by the width of the paw.

We have attained the highest terrain, and now we are glassing in search of our quarry. The long ridge runs roughly to the west, descending slowly. There are numerous pockets where goats can hide, and droppings are everywhere.

At last we find a nanny and a kid, so close in the fog below us that we could easily cast a stone at them. They are standing on a hump of solid ground in the center of a collapsing slide that drops like a plumb line in every direction. The female has true trophy horns of better than ten inches, by Kevin's estimate. We back away from the edge and leave them undisturbed. It's just as well it isn't a billy, since we could never have extracted him from the plunging shale slope.

There is heavy timber off one side of the ridge, and we figure that the billies are hiding in the dense forest. Disappointed and soaked to the skin, we turn back toward the horses, the configuration of the mountain requiring that we climb considerably before we can descend to them. The fog grows ever thicker, and I am disoriented in the confusing and irregular terrain. We are truly in a whiteout now, and I wonder if we can locate our objective. Even Kevin appears confounded to a degree. I am becoming very tired, although not exhausted, and I wonder about the possibility of hypothermia.

We expend more than an hour cruising the ridge, seeking the place where we ascended from the horses. The landmarks are repetitive and uncertain, a large boulder here, a scattering of small trees there. If we descend in the wrong place we could miss our mounts and find ourselves spending the night without food or shelter.

I have been in a few tight spots in my hunting career, most of them due to weather and terrain. We now find ourselves facing some of the worst of both, and the unyielding fog seems determined not to release its grip on us. I sense a hint of despair in my young companion, though he is brave and determined. I have a well of strength outside myself, and in that trying moment I lift a silent prayer to God to give us the direction we need. I make mention of my prayer to Kevin, and even as I speak the fog lifts briefly as if by some giant hand. Visibility is superb for the moment, and we are easily able to see the horses waiting serenely a half-mile below. Then, as quickly as it lifted, the fog descends, obscuring even Kevin. But the descent to the horses is uneventful, and my young friend and I are silent in thought.

By the time we arrive in camp I am shivering from the damp of the cold rain plus several hours of my own sweat. We start a fire in the shepherd's stove in our kitchen, a most welcome warmth, and soon I am in dry clothes and comfortably enjoying a meal of canned moose meat. Thank God for blessings large and small.

We awake after a restful night under our fly tent to find that two inches of heavy, wet snow have fallen overnight. There is continuing precipitation as well—spitting snow mixed with rain. We figure that the goats will probably stay sheltered in the timber, and it seems foolhardy to venture out. We elect to stay in camp and hope for a break in the weather.

There is always some joy to be found, even in sharing close quarters with a guy half your age on a rainy day. Kevin is a skilled craftsman in many ways, and solely for my entertainment he constructs an old Indian puzzle using a piece of rope and two pieces of wood. I find it challenging, and some hours into the long day, while he constructs new halters for the horses, I hit upon the solution. Kevin grins as he concedes that I might be pretty smart for a white man.

By nightfall the rain and snow have stopped, and there are tentative breaks in the overcast. I am well rested now. Tomorrow we will return to the mountain.

We park our horses in the same spot, and I marvel at the change in the view. The whole mountain range now spreads out before us. The climb to the ridgetop is no less fatiguing, but it seems easier without the heavy rain gear. In only an hour we are on the gently inclined summit. Now, however, there are eight inches of fresh snow on the ground.

Despite all our trouble, there are no decent billies here. We spot a small band of Stone rams and perform a mock stalk on them, getting incredibly close before they lunge down the mountain. Sometimes even sheep will go downhill if they spot you above them.

The long ride back to camp is tainted with discouragement. The weather is now beautiful, and the melting snow gives a nice contrast to the fall colors. But I am here to take a mountain goat. We decide over supper to pack back out to the main camp on the river and try again from there.

A few days later I am standing beside the tumbling Turnagain River, gazing upward at the same cliffs that so intimidated me a week ago. I had hoped to avoid climbing this particular

Goat camp high in the mountains.

mountain, but it increasingly appears that it is here or nowhere that I will succeed. Goats are now visible in abundance, including a couple of promising billies near the summit. The loners are usually billies, and the ones we see through the spotting scope appear to be dandies. We are too far away to be sure, though. We must work our way closer through dense poplar and spruce forest, wending slightly uphill for a half-mile or more until we can see better. The spotting scope reveals what I had both hoped and feared: we must climb.

The big timber ceases where the cliff begins, and brush-covered rock looms ahead. The climb is arduous, and only the spindly alders provide handholds as we move from ledge to ledge. As firm anchors among the sparse vegetation become infrequent, I am increasingly aware of just how close to death the mountain goat lives. After a couple of hours of uninterrupted climbing, looking down from any vantage point is dizzying.

Now we are truly in goat country. A nanny and kid stare at us across an unbreachable chasm, hardly any fear evident as they amble lazily out of sight. Two young billies lounge on a rocky outcrop not far above them, and the spotting scope confirms that they are not what we seek. Ever higher now my aching legs take me, and I stop frequently to allow my surging chest to catch up.

We have now climbed for four hours, and the top of the mountain seems to be ever receding from our sight. Each new shelf reveals only another above it. I question Kevin about how much farther we must climb, showing my inexperience. He can't possibly know, because these mountains don't have tops, and the goats don't stay put. "Not much farther" is of little comfort. Glancing back toward the river during a brief rest, I can see our boat beside the Turnagain, over a mile off. The silver thread of the river disappears near the horizon to our east.

We reach the six-hour mark, and my legs are feeling every minute of it. I am beginning to wonder how anyone ever takes a mature billy. Just as my melancholy mind-set begins, though, Kevin motions me to get down. He's seen something ahead, and up here it is obviously a goat. Nothing else in God's creation would be on these dreadful cliffs—except a crazy hunter.

"There are our billies," he says quietly, pointing across a gigantic ravine. I see two white spots, immobile and distant, each on a jutting promontory. They are a hundred yards apart, and either oblivious to or unconcerned about our presence. I judge the distance to be over four hundred yards.

To get within reasonable range, we must move laterally a couple of hundred yards, not an easy task in this perpendicular terrain. In closing the distance we cross several of the perilous gullies we saw from below, each filled with loose rock that tumbles downhill with every step, giving one the uneasy feeling of being part of an impending avalanche. Kevin seems to be in his element, however, and shows no fear, moving like an agile gazelle. He occasionally looks back to see how I'm doing. I keep up, with some difficulty.

Three hundred yards from our goat, we stop to assess the situation. I look through my riflescope, and the shot still looks too long. This is as close as we can get from this approach, though, because another monstrous gulch blocks our way, and our quarry is on the far rim. So I remove my pack to use it as a rest and take my time getting ready to squeeze off the shot. When the round explodes, the animal leaps to his feet and disappears. I know immediately I have connected by the resounding smack of the bullet, but I quickly squeeze off another round at the receding figure.

"You hit him too far back," observes Kevin, dissatisfaction in his voice. "Let's work our way over there."

The approach to the wounded goat is an acrophobic's nightmare. The gully we must cross leaves us no option but to tempt fate, to put ourselves truly in the hands of God. Each side of the vertical gorge is a cliff unto itself, complete with precarious rocky ramparts and horrendous drops of 500 feet or more. I manage to make it to the bottom alive, only to be entrapped in another shifting shaft of vertically stacked rock, the worst yet. In attempting to attain the other side, I find myself on a narrow granite shelf about a foot wide with nothing but air below me for hundreds of feet. Kevin is as nimble as any squirrel, and he leaps up to the next ledge, utterly heedless of danger.

"Give me your pack and rifle!" he commands. As I readily comply, I say another of my frequent inaudible prayers. I try never to bargain with God, but in this circumstance I am sorely tempted.

I have never before had an experience like this. Kevin extends his hand and offers to pull me up, the alternative being to stay on the stone wall for the rest of my life. I must relinquish my steel-trap grip on the crumbly rock and depend entirely on an Indian boy's arm. *God help me!*

With nothing but air and rock below and a firm helping hand above, I scramble upward to relative safety beside my guide. He grins as though this is great fun and hands me my pack and rifle. Soon we are above my goat, which is sprawled on a grassy shelf some forty yards below, wounded but still alive.

"I'll have to shoot him again, I guess."

"He'll jump," says Kevin matter-of-factly, suggesting that he has been in this situation before.

I survey the endless expanse of stratosphere on the other side of the animal, wondering if Kevin is right, and what such a fall might do to the animal. The pelt and horns could be ruined, as well as the meat.

Look closely and see the beauty all around you.

"What if I break his neck?"

"He'll jump. Too bad we can't get a rope on him."

I contemplate my alternatives. Nothing comes to mind except another shot. I carefully place the cross hairs just in front of the shoulders, hoping to anchor the creature in place. Perhaps the width of the resting place will contain him, since he is several feet from the drop-off.

At the report, the goat leaps into the broad abyss, doing a series of barrel rolls that would make a mourning dove envious. Quickly he is out of sight.

"He jumped!" I gasp.

"I know."

Down we climb off the face of the cliff, moving carefully from ledge to ledge. In my

A long horseback ride puts us in new country and brings us back out.

mind are visions of a ruined animal, an outcome I had hoped to avoid. Every hundred feet or so there is telltale blood or hair where the descending goat has bounced. Perhaps a thousand vertical feet from my last shot, we find him. I breathe a sigh of relief that the animal is still intact and little the worse for the experience, except that one horn is dislocated; fortunately, it is still attached.

Pictures, caping for a full body mount, and quartering the animal consume a couple hours. Descending with heavy packs is not quite as precarious—though it is more laborious—than

what we have already endured. Somehow we reach a little deeper when we must, and I am able to make it back to the boat, weary but fulfilled. I now fully appreciate why my guide was reluctant to climb this mountain unless it was necessary.

While I was hanging by one hand over eternity, I promised myself I wouldn't do any more goat hunting. Now that I've returned to earth the issue isn't so certain. I'm glad I didn't do any bargaining with God over it. I may hunt goats again someday, but before I go I'll do lots of physical exercise to strengthen my grip and a lot of spiritual exercise to strengthen my faith.

Plains bison. (Photo from the author's collection)

PLAINS BISON
(Bison bison bison)

On the last day of September, 1871, I joined my regiment,
then in camp near Fort Hays, Kansas. . . .
We broke camp and took up our line of march to the west.
As evening came on, small groups of buffalo were seen dotting the plain.
At sunrise we saw hundreds. From the higher points of our route,
when the horizon was distant from ten to twenty miles,
hundreds of thousands were visible at the same instant . . .
spread out with great regularity over the entire face of the land.
For six days we continued our way through this enormous herd. . . .
It is impossible to approximate the millions that composed it.

—George S. Anderson,
American Big Game Hunting, 1901

The stunning spectacle of immeasurable herds of bison was common in the West before the invasion of the white man. The end of the War Between the States, a mighty U.S. military with no further objective to pursue, the construction of railroads and telegraph lines, and an increasing demand for land by restless settlers all placed the noble and proud Native Americans of the Great Plains squarely in the way of the encroachments of civilization. The bison were the Indians' principal game animal and the source of much of their strength, and by all accounts the creatures were as innumerable as the stars of a clear prairie night. Trains were halted by the measureless herds, for waiting out the bison was the most prudent course of action for locomotive drivers. Attempts at ignoring them as often as not ended in derailment.

That state of affairs didn't last long. Slaughter of the plains bison by the white man obliterated the species from the American West with astounding rapidity, and in the process annihilated virtually the whole culture of the Plains Indian. Some bison were shot for their hides and tongues, but many were slaughtered simply for the perverse pleasure of killing. Much of that shooting was done from moving railroad trains, so making any use of the felled beasts was not even remotely possible. For centuries the Native American had depended on the meat, hides, bone, and sinew of the bison. When that bounty vanished, so likewise did the Indian's ability to resist the federal government's policy of expansion, our "Manifest Destiny."

By 1889 there were only 541 living bison within the boundaries of the United States. Some of the greatest conservationists of all time, men of vision and determination like William T. Hornaday, united to save the remaining "buffalo." As a result of a continued conservation effort, today there are some 200,000 plains bison in the United States and Canada. True free-ranging herds are unusual in the Lower Forty-eight, primarily because the creatures refuse to pay much attention to man's flimsy barbed wire obstacles. Yellowstone National Park has a herd of unrestricted plains bison, as do the Henry Mountains of Utah. In Canada and Alaska, several herds thrive and roam free.

In most other locations and with all private herds, barricades are necessary to prevent the animals from roaming. In fact, the annual bison pilgrimage to wintering grounds on private property outside the confines of Yellowstone Park is an ongoing problem. A high percentage of the animals in the park are infested with brucellosis and therefore pose a very real threat to cattle. During a recent winter almost one-third of the herd had to be destroyed by government agents for trespassing. That is not only bad for the bison but is terrible publicity for the agencies involved and provides bothersome ammunition for the animal rights fringe.

In Custer State Park, South Dakota, a disease-free herd of some 1,000 animals subsists handsomely in a massive 71,000-acre enclosure. The area is highly typical habitat for the plains bison: an expanded transition zone where the endless prairies to the east blend with the ponderosa pine forests of the Black Hills. The park maintains the superlative herd of plains bison for aesthetic, public education, and scientific purposes, as well as to provide an economic base for park operations. There is also an ongoing program of genetic research on the bison. Sales of excess bison stock to outside interests account for about 20 percent of Custer State Park's revenues, almost $1 million annually in recent years.

Plains bison once ranged from the Appalachian Mountains as far north as New York and as far south as Georgia, westward to the Rocky Mountains and all states in between. The southern extent of their range was in northern Mexico, and to the north they extended into upper Manitoba, Saskatchewan, and Alberta, where they intergraded with the wood bison, which inhabits forested meadowland. This latter subspecies was originally a nonmigratory animal that rutted to the north of the region between the Saskatchewan and Athabasca Rivers in Alberta; the rutting area of the migratory plains bison was on the Great Plains to the south.

The North American bison is not actually a buffalo. True buffalo don't exist in North America, and hunters, who are more aware of the true buffalo, should lead the way in clarifying that fact. The larger head and neck and the prominent hump, as well as the long, thick hair, serve to distinguish bison from buffalo. Also, a genuine buffalo has thirteen pairs of ribs, whereas our bison have fourteen. There is an Old World bison, the closely related wisent of Eurasia. Extinction once stalked that creature as well, but now they are protected, secure, and thriving.

An especially large bull bison may weigh as much as 3,000 pounds, although 2,000 pounds is a much more common number. Cows seldom weigh more than 1,100 pounds. The hair is dark brownish-black in front and fades to a lighter brown toward the rump. The head, neck, and hump have much longer hair than the rearward portions, and there are even longer strands on the neck and chin, forming a rather attractive and distinctive beard. A big bull may stand six feet high at the shoulders and span more than twelve feet from nose to tail.

Bison are sexually mature as yearlings, though most cows breed at two years of age. Young bulls are capable of breeding in their second summer (when fifteen to sixteen months old), but in free-ranging herds most mating is the work of dominant bulls five to nine years old. After that age they decline significantly in productivity, though they may live for twenty years or more (and sometimes much longer in captivity). The rut for plains bison is from July to October, although the peak is usually in late July and August in most areas. The animals wallow year-round but do so especially during the rut, and, like many other ungulates, bulls may urinate in the disturbed soil to advertise their presence and availability.

During the rut the animals aggregate into larger herds. Dominant bulls tend to stay close to the cows they are tending. When two dominant bulls challenge one another over the same cow, brutal fights often break out, frequently characterized by a preliminary roar, aggressive pushing, and vicious hooking of the horns. Occasionally a bull will expose a flank, and the conflict can turn fatal. The great horns can easily penetrate the abdominal cavity, shoulder, neck, or lungs of an adversary, producing a wound that can lead to lethal infection.

Bison are capable of making innumerable grunting, snorting, and bleating sounds at any time of the year. A prominent and unforgettable feature of the rut is the bull bison's "roar," a lionlike noise that is audible for up to five miles on a still day. Bulls may roar while tending cows, when a rival is encountered, or sometimes simply in answer to a similar call by another bull.

Cows leave the main herd to give birth to a single calf, which can be born anytime from April through August. They produce an average of two calves every three years in unmanaged free-ranging herds, although in more ideal conditions, such as Custer State Park, the annual weaning rate for cows three years old is often above 90 percent. Gestation averages between 270 and 300 days. Calving in most areas peaks in May, tending to be later the farther north the animal lives. The calf is a light reddish-brown, usually weighing thirty-five pounds. Twins are uncommon, and albinos are so rare that Plains Indians believed their advent to hold special prophetic and religious significance.

Newborn calves can soon stand and walk, and within a couple of hours they can run with the herd. Both bulls and cows will come to the aid of a calf threatened by predators, chief among which even today is the wolf in the more northerly parts of the bison's range. Wolves are proficient at attacking even large bison, although they have a preference for calves and very old adult males.

Consummate grazers, bison digest and utilize the native grasses of the American West more efficiently than domestic cattle. They also eat sedges, and 10 percent of their diet comes from browsing on forbs (annual broadleafs). In a desert environment like the IIcnry Mountains of Utah, such browse is a larger percentage of their total intake. Although bison compete with cattle for food, they tend to graze steeper slopes than cattle. Also unlike cattle, bison show a natural tendency to vacate an area rather than overgraze it.

Emblem of Custer State Park.

Bison were an integral part of the original prairie ecosystem. They helped maintain the shortgrass prairie, both by scarifying the soil and by enriching it with their copious droppings. The animals tend to graze selectively on those species of prairie grass that thrive best when cropped, and they hinder the encroachment of woodland into the open prairie by damaging trees that attempt to grow there—either by rubbing against them or by using their horns.

Bison are the dominant ungulate in almost all situations where they coexist with other ungulates. Even a healthy bison calf demonstrates dominance over mature elk, and mule deer and antelope give the bigger creatures a wide berth.

What is a great bison trophy? In my opinion it is an ancient bull with massive horns, its muzzle grizzled from fighting and the tips of its horns blunted or broomed. Very old horns have an impressive buildup of annuli at the base. A truly old bull will develop a whitish film on its horns that is not present in younger bulls and cannot be polished out without damaging the structure. Such an animal meets my definition of a genuine trophy.

Bison are generally not spooked by loud noises such as a rifle report, and therefore a "buffalo stand" could sometimes allow a single rifleman to wipe out an entire herd. Such carnage is today anathema, but at one time it was an honored occupation, inspiring many a romantic Wild West tale in the dime novels of the day. Entrepreneurs like Buffalo Bill Cody made fortunes portraying for the crowds back East buffalo hunting and other activities of the Wild West.

In the days when the Plains Indians ruled the West, hunting bison no doubt was arduous, especially before the advent of horses and modern firearms. Native American hunters developed intricate techniques for driving frenzied herds over cliffs, and such "buffalo jumps" are still littered with the bones of unlucky bison.

Today, we can hunt bison with a minimum of specialized gear, though many historically minded hunters opt for buckskins and muzzleloaders (or breechcloth and bow). Just keep in mind that temperatures in most present-day bison ranges can be extremely frigid. Hunting on the Great Plains in December or January may be occasion for the best in cold weather gear, and there may be extensive walking before you locate a good, mature bull.

Any firearm capable of delivering a healthy punch will kill a bison. Getting close is usually not a problem, although hunters report that the herds in northern British Columbia, northern Alberta, and the Henry Mountains of Utah are quite unapproachable if they sense your presence. Even in Custer State Park, where my hunt took place, I had to make a true stalk to get a one-shot kill.

I remember a successful fund drive in Albany, Georgia, long ago, to acquire a single bison for the local zoo. Children were urged to donate their "buffalo nickels" toward the purchase, and it was indeed a thrill for me to gaze upon the buffalo, the fruit of that labor of love. There were reportedly some four thousand bison in the world on the day I admired the shaggy beast. Just to see a living legend was a moving experience.

Bison hunting was not an option in those days. Today it ranks near the low end of the big-game spectrum—but only when it comes to its cost. In terms of history, depth of feeling, and a sense of attachment to the hunted animal and its habitat, bison hunting is still one of the high points of any sportsman's career. All big-game hunters should do it at least once.

PRIDE OF THE BLACK HILLS

Looking out over the undulating ponderosa pine forest, I can see dark woods stretching up to a massive deadfall. In 1988, a wildfire here created thousands of acres of arboreal graveyard.

I am hunting plains bison in Custer State Park, South Dakota, with Vern Ekstrom, park ranger and manager of the resident bison herd. My woolens are too warm, and I am heating up despite the cold temperatures. My pac boots are out of place, too. It is the day before the winter solstice, so there should be plenty of snow by now. Another miscalculation.

The Yellowstone Park fires of 1989 struck here the year before, and young pines and brushy vegetation are virtually everywhere—a bonanza for the park animals. Quality forage resulting from the blaze has led to an explosion of the ungulate population in the park, so much so that hunting is a virtual necessity for certain species, including elk. Unhindered by the near-lunatic aversion to sport hunting that pervades our national park system, the much more pragmatic state of South Dakota allows Custer State Park to hold hunts as necessary to manage populations.

The park is hardly pristine, and everywhere is evidence of man's intrusion. Before the birth of the park this was ranchland, so two-track roads, fences,

Stalking close in the fog and snow.

Loading the kill onto the truck for the ride to the processing plant.

and a few buildings remain. Nonetheless it is beautiful beyond description, representing the rolling Black Hills at their best. The grass is knee deep, and during winter the brown tones contrast perfectly with the darker forested slopes. In the burned areas, the stark skeletons of dead trees stand like sentries. They slowly decay in the dry climate and then topple, making walking among them a chore.

The bison here are considered free ranging, and I am hopeful that we can locate the park giant, a massive twelve-year-old bull that Vern has sought unsuccessfully with eight hunters who preceded me. The bull is past prime and is a candidate for winterkill, or simply becoming so mean that he attacks the other, more peaceful bison. Every bull harvested is in this age classification, give or take a year or two. I would like to be the hunter blessed

with the privilege of taking the grand one. But I have only three days, and there are hundreds of bison and thousands of hiding places. Vern relates the tale of this particular bull and how elusive he is. No one has seen him since the bison season began, weeks earlier, the wise oldster having faded into the backcountry with the first frost.

The huge burned area is the favorite winter haunt of this particular bull. We spend several precious hours searching, and we actually find six bulls a mile off. We approach, climbing over fallen trees and working up a considerable sweat. To our great surprise, the big boy that has eluded Vern all season is the lead bull.

Unfortunately, Vern never allows a first-day kill. The first day is always for looking, and my rifle is safely stowed at park headquarters. We couldn't

Bison on the plains of South Dakota.

shoot the bull here, anyway, Vern advises, because it would take a heavy-lift helicopter to extract him from the impossible terrain. To boot, the meat inspector must check the animal on the hoof before we can take him. My heart sinks at the thought that by tomorrow he may be gone.

Photos are the order of the day, and I shoot a roll of film before we leave the group relatively undisturbed, hoping not to spook them deeper into the tangled deadfalls. I pray that they move in the opposite direction, so that I can take this impressive bull.

We ride with the windows down in the pickup as we look for other bulls. Around me is open prairie interspersed with patches of evergreens, and above a clear sky. As we drive we talk—about issues as basic as bison and as intangible as our life perspective. I discover that Vern shares my faith in Christ, and the bond of brotherhood is cemented under a backdrop of God's infinite creation.

Several younger bulls are mingled among huge groups of cows and calves. Two five-year-olds that Vern has christened "the Longhorns" already have headgear that would make the Boone

and Crockett record book. Some lucky hunter may have an opportunity to take a new world record in five to seven years.

Photo safari is not normally my game, but today it is the main event. A feisty white-tailed buck with five does, a virtual harem, poses willingly for my telephoto lens, his tall tines glistening in the late-morning sunshine. Elk are everywhere in the burned area but absent on the open prairie, where most of the cow bison are located. And antelope are plentiful, although the bucks have already shed the outer sheaths from their horns. They are nevertheless beautiful to watch and photograph.

While taking one spectacular shot of perhaps two hundred bison, I remark to Vern that the picture would have looked almost the same two hundred years ago, but for the contrails in the sky. At close range we hear the grunts of the animals, a sound more nearly like that of a pig than I had imagined. Bison stretch virtually to the blue horizon, grazing and lazing, calves frolicking and suckling. Watching them is like stepping back in time. I think of the early mountain men, and later the wagon trains of settlers moving west. Buffalo chips litter the ground, and buffalo wallows are everywhere, throwbacks to an epoch when tens of millions of bison ruled these plains.

As late afternoon approaches, I sense a shift in the weather, that creeping feeling of a change in the air and the appearance of the sky. A fog rises to the east, flows steadily in our direction, and soon engulfs us. We grope our way through the park now, relying on Vern's intimate knowledge of its geography. We have seen only one bull that is a taker, save one slightly younger bull with splintered horn tips.

We turn south, to a place near the park border where the fog is less dense and a ranger has reported seeing an eleven-year-old bull. No luck. There are bison on the next hillside, but they are mostly cows and calves. We climb for a closer look but don't find what we seek. Then, below us, two black spots emerge from the thinning fog, far up a dry creek bed.

"There are two down there," I call out to Vern.

"One looks good. Let's go down for a closer look."

One is indeed good: eleven years old, by Vern's estimate, with massive horns, one slightly shorter than the other, and a brilliant and luxurious winter coat unscathed by fighting. Vern is sure that he is not the bull we are seeking, but he is just as good. What's more, he is in a place where we should be able to find him tomorrow, if need be.

As darkness threatens, we drive through a heavily timbered draw into the park's fabulous bighorn sheep habitat. The bare knolls and steep cliffs are ideal for sheep, the terrain being reminiscent of areas I have hunted in Montana. We don't see any bighorns, however, and we move on. In the failing light we discover one more mature bison bull, which Vern believes to be a ten-year-old. We may not be able to find him again, because he is feeding along the edge of some of the thickest timber in the park. We nevertheless mark the spot, just in case we fail elsewhere tomorrow. Now it's time to call it a day.

Following a fabulous Mexican feast at Tortilla Flats in Custer, I find sleep a bit elusive. My stomach is too full of enchilada, and my head is too full of a massive bull bison on a deadfall-littered ridgetop. Will we be able to locate him two days in a row, despite the fact that the best buffalo man in the West couldn't find him on some twenty previous tries?

We plan to take a bull today, so Vern meets me at daybreak, an hour earlier than yesterday. The meat inspector is standing by with Park Superintendent Ron Walker, ready to come at our call. A light dusting of snow overnight has turned the park into a fairyland, and it's still snowing as we leave park headquarters. I will need my woolens and pac boots today. We cross the rushing creek with the locking hubs of the pickup engaged and start up through the big burn, passing a young bison bull.

We retrace yesterday's route. The black snags that dominate the burn are today outlined with a frosty rim of snow. To my disappointment, the area where yesterday we saw the group of bison is now deserted. Again we pass numerous elk, as well as mule deer. They look at us inquisitively before warily moving off. My bull is somewhere deep in that impenetrable black and white forest.

Several huge vistas open up, but none with bison. Vern is on the radio with Ron, telling him that we may be heading south to seek our second-choice bull. "The old boy is too smart for us again," I hear him say with frustration in his voice.

But I'll probably still take a good animal, I console myself. The fog could be a problem, but at least it isn't pea soup. We should be able to locate the other bull.

"Vern, look! Bison!" I almost shout, as several dark shapes materialize out of the haze ahead.

"I see them. Maybe he's there. They're in a good place, if he is." A look through his binoculars confirms in an instant what I have been hoping. He's the big male.

We descend from the vehicle after a quick call to headquarters and maneuver ourselves into position above the bison, getting between them and the impossible burn. They are feeding on the edge of dark, unscathed timber and start wandering as soon as they become aware of our presence. We move with them, trying to keep up, awaiting the meat inspector. Soon I spot an approaching park vehicle, and a man quickly descends to assess the animals. He is satisfied that they are healthy, and I have the OK to shoot.

In the park, bison are harvested with a shot to the head, a humane and painless placement of the

Plains bison. South Dakota, December 1995.

bullet that wastes no meat. The target is four inches behind and two inches below the base of the horn, and the preferred impact zone is six inches in diameter—about the size of a grapefruit. Achieving that compassionate and certain kill is sometimes harder than it looks, and every year a few hunters require multiple shots to down their buffalo. I am determined to use only the one 200-grain Nosler handload that's in the chamber of my old .30-06, so I put no additional cartridges in the magazine, although I keep several handy. The bull, however, refuses to cooperate, hiding first behind another bull, then facing directly toward me or directly away. My frustration rises as I move several times to set up the perfect shot

Finally the bull presents broadside. I rest on a blackened snag at forty yards, flip the safety, and

squeeze off the shot. The bull crumples into a lifeless pile.

We approach cautiously as the other five huge creatures linger, moving away only grudgingly at our approach. When they decide we might be a threat, they break into a full run. For animals that weigh a full ton, their agility and speed are astounding.

What a beauty! I am elated as I admire the massive horns, which at their base are too large to reach around with both hands. The biggest bull in the entire Custer State Park herd, and now he's mine. Handshakes, backslapping, and jubilation reign, followed by a joyous picture session in the falling snow.

Driving west out of Rapid City, I carry the cape and horns in the trunk of my rental car. Tom

A big plains bison bull feeding in a burned area.

Hardesty of Atcheson Taxidermy is driving over from Butte to meet me in Billings. All around me is the grandeur of the prairie country, the rimrock buttes and sagebrush hills that dominate this part of South Dakota, Wyoming, and Montana. Now it has been painted white by the snow. Mule deer and antelope teem here, but in my mind I see only bison. Once this was their country.

I pass Custer Battlefield National Monument, where Sioux and Cheyenne warriors enjoyed their most celebrated victory over the U.S. Army. I motor then through the Northern Cheyenne and Crow Reservations and feel a hint of sadness. Is it the knowledge of the brutality that shaped this frontier? Or is it just knowing that a way of life, for the Native Americans as well as for their bison, has ended? As I reflect on these questions, I begin to understand some of my inner feelings and resolve to do my part to contribute to a better future.

Gladness fills my heart as I think of the magnificent bull. I have become part of the history of this region, joining with all the Indians, white buffalo hunters, and others who have partaken of the bounty of the plains. Yes, I am glad—proud— to be a buffalo hunter, a modern, conservationist buffalo hunter. God help me to appreciate how much of a privilege that truly is.

Wood bison. (Photo: courtesy of Dr. Cormack Gates)

WOOD BISON
(Bison bison athabascae)

Buffalo . . . were very plentiful. . . . The buffalo in those parts,
I think, are in general much larger than English black cattle;
particularly the bulls, which, though they may not in reality
be taller than the largest size of the English oxen,
yet to me always appeared much larger.

—Samuel Hearne, *Arctic Dawn,*
Journey to the Great Slave Lake, December 1771

Fort Providence, Northwest Territories, Canada, is near the center of the universe for the wood bison. The tiny hamlet on the banks of the mighty Deh Cho, or Mackenzie River, is the "Home of the River People," the native Slavey Indian tribe. It is also the gateway to the Mackenzie Bison Sanctuary, a vast boreal prairie where the largest and purest herd of the giant bovines is located. Almost two thousand of the creatures inhabit the sanctuary and range freely back and forth across the paved highway that leads to the capital of Yellowknife, some two hundred miles to the north.

Had the white man been present early enough in the history of North America, he would have seen the magnificent wood bison as far west as the Chukchi Sea off western Alaska. Even today, stories of bison hunting persist among Alaskan native elders, and the veracity of those tales is vindicated by copious hard evidence. Just a couple of years ago a well-known hunter discovered a bison skull—from a monstrous bull, buried in the tundra in the Yukon Flats region—and such remains continually turn up. Unfortunately, there is no written documentation of the presence of live animals in Alaska; early native peoples may have hunted the wood bison to extinction, or perhaps they succumbed to some natural disaster. Estimates of the most recent inhabitation of Alaska by wood bison range from two hundred to four hundred years ago.

Today the wood bison occupies only about 3 percent of its former range. At least a portion of that decline can be attributed, unfortunately, to subsistence hunting, which puts bison in danger of being overhunted. Estimates of the number of bison in North America at the time of European contact range upward of 100 million, a staggering figure that may well represent one of the largest concentrations of animal biomass in one terrestrial species in the entire history of the planet.

Most people are familiar with the story of how the plains bison was unmercifully slaughtered. The wood bison was a bit more remote and a lot more reclusive—and hence somewhat later in its demise—but eventually it suffered a similar fate. In addition to hunting pressure, the animal may also have felt the effects of several unusually severe winters in the late 1800s.

Because of the decline in the wood bison population, in 1897 Canada moved to ban hunting of the species, at a time when there were probably only about 300 remaining. Wood Buffalo National Park was established in 1922 in northern Alberta and the Northwest Territories to protect the remaining bison. At that time there were some 1,500 bison in the park. Unfortunately, the government of Alberta made the mistake of transplanting 6,673 plains bison into the park between 1925 and 1928, thereby diluting the gene pool and introducing bovine brucellosis and tuberculosis into the herd. It appeared that the wood bison as a subspecies might disappear entirely, since the new arrivals considerably outnumbered the original animals.

There was some interest in maintaining the wood bison as a separate subspecies, but until 1959 the animal was considered extinct. Then a careful search in a remote area of Wood Buffalo National Park turned up 200 animals that had been isolated from the other bison and unquestionably bore all the characteristics of true wood bison. Eighteen were transplanted to an area west of the Great Slave Lake

Wood bison. Northwest Territories, February 1997.

in 1963 to establish a distinct and disease-free herd. That small group has given rise to the largest and purest herd of wood bison in existence, and they remain to this day free of both brucellosis and tuberculosis. There is a bison-free buffer area between the Mackenzie Bison Sanctuary and Wood Buffalo National Park, to prevent admixture of the herds.

Like all bison, *Bison bison athabascae* are susceptible to sporadic outbreaks of diseases such as anthrax. Unlike the bovine brucellosis and tuberculosis organisms, the bacterium that causes anthrax is not endemic to the animals but resides in the soil as spores that under certain circumstances can become active. Anthrax killed 173 bison in the Mackenzie Bison Sanctuary in 1993, the first time that such an outbreak had occurred there, and the disease has ravaged other areas from time to time as well.

The range of the wood bison seems to be expanding naturally, and there are now some 500 disease-free animals in the Yukon, which has established a harvest plan for surplus animals. I have observed several dozen bison northwest of Whitehorse while hunting there for grizzly bear, and their westward expansion seems to be following the route of their previous range. This expansion is highly desirable, since only around 39 percent of the animal's former range is available for such repopulation. Plans are also in the works to reintroduce the bison into the Yukon Flats of Alaska, where there is range sufficient for up to 2,000 wood bison. Unfortunately, there may be resistance to that strategy from the U.S. Fish and Wildlife Service on a number of technical grounds, all of which appear questionable to me. Russian Siberia also has historical bison habitat, and negotiations are under way to establish a herd there. Transplant animals come from a captive, semiwild herd at Elk Island National Park in Alberta, where their health and genetic purity can be monitored and confirmed.

Canada placed the wood bison on the endangered species list at the first CITES convention in 1973, despite the fact that there was no international trade in the species nor any contribution to their original decline that could be attributed to such activity. At the 1997 CITES conference in Zimbabwe, the wood bison was downlisted to CITES Appendix II at the request of Canada, to which there was no dissent by any of the party nations. No one now considers the wood bison to be endangered. There are more than 6,000 of the animals all told, some 3,500 of which are disease free and essentially nonhybridized. Almost 2,000 of them are in the Mackenzie Bison Range, where I hunted, and 700 more are in five other free-ranging herds, the largest of which is in the Yukon (with 500 or more animals, and growing at 13 percent a year). Almost 800 more are in captive herds, including in excess of 400 in the Elk Island National Park. In the Slave River lowlands of the Northwest Territories and in northeastern Alberta there are about 2,800 wood bison infected with endemic tuberculosis and brucellosis.

Hunting the largest population, those in the Mackenzie Bison Range, began in 1988. Currently, forty-seven animals are harvested each year, all but nine by local residents for food. The nine animals taken by nonresidents are sport hunts marketed for the benefit of the local people, who get the meat for their own consumption. During the 1997–1998 season, hunters received thirty permits for either sex and harvested six bulls.

The wood bison is the largest land mammal native to the Americas, large bulls weighing in at up to 2,200 pounds in the wild. At Elk Island, though, wood bison bulls have tipped the scales at an incredible 2,500 pounds. By contrast, the average plains bison bull is a few hundred pounds lighter, with shorter legs and more weight in the head and hump. Wood bison are darker in color

Warning along the highway between Yellowknife, Northwest Territories, and Fort Providence.

and have a number of other distinguishing characteristics, some of which are fairly subtle. The most obvious difference between the two subspecies is the size and position of the hump, which is much taller relative to body size in wood bison and is slightly forward. The plains bison appears to have a relatively round back when placed beside a wood bison.

The horns of mature bulls generally tower above the head hair, something rare among plains bison. The wood bison's tail is longer and more heavily haired, while the penis sheath in bulls is shorter. The beard is more pointed in the wood bison; the neck is longer and thus much more apparent. Contrary to what one might think, the hair of the wood bison is much shorter along the underside of the brisket than that of the plains bison.

One more distinguishing feature of the wood bison is its reclusive nature, making a hunt for one of these northern monsters nothing like the relaxed hunt one expects for plains bison. They live in open sedge meadows, but always nearby are impenetrable thickets of willow and spruce. The

animals quickly learn to retreat there for safety. It becomes a matter of hide-and-seek, a serious hunt that is highly demanding of the hunter and in which all the odds favor the wood bison.

Bulls of eight years and older do most of the breeding, and recent research shows that the oldest bulls sire the most calves. Cows are sexually mature at two years of age, and a high percentage breed at that time. The rut is in late summer and early fall, gestation being nine to nine-and-a-half months. Brucellosis affects the ability of cows to carry to term, so in infected populations the calving rate is correspondingly lower. Calves are born in late spring through summer, weigh about fifty to sixty pounds at birth, and may grow to twice that weight in only two weeks. Except in rare instances, calves are single births. The wolf is a threat during the first days of life, but as bison age the hazard of predators wanes considerably. Wood bison seldom live beyond twenty-one years in the wild.

The food of the wood bison in winter is primarily slough sedge, with lesser quantities of reedgrass and other types of graze. During

It gets cold when you hunt wood bison in the Northwest Territories in February.

A chilly dawn on the workhorse of the Northland.

summer they eat a wide range of protein-rich plants, particularly willow leaves, which may make up half their diet during the warm months. When willow is dormant the animals disdain chewing the woody buds, even in the face of starvation, preferring to dig in the snow for dry grasses and sedges. Wood bison, like the plains bison, are quite selective in their choice of food and have an uncanny ability to pick the most nutritious plants for consumption.

A true trophy wood bison is at least twelve years old, an animal at its full maturity. The horns should tower above the shaggy head, and ideally the slight blunting characteristic of older animals should be present. The mass of wood bison horns is awesome, and I have seen bulls that I believe would crack the top ten in the record books. (Mine is dwarfed by a giant I photographed at close range in the Yukon eight months before I shot my trophy in the Northwest Territories.) The Mackenzie Bison Range has a huge population of breeding age bulls, all competing for cows, and good management requires that some be removed annually.

One should keep in mind that the record books do not divide bison into their two subspecies. Let's hope that one day the wood bison will appear as a separate entity, adequately available to sport hunters to require a distinct category.

Hunting for wood bison almost invariably involves snowmobiles. The deep freeze of winter in Northern Canada makes them indispensable, and the sleds they pull can take out all of the edible meat. Cold weather is a factor that any southern hunter should consider carefully before embarking, because hunting the wood bison in February in its native Athabascan habitat is a true deep-winter experience. The very best in Arctic clothing is required, and be prepared to spend long hours astride a snow machine, sometimes for days on end. The wood bison has learned that snowmobiles signal danger, and at the first sound of one the entire herd retreats into impenetrable thickets. One sees many fresh tracks on such a hunt but precious few bison.

I recommend a down Arctic parka with a fur ruff around the hood, down underwear, the best pac boots, down pants, and fur gloves (I've used wolf and caribou skin gloves, and both are excellent). Be prepared for temperatures that may plunge to 45 degrees below zero, cold enough to turn whiskey into syrup. Be sure to degrease your rifle completely, as one would for any subzero hunt.

The North American hunter needs to be reminded of one important fact. It is illegal to use anything smaller than a 200-grain bullet. Fortunately, I had my rifle tuned up with 200-grain Nosler handloads, so I just met the regulations. Expect a thorough and mandatory briefing by wildlife personnel before you embark on your hunt, because they want you to make a sure kill by hitting the animal low in the vitals. The heart rides low in the rib cage in the wood bison, so that is the preferred point of aim. The lungs are so large that a pure lung shot may result in prolonged tracking.

I left the wildlife office in Fort Providence all fired up. They showed me a fine video with fantastic shots of the bison, and explained that taking samples of tissue (liver and lung) and blood were required. We accomplished all that without difficulty; I filled the blood tubes and carved off pieces of the required tissue myself.

Be prepared to help with the heavy work. Your native guide and assistant guide do most of the skinning, caping, and quartering, but they appreciate a helping hand. I wore my glove liners, and they rapidly became soaked with blood and went into a plastic sack for the trip back to Georgia. One doesn't work in such temperatures with skin exposed, though.

Don't complain about the many miles and hours aboard a snowmobile. Plan on at least a week of actual hunting, and don't be surprised if the bull you take is the only bison you see. The work is hard, the days are long, and arrival back in camp in the dark of evening is inevitably welcome—but the rewards are great. Above all, keep a positive attitude and remember that there are hundreds, perhaps thousands, of the animals in the snow-covered countryside, regardless of how scarce they may seem.

Canada is to be heartily congratulated for their immaculate wood bison recovery program. The Wood Bison Recovery Team, chaired by Dr. Cormack

Gates of Calgary, Alberta, has done a masterful job of ensuring the future of this unique and noble creature. To have participated in a wood bison hunt is to have experienced the north country, with all its history and legacy, at its very best.

BEHEMOTH BULLS OF DEH CHO

The cold slipstream whips my exposed face as the snowmobile grinds onward, cutting through crunchy snow as night closes in. The machine has no handle grip warmers, and a creeping numbness stiffens my fingers as we motor along, a pink sunset at our backs. My Slavey Indian outfitter, Edward Landry of Fort Providence, Northwest Territories, Canada, calls for a break, and we pause on the shore of Calais Lake. Bare willow bushes cloaked in a thick layer of hoarfrost stretch to the horizon along the edge of the icy shore, the whole scene frozen in the iron grip of winter.

There is no wind. The exhaust fumes from our chugging machines linger around us like a blanket in the still air, low to the ground. I find myself immersed in the clinging, smoky cloud and dismount to get into clean air and to stretch away the kinks in my legs. Only with some concentration can I make the muscles loosen and uncoil. I think back to lengthy snowmobile hunts for a half-dozen other species, and memories flood back of the deep weariness such travel engenders.

Edward's people inhabit Fort Providence, a place his people call Zhanti Koe, meaning "house of the priest." The Slaveys were evangelized by the highly regarded Roman Catholic order of Oblate missionary priests a hundred years ago, and most are still faithful to the church and its teachings. They are known as the "People of the Big River," denizens of the great Deh Cho—in English, the Mackenzie River—and its tributaries. Here they have subsisted for millennia, partaking of the natural bounty. They have always been notably less inclined to landlocked pursuits than their kinsmen, the Dogrib and other Dene peoples.

We are here to hunt the purest wood bison in the world. The Slavey people have inherited this resource and benefit the most from it. Edward's parent business, Deh Cho Wilderness Tours, conducts all manner of backcountry

A coating of frost shrouds all vegetation.

the North Star, my usual points of reference, are much higher overhead than they ever appear back home.

The heavens are not the only lights I see. The snowmobile headlights illuminate innumerable crystals in the fairyland forest around us that gleam and glitter like diamonds. The enchanting display mesmerizes me, and for a moment I forget my aching fingers—but only for a moment. I have no choice but to roar onward and hope to reach camp before frostbite sets in. Oh, the treachery of inadequate gloves!

We finish traversing the vast lake and enter dark woods of dwarf spruce, where moguls of snow, exposed rocks, and the occasional new-fallen log make staying on the narrowing trail difficult. I see huge ungulate tracks here and there, but whether of moose, bison, or caribou I cannot tell.

It was not without some sense of apprehension that I embarked on this midwinter trek. I have hunted in temperatures approaching 50 below zero on one other occasion, and in cold almost as severe several other times. What I fear is that one of the gruesome Arctic high-pressure systems with readings of 70 below may fall upon us, a distinct possibility during February in the Northwest Territories. So far, everything is cozy, though, with the thermometer hovering just below zero. It is forecast to drop quite a bit during the clear night, but not to the dreaded extremes. I have petitioned the Lord for tolerable weather and a good bison bull, and so far the weather is shaping up as a welcome answer to that prayer.

The lights of camp emerge from the darkness almost unexpectedly, and a welcome array of cozy cabins soon fills the headlights. Several more Slaveys appear in the doorway of the cookhouse, and without delay they unload the gear from our heavily

trips in and around the bison refuge, including sport hunts.

During our foggy respite I mention my freezing fingers, but Edward assures me that we are just across the lake from his base camp. I automatically fear the worst. "Not far" in this part of the world has an uncanny way of stretching into hours, not the mere minutes the phrase implies in temperate climes. We push onward in the gathering darkness, the deepening chill of a starkly clear winter's night descending fast. The transparent atmosphere reveals an awe-inspiring expanse of starry heavens, and I note that the Big Dipper and laden toboggans. I have my own small cabin with a wood stove, as does the other hunter in camp.

My companion on this hunt is Arvid, a delightful chap from Norway who runs a Mercedes Benz dealership there. He arrived yesterday and has been out hunting wood bison all day. Around the supper table we partake of a belated meal as he and his guides relate the tale of their day, a fruitless journey that revealed hundreds of fresh tracks but only two wood bison. What I have heard of these animals appears to be true. I recall the dense stands of aspen, birch, jack pine, and spruce that I observed on our journey in and marvel that anybody ever takes one. Edward tells me that the largest concentrations of bison are in the inaccessible dry lakes that abound in the refuge, places where the forests on all sides are so dense that snowmobiles cannot enter.

Elsie, the camp cook, serves up a feast of homemade soup followed by thick and juicy bison burger. The meat has no wild taste at all, not a surprise to me but quite so to my Norwegian companion. I tell the cook *maksi* (thanks) and step outside.

A band of aurora borealis streaks the heavens, undulating cheerily, and the sky seems near enough to touch. I watch until the cold forces a retreat into the warmth of the cabin.

My .30-06 is stowed in a soft case outside the cabin so it doesn't pick up condensation moisture. The specter of a failure to fire is always there when hunting in extreme cold, though I did have the weapon professionally degreased before leaving home. I have confidence in my rifle and only hope I get the chance to use it.

I feel now as I often have while hunting wilderness elk, which inhabit equally thick terrain. But unlike Idaho and Colorado, this dense region is as flat as my native south Georgia, and I don't understand how it's possible to spot a wood bison before it is at arm's length. Two hunters here were shut out last year, and only two bulls fell to sport hunters. Fifty percent seems a high success rate for hunting conditions like these. If I am successful I will be only the second U.S. hunter to take a wood bison. I say a special prayer for success before retiring to sleep.

My guide is an experienced hunter, Greg Elleze, who is intimately familiar with the Mackenzie Bison Refuge. He is assisted by an expert snowmobiler and hunter named Ronald Squirrel. Both are proud of their heritage, proud of their hunting tradition, and pleased to be on this excursion. They are determined to show this white hunter that they know their business. Out of

It's a cold, rough trip to the hunting area over unplowed trails.

courtesy, they refrain from using their native tongue in my presence, since both know English extremely well. Edward directs them to take me to Tuaro, as the Great Slave Lake is known in Slavey. It is over forty miles distant, but native hunters have spotted a big bison bull on the vast shoreline. The native hunters had passed him up because they wanted a younger animal for meat. He sounds like exactly the wood bison I want.

For some ten miles, four snowmobiles travel in tandem toward Falaise Lake, a prime bison feeding area. This is where the Norwegian spent the day yesterday, and the place is crisscrossed with bison tracks. The forage here is bison heaven, with copious grass that makes for prime grazing. In addition, the serrated edge of the dense forest is nearby, affording a vital haven to the animals. No one can follow them into that jungle of stunted trees except laboriously and on foot, a tactic that is increasingly imperative in hunting wood bison.

Not far from camp we encounter the first of hundreds of fresh wolf tracks. The packs follow the snowmobile trails because the footing is so good, making me wonder if the snowmobile might not be contributing to the exploding wolf population. Expending less energy by navigating the packed trails makes the animals much more vigorous in pursuing their quarry, and they eat perhaps hundreds of wood bison, mainly calves and weaker animals, each year. In places their tracks merge into a confluent ribbon of footprints almost a half-yard wide.

Our companion group of two snow machines goes north, while we motor southeast toward the nearest shore of Tuaro. Moguls in the trail pound us mercilessly as we travel, an effect compounded by the rebound jerking of the toboggan behind. Finally, dead ahead, stretching out of sight to the horizon, we see the gigantic frozen lake. There is a fishing camp where we emerge from the bush at Deep Bay, but the fishermen have gone out on the ice for the day. Not far to our west the mighty Mackenzie River drains eternally from the immense lake, eventually spilling northward into the Arctic Ocean.

We elect to park the snowmobiles and do some walking, since there are fresh wood bison tracks coming down the trail we have just traversed. I unpack my rifle and strap it on my back. The sun is shining brightly, and the reflection off the frozen lake is blinding. It seems prudent to stop a moment and apply sunscreen to my face. Despite removing my parka, I am soon perspiring from the heavy labor of footwork in the snow.

We have scarcely traveled three hundred yards when we come upon a bull wood bison. Apparently he is somewhat accustomed to the movement of snow machines on the lake, and our noise has not frightened him. The bull stands in a willow thicket approximately fifty yards off, watching the approaching ghostlike figures in their white apparel. We stand still, hoping he will tarry long enough for a good evaluation, and I raise my binoculars. I am astonished at the proximity of such a grand beast, but my mind is clear as I evaluate the creature. I note that the black horns, sharp and high, rise well above the hair on top of the massive head. If this animal were a plains bison, he would indeed be a trophy. But the horn color is the giveaway—he should have lighter horns if he is a breeding bull, and more mass.

Before I can make a firm decision to pass, the 2,000-pound animal is gone in a spray of flying snow and flashing hoofs, thundering away through the willows with the agility of a rabbit. Second thoughts abound, but in all I am not sorry I didn't fire. I remain hopeful we will find a mature bull, and jump shooting them like game birds is no way to accomplish our mission.

We negotiate another laborious half-mile through the deep snow, sticking as much as possible to an old snowmobile trail. Disappointed to see no more fresh tracks ahead, we turn around reluctantly. We will retreat to the fishing camp and try another direction. The shore to the north along the coast of Deep Bay is another possibility, but we will have to move cautiously to avoid overtaking nothing but hot tracks.

It seems an eternity. We motor slowly and alertly through miles of smooth, unbroken snow, punctuated here and there by the tracks of the snowshoe hare. Ungulate tracks are notably absent, the tranquil surface mocking us with its monotony and serene beauty. There appear to be no wood bison anywhere about, and I feel a rising tide of discouragement.

Along the shore of Tuaro, we finally find tracks in the snow. Wood bison have been feeding here on lush sedges. Most of the tracks are large and fresh, indicating the presence of a grand old bull, but he will be wary and wise, perhaps unapproachable. Happily, the wind is out of the north and in our faces.

We ease along slowly. The bull has been here recently, his monstrous imprints left behind in the snow. We glass the shoreline as far as we can see. Thick vegetation along the edge of the lake makes it impossible to see very far inland, and our chances look grim.

It is already afternoon, and we are tiring rapidly. Breakfast was many hours ago, and Ronald, riding in front, turns to suggest we return to the fish camp, now a number of miles behind, for lunch and a rest. I agree, hesitating only momentarily as he initiates a wide turn.

What is that? Snow falling from a tree along the shoreline? There is only a light wind, and I raise my binoculars to look. Snow again cascades from a towering aspen. Something is moving, something black and brown and massive.

"Ronald, Greg, look here," I whisper excitedly. Greg pulls out his binoculars and, as if on cue, a mammoth bull bison gallops like a frolicking colt out of the willows and stops, standing broadside, some 175 yards away. The horns are massive, high, and covered with the characteristic white frost that signifies an ancient animal. I excitedly chamber a 200-grain Nosler handload and try to sight in on the bull. He is galloping around, perhaps relishing the cold temperature and the lack of insects, presenting an unstable target. I am unable to get a decent rest, and my opportunity is suddenly gone. Without warning the bull disappears once again into the thick willows, and my heart sinks.

"That's a good one," says Greg, "and he doesn't know we're here."

"Is he gone?"

"No. He hasn't seen or smelled us. He won't go far. Just get ready and wait."

I do just that, determined not to blow what could easily be my only chance. I work myself into a better shooting position.

"He's back where you first spotted him," says Greg a moment later, peering through his binoculars.

"I see him, too," I reply in a whisper. Only the dark color is visible, however. Where do I aim? There is another bit of movement, and suddenly I realize that I'm looking at his tail. Now if I can only figure out where the chest is.

All at once I see the lower part of the enormous chest cavity through an opening in the willows. I rest solidly, and then, without alerting my companions, squeeze off the shot.

There is a thunderous explosion, and the animal reacts immediately, galloping once more into the open, presenting the other side of his body. I work the bolt of the .30-06 and deliberately, but more hurriedly, fire again. This time the animal disappears, but we can easily follow his retreat as he shakes trees and runs through the snow into the lakeshore forest.

As we walk up, we see blood on the willows at chest height, but where I hit the animal is still unknown. Only a spot of blood shows here and there, and the ground should be covered if indeed I hit the kill zone.

With rifle at ready, I ease through the tight thicket, moving now into more open spruce forest. Up ahead, I suddenly see a dark form, still but nevertheless upright, with massive shoulders and hump visible. Great billows of condensation cloud the air from the creature's voluminous respiration, although the head is hidden from sight by a snow-mantled spruce. I quickly place two more shots in the animal before he lumbers off through the evergreens.

In moments we are standing in awe of the sheer size of the beast, a small mountain of brown and black hair lying in the snow. Satisfied that the bull is going nowhere, my two companions trek back to retrieve the snowmobiles before we begin the picture session. They will have to carve a trail through the dense willows with a chain saw before we can retrieve the animal.

The picture session consumes thirty minutes and four rolls of film. I am amazed at the horns on this colossal bull, which we measure at 18 inches long with 17-inch bases. No wonder they classify these giants as a separate subspecies. I kneel, place my hand on the animal's head, and thank God for His grace in providing me with this marvelous trophy. My guides seem to understand and respect my simple act.

Butchering a bison is no small task, and it takes almost three full hours. It is already dark by the time we have the last scraps of edible meat aboard and drive off on the snowmobiles. Riding double through the thicket in the dark, I cover

Greg Elleze, my Slavey Indian guide from Fort Providence, Northwest Territories, Canada.

my head with my parka hood and pray we will make it back with our heavy load. I relax only when we break into the open once more. Even on the smooth lake the added weight strains the snowmobile engine, which whines in protest each time we encounter any added resistance. It is a sound I will hear for hours.

The far north throws great distances at the hunter. We are forty miles from camp, riding in the blackness with the whole of heaven overhead providing but dim illumination. By my friend the North Star, I know the direction—first north along the shore of Tuaro, then southwest. Finding the appropriate trail, which amounts to no more than a gap in the brush, is beyond my ability. But Greg navigates the maze with ease, and three hours later we are back in camp with our prize safely home. All of us are weary but content.

The other party has seen no bison today. They examine my trophy with interest and politely question us about our resounding and rapid success. Arvid, the Norwegian hunter, seems greatly encouraged and not at all envious.

There is an old Slavey song:
Our forefathers left us with pride . . .
with wisdom and courage to fight. . . .
We are standing all as one. . . .
To fight for our rights and our land.

Indigenous peoples continue to seek dignity and usefulness in a world dominated by the white man and his seemingly indispensable goods. The bison in many ways symbolizes the Native American, and depriving them of the animal was part of a strategy to disenfranchise them. On a small scale, the wood bison is contributing to a comeback of the native people, and a rebirth of their self-respect and cultural heritage. I have seen it firsthand. Let us hope that this is only the beginning.

Greenland muskox. (Photo: courtesy of Erwin and Peggy Bauer)

GREENLAND MUSKOX
(Ovibus moschatus wardi)

You have spoken very well, Father.
You have told me that Heaven is very beautiful.
Now tell me one more thing.
Is it as beautiful as the country of the muskox in summer,
where a mist rises over the lakes, and the water is blue,
and the loons cry very often?

—Saltatha, Dogrib Indian guide for early hunter Warburton Pike,
speaking to a nineteenth-century missionary priest, circa 1891

Greenland muskoxen differ from barren ground muskoxen (*Ovibus moschata moschata*) in several ways, although differences are admittedly slight. It has not been resolved whether the subspecies listing is biologically valid. They have the same basic features, being squat and blocky with a shoulder hump sloping downward to hindquarters that are slightly lower than the forequarters. Some feel that the dense wool and long guard hairs are slightly more luxurious on this subspecies, presumably the result of the harsher climatic conditions in which they live. The distinctive features of this subspecies include slightly smaller size (600 pounds for the average bull, compared with 750 pounds on the mainland), often a white saddle, and a white face and stockings, features that are usually no lighter than cream-colored on mainland muskoxen. In the high Arctic, bulls' horns are lighter in color, being frequently white except for black tips. Horns of the Greenland subspecies certainly reflect the smaller size, as a check of the record book easily demonstrates. Safari Club International recognizes this difference and lists the subspecies separately, but Boone and Crockett lumps them together, with the result that mainland bulls dominate that record book.

In prehistoric times, muskoxen were distributed in circumpolar fashion around the entire Arctic. By the time of recorded history, these unique animals had disappeared from all of Asia and Europe, leaving only the population in North America intact. Hunting by early humans may have been a significant factor in the elimination of the Eurasian population, whereas in North America inhospitable offshore islands extended farther north than hunters generally ventured, perhaps offering the animal a sanctuary. However, we still know relatively little for certain about the effects of prehistoric hunters on muskoxen (or other species).

During the Ice Age, a large sheet of ice may have separated the North American muskoxen into two separate populations, a northern and a southern group. The isolation of the two populations from each other, whether by an ice sheet or simply by distance and icy waters, allowed the development of subspecies. Greenland muskoxen are the more northerly of the two.

Today, muskoxen living on the Arctic islands, Greenland, and the transplanted populations in Alaska are of the Greenland subspecies. There may, however, be some interbreeding between these modern populations, because muskoxen will cross the sea ice between the islands and the mainland, as well as between various Arctic islands of Canada.

The more northerly climes differ significantly from the mainland, primarily in availability of browse and grassland. Forage quality is as good on the Arctic islands as on the mainland, but cooler summers and a shorter growing season result in less food there—small patches rather than large meadows. Because of differences in the quantity of food, Greenland muskoxen tend to subsist in smaller herds than their mainland cousins. Population dynamics also are different, primarily because of the unpredictable annual

Greenland muskox, Northwest Territories, March 1993.

climatic variation on the islands. A less important factor in population fluctuations for Greenland muskoxen may be barriers to dispersion of this subspecies when food is in short supply.

Like the barren ground muskoxen of the mainland, the Greenland subspecies subsists on a summer diet of sedge, willow, and occasionally grasses; in winter the diet is mainly sedge, a coarse, grasslike plant that grows in tufts on marshy ground. Areas of quality grazing in the high Arctic are much more limited than on the mainland, and the willow is much smaller. Winterkill may be catastrophic for Greenland muskoxen during certain conditions, most notably severe crusting of the snow and freezing rain. Freezing rain is particularly devastating, for it can trap the animals in their beds by freezing their long guard hairs to the ground, resulting in starvation or easy predation. In crusted or deep snow, the animals expend so much energy foraging that they may succumb to malnutrition. Muskoxen prefer areas with fewer than twenty inches of snow annually, which may be the main reason that there has been no historical population on giant Baffin Island, with its heavier snows. That harsh winters and difficult snow conditions kill Greenland muskoxen was dramatically demonstrated in the winter of 1973-74, when some 500 muskox carcasses were spotted on Bathurst Island, where I took my Greenland muskox in 1993. The quota there remains only 5 animals per year, reflecting the susceptibility of high Arctic muskoxen to harsh winters, and the slow recovery that sometimes follows.

Like barren ground muskoxen, the Greenland subspecies received complete protection from the Canadian government in 1917. One might suppose that the remoteness of the high Arctic would have offered adequate protection, but that has been true only for islands like Ellesmere, which has seen little encroachment by man. On many of the islands muskoxen are completely absent, exterminated by severe winters, early hunters, or a combination of the two. Because there has been only limited trading of skins on the Arctic islands—mainly in low quantities to whalers—overhunting has been more of a factor on the mainland.

The Greenland muskox played an important role in the exploration of the Arctic and the search for the Northwest Passage in the nineteenth century. Many documents from that era tell of explorers being saved from starvation by the presence of the animals. Interestingly, the expected fluctuations in muskox numbers have often been verified by the writings of those early explorers. They apparently reflect the natural fluctuations of a volatile population.

Today, muskoxen on the Arctic islands and on the mainland are under the protection of the same quota system. Observers in airplanes count both live animals and carcasses, which are easily visible from the air on the frozen tundra. Such surveys are expensive, and they must cover vast tracts of terrain to be comprehensive and effective. The local Inuit Hunter-Trapper Association determines use of the assigned harvest quota, which may go toward local consumption or to sport hunts for nonnatives. That is virtually the same as the polar bear quota system, in that the indigenous people receive the benefit of the resource, and they make the decision how to utilize it. The system works well, and the Inuit participate in every phase of management, benefiting both themselves and the muskox.

In 1935, Greenland muskoxen were transplanted to Alaska's Nunivak Island, where they thrived. Indeed, the herd expanded so much that a sport hunt is now standard, and the herd has supplied animals for transplant to northern Alaska. Nunivak Island is much more temperate than the Canadian Arctic islands, and it provides abundant and nutritious forage. Predators are absent, so control of the herd is essential.

Hunting Greenland muskox is perhaps the coldest big-game hunting in the world. Late winter is the normal time for such hunts, and the cold in the high Arctic at that time of year can be severe—especially for a hunter from Georgia. I traveled to Resolute Bay for my hunt and experienced a temperature change of about 110 degrees Fahrenheit. Talk about a shock! When I began my Greenland muskox hunt on Bathurst Island, temperatures were about 45 degrees below zero. Add to that the 40- to 50-knot wind, and you get the idea. Caribou skin clothing makes life much more comfortable, and it's a true necessity for the high Arctic.

Most hunts are by snowmobile, although Canadian law mandates that the final stalk be on foot. The law specifies that a sport hunter may approach muskoxen by snowmobile no closer than 3.25 kilometers (about two miles). One must rely on the guide to determine where to stop the snowmobile; he is the driver, and the hunter is usually riding in the sled, or *qamutik*. When muskoxen appear one may already be as close as the law allows, or there may be a strategy session to decide how best to approach. Often, as on my

Putting on caribou-skin clothes is essential in this cold, but it's difficult work.

hunt, the wide-open terrain makes a conventional stalk all but impossible. If muskoxen were more skittish, specialized techniques of approach would be needed. As it is, they assume the characteristic defensive circle—unless they have been hunted a lot—allowing the hunter to approach to within rifle range. One can only speculate whether they will continue to employ this behavior. It is an extremely effective defense against wolves, but not much good against a modern firearm.

Currently, Greenland muskoxen are in extremely good condition, with only a few local exceptions. The successes far outweigh the areas of concern. A notable example of the burgeoning population is that on Banks Island, which had no muskoxen at all earlier in this century. The quota there is 5,000 animals for harvest, out of a total population of some 60,000 in 1994, an unbelievable recovery with no assistance from man except for protection and management.

The experience of Canada's high Arctic for a Greenland muskox hunt is one no sport hunter should miss. It is also a highly affordable venture, especially when compared with the other species available here—the polar bear. Take your warmest down clothes and insulated boots, but expect to hunt in caribou-skin clothing, if it is available. Book with an outfitter committed to keeping you as warm and comfortable as possible, and trust your experienced Inuk guide to find your quarry and get you back home from the trackless and confusing Arctic back country. This a real adventure that harkens back to the time of the early Arctic explorers. Keep your feet warm, and you won't be sorry you went.

HIGH ARCTIC ADVENTURE

A howling, icy wind greets me as I descend from the plane. This is my first experience with the high Arctic, and I am standing on the southeast corner of

Bitter cold greets the hunting party as we disembark.

Bathurst Island, somewhere near the magnetic North Pole. Bathurst is a frozen chunk of tundra 65 miles west of Resolute Bay, Northwest Territories, Canada, and almost 600 miles north of the Arctic Circle. As the Twin Otter lifts off the sea ice and thunders away, I suddenly sense a wave of doubt about my sanity. I have always wanted to experience the raw Arctic. Here I am.

Human beings may feel great uneasiness in the face of the unrelenting cold and wind. Our quarry, on the contrary, is perhaps the ultimate example of adaptation in this frozen world. As I gaze at the bleak landscape, I marvel that anything living can survive here, never mind thrive. The only visible vegetation consists of a few clumps of moss and lichens, clinging to life amid the rocks on windblown ridgetops. The temperature hovers at 45 degrees below zero, and the air stings exposed skin with a thousand needles: vicious weather, but not at all unusual here. I struggle to bring even my nose and eyes into the protection of my tightly drawn parka hood. Breathing so burns my windpipe that I draw my breath from inside my face mask, and the warmed air grabs the fabric as it exits, forming a crusty ring of condensation. I remember outfitter Jerome Knap's last word to me on the phone in the Narwhal Hotel in Resolute Bay, assuring me that all will be well when I don the caribou skins. I am dressed in wool, down,

and high-tech fibers, but still I feel frozen to the bone after only a brief exposure. I hope Jerome is right about the skins.

We quickly make our way to camp, a ragtag assembly of prefabricated buildings flown in by C130 aircraft twenty years ago for a mining exploration encampment. Some have been almost swallowed by the permafrost, a consequence of melting that takes place underneath all man-made structures in the Arctic. Most have completely filled with snow, their doors caved inward. The two usable structures are miraculously intact, and ours even has a pair of double-decker bunk beds left over from better days.

Adam Kalluk, my young Inuk guide, arrived earlier by snowmobile from Resolute Bay, and he has remarkably comfortable quarters prepared for us. A happy torpidity fills the tiny room, soothing heat emanating from a kerosene heater in one corner. I savor the welcome relief for my numb fingers and face, heralded by a distinct tingling of the nerve endings. We all back up to the heater with obvious gratitude and enjoy the smell of the caribou stew Adam is cooking on a gas stove. After thawing out, we retrieve our gear and spread our Arctic sleeping bags on the bunk beds.

I contemplate the weathered faces of our four Inuit guides, especially that of renowned craftsman and carver Simeone, who is to guide one of the other

The village of Resolute Bay, Northwest Territories, where the hunt originates.

hunters. He has seen his share of the high Arctic, and the harsh life shows in the chiseled lines of his copper-colored skin. Like most older Inuit, he sports scattered facial hair, classic in both color and distribution. His eyes are typically Oriental, deep brown and narrow with irides of mahogany brown. In their winter clothing, these men could be Inuit of the recent past, people who survived off the land, with neither help nor hope from the temperate world. I marvel at the quiet dignity of these survivors, who, still lovers of the great land, remain a mystery to much of the uncaring outside world.

There are four muskox hunters in camp, all of us new to such ferocious weather. My own guide, Adam, will share our quarters. Over lunch we get to know one another, and soon we become aware of the unbelievable language distribution in our small group. Of the five people sharing our cabin, each has learned a different native language. Adam speaks Inuktitut, the Inuit tongue; the other hunters include a Cuban-American, an Italian, and a German. I am in a distinct minority as a native English-speaker. Everyone speaks at least one of the other languages, so we frequently

have conversations going on in three or four tongues, especially when the other guides are present and conversing in Inuktitut.

Whatever the language, the discussions are centered on the muskox, the cold, the wind, and the indomitable Arctic. We wait another full day for the vicious gale to die down, and I pass the time getting to know my new friends. The hours seem endless, so I have plenty of time for reading Berton's *The Arctic Grail,* the story of those who first explored the Arctic. The book is a veritable encyclopedia of hardship, deprivation, and death, as ill-prepared men tried to cope with conditions just like the ones outside the thin walls of our shelter. In 1846, I learn, the doomed Franklin expedition passed only a few miles from our very position before disappearing forever into the unforgiving cold.

Late on the second day, too late to go hunting, Adam borrows my binoculars for a quick scouting trip by snowmobile. Our spirits soar at his report of several bands of muskox just over the low mountains behind us. A quiet darkness settles slowly over the bleak landscape, and the gale subsides ever so slightly. We hope for a break in the storm.

By the third day the wind has finally died sufficiently to allow us to hunt, so we prepare our clothing and gear. With some bewilderment I assemble and inspect once more the carefully crafted caribou-skin clothing. How in the world can it be that simple animal skins are better than the technological marvels I order through my favorite catalogues?

First come the inner boots, with the hair turned out, extending up to the knee. Then the outer bootie, only ankle high with skin turned in, fits over the inner bootie and is tied on securely. Surprisingly, only a regular wool sock and liner are needed under these, not the triple or quadruple layers I had imagined. Then come the "Bermuda shorts" with suspenders, hair outside. After that the lined coat with hood, hair outside, goes on. Caribou-skin mittens, again with the hair outside, come last. And all of that fits over a conventional inner polypropylene/outer wool arrangement. I know it is good when, for the first time, I have to retreat outside. I cannot even feel the terrible cold while wearing this outfit. Now I understand why those fur-clad figures of the Arctic, so familiar to all who are even superficially familiar with the region, seem so immune to the cold.

Today, hunters pursue muskoxen by snowmobile. Hunter, gear, and game ride behind the snowmobile in the *qamutik*. These sleds can move amazingly heavy loads, the only drawback being the significant pounding the riders take, especially over rough ice or snow.

My old Remington .30-06 rides in its padded case in the *qamutik* with me. I have completely degreased it to prevent malfunction in the cold. The sled tosses me around like a rodeo rider as we cross the irregular frozen bay. We head for the highest promontory on the opposite spit of land, a dark rocky butte that contrasts sharply with the white lower hills. I strain to observe the terrain, but my frosty breath has clouded my ski goggles. Despite my struggles to see I am engrossed by the Arctic scene.

As we enter a small inlet, I see my first muskox. About thirty animals stand gazing at us from the top of a ridge a couple of miles distant. All four snowmobiles stop for a discussion of strategy, which mainly involves the guides, who speak in a language that is unintelligible to me. While we pause, the herd silently retreats over the top of the hill and out of sight.

Apparently there are several acceptable bulls in the group, because the guides motor in a large circle to intercept them. When next we spot the animals, they have "rounded up" on a small knoll, some nervously milling in and out of the group. The defensive formation is so classic that for a moment I am tempted to abandon hunting and concentrate on photography.

As we maneuver the snowmobiles into position we become separated from the other hunters, so the stalk proceeds from two different angles. My Cuban friend, Alberto, is with me, while the two European hunters are together and momentarily out of sight. Muskox hunting is like a frontal infantry assault. We simply march toward the herd in full view, an approach utterly new to me. Walking in our bulky garb makes the long trek no small task. As we labor along, I feel like a lumbering Ice Age beast, plumes of white mist billowing from my lungs into the icy air with each step.

Nearing the herd, we see the German and Italian hunters already in position to shoot. Both are apparently excellent marksmen, and two bulls immediately do down. At the shots, the animals begin milling and mixing, making choosing a target difficult for Alberto and me. I finally get my sights on a good bull, but he is standing directly in front of a cow. This presents a dilemma of muskox hunting— the real possibility of killing two animals with one shot. I hesitate, as does Alberto, and when the herd suddenly bolts we rightly elect to hold our fire.

The bulls that our European companions have taken are excellent, and we pause to admire the long curving horns and thick dark capes. It appears to my untrained eye that they may not be the best in the herd, however, and my excitement rekindles as we head out on foot. The snowmobiles are soon miles behind, and I find myself drenched with sweat in the heavy clothing.

The herd finally stops in a small valley, out of our view until we are quite close. This time we are dealing with very agitated animals, so we attempt to stay out of sight as we approach. Open terrain makes this a challenge, and, despite our efforts, the group spots us and begins its nervous milling. We must hurry our shots before the entire herd takes off. I put my scope on what appears to be the largest bull in the herd, and I confidently squeeze off the shot, carefully avoiding the surrounding cows.

More rough riding by snowmobile and qamutik.

Alberto fires almost simultaneously, and as the herd flees, two animals lie silent in the snow.

My bull is excellent, with long, curving white horns tapering dramatically from the massive frontal boss downward and outward to ebony tips. While the horns of the Greenland muskox in the high Arctic are not usually as impressive as those on their barren ground cousins of the mainland, other attributes more than compensate. For one thing, the cape is truly amazing, twenty-inch outer hair guarding wool underfleece so thick that a knife can hardly cut it.

While I am celebrating, I become aware of the downcast countenance of my friend and discover that he has accidentally shot a cow. I can see how easily such an error could occur, but Alberto is understandably disgusted. I truly feel for him, and no less for his Inuk guide, who also takes the mishap pretty hard. Both are gentlemen, however, and each tries to take the blame on himself.

Dead animals quickly freeze solid at 40 below, making skinning impossible, so we set about it immediately. I marvel at the Inuit skill with a knife, as the flashing blades efficiently slice the hide from the body. I want my bull skinned for a full-body mount, and after doing the job we hurriedly quarter the carcass before it freezes.

We wait for the snowmobiles and sleds, an interval that would be deadly without the caribou-skin clothing. As I break out a thermos of hot coffee from my pack, I note with some degree of concern the dim Arctic light. One can't help but feel uneasy so far from the safety of the warm cabin.

The ride back is bittersweet and bumpy, my mind alternately rejoicing at my own trophy and grieving with my friend Alberto. Oh, well, that's hunting. I hear the phrase in at least five different languages that night, but no matter how it is expressed it does little to diminish my companion's pain. He gives the magnificent cape to his guide and elects to do a European mount of the skull as his only memento of a disappointing hunt.

The original plans called for a nine-hour *qamutik* ride to Resolute Bay, but a broken snowmobile necessitates calling in an airplane, so Alberto and I happily change our plans. We leave the other two hunters behind to embark on a

It's cold, but we load the sled to hunt Greenland muskox on Bathurst Island.

polar bear hunt from our same camp, testing the shifting ice of Viscount Melville Sound.

One learns much on an adventure like this. John Ross spent four years stuck in the Arctic ice, from 1829 to 1833, unable to extricate his ship. He and all but one of his men survived because they adopted the ways of the Inuit in food and dress, a helpful Arctic survival lesson never learned by the Royal Navy in those times. More than a decade later the Franklin Expedition left England for this same area, and all 134 men perished by holding resolutely to European survival tactics and dress.

The Inuit know their land and their animals, and they know from millennia of experience how to live there. With confidence, I anticipate a return to muskox country someday to enjoy its beauty, its bounty, and its blessings.

Barren ground muskox. (Photo: courtesy of Lon Lauber)

BARREN GROUND MUSKOX
(Ovibus moschatus moschatus)

[T]he treeless tundra . . . Here, if anywhere,
lie all the majesty and mystery of the north,
for the stillness of death hangs over these barrens. . . .
They put men in awe.

—Pierre Berton, *The Mysterious North*, 1956

Muskoxen have always been inhabitants of those awesome barrens, a land that stretches for a million square miles in a broad swath across the top of Canada, encompassing all the vast Arctic coast lands except for the Mackenzie River delta. Muskoxen once claimed the circumpolar north country as their own. We find their fossils in northern Europe and Asia, all across Siberia and into Alaska. In the past few hundred years (at least), the only surviving populations have been in North America, confined to the central mainland of Canada's Arctic (the barren ground muskox), the Arctic archipelago, and Greenland (the Greenland muskox). As a result of physical barriers, most likely a huge sheet of glacial ice during the Ice Age, the animals split into northern and southern populations. Those muskoxen confined to the mainland have developed characteristics that distinguish them from their northern Greenland cousins.

The Canadian mainland produces more forage than the Arctic islands of Canada, and muskoxen prefer sedge, although willow is an important summer supplement. Just like the Greenland muskox, barren ground muskoxen favor areas that receive less than twenty inches of snow per year. More snow than that can make foraging so difficult that the animals starve, and freezing rain can cement their thick coat to the ground.

Today, hunters of the muskox are mainly human, but wolves have been their principal foe for millennia, and they still take far more than any other predator. Both polar bears and grizzly bears eat muskoxen at times. The characteristic defensive circle that muskoxen form when threatened is good protection against the wolf. Standing in a circle with horns pointing outward and the calves safe in the center, they present a formidable obstacle to hungry canines.

Herds of barren ground muskoxen tend to be larger than those of the Greenland subspecies, presumably because of the better and more consistent forage; body size also reflects that difference. The rut occurs in August for both subspecies, with the dominant bull in the herd breeding most of the cows, at least until he is exhausted, at which time another bull may breed. The rut is accompanied by a significant mortality for the bulls, partly because of fighting but mainly because the dominant bulls emerge in a weakened condition and may not survive the winter. Cows breed for the first time between the ages of two and four, depending in part on the quality of summer feed. They almost always bear a single calf, although twins occur rarely. Calves are born in April or May, and many enter the world to be greeted by temperatures of 20 to 40 below zero. Muskoxen may live more than twenty years, and adult survival is high during normal winters.

There has been some concern about burgeoning numbers of muskoxen and the possible effect they might have on the caribou that share their habitat. So far, there seems to be little competition between the two species, at least on the Arctic mainland, because they favor different forage. Moreover, muskoxen tend to stay on the valley floor and the caribou on the slopes, minimizing overlap of grazing areas. When the snow is deep, however, muskoxen may move onto the slopes to browse in areas where the snow has blown off.

Muskoxen wear the finest wool in the world, with strand length considerably longer than that of any other animal. Unlike the long guard hairs, which are permanent, the wool sheds each summer. There has been a small amount of commercial use of the animals' coats.

The horns of muskoxen are highly interesting to the hunter, being almost sheeplike in appearance. Barren ground muskoxen have longer and darker horns than the Greenland subspecies, but the merging of the heavily ridged midline boss in mature bulls is the same. As in all bovids, the horns have a bony core. They stop growing in length after age six, and subsequently only the boss grows, providing a measure of the animal's maturity.

Muskoxen are a true conservation success story, one of many in the world today that follows on the heels of a man-made catastrophe. Lack of protection in the nineteenth century led to virtual extermination of all but the most inaccessible populations. As has often been the case, commercial exploitation was to blame. Recognizing the imminent demise of the species, Canada took early steps to protect the animal. The Unorganized Territories Game Preservation Act of 1894 established a closed season, and the Northwest Game Act of 1917 protected the species entirely.

Recovery was extremely slow. No modern game management techniques were applied to augment the protective effort, which consisted only of closing the muskox season and establishing certain sanctuaries. It is estimated that in 1930 there were only 500 barren ground muskoxen on the Canadian mainland. That number had increased to only 1,500 by 1958. The present quota system of harvest was established in 1969, with all quota tags allocated to the native communities. Sport hunts are taken from the community quota to augment revenue. Today barren ground muskoxen are plentiful in central Canada, and the animals inhabit all of their original range.

Sport hunting for barren ground muskoxen is usually in the late winter and early spring, when the animals' coats are prime. Temperatures can be brutally cold, so down-insulated parkas and pants are essential.

Barren ground muskox. Northwest Territories, April 1996.

Caribou-skin clothing is generally not available for mainland hunts, so buy the warmest garments you can. Many of the Hunter-Trapper Associations have Arctic parkas for their clients to wear, so check with your outfitter.

Hunting is usually by snowmobile. Because by Canadian law a sport hunter may not approach closer to a muskox than 3.25 kilometers (about two miles) on a snowmobile, the final approach is by conventional stalk over open terrain. Stealth is often unnecessary, however, as the herd characteristically assumes the defensive circular formation at the approach of predators, whether animal or human.

It can be brutally cold during a muskox hunt, but there is an alternative. A relatively balmy fall hunt for barren ground muskox is available in some communities. The coats may not be quite prime at that time of year, but they are nevertheless impressive and beautiful.

The muskox may not be the most elusive of animals, but the vast country they inhabit is their protection. You will have to travel many miles to find one that is a top-quality bull. Relax, stay warm, and enjoy hunting with your Inuit hosts. It is a hunt that I intend to make again soon.

QUEST IN THE INFINITE ARCTIC

It is with some degree of misgiving that I inspect the powerful Polaris snowmobile that will be my pony for the next week or two. My Inuvialuit guide, James Pokiak of Tuktoyaktuk, shows me the ignition sequence and how to kill the engine instantly if necessary. I observe his instructions keenly, knowing that mastering these skills may save me untold misery. I encountered an elderly Eskimo in the airport yesterday who was on his way to Inuvik to have his leg cast removed. Some time ago he suffered a severe fracture from an accident with one of these machines. I am familiar with four-wheel ATVs, and the knowledge transfers handily. Many miles away lies the land of the barren ground muskox, 150 miles to the east as the raven flies.

Tuktoyaktuk, in the Inuvialuktun language, means "place of the caribou crossing." For thousands of years, the peninsula on which the hamlet is situated has been home to countless

tuktu, or caribou. There have always been plenty of animals here, as well as the bounty of the adjacent Beaufort Sea, a prolific and relatively fertile tundra, and an endless supply of driftwood spilling from the mouth of the nearby Mackenzie River. These attributes have combined to make the Tuktoyaktuk Peninsula a historical gathering place for the Arctic peoples.

Western Canada's mainland Arctic is different in many ways from the eastern Arctic, its history and its primitive culture having been modified by the white man much earlier. The fur trade up the Mackenzie, occasional whalers, and Arctic explorers all influenced the people, their traditions, and their language. One can hardly fail to notice that the natives speak to one another in English, a phenomenon unusual in the east, where the similar Inuktitut language is commonly spoken even today. The sled behind my snowmobile here is not a *qamutik,* as it is in the east, but a "sleigh" or "sled."

Despite the favorable conditions, muskoxen have apparently never lived on the Tuktoyaktuk Peninsula. To find a muskox by hunting from Tuk, one must travel to the Horton River drainage; the creatures are plentiful from that point eastward. We are a full twelve hours of snowmobiling away from the best muskox hunting.

One should never presume to enter the Arctic with less than boundless time to spend, unless you are willing to settle for the routine tourist experience. In the constant daylight of late April on the Arctic coast, time has little meaning. Without the separation of darkness the days meld together, and only sleep divides life into manageable segments. In a strange twist, I feel myself caught in the disharmony between the local outlook and my hurry-up daily world. I actually have only four days, including our travel day, before muskox season closes on 30 April. I have a nagging worry that it won't be enough time, although everyone has assured me that three days of actual hunting is sufficient.

James and Maureen Pokiak are an interesting couple who, in a slightly convoluted manner, embody the very tension I feel within me. James is a thoroughbred Inuvialuit Eskimo, born and raised in Tuk, and half the town's population is related to him in some way. Maureen, on the other hand, is equally pure Caucasian, a native of

Muskox camp near the Horton River on the Arctic coast of Canada.

Saskatchewan. She came to Tuk as a young teacher in the early 1970s, fell in love with James, and never left. The pair have three children, two of whom are presently away at school in Inuvik; they also have a teenage daughter off fishing with friends in the back country.

The comfortable Pokiak home sees a never-ending stream of new faces, for they hospitably take in everyone from tourists to troubled youths. Their guests tonight include a young Frenchman who drifted into town in a quest for adventure, seeking experiences that will make him a better writer. A high school senior from Australia, an exchange student, will be here for the entire year. These young men will experience an alien culture, broadening their horizons and expanding their minds. I am exhausted from two solid days of travel, so I break away from the conversation early. It is time to settle in for some fitful sleep in the ceaseless daylight.

Sam Pingo, the assistant guide, shows up early the next morning. Maureen tells me that he is widely respected as a hunter and will be an asset on our hunt. He roars in from the direction of town, and now I have two highly experienced companions instead of one. Both men know the area well, and my only doubts have to do with the ever-ticking clock.

The powerful surge of the engine beneath me feels strangely familiar, and riding the bumps is surprisingly similar to driving an ATV. To my dismay and embarrassment, however, my hat blows off a couple of times. Sam, who trails me, scoops it up and returns it each time. Finally I hit on the right combination of goggles, hat, balaclava, and parka hood to keep everything in place. We're off and running, the miles slipping behind us like the flow of a great river. In time the constant pressure of my hand on the throttle and the pounding of the bumps begin to induce a gnawing fatigue. James and Sam seem unaffected, though, and I can't help but wonder if our Creator didn't endow them with more powerful right thumbs and more resilient backbones.

We are heading due east, crossing the Tuktoyaktuk Peninsula, weaving, bobbing, and bouncing. A flock of ptarmigan in the brown transition plumage of spring flushes at our noisy intrusion. They fly away like ghosts, with no sound of their wing beats audible over the roaring engines.

My Remington .30-06 is in its padded case atop Sam's sled, and I am concerned lest the incessant pounding damage it. It's never before experienced this amount of abuse. Even a rugged backpack hunt or a couple of weeks in a saddle scabbard are minor by comparison. I can only hope that it will function accurately when the moment arrives—assuming that we can find a good muskox bull in the allotted time.

James notices that my machine isn't tracking properly, and we pause on the shore of Eskimo Lake, with the long peninsula crossing behind us. A bolt has sheared off from the shaft, a problem that will eventually lead to a disastrous dislocation of the main drive belt. The spare parts we carry do not include the essential shaft, so James roars back to town to retrieve one. The hours crawl by as I chafe under the stress of lost time, but my host returns in only five hours. The repair requires quite a feat of engineering, but we are finally off again. Now I relish the cold wind as it stings my face. Maybe we can start the hunt tomorrow as planned, despite the delay.

The journey before us now is the roughest part of the entire trip, some twenty-five miles of irregular frozen ice that bludgeons me without pity. Eskimo Lake is actually a tongue of the salt water that separates the Tuk Peninsula from the mainland. The ice here is the most irregular I've ever seen, except for the chaotic multiyear ice on the open sea. Within a couple of hours I spot the Atkinson Point DEW Line station to our north, a landmark that signifies we are nearing Liverpool Bay, another broad body of salt water. If Eskimo Lake is this bad, I dread a wider body of salt water.

To my pleasant surprise, Liverpool Bay is glasslike in comparison to Eskimo Lake, and I am now able to appreciate the abundant power of the sturdy Polaris. Visibility fades with the decreasing angle of the sun behind the overcast, and a peculiar combination of opaque clouds and incident light diminishes my depth perception. I am glad it is smooth here, because the occasional bumps come as a complete surprise in the whiteout.

An imposing Arctic cliff looms ahead where we intersect the mainland. In places the snow has melted away exposing bare tundra, the vertical faces even losing some of their thin soil to expose awesome permafrost massifs. In most places this peculiar product of the Arctic is pure ice, with only rudimentary streaks of soil, not the frozen dirt I had imagined. The adjacent beach is even smoother than the bay, and we thunder onward. Occasional gaps in the sheer wall that parallels the seashore reveal lush tundra stretching to our south, mysterious country that I long to have time to explore.

The ache in my right thumb and forearm grows worse, and I am beginning to wonder how long I can keep going. We have now been traveling for nine hours, in addition to the five-hour wait for the spare part. James has been on his machine an incredible fourteen hours, counting his dash back to Tuk. The beach we are navigating has that peculiar endless quality that seems to typify the Arctic: another landmark enticingly appears each time we reach what had seemed the end.

Finally we break around the last point and cross a narrow isthmus to Nicholson Island. Here another sentinel DEW Line station stands in mute testimony to man's intrusion. All the DEW Line

A very tired guide after a twenty-hour day.

The ingenious Inuvialuit can fix anything that breaks—usually.

stations, however, are now completely automated and unmanned.

We will camp here on the south shore of Nicholson, just across Wood Basin from the mouth of the Anderson River. We are some 120 miles from Tuk, according to my Magellan GPS. It is now after midnight, and the eerie Arctic twilight descends upon us, though the daylight never completely dies. The two Inuvialuit rapidly pitch a comfortable tent, complete with heater, and anchor it between the sleds. Caribou skins cover the floor. I fill my stomach with caribou stew and hot tea before gratefully climbing into my sleeping bag.

We have seen little animal life thus far, and certainly no sign of muskoxen. James tells me that none of the species live west of the Anderson River, so I should not be surprised. Still, I have only three days for this hunt, and we must snowmobile thirty miles more to reach top muskox habitat. My guides sleep while I fret.

I finally manage a few hours of rest before it is time to move on. Camp comes down in a hurry after breakfast, and we move out onto the sea ice for a dozen miles. Approaching the north shore of the mainland once again, we encounter a colorful trio of polar bear guides mushing dog teams back to Tuk. Their sport hunter became ill and had to be airlifted back to town. They have been out on the ice the whole time, so they have no news regarding muskoxen.

At last we begin a slow ascent from the edge of the frozen sea into real muskox country. A fine snow is falling, and a misty haze limits visibility to a few hundred yards. To my great disappointment, we discover no sign of muskoxen, not even so much as an old track or droppings. By midnight it is time to camp again, this time in a sheltered inland depression just out of sight of the Horton River DEW Line station to our east, the fourth such installation we have seen. Here in the shelter of the low hills we are protected from the icy wind flowing off nearby Amundsen Gulf.

Neither James nor Sam seems concerned, but I can't shake the ominous feeling that I might be the unlucky hunter who doesn't get a barren ground muskox. After all, I'm the same guy who took three trips to get a cougar and three trips for a Sitka black-tailed deer. Why didn't I plan more time? It's an expensive commodity back home, but how abundant it seems here in the Arctic.

"Don't worry, we get him by four o'clock tomorrow," James assures me.

"I hope so." I try hard not to let my natural tendency to worry show.

"Bad whiteout. Can't see too far. We find them when it clears some."

But what if it stays this way for the next two days? Then it will be a very long ride home.

Sam's snowmobile is frozen in reverse as we prepare to break camp. He places the finicky machine in the now-familiar snowmobile-on-its-side position to make repairs while James and I zoom off to explore the country to our north.

Only five miles from camp, we find the fresh tracks of a lone muskox. The animal has been on a bare ridgetop, and by all appearances it has dropped off into a deep draw leading toward the coast. We elect not to follow into the inhospitable terrain and motor onward. Visibility is improving, and I am encouraged that at least one animal inhabits the area.

Now James has spotted something. Through my binoculars I see the herd of muskox, feeding on tundra grasses a few miles away. We motor close enough to inspect the group but find only one immature bull among the animals.

"What next?" I exclaim under my breath. "Why does the only herd of muskox in this part of the Arctic lack even a mediocre bull?" But I can't answer that question, and I recognize the emerging thought pattern. *Lord, forgive me and help me to think positively*, I pray silently. I truly am enjoying being out here, and I resolve to put my success orientation out of mind as best I can.

After carving a thirty-mile circle, we return to camp for a lunch of dried beluga whale and bannock. Sam is now mobile again, his machine ready, but it is already early afternoon. Considering the hour, we decide to camp in this same spot again tonight. This afternoon we will scour the territory to our east and south, along the west bank of the Horton. Visibility still isn't the best, but it has improved considerably.

Motoring across the endless barrens, I marvel at the absence of large animals. The only mammal tracks we see are those of the Arctic fox, which, like the animals themselves, are everywhere. Ptarmigan are relatively plentiful as well, as are the ubiquitous *siksiks*, or ground squirrels. But the muskox, like the caribou, are nowhere in evidence.

To our east we see the famous smoking hills, where hell seems to bubble to the surface of the Earth. For hundreds of years, perhaps even thousands, the sulfur-laden peat deposits within the hills have burned, a natural phenomenon that defies explanation.

"When the wind is right, you can smell the sulfur," James tells me.

Atop a high hill we find disturbed soil, perhaps the work of a herd of muskox. We dismount for a closer inspection, but much to my disappointment the "tracks" are the work of an industrious flock of ptarmigan scratching for food. We climb back aboard and continue on.

As we stand on a breathtaking bluff above the river, Sam points unexpectedly and chatters unintelligibly to James, indicating something far to our south.

"Muskox!"

I scan the area but see nothing. He describes where he sees the animals, and finally I discern them. They are mere dark spots on the white snow, invisible to all but the most practiced eye. Surely they must be ten miles away, mere specks.

James and Sam unhook their sleds and are off and running, while I bring up the rear, somewhat encumbered. They want me to bring my lighter sled in case we need it. It takes a full twenty minutes of motoring wildly across the tundra before we are in position to approach the herd. There is, indeed, a decent bull, and I determine that I must try to take him.

Stalking muskox is work, though perhaps not as challenging as stalking a bighorn ram or a pronghorn. In remote locations, the animals may eye you, circle up on a parcel of high ground, mill about nervously, and perhaps run a short distance. But there is seldom any element of surprise.

I take great care to be certain I am targeting the right bull and that he is in the clear. The herd has several bulls, but only one is of reasonable trophy quality. Finally the animal presents broadside about a hundred yards from me. He stands sufficiently apart from the other animals, so I chamber a round. Steadying the rifle as best I can under the circumstances, I squeeze off the shot, aiming just behind and below the base of the horn for what should be a painless and bloodless kill.

To my great surprise, at the report the brawny bull only bounds a few yards and stops again, looking highly puzzled. After working the bolt, I aim slightly lower. At the explosion, the bull collapses into a lifeless heap.

The rest of the herd gallop away for parts unknown as we approach our prize. The bull is an

The long ride back to Tuktoyaktuk.

excellent example of a barren ground muskox, though he measures a bit smaller than I had hoped. The thought triggers a question in my mind: *You're never satisfied, are you?* I forthwith say a prayer of thanks, in gratitude that there was indeed a trophy bull here after all.

James interrupts my thoughts by saying, "Hey, partner, look at your watch. What time is it?"

I look at my timepiece, then reply, "Five after four. Why?"

"What did I say?"

"Oh, yeah, you said we'd have him by four o'clock." It must have been about a minute or two before 4 P.M. when I made my shot.

Retrieving our vehicles, an extended picture session, and skinning our prize take almost three hours. While the two guides complete the caping, I do the quartering and remove the meaty backstraps. The sled is soon laden with meat, hide, and horns. By seven o'clock in the evening we are back in our camp.

Morning breaks overcast and white, with a spitting of snow and a drab layer of low fog. Visibility for the twelve-hour ride back to Tuk gets worse as time passes. I had already forgotten the brutal bumps on Eskimo Lake, but I remember them as we tackle that part of the journey once more. By the time we arrive to a hot supper of freshly cooked goose at Maureen's kitchen, the odometer on the snowmobile shows 705 kilometers traveled, 437 miles. Happily back in bed indoors again, my sleep is now sound and my mind at ease. I challenged the harsh Arctic, and by God's grace I got my bull.

Maureen and James conduct hunts for polar bear, barren ground grizzly, muskox, and caribou, and they also do river trips and fishing in the summer. Tourists flock to Tuk because nowhere else in the western Arctic of Canada is a town situated directly on the seacoast. This brings in a steady flow of tourists, and Maureen conducts local tours for a small fee. I accompany her on one such excursion before my departure and hear about the region's pingos, permafrost, and people. The tour ends in Maureen's home, where she serves dried beluga whale meat dipped in whale oil, *muktuk*, and smoked whitefish, all local favorites.

The Anglican church in Tuktoyaktuk, oldest in the western Arctic.

James treats me to a ride on his dogsled, demonstrating a control over his team I had thought impossible. His dogs are much more friendly and gentle than others I have encountered in the Arctic, and he seldom uses a whip.

I leave Tuk after resting for a day, happy the hunt was successful but sad I hadn't planned better to avoid the time crunch. I must try to remember what I already know: never go to the Arctic and attempt to do things in a hurry. In fact, it is better never to be in a hurry.

I rush to get to the airport in time for my flight to Inuvik, the first leg of my journey home. Looking back, I wave an enthusiastic farewell to my new friends.

I am sprinting back to my hurry-up world. Already I am forgetting the recent lesson, as I wonder uneasily about connections, reservations, and my schedule. As the plane lifts off from the frozen runway, it suddenly occurs to me that the life in this remote corner of the continent isn't all that bad. I find myself envying James and Maureen Pokiak.

Dall sheep. (Photo: courtesy of Eric J. Hansen)

DALL SHEEP
(Ovis dalli dalli)

There's a land where the mountains are nameless,
And the rivers all run God knows where;
There are lives that are erring and aimless, and deaths that just hang by a hair;
There are hardships that nobody reckons, there are valleys unpeopled and still;
There's a land—oh, how it beckons, and I want to go back—and I will.

—Robert W. Service (1874–1958), *The Spell of the Yukon*

Dall sheep live in enchanting country. For many hunters they are "Sheep 101," and it is easy for that first experience to develop into a burning passion known as "sheep fever." Much of that attraction is tied not to the animal as much as to the terrain: seemingly random mountains and rivers, terrifying heights, imminent danger, and unending adversity. The rewards of such a hunt are great when success finally comes, but seldom is it easy. Usually the most difficult part is negotiating the vertical slopes where the white sheep live. It is my estimation that as a rule none of the more southerly types of sheep inhabit such precipitous country. But before we tackle that interesting aspect of these animals, let's identify the Dall's delightful physical characteristics.

The first scientific description of the Dall sheep was the work of the American naturalist and explorer W. H. Dall in 1884, although the sheep had been well known long before his expedition. Dall's research took place south of the Fort Yukon area, most likely in the region of the Tanana Hills. He named the new specimens *Ovis montana dalli*, a designation that was later to become *Ovis dalli dalli*.

The Dall sheep, like all mountain sheep, is somewhat blocky in appearance, the corners of its body becoming more acute at maturity. The coat is flawlessly white, though some Alaska Dall sheep have a few black hairs around the tail and rump. Record-keeping organizations would technically identify these animals as Stone sheep if they lived in the southern Yukon, but in Alaska they are Dall. It is not uncommon for the white coat to become stained, for example by the soil on which the sheep lie during summer.

Every sheep hunter is familiar with the amber horns and wide flaring tips that characterize this sheep enthusiast's dream. The eyes are deep yellow, and the hoofs and nose are black. Rams weigh in at 200 pounds and ewes at 120, on average, although there are larger animals, and some authorities would put the average weight of a mature ram in some populations at nearer 300 pounds. The horns of adult males account for about 10 percent of the total body weight, equivalent to an average man's wearing a seventeen-pound hat all day. It is from the longer and more slender configuration of these horns that the Dall sheep acquires its classification as a "thinhorn" sheep (the other is Stone sheep), as distinguished from the more massive horns of the "bighorns."

There is another subspecies of Dall sheep, those of the Kenai Peninsula, which I should mention for completeness. Those creatures are the *Ovis dalli kenaiensis*. Most taxonomists, however, generally lump them into the same category with the other Dall sheep.

A Dall ram, like other mountain sheep, becomes a true trophy in the last years of its life. At that point, the potbelly has become apparent, horn growth approaches maximum, and the animal is perhaps eight to ten years old. Viewed from the side the horns form a full curl, and the best rams carry much of the basal mass well into the middle third and farther. Ideally, when you check the teeth one or two jaw teeth will already be missing, indicating that the upcoming winter would likely have been the animal's last.

Hunters seldom observe the rut of these sheep because it occurs in late November and December, well after the close of the season. Moreover, in some portions of the Dall range, it is mostly dark at that time of the year. Rams usually travel in small groups of five to ten, although in Jack O'Connor's time there were groups of up to a hundred. There is a well established dominance order among the rams; nevertheless, battles are common during the rut. Rams rarely mix with ewes except during breeding.

Gestation lasts about 175 days for all mountain sheep of North America. Ewes move into rugged areas to give birth to a single lamb, with most births occurring between May 10 and May 25. Newborn Dall lambs weigh about ten pounds, and it is at this stage that they are most susceptible to predators. I have observed newborn lambs scampering as a unit within a band of ewes, and it amazed me to see such tiny creatures moving so well. Whenever a golden eagle flies over the lambs seek the shelter of the ewes, the shape and movement of the predators apparently being imprinted in them genetically. One spring I observed a band of perhaps fifty animals in the Yukon. Eagles made numerous passes over them, but I never saw one of the birds attempt to catch

one. That was probably because the lambs had already become proficient at remaining among the ewes. Had I been there a week earlier, perhaps I would have seen the less hardy and the slower learners picked off.

A recent study of lamb mortality in Alaska revealed that 50 percent die by the end of their first year. Of those killed, coyotes took 43 percent and eagles 22 percent. Wolverine and bear accounted for 4 percent, and 17 percent died of unknown causes (probably wolves or coyotes).

The lambs grow quickly and can eat plants within two weeks of birth. By the end of their first summer they are as agile and fleet as the adults, and by fall they weigh close to eighty pounds. They are sexually mature at eighteen months, although young rams may not breed until they are much older because of dominance by mature animals. They live twelve to fourteen years, the rams generally a few years less on average than the ewes. Winterkill is common after age ten, when the ravages of time begin to take a toll.

Like most ruminants, Dall sheep eat a variety of plants. The sheep feed early and late in the day, and only reluctantly feed at night. During summer they prefer fescues and sedges, especially the

Dall sheep. Alaska, August 1990.

nutritious seed heads, and they also feed on saxifrage, horsetails, fireweed, and willow. In winter their diet shifts to dried grasses and small quantities of lichens and mosses, which they dig for on windblown ridges where the snow isn't deep.

The remoteness of the white sheep's habitat protects it from man's encroachment. They continue to occupy virtually all of their original territory, from the Brooks Range of Alaska's Arctic throughout the Alaska Range, the Chugach and Wrangell Mountains, the St. Elias Mountains, most of the mountains of the Yukon, and the Mackenzie and Richardson Mountains of the Northwest Territories. Since the southern tip of the St. Elias Range extends into British Columbia, three Canadian provinces can claim Dall sheep populations. They are the most numerous of the native mountain sheep in North America. Estimates for Alaska alone range as high as 73,000 animals, with 26,500 estimated to be in Canada. Numbers decline during severe winters but recover quickly when winters are mild. Periodic counts of targeted populations and monitoring of the harvest are the usual management tools. Ongoing research projects focus on important habitat areas, growth and reproduction, mineral licks and their impact on sheep health, the effects of predators, and monitoring for various diseases.

Hunters take about 1,400 of the white sheep annually in Alaska, and proportionally less from the Canadian populations. I have taken both my Dall rams in Alaska, one from the Brooks Range and the other from the Alaska Range. I got my first taste of sheep hunting in the Brooks Range, and I have been an enthusiast ever since. Although I don't consider myself a "sheep nut," I do know how they must feel.

Many a man has waxed poetic when transported into sheep country for the first time. There is a magical quality about moving quickly from the world of cars, streetlights, warm houses, and electricity to a scary landing on a gravel bar or ridgetop far from civilization. The transition is astonishing, and the novice may be dismayed and uncertain about the challenge that lies ahead. The successful completion of such an adventure tends to produce a desire for more. On the other hand, the unsuccessful hunter or the hunter who has

overestimated his endurance may come to dislike sheep hunting. One acquaintance told me that he labored for hours to climb one mountain in the relatively rolling Brooks Range. When the guide informed him that they had to climb the next mountain too, he broke off the hunt. He told the guide, "If you'll get me home, you can have that $5,000."

As a group, sheep hunters are the most highly motivated and best prepared of the hunting community because they know from discussions with other hunters something of the requirements. The high terrain is daunting, the effort required is often colossal, the dangers are very real, and the whole concept is quite inexplicable to the uninitiated.

The difficulty of hunting sheep varies directly with the steepness of the terrain. In the Brooks Range there are few real cliffs compared with the Alaska Range, the Wrangells, and the Chugach. My "cliff-hanger" ram lived in some of the steepest sheep habitat in North America; it was completely safe from human predation until it moved out of its niche. Most Dall sheep habitat has its share of rock slides and steep cleavers of semisolid rock on which vegetation grows with varying degrees of density. Climbing in such country is indeed a challenge, but once one has scaled the heights to look down through clear air at a distant, serpentine river, the feeling of satisfaction is addictive.

Because of the remoteness and inaccessibility of most Dall sheep range, quotas and a drawing system have been unnecessary. There are areas in Alaska where a successful draw is necessary to hunt, mainly for highly accessible populations near urban areas or in "limited entry" trophy ram areas. Hunting pressure is seldom if ever a factor in population dynamics, due to the difficulty of the hunt and the age class of the animals harvested.

Populations of Dall sheep do fluctuate, however. When winters are mild over several years, sheep numbers increase. Deep snow, drought in summer, or a very wet spring contribute significantly to mortality. Predation on adult sheep is mainly by wolves. Bears, lynx, and wolverine seldom take adult sheep. In general, predators have a minor impact on Dall sheep populations. Disease is unusual, but cases of "lumpy jaw," a bacterial disease of the soft tissues, have been problematic at times. Since domestic animals have been rare in their habitat, Dall sheep have so far escaped the lungworm pneumonia complex that has devastated so many of their more southerly bighorn cousins.

Hunting techniques vary little among the subspecies of *Ovis*. As Jack O'Connor wrote, one "must see the sheep before the sheep sees him. Then he must select a route where the wind is right and where he can stay out of sight of the sheep. Then he sneaks up and shoots the sheep." Nothing to it. O'Connor understated the facts, but still accurate they are. Reaching that final position can be a highly torturous proposition, though, involving many airplane miles for most of us, then gradually smaller planes down to the Super Cub or float plane. Many days of hiking, climbing, and glassing, and then many hours on the final stalk, also intervene.

Although the classic stalk is the most common way to take the sheep, it also works well to wear white coveralls and approach them directly. That type of stalk is useful when there is no other way to get close enough for a shot. The hunter simply meanders in on a slow, erratic path toward the target until he is in range.

My favorite sheep hunting clothing is a pair of Patagonia climbing pants with suspenders and a belt, leather boots, a light wool or chamois shirt, and polypropylene underwear, topped with a mesh-back cap for good cooling while climbing. On backpack hunts I always carry a pack with a special hook on which to hang my rifle, a most useful setup designed by Jack Atcheson Jr. of Butte, Montana. In the pack are essentials: a waterproof down parka with hood, a down vest, a set of lightweight rain gear, gloves, and a foam pad on which to sit while glassing. Also I include survival gear: a space blanket (the kind made into a sleeping bag weighs only a couple of ounces and can save your life), a small flashlight, fire-starting materials, a little food, and a water bottle. One also needs to pack extra ammunition, a spotting scope, binoculars, moleskin for blisters, a knife, and a couple of plastic bags.

A happy guide celebrates the hard-earned victory.

Cameras have to fit somewhere as well. Don't forget them, and don't wait until you have your ram down to use them. Every step of a Dall sheep hunt is irreplaceable, so record as much as you're able.

CLIFF-HANGER RAM

As we negotiate the vertical walls of the mountain pass in the big yellow Otter, pilot and outfitter Jim Harrower deftly maneuvers the plane between rock faces and meandering glaciers. The giant radial engine growls as we gaze out the window at the magnificent land below. The lower fingers of the wandering rivers of ice give rise to silt-stained streams that fan out below us, milky white and running fast. Interlacing branches look like a terrestrial vascular system, with multiple channels in each broad, rock-strewn riverbed.

There is a strange black coating on the white ice of the parent glaciers, a dusting that at first glance appears to be soot or some other particulate substance. The sight is peculiar, but this is Alaska, where impressive and inexplicable phenomena are commonplace. The view from the plane instills a deep sense of amazement at the landscape below, however, so I ponder the polluting material only momentarily.

As we fly toward Harrower's Stony River Lodge, I reflect on how I came to be here on another quest for Dall sheep. I had called my friend and sometimes outfitter Jack Atcheson Jr. and asked where I might perchance find a truly exceptional Dall ram. Years ago on my first sheep hunt I had taken a little one, and Jack assured me that this is the place I would find a trophy.

The rugged terrain over which we are flying has a terrifying aspect. I remember a goat hunt in such country some years ago, the experience having marked me for life because of the close escapes and the ever-present danger of falling. One understands one's tenuous grip on existence when hanging precariously hundreds of feet above the next horizontal real estate. I obviously want to hunt these sheep, or I wouldn't be here. Nevertheless, a certain dread fills me as we pass over those awful sheer walls below.

Many areas are impossible to hunt because of the precipitous cliffs. Glaciers are everywhere and intimidating here in the Alaska Range, and hidden dangers abound on their surfaces. Monte Stadtler, who will guide me on my hunt, points to a broad stretch of gravel bar in a side canyon where tomorrow we will begin my quest. The timbered lowlands quickly give way to tundra-covered highlands, and lush August green fills the lower valley. Above that, nothing but gray and red rock stretches as far as the eye can see. The erect walls of the valley are almost unbroken as they disappear into the distance. My heart sinks as I realize that I will most likely have to climb those imposing monoliths. Visions flash through my mind, gruesome thoughts of dangling from a rope, a tenuous linchpin wedged in a faltering crevice, hunting sheep as a rock climber might assault El Capitan. No matter—I will do whatever it takes to get a truly good Dall ram.

Four hours of climbing a rocky ridge put me on top of the world.

Harrower expertly guides the big workhorse airplane to the sandy riverbank strip near his lodge, putting it down where there is no margin for error. I say a silent prayer of thanks to have arrived safely at the Stony River Lodge. An ATV delivers the incoming hunters' baggage to the cluster of buildings.

The lodge has all the modern conveniences and is among the best I have ever encountered. We sit down to enjoy a sumptuous meal and get to know each other. I usually travel alone on such hunts, which denies me the companionship of longtime friends but opens opportunities to meet new ones. Among the guests is Jack Atcheson Sr., whose son booked this hunt for me. Coincidentally, he is here to hunt a little and observe a lot, studying the level of service in one more hunting camp.

After our meal, Jim briefs us on the upcoming hunt. There are several sheep hunters, and I hope silently that Jack Jr. has sent word that I am not here to hunt just any ram. I already have one of those. I want a beauty, and I am relieved when the outfitter explains what he has in mind. This will not be a hunt for sheep in the plural. I will not be inspecting sheep until I find one I want. Instead, I will be hunting one sheep, a beautiful loner of a ram that lives up the valley I studied as we winged

our way here. I will most likely see my sheep the first day, and my guide and I will spend my trip trying to calculate how we can get to him. He is ancient, heavy of horn, and almost as cagey as a whitetail buck. Jim's hunters approached the ram only once, and they haven't seen him leave the impressive cliff face where he dwells since then. The ram is getting old and will likely not survive the upcoming winter, so someone needs to do everything possible to get him before he is lost forever. I like the quest, even if I dread the formidable terrain.

My guide is a solidly experienced and mature man who is comfortable with backpack hunting of the most arduous sort. He is ten years my junior, but his intensity and sincerity appeal to me. I discover that he has come back from a severe knee injury a few years before that required extensive reconstructive surgery with complicated tendon transplants, the kind of disability that drives many men into early retirement from demanding physical pursuits. But not Monte. He still works as a river rafting guide, a ski instructor, and a hunting guide, depending on the season. Monte assures me that his physical problems will pose no obstacle to our hunt. He clearly has an

A night in "alder hell" leaves guide Monte rested and ready by morning.

The indispensable Super Cub deposits hunters and gear on a remote gravel bar.

indomitable nature, and he expresses his excitement at the prospect of our pursuing this particular ram. I sense immediately that we will get along famously.

In mainland Alaska, there is always a Piper Super Cub in the hunter's future. After a good night's sleep, we embark on our quest for the cliff-hanger ram. By noon I am standing on the remote gravel bar, the looming rock walls even more impressive and intimidating than they had appeared from the air. The Super Cub thunders away, leaving Monte and me in utter silence.

We stand for a long moment savoring the tranquillity, the wilderness peace I had almost forgotten. It is always a special time when thoughts of civilization recede and the hunter's focus on his task becomes as intense as a laser beam. Determination floods me. We will hunt this ram and we will take him, by God's grace. We shoulder our copiously stuffed packs and head upstream toward the headwaters of the rushing stream.

The tortuous river flows brown from an unusually heavy load of glacial silt, as stained as a Georgia creek after a thunderstorm. The water level here rises in direct proportion to the air temperature because of melt from the myriad glaciers upstream. This year the level is even higher than usual, because an explosive eruption of nearby Redoubt Volcano has tainted every glacier in the region with volcanic ash. That explains the black dust I spotted yesterday from the plane. The ash not only dirties the melt water but also causes the ice fields to absorb more heat than usual, the result being that every river in the area is an absolute stew of ground rock and pumice. The water looks like a chocolate milkshake. We will have to drink that water, a prospect almost as daunting as that of having to cross those raging torrents.

No matter how much one conditions for a backpack hunt, the first miles are always tough. In these struggles humans are but tiny laborers pitted against the vast wilderness, and I always feel woefully unprepared. In no time I feel the sweat running down my forehead and a dampness under my pack.

The river is negotiable in places, and we walk repeatedly on unsteady legs through the dark, boiling waters. The furious flow undermines the river bottom, threatening to capsize anyone who is not diligent and determined. The water is colder than iced tea, so a spill could be disastrous. We are wearing the hip boots that are required in most of Alaska, but the water flows so swiftly that one can actually hear rocks rolling on the bottom of the stream, an added danger to the footing. Rather than go it alone and take our chances, Monte and I join hands and alternate walking in the deeper, more treacherous sections. That simple maneuver is impressively helpful.

We are only an hour or so upstream when we spot a solitary white speck high on a cliff several miles upriver—a Dall ram. Our quarry reportedly lives in those high cliffs, so this could be the one. The distance is so great that the most we can do is confirm the animal's sex, although the thought that this might be the very ram I am seeking is deeply exciting. Even from miles away we begin to speculate how we might approach. The high mountain is terrible and forbidding, a demonic place where no sane man would venture. My worst fears about the vertical terrain are already unfolding, but perhaps the ram doesn't stay up there all the time. Perhaps he comes down, or changes mountains. We have a full week to find out, and the very sight of the ram buoys my hopes.

This country is excellent habitat for both black bears and grizzlies, as evidenced by copious tracks in the sand along the river. We don't see any grizzlies, but we do spot blacks at several locations. With all the bear sign, we ponder whether the threat of predation might not be the reason why the sheep keep to their cliffs.

After several hours of grueling toil we arrive at a point exactly opposite the ram. A cliff on our side offers some protection from the ceaseless wind, and there is a small branch of the river nearby that is relatively free of the awful silt. We can see well from here, so we elect to camp. Before we erect our tent we set up the spotting scope and evaluate the ram, still visible on his perch some 4,000 vertical feet above us. He is definitely our desired prey, as evidenced by heavy headgear and dramatically upshot tips. Now we need a plan.

After getting everything ready for the night, we maneuver closer to the ram and set up the spotting scope again. I have never seen a more beautiful creature. Monte assesses the ram at better than 38 inches, a little shorter than his age and mass would dictate because the heavy horns curl so tightly. Both tips are intact and directed upward and outward in classic fashion. The ram's location, however, is even more impossible than I had thought, the steep cliff in front of him absolutely unclimbable by conventional means. On all sides are vertical drops of more than 1,000 feet that would give the most stalwart mountain hunter a bad case of acrophobia.

The white ram is positively unapproachable unless he moves, so we may be in for a long siege. To make matters worse, he moves only to feed, a sign of age and contentment, perhaps. Either way, it bodes ill for our chances of catching him on more accessible terrain.

Sleep is fitful in the crowded tent. Visions of trying to climb that awful face haunt my dreams, and I awake several times to find myself clinging to a tiny ledge thousands of feet up, a yawning chasm below, and the ram always out of reach. The patter of raindrops against the tent fly lulls me back to sleep as I remember that Monte has already said we won't climb up anything we can't descend intact.

Our ancient ram doesn't move the next day, merely wandering a few yards. In mild frustration we lighten our packs and, leaving camp intact, move upstream to scope any other resident rams who might live in the drainage. During a four-hour trip in intermittent rain we see a half-dozen rams, but nothing worth taking. Finally we reach a place where the boiling waters combine into a single surging and uncrossable torrent. We head back, walking another four hours before arriving at camp.

The most telling information we have garnered from our trek is that the ram's home is a veritable fortress. Between our camp and the ram is a ridge, and behind that steep monolith lies an abyss, horrifying beyond description. The walls on either side are vertical, and the bottom is littered with blocks of ice the size of houses. Waterfalls cascade off the cliffs, creating additional obstacles. Unless the animal moves, we are defeated. I detect within me that old familiar feeling of helplessness in the face of insurmountable obstacles. Nevertheless we must hunt this old monarch or go home empty-handed. There is no other outstanding ram in this valley.

We awake the next day to intermittent rain and savor the welcome rest after our long walk. Pleasant sunshine breaks through at midmorning, and we spend the rest of the day observing the ram through our spotting scope. A deep longing to be closer gnaws at me, a yearning that I can quench only by taking him, touching him, and admiring those massive horns closeup. Despite the potbelly and the infirmities of age, the creature nimbly negotiates terrain impossible for a man. The animal has spent his life one step from oblivion—a psychological advantage no human can claim.

As we rest on a grassy knoll, we feast on the lush blueberries that grow in profusion there and enjoy this day of relaxation. We return to camp undaunted but with no new ideas—except to wait and hope. Old Mr. Tight Curl has moved scarcely fifty yards since we first spotted him two days ago.

Another night passes without incident, except for a close encounter with a local bear that wanders through the camp, and we arise for another day of watching. This kind of sheep hunting is new to me, but we must adjust our tactics to the conditions. The ram shows every sign of staying put, so we will trek downriver to where our pilot is planning to meet us for a check and fresh supplies. I don't believe we will miss anything but a lot of waiting, so I elect to accompany Monte instead of manning the spotting scope. Monte decides to take the tent with us, and on arrival at the strip we conclude it was a good decision.

Nature's bounty—and a nice addition to breakfast.

The plane fails to arrive. A date with a Super Cub is always no more precise than forty-eight hours or so, and we spend the night in our original landing spot. No matter. We can still see the old ram through the spotting scope, a stationary white spot five miles away.

Traveling upriver after our rendezvous, we mull the news that Dee Harrower, Jim's wife, says we will be successful. I don't believe in intuition, but it's encouraging nevertheless. She said that the ram will move into position where we can take him, but so far that has not happened.

An ominous warmth pervades the land and a soft rain falls as we labor back toward our campsite. The river is rising and rushes ever more insistently, flooding more of the previously dry channels. The main channel has become a furious, powerful stream reminiscent of the Colorado River in spring—churning, leaping, and lashing at the air. We have no choice now but to stay to the west side, where the ram lives, because we might not be able to cross back over higher up where the river channel narrows. Moreover, we could become trapped on the wrong side.

Our late start from the strip means that we must hurry to reach the new campsite, across the river from our first camp. About a half-mile from our destination the river curves acutely to the west, abutting a steep bank wickedly undercut by the roaring main channel. The high wall of dirt is topped by the scourge of Alaska—the ubiquitous alder. We can't cross to the easy walking on the gravel bar, so we traverse the top of the slope and battle the dripping alders in full packs. Another half-mile up the river we see our destination gravel bar, but it is unreachable without toiling through the maze. We ascend the slippery bank with difficulty, making an all-out assault to reach the inviting bar.

Dark is falling as we struggle against the treacherous interlacing branches. Like demons, the boughs grope for us and our gear with unyielding fingers. My dry mouth craves refreshing liquid, but I have finished the last of my scant water. The deafening sound of the flooding cataclysm at the foot of the slope summons me. But I know that the nearby water cannot be reached without unacceptable danger, particularly in the dark. Flashlights are no match for a moonless Alaska night, yet in their feeble beams we labor onward.

After two hours, we finally succumb and call a halt. We have covered perhaps only a few hundred yards of "alder hell," but our legs and arms are leadened from the effort. It will be necessary to find some kind of opening in the dense thicket and spend the night. Rolling out sleeping bags and tarps, I am grateful the rains have ended and the stars shine overhead. Monte has a swallow of water for each of us before we collapse in exhaustion.

Awakening to find the tiny glade awash with welcome sunshine, we dry our gear and prepare to move on. A lone cottonwood tree stands nearby, and scaling it I chart a course to our destination. By noon we are setting up our tiny tent near crystal-clear water that seeps from the mountain where our ram lives.

The ram is much nearer us now than before, though he has not moved from his place on the mountain. For six days the old monarch has remained stationary, teasing us from his lofty perch. All I can do is watch as the ram of my dreams tempts me to make a suicidal climb. My hunter's heart burns to take him before he is lost forever to the coming winter. Monte and I discuss every possibility, calculating how a stalk might be possible if the ram moved this way or that, up, down, or to either side. I ask God to move him somewhere more accessible, feeling a bit selfish in my request.

Late that day, without fanfare, the old ram finally makes his move. We are glassing from the bottom of a treacherous rock slide near camp when the miracle begins. Ambling down from the rock face, he makes a resolute walk to our left and disappears behind a ridge near the head of the frightening gorge. For thirty minutes we sit wondering where on earth he has gone, and at last he emerges on the ridge nearer us, on the proximal side of the unfathomable crevasse. The ridge he is now on is also probably unclimbable, but at least he has moved. Hope wells as never before. He is still perhaps 3,000 feet above us, but a rock slide below appears negotiable, though extremely steep.

"Look! More rams!" Monte observes, as three decent rams arrive from upriver, perhaps the same ones we saw on our long walk to the headwaters. They cross slowly beneath our ancient ram, while his gaze remains riveted on the trio. Another, a small sickle-horned youngster, passes much closer to our ram, which shows uncharacteristic interest in that animal as well. All four disappear before nightfall, but our old monarch remains in his new position atop the vertical fortress.

"Tomorrow we climb," Monte comments as the lingering twilight fades.

"Where to?" I ask, hoping that the ominous ridge below the ram is not what he has in mind.

"Up the ridge or up the slide. Depends on where the old guy goes—if he goes anywhere at all."

Another fitful night in the sleeping bag follows, my heart silently praying that the ram will descend. In my dreams he comes right down to our camp and offers himself to us, an unlikely possibility to say the least. The easy dream kill is inevitably followed by nightmares of vertical rock faces, long falls, and broken bones.

First light on my last scheduled day in the back country finds us scrambling to eat early so we can go to our glassing place immediately. It is fortunate that we arrive early, an answered prayer of the highest magnitude. The old ram is indeed lower, perhaps only five hundred feet above the top of the rock slide. We quickly surmise that he would be irretrievable there if he lodged after a long shot and destroyed by the fall if he did not. We begin to plan a stalk that will put us as close as possible for a day of watching and hoping.

Without fanfare, the small sickle-horned ram from the night before appears, quite near us, just at the bottom of the rock slide. He begins a slow and methodical ascent of the steep boulder field, and we watch with anticipation for the old ram's reaction. As he did yesterday, the ancient king focuses completely, inexplicably, on the youngster, intently watching him ascend. The whole process consumes perhaps thirty minutes, and our adrenaline spikes when the grand patriarch starts to descend. This lowly sickle-horn has become the bait that will attract our prey. We rejoice perhaps prematurely, but we may yet have a chance.

We watch as both animals disappear behind a ridge that dominates the left side of our field of view, the broken cliff from which much of the slide originated. We will have to climb the bulge of that steep ridge, and for the first time on this hunt I now feel as though I'm really hunting sheep.

The slope we traverse resembles a giant, narrow pyramid. There is a steep rock slide on the right of the ridge and a nearly vertical crevasse in the sheer face on the left, its bottom strewn with ice blocks the size of icebergs linked by intermittent white water. We climb with a close-up view of that alarming chasm, but at least now it is not between us and the ram. At first we try climbing the rock slide but quickly see that it is too steep and the footing too unstable. Similarly, the cliff on the left side of the slide, rising on gigantic pillars of stone, is unassailable by mere mortals. The only way up is to mount the steep ridge, staying where there is vegetation.

Scrambling up a narrow tongue of gravel that spews from the ridge, we finally surmount the rock slide and reach terrain where grass and dwarf alders grow, indicators of relatively stable earth. It is nevertheless gruelingly steep, and a comparison with the adjacent ridge, where the old ram had been, demonstrates the utter folly of our even thinking we might have climbed there.

It takes four hours of climbing to get near the top. We turn and survey our campsite in the river bottom, 3,000 vertical feet below, our tent a toy in the distance. The ridge narrows as we ascend, and we gasp at the vertical cliffs that yawn on either side—at least 1,000 feet to the bottom on the right, perhaps twice that on the left. As we run out of real estate near the pinnacle, Monte motions me down suddenly. There they are!

The two rams are visible a scant 400 yards away. The knoll on which they are feeding appears to be a solid extension of our narrow ridge, perhaps connected to it. We work closer, keeping low, and approach to about 300 yards. The ancient ram is lying on the very crest of the skyline, his head just visible and facing the other way. The smaller ram is up and feeding nearby, entirely unaware of our presence. I go through my usual pre-shot sequence, pulling down my bipod legs and chambering a round, incredulous that we are finally getting an opportunity.

Monte is much more cautious. He silently surveys the overall situation and decides that he needs more information on the intervening terrain. The ram will have to stand before I can shoot, so we have some time to study the location.

"We might not be able to retrieve him. There might be a ravine between the ram and us," he says. "When the little ram feeds out of sight, I'll crawl up and look."

The sickle-horned ram finally disappears, and I wait apprehensively as Monte crawls out of view up the slope. I keep my scope on the big ram, ready but uncertain. My excitement is difficult to contain as I observe the magnificent specimen through my old Redfield scope. I am uneasy as Monte slides back to my side.

"Mighty iffy. The ridge we're on peters out to a knife edge maybe thirty yards from the knoll they're on. It's steep off each side, almost vertical. And the knoll itself has a cliff to ascend before we reach them. And if he rolls. . . ."

"Can it be done?" I whisper.

"Maybe. I just wish we had a good rope. That knife edge has loose rock all along it."

I gulp hard. What should I do if a clear shot presents? If he walks this way, I'll shoot. If he walks the other way, I won't.

Another hour passes as the chill of the elevation, the persistent wind, and my sweaty clothes combine to cause me to shiver. My eyes are getting sore peering down the tube of the rifle scope, and the ram is so still I wonder if perhaps he has already died. Finally, he stirs, rises to his feet, and presents broadside on the horizon, magnificent against the crystal-blue sky. I hold my fire and wait, confident that a touch on the trigger would end his life. He then turns and walks resolutely away, presenting a rear view as he disappears over the crest. I feel a deep sense of both disappointment and relief as we wait to see if he will reappear. He is gone.

Now we can relax and talk freely. The hunt has been intensely interesting, one to remember. I have been defeated before, so the experience is not new. We eat our lunch after climbing to the apex of the ridge. I am aghast at the knife edge separating us from the ram's perch. A formidable boulder sits halfway across it, and the vertical plunge of the cliff makes me shiver. The place the ram could have fallen into is still worse, so I conclude that I made the right choice.

The sun is shining brightly as we eat our sandwiches and lick our wounds on the lofty ridge, swirling clouds just over our heads. We savor the fantastic view, the silver thread of the river far below, the soaring cliffs surrounding us. This is what sheep hunting is all about, ram or no ram. It is good to have participated in the quest, bittersweet in that the terrain has defeated us, satisfying in that we have given it our best effort.

We begin our perilous descent to camp, and the extreme steepness is even more apparent on the trip down. In several places I call on the hardy alders to keep myself from falling headlong. Several hundred feet below our apogee, Monte stares off toward the mountain on the other side of the chasm. In silence he gazes, and then purses his lips. I follow his look.

"Our ram! Look at him!"

The master ram remains out of reach, but there he is for us to ponder. He has descended the deep ravine after leaving the high terrain and now stands silhouetted against a strip of snow. A long moment passes, then he turns and walks straight up the white chute and disappears. I bid the old king of the mountain farewell and hope that by some miracle he will survive the winter. My heart aches a bit at the knowledge that I will never see him again, but I am grateful for this one last view.

Three hours later we arrive back in camp, weak in spirit but satisfied with our effort. Reclining against a rock, I drink copiously to rehydrate myself and have a bite to eat. I gaze downriver at the tangle of alders we must cross once more to reach our pickup point, the surging river more ominous than ever. We dread the alders, knowing that they will yield no quarter. Neither Monte nor I am in a mood for conversation. I can't shake that last image of the old ram. I can hardly stand the thought of such a magnificent creature's ending his days as carrion, food for ravens and magpies.

Then Monte glances up the mountain and makes an offhand comment that he sees a sheep. I glance up and I see the animal too, at the top of another gigantic rock slide. The ram is on the side of the mountain opposite where ours disappeared, and almost as high up the slide as the steep ridge

Imposing rock walls tower on all sides of the gravel-strewn riverbed.

we have just descended. We begin glassing intently, and we spot five sheep, all feeding in an accessible area at the top of the slide. Could these be the same five sheep? Could our ram be there?

We scramble madly to reassemble the spotting scope, and hope rises as we confirm that our ram is among them! We are near exhaustion already, and it is already 5 P.M., leaving only four or five hours of daylight. The sheep seem disinclined to move, feeding contentedly. We've got to try. Methodically we repack our gear, resupply with granola bars and candy, tank up the canteens, and set out. We check the rams once more through the spotting scope and find our ram engaging in a sparring match with the largest of the other four. They bed in the rocks as we shoulder our packs and set out toward them, the sinking sun edging toward the highest peaks.

My legs are heavy from our earlier trek, and as we walk I petition God for adequate energy for the task before me. A verse of Scripture, as familiar as an old hymn, cascades into my thoughts as we labor through the alder tangle: "Those who wait on the Lord will gain new strength; they will mount up with wings as eagles, they will run and not get tired, they will walk and not become weary." A surge of new energy courses through my body as I recite the words aloud.

The alder flat that separates our camp from the slide is perhaps a thousand yards wide, and we negotiate it in less than an hour. Another hour of trekking up a cascading stream and we are at the base of the slide. We can see the sheep some eight hundred yards above. We can't tell if we have time

before dark to get within range, as the light is already beginning to fail. The wind is contrary, blowing on our necks most of the time now. Most of our water is already gone, and we have a dizzying maze of loose slides to negotiate. Nevertheless, the thrill of the hunt drives us, the smell of victory tantalizing us.

The two larger rams are preoccupied with their pre-rut dominance ritual, the lesser ram continually annoying the old ram, perhaps sensing the end of his reign. They seem to be ignoring the noise we make as columns of rock shift wholesale down the mountain at our step. Feeling the footing give way is a spooky sensation, and I step as gingerly as possible as we ascend. The wind is perhaps a bit more crosswise now. Perhaps they won't detect us.

No such luck. The three smaller rams have spotted us and stand staring. Shortly thereafter all three flee up another cliff and disappear. Fear grips us that perhaps the others have gone as well, as we are now in a pocket out of sight of them.

Easing up over the last rock wall, Monte emits an audible gasp. There are the rams! A scant three hundred yards away, within range, and standing where a successful shot will produce a retrievable animal. To make matters even better, neither is aware of our presence.

The shot is anticlimactic. The old ram tumbles in soft barrel rolls down the slide and comes to rest where we can easily reach him. Monte sticks out his hand and clasps me in congratulations, sporting a grin as big as all outdoors.

Stone sheep. (Photo: courtesy of Jeanne Drake)

STONE SHEEP
(Ovis dalli stonei)

Though far be the glacier-filled fountain,
The foot of the hunter is free.
Though high be the ram on the mountain,
The hunter climbs higher than he.

—William T. Hornaday, *Campfires in the Canadian Rockies,* 1927

Sometimes it is difficult, if not impossible, to outclimb the dark sheep of British Columbia and the Yukon. The terrain can be fiercely steep, glaciers are frequent, and the top of the mountain may be unattainable without mountain-climbing gear. But ideally the sheep hunter should heed Hornaday's admonition whenever possible.

Stone sheep are named for an American from Missoula, Montana. Andrew Stone first described the subspecies in 1897, after making a scientific foray into the headwaters of the Stikine River of British Columbia. The existence of thinhorn sheep (Dall and Stone) is probably the result of the well-recognized Rocky Mountain gap between them and the bighorns. In a hundred-mile-wide swath of terrain southwest of Fort St. John, British Columbia, there are no wild sheep at all. That stretch of mountains has a slightly different angle of incline from the rest of the Rockies, and as a consequence snow tends to remain on the exposed eastern slopes. This seemingly insignificant difference in terrain is critical, and renders the region devoid of sheep.

A separation does not exist between the two thinhorn varieties, however, which freely interbreed where their ranges overlap. Stone sheep occupy only the northern part of British Columbia and the southern part of the Yukon, and are the most limited in geographic distribution of the major subspecies of North American sheep. There are approximately 14,500 Stone sheep, of which about 3,000 are in the Yukon and the remainder in British Columbia. Ignoring the differences between the various desert sheep subspecies, Stone sheep are the least numerous, except for the California bighorn. That is in contrast to their close cousins the Dall sheep, which are easily the most populous variety, approximating the numbers of all other North American sheep combined.

In 1901 a separate subspecies known as the Fannin sheep was recognized, mainly on the basis of body coloration, and Hornaday proposed it for classification. We now know, however, that coloration is the least reliable of distinguishing characteristics among North American sheep, and this intermediate color phase is now acknowledged to be a Stone sheep. In fact, all thinhorn sheep with any dark hair are technically Stone sheep. In many transitional herds of Dall/Stone sheep, it is frequently observed that very dark and very light animals coexist in the same herd. The two subspecies share most habits and basic characteristics. I have seen this variation firsthand on several Stone sheep hunts, and have even had to choose between a coal-black ram and a salt-and-pepper cohort with nearly equivalent horns. Darker Stone sheep seem to predominate in the southern part of their range. The dark rams among these southerly sheep may also weigh about twenty pounds more than a typical Dall ram.

On a grizzly hunt one fine spring day in the Yukon, I observed a herd of my outfitter's dazzling Dall sheep high on a mountain where we had hoped to find a mature bruin. Lacking any bears to look at, we assembled the spotting scope and checked out the numerous rams, all of them unquestionably well within the geographical area recognized to belong exclusively to the Dall. One of the finer specimens had a black tail, a feature that my host had noticed on the animal when it was a youngster. Was this a Stone ram living a hundred miles deep into Dall territory? It was by the record-book definition, even though the rest of its coat was virgin white, as were all its fellow sheep. But who would ever know about the black tail anyway—particularly if one orders a shoulder mount? It depends, at least to some degree, on what the hunter really wants to call his trophy.

This simply underscores the close kinship between the thinhorns. Stone sheep tend to have slightly larger horns overall, though the difference is mostly negligible. Overall scores, horn length, and base diameters are slightly greater on average than for Dall rams. One will not detect this, however, on a cursory examination of the record books of the Boone and Crockett Club or Safari Club International. Keep in mind too that far more Dall rams are harvested each year, which tends to skew the listings in favor of Dall sheep. But for the top twenty-five animals in the record book, an analysis of mean horn length and base diameters reveals Stone sheep to be slightly larger.

Despite the neck-and-neck appearance of the listings, it is the one at the top that is most dramatic.

The famous Chadwick ram is widely regarded as the finest North American hunting trophy of all time, the only sheep from this continent to have a documented horn length of more than 50 inches. Taken in 1936 by L. S. Chadwick in the Muskwa River drainage of British Columbia, it scored 196⁶/₈, with both horns over the magic 50-inch mark. It sits as authoritatively on top of its classification as any animal in any record book. The next largest thinhorn sheep was a Dall ram taken by Sherwin Scott in 1984. It scored 191³/₈, but horn length on that magnificent creature averaged four inches shorter than that of the Chadwick ram. Hardly any of us will ever focus a spotting scope on anything nearly as magnificent as the only thinhorns ever to top 190 points.

The splendid curving horns of Stone sheep are well known to most avid hunters. These grand adornments grow throughout life, and in Stone sheep brooming is unusual, more uncommon than in any other North American wild sheep. I had always thought that might be because the

Stone sheep. British Columbia, October 1993.

extremely wide flare of the horns makes brooming unnecessary to maintain good peripheral vision. Biologists, however, believe that most breakage occurs during fights associated with the rut, and that the naturally wide flare simply puts the horn tips out of harm's way. The greatest annual growth occurs during the second summer of life; it then tapers off each subsequent year. During the last few years of the animal's life there may be very little growth, and the yearly rings may be hard to detect. Growth occurs only at the interface of the conical bony skull appendages that fit up within the base of the horn.

Outfitter tags are apportioned by the government of British Columbia for use by nonresident trophy hunters, who pay a fee for the privilege. It isn't cheap. In fact, this is the third most expensive hunt in North America, after desert bighorn sheep and polar bear, though a few Rocky Mountain bighorn hunts and Alaska brown bear hunts are close behind. With the economic stakes so high, it is no surprise that those concerned closely guard the health of the resource. Outfitters receive permits for nonresidents according to an established harvest schedule, but the number can be increased if older rams are present in sufficient numbers in the season's take. Conversely, if younger rams are taken, the outfitter's quota can be reduced. I know my outfitters have been strict about making absolutely certain that any sheep harvested is old, even insisting on counting rings to avoid mistakes. We knew my last Stone ram was at least ten years old before the shot, and he turned out to be a good twelve and a half, perhaps older. He had already lost jaw teeth, and was almost certainly entering his last winter.

About three hundred outfitter tags for Stone sheep are available in British Columbia each year, although the exact number fluctuates. Residents of British Columbia are restricted to one Stone sheep every few years, depending on the area, and they take about 175 rams each year. The success rate runs about 66 percent for Stone sheep hunts by guided nonresidents, or about 200 rams per year. The success rate for residents, who are usually unguided, is much lower. A few tags for Stone sheep are available to hunters in the Yukon as well.

The country inhabited by Stone sheep isn't quite as precipitous as the Wrangell or Chugach Mountains, nor is it generally as gentle as the Brooks Range—all of which provide habitat for Dall sheep. Most mountains in Stone sheep country are climbable with pack and rifle. These sheep tolerate lower country, in general, than do Dall sheep, and favor the moderate hills on the northeast side of major mountain chains. Those areas are periodically warmed by chinook winds that expose forage in winter. The terrain is also gifted with high precipitation, which makes for good growing conditions for grasses and forbs during summer.

My best Stone sheep came from an area of gentle hills just above timberline, several miles from the kind of cliffs the animals usually prefer as escape cover. Folded Mountain was the major feature of a string of high, rough mountains to our southwest, so the location fit the Stone sheep habitat type. I have also taken a Stone ram from a talus slope above which towered a rocky monolith that would make even a mountain climber shudder. Even there the sheep seem to prefer the far less intimidating topography to the northeast, staying close to the rough escape cover nearby. Stone sheep more often go to subalpine brushlands and even forests than do their Dall cousins.

The diet of Stone sheep is similar to that of Dall sheep. In most regions they consume between 50 and 120 kinds of plants. In winter, grasses amount to 87 percent of their diet, so the sheep seek them on exposed slopes warmed by the chinook winds. In summer the percentage of grass declines, though it is still the major part of the diet. Succulent forbs that grow rapidly during the warm season, as well as tender shrubs, then supplant the grasses. When food is scarce the sheep will consume low-nutrition lichens and mosses, although they probably do not provide an important source of nourishment.

Stone sheep are especially fond of graminoids (grasses) such as wheatgrass, bluejoint, ryegrass, bluegrass, and various sedges and fescues. They also consume many types of annual forbs, especially during the spring and summer, changing altitude and terrain to stay with the most tender emerging plants. These sheep will readily eat many shrubs, including bearberry, juniper, soapberry, wild rose, willow, birch, blueberry, and lingonberry.

Stone sheep, like all North American wild sheep, feed mainly during daylight hours. When days are long and summer plant growth is in full swing, they may feed all day long. When the days shorten and the weather becomes severe, feeding time is short, with conservation of their energy as important as foraging.

Fire helps Stone sheep habitat by eliminating thick coniferous areas that suppress the growth of edible plants, and the animals use the resulting open areas heavily. British Columbia's burning program has significantly improved Stone sheep habitat. The results have been impressive, with increased lamb-to-ewe ratios, better horn growth, and decreased loads of parasites. Good food production leads to good fat stores and better winter survival.

The rut occurs from mid-November to mid-December. The peak of activity seems to be later than that of Dall sheep, and it may extend longer. By the time of the active rut, dominance orders have long been established, so few serious battles occur. The rams move among the ewes checking to see if they are receptive and breed when the ewe is ready. These sheep do not gather or tend harems as do bull elk and certain other ruminants.

A dominant ram is capable of breeding many ewes, but sometimes younger rams may do some of the breeding near the end of the rut.

The gestation period of the Stone sheep is probably the same as that of Dall sheep, about 175 days. Like other sheep, the ewes enter the roughest, most inaccessible country available to give birth, a strategy that is generally successful. At birth lambs weigh 7 to 10 pounds, and they are highly mobile within days and eating solid food shortly thereafter. Most births occur between 23 May and 16 June. The ewes go away alone to give birth, but when they return, the lambs of the previous season join them to form sizable groups.

Lamb survival depends on many factors, such as summer nutrition, the severity of their first winter, and the effects of predation. Studies have shown that the number of Stone lambs declines to 47 lambs per 100 ewes by age 2 to 3 months; 35 lambs per 100 ewes by age 9 months; and 15 lambs per 100 ewes by 21 months (which would carry them through two full winters). Biologists feel that about 26 lambs per 100 ewes at the end of the first year of life is necessary to maintain a stable population.

Backpacking into Stone sheep country—always a long climb.

Stone rams abound—but are there any takers in this band?

The ram-to-ewe ratio is normally about 35 to 100, even in unhunted populations. The stress of the rut on rams probably accounts for their susceptibility to predators. In a recent incident, British Columbia biologists discovered three mature Stone rams killed by wolves within a single week. Rams are not as fleet as ewes—perhaps because of the rut, or their more stocky body size and heavy headgear. In addition, rams congregate in smaller groups, spreading themselves over more territory and thus making encounters with wolves more likely. Wolves are the main limiting factor on Stone sheep populations. Initially wolves prey on the sick and the weak, but when those are gone they may readily consume the rest as well. Quantity and quality of forage may have some effect on populations, but biologists report that they have never seen a single animal that starved to death.

The Stone sheep's primary defense against wolves is the steep terrain into which it flees. Biologists have often seen wolves climbing the cliffs to drive sheep into the jaws of their waiting brethren, and both pursuing wolves and Stone sheep occasionally fall to their deaths. More frequently, wolves simply surprise the sheep a couple of hundred yards from escape cover and catch them before they can reach safety. Steep terrain will protect small populations of Stone sheep, but when the population increases so that the animals must seek food away from the cliffs, predation begins to take its toll. Golden eagles get some newborn lambs, and in some areas both young and adults fall to coyotes, wolverines, black bears, grizzly bears, and occasionally lynx.

The effect of wolves on Stone sheep populations can be extraordinary. In one period of a few years, biologists moderately reduced the number of wolves, and hunter harvest of rams went up by 50 percent. The average age of harvested rams also increased dramatically. Recruitment of surviving lambs into the population also improved significantly when wolf numbers declined. When the wolf control program ended, everything reverted to preprogram levels within a few years.

Disease is extremely rare among Stone sheep. Lumpy jaw, or mandibular osteomyelitis, was reported in these animals in 1930. The scourges of the bighorns, such as scabies and pasteurella pneumonia, are rare or nonexistent. The isolation of Stone sheep from human activities, and especially from livestock ranching, has no doubt contributed to their excellent health. Tooth problems are not uncommon, however, and seem to result most often from coarse seeds getting stuck between the tooth and gum.

My clothing and equipment recommendations for hunting Stone sheep are almost identical to those for Dall sheep, so I won't repeat them here. If you are backpacking, a sleeping bag, cooking gear, food, and a tent must fit in somewhere. Stone sheep live in spectacular country, so don't forget a camera and plenty of film, and be sure to store them in plastic bags for protection against moisture.

Stone sheep are getting more expensive to hunt as each year passes, and expanding wolf populations and public rejection of wolf-control measures may result in fewer hunting opportunities. Even if I had to take out a mortgage, though, I'd do this hunt once. It's worth it, and you'll agree with me when you admire your Stone sheep trophy with its sweeping, full-curl horns. Take plenty of photos in case you never pass that way again.

A RAM FOR HARVEY

Luck seems to have run out for my friend and guide, Harvey Daniels. We have combed the numerous tributaries of the Toad River of northern British Columbia for thirteen days, seeking the exceptional Stone sheep I want. We have seen perhaps fifty, but few are old enough and none sufficiently heavy or long of horn. And that on the heels of a fourteen-day hunt last year that was even worse—eleven immature rams spotted, but no takers. We are on the verge of another defeat. My weary legs ache from a dozen lung-bursting climbs into fantastic sheep basins, where we have viewed and photographed everything except what we are seeking. We have seen scores of sheep, as well as moose, caribou, wolf, and wolverine. But the ancient ram has thus far eluded us.

I took a 38-inch Stone ram several years ago, so I am seeking a truly special animal this time. But Harvey and I can scarcely find a mediocre one. We stalked one ancient ram with a missing left horn on the tenth day, but I elected to pass despite its advanced age. A unique trophy, yes, but not the ram of my dreams. I will find another, equally old

but with undamaged horns, or I will harvest nothing. Harvey seems to understand, although he says that he would have taken the one-horned ram without hesitation. One hunter's trophy is another's reject.

Day fourteen dawns clear, cold, and windy but without a hint of the snow normally prevalent this time of year. The lack of winter weather has been a concern for the whole trip. The biggest sheep will not move into the area we are hunting until deep snow forces them from their summer ranges. It's beginning to look like our bad luck is going to persist.

We drive out of camp on a Japanese pony, as Harvey disdainfully refers to our ATV, heading for a basin we have climbed twice before. He despises the vehicle so much that he insists that I do all the driving, a task I don't mind. We leave it at the end of a logging road and plunge on foot down a barely perceptible trail that leads to the gateway to sheep heaven.

An hour later we traverse a deep creek with much effort and ascend the opposite timbered slope toward open sheep country. The ominous drone of an airplane engine fills the sky, and we see a small yellow Super Cub come into view. It appears for all the world to be probing every pocket of the gigantic basin in which we are hunting. I can't help but wonder if the plane is seeking us. Or perhaps the pilot is a resident hunter trying to pinpoint a promising band of sheep.

We are still climbing but haven't yet cleared the dense timber, so we are unable to attract the attention of the airplane. I feel a sense of frustration as the pilot heads down the valley and disappears. An ominous foreboding comes upon me. Is the outside world trying to contact us? Harvey's mother has been quite ill recently, and I cannot help but feel concern about my own family.

We have no choice but to continue uphill and clear the timber to a pinnacle overlooking broad sheep basins, deep and inviting, on both sides. A lone wolverine traverses the valley to our right, a moving speck in the distance. Breaking out our lunch, we huddle behind a large boulder for protection against the wind and enjoy the breathtaking view. It is a couple of hours before I spot a lone ram far up the valley to our left. He appears no more than mediocre, like several dozen

Wildflowers produce an explosion of color on early hunts.

others we have inspected, but I dutifully point him out to Harvey.

"Let's go check him out. There might be some others with him," he counsels.

We shoulder our gear and prepare to depart. Suddenly, the unmistakable sound of a helicopter bursts upon us, a menacing sound that immediately brings back a flood of Vietnam memories. Now, however, it conveys a different kind of terror, in the form of raw uncertainty. Combined with the earlier visit from the light aircraft, it can only mean an emergency for one of us, some apocalyptic development back home.

Dale Drinkall, outfitter and sheep guide par excellence, rides as a passenger in the chopper, and his sharp eyes spot us immediately. Dale is in the aft seat, motioning us to a good landing spot perhaps a thousand vertical feet below on a flat bench. Harvey plunges off at a dead run, so fast that I can by no means keep up, and arrives several minutes before me. When I arrive, out of breath, I see him leaning into the affectionate arms of Sandra Drinkall, Dale's wife. He has hot tears streaming down his weathered cheeks. Dale walks toward me as I approach, keeping some distance between us and Harvey.

"What happened, Dale? Did his mom die?"

"No, it was his wife. She died suddenly. Ruptured brain aneurysm or something like that."

The news strikes me like a bolt from the sky. Irma was only forty-two years old and had appeared as healthy as could be when I met her in Calgary only six months ago. She had died quietly and without pain, a merciful bit of information in an otherwise bleak tale. Slowly and thoughtfully I remove my sweat-soaked hat and clutch it to my breast, turning away in silent prayer for my friend and companion. I almost feel guilty about my deep sense of relief that the news wasn't for me.

Harvey and Dale exchange places in the chopper. After a simple "God bless you, Harvey," he is gone. My new guide unloads his gear onto the ground, lightening his pack so we can take a closer look at the ram I've spotted. We will retrieve his excess gear on our way back to camp.

Dale and I resolve as we walk to do our best to finish this hunt successfully, as much as a tribute to a great sheep guide in mourning as to anything

else. We find that the ram I saw, as well as his five companions, can be no more than seven years old. We return to camp with an overriding sadness, the lack of a harvestable ram taking on a much-reduced importance in our sharing of Harvey's grief. I repeatedly thank God that my family back home is uninvolved, and I ask for a light of comfort and mercy to shine into the life of my bereaved friend.

That night in our tent Dale and I do some real soul searching about what course of action we should take at this late date in the hunt. We decide to move to another location more familiar to Dale than the timbered drainage we are now in. Harvey and I have already combed all the adjacent basins for two weeks, and my departure date is just three days off. Dale recommends an area he knows intimately, and I heartily agree to make the move.

Until I met Dale, Harvey was my most experienced sheep guide, having taken some 74 rams in the course of more than twenty years of guiding. Dale claims to have stalked and killed 92 rams, including a few he has taken himself. Being only thirty, he could be on track for taking over 200 rams in his career, a phenomenal figure. But can he push this unlucky hunter to one more ram and make it 93 to close out the season? This has already been an unbelievable year for him, and he has led clients to two rams that qualify for all-time Boone and Crockett listings. I am not necessarily looking for a book sheep, but I won't complain if we find one.

We spend the next day packing out, arriving in Dale's familiar hunting grounds in the evening. We glass into basins that are accessible without a lot of effort. Mercifully, Dale doesn't suggest we do any climbing, despite the short time remaining. I have two more days, and I know I will need all the strength I can muster for the final push. Unfortunately, we spot no good rams.

That night at supper Dale sketches out our final two days. We will use horses to get as high as possible into sheep country and leave the mounts at timberline, shortening the required climb by at least half. We will start on a mountain where one of the Drinkall moose guides has spotted an old ram, broomed on both sides. I really want one with classic flaring tips, but any really old ram with heavy bases would be quite a trophy. We'll spend the last day on another mountain taking a shot in the dark if we are unsuccessful tomorrow. My hopes are sagging by now, but I will not give up until the hunt is over.

The horses carry us to timberline, their strong legs giving mine some much-needed relief. Soon we spot a band of young rams, so we dismount and hitch the horses, hoping that the fickle breeze will not alert the band.

Despite the respite, I still find the climb grueling. Even on day outings my pack and rifle weigh nearly fifty pounds, because I carry several heavy cameras and lenses. Just as we creep over the top, we are in time to see nineteen rams parade from our mountain, cross a ravine, and disappear. The wind has given us away. Dale inspects each one through the spotting scope and pronounces all of them too young. Same song, umpteenth verse.

We spend the remainder of the day glassing adjacent high terrain. Dale locates one heavy-horned old monarch, nearly two miles away, that he feels merits a closer inspection tomorrow. The ram is in a group of nine, and he may well represent my last chance this year.

The weather for my last day of hunting dawns bright and unbelievably warm for mid-October in the Toad River country. I have been blessed, or perhaps cursed, with unseasonably excellent weather for most of the hunt. Where snow normally drifts several feet deep, blueberries offer themselves for the picking. As I stow my camouflage woolens, I realize that I have not needed them at all this trip, an indication of how unpredictable weather in the northern country can be this time of year.

Again the horses carry a tired hunter up the mountain, on the last ascent of a very long season. I am able to climb better now, on legs that are partially rested, and soon the horses are far below and we are in a saddle near the spot where we saw the old ram yesterday. Dale is ahead of me by perhaps thirty yards when I see him glance over his left shoulder and then drop like a toppled

Headwaters of the Toad River—land of giant rams.

tree to the rocky ground. I follow with no hesitation, realizing instinctively what it means.

A thousand yards away, on the next ridge, is the band of rams. They've moved some distance since yesterday. One of them has obviously spotted us, and he stares in our direction for an eternity. Both Dale and I remain motionless, and finally the ram resumes feeding.

We have passed test number one. We watch fascinated for another thirty minutes but are too far apart to talk. My mind is racing, wondering if this band contains a sheep that will meet the exacting specifications of Folding Mountain Outfitters—as well as my own expectations. Finally, after peering interminably through his spotting scope, Dale flashes me a thumbs-up.

Now we simply wait for our opportunity. Thankfully the wind is favorable, so we need not hurry. At last all the rams feed out of view around the brow of the mountain, except for one that has bedded in sight of us but is facing away. We hurriedly move five hundred yards closer, but we stay ready to halt instantly if necessary. We are in broad view if the ram should turn around. As soon as we reach our destination he does exactly that, almost catching us in motion. We dare not move for another long interval as the wary creature stares suspiciously in our direction. When the ram eventually looks away, Dale deftly sets up the spotting scope.

"He's old enough, at least eight or nine by the rings I can see from here. He's over thirty-eight, maybe thirty-nine. What do you want to do?"

"Any hope he's older?"

"Hard to say at this distance. Lots of little rings at the bases. Could be eleven or twelve. We can see a little better when we move closer."

"Let's take him."

The nice flare of the tapering tips weighs heavily in my decision,

and I have the distinct feeling I will be very happy with this fellow. Now if he will only get up and turn around again so we can move in without being detected.

The passage of time seems endless, a common feeling on any hunt in which patience is tested. Animals are never in a hurry unless they sense danger, which generally sends them off in the opposite direction. The brisk October wind is picking up once more, and I feel distinctly chilled. Because the animal is staring right at us, however, I can't even break into my pack for more clothes.

Reflecting on a previous unsuccessful Stone sheep hunt.

Will the creeping cold and my shivering affect my ability to shoot straight?

Finally the oldster rises to his feet, pivots 180 degrees, paws intently at some unseen irritant in his bed, and lies down facing the opposite direction.

We drop silently into a depression where we are out of sight, thankful for a face full of breeze. When we ease up to the ridge above the rams, all nine are visible below, the ancient monarch by himself to our far right.

Dale methodically checks the ram again to be sure, and after giving me time to get set, he whistles to get them to stand. The whole band looks about inquisitively, as if pondering what kind of strange bird could be making that odd noise, but amazingly they all remain in their beds. My time has finally come. One hundred and fifty yards away lies a ram in full view. I can't miss. Gently and confidently I squeeze off the shot.

My prize leaps to his feet, obviously hit hard, but he is not yet immobilized. I put a second quick shot behind his shoulder, anchoring him firmly to the spot.

The other sheep stand about, apparently wondering what has happened to their quiet world. Their delay is my opportunity for some wonderful telephoto shots of a completely transfixed band of rams.

The Stone ram I have taken is a great trophy, truly a black beauty, and nearly meets my highest expectations. He turns out to be twelve and a half years old by the biologist's calculation, very probably a couple more, and carries an honest 39 ½ inches of horn with broad, flaring tips. His teeth are terrible, several being missing, and he likely would not have survived the upcoming winter. The ram is not record class, but misses it only narrowly, like so many outstanding trophies.

I dedicate this one immediately to Harvey Daniels and his departed wife, Irma. May God comfort Harvey, welcome his wife to eternity, and grant my friend recovery and comfort from his loss. And may He also grant that Harvey return once again to Stone sheep country, to the far reaches of the Toad River and its tributaries, to guide hunters to these amazing animals.

Rocky Mountain bighorn sheep. (Photo: courtesy of Jeanne Drake)

ROCKY MOUNTAIN BIGHORN SHEEP

(Ovis canadensis canadensis)

One-fifth of all the rocks in the world are in the
Montana Unlimited Sheep Areas.

—Jack Atcheson Jr., to author on 13 September 1991

Things haven't changed much over the centuries when it comes to hunting the sheep of the high mountains. The terrain has always been challenging. Almost one hundred years before my conversation with Jack Jr., Archibald Rogers described it this way: "In pursuit of the Rocky Mountain sheep, the hunter, to be successful, must have a fondness for the mountains, a sure foot, a good wind, and a head which no height can turn. These requisites, with patience and perseverance will, sooner or later, reward him with ample returns." (*American Big Game Hunting,* edited by Theodore Roosevelt and George Bird Grinnell.)

The hardships are indeed worth the effort. Even as I write this I'm planning an excursion to Alberta to try for another, despite the fact that I've experienced my lowest success rate hunting the Rocky Mountain subspecies. On four trips, I've harvested only one.

Some of my miserable success rate on Rocky Mountain bighorns is due to the places I've hunted them—the Unlimited Permit areas of Montana on three occasions, and once in fabulous Area 438 of Alberta. In the former, the habitat is so remote and success rates are so low that I am fortunate to have taken a single ram there. In Alberta the nonresident hunter is at an unreasonable disadvantage because the first and the last two weeks of the season are open to residents only.

The first specimen of a Rocky Mountain bighorn used for scientific study was harvested by zoologist George Shaw. It came from the upper Bow River area of Alberta in 1800. Lewis and Clark encountered numerous animals during their expedition of 1804–1806 that were likely of both the Rocky Mountain and California subspecies.

The classification of wild sheep in North America has always been controversial, and in great part without scientific consensus. In this book I recognize eight subspecies of bighorn sheep in North America, of which one (the Audubon, or Badlands, bighorn) has been extinct in the Dakotas since 1905 and in eastern Montana since 1916. Avid hunter and naturalist John James Audubon first described that animal in 1843, and controversy continues as to whether it was truly distinct from the Rocky Mountain bighorn. Five of the living subspecies are lumped together as "desert bighorn sheep," the other two being the Rocky Mountain bighorn and the California bighorn. All these animals carry horns characteristically heavier than those of the thinhorns (the Dall and Stone sheep).

Rocky Mountain bighorns exist today in eleven Western states and two Canadian provinces. In the Dakotas, they live in habitat formerly occupied by the Badlands bighorn. They have also been introduced into other nonnative areas, and they are thriving wherever predation is minimal and there is scant contact with disease-bearing domestic sheep and goats. There is no question that the bighorns have been more affected by human habitation and livestock than have the thinhorns of the far north. For that reason, much of today's management activities, transplant programs, and habitat improvement projects concentrate on the bighorns.

About 25,000 Rocky Mountain bighorns inhabit the Lower Forty-eight, and there are about half that number in the Canadian portion of their range. That makes this subspecies the second most plentiful of the five varieties of mountain sheep in North America, although they are only about one-third as numerous as the Dall.

Some of the finest herds are introduced from elsewhere, even within the same state. Montana is the classic example, with transplants from the Sun River stock reoccupying much of their best habitat. In fact, thirty of forty-two herds in that state are the result of transplantation, creating one of the most dynamic populations of bighorn sheep anywhere. Not all such efforts have been resounding successes, however; eight other transplanted herds have failed to thrive for a variety of reasons. Nevertheless, Montana has perhaps 5,000 Rocky Mountain bighorn sheep, with the Sun River stock being the most prolific and carrying the most impressive headgear.

In the purely native herds, such as those I have hunted in the Unlimited Permit areas, the sheep seldom attain record-book size. One reason for that is the extremely high, inhospitable terrain in which some of them live, but other factors also may be involved. Inbreeding may be a problem in some very small and isolated herds, although a population that fails to thrive usually has more problems than simple inbreeding: some of the best herds in Montana started with fewer than fifty animals.

Wild bighorns are not known either for adaptability or for tolerance to inhospitable conditions. They need ecologically mature habitat, far from human disturbance and competition with domestic stock. They are highly susceptible to livestock diseases, their isolation having afforded them little immunity to Old World microorganisms. Many biologists believe that this susceptibility is also attributable to their being of the bovine family, like domestic sheep, goats, and cattle. Diseases that afflict those animals readily find a home in native wild sheep. Moreover, mountain sheep tend to remain in a localized area and disperse only minimally, making it difficult for them to colonize new habitat. Nevertheless, wildlife managers in many states have achieved outstanding success in reestablishing vibrant herds.

Rocky Mountain bighorns are easily the heavyweights among the sheep of North America, and indeed are among the largest of the world's wild sheep. It is said that the bighorns of Alberta are slightly larger than those elsewhere. Most mature Rocky Mountain bighorn rams stand some 42 inches at the shoulder and attain occasional body weights of 300 pounds or more. The Audubon subspecies reportedly weighed about 40 pounds more than that, although many biologists dispute the assertion. Mountain sheep are genetically

Glassing on top of the world in Montana's Unlimited Sheep Area.

similar to domestic sheep, and can crossbreed with them, producing fertile offspring.

The horns can weigh up to 40 pounds, as much as 12 percent of the total body weight, a tremendous load. The horns curl quite tightly compared with those of the thinhorns, and they seldom exhibit argali-type flare of the tips. More often than not the tips are broomed in mature rams. The distinctive feature of a truly outstanding Rocky Mountain ram is the persistence of mass throughout much of the length of the curling horns.

The pelage varies little except for the depth and intensity of the color, which can run from light to dark chocolate brown. The animals of Alberta are darker on average, though in the Yellowstone ecosystem and surrounding areas there also are sheep of a dark chocolate. There is white hair around the muzzle, and the rump, the rear part of the belly, the inner aspects of the hind legs, and the back of the front legs are creamy white. The tail is dark, much like the upper portion of the coat. Individual hairs trap air within a hollow shaft for thermal insulation.

Most ewes weigh no more than 150 pounds. The females, lambs, and young rams live apart from the mature rams, in herds that range in size from a few animals up to 30 or more, except for the brief period of the rut. The rut occurs in December, and bighorn rams demonstrate the amazing ability to mate with several ewes within a few minutes. There follows a gestation period of about 180 days. New lambs weigh approximately 12 pounds and are born in May in most locales. Twins occur less than 2 percent of the time. The tiny animals become mobile rapidly, but during the first few days of life they are susceptible to predators, most notably coyotes in the parts of their range where wolves are absent. In one Montana herd, lamb survival was only 25 percent, with 67 percent of the mortality caused by coyote predation within three days of birth. Within two weeks of birth, bighorn lambs are eating grass and other tender vegetation.

In some areas cougars are the most important predator of Rocky Mountain bighorn sheep. Most cougars kill few, if any, bighorns. However, a few cougars seem to learn how to hunt and kill the sheep, and if that occurs an individual cougar can become a real threat. One female cougar in Alberta took 9 percent of a single bighorn herd,

along with 26 percent of the year's lamb crop, in just one winter.

Montana biologist Mike Frisina feels that some eagles are specialists at taking newborn bighorns. Such predation causes the sheep to be watchful of the sky, making them harder for humans to stalk by climbing above them.

Young rams remain with the ewes for the first two years of life, then leave their mothers to join the bachelor bands characteristic of the male of the species. These groups may consist of only a very few animals, although they may encompass as many as thirty or more. Very old rams are sometimes solitary, an indication that they may be losing interest in the opposite sex.

Bighorn sheep, like their thinhorn cousins, are not very vocal, but they do communicate effectively. Bleats and blats are common between ewes and lambs, and at times rams will grunt and snort. An agitated ram may grind his teeth audibly. Rams establish dominance not by vocalizations but by body posturing and physical contests, with horn size playing an important role in establishing the pecking order. Rams may horn one another, do a front leg kick or horn display, or perform a low stretch in which they cock and twist the head to show as much horn mass as possible. In that way they often avoid the need to expend energy in dominance fights.

The clash of rutting bighorn rams can be heard for two miles, the animals launching themselves with full force at one another to slam their heads together. I heard that sound on my first bighorn hunt, and it is highly distinctive. Most of the energy of these shocks is absorbed by the fibrous nuchal tendon at the base of the skull behind the horns. In addition, the forehead skull below the horn cores is thick and has air pockets that act as shock absorbers. Thanks to these specialized mechanisms, rams do not destroy their central nervous system in such conflicts. Fights often break out when a subordinate ram challenges the dominant ram by giving him a shove from the rear.

Rocky Mountain bighorns graze on grasses, including certain sedges, bluegrasses, wheatgrass, and fescues. They often browse on sagebrush, willows, rabbitbrush, curlleaf mountain mahogany, winterfat, bitterbrush, and green ephedra. They also consume a variety of forbs including phlox, cinquefoils, twinflower, dandelion, and clover. They can eat with impunity conifers and other plants that are toxic to domestic sheep. In Montana, the largest bighorn rams come from areas where native bunchgrass species are the predominant vegetation. For an area to qualify as prime bighorn habitat, there must be little competition from domestic stock, because both domestic cattle and sheep also prefer bunchgrass over other plants. The bunchgrasses are high in nutrients, especially protein. In Alberta, reclaimed areas of a coal mine have been fertilized and planted with nutritious grasses, producing a large number of big rams.

The world record bighorn ram was taken in Blind Canyon, Alberta, in 1911. It scored an awesome 208 1/8 points. Many believe that Area 438 of Alberta has at least one ram that would beat that record, and it is the dream of many a hunter to find it. Probably the largest bighorn ram ever taken by a hunter was the Phillips ram of 1939, which measured more than 50 inches on each horn. A photo of that ram's horns survives, but the actual horns were destroyed in a fire before they were officially measured. That loss leaves the Chadwick ram of Stone sheep fame as the only North American sheep with horns that officially top 50 inches. Experts agree that the Phillips ram would likely be the world-record bighorn, with a score of about 214, had not fate intervened. Youngsters killed it just north of the Montana border near Grasmere, Alberta, using .22 rifles.

Alberta holds the standing record, but today most record heads come from Montana, where each year some thirty-five rams meet Boone and Crockett minimums. Only one ram from the United States has ever netted more than 200 points on the Boone and Crockett scale, however, that being one taken in 1990 by Lester Kish. That animal, which fell just one-eighth of an inch shy of 201, had unusually flared, unbroomed horns that measured almost 50 inches. As of this writing it is still the U.S. record. It was taken in the South Flint Creek area of Montana (Unit 213), which has been the source of many enviable trophies. The area produces bighorns with long horns yet light bases. In April 1992, Jack Atcheson Jr. found a long-dead ram he named "the King." Its horns scored 203 5/8 points despite two years of exposure to the elements. Many believe it would have been a new

world record had it been taken by a hunter instead of dying of old age, winterkill, or disease.

Unfortunately, the draw areas of Montana are notoriously difficult places to obtain a permit. Odds are near 1 percent in the best units. There is some movement in Montana toward establishing a preference point system, although such an arrangement has not aided me in drawing a permit, at least not yet. I've been participating in such a system in Arizona and Nevada for many years, seeking a desert bighorn permit. I've spent over $1,000 on licenses to keep up with the pack and gain a bonus point, but still without success. The Unlimited Permit areas offer relief from the hard luck of the draw, but the rams are notably smaller and the hunts can be absolutely brutal.

Other famous big sheep areas of Montana include Upper Rock Creek (Unit 216), the East Fork of the Bitterroot (Unit 270), the Missouri Breaks (Units 622 and 680), the Highlands (Unit 340), Thompson Falls (Unit 121), St. Regis Cutoff (Unit 122), and Perma Paradise (Unit 124). A bighorn tag in any of these areas is worth all the gold you can stuff in the pockets of your hunting pants, and maybe more.

All these herds are transplants of sheep captured and relocated from the Sun River herd (Unit 420), which is not particularly known for big rams. Placing these genetically superior sheep in luxurious, pristine habitat helps them grow big rapidly. In the Sun River area the sheep endure strong winds, heavy winter snow, biting cold, and in places poor winter range conditions. Rams there seldom live long enough to become truly outstanding. When placed in ideal grassy habitat with intervening stands of thick timber, these sheep undergo phenomenal horn growth. Units 213 and 216 produce such big rams that half the annual ram harvest usually qualifies for the Boone and Crockett record book.

It is an unusual quirk that the most exciting herds of bighorn sheep in Montana are the rapidly growing sheep in these transplanted herds. In Unit 213, the rams grow a horn volume of 285 cubic inches during their first four years of life. In the parent Sun River region, the growth is only 174 cubic inches over the same span. Habitat can make an amazing difference in horn growth. Conversely, it has been conjectured that animals in rapidly growing

Here's a great place to camp next to a trout-filled high-country lake.

herds of sheep (in terms of numbers of animals as well as horn mass) may experience relatively short life spans, sometimes averaging only six to seven years, although that has not been well documented.

Nevertheless, many rams in such vigorous areas as Units 213 and 216 may score over 190 points and be only six years old. A hunter has to fantasize about what kind of ram might result if such sheep lived twice that long. The growth rings of an older ram are always contracted somewhat near the growing base, so longer life span might not translate into a tremendous amount of additional length, but the possibilities are nevertheless fascinating to contemplate.

Rocky Mountain bighorn sheep are affected by many diseases and are unusually susceptible to severe die-offs under certain conditions. An outbreak of pasteurella and pneumonia complex in 1991 killed off the majority of the sheep in Montana's fabulous Unit 213, a tragedy of monumental proportions that many sheep enthusiasts still lament. Duncan Gilchrist, in his book *Giant Rams of Montana*, reports sighting 88 rams in one band in that unit before the die-off, and 225 rams on just one visit. From a herd of several hundred sheep, only 144 were counted in the spring survey after the dust settled. Gilchrist quotes well-known guide Tim Magnessas

lamenting, "Disneyland has burned down." Pasteurella is a common and widespread bacterium in bighorn sheep, but only in certain situations does it combine with other factors to cause mortality. Contagious viral diseases, nutritional stress, crowding, and the like can trigger the onset of this devastating complex.

Another problematic disease among bighorns is scabies, which is caused by a tiny mite. It is most problematic in the southern parts of bighorn sheep habitat. Scabies was one of the first diseases known to kill bighorn sheep, probably being transmitted to them by domestic sheep. The mite causes severe itching, inducing licking and scratching that lead to hair loss and scabbing sores. Major historical die-offs are attributed to the disease, as early settlers described wild sheep that were infected with the characteristic sores.

In many locations, the most significant disease of bighorn sheep is lungworm-pneumonia complex, initiated by a parasite that infests the bronchial tubes and lungs. These worms embed themselves inextricably in lung tissue and the lining of the main air passages. Scientists call them *Protostrongylus*, of which there are several important species. The worms infect many, if not most, bighorns in some locations, and when

Rocky Mountain bighorn sheep. Montana, September 1987.

combined with certain environmental stresses their presence can cause, or at least facilitate, a fatal pneumonia. They are a serious problem only for Rocky Mountain bighorn sheep, though they also show up in desert bighorns, California bighorns, and Dall sheep. They require a type of terrestrial snail as an intermediate host to complete their life cycle, and sheep ingest the snails while foraging.

Botflies often deposit larvae in the nasal passages of bighorns, which can lead to fatal sinusitis, but that apparently does not affect the Rocky Mountain subspecies as much as it does desert sheep. The reason could be the fewer insects in the more northerly habitat, or perhaps the desert sheep's greater susceptibility to nasal and mouth irritation because of the spiny foods they ingest. In similar fashion, Rocky Mountain sheep are less susceptible to leptospirosis, another bacterial disease common in desert sheep. The viral diseases epizootic hemorrhagic fever, bluetongue, and contagious ecthyma also can occur in Rocky Mountain bighorns, but again they are not as significant as in the desert subspecies.

Hunting the magnificent bighorn inevitably involves climbing, glassing, and days of hard work. The only opportunity in the world to simply buy a tag and go hunting bighorn sheep is in Montana's Unlimited Permit areas, but that is perhaps the most difficult hunt of any kind anywhere. In Canada one can purchase a permit and hunt without a draw, but only through an outfitter's quota of tags in either British Columbia or Alberta. About 25 percent of Alberta's sheep harvest goes to nonresident hunters. Many hunters will never harvest a Rocky Mountain bighorn sheep unless they are fortunate enough to draw a permit in one of the Western states that allow them to apply. The Unlimited Areas and Canada are simply beyond the abilities of many, for reasons both physical and economic.

However you plan to hunt these animals, I strongly recommend the services of a competent guide. Even if you are fortunate enough to draw a tag in Montana or Wyoming, a guide will be a big help. Most guides relish the opportunity to scout for a trophy sheep and will inevitably have done much of the work for you ahead of time. Most of the time Rocky Mountain bighorns stick close to thick timber, but you need to know where to look. Often one must poke along in a likely spot, seeking a telltale patch of brown that reveals a resting ram. Bump into a mature ram and scare him, and you may never see him again. A good guide knows where the sheep are usually found, and can prevent many mistakes.

Judging a trophy bighorn ram is not too difficult for the person who has looked at a lot of specimens. But when one is hunting in Montana with a once-in-a-lifetime draw permit, or on a very expensive hunt in Alberta, a group of rams may be extremely hard to separate into the just good and the truly outstanding. There, also, an experienced guide is your best insurance against "ground shrinkage."

Always view a ram from the side before making a decision. Most of the time there is no great hurry if you've spotted a band from afar. Try to estimate the tightness of the curl. Jack Atcheson Jr. and Tim Magness recommend visualizing passing a ball through the opening created by the circle of the horns. The larger the ball, the higher the animal will score. If that's too hard to envision, make sure the horns drop below the jaw line and carefully check the mass of the horn at the junction of the inner two-thirds and the outer third (it should be almost as thick there as at the base).

Terrain and weather in sheep country vary, but one can always count on vertical inclines. Up on top it can be relatively flat, and one can actually wind up hunting downward, which is always preferred. Sheep expect danger from below and are less likely to look upward. I've hunted bighorns on fabulous blue sky days on top of the world, with fresh snow a foot deep all around me. I've hunted them in driving rain, in subfreezing cold, and in heat that felt like summertime in Georgia. Go prepared for anything. I'd recommend that you have a waterproof down parka and rain pants, a space blanket sleeping bag, a full water bottle, and a little survival food with you at all times.

My sheep hunting pack is a North Face Snow Leopard modified in Jack Atcheson Jr. fashion with a metal hook bolted to the only hard part of the frame. This is doubtless one of the best backpacking and hunting arrangements of all time, as it allows you to sling the rifle to the pack, leaving both hands free for hand-over-hand climbing. The neck of this pack extends out from the ample cargo compartment for extra big loads.

The classic sheep rifle is probably the .270. Sheep are not hard to kill, so any legal rifle capable of making a 300-yard shot is adequate. You should be able to hit the vitals of a sheep-size target consistently at that distance. It is disheartening to find oneself unable to get any closer, but sometimes

that occurs. Don't get caught with a 300-yard shot you have never practiced.

When your chance comes, you won't blow it if you've done your homework, whether that involves saving money to go to Canada, getting in shape for one of Montana's rugged Unlimited Area hunts, or waiting out the long draw. Go prepared, and I hope you take a superlative ram. For all but a tiny minority, it will happen only once in a lifetime. Make the most of it.

UNLIMITED SUCCESS

The high mountain air is as thin as it is crisp and clean. As I catch my breath after putting six miles of trail behind me, I dip my water bottle into the crystal stream that crosses the trail ascending high into the Absaroka-Beartooth Wilderness. Water is plentiful here. It's a good thing, because so is perspiration when one tackles this stretch of real estate.

My guide is Gary Mandic of Butte, Montana. Gary works this time of year for Jack Atcheson Jr., who outfits bighorn sheep hunts in this primitive area. Gary is dripping with the sweat of hard walking, and both of us savor the cool of the shade while we down a couple of sandwiches, the last such food we will see for perhaps a week. We then shoulder our packs for the ascent into the high basin where we will camp our first night. Gary's prediction of what we will face between here and there has me dreading the remainder of the day. Up to this point we have been on a trail, but there is none where we will be hunting.

This is brutal, bewitching country. The terrain will kill a person who is not in shape, and it will unmercifully bludgeon even the hardiest of souls. The odds of actually harvesting a sheep here are about as remote as the odds of drawing a permit in a more desirable area—unless one hires an outfitter with the experience and knowledge of Atcheson. His hunters enjoy an enviable success rate of better than 50 percent.

The heavy pack tugs at my shoulders, and even before we leave the trail I am feeling the strain on my legs. I have exercised long and hard to prepare for this trip, and I am able to keep moving despite the discomfort. But I find myself wishing I had spent even more time conditioning.

Packing out the kill—only thirteen miles to go.

We leave the trail behind where another rushing stream feeds the lake below and begin threading our way through thick evergreens and intermittent deadfalls. The terrain is now sharply steeper, and I must stop often to catch my breath. Gary is a tireless workhorse, and he waits patiently and compliments me on how well we're doing, keeping my spirits up. He says it took him two days to get his hunter this far last year.

Topping out hardly ever happens in the Unlimited Areas, but the ground levels somewhat after two long hours on ascent. Our progress is slowed by increasingly massive deadfalls, however, so the required effort is still considerable. In addition to the fallen timber, rock slides abound, blocking our path and requiring creative maneuvering. Gary unerringly pilots us through the maze, drawing heavily on his intimate knowledge of the terrain. We can now see above timberline, and we begin to glass methodically for sheep whenever we can gain a new vista or stop to rest. None are in evidence, but it is heartening to know that Gary has seen them here often in the past.

As nightfall nears we arrive at a beautiful lake near timberline, and high rocky peaks reflect brilliantly in the quiet waters. It is heavenly to camp in the midst of such grandeur, and from our tent we can easily glass into three treeless basins. Rock marmots whistle at our intrusion and ravens protest mildly, but no other life is visible.

A merry fire is soon crackling and steaks sizzle upon it. We have ascended 5,000 feet in eleven miles carrying heavy packs. Despite extreme weariness, sleep is difficult to attain. It is unseasonably warm in the high country for mid-September; inside my down sleeping bag I am roasting, but outside it I am freezing. That discomfort adds to the day's grueling physical exertion, the high altitude, and the excitement of being in bighorn sheep country for the first time. I prop the bag open but keep inside, and finally I get some sleep.

At dawn, sunshine filtering through the tent wall awakens me. A heavy frost covers the ground, but the day is bright and blue. I feel a deep sense of gratitude toward my Creator for the beautiful weather, because bad weather can come up quickly in this remote high country. We are prepared, but who wants to use rain gear? Half the hunts up here are either ruined or hampered by bad weather, more often snow than rain at our 10,000-foot elevation.

Glassing the surrounding basins is again unproductive, except for an outstanding billy goat that feeds undisturbed on a gentle alpine slope behind our camp. I reflect on my own mountain goat hunt some years earlier and note the marked contrast in terrain between this animal's habitat and the Cassiars of British Columbia. From this campsite a goat would be simple. But on second thought, getting here wasn't exactly easy.

After breakfast, we elect to move over a couple of basins to one of Gary's favorite areas. Getting there will take all day, but we can make the trek up and over one of the 11,000-foot saddles to our south. That way we won't have to descend through the horrible deadfalls between us and the trail far below, since the country we will traverse is virtually free of vegetation.

We plan to cover only about five miles, but the rough terrain and massive boulder fields make the going slow. As I negotiate a steep slide with my pack and rifle, I become aware that any slip in this country could be disastrous. How would an injured hunter get out of here? Up and up we go, hopping from boulder to boulder and avoiding the loose scree. Net gain in altitude will be only a thousand feet or so, but an intervening pair of ridges we must ascend and descend will perhaps triple the climb. Although that's still well short of what we covered yesterday, my pack and rifle feel heavier.

Topping out on the final summit, we can see lofty Granite Peak, the highest point in Montana, to our east. In the remote distance to the south are the craggy peaks of the Grand Tetons, meaning that we are looking across the entire width of Yellowstone Park. Below us spreads one of the most fantastic basins in existence anywhere, its upper reaches ringed with stony ramparts, and with two pristine lakes far below us. A more spectacular view doesn't exist in North America, and perhaps the world.

The view isn't the only cause for excitement. The ridge is literally crisscrossed with the tracks of sheep, and they appear quite fresh. There are fresh droppings, and occasional shed sheep hair. For the first time since we left the trailhead I have the distinct feeling that we are in the right place.

Gary points out in the distance the picturesque meadow in which we will camp tonight. To reach it we must descend a treacherous shale slide where we virtually ski on the loose rocks. On reaching the valley floor we turn to survey our course, and to our surprise we see a band of a dozen or so ewes and lambs standing almost exactly where we crossed the spine of the ridge. This is the first time I've seen Rocky Mountain bighorns on an actual hunt, and I view the group with admiration. No rams show up, so we move on across the basin.

Our new campsite is strikingly similar to the first, fairly glowing with beauty. A major difference is the adjacent lake, which is much deeper and teems with hungry cutthroat trout. There is some kind of insect hatch in progress, and the fish feed furiously, some of them clearing the surface in their frenzy.

We again have a great vantage point from which to survey the rocky territory above timberline. We spot another fine mountain goat that evening, but no rams present themselves. The band of ewes is still feeding on the ridge, however.

Despite the fact that we are now down to preserved foods, Gary does an admirable job of feeding us. Sleep comes more easily as radiational cooling lowers the temperature of the clear night air, and my tiredness seems to be catching up with me as well.

We arise early and light a campfire, huddling against the morning chill as we down our instant oatmeal. The cool air feels refreshing as I gulp hot coffee and contemplate the upcoming day. We plan to leave our camp intact so we can cover more ground with lightened packs, and then to return here tonight. The lighter pack is an unanticipated treat as we depart in the breaking dawn.

The haunting terrain fascinates me as I watch shadows flee the coming sun. The captivating basin has apparently in times past been the home of an immense glacier, which has left behind innumerable moraines of boulders. We crawl and climb over each giant pile like a couple of ants on a hill of sand, crossing unbelievable aggregations of rocks arranged in ridges across the width of the valley. I ponder how thick a sheet of ice would be necessary to accomplish such a feat, and how much man-made machinery it would take. Humbled by such thoughts, I trudge onward and upward toward the head of the basin, where there is a climbable slide. Gary is confident we can top out there and be in position to view the other side of the mountain. As we hopscotch from one rock to another, I am doubly thankful for the lightened pack.

The light gradually improves as we walk, and we begin glassing this extraordinary valley. Spreading in three directions around us is sheep country. The place where we entered the basin is now far to our west, and I spend precious time glassing to see if I can still spot the ewes.

We are an hour above camp now, and all at once Gary stops short and looks intently ahead toward the slide. Lowering his binoculars, he turns to me with a grin that conveys instant excitement. I know immediately what he has seen.

"A ram," he exclaims softly. He points out the sleeping animal, and a tingle of excitement causes me to shiver.

"He's a dandy! Look at him, he's sleeping on his horn."

Gary soon finds another smaller ram nearby, resting but in an alert posture. Two immature rams are feeding. We set up the spotting scope for a closer look, and Gary confirms his initial impression of the larger animal. I gaze with intense interest at the magnified image. Soon the smaller ram begins feeding, and the larger raises its head and gets up, moving about and affording us a fine view of his horns from every angle.

Often a stalk on a ram requires a lot of forethought, planning, and cautious execution. In our case there is little we can do except take a frontal approach. The animals occupy the only location we might be able to ascend to get above them, and the sheer distances involved in any other direction make that out of the question. Too, the broad sweep of the basin walls would place any hunter plainly in view. All we can do is use the jumble of glacial boulders as cover and try to move in closer. Thankfully, the friendly wind is in our faces and the bright sun is at our backs.

All four rams are now feeding down toward us, so even if we could reach the top we might be in a poor position to shoot by the time we got there. They are now moving ever closer, and we manage to stay out of their sight in the rock pile as we slowly and carefully close the distance. Another half-hour and we have made measurable progress as the animals feed leisurely across the steep slope, completely unaware of our presence.

"We've got a problem here," whispers Gary, pointing to a wide expanse of barren soil stretching for a hundred yards in the direction of the sheep. Our objective is a jumbled pile of boulders about three hundred yards from our prey, but to reach it we must cross this open space. My heart sinks as I contemplate those powerful eyes sweeping so close I can practically feel them.

We survey the situation. The expanse of open soil and grass has us completely stymied. It looks as though the sheep will pass us by, far above. Gary fidgets and looks at my rifle.

"Look through your scope," he says. "Can you hit him from here?"

Hesitantly complying, I can see right away that I'm not likely to put a bullet from my .30-06 in exactly the right place, so tiny does the ram appear. Still, it's a privilege to be sighting in on a Rocky Mountain bighorn.

"Got to be over 400 yards, Gary. No way, unless it's the only chance. Any other options?"

The wind and sun remain in our favor. Our only alternative is to move forward and hope the animals don't see us. I say another silent prayer, the gravity and seeming impossibility of the situation heavy on my mind. One more look through the binoculars, and then we'll move out.

The instant the lead rams come into focus, there occurs one of those mysterious events that highlight many a hunting trip. The band is moving across the steep slope, intermittently feeding and alertly watching below, when the smaller ram suddenly becomes aggressive, for reasons unknown. Perhaps this is the first burst of energy that signals pre-rut dominance rituals. He lowers his head and gives the larger ram a swift butt in the rear, knocking the leader off balance and nearly toppling him down the slope. The larger ram immediately swaps ends and meets his aggressor head on, and a tremendous clash of horn upon horn echoes throughout the basin. First the rams' heads come together silently, then the sound reaches us. For the moment I forget that I am a hunter and become merely an observer of this classic battle.

My guide, however, has kept his wits, and he immediately recognizes the opportunity this presents. He motions me up and points forward.

"This is our chance!"

More electrifying crashes follow, the reverberations tempting me to stop and watch. True to Gary's prediction, all the animals are focused on the fight, and we achieve our goal easily. We catch the tail end of the action after safely diving behind the pile of rocks, and then I get ready for the shot. We are within 350 yards now for certain, perhaps even as close as 325 yards. Taking my ram is now a distinct possibility.

Is there a top to this mountain?

The contest between the two animals has lasted only a minute or so, and with the pecking order reestablished the band resumes business as usual. Gary watches them through his binoculars and exclaims softly, "What a beauty that big guy is."

I feel a case of nervousness coming on as I prepare to shoot. There is no hurry, though, as the animals are oblivious to our presence. I resolve to do my best, and to be certain that I settle myself before touching off the round.

Gary whispers last-minute instructions. "He's the ram on the left. Don't elevate over him, easy does it, and he's yours."

At the crack of the rifle, a healthy whack tells me the bullet has found its mark. The ram spins around to face the opposite direction as Gary instructs me to shoot again. On the second shot the animal rolls topsy-turvy down the steep slope before coming to a halt halfway to the bottom.

Jubilation! Exhilaration! An incredible wave of joy rolls over me with this sweet success. The harder one works, the deeper and sweeter the joy. The picture session after the kill with my Unlimited Area ram is one of my most memorable moments.

Montana is extremely finicky about wasting meat taken by a sport hunter, and in addition the hunter must present the entire, unaltered head to the Department of Fish, Wildlife and Parks. We have quite a load to haul a very long way. We will leave all our equipment, including my precious rifle, in the backpack tent and carry sixty-five pounds apiece thirteen miles back to the vehicle at the trailhead. Tomorrow we will walk back in to claim our gear, then make as much progress back out as we can. After a little calculation, I figure that comes to almost fifty miles of backpacking. It is quite a price to pay, but I count it all joy. I got my ram!

Desert bighorn sheep. (Photo: courtesy of Eric J. Hansen)

DESERT BIGHORN SHEEP

(Ovis canadensis cremnobates,
nelsoni mexicana, and weemsi)

The mighty pyramids of stone
That wedge-like cleave the desert airs,
When nearer seen, and better known,
Are but gigantic flights of stairs.

—Henry Wadsworth Longfellow (1807–1882),
The Ladder of Saint Augustine

One stands in summer on the rim of the Grand Canyon and gasps in awe at the sight, overwhelmed at the raw power and beauty of the natural world. From more southerly Tucson or Phoenix, from Las Vegas or Lake Havesu, distant purple desert mountains shrouded with halos of cumulus display an allure that borders on the magical. During winter, when the air is as transparent as a flawless diamond, the violet color clarifies to reveal details of rock and vegetation, a desert environment that changes dramatically with the seasons and with elevation. To the hunter, such sights serve also as reminders that a magnificent animal dwells here. This land is home to the splendid desert bighorn sheep.

For sheer fascination, and reverence from the hunting community, probably no animal in North America surpasses the desert bighorn sheep. All wild sheep are greatly esteemed, but the scarcity of the desert bighorn has made it the darling of the hunting world. The fondest dream of many a hunter is to draw a tag for one of these animals in the places where they are available on a limited-entry basis: mainly Arizona and Nevada, where nearly two score nonresident permits are allocated each year. California and Utah have added nonresident opportunities, although the total number of nonresident tags combined can be counted on the fingers of one hand. Huntable populations also exist in New Mexico, Colorado, and Texas, but tags are so few that nonresidents need not apply.

The only certain permits are available in Mexico, where I hunted my desert ram. I was fortunate to hunt before prices there skyrocketed, but even then it was my most expensive single hunt. The location of the hunt, the state of Baja California del Norte, has since been closed to legal hunting of desert bighorns, though limited moves have been made to reopen the season on a highly restricted basis. And a few permits are still available in Baja del Sur, farther south, where the animals are numerous but smaller. The U.S. Fish and Wildlife Service came very close in 1997–98 to listing the Baja Peninsula populations of desert bighorns as endangered, a move that might well have spelled their eventual extinction. The proposal was withdrawn when helicopter surveys revealed a surprisingly robust population in the area, with a healthy ram-to-ewe ratio.

It is encouraging that in this case the U.S. Fish and Wildlife Service gave weight to scientific findings instead of blindly applying a dangerous "precautionary principle." When such a valuable creature becomes merely meat, it can be very quickly eliminated by lightly policed locals eager to fill their stew pots. With legal hunting in place, game wardens funded by hunting income are available to protect the animals. Also, in Mexico auction funds for desert bighorn sheep permits go to community action projects that benefit the local people and give them a sense of ownership and an incentive to protect the sheep. Such innovative programs ensure a future that is likely to be secure for the *cremnobates* subspecies of the Baja.

Sonora is today's hot spot for people of means to hunt the desert bighorn. The rise of modern game management, allowing landowners to supervise their indigenous wildlife and benefit from it, has been a true shot in the arm there. Unlike the Baja Peninsula, most of the land in Sonora is privately owned.

Permits are prohibitively expensive for all but the most well-off hunter, costing around $50,000. Permits also are available annually by raffle through several hunter-conservationist organizations.

Another offshoot of the current management program in Mexico is the reintroduction of desert bighorn sheep into areas from which they had been eliminated. Ongoing negotiations may allow sheep from the herd on Tiburon Island to be placed back into the state of Coahuila, far to the east of any present-day desert bighorn range in Mexico. There is almost unlimited habitat there, and new sport hunting opportunities could someday arise. Chihuahua is another state with extensive historical desert bighorn range, and discussions of restocking are going on there as well.

"A big desert ram which pops up on a ridge above you—strong, brave, fleet, and defiant, with those great horns of his cutting circles against the sky—is to me one of the most thrilling sights in nature. He seems part of those fantastically lovely desert mountains, and the merest glimpse of one makes my heart pound and my breath catch in my throat." Why are people so fascinated by the smallest of the North American bighorns? Their scant numbers have fueled much of the interest, no doubt. The difficulty of securing a chance to hunt them is legendary. To receive notification that the draw in Arizona or Nevada—or anywhere—has yielded you a permit must be comparable to winning a state lottery. Indeed the creatures have a certain mystique that holds one spellbound. The late Jack O'Connor stated it well when he penned the above words more than a half-century ago.

The desert bighorn is one of three types of generally recognized bighorn sheep (as opposed to the thinhorn, Stone and Dall sheep), along with the Rocky Mountain and California bighorn. The desert variety actually comprises five recognized subspecies, though from the standpoint of morphology there is little to separate any of them from their slightly larger cousins except for the notably smaller body and lighter coat. The main distinguishing feature is the striking adaptation to a harsh desert environment, and, for the hunter, the challenge of an absolutely unique type of sheep hunting. Here are the usual steep mountains and lung-bursting ascents, but to the normal hardships are added dangerous vegetation and reptiles, a parching lack of water, and midday heat that, stated plainly, can kill you.

The desert bighorn sheep was decimated, as were the other bighorns, by the twin forces of market hunting and livestock disease. Their numbers today have recovered to approximately 25,000 animals distributed over the desert Southwest of the U.S. and three states of Mexico. The most current count shows some 6,500 in Arizona, 5,500 in Nevada, 3,500 in California, 2,500 in Utah, 500 in Colorado, 300 in Texas, and 200 in New Mexico. South of the border, there are 3,500 in the two states of the Baja California peninsula and 2,500 in Sonora. In a recent year, 100 rams were harvested in Arizona, 102 in Nevada, 29 in Utah, 14 in California, 5 in Colorado, 2 in New Mexico, and 1 in Texas.

Desert bighorn sheep. Baja California del Norte, January 1989.

Success rates are excellent for the hunter who is able to obtain a permit. Securing that permit is perhaps the highlight of any big-game hunter's career, and inevitably many will never have that thrill. Fewer than 5,000 desert bighorn rams have been taken by sport hunters since 1952, and in a recent year in Arizona there were 6,842 applicants for the 108 permits, a draw odds of 1 in 63. Perhaps all of us who continue to try to draw a tag should concentrate at least some of our efforts in the area of desert bighorn conservation, especially transplantation efforts and water-hole projects that are likely, in the long run, to open up additional hunting opportunities. The individual who does that may well see desert bighorns in their prickly and bewitching habitat, and will have the satisfaction of contributing more than goodwill to their well-being.

Desert bighorn sheep are the smallest subspecies of wild sheep in North America. A big ram will seldom weigh more than 200 pounds. Ewes average only a little more than 100 pounds but may weigh up to about 130 pounds. With their smaller bodies, one would expect smaller horn measurements, and that is in fact the case. But the difference is nowhere comparable to the disparity in body size, making the small ram with the huge horns a stunning reality. At the top end, the world- record desert bighorn sheep was taken in Baja California and scored 205$\frac{1}{8}$, while the top Rocky Mountain bighorn scores "only" 208$\frac{1}{8}$, a minuscule difference. Biologists believe that the outsized horns, which are penetrated by a highly vascular core, have differentiated in these desert creatures as a means of dissipating heat, in addition to their more conventional functions.

The rut for desert bighorn sheep is much earlier and quite a bit more protracted than it is for other sheep. Breeding may occur from June into October, with the peak in August for most subspecies. The rams don't tend a harem of ewes intensively, nor do they band together. They move about in solo excursions from one group of ewes to another, attempting to breed as many as possible.

After a gestation period similar to that for other wild sheep (179 days), the ewes give birth to one, or occasionally two, lambs. Births occur from January to April. Newborns weigh eight to ten pounds, and about half of them die during their first

six months of life. Their major predators are golden eagles and coyotes, though in mountain ranges with sufficient deer to support a population of mountain lions, those cats can become efficient killers of desert bighorns as well. Rams move around more than ewes and are often far from escape terrain; hence they suffer a higher rate of death, due to predation, accidents, and losses related to the stresses of the rut. Mortality is nevertheless fairly low until around age ten, after which it increases exponentially each year. A desert bighorn more than fourteen years old is ancient, a statistic that squares well with that of other wild sheep.

Desert bighorns are well adapted to the forage in their harsh environment, and when food is readily available they can consume several pounds of vegetation at one feeding. They prefer grasses and sedges, but at certain times of the year browse plants become extremely important. The animals will eat jojoba, desert holly, fairyduster, sagebrush, willow, rabbitbrush, curlleaf mountain mahogany, winterfat, bitterbrush, and a variety of low-growing forbs. Although they can go for months without water, having developed a capacity to store and conserve their bodily fluids, they drink huge amounts when it is available and eat a variety of water-storing cacti when it is not. Desert bighorn sheep can drink up to two and a half gallons of water a minute, a rate comparable to that of a horse.

The flesh of desert bighorn sheep was a favorite of the aboriginal peoples of North America. In the desert Southwest, the bighorn sheep is the most frequently portrayed animal in pictographs left by ancient Indians. Even today sheep meat remains a rare delicacy, and that toothsomeness unfortunately made the animal a preference among market hunters early in our nation's history.

Westward expansion introduced domestic sheep and cattle into the ranges of the desert bighorn, and with them new diseases. Scabies was an early killer. Later, sinus disease mediated by botflies was discovered to be much more deadly to the desert bighorn than to domestic sheep, because the wild sheep have extensive sinuses that are highly susceptible to such infestation. Viral and bacterial pneumonia also took a toll. Bluetongue, a viral disease also known as malignant catarrh fever, is carried by gnats and has been reported in desert bighorns as well.

The big boy of Baja is finally down and out.

Hunting techniques and equipment for desert bighorns are quite similar to those for the other sheep of North America. I select cooler clothing for the hunt, plus a parka for sitting on a high ridge in a brisk December breeze. It warms up in most of the animal's range as the day wears on, so layering is the best approach. I like tough khaki pants of the kind made by Patagonia, and as always my red suspenders and a colorful chamois shirt. Leather boots, well broken in, are a necessity to protect against the thorny plants that abound in the desert Southwest. I like wool socks with polypropylene liners. Take along moleskin in case of blisters, good advice on any walking and climbing excursion. The dry season is on during the hunting season throughout most of the range of the desert bighorn, so rain is unlikely, but nevertheless take a waterproof parka and rain pants.

Speaking of water, seldom can one find a stream with drinkable water in the desert mountains. My own hunt was a notable exception, and the rivulet that cascaded down from snowfields high in the San Pedro Martirs was as pure as any water in the world. But the opportunity to drink stream water safely is rare for the desert bighorn hunter, so take along plenty of water and be sure to rehydrate yourself each night. Water is always best—not your favorite hard or soft drink.

You will want the best in optics for locating the ram of your dreams amid the mountain mahogany and saguaro cacti. The sandstone-tan desert bighorn ram that I eventually harvested was the most difficult animal to spot of any I encountered in my North American hunting career. The creature blended perfectly into his boulder-strewn feeding grounds. A good spotting scope is a small investment compared with the cost of a desert bighorn sheep hunt, and it's required equipment in most localities. A 20X or better spotting scope could save many miles of walking and many hours of climbing.

Any desert bighorn ram that meets the legal requirements of the principality in which you are hunting is a real trophy, but as with all sheep, the older the ram the more satisfying the experience. Sheep live relatively long lives by ungulate standards, and taking young rams does nothing good for population health or dynamics. Some states require that the hunter (or the hired guide) take a course prior to taking to the field. In Nevada, for one example, the ram must be seven years old or score 144 Boone and Crockett points, a fairly minimal requirement that every hunter wants to beat. The punch line is that you don't shoot the first ram you see unless it's a real dinger, and you never shoot a marginal ram unless the clock is running out (and then only if you're certain the animal meets the mandated requirements).

The desert bighorn is an animal of mystery and intrigue, one that few of us will ever be privileged to hunt. I feel deeply blessed to have been able to do so, and I hope to again someday. I buy bonus points in Arizona and Nevada each year by purchasing a never-used nonresident license in both states. I may have more bonus points than any other person alive if I live to be ninety, but I'll never stop trying. Yes, I already have a desert ram, and perhaps that will suffice. But every real hunter knows why I can't stop applying.

BAJA BIGHORN

Desert bighorn sheep! I contemplate the meaning of the phrase as I sit in the canyon, glassing for them. The hours before sunrise in a desert are cold, even as far south as the Baja Peninsula of Mexico, and I welcome the rising sun. Soon the desert will begin to warm.

I am in the middle of a big arroyo, one of many deep gulches that split the sides of these arid mountains. The irregular spine to our front bears the name San Pedro Martir, Saint Peter the Martyr. This particular canyon is south of the high point of the range, Diablo Peak, in what is known as the Algodones area. The word means "cotton" in Spanish, but I see nothing here that remotely resembles that plant. My six Mexican companions are chattering excitedly, and my Spanish, though usually adequate, is not up to following their rapid-fire exchanges.

"*Borregos?*" I ask, using the Spanish word for rams. Their tone tells me my suspicions are correct, although I certainly can see no sheep amid the brown jumble of boulders.

"*Si, tres borregos!*" replies the head guide, Jorge, pointing a tanned, bony finger toward the apex of a long, irregular draw that stretches close to the top of the nearest peak. Desert vegetation in the ravine combines with the naturally camouflaged sheep to make the animals nearly invisible to me. The guides accommodate their

Beautiful and wild Diablo Peak in the San Pedro Martir Mountains (highest point on the Baja Peninsula).

gringo hunter by setting up a spotting scope. Sure enough, there in the center of the field of view are three beautiful desert bighorn rams. I still can't find them through my binoculars, even though I now know exactly where they are. I am using the latest in optics, making it all the more amazing that my Mexican friends can find them so easily.

Sitting in the warming sand as the desert awakens, I can't help but reflect on the events that have brought me to this place and time. I already have three of the North American wild sheep, and this is to be my "grand slam" hunt. One should never assume that things will go as planned, but this sighting fills me with hope. Those rams look good.

Diablo Camp, where hunters relish the ample tent accommodations, is comfortable enough for a sheep hunter, although it is Spartan by many standards. The Mexican government provides all meals, transportation, and guides for me and the other hunters in the Diablo Peak area. There is no shortage of help, and I am accompanied by a chief guide, an assistant guide, a spotter, two packers, and a government biologist. One of the packers carries my fairly heavy load, thus making this a backpack trip in name only for me. I have skipped along up the dry arroyo feeling as frisky as a kitten, carrying only my rifle.

The guides report that the rams are feeding. I naturally want the biggest desert bighorn ram ever taken in Baja del Norte and have made that as clear as my Spanish will allow. No, I'm only kidding about the biggest—but I do try hard to set a high standard. After all, this will be my grand slam ram, so I don't want a squeaker if I can help it.

Jorge assures me that one of the rams will be to my liking, and he plots out a way to get in closer. The plan is to climb (isn't it always?) a long, sloping ridge to our left, ascend to the ridgeline just this side of the group, and perhaps even attempt the shot from there. It will depend on what appears feasible, and whether the best ram looks good enough upon closer inspection. Jorge and I will be accompanied by the assistant guide and the biologist, while the others will stay in the arroyo with the packs, waiting and spotting while we climb. I look around for my pack, stuffed with gear and accessories. I never go anywhere without

Glassing for desert bighorn sheep with Mexican guides amid desert splendor.

some of the items in it, and at first I am unwilling to leave it behind. Still, this is just a short climb, so maybe I can do without them.

We depart the sandy bottom and begin our ascent, leaving everything except my rifle, binoculars, a few extra shells, a small pocket camera, and the clothes on my back, which I've pared down to climbing minimum as the temperature rises pleasantly. Even in January it gets quite warm at midday in the Baja desert, and the warmth lulls me into a lamentable complacency.

The terrain we are negotiating is as vertical as any sheep country, and it has a most unconventional and mesmerizing beauty about it. Instead of the hordes of smaller rocks, so familiar in virtually every other sheep habitat in North

Finally in position for a long, dangerous shot (note spiny plants).

America, here are mountains of boulders, the texture of which reminds me of a coarse whetstone. The rough material gouges my pants and gloves, doing considerable damage to the latter.

The house-size boulders over which we are laboring harbor another menace, potentially even more harmful. Every crack and crevice is full of vegetation laden with sharp stickers and deadly spines. The most menacing of these is a kind of century plant, the leaves of which resemble the sabers once carried by mounted cavalrymen. Uncannily, and doubtless the work of some demonic force, they seem to be in the places most likely to result in grief to any unlucky sheep hunter who ventures by.

Other vegetation is only slightly more forgiving, and I constantly fight the spiny assaults of cholla, prickly pear, barrel, and even giant saguaro cacti, not to mention many other plants more than capable of penetrating even the leather boots of a careless climber. The most sinister is the vicious *uña de gato* (cat's claw) plant, the curved talons of which rip both flesh and fabric. My leather gloves are soon worn through, and I wish repeatedly that I had brought a couple of extra pairs.

The day wears on, and by noon there is no end in sight. I am getting thirsty, but I left my water bottle in my pack. Jorge has a little, and we share it until it is gone. Hunger pangs set in next, but I have failed to put even a candy bar into my pocket, anticipating that we would be back in the arroyo by now.

Our two-hour climb stretches into nearly eight as cliffs and oversized boulders slow our progress. The government biologist, who is actually a student at the university, is on his first such expedition. He sticks it out for a few hours before electing to return to the waiting group. Only Jorge and an assistant guide continue upward with me. I am by now kicking myself for having left all my survival gear at the base of the mountain, including even my water bottle. How could I have been so stupid?

It is near 4 P.M. when we finally reach the ridge. We are lying among the thorns looking into the very basin in which we saw the rams early this morning, but no sheep are in evidence now. *If we can't find them, let's head down to the creek for a drink.* My raging thirst must be clouding my judgment, bringing up such a thought when there are desert bighorn rams about.

Finally, Jorge points to a tangle of brush opposite us, between two massive boulders. The rams! They have been lying down, but now they are on their feet and visible.

"El grande es más bajo," comments Jorge softly, indicating the position of the best ram. This time I can see them easily with my binoculars as they begin feeding once more.

Shooting distances in the Baja are often quite long, even by sheep-hunting standards, because the rough terrain hides the sheep unless one can look across a canyon at them. We move in as close as possible, finally setting up on one of the numerous boulders. Here the terrain begins to fall away into the deep canyon, so a closer frontal approach is not possible, and the sheep are protected from above by massive rocks. Our only option appears to be here and now.

Jorge insists that the distance is under 350 yards, still a very long shot. The larger of the rams appears quite respectable, with massive bases and good length. Despite the distance, I elect to try for him. I am fully aware of Mexican policy that a wounded ram is your ram, a policy I fully endorse. I am confident that, with a good rest and my bipod attachment, I can be successful. I establish myself in position and get a rock-solid rest fore and aft. Although I'm certain I can do this, the animal looks mighty small in my scope.

I carefully and gently squeeze the trigger, and my shot hits under the ram, kicking dust into the air. It is a certain miss. The bullet drop confirms my own estimate of the distance at 400 yards or more. Rather than perhaps wisely backing off, I simply elevate a bit more and touch off another round, holding at the top of the back. This shot breaks the front leg at the shoulder and momentarily rolls the animal over. The ram hobbles away from us behind dense cover, and when he appears again at a considerably greater distance, I shoot two more times before he disappears. Jorge confirms my suspicion that both shots missed.

I now have a real problem, one born of inappropriate pride in my shooting ability and the overwhelming desire to complete my quest. A series of bad decisions has now placed a priceless game animal at peril of being lost wounded, the worst of all possible outcomes. Only an hour of daylight remains, so we must act quickly.

We take off running through the treacherous terrain in a desperate attempt to get to the spot where the ram disappeared. This involves climbing perhaps another five hundred feet through some of the steepest, most dangerous terrain I have seen so far in this hellish country. I am already exhausted and have had nothing to eat for many hours. By some miracle I reach deeply within and come up with just a little bit more. For almost an hour we ascend rocks of gargantuan proportions, at one point climbing under a boulder to emerge through a narrow crevice. We arrive just before dark where we last saw the wounded animal.

As we ease along I keep my rifle at ready, hoping and praying that we can locate our quarry. Suddenly Jorge wheels and grabs my arm excitedly, thrusting me forward.

"Alli está," he whispers with electricity in his voice, pointing into the jumble of rocks below. I immediately spot the ram, standing broadside perhaps a hundred yards away, looking at us.

After the extreme effort of the last hour, I am a bit shaky as I crawl into position. The solid rest of yet another great rock fuels my confidence, and I am resolved that this time the shot will not be in vain. I ease a cartridge into the chamber and assume shooting position, placing the cross hairs securely on the ram's shoulder. At the crack of the rifle the ram wheels and runs away once more, disappearing into the moonlike boulder field.

We scramble forward over the boulders, again on the move across treacherous terrain, dodging prickly spines and leaping from rock to rock. Prominent speckles of blood lead us along the path the ram took in his flight, and my faith soars.

The trail leads quickly to the downed ram, which is piled up under a piñon tree at the edge of a bottomless drop-off. A few more steps and the creature would have reached thin air and possible destruction, far below.

The events of this day have not been as I expected. For years I have looked forward to colossal exhilaration and a towering sense of accomplishment upon completing my grand slam. It turns out to be a strangely quiet moment.

Perhaps I am simply too exhausted to celebrate. To be sure, I have a happy feeling down deep, but here we are in the dark, several thousand life-threatening vertical feet from our gear. We have no food or water. We have no clothes in which to weather a subfreezing night on the mountain, and we have no light with which to make a descent. I mentally kick myself in the rear once more for being so nonchalant

Looking over our rams before we decide to take one.

about leaving my carefully prepared backpack behind. Never again.

I do have my pocket camera, though, and I dutifully take a few flash pictures before we embark on the laborious return to the arroyo where the others must have enjoyed a ringside seat for our adventure. He really is a beautiful ram, even if I am so exhausted that I can't fully appreciate the fact. We cover our prize with limbs to discourage scavengers before we set off down the mountain.

I say a prayer of thanks as we begin our electrifying plunge into the darkness. I am grateful for the success, for the safety so far, and for the beautiful half-moon that is rising out of the Gulf of Baja California. I also petition for protection on our trip back to the safety of the arroyo below, recognizing the very real potential for serious injury. I suffer two more or less major spills as we descend, and several minor ones, but by God's grace I miss breaking any bones or impaling myself on the century plants. I do sustain some painful bruises and scrapes on both legs that will remind me of this hunt for weeks to come. And I smash my camera during one of several terrifying falls, although breaking the camera happily does not damage the film.

We can see, far below, the campfire our relaxed companions have built, tantalizing in its nearness and yet so distant. When we finally arrive in camp, we bask in the glow of that fire while I change out of my sweat-soaked clothes. We drink from the rushing stream in the arroyo—yes, you can drink the stream water in Mexico, at least in this pristine location—and I fill my empty stomach with some kind of delicious Mexican canned food, a sort of hominy.

The next morning we ascend once more, this time taking a more direct route, although it is even more steep and treacherous than our ascent of yesterday. My legs have recovered sufficiently to allow me to make good time. We plan ahead a bit better for this climb and are able to enjoy a great lunch on a sun-washed bench near my trophy. Thankfully, it has lain undisturbed overnight. I take several rolls of pictures with my remaining camera (resolving henceforth always to carry three).

What is the lesson of this hunt? Always assume you'll be gone all day—and maybe all night—when you head out in the morning. That is pretty basic. In an unfamiliar situation one may be tempted to violate even such common-sense rules, but if you do so often enough, expect to pay a price. Sooner or later, the cost of indiscretion is disaster. It was by the grace of God that it was not so on this hunt.

California bighorn sheep. (Photo: courtesy of James L. Davis)

CALIFORNIA BIGHORN SHEEP

(Ovis canadensis californiana)

Forty-five miles to water.
Seventy-five miles to wood.
Two and a half miles to hell.

—Sign seen by Owen Wister in the Okanagan Country, 1880

California bighorn sheep look amazingly similar to desert bighorns. I noticed that the first time I glassed a band of rams, their light coats and their desertlike environment reminding me of Baja California. Owen Wister was doubtless aware of the dry, thirsty nature of the Okanagan region. Typical California bighorn habitat is arid in most areas, warmer than the realm of the Rocky Mountain subspecies, and it has a higher proportion of grassland with lower alpine habitat. These sheep typically inhabit lower mountains where there is more volcanism, hence the terms "lava bed bighorn" or "rimrock bighorn."

Not everywhere in California bighorn country is this description entirely accurate, but that is the general situation. Like all sheep, the California subspecies requires a certain amount of pristine habitat with minimum competition from humans and domestic livestock, as well as adequate forage and escape cover. Their original range encompassed only one Canadian province and four states of the United States. The animals were found from the coastal and interior mountains of southern British Columbia, southward into Washington, Oregon, and into the Sierra Nevada of California as far south as 37 degrees latitude (about the location of Kings Canyon National Park), and eastward into Idaho. Although they became extinct throughout much of southern British Columbia by the middle of the twentieth century, transplantation efforts now have returned populations to many parts of their original range. In addition, California bighorn sheep now occupy a portion of Nevada and have been introduced into North Dakota, where the extinct Audubon bighorn once roamed.

D. Douglas first described this subspecies in the *Zoological Journal* in 1829, but it is unclear where he collected his specimen. It was either from present-day Oregon near the mouth of the Deschutes River, or farther north in Yakima County, Washington, near Mount Adams. Surely Lewis and Clark, on their exploratory journeys a quarter-century earlier, encountered this bighorn as well.

The conventional wisdom has always been that these sheep are smaller than their Rocky Mountain cousins, and almost as small as desert bighorns. The few studies that have been done fail to confirm that, and indeed California bighorns may be virtually the same size as the Rocky Mountain subspecies. They may average just a shade smaller in all age classes, but the difference is certainly not dramatic. The males grow faster and for a longer period than the females, which reach their maximum weight by age three or four.

California bighorns are different from Rocky Mountain bighorns in other ways, however. They are lighter in color, and their coat has a dark stripe that runs down the center of the back, across the white rump patch and onto the tail. The pelage is much less dense, with shorter hair, making it distinctly reminiscent of a desert sheep. In yet another similarity to the desert bighorn, the ears are slightly larger, for heat dissipation. The horns, that feature of most importance to the hunter, are undeniably smaller than those of any other bighorn.

California bighorn sheep are the least numerous of the North American wild sheep. There are fewer than 10,000 on their present range, more or less evenly divided between the United States and British Columbia. It is a shame that the only range state without a hunting program for these sheep is its namesake, California. There is no hunt for some local populations in other states as well, as a result of insufficient numbers and other factors. In British Columbia there are a total of 162 resident permits for

California bighorn sheep. British Columbia, September 1996.

California bighorns (55 in the Okanagan, 97 in the Ashnola area, and 10 in the Junction area). Approximately 30 nonresident permits are available through licensed outfitters in British Columbia. All these numbers fluctuate on the basis of the annual scientific data. Success rates for residents are quite low, although in recent years guided nonresidents have experienced a success rate of about 50 percent. All hunts for California bighorns in the United States are on a draw basis.

The dry nature of their habitat would make one suspect that California bighorns might be able to survive on very little water. The scarcity of water-storing plants in most places they inhabit seems to bolster that argument. But while California bighorns are seldom observed to drink water, they are usually not far from a reliable source, suggesting that they do. Because of the stresses associated with the rut and with lambing, you are most likely to observe the animals drinking during November and April. California bighorns also use mineral licks more intensively during those times of the year.

These sheep may utilize separate summer and winter ranges, but because of the generally lower

elevations and more moderate annual extremes of temperature, they may tend to use the same areas year-round. In some places they may occupy separate rutting, lambing, and mineral lick areas as well. The recent volcanic activity in much of their range makes for excellent mineral content in the soil, so these animals are not as dependent on mineral licks as are their Rocky Mountain relatives. More often they traverse the mountain in response to changing forage conditions, following the fresh green-up in the spring and moving the other way in fall, according to snow accumulation. They may occasionally make brief visits to very low elevation mineral licks in some places.

California bighorns generally eat grasses, forbs, and browse more according to their availability than any other factor, such as nutritional content or palatability. Thus they could be labeled random, rather than selective, feeders. They eat grasses and shrubs in a relatively constant proportion year-round, except for some increased consumption of shrubs in winter when grass may be under snow. Forbs are spring and summer foods that are of less interest in fall and winter as those plants begin to decay. California bighorns like rough fescue, prairie June grass when it is greening in spring, needle-and-thread, and Kentucky bluegrass. Among their favorite forbs are silky lupine and Thompson's paintbrush. They browse on a large number of shrubs, some of the most important being pasture sage, Wyeth buckwheat, and snow buckwheat. In all locations they select new growth over old, flower heads over other parts, and leaves over stems.

Like other wild sheep, California bighorns feed mainly at dawn and dusk, though when undisturbed they may feed twenty-four hours a day with frequent bedding periods, particularly in the spring and late fall. Like most wild sheep, they tend not to feed at night, and they travel more in winter. During extreme cold (below zero Fahrenheit), which seldom occurs in most of their range, the metabolic rate of the animals rises to ward off hypothermia. Under such conditions they may bed longer than usual to conserve energy and minimize heat loss.

The smaller horns of California bighorns are likely the result of both genetic and environmental factors. As with all mountain sheep, the horns arise from a conical projection of the bony skull plate and grow like a series of keratin ice cream cones stacked inside one another. Rocky Mountain bighorns uniformly outscore California bighorns, and few of the latter ever reach Boone and Crockett minimums. Safari Club International has established a separate category in its record book for California bighorns in recognition of this difference.

The horns of California bighorns seem to have a bit more of a flare than those of the tight-curling Rocky Mountain subspecies. They are often broomed, which might improve side vision, and the sheep put them to a variety of uses ranging from fighting to digging. Brooming can remove up to three years of horn growth, though usually it involves mainly the lamb tips. Growth rings on ewes are as visible as those on rams and are a reliable way to determine the age of ewes up to about five years. After that the annuli become so tightly packed that the method becomes impractical, and other ways to determine age are necessary. For males, determining age by horn annuli is quite precise up through age ten or so.

As is the case for all wild sheep, establishing dominance is an ongoing matter. For males, the hierarchy is well understood before the November rut begins. Age and horn size, along with individual health and vigor, determine the pecking order. The rams remain separate from the ewes until the rut, which can begin as early as October, although it seems to peak in November and taper off through the first half of December. As with most ungulates, the rut is initiated by decreasing photoperiod, consequent hormonal changes, and the subsequent intermingling of males in the female population. The rams continually test the receptivity of the ewes, and when the ewe is ready breeding takes place.

Among California bighorns virtually 100 percent of ewes are impregnated, a higher rate than among other subspecies. One ram can breed ten to twenty ewes. The gestation period is 175 days, and lambing is earlier in some populations than for other mountain sheep, peaking in late April instead of June. In British Columbia's Ashnola area, lambing occurs most often in mid-May. That area is farther north than much of current California bighorn habitat, and early lambs tend to perish there. The ewe seeks solitude in terrain that is relatively inaccessible to predators, entering a labor of twenty minutes or less before delivering the newborn. New lambs weigh about the same as those of Rocky Mountain bighorns, about eight to twelve pounds. Usually the births are single, but some say that twins occur more frequently in California bighorns than in other subspecies. However, other biologists feel that instances of apparent twinning are simply "babysitting."

The lamb stands just minutes after birth, and walks soon after that. Suckling begins within an hour or two. The ewe and lamb bond quickly, and one of the functions of the birth isolation phase seems to be the establishment of this relationship. The ewe initially learns to recognize the unique smell of her newborn, and later both visual and auditory identification are in place as well.

The major predator of newborn lambs is the coyote, which is prevalent throughout the range of California bighorn sheep. In the Ashnola and Junction populations of British Columbia, up to 80 percent of lambs are lost to coyotes in some years, the deaths occurring after the ewes leave the lambing grounds to join the large maternity groups characteristic of the species. The highest losses involve early lambs whose ewes return sooner to the larger group.

The heaviest losses of lambs to coyotes usually occur where escape cover is limited, and such areas are usually populated by transplanted sheep inhabiting country that is not original range. Wolves are mostly absent, except in northernmost California bighorn country. Cougars may prey significantly on some populations, especially on rams just after the rut, when the sheep are in a weakened condition. There is little mortality between the ages of one and two years, but in rams it increases gradually thereafter and peaks at age thirteen or so, the expected maximum life span. Ewes may live longer, though overall only a tiny fraction of the sheep population lives to be older than thirteen years.

California bighorn sheep are susceptible to most of the diseases that have decimated all bighorn populations. Perhaps the major killer is the bacterial disease pasteurella, of which several types infect these sheep. The disease causes fatal pneumonia, striking most often in populations stressed by overcrowding, poor forage, heavy snow, high levels of dust, poor escape cover, harassment by humans or domestic dogs, or competition with livestock.

Lungworms are common, and high burdens of that parasite also predispose sheep to fatal pasteurella pneumonia. The intermediate host of lungworms is a land snail that clings to vegetation sheep ingest. Another disease is scabies, caused by a mite, which can lead to loss of hair, sores, and resultant weakening and sometimes death. Chronic sinusitis is related to nasal botfly larvae infestations, and up to 20 percent of California bighorn sheep may have that disease. The sheep also carry a variety of intestinal roundworms, but those are usually asymptomatic.

The biggest California bighorn sheep, in terms of record-book scores, come from British Columbia. Several scores are over 170, which is a darn good ram of any subspecies. My own California bighorn, which came from British Columbia, actually outscores my Rocky Mountain bighorn, which came from a native population of Montana sheep not noted for high-scoring rams. I can find no listings for California bighorns higher than the low 170s, so some thirty inches of horn measurement separate the high-end scores of this subspecies and those of the Rocky Mountain variety.

Hunting California bighorn sheep, like any hunting, is an experience requiring patience and persistence. Expect to do extensive glassing of heavily timbered terrain, and concentrate your

Great scenery in the Okanagan country.

searches during early morning and late evening feeding times. Locating a band of rams during preseason scouting does not ensure that the animals will be there when you come back, but they will likely not move far away, at least not quickly. If you are hunting in Canada, where outfitter tags obviate the need for a successful draw, your host will likely know where the sheep are. If you are among the fortunate few privileged to hunt California bighorns in the Lower Forty-eight, hire a guide who is very familiar with the area you will be hunting. A band of rams can hang tight in a small place, and finding them can be a task unless you know where to look.

Gear for hunting this subspecies varies little from that needed for the other bighorns. The dry, lower region is more prone to harbor rattlesnakes than most sheep country, so exercise caution in crawling around on rocky outcroppings and uneven slopes. Good leather climbing boots, a sturdy backpack, a spotting scope, and good binoculars are the most essential items. Use your favorite sheep rifle in most any centerfire caliber that is legal where you are hunting.

About 250 California bighorn permits are available each year, and many of those go to residents of the range states and British Columbia. If you are privileged to hunt this subspecies, make the most of it. Take a pair of cameras and keep them rolling. Film is cheap, and this is likely to be the only time you will hunt California bighorns. Make sure you never forget it.

RAM OF THE OKANAGAN COUNTRY

The small rental car breezes along the road between Spokane, Washington, and the small town of Omak, where I hope to have supper. The wheat fields are endless, stretching to the horizon. Harvest is over, and the stubble has been cropped short. Already farmers are preparing the fields for the fall planting.

Vast deposits of loose rock punctuate the wheat lands at intervals, the residuum of the original bedrock, splintered over time by geological forces. Rocky outcrops rise along the way, revealing the intact portions. Man has left them unmolested from time immemorial because the ground is impossible to farm; it yields to cattle ranching only

grudgingly. Around the base of each formation are formidable slides of picturesque, undisturbed scree, giving every appearance of having been just as they are now since before the time of Christ. Bunch grass, a plant that feeds numerous ungulates, thrives on the flat tops of the promontories. In many places the mullein plant grows, its coarse, fuzzy leaves emerging from a tall stem topped with a long seed head reminiscent of some type of grain. Both plants are a favorite food of the California bighorn sheep.

Passing by the giant Grand Coulee Dam and Lake Roosevelt, I now enter habitat typical of this bighorn sheep. Crumbling rock cliffs line the Columbia River and grow in prominence and elevation as I motor westward. The magic sheep country known as Okanagan looms ahead. I am approaching the center of the world for the California bighorn sheep, despite the more southerly name attached to the animal.

A friend I knew in the army while stationed at Fort Lewis, Washington, drew a tag in the limited entry drawing that qualified him to hunt the California bighorn in the rugged hills on the south side of the U.S. border around Omak. He took a magnificent ram, and my heart ran amuck with envy when I saw the mount. It was an impossible dream for me back then, but one that I cherished over the years with quiet determination. My hopes came to fruition with a score of North American sheep hunts in other places, for other kinds of sheep. But this is the first trip to the birthplace of my passion for hunting the kings of the high country.

I am scheduled to hunt with Jim Weins of Vaseux (rhymes with "lasso") Creek Outfitters, based in Oliver, B.C. His operation has a reputation for being one of the best for this subspecies, and I heartily look forward to it.

The small hamlet of Oliver is as charming as any I can recall. The neat shops and clean streets are appealing, and imposing cliffs surround the town as a continual reminder that sheep country is only a look away. Indeed, signs on the busy highway caution motorists to watch out for bighorns, which winter in the low country and often wander into town. The sheep share their historical winter range with myriad buildings, livestock, and people, and they are cherished and protected to an astounding degree.

Caping out the trophy back at the comfortable camp.

up, complete with a front deck for lounging and a generator to power the refrigerator and freezer.

Five other sheep hunters are here, one from Texas, two from Washington, one from Connecticut, and one from Germany. All are likable, some of them younger and some older than me. We spend the first afternoon checking our rifles to be sure they are shooting straight and sampling the fine red wine offered by local vintners. We are all encouraged that the guides have done their homework and know where the sheep are concentrated.

I discover that my comrades are quite focused on the possibility of running into a rattlesnake, found here in considerable numbers. Nowhere else in Canada, it seems, do sheep and rattlesnakes coexist. It will take more than a rattler to rattle me on this sheep hunt, though. Still, when climbing among the rocks, I'll keep my eyes peeled for the sinister zigzag pattern of scales, a precaution one can usually dismiss when hunting sheep.

The season opens tomorrow, and a scouting trip seems in order to check a group of three rams that Ross has been watching for over a week. This drive is my first chance to speak alone with my guide. He answers numerous questions about the hunt, and tells me that two years ago the rams all melted into the dense timber because of hot weather and the whole camp was shut out. Weins has a great success rate, but not because the sheep are predictable or easy to hunt. Last year the success rate climbed to about 75 percent.

We drive through steep mountains surrounded by rocky cliff faces that rise above thick pine forests. Most of the lower slopes are covered with vegetation thick as fleece, hiding any wildlife that might bed there. The temperature is unseasonably warm and getting more so by the day, and foreboding fills my thinking as I contemplate the shutout disaster of two years ago. Maybe the weather will change

I meet Jim Weins in person at the motel, and he introduces me to the guides and the other hunters. My guide will be a robust thirty-three-year-old carpenter who takes time off every sheep season just to hunt the animals. Ross Janzen is tall and tan, with shoulders at least twice as broad as my own. He looks like he is made of cast iron, if not annealed steel. He has spent many seasons as a spotter and guide for Weins and boasts an excellent success rate.

Camp is fifteen miles from town in a secluded grove of ponderosa pines, where the gentle breeze and clear mountain air lull one into a sense of peace difficult to find in the hurried world back home. Unlike some more uncivilized camps, we will be sleeping in an assortment of campers Jim brings up every year to accommodate his hunters and guides. A comfortable and spacious kitchen is already set and bring in the seasonal cool that heralds the onset of fall in the Okanagan.

We are planning to glass the timbered draws and bare ridges of Grouse Mountain. For the best vantage point we hopscotch from rock to rock across Vaseux Creek, a cascading whitewater stream as clear and clean as a fine brew, then begin an arduous ascent. Shortly I am in my summit step, moving from one foot to the other in rhythm with my breathing. Thirty minutes later, spread before us is a huge expanse of sheep habitat that disappears to the east around a sweeping bend in the rushing creek. The lengthening shadows signal it is time for rams to be up and feeding.

My luck seems unchanged. Of my last five sheep hunts, I was shut out on three and took last-day rams on two. This night Ross's rams, which have been reliably appearing near dark in a sharply inclined distant meadow, fail to show. Disappointed, we retreat down the trail as darkness descends, while unseen obstacles grab at our feet.

As we drive back to camp, I feel disheartened. I'm coming off a major defeat at the hands of the Quebec-Labrador caribou, having failed in a week of hunting to see a single decent bull. I had a long period of unsuccessful hunts three years ago, too, and I can't help but wonder if I'm not in for another.

The timber in which these animals hide is intimidating, and I am totally unaccustomed to hunting sheep in such conditions. Ross, however, is unperturbed and optimistic. We can spot the sheep in the timber if necessary, and stalk them as well. Perhaps the rams he saw earlier will show up tomorrow and the question will be moot.

Jim Weins's mother, Faye, is the head camp cook, and we are treated to a feast when we return to camp: savory spaghetti with all the trimmings, as tasty as in any restaurant. I retire to bed, uncomfortably full of pasta and spinning with conjectures about where those rams might be. The bed, I discover, is almost as good as my own back home.

Breakfast is at 4 A.M. Splashing my brain awake with hot coffee, I wolf down pancakes and eggs and bolt hurriedly back to our camper for my gear. It is imperative that we be in position at first light or we might not find our rams, even if they are still in the area. We are soon bouncing down the boulder-strewn lane once again.

We elect to go directly to the last place Ross saw the rams. There is a good deal of resident pressure on the sheep here, and we want to find the trio of sheep before someone else gets there first or spooks them out of the area. We drive as far as we can up the awful range road to where we can park our vehicle unobtrusively. Despite the

Packing out the kill, surrounded by tall mullein plants, a favorite food of the California bighorn.

weight of pack and rifle, the thrill of hunting sheep once again energizes me.

The light is barely adequate for walking. In several places deadfalls block our path, necessitating irritating detours. We snake our way eastward toward the last known location of the rams, hoping to catch them feeding at first light. A capricious breeze caresses the back of my neck, the hunter's sign that all is not well. Wafting as it is toward the assumed position of our quarry, it is likely to reveal our presence long before we arrive. It will be better to stop here and wait for the dawn.

We wait in silence. After a long half-hour, we sense a subtle shift of wind to the opposite direction; soon it becomes a reliable breeze. The light has also improved, so we shoulder our packs and move out cautiously.

We are moving through a series of grassy meadows where the bunch grass and tall mullein are plentiful. Here and there the trail is littered with sheep droppings and tracks, but they all appear quite old. Between the meadows are intervals of dark pine timber, sanctuaries that defy prying eyes. We glass with extreme diligence, hoping to spot the sheep before they spot us. I check the Remington .30-06 repeatedly, and as we move along, Ross tells me to go ahead and chamber a round. I am unaccustomed to doing so before sighting my prey, but in this thick cover a quick shot might be all I get. I comply only a trifle reluctantly, but I check the safety twice before moving on.

Now we are entering more open land. We scrutinize each successive ridge and move cautiously forward to gaze into each deep draw. Finally we find abundant sheep droppings and fresh tracks. Several beds look recently used; this is the exact spot where Ross observed the band bedding down at this precise time early yesterday morning. I am beginning to have my doubts, though, that we will be able to find them. Hastily I put my such pessimistic thoughts aside.

"Maybe they moved over a few ridges," Ross whispers. "This is definitely where they were. Now where did they go?"

"Maybe they got spooked out," I offer.

"We'll see. Be ready, though."

Ever more cautiously, we ease forward. Up ahead a large boulder marks a drop-off into a steep canyon with a broad vista beyond. We move slowly ahead to the brim of the ravine.

"Get down!" Ross exclaims, the urgency in his voice quite familiar to me. I immediately fall to the ground while he moves slowly off to my side. I gaze intently into the valley but am unable to see anything.

"Down by that big tree. To the right is a bedded ram, and he's got us pegged. Don't move."

I see them now, a white rump patch glowing through the lower branches of a lone pine near the bottom of the ridge across from us. I quickly spot the other ram as well, now standing and looking nervously at us. I will have to shoot quickly if I am to shoot at all. The distance is more than 200 yards, and I will have no time to find a rest of any kind except for my own wobbly knees. I am unsure of my rifle, since my gunsmith bobbed off two inches of the barrel last week, and it is untested at long distances. It has likely lost some important muzzle velocity. The shot feels extremely uncomfortable at a steep downhill angle. When I lean forward to peer through the scope normally, I can't rest the rifle at all. When I lean back to rest adequately, I can see only a central spot through the instrument. *From this position a scope would need a foot of eye relief,* I fret silently.

"That one on the right is the big guy. Take him!" Ross advises.

It's now or never. The animal is walking resolutely away from us and will top an obscuring ridge in short order. I hold as steadily as I can, combining best rest with best optical effect, and I squeeze off the shot. At the report the ram swaps ends and runs headlong toward us! He is obviously unhurt, the bullet having gone over his back by all indications. Since he is moving our way, I elect simply to wait until he is closer, so I work the bolt and hold my fire.

The animal is momentarily obscured by a pine tree, and when he emerges with his two companions he is in full run. Somewhat confused, they hesitate in an opening perhaps fifty yards closer than before. My shooting rest is unimproved, but the distance is tremendously better. I squeeze the trigger again, and this time I hit him. One more shot spins him around before he can disappear into the deep intervening draw.

We move up cautiously, hoping our animal is dead. The two smaller rams look perplexed as we approach, and the pair move away warily, looking alternately at us and down into the draw. Soon we see the ram, lying dead against a boulder. We watch his two companions depart after they stand broadside, looking at us for several beautiful moments. I unload the cartridges from the rifle as soon as it becomes obvious I will need them no more on this hunt.

"What a dandy!" exclaims Ross as we approach. I concur, and I remove my hat and drop to my knees to give God thanks for the animal and our victory. Handshakes and backslapping are then the order of the hour.

For a California bighorn, this specimen is indeed a beauty. After all my last-day successes (and failures), it sure is nice to have a first-day win to my credit.

I relax on the comfortable deck of the kitchen, the cliffs and bunch grass meadows of California bighorn sheep habitat surrounding me as the sun slowly sinks. A fragrant aroma of cooking elk roast wafts from the stove. It is wonderful to be alive in this beautiful world, and to be enjoying the magic of Okanagan country. I feel a pervading satisfaction and joy that transcends the hunting experience.

Leaving the comfortable confines of the sheep camp, I motor down the rough logging road on my way homeward. Dust swirls underneath the vehicle like a cyclone, and winding across the road in its familiar zigzag, I spot an evil ornament of danger. My heart jumps. It is a rattlesnake, making its way through the dust toward the safety of a rocky face on the shady side of the road. Everything has gone my way on this trip. I didn't see even one of the venomous creatures while hunting, yet here one is to bid me farewell.

As I cruise along the beautiful Okanagan River, the sinking sun casts long shadows across the valley. I marvel once more at the rocky cliffs, so steep that I don't know how sheep can live there. I am basking in the grandeur, and taking a California bighorn home as well.

Alaska-Yukon moose. (Photo: courtesy of James L. Davis)

ALASKA-YUKON MOOSE
(Alces alces gigas)

Not far from where [J. C. Dun-Waters] had killed his moose,
we, in 1908, killed the record head of British North America,
having a spread of 69 and one-fourth inches. . . .
Many offers were made for our record head . . . but it was not for sale,
and can be seen in the Golf Club House at Aldeburgh in Suffolk, England.

—Major Neville A. D. Armstrong, *After Big Game in the Upper Yukon*, 1937

Today, that head would likely be well down the list in the Boone and Crockett Club record book. I assume the record was "unofficial" in those days, since general acceptance of the Boone and Crockett book was some time in coming. Moreover, the current record book lists almost 150 Alaska-Yukon moose taken since then that have wider spreads, the only measurement given in Major Armstrong's book. But cut it any way you wish, a moose with a spread near seventy inches is a whopper, whenever it was taken. I hope those magnificent antlers still grace the clubhouse of that English golfing fraternity, giving the patrons of the manicured greens at least a glimpse of true wilderness.

Four kinds of moose inhabit North America, of which the Alaska-Yukon subspecies, also called the tundra moose, is the largest. They are distinguished from one another primarily by skull characteristics and, to some extent, the antler configurations of the bulls. For record-book purposes, both Safari Club International and the Boone and Crockett Club recognize any moose from Alaska or the Yukon as an Alaska-Yukon, as is any moose from the Mackenzie Mountains of the far western portion of the Northwest Territories. Biologists recognize an intergrade area between this subspecies and the western Canada moose (*Alces alces andersoni*—also known as the woodland moose) in the southern Yukon, although the line of mixing appears to me to be broad and somewhat indistinct. While I recognize the biological facts, it is nevertheless much simpler to use the hunters' classification for my purposes. After reading much literature on the subject, I believe that my Yukon moose came from slightly south of the biologists' line, but it had all the characteristics of the larger subspecies.

The Alaska-Yukon moose is not only the largest moose; it is also the largest member of the deer family. Bulls can weigh over 1,800 pounds, while cows commonly weigh 800 to 1,200 pounds. Calves weigh approximately 35 pounds at birth and must grow rapidly to survive the winter. An adult bull moose may stand 7 feet high at the shoulders, while cows may stand almost 6½ feet.

Moose are typically rust colored at birth and may be anywhere between light tan and quite black as adults. Older animals tend to be darker, though sometimes a very mature moose may have a remarkably light coat. The coat consists of two kinds of hair, long outer guard hairs and a fleecy undercoat. In addition, there are two specialized types of hair in the eyelashes and tactile whiskers, or vibrissae, around the nose and mouth. Cow moose have a distinctive patch of white hair around the vulva that is quite useful in determining sex, especially after the antlers shed, because light hair in that area is almost uniformly absent in bulls.

One interesting physical feature in moose is the distinctive bell, or dewlap of skin and hair, underneath the chin of both bulls and cows. Some moose also have a long "tassel" attached to the bell. This tassel on my Alaska-Yukon moose was eighteen inches long and contained a long nourishing cord about a half-inch in diameter that extended to near the end of the appendage. This ornament is apparently more common on younger moose, because an especially severe winter can freeze it solid and cause the animal to lose it to frostbite.

For the inexperienced moose hunter, the appearance of any tracks may cause excitement, because even cows leave prints suggestive of an animal of great size. Discrimination between the tracks of a prime bull and those of cows or younger animals is possible on the basis of size, however, a difficult task with most other ungulates. A trophy bull will have tracks greater than five inches in width, while those of cows are little more than four inches wide at most. Cow moose tend to have long, slender tracks, with the points straight ahead or converging, while a big bull's may be splayed apart or diverging.

There are about 155,000 moose in Alaska, with numbers fluctuating according to the number of predators and the severity of the winter. The latest figures from the Yukon Territory show about 63,000 moose. Moose are the most hunted big game in both Alaska and the Yukon, constituting 60 percent of the total big-game harvest. Hunters take some 5,000 to 7,000 moose each year in Alaska, while the Yukon harvest, including native subsistence and outfitter clients, totals about 1,100 to 1,200 animals.

The distribution of moose is anything but uniform, varying dramatically with habitat. Densities are highest in forested river bottoms, and also are high in many of the brushy subalpine areas above timberline. In the northernmost parts of their range moose tend to stick to the lower terrain, but they are also present on true tundra where the only trees are low willows. I have observed the animals in the Brooks Range of Alaska, where they are numerous along certain river drainages. The very best moose habitat supports more than three moose per square mile, while poorer areas may have only a single moose per five or ten square miles. Their range in Alaska has expanded dramatically in the last fifty years, and the animals have become common on the Alaska Peninsula

Alaska-Yukon moose. Yukon Territory, October 1989.

north of Cold Bay and on the Seward Peninsula, both of which had few or no moose previously.

Moose are browsers, consuming nearly fifty pounds of leafy and woody vegetation per day. They prefer aspen and willow but also ingest birch and other plants. They will sometimes consume spruce, but only when alternatives are not available. Their feeding tendencies may have inspired their name, which means "eater of twigs" in the Algonkian Indian tongue (it is also said that *moose* in Ojibway Indian means "to cut smooth," as in browsing twigs). During summer they covet aquatic plants and will wade extensively to find them, even putting their entire head under water for several minutes at a time to retrieve them. They feed extensively on a variety of forbs but consume grasses sparingly. The higher fiber content of their winter diet produces droppings of oblong hard pellets dramatically different from those produced by the richer foods of summer. Instead of hard pellets, summer food produces semiliquid "cow pies" similar to those of domestic cattle. Small and large pellets together indicate a cow-calf pair.

Like all cervids, bulls develop antlers annually, the velvet-covered bony growths extending from pedicles similar to those of other members of the deer family. A bull moose has no true antlers in the first year of life, though male calves do have small, velvet-covered antler pedicles up to two inches long that they keep all winter. Yearlings grow a set that may be simple spikes or have small palmations. A three-year-old has antlers configured like those of an older moose but smaller, and it is highly useful to compare the antler width to the ear length when judging trophy quality. The length between the tips of the ears on a bull moose averages 24 to 30 inches, so the hunter seeking a special trophy can use that as a measuring device. I have never worried much about the width of the antlers of any moose I've taken, though. Big looks big, and all of mine are big enough, with wide palms and plenty of points, the makings of true trophies in my mind. The massive antlers of a terrific Alaska-Yukon bull moose may weigh upward of seventy pounds.

Antlers are made primarily of a mineral known as calcium hydroxyapatite. The largest antlers occur in bulls of approximately ten years of age, when size plateaus for three years or so; then a gradual decline begins as advanced age sets in. The growth of these remarkable appendages is so rapid that bulls may become severely deficient of calcium, so much so that osteoporosis may develop. That condition seems to affect the ribs more than other bones. The weakening of older bulls, which occurs more as a result of intensive rutting than anything else, may allow smaller bulls to become dominant over males with larger antlers late in the rut. The big guys are simply worn out, but they may also be severely calcium deficient and prone to lack of energy, bone fractures, slow healing, and the like.

Antler growth stops in late August or September, and the bulls polish their antlers in preparation for the upcoming rut. Following the rut, the cumbersome antlers drop in late November or December, and they start to regrow the following March or April.

As with most antlered animals, mating occurs in the fall, and the rut usually is in full swing in late September and early October. Bull moose act somewhat like white-tailed deer in that they make wallows with many of the same characteristics as a buck scrape, including depositing urine. Cows come calling, and the receptive ones are bred. Fierce competition can develop between bulls seeking the affection of an estrous cow, and battles can erupt. Some bulls move around seeking cows, while others hole up in a subalpine area with several cows, avoiding conflict unless another bull tries to evict them.

One recent study in Alaska showed that 81 percent of the breeding-age cows were pregnant after the rut. Gestation is about 205 days. Twins are born about 38 percent of the time, but triplets are unusual. Calving is usually between 18 May and 15 June, centering on 1 June. The calves must gain about five pounds per day before fall arrives if they are to be at the average calf weight of four hundred pounds at the start of winter. They then maintain their weight but grow little until the following spring.

In Alaska and the Yukon, the major predators of moose calves are grizzly bears and wolves, which may get up to half of the total calf crop the first year. For tundra moose overall, wolves are the more important predator. Most of the bear kills come before the calves are eight weeks old, after which they are far more agile and able to escape. A cow moose will vigorously defend the calf against all adversaries, presenting a formidable set of flying hoofs that can kill and maim. Despite the cow's efforts, though, bears and wolves take up to 90 percent of calves during their first year in some localities. In fact, 75 percent of total moose mortality is due to animal predators, and less than 10 percent is the result of hunting, though that figure varies considerably from place to place. Subsistence hunting can certainly have a sizable impact on populations. Disease, old age, accidents, and the like account for the rest.

Biting insects heavily harass moose during the summer months, the loss of blood and energy-draining evasive movements taking a serious metabolic toll. The animals wade into the water or climb high into the subalpine region to attempt to escape the onslaught. Fortunately, the severity of winter renders ticks uncommon in both Alaska and the Yukon. A variety of intestinal parasites are occasionally found in Alaska-Yukon moose, though the incidence is lower than in temperate climates.

Moose sometimes get "lumpy jaw," a bacterial infection of the jawbone most common in wild sheep and elk; it's similar to an abscessed tooth in humans.

A good part of moose management involves the use of harvest statistics and aerial surveys. Aerial work is usually conducted in Alaska and the Yukon in November, after the leaves are off the trees and there is snow on the ground. Additionally, the bulls usually haven't lost their antlers at that time of year, making sex determination easier. Flying a grid pattern over the selected area yields data from which scientists can extrapolate moose numbers for setting desirable harvest levels. When predation is not a major factor, hunters can remove up to 10 percent of the moose population annually without affecting its stability.

Hunting methods are mainly spot-and-stalk, although calling works well for almost everybody except me. I did have a moose come to my guide's call in British Columbia once, but it was after I already had my moose. Still, it was thrilling to see

Off the horses and looking at a nice bull moose.

A refreshing spot of tea to warm us up.

the fire in that bull's eyes as it came charging in to the lowing of a cow moose. Spotting a moose isn't hard when the country is open, but getting into position to make a clean and humane kill can be next to impossible. Even tundra moose can sometimes have an affinity for deep brush, and unless they will come to a call they can be very difficult to get into your sights. I have hunted moose in the Yukon twice, both times with the aid of horses, and I have seen many moose both times. Other means of transportation include boats, and for late-season hunts, snowmobiles. In many areas hunters are dropped in by airplane and conduct their hunt on foot. This is advantageous because it spreads human hunting pressure over a larger area than would be possible otherwise.

The best time to hunt is during the rut, naturally. The animals tend to respond to a well-voiced cow call, and they are also moving around much more and therefore are more likely to be visible. Prime time in Alaska and the Yukon is late September and early October.

There have been thousands of moose taken over the years with the venerable .30-30. At close range and with the bullet well placed, that caliber will do the job. Most hunters want a little longer reach, though, so I would put the .30-06 down as the minimum moose medicine. I took all of my moose with 165-grain Nosler partition bullets, though that is probably a bit light.

Go moose hunting prepared for two inevitable circumstances: bad weather and heavy work (the latter after the kill, and the former always). I like woolens in the brush because they are quiet and stay warm when damp. Bring good rain gear even if you go when it's more likely to snow. Perfect

Moose camp at Hyland Lake, Yukon Territory.

camouflage isn't necessary for moose hunting, as their eyesight is secondary to their hearing and sense of smell, but I'd wear it anyway.

The heavy work after the kill involves skinning the animal, quartering it, removing the antlers, and packing it out. Neither Alaska nor the Yukon will allow you to waste edible meat, even when there are hundreds of pounds of it, so plan on getting it out. A guide who uses horses can be a great help, though horseback hunts in Alaska are hard to find. A boat is handy for a moose shot near the water, but unless it dies at water's edge there will be more packing than one likes. Getting a big moose out of a tight place by small aircraft can be tricky, dangerous, costly, and even impossible, so consider that before having yourself dropped off.

Hunting for the animal with the largest set of headgear in the world has its drawbacks. But the rewards are great, and the payoff comes in a grand set of antlers on your mount, delicious

moose meat at dinner, and the satisfaction of playing by the rules and winning.

THE GIANT OF HYLAND LAKE

I remember reading the autobiography of General Chuck Yeager, who broke the sound barrier in a rocket plane called *Glamorous Glennis*. In his book *Yeager,* the general talks about the advantages he had over the German pilots during World War II, particularly when it came to eyesight. He could spot the black dots of German planes long before they could see him. Yeager had the element of surprise on his side, something that comes in pretty handy in hunting as well.

Like Yeager, I too have been blessed with excellent eyesight, though I am reluctant to claim vision as good as his. Many times I have been able to spot animals that my guide has failed to see, though in fairness I believe that most of my guides have spotted more than I by hunt's end. On some occasions the animal we took was the one I myself discovered, a most satisfying end to a hunt. That happened perhaps a score of times during my quest for the North American big-game animals.

My guide on this hunt is Ted Neufeld, who lives and works in northern British Columbia and the southern Yukon and is currently employed by Terry Wilkinson of Caesar Lake Outfitters. A workhorse single-engine Otter deposited us at this remote location three days ago. The jumping-off place was Watson Lake, Yukon Territory, and we now are a hundred miles north of there, hunting country that is virtually inaccessible except by float plane. It is early October and the moose rut is over, so most of our hunting will be my favorite kind, simple spot and stalk. Moose seem to be immune to calling when I'm the hunter (come to think of it, so are elk, white-tailed deer, and wild turkeys). Maybe that's why I feel I have a better chance on a later hunt when calling is not a factor.

The departing hunters we met a few days ago when we disembarked from the plane all had good moose, so my hopes are high. In all honesty none of their animals sported the broad palms and innumerable points I have envisioned for my Alaska-Yukon moose, but they all shot the first decent animal they saw. We have already passed up two fairly dandy bulls, one far upriver above Hyland Lake and another down the winding, cascading river that flows from its lower end. Ted discovered both of those animals from the horse trail, and the spotting scope revealed that they were good but not trophies.

The camp at Hyland Lake sits amid spectacular scenery so characteristic of the Yukon. I have never hunted with Terry Wilkinson's outfit before, but he comes highly recommended. His wife, Ruth, met us at the airport, even inviting us over for supper that first night. On this hunt I am accompanied by a nonhunting shadow, my good friend Bob Walker, who wants to do some backcountry fishing after my hunt for a moose. He will act as photographer, since he is more talented in that department than most guides.

We are sleeping in a comfortable tent not far from the main cabin. There is a bow hunter in camp as well, and the tiny cooking area lacks room for all of us. A shepherd's stove keeps the tent warm enough, though when it goes out at night the cold creeps in. A grizzly has been about—there are fresh paw prints along the lake—but we are unconcerned. Both the bow hunter and I have the ultimate grizzly repellent in our pockets—grizzly tags.

The ground is covered with snow, though it is only a few inches deep here in the broad valley. To our northwest we can see the tops of snowy peaks in the Northwest Territories. To our southeast the roaring Hyland River disappears in the direction of Watson Lake, though this far upstream it is hardly navigable. We will have to leave camp at hunt's end by horseback instead of float plane, because each morning the ice on the lake is a bit thicker and extends a bit farther from shore. By mid-October the iron grip of winter settles onto this land, holding it captive until the following May.

I do not like to waste time, and I am glad when I hear the horse bells approaching in the predawn darkness. Ted has rounded up the animals so we can pursue caribou today, taking a break from the moose hunting of the last couple of days. After a hearty breakfast we will ride up near the high mountain basin immediately behind camp, where the mountain caribou bulls may be in a rutting frenzy.

While Ted makes things ready, I do some glassing of the countryside. I first peruse the sprawling lake, noting that most of the waterfowl that greeted our arrival have now departed. A beaver stirs up the water near the upper end of the lake in an area riddled with beaver dams and houses. A bald eagle soars overhead, ever vigilant for a meal, hoping, no doubt, that our moose hunt will provide him with one before the winter famine.

The upper end of Hyland Lake is some of the best moose habitat in all of Terry's area, and he hunts it only every two or three years so the bulls can reach full maturity. An open marsh spreads for miles along the headwaters of the Hyland, and tangles of spruce and willow on the adjacent slopes provide food for the huge animals even when the snow is deep. Thus far we have hunted only along the river because the interlacing trees on the steep slopes are not conducive to spotting or stalking a moose. Nevertheless, the area looks promising, and I instinctively swing my binoculars along the vast expanse of dark green and patchy gray.

As I sweep along, an irregular burst of white catches my eye, although at first I fail to recognize

The glassing never stops when you're hunting moose.

it as anything more than a sun-bleached snag. Curious, however, I return the glasses to it and at first have trouble finding it again in the awful alpine jungle. Then, there it is. White tips sticking skyward in a most conspicuous fashion, unmoving but definitely suspicious. I move back to one of the hitching rails to steady my binoculars. Ted is having to work around me as he finishes putting the last saddle in place.

Resting the binoculars on a post, I can now make out what I believe to be a palmated antler, perhaps of a very large bull moose. I can't be certain yet and I don't want to cry wolf, so I wait and watch. Too many times in the past I have asked a guide to evaluate something that turns out to be a stump or a rock.

Now there can be no doubt, the white-tipped antler slowly becoming paired, then drifting once more back to a single antler. That has to be a moose. I rivet my binoculars on the spot and call out to my guide. "Ted, come here. I see a moose."

"A moose? Where? Is it a bull?"

"For sure. Just look where I'm looking, three ridges up the lake. He's up in the heavy timber."

Ted's sharp eyes soon find the spot and he scrambles for the spotting scope, already stowed in the saddle bags. He sets it up on a fuel drum while I wait eagerly for his evaluation, hopeful that this is the break we have been needing.

"Wow. What a bull. We saw him a couple of weeks ago, but we couldn't get up on him. He wouldn't respond to calling. He's probably still got three or four cows. The caribou can wait."

I peer through the high-powered scope. Wide palms and innumerable long points adorn the massive set of antlers, a moose hunter's dream. We mount up and head around the lake after making certain all the essentials, including my Remington .30-06, are aboard. It is loaded with 165-grain Nosler Partition bullets in anticipation of caribou, but the lighter loads will do the job on a 1,700-pound moose if I place them right.

We pause periodically on the two-mile trip up the lake to check our quarry. The moose is roaming the dense hillside, feeding in the early morning sunshine, and we repeatedly have to search for him. The lake is glassy smooth and rimmed with early ice, the mountains inverted in its surface in the manner of an impressionist painting. Near the end of the lake we dismount so Ted can try calling. His best and most passionate efforts, however, elicit no response. He offers an alternative plan.

"We'll have to pick our way across these beaver flats and get closer. The bull might be in range if we can spot him in that thicket. That was the problem before, he just wouldn't give us an opportunity. I don't reckon he's any less smart now."

The crossing is treacherous, but the surefooted horses make it merely memorable and not lamentable. On reaching the steep bank on the other side we plot a course up to the giant, or at least as near as we can safely advance. There are several small but steep glacial hills at the base of the slope, and perhaps from the top of one of them we might get a glimpse of our moose. By now we have seen brief views of the harem of cows, so we are not surprised that the bull refuses to respond to calling.

We leave the horses tied to the willows near the lake and start a treacherous ascent up the steep hillside. The wind is in our faces. A timbered hillock looms ahead of us, and we negotiate many deadfalls before arriving on top. To my disappointment, I can't see anything on the main slope but acres of tangled willows and evergreens. How in the world can anyone extract an animal from a jungle like that?

Ted has some ideas, none of which seem practicable. He calls once more, but there is no response. We hear the animals walking in the snarl of alpine vegetation, but we can't see them. We descend from our hillock to see if the next one offers a better view, once more fighting deadfalls and uncooperative willows. The hill ahead is a bit higher and has fewer trees on top; maybe it will offer what we need.

One big spruce has sturdy limbs near the bottom, and I break some away to clear a shooting lane, just in case. All at once I can see the very top of the bull's antlers again, some 350 yards up the sheer slope. I tell Ted that I can see antlers but not the body, and that the distance is probably too far for my light loads. Ted calls again, and still there is no response. We seem to be running out of options.

"Maybe if lust won't get to him, jealousy will," says Ted.

With that he begins making rutting, raging sounds and beating the brush like an angry bull. I keep my rifle resting securely in the spruce tree, the cross hairs trained on what I believe to be the moose, although the intervening foliage makes it hard to be sure. The massive antlers move, but the white tips are all I can see.

Suddenly the bull takes a step forward, and for the first time I see the body. There is a lot of material in the way, but this may be my only chance. An enormous chest looms in my scope, and I gently squeeze the light trigger of my rifle. The thunderous explosion rips through the silence like a bomb. A follow-up shot would be futile, because all I can see now are limbs and leaves. A tall spruce tree high up the slope abruptly shakes and then disappears completely from view, while another trembles as if some unknown force were trying to vibrate the needles off it. The crashing of running animals makes me wonder if my shot hit a moose or a tree limb. I pray that I have not wounded this fine creature, but that I have either missed cleanly or killed him humanely.

The vegetation is some of the thickest I can remember hunting in the north country. Ted knows the task we face in simply finding the animal, if he is down, so he instructs me to stay at my rest while he climbs the hill. Directing him to the place I last saw the bull isn't as easy as it sounds, because my guide becomes completely invisible to me from the moment he leaves the hillock. We communicate with intermittent shouts and an occasional hand motion at those rare times when we do see each other. I am still not certain I hit the moose, but the shaking tree and the one that fell are good signs.

Finally, a whoop of joy fills the air as Ted stumbles onto our downed moose, an hour after my shot. Bob and I then begin to make our way up

My bull does a little land clearing when he falls.

the impossible hillside, and both of us are amazed that anything could live in such a tangle. We call repeatedly to our guide to avoid becoming lost in the overgrowth, and we follow his voice to the kill site. I am gratified that I have been successful, but I don't understand how the bullet got through all the obstacles.

As I approach the grand old bull, my heart leaps with joy at the sight. The broad palms are fully 17 inches wide, and the spread is a healthy 54 inches, not all that wide but certainly an exceptional animal with amazing mass. He scores only a couple of inches short of Boone and Crockett, as a whole host of my trophies do. I am completely satisfied. I inspect the fine animal as we prepare for a picture session, noting an unusual 18-inch tassel extending downward from the symmetrical bell under the chin.

The unique configuration of the bull's coat is an unexpected bonus, and I drop to my knees and thank God for the success.

The bull traveled only twenty yards after being struck through both lungs by my bullet, which obviously had eyes as it made its way up the obstacle course and into my moose. When the creature fell, he knocked over a spruce tree six or seven inches in diameter. It was a painless and humane one-shot kill, the kind I always feel good about.

The picture session consumes an hour or more, and then it is time to begin the real work. While Ted sets about caping out the animal for a shoulder mount, Bob and I retrieve the horses, blazing a trail as we descend so we can relocate the site without undue difficulty. In three hours we have completed the necessary work and

The day after the kill and back in camp.

begin loading the quarters and gigantic head aboard our mounts. This is my first moose, so I have nothing with which to compare him, but it appears to me that moose quarters weigh at least half a ton. The horses buckle slightly under the weight, so we carefully balance it. Fortunately, the terrain is mostly open after we get off the wooded slope.

Terry is already in from his bow hunt by the time we arrive, and he examines the animal with admiration. He is the largest moose Terry has seen anyone take in some time. I am a happy hunter to have taken such a grand prize.

We will have to pack the massive antlers and the hundreds of pounds of meat all the way to the trailhead, some twenty-eight miles away, where an ATV awaits. From there we will trailer it another twelve miles to the road. We still have a caribou hunt to accomplish, but the trip is already a success.

I am acutely aware that the hunt could easily have turned out differently, and I overflow with gratitude as I consider God's grace. As Coach Joe Paterno once said, "I just thank Him for all the good things that keep happening to me."

Meanwhile, I must concentrate on the caribou hunt at hand. Perhaps I will have success there as well. I will hunt Hyland Lake again someday, perhaps for grizzly or another moose, but for now I am satisfied. The giant of Hyland Lake is mine.

Eastern Canada moose. (Photo: courtesy of James L. Davis)

EASTERN CANADA MOOSE
(Alces alces americana)

*The dense forests, and closely shaded swamps of these regions,
are the favorite resorts of this animal, as there the most abundant supply
of food is to be obtained with the least inconvenience.
The length of limb, and shortness of neck, which in an open pasture appear
so disadvantageous, are here of essential importance,
in enabling the moose to crop the buds and young twigs of the birch, maple,
or poplar; or should he prefer the aquatic plants,
which grow most luxuriantly where the soil is unfit to support other animals,
the same length of limb enables him to feed with security and ease.*

—Frank Forester, *Frank Forester's Field Sports*, 1849

It is more than likely, almost a certainty, that the first variety of North American moose discovered by Europeans was of the eastern Canada subspecies. French adventurer Jacques Cartier reported their presence while exploring the St. Lawrence River system, confirming the sightings with fairly accurate drawings. Another explorer, Lescarbot, reported in 1609 that the moose was the most abundant terrestrial game species available to the natives. Abundance and utility made the moose a valued item of trade in those early days. We read that in 1672 the Indians of French Canada traded to the whites some 6,000 moose hides annually. Even prior to European contact, some one hundred aboriginal tribes and ethnic groups utilized the moose. They developed ingenious schemes to take the animals by means of primitive weapons and snares, catching them in open water and dispatching them, or entrapping them in deep, crusty snow.

The eastern Canada moose is the first of the taiga subspecies in this book, the western Canada (*Alces alces andersoni*) and Shiras (*Alces alces shirasi*) being the other two. The taiga moose inhabits the boreal forests virtually from coast to coast in North America. Only Safari Club International delineates the eastern Canada moose in its record book; the Boone and Crockett Club lumps the eastern and western subspecies together. The dividing line between the two subspecies is in Ontario, a straight line from the northwest corner of Nipigon Bay on Lake Superior to Fort Albany on the James Bay. That is an artificial demarcation, but it had to be somewhere. Moose to the east of the line, including those of New England and Newfoundland, are considered eastern Canada moose.

A prime bull of the eastern subspecies can weigh up to 1,350 pounds, making it the next smallest after the Shiras moose. An adult cow will weigh perhaps 900 pounds. A bull will stand slightly over 6 feet high at the shoulder. Antlers are seldom more than 65 inches in width and weigh no more than 40 pounds, although a bull of considerably lesser dimensions is a true trophy of the eastern subspecies. One could hunt a lifetime and never see an animal of such proportions. The front palms are not usually as developed as on other subspecies, more often consisting of three or four front points instead of palmation. Bulls grow only spikes or forks the first year of life, and maximum antler development is at age ten to twelve years.

All the senses are extremely well developed in moose. Forest-dwelling moose, and particularly those of the eastern subspecies, are almost as crafty and reclusive as white-tailed deer, and they use their acute senses of hearing and smell to avoid predators. Unlike the tundra moose, these animals retreat

Eastern Canada moose. Newfoundland, September 1998.

into the thickest cover available to escape predators, and getting one requires both the utmost skill as well as a few breaks.

These moose do not form large breeding groups, as does the Alaska-Yukon variety. One bull will often tend a single cow, which lures the bull to its territory when she comes into season. Bulls are not territorial, moving around extensively during the rut, although they may temporarily claim ground and make rutting pits like their tundra cousins. Because taiga bulls breed fewer cows, there must be a higher bull-to-cow ratio than for tundra moose to ensure that all cows are bred. If a cow fails to mate, it cycles again in twenty-eight days. If it misses more than one cycle and is bred late, a cow may give birth to a late calf, which has little chance of surviving its first winter.

The forests of eastern North America provide abundant browse for moose. White birch, eastern white and red pines, hemlock, yellow birches, sugar maple, red maple, basswood, white elm, white cedar, aspen, beech, white oak, butternut, and white ash are important species. In Newfoundland the most important winter browse species is balsam fir, which almost all moose eat. Moose in New England, northern Quebec, and Isle Royale of Michigan—and in fact in all areas where the tree is the most available part of the browse layer—favor the balsam fir. The most important deciduous browse in Newfoundland is the white birch.

The forests of New England are ideal moose habitat, as is most of boreal Canada. Apparently the extent of moose range to the south of New England and upstate New York is limited by heat, as the animals do not tolerate temperatures over 60 degrees Fahrenheit very well. To the north of the boreal forests the animals are limited by the lack of food and cover, although they live far north into both Quebec and Labrador along riparian corridors where trees persist.

The moose is not a native of Newfoundland, a surprising fact many hunters may not know. Six of the animals, introduced there between 1895 and 1904, colonized virtually the entire island. Prior to that the caribou was the only native ungulate in Newfoundland. Surprisingly, little competition exists between the caribou and the moose, which have minimal overlap in their diets. Neither is there any adverse parasitic relationship such as exists

between moose and white-tailed deer, so caribou and moose coexist quite well. There are now more than 125,000 moose in Newfoundland.

Such an increase in numbers isn't bad, but in most of the range of the eastern Canada moose the story hasn't been as positive. Because moose were once rare in Labrador, supplementary introductions were made in 1953, and those moose have done well. Years ago they gradually disappeared from Pennsylvania (1780s), Massachusetts and Connecticut (early 1800s), and New York (1860s), as well as Vermont and New Hampshire (around 1900). Protective measures were finally instituted where the moose still existed, and that set the stage for a remarkable turnaround. Hunting was closed altogether in New Brunswick in 1937, in Maine in 1935, and in New Hampshire and Vermont about 1901.

With the new wave of conservation instituted principally by America's hunters, populations began to recuperate. Most of the recovery has been by expansion of existing populations rather than transplantation. New Brunswick reopened its moose season in 1960, Maine and New Hampshire in 1980, and Vermont in 1993. The New England population of moose continues expanding southward into former moose range, and there are now moose in both Massachusetts and Connecticut as well as in upstate New York.

The are several reasons for this resurgence. Protection from overexploitation by hunters and the cooperation of local people have been paramount. The extirpation of their natural enemies from the recovering ranges has allowed unchecked population growth as well. A lot of farmland has been allowed to revert to woodland, creating excellent conditions, and logging operations have created beneficial clear-cuts sometimes configured to maximize productivity for the benefit of moose. Additionally, wetlands have grown up where none existed before, mainly as a result of increased beaver activity. People seldom trap these prolific rodents as in former times, and beaver ponds provide prime moose habitat.

More than 300,000 moose of this subspecies now live within the range east of the line in Ontario. By far the highest population is found in Newfoundland, with Ontario and Quebec having the next highest numbers. Maine has a healthy population of over 40,000 moose, the most of any state except Alaska.

Approximately 45,000 eastern Canada moose are harvested by legal hunters each year, with well over half coming from Newfoundland, which had a quota of 28,320 for the 1998 season. Success rates are high in that province. Nonresidents must book through a licensed outfitter, who has a share of tags allocated to his operation. Residents of Newfoundland must apply for a drawing, and their take is by far the greatest percentage of the kill. Even with the necessity of a drawing for residents, I have encountered no evidence of jealousy regarding nonresident participation. Newfoundlanders know that outsiders pay well for the privilege of hunting there, and the local economy benefits.

It is a different story in Maine and most other locations, at least as far as getting a permit is concerned. I've tried for years to draw a Maine moose tag to no avail. The year I took my Newfoundland moose, I pulled out all the stops and had my wife and six friends apply for a Maine moose tag, putting me down as subpermittee (a designation that would legally allow me to do the hunting, with the actual permittee only tagging along). I also bought extra chances, as allowed, and thus my name was in the computer fifty-four times. Same result. I went back to Newfoundland.

Success rates vary greatly. In Maine the kill rate is well over 90 percent most years, even though the season lasts only seven days. On guided hunts in Newfoundland, many outfitters claim 90 percent, but I am skeptical. The official kill rate for nonresident hunters (all of whom must have an outfitter) is 75 percent, although opportunity levels may approach 90 percent. The highest success rates in Newfoundland are on the Northern Peninsula and along the west coast (Region 4, consisting of Areas 1, 2, 40, and 45) and Region 7 of the east coast. Unfortunately, few nonresident opportunities exist in those areas as a percentage of total available quota.

Where strict limited-entry drawings are held, such as New England and the Maritime Provinces (other than Newfoundland), success rates are generally very high. In some localities, such as Quebec and Ontario, success rates appear to be as low as 10 percent.

The spot-and-stalk technique is typical of all moose hunts, but more often the hunter eases quietly through the dense cover to get a look at a bull. Calling is worth a try and works for some. Cruising old logging roads is a common method in Newfoundland, Maine, and elsewhere, and offers the benefit of a vehicle to help with the heavy work. Aesthetically, though, it isn't very attractive to me. As long as you have a valid license, you can step off the pavement and shoot a moose most places in Newfoundland (but don't shoot across or toward the highway), because such roadside moose are an ever-present danger to human life and property. Removing them makes good sense from a number of standpoints.

The main disease of eastern Canada moose is caused by the meningeal worm, with infestation resulting when game animals eat the cysts. This parasite can complete its life cycle in the white-tailed deer without killing the animal; that the host survive is necessary for its propagation. In moose, however, the disease has a high rate of mortality; thus completion of the life cycle of the worm is seldom possible. Because deer are only somewhat affected by brain worms, the parasite is able to reproduce and contaminate the environment. The main adverse effect, thus, is on moose that share habitat with whitetails. Fortunately, where moose browse is optimum and deer populations are relatively low, the rate of infection of both species is minimal.

Predators of the eastern Canada moose are few. Black bears doubtless take a toll on calves in the spring for a short time, and wolves are an important factor where they are present. A major unnatural source of mortality is the vehicle, which kills an estimated 35,000 moose in North America each year, probably most of them in heavily populated areas. Such collisions usually result in death for the animal, and striking a moose is also tremendously hazardous to the vehicle's occupants.

When should one hunt eastern Canada moose? Not a hard decision if you draw a tag in Maine or New Hampshire. The season is winking short there. If Newfoundland is your destination, my advice is simple: go as late as your outfitter will allow. Forget the rut, which is supposed to occur in September. It will be so hot the bulls will be active only at night or very early morning. October is far better, and I'm told that November is the best.

Searching the bog edges for moose.

I've said it before and I'll say it again. Waterproof rain gear and rubber boots are necessary when hunting Newfoundland, and probably for most of the eastern Canada moose range. I remember riding an open Argo down alder-choked logging trails with a steady rain falling and a lapful of extra water pummeling me at every dripping limb. Don't leave home without the best.

When it isn't raining you need the quietest clothing possible. It's hard to beat some of the new camouflage wool outfits, but unless you're going in October I'd opt for cotton for the sake of coolness. Take a set of long johns, just in case, but be prepared to leave them in camp most days. Remember to pack insulated rubber boots no matter when the hunt.

Bullet placement, as always, is paramount. Never take a tail shot at a moose, regardless of the kind of cannon you are carrying, because you'll likely not reach the vitals and might well lose a wounded moose. At the very least you'll probably spoil some of the best meat in the world. A standing broadside shot is perfect positioning and is worth the wait.

And when the moment comes, when you're bone weary and the rain is falling and creeping moisture is penetrating through every pore, remember what a privilege it is to hunt a moose in this part of the world. Less than a century ago, it was a virtual impossibility.

BULLS OF BEAR LAKE BOG

Hunting in Newfoundland has been mixed for me. I reflect on my experiences of the past two years as the four-wheel ATV rocks and bumps us through the cold blackness of early morning. The bouncing results from the innumerable rocky outcroppings in the road bed, unavoidable obstructions in the rugged backcountry road. Although my guide, Brian Peyton, expertly maneuvers the vehicle to avoid the worst obstacles, the pounding is hard on my backbone. Alders choke the old road in places, lapping toward the middle in a determined effort to strangle access to this stretch of wilderness.

I have already seen a moose, a dusky ghost in the ATV headlights that quickly retreated into the dark timber. This early sighting seems to me a positive sign. I have hunted Newfoundland south of here for the past two consecutive years, and there merely catching a glimpse of a cow had amounted to a relatively successful day. This year I am with Horace Lane's operation, Riverrun Outfitting and Tours, Ltd., and I'm hoping for a more productive outing. My guide, proficient and familiar with the area, has a small cabin that we will use as a rest point at midday. He snowmobiles frequently each winter in the vast wilderness to the east of Norris Arm, a small nearby hamlet where he lives with his wife and family.

Brian's last name has intrigued me since we were first introduced. As we ride I question him about a possible connection to a family featured in a historical book about these environs, *River Lords*. Brian is indeed descended from the early pioneer John Peyton, for whom a mountain to our east is named. John Peyton's son, John Jr., was host and friend to the last original Native American of Newfoundland, a melancholy maiden named Shanawdithit, who was given the English name of Nancy April. She had sought refuge with John Peyton in 1823, along with her mother and sister, after the few remaining members of their Beothuck tribe had perished. Although her two relatives died shortly thereafter, Nancy lived for five years in the isolated house of my guide's ancestor and his family, located on Burnt Island at the mouth of the nearby Exploits River. There she learned English and was relatively happy, apparently, but she was subsequently spirited away by the authorities to Twillingate. The governor apparently believed that the woman's well-being had to be sacrificed to learn more about her reclusive and poorly understood tribe. While she did indeed furnish much of the information known today about the Beothuck, in Twillingate she encountered large numbers of people for the first time and shortly afterward died of consumption, the antiquated name applied to any number of the white man's many diseases. The last survivor of the Beothuck tribe, the aboriginal people of Newfoundland, thus lived and died in the midst of tragedy.

I find myself in the thick of a kind of tragedy of my own, though of much smaller proportions. I can't seem to get an eastern Canada moose, no

Telltale evidence that our quarry is somewhere about.

Four-wheel ATV transportation along old logging roads is a regular method of hunting.

matter what. But I'm hopeful that this present excursion, a foray into a small slice of Newfoundland where the streams all flow into the mighty Exploits River, will give me a victory that has so far been elusive. Glimpses of wildlife in the predawn darkness seem to portend a fruitful trip, if rabbits are any indicator.

After nearly an hour of jarring impacts and intense jostling, we reach the end of the alder-choked trail, where we will leave our Japanese pony. I slide four of my premium handloads into the magazine, carefully closing the bolt to leave the chamber empty but ready. In Newfoundland, it is a grave offense to ride in or on a vehicle with a round in the magazine, for such a weapon is considered loaded. A wildlife officer will seize your rifle if he discovers it.

We are immediately in the bog country for which Newfoundland is famous. The ground floats on top of a bed of mud, and one dare not step on a bare spot. Unless vegetation grows on it, the ground is unreliable as footing. Underneath the vegetation the soil is semiliquid, and walking over it is like traversing a lily pad pond. If your foot

misses a pad, you go in over your boot most places. A stiff breeze blows in our faces, and the long yellow grasses and sedges that populate the bog shimmer in its unrelenting blast. The soft earth is as difficult to negotiate as plowed ground, and the effort shortly has me sweating. I pause to remove my vest, stowing it in my backpack.

Between bogs we pass through stunted forests of fir and tamarack, the small trees clinging to life on rocky ridges. In the distance, more substantial trees populate the higher terrain. The old snowmobile trail we are following has become difficult to see out on the open shifting bog, but in the occasional thick trees it stands out clearly. As we ease toward the brink of yet another of the endless series of naked expanses, we detect movement ahead, big black bodies partially visible in the timber on the far edge of the bog.

"Get down! Moose!" Brian whispers excitedly.

My heart leaps at the announcement. Two moose are on the opposite edge of the bog. Both are cows, and no bull is with them, as far as we can tell. The animals look at us with eyes and huge ears focused intently, and then fade into the dense thicket that surrounds the swampy expanse. Within seconds they are gone. We move on expectantly as the light slowly improves.

The day is gray and threatening, and the southeast wind suggests imminent rain. The downpour isn't long in coming, thin but persistent sheets of icy dampness that send me scrambling to unpack my rain gear. My old .30-06 becomes completely soaked, causing me no small amount of anxiety. It has been drenched innumerable times in the past, but the rifle is now approaching twenty-five years of service. Tape situated strategically over the end of the barrel prevents water from entering there, at least.

We are hunting through a succession of open bogs surrounded by impenetrable thickets of fir, balsam, alder, maple, birch, and aspen. High ridges rise from the valley floors in a swirl of color—yellows, fiery reds, pinks, and greens. First the maples of Newfoundland become opulent red or vivid yellow, then the birches metamorphose into a rich gold. The ubiquitous tamarack trees of the bogs are various shades of yellow. Autumn's chill has cast its spell on the trees of Newfoundland.

Stark skeletons of tamarack and fir long dead stand over each of the bogs, victims of the thin sustenance offered by the trembling semiliquid subsurface. Nearer the edges the trees thrive on more solid ground in compact and impregnable forests. Each step across the bog is an adventure. The soft surface is marred by each step to a depth of several inches, and a ripple of disturbance betrays the water below. Here and there narrow drainage channels cross the bog, and one can glimpse what awaits the unwary. The inky water appears to be several feet deep, and looks as if it might swallow one completely. We step gingerly across these natural traps, carefully placing heavily booted feet on firm vegetation at the edge. Brian cautions me that to step into one of the channels is to go in up to the hip, at least. In places one must jump slightly to clear a particularly broad trench, and the give of the far bank is unsettling.

Now we can clearly hear the insistent call of a cow moose on a thick timbered ridge to our east. We in fact spot a lone cow momentarily in the dense vegetation on the colorful hillside, but it fades away just as quickly. At least two or three

cows are hidden from our view, and a deep-throated bull makes its presence known as well. The sound of antlers grinding against trees is unmistakable, intriguing, captivating. We maneuver to try to locate the animal, but the tactic is hopeless. For perhaps a half-hour the sounds emanate from the tangled thicket, but the bull will not respond to Brian's calls. The bull already has a very adequate complement of females.

Approaching in the noisy underbrush would bump the moose out of the area. Perhaps we will have a better chance later in the week. We move down to the last two in this series of bogs to see if there is any activity there.

As we emerge from the timbered ridge and move toward the open grassland, another disturbance immediately becomes apparent. A cow moose is crossing the bog, and we can see another animal following her, though only the form is visible through a dense stand of dead tamaracks. My heart leaps at the thought that the cow might be pursued by a lover with a head full of antlers.

"Get ready! Could be the bull!" whispers my guide.

I chamber a round as quietly as possible and edge toward a snag that could serve as an improvised rest. The second animal creeps into view, but it is only a huge calf, and no other creature seems to be accompanying the pair. Disappointed but mesmerized, we observe intently as the two lumber past within perhaps thirty yards of us. It is amazing to watch the dark creatures expertly distribute their great weight, sinking only minimally into the surface. The cow is especially adept, moving only one foot at a time while keeping the other three firmly planted, never making a mistake. The pair negotiate the bog quickly and smoothly, and I can only marvel.

Our crossing of the marshy expanse is not nearly so unfaltering. Because Brian knows where the firmest footing is, we have only minimal difficulty, though we doubtless expend maximum energy. As we labor, an osprey sails easily overhead.

The rain is a continuing annoyance, and it finds all the chinks in our gear. Sweat accumulates as well, creating a warm wetness within. A bull grunts from the hillside thicket once more, his baritone voice bespeaking trophy potential. But for now any attempt to reach him seems destined to fail. By the time we arrive at the end of the last bog, all has fallen silent, save the whistling of the stiff wind and the patter of rain on the hood of my jacket.

We slowly work our way back the two long miles to the ATV, but nothing shows itself except a few birds, a couple of red squirrels, and the gorgeous fall colors. In the absence of moose, I turn my attention to the plants and immediately notice abundant pitcher plants scattered across the bog. All are filled with water and most have turned red in the early frost. Some have a single shoot arising from their center, perhaps a foot in length, which is topped by a lovely pinkish flower. Brian points out that the bog is so typical of Newfoundland that the pitcher plant, and especially its flower, appear on many official documents.

We have just mounted the vehicle once more and headed out when a juvenile bull moose steps out of the alders and into the trail in front of us. Brian begins yelling at the animal, most unusual behavior to my thinking, and instead of spooking away the animal paradoxically stops to stare at us. Just behind the animal is his twin, both of them sporting short forking antlers that would be no trophy even were they growing on a Coues deer. We jump off the ATV and search vainly for a bigger bull that might be in their company, but no luck. Both the youngsters soon trot off, stopping to look back several times. Brian keeps up a dialogue with them, asking questions and shouting instructions that strangely seem to hold their attention.

"Great meat bulls. And close to the road. Lot of locals would love to see them here," comments my guide as we remount the ATV.

"Why were you talking to them?"

"Oh, just to keep them interested. I ask them where their grandpa is, and how'd they like a nice surprise, and where they're going, and the like. Even a big bull stops and listens out of curiosity."

Interesting. Stealth is the word up to a point, then talk to them loudly when they do appear. Quite an unconventional system, but it apparently works.

We motor to a point perhaps a half-mile from Brian's cabin on the shores of Bear Lake and then walk the remaining distance. There we rest and have lunch, awaiting the more opportune hours of late afternoon before resuming our hunt. The lake is a restless caldron of whitecaps in the wind, its deep waters stormy and dark. We shortly are basking in the glow of the wood-stove fire and enjoying sandwiches as the rain and wind howl maliciously outside. There is even a bunk bed for a much-needed nap. I got into bed after midnight last night and had to be ready to hunt only four hours later. A restful nap will put me in better condition for this afternoon.

As we sleep the sound of the rain gradually diminishes, and by the time we emerge for the evening session we need rain gear only because of the wet leaves. We return to the four-wheeler at 4 P.M. We probe into several boggy areas, none of which is far from the system of interlacing trails Brian knows so well. We see no moose, though, despite several hours of searching. Doubts begin to cloud my mind, but the happy memory of abundant action this morning reinvigorates me. By the time we arrive back at the main camp, I am tired but hopeful about our prospects for tomorrow. The forecast is for clear skies. Perhaps the moose will finally cooperate.

We arise in the predawn darkness once more, and after breakfast we head out. As we motor rapidly through the maze of boulder-strewn back roads the morning air is ominously warm, so much so that I have left my parka behind as an unnecessary burden. Soon we are traversing the same bog where we spent so much time yesterday.

Nothing. Absolutely nothing. The wind is completely calm, and we are both surprised to hear no sound from the moose we are certain are lurking in the nearby thicket. The snapping of twigs betrays the presence of a large animal walking in the timber, but it makes no other sound and fails to respond to a cow call.

Finally we spot a lone cow far up on the ridge, but it is tranquil and has no company, as far as we can see. We jump another fork-horn bull out of his bed at the lower end of the last bog, but he also is alone. The animal is nevertheless beautiful to behold, and Brian does the same playful shouting to keep his attention.

Our daily retreat to the cabin for lunch is a pleasure. The lake is now tranquil, and no fire is necessary. The calm wind and the warm sunshine are pleasant, but this good weather is of no use for moose hunting. A gray jay entertains us after lunch, and we playfully establish a trail of bread fragments to see how far inside the cabin we can entice it.

The bird advances all the way to the center of the main room, scooping up whatever its mouth will hold before scurrying back out the door on the fly. The morsels are too many to consume, so we are certain it will cache them in preparation for winter.

Nap time today brings a most unusual dream, that we spot a big bull moose and my old rifle disintegrates when I try to shoot. The stock breaks off just behind the receiver, and the metal parts disassemble suddenly and completely in my hand. I awaken as I am trying to figure out how to put back together enough of the useless firearm to get off a shot. It is an illusion so real that I immediately check the old rifle. All seems well, but I manipulate the bolt and look through the scope before I am satisfied.

While Brian finishes his nap, I spend a little time down by the shore of Bear Lake doing some thinking and praying. It will take divine intervention to get that moose, no matter how much effort I put into it, especially with the unanticipated turn of the weather to sunny and warm—no, hot by late-September standards. I strip to my T-shirt while the gentle breeze ripples the lake's blue surface, rustling the fir trees. The distant shore is a riot of yellow, red, and green with the changing season, and the stark white of the aspen trunks contrasts with the black fir stems. The skyline is deep azure punctuated by fluffy white cumulus. The only sounds besides the gentle wind and the rhythmic lapping of the waves at my feet are a scolding red squirrel and the wistful call of a loon across the lake. Awash in tranquillity, I have a difficult time maintaining a positive attitude about my chances of taking a moose. In the back of my mind is the lingering thought that a fourth trip to the island of bogs and dense forests might be necessary. I even find myself searching in my mind for a place to fit another excursion into my schedule. No, I won't give in to such thoughts just yet. We will put every effort into making this trip draw to a successful conclusion.

This afternoon is no more productive than yesterday's. We climb a high hill near the bog we have walked two mornings in a row, but neither a sound nor a sighting of moose is forthcoming. The high terrain is beautiful, requiring a walk of

Midday respite in the guide's remote cabin.

perhaps a couple of miles through dense fir to reach. The pungent aroma of the thicket reminds me of Christmas. Deep moss covers the ground like a lush carpet, green and luxurious. We spot another small bull on the way out, but he is of only passing interest.

That night I manage three hours of restless sleep, but by wake-up call I am ready to arise. Soon we are back in the wilderness; the bog is no easier to walk than before, nor is it any less intriguing. The sky behind us is beginning to brighten as we start out, and red clouds attending the sunrise portend a change in the weather. Colder temperatures may come too late to help me, though. At least the wind is still in our faces.

The bull near the timbered ridge is still silent, but a cow calls on a couple of occasions. Brian swears the bull is walking in the thicket again, but I can't be certain. After a couple of fruitless calls, we move on. Two bogs later we still have seen no moose, but a cow calls once more from a different location. Then, there it is—the unmistakable grunt of a bull moose! The bog is nearly a half-mile long, and we can't see the other end, so we move along slowly, trying to locate the source of the sounds. Brian gives a cow call, which the bull immediately answers.

"Load your rifle. He might come over," Brian says, and I quietly slip a cartridge into the chamber.

The specter of the disintegrating firearm briefly arises as I lock the bolt into place. *Couldn't happen, not even with this antiquated rifle. Now if only I can get a look at this bull.*

"I see a cow," Brian whispers, pointing to an opening to the left of a small head of timber that protrudes into the bog.

I immediately spot the animal some 150 yards distant, its radar ears pointed in our direction. We freeze and the cow looks away, momentarily forgetting us. The wind is light, and it is still in our faces.

I can see a dark form in the brush behind the cow, and I ease toward a sturdy tamarack snag to use as a rest, just in case. I scan the area with my binoculars and note with deep disappointment that the emerging animal is another depressingly small bull, one with only forks for antlers. He looks exactly like the one we jumped in this precise location yesterday. Isn't there anything in Newfoundland but fork-horn bulls? Another animal comes out, yet another cow. I scan desperately for more moose.

Suddenly, a dark form materializes from the brush. I can see only a couple of legs and one flank, but the body seems large. The creature is moving slowly and is reluctant to come out of the deep timber. An abrupt movement of the head reveals white antler tips in the brush, and just afterward palmation is visible. A mature bull! I ready the rifle on the rest and flip off the safety. Please come out, I plead in my mind, my heart racing. I finally have a trophy eastern Canada moose in my sights. Now if only he will cooperate. These creatures can be unexpectedly crafty and will sometimes pull the well-known trick of fading back into the thicket without ever presenting a shot opportunity.

He's moving forward! I can see all four legs now, and gradually the entire animal. I see the antlers only in profile, and the bull refuses to turn his head toward me. He will be gone in a few more steps, the small opening being perhaps a mere dozen yards wide. It is now or never. I place the cross hairs behind the front shoulder and squeeze gently. The recoil rocks me backward mildly. The animal spooks straight away from us, and the four moose mix and mingle. I thought I heard the thump of the bullet entering flesh, but it is impossible to be certain. Immediately I chamber another round. Brian is beside me, and he reports that the animal is hit and staggering.

"Be careful! There's a cow in front of him. For God's sake, don't hit her!"

Indeed there is a cow between us and the bull, both of which are standing unmoving in the center of the small tongue of bog that tails off into the forest. I wait. Nothing moves, but the cow is getting nervous. As the second cow and the small bull bolt, the cow finally moves clear, and the big bull turns slightly to present broadside once more. Only the neck and head are visible, but I've got to get one more bullet in the animal. I take what I can get, the right side of the neck, and squeeze off another round. This

Moose never respond to calling when I'm along—but it's fun to try.

Bear berries are plentiful and colorful in the forests of Newfoundland.

time the bull goes down for good, piled up resoundingly. Brian lets out a whoop and extends his hand to me in congratulation.

We approach cautiously as the other moose scatter and quickly disappear. This is a fine bull, not as large as I had hoped, but certainly a representative specimen. I am deeply appreciative and openly express my gratitude for the success.

With great joy we cape and quarter the moose, remove the loins, and prepare the whole carcass for packing out. We will return tomorrow, bringing strong help and sturdy pack frames. In the meantime we lay the quarters in the shade and cover them with fir and tamarack boughs.

As I leave Newfoundland, the sun is still shining and the threatened change in the weather hasn't occurred. Until the coming of cold and snow, hunting here will be hard. I am grateful to have avoided a third consecutive shutout. But I am most grateful that my daytime nightmare didn't come true. The vintage rifle has performed flawlessly once more, despite its age. On my way home to Georgia, I look forward to the future with renewed confidence.

Western Canada moose. (Photo: courtesy of James L. Davis)

WESTERN CANADA MOOSE

(Alces alces andersoni)

After a good meal the men hunt moose.
When all the wood around camp is gone we move on usually to the place where
a moose has been killed. We make a teepee again and live there.
That's the way it used to be and when I am alone I think about these things.

—Liza Loutit, Slavey Indian elder of Fort Providence, Northwest Territories,
quoted in *Nahecho Keh: Our Elders*, 1987

The moose was immensely important to the livelihood of the northern aboriginal peoples. A review of stories from the past—as told by thirty-eight native elders in the above publication—is highly insightful. A tally reveals that two-thirds of them mention the moose or some moose product in the course of everyday life during their younger days, early in the twentieth century. The moose of the north country continues to be a mainstay of the diet of both aboriginal and nonnative peoples.

Safari Club International (SCI) recognizes the western Canada moose as a separate entity, but the Boone and Crockett Club (B&C) lumps the *andersoni* subspecies in with the *americana* animals of the east. There is some support for the B&C position, as many authorities feel that the *andersoni* subspecies listing is invalid. Currently, however, official taxonomy does indeed recognize the two as separate.

The eastern line in Ontario is admittedly somewhat arbitrary, and the same goes for the west. The northern extent of western Canada moose range is at the Arctic Ocean in the Northwest Territories, and at the border between the Yukon and British Columbia farther west. Moose of the Mackenzie Mountains are considered Alaska-Yukon for record purposes, but all others of the Northwest Territories are counted as western Canada moose. To the south, B&C draws the southern extent of Canadian moose (in the west) at the U.S. border, while SCI excludes the moose of southeastern British Columbia east of the Duncan River and south of TransCanada Highway, and those of southwestern Alberta south of the TransCanada Highway and west of Highway 2. SCI counts the latter as members of the Shiras subspecies. Under the SCI system, the moose of Michigan, Minnesota, and North Dakota are western Canada; they are simply Canada moose under the B&C system.

From a scientific standpoint, Canada moose and Alaska-Yukon moose intergrade along a line in the southern Yukon, meaning that moose of the southeastern Yukon may be of the *andersoni* subspecies. Studies have attempted to delineate accurately the area of intergrade, but for our purposes it is necessary only to use the Yukon/British Columbia border as the dividing line. Admittedly, an occasional moose from the northern part of B.C. will show Alaska-Yukon characteristics, and just as likely a moose from the southern Yukon may sometimes fulfill all the criteria for Canada moose.

The size of western Canada moose is similar to that of the eastern subspecies, except that in areas of intergrade with Alaska-Yukon moose the average size tends upward, as do the antler scores. For that reason northern British Columbia dominates the record books for this subspecies. Of the top fifty animals in the current SCI record book, all came from northern B.C. except three, two from Alberta and one from Ontario. There are no entries from the Northwest Territories, Saskatchewan, or Manitoba under this subspecies heading. The latter two provinces are somewhat vindicated by the B&C book, though, with two from each location among the top listed for the broader category of Canadian moose. Nevertheless, British Columbia heavily dominates the B&C record book, with well over half of the top fifty coming from that province.

Aboriginal peoples have known this subspecies for millennia, but the first European to see one was probably English explorer and navigator Henry Hudson, who arrived in 1609 on the western shores of the inland sea that bears his name. If it wasn't Hudson, it was probably Thomas Baffin and William Button, adventurers who entered the western side of Hudson Bay in 1612. Possibly contact awaited the penetration by French explorers and missionaries into the western Great Lakes region, half a century later. Nobody seems to have recorded exactly who first encountered *andersoni*, quite likely because it wasn't understood as a separate subspecies. After all, moose were just meat back then.

While the size and most physical features are similar to those of the eastern subspecies, there are differences. Skull features seem to be the most consistent distinction. The western Canada moose tends to have a wider palate than its eastern Canada cousin, and a narrower palate than the Shiras and Alaska-Yukon subspecies. Western moose also tend toward more palmation on the front of the antlers, a characteristic more like the Alaska-Yukon subspecies than the eastern moose.

Moose are relative newcomers to North America as ungulates go, having arrived as recently as two thousand years ago. They have been present for most of that time in the northern portion of B.C., but they moved down the spine of the province to the south much more recently. They have been in the prairie provinces of Alberta, Saskatchewan, and Manitoba for hundreds of years.

The habitat of western Canada moose is typical of woodland moose, open areas interspersed with copious thick cover being what they prefer. Logging operations in the boreal region can greatly benefit the moose, if excessive use of herbicides and large clear-cuts are avoided; smaller clear-cuts with abundant edge are much more desirable. An unfortunate side effect of logging is improved vehicular access, which tends

Rutting pit dug by a feisty bull moose.

168

Glassing for moose along the Toad River.

to offset any benefit that clear-cuts offer to the moose population. There is a special type of natural habitat in the prairie/boreal transition areas of Minnesota and North Dakota, where islands of suitable vegetation exist for habitation by moose.

Moose consume up to 221 different kinds of woody vegetation across their North American range, eating only a few varieties extensively. Those include aspen (the predominant deciduous tree throughout the western Canada moose's range), birch, and especially willow. Summer diet is primarily green leaves, but the pattern changes to fallen leaves, twigs, and branches from living plants in winter. Freshly fallen leaves have more protein and are more digestible than woody twigs, so in autumn and early winter they are extremely important to moose. As snows become deeper, the diet shifts more toward standing browse plants. These western moose seem to browse evergreens,

such as balsam fir, more sparingly than their eastern counterparts. Grasses account for only a small percentage of food intake. When food is scarce, hungry moose may strip bark from trees.

The rutting behavior of western Canada moose is typical of taiga moose, with small breeding groups of one bull and one or several cows. Subordinate bulls often linger around the periphery of the breeding site. Calves may be allowed to remain with the breeding pair or group, as is characteristic of the subspecies.

Because much of the range of the western Canada moose has remained relatively pristine, these moose have maintained generally good numbers, with few exceptions. They were nearly eliminated from Minnesota, only recently reoccupied North Dakota, and are increasing from historical lows on the Upper Peninsula of Michigan. In the parts of their range shared with extensive human populations, they have recovered

Hauling the kill back to civilization by four-wheel ATV.

remarkably well with increased protection during the twentieth century.

Over the past fifty years or so, the number of moose in western Canada has fluctuated for a variety of reasons. In the 1950s and 1960s, before the environmental and animal rights movements began to pick up steam, wolf control in much of the back country dramatically increased moose populations. The increases were more modest in highly settled areas because the numbers there were kept down by hunters. Starting in the 1970s, lack of wolf control has resulted in a declining moose population. Density currently stands at roughly 0.5 moose per square mile where no cow harvest is allowed and perhaps 0.2 moose per square mile where it is. Where native hunters exercise their aboriginal rights to harvest unlimited moose, the population may be dramatically lower. Because there are fewer wolves in settled areas, moose have increased in numbers there, aided by more conservative hunting regimens. The focus

for moose management in western Canada now is the aspen belt that fringes the agricultural zone. There are perhaps 300,000 western Canada moose today, two-thirds of them in Alberta and British Columbia. Of the taiga moose subspecies, the western Canada population is the most affected by predators, so it appears that prudent wolf control measures are in order. Any reduction in sport hunting for grizzly bear in British Columbia will likely contribute to further moose population declines, since older male grizzlies may be efficient predators of newborn calves.

Hunter success on this subspecies is highest in the Northwest Territories, where outfitted hunting by nonresidents and subsistence hunting by natives are the primary human take. Success there approaches 100 percent. Many outfitters in British Columbia and Alberta also claim 100 percent success rates, although the overall figures in those provinces are no better than 25 to 30 percent, slightly higher in B.C. than in Alberta.

Disease and parasites are not particularly prevalent in western Canada moose. The brain worm, virulent in the eastern part of North America, is not present in western moose. On the other hand, leg worms, which occur in the tissue underneath the skin of the legs and brisket, are found most often in western moose. These worms are not fatal and do not affect the edibility of the meat, though they can be present in large numbers, and be a disgusting sight, in some animals. A variety of intestinal parasites also sometimes appear, though they are usually of little consequence. A muscle parasite known as *Taenia ouis krabbei* can form an intermediate cyst known as a cysticercus in the muscle of moose. It is actually quite common, though it cannot infect humans and cooking eliminates it.

Winter ticks, also known as moose ticks or elk ticks, occur predominantly in the range of the western Canada moose. These parasites can threaten the survival of heavily infected animals, and more than 50,000 have been found on a single animal. Loss of blood and energy, as well as hair loss due to scratching, can add to the burden of the infested moose. Such moose may appear white to the observer and are referred to as "ghost moose." The ticks are most prevalent in the aspen zone, south of 60 degrees latitude, but are not present in the Alaska-Yukon subspecies or those in Newfoundland, at least so far. Nasal bots, deposited by flies, are not considered a major mortality factor. Biting insects abound in all moose range in warmer months, robbing the animals of vital energy by sucking their blood and by impelling the moose to try to shake them off or otherwise escape them. Moose even have their own namesake fly, an otherwise benign insect that accompanies all moose and feeds on no other cervid. The pests reproduce by laying eggs in moose droppings.

Hunting techniques and equipment are by no means unique for this subspecies. You must always hire a licensed outfitter, except for Canadian residents and residents of Michigan, Minnesota, and North Dakota fortunate enough to draw a permit. I have hunted these moose in dense forest, open hillsides, and riparian corridors. It is generally more

Resting up in camp the day after the heavy work.

open hunting than you encounter for the eastern Canada moose, although the animals are often in pockets of dense cover.

It's highly workable to hunt this moose in combination with caribou, sheep, grizzly, or mountain goats. That applies to the Alaska-Yukon subspecies as well, but only on a limited basis to the eastern Canada and Shiras subspecies.

Particularly in British Columbia and Alberta, these moose inhabit some of the most mountainous terrain in all of North America, so be prepared to climb. The best moose seem to be up high, so be in good shape before hunting the animal. Furthermore, hunts for these moose are often horseback affairs, so wear your best riding boots, made of rubber and well insulated. But above all, enjoy the beauty of western North America. You'll be glad you went, even if the massive bull with dozens of points and the wide palmation eludes you.

HARVEY'S LAST MOOSE

Chest-high willows claw at me from every angle, tangling my feet and tiring me rapidly. My guide and friend, Harvey Daniels, urges me onward and upward, telling me through gestures and whispers that our quarry might be slipping away. In the rugged terrain, keeping our eyes on the monster bull we have spotted is a task that is all but impossible. We saw the animal not far off only moments ago, but after regarding us tantalizingly, he nonchalantly turned and faded into the brush. He has refused to respond to a seductive call from my guide, and now we have little choice but to follow.

We are hunting along the cascading Toad River in northern British Columbia. These grand ungulates are numerous enough, and we have already seen some twenty bulls in only a half-dozen days. Selectivity thus seems to be in order. Harvey is a superb sheep and goat guide with scores of kills to his credit, and he makes no secret of his disdain for hunting "swamp donkeys." Indeed he agreed to take me on this hunt only because we formed a friendship on past hunts. Nevertheless, agitation shows on his face as we push on, a visible consternation at the prospect of losing this moose.

"Never been outsmarted by a swamp donkey," he mutters under his breath as we struggle upward. "This isn't going to be the first time!"

Nice palms!

Packing a very big kill down a steep mountain—never again, says my guide.

The rut is in full swing, and uneasy males abound. As we move ever higher up the slope, any small opening on relatively flat ground is likely to hold a scrape made by amorous moose, and one can easily see the resemblance to whitetail scrapes. The scooped-out depressions are pungent with the scent of urine, advertising the bulls' availability to any willing cow. Damaged willow saplings bear testimony to where the creatures have rubbed the velvet from their antlers. During the October peak in mating activity, the bulls ordinarily come to a call without hesitation, but the cagey one we have spotted is an exception.

We are hunting with Folding Mountain Outfitters, based in Toad River, B.C. I spent the first night in their beautiful lodge at Mile 419 of the Alaska Highway, and on the following day Harvey and I motored by four-wheel-drive ATV into our remote hunting area. Most hunts here are by horseback, as roads are few. The place we will hunt, however, is accessible by an old mine road that is a nightmare of washouts and harrowing creek crossings. By being scrupulously careful on our machine, we have been able to ascend farther into the mountains than I would have dreamed possible. On reaching the end of the road, we continued up the broad creek bed for many miles, picking our way between deadfalls and boulders, until we arrived high in the trackless back country. Our camp is some thirty miles from the Alaska Highway, and Harvey has erected a comfortable pyramid tent with cozy wood heater, propane lights, and a cook stove. From here, we must do most of our hunting on foot.

Soon after arriving we found tracks, scrapes, droppings, and antler rubs. That first day we saw a couple of small bulls and several cows before darkness forced us back to camp.

Harvey's strong points include his cooking, although admittedly it is one of his lesser strong points. Each night we have returned to the tent, where he displays his skill on the wood stove. The memory of Sandra Drinkall's incredible cooking fills my mind and may be prejudicing my judgment. As the recollection of that terrific spread at the base lodge fades, however, Harvey's cooking seems to improve. I have made the mistake of bringing an air mattress instead of a foam pad, and each night I sleep restlessly because of the cold. I won't make that mistake again.

Bright October sunshine accompanied our trek up the creek to this site, but the weather has turned. The cloudless day of our arrival is just a memory. Now we have a prolonged siege of inclement weather, and a cold, stiff wind sends shivers up and down my spine. On our first day here we climbed a steep ridge across from camp, and a soaking drizzle fell most of the day. From among the evergreens we watched the downpour change from rain to snow and back to rain, over and over. My rain gear held, though, and I returned to camp that night wetter from sweat than rain.

Despite a gorgeous view of the rain-swept valley, we saw only a couple of mediocre bulls with cows. Rutting activity that first day had been much in evidence, though, and it had seemed like only a matter of time until a truly good animal showed up. In the meantime I enjoyed looking at the gigantic moose we rejected, a youngster sporting a huge tassel that extended down a full two feet from his bell. The object hung like some outlandish ornament below his knees, bumping along rhythmically as he walked. I long to see what that bull will look like after his 30-inch antlers are fully mature, but Harvey is pessimistic that the tassel will survive the cold of winter.

Several days of hard, brushy climbing have left my legs tired, but my mind is resting in the joy of the chase. The moose in this valley have shown us plenty of activity, even though so far we've not been able to locate a truly dominant bull. A hunter we talked to earlier saw a good bull with a spread of about 48 inches somewhere up this creek, so we are scouring the area. My heart's desire is a 50-inch bull, but who could quibble about a measly two inches?

Earlier this morning we set up near the valley floor, just high enough to see over the willows on the other side of the creek, where the bull was supposed to be. We saw yet another young bull, but no mature animal. I climbed a bit higher to see over a knoll blocking a portion of the creek bed, and as soon as I topped out, the very animal I sought materialized through a clinging mist, an apparition in the early morning fog. The distance was much too great for a shot, but I immediately knew that this was what I wanted.

"Harvey! There he is!" I whispered, clambering down like an excited school kid. "We can get him in the creek bed if we hurry!"

We hastened back down the rocky expanse. Long before we came within range, though, the animal had melted into the thick alders and out of view. We tried both calling and waiting, but he refused to reappear. Disappointed and frustrated, we resumed our watching and glassing from a slightly different vantage point.

From that new vantage point we discovered the bull we are now looking for. About midafternoon the giant charged into our field of view about a mile upstream. I first caught sight of a moving black dot that the experienced hunter instinctively interprets as a traveling animal. I had swung my binoculars to the spot without hesitation, and my eyes had widened at the immense antlers on this monster. They are broadly palmated both up top and in front, and carry a tremendous spread and innumerable long points, definitely a trophy animal. My standards had been ratcheted up several notches at the mere sight of such a world-class bull.

We had spent only a short while watching, waiting, and plotting our next move. The massive animal had been charging all over the mountainside in a frenzy of rutting activity, though we saw no cows. The bull had been covering so much of the heavily vegetated terrain that we hadn't known how to go about putting a stalk on him. No matter where we might go, by the time we could get there the animal would be somewhere else. When the bull had disappeared over a ridge into a small basin, we had decided to move in closer.

It has taken us a good thirty minutes of rapid footwork to reach the basin. The hill over which the bull disappeared is much steeper than it

Western Canada moose. British Columbia, October 1993.

seemed from a distance. We have succeeded in ascending it rapidly and quietly, but as we had topped out, lungs bursting, we could not find the animal. A chance glance up the steep adjacent mountain revealed his location, a shocking and difficult quarter-mile from where we expected to see him. There he had stood in all his magnificence, staring with unconcealed disdain at these two weaklings who dared to pursue him. He had remained there motionless for a time. Perhaps he had been merely puzzled. Harvey had tried the moose call once more, but it had utterly failed to elicit anything more than a tentative step forward. Frustrated, Harvey switched to a bull call, and the sound immediately put the animal to flight. We had stood for a fleeting moment, mystified by the bull's behavior. Perhaps he has just had his tail whipped by a bigger bull and doesn't want to tangle again. We had watched as the bull whirled and vanished over the crest.

Now I am completely engulfed in willows, the tenacious plants poking and jabbing like a boxer, seeking my eyes now, my face now, my hat, my feet. Struggling upward and fighting the impulse to curse the unrelenting branches, I pause to catch my breath in a small clearing as Harvey pushes me onward. In the back of my mind I can see us shooting a big moose a mile or more from the creek bottom and finding ourselves with two days of packing to retrieve the meat. No matter, I decide, this one looks good enough to be worth it, if we can just catch up to him. Harvey is only a little reluctant, despite his persistent and repeated mutterings about the worth of swamp donkeys. I credit him with willingness, if not with enthusiasm.

As we peek over each stairstep ridge, I half expect to see our quarry standing and looking back at us. Near the crest the willows abruptly cease, providing unaccustomed visibility and freedom of movement. I follow my guide as he instinctively drops back to our left, toward the creek bottom.

"No reason for him to go into sheep country. Moose like the willows. We'll drop down slowly and hope he stopped somewhere. Let's be quiet. Damn swamp donkeys."

Just as I am about ready to give up the chase as a lost cause, powerful antlers and a coal black body loom out of the willows 150 yards below. We are skylined, and the bull sees us as soon as we see him. He rises to his feet. The moose appears to be in no hurry now, though, and he stares arrogantly at his persistent pursuers.

The moose might not be in a hurry, but I am. I scurry to set up for a shot. I ask Harvey to scope him out one more time, just to be certain I've got the right animal. He confirms with a look and a nod. Resting on a spindly spruce tree that is the only available prop, I chamber a round and sight in on the animal's ample shoulder. The wind gusts up suddenly, and I must delay the shot until it dies a bit, all the while anxious lest the bull plunge down the mountain before I can fire. Finally the cross hairs settle and I squeeze gently until recoil rocks my shoulder and the quiet is shattered by the blast.

As the Remington 700 .30-06 speaks, the bull reels backward, collapsing down the steep slope as if shot with a cannon. By the time I have regained my view I can see nothing except a huge pair of back legs kicking in the air like those of a dying insect. A follow-up shot is neither necessary nor possible, but I chamber another round just in case. I then rise and start down the hill while Harvey stays put to direct me to the animal in the thick brush. Soon I am standing proudly beside the huge bull, all smiles.

The bullet has done a masterful job. As we cape the animal, we find that the bullet entered the brisket presentation slightly higher than I had intended and broke the neck, a not unexpected result in view of the acute downhill angle of the shot. Harvey belatedly bemoans the fact that he doesn't have his video camera to document how rapidly an animal the size of a moose can succumb.

The bull measures a quite respectable 53 inches and has massive front palmation. He scores very near the book minimums for Boone and Crockett. This is a truly fine trophy, earned the hard way. I am elated.

Getting the cape, antlers, and meat off the mountain consumes almost a full day. Fortunately,

Folded Mountain along the Alaska highway near Toad River, British Columbia—from which Folding Mountain Outfitters derives their name.

the steep grade drops straight down to the creek bed, and with some creative driving I am able to get our trusty ATV in close. I am deeply grateful that we don't have to pack the animal, piece by piece, a couple of miles back to camp. Harvey asserts repeatedly that one shouldn't hunt animals that can't be backpacked off the mountain in one trip.

The biggest laugh of the season comes when we complete the snowy trek back out along the old logging road to Harvey's truck and finally to the lodge. Everyone turns out to admire our marvelous antlers while we fill them in on the details of the hunt. When the other guides get wind of the fact that Harvey backpacked a whole moose off a mountain, they won't get off his case for a truckload of beer. It's something he had

vowed he'd never do again, but this time he made an exception. Just for me, thank God.

We will have excellent documentary photos. I agree to send back an enlargement of Harvey backpacking those huge antlers off the mountain for all to see. With just a little bit more on his back, perhaps he could have gotten that moose off in only one trip. But I don't think so.

I can hear my ol' buddy Harvey still, growling under his breath as we slip and slide down that willow-covered incline, the wind whipping and the branches grabbing at us and our burden. "Backpacking a swamp donkey. The first time, the last time, and never again."

Every time I look up on my wall at that great trophy, I just can't help but smile.

Shiras moose. (Photo: courtesy of James L. Davis)

SHIRAS MOOSE
(Alces alces shirasi)

The best moose is the one that falls on the uphill side of the road,
and as darned close to the pickup as possible.

—Jim Zumbo, *Fair Chase*, summer 1997

It has certainly worked out otherwise sometimes. On the other hand, my Shiras moose in Utah proved to be the epitome of a good moose, by Zumbo's definition. We simply skidded the animal down a small hill and into the back of the pickup. A very good moose indeed.

According to the Boone and Crockett Club, the Shiras moose inhabits only the Rocky Mountains of the United States. Safari Club International recognizes as Shiras moose those that inhabit southwestern Alberta west of Highway 2 and south of the TransCanada Highway, and those of southeastern British Columbia east of the Duncan River and south of the TransCanada Highway. I am not certain why B&C maintains the line at the U.S. border, because scientists uniformly classify the Canadian portion as Shiras moose.

The Shiras moose has been expanding its range dramatically for many decades, probably beginning in the 1940s. Lewis and Clark killed not a single moose on their travels, a journey that relied heavily on subsistence hunting and carried them through today's prime Shiras moose terrain. They wounded a moose near the Continental Divide on 7 July 1806, but that was their only such report and probably the first time a white man had ever seen the subspecies.

Another early contact between the white man and the Shiras moose occurred in the 1840s when Jesuit priest Nicholas Point was ministering to the Indians of the upper Missouri River. He reported that the Blackfoot, Flathead, and Couer d'Alene Indians all deemed moose flesh to be "in the quality of its meat . . . almost the equal of buffalo." Despite the near absence of moose when Lewis and Clark passed through that area, moose were abundant enough in some localities to be a significant part of the aboriginal diet.

This animal has the distinction of being the first subspecies of moose killed by President Theodore Roosevelt. While hunting in the Bitterroot Mountains on the Montana-Idaho border in September 1887, he used a Winchester .45-90 that he carried on many other hunts to take his first moose. He describes the experience in detail in his book *The Wilderness Hunter* (1909).

The U.S. Biological Survey chose the name Shiras for the subspecies in 1914. George Shiras III was a congressman from Pennsylvania who had traveled extensively doing wildlife photography and promoting conservation. He was extremely knowledgeable about moose in many parts of North America, and in honor of his contributions his name was attached to the moose of the Rocky Mountains. In some circles the same moose is also known informally as the Yellowstone or Wyoming moose.

The Shiras moose is the smallest of the moose of North America, though it is still larger than its European counterparts. A big bull will on occasion weigh up to 1,200 pounds, though many are smaller, and cows average 600 pounds or so. From the taxonomist's viewpoint, a major difference is in the skull, where this subspecies has a relatively wide palate compared with the western Canada moose. The nasal apertures are also wider, perhaps as a cooling mechanism for these more southerly animals. The pelage tends to be lighter on the top of the back than that of other moose during winter, though the animals vary from a rusty or yellow-brown color all the way to coal black. The ears on Shiras moose are said to be paler than those on other subspecies. The antlers also are smaller and score correspondingly lower, by whatever system one chooses to use.

Today Shiras moose occupy most Rocky Mountain states, and their numbers total approximately 60,000 if one includes those of Alberta and British Columbia. The largest population in any single state

Shiras moose. Utah, September 1992.

is in Wyoming, where almost 15,000 moose dwell. Other states with excellent populations are Montana and Idaho, with approximately 6,000 each. Northeastern Washington State has enough to allow hunting. The moose of Colorado came as transplants from Utah, and they have done extremely well.

The best chance of drawing a Shiras moose tag is in Wyoming, where the draw system is eminently democratic. Perhaps the best opportunity to hunt them, though, is in Utah, where a hunt was instituted for the first time in 1950. In that state private landowners control a few permits and can offer them to nonresidents. And Idaho is considering changing a long-standing policy of allowing only residents to hunt moose. If you are like me and can't draw a permit, and you don't really care whether the Boone and Crockett Club will list your moose, reasonable hunts for this subspecies exist in Alberta and British Columbia.

Shiras moose eat essentially the same foods as moose elsewhere and tend to concentrate on willows where they are available. They apparently have a lower reproductive rate than their northerly cousins, as evidenced by a significantly depressed twinning rate. This reduced productivity is probably not genetic but seems related to more stable habitat and reduced pressure from predators. In the far north bad years are more frequent, creating a greater need for rapid replacement. Shiras moose, however, don't face nearly as many population-depleting threats, so they don't need such rapid repopulation. At least that's the way I understand it.

The well-known brain worm complex, associated in the eastern part of North America with the proximity of moose to white-tailed deer, so far hasn't arisen with the Shiras moose. Perhaps that is because these moose tend to be on the mountainsides, while the nearby whitetails are in the river flats and creek bottoms. It could be that the infectious agent simply isn't present in their range. Ticks are a problem at times, as are intestinal worms and botflies. None of these factors seem to have a significant effect on populations, however. While predators are a minor problem in most Shiras moose country, black bears will take an occasional calf, as do grizzlies in those areas where their ranges overlap. Ongoing reintroduction of wolves into Shiras moose range may assume increasing importance.

Any rifle that will take an elk is adequate for Shiras moose. Shots are seldom long, but a good bit of knockdown energy is required for such a big animal. I'd recommend a .30-06 or similar caliber. You'll have only one chance to hunt Shiras moose in a lifetime, if you're the average hunter, so don't risk wounding and losing a valuable creature by going too light. And use the heaviest bullet the rifle shoots well.

Hunting Shiras moose generally does not require rubber boots. My Utah hunt was in the driest of conditions, and leather boots were perfect. The hunt is in September in most localities, so expect cool mornings in the high alpine country. Often it warms up later in the day. The autumn colors are brilliant, and the overall experience is one of the most pleasant on the North American hunting scene. I can imagine that the weather in the Bob Marshall Wilderness of Montana or along the Lochsa River of Idaho could turn nasty, though, so take along gear for cold, wet weather just in case. It's for certain you won't enjoy the view if it begins to drop wet snow and you've brought along only cotton camouflage.

BULLWINKLE FROM PARADISE

Easing through a forest of quaking aspen turned gold by the September chill, we spot a movement in the glen ahead. Gigantic antlers loom in the opening, turning as the big bull looks our way. The cool breeze carries our scent away from him. Just beyond is a pair of cows, a harem, it seems. I scope in on the bull, resting on a convenient tree, and look over the headgear with a critical eye. In a whisper I consult with my guide, David Leishman, who likewise is sizing up the situation. It is our first day out, so we don't want to be hasty.

The first Shiras moose I ever saw was in Idaho on my first hunt for Rocky Mountain elk. The time was the late 1970s, and back then I was ignorant of the different classifications of moose. I was fascinated by the huge creatures, though, and spent hours watching their lumbering

High alpine aspen groves are prime moose habitat in Utah.

movements among the overgrown willows of the Selway-Bitterroot Wilderness. I saw a lot more moose than elk on that trip, since the ponderous beasts inhabited every salt lick and every hillside. The animals seemed indifferent to our presence on horseback, perhaps possessing some sixth sense that we were no threat. Watching the moose of the Selway sowed in me the implacable desire to hunt them.

Aspirations to hunt Shiras moose are a lot easier to cultivate than to realize. I tried for years to draw a permit everywhere they were available to nonresidents, but as in the case of every other limited-entry permit I have ever sought, each year I received my money back with a nice letter informing me that I had been unsuccessful again. All I could do was keep trying.

After years of frustration, I finally heard about Utah. That state, a relative newcomer in the Shiras sweepstakes, contains excellent habitat and a good population of moose. Unfortunately—or fortunately, depending on your point of view—much of the moose population inhabits private land, making it necessary not only to draw a permit but also to get permission to hunt. That uncomfortable impasse dissolved when the state began to allow landowners a certain number of permits in exchange for permission to hunt for those who drew them. Now that's a sensible arrangement.

I booked a hunt with Roland Leishman of Porcupine Adventures, based in Paradise, Utah. Roland leases the rights to several large ranches near his home and manages them superbly for moose, mule deer, and elk. He generally takes three bull moose per year for his hunters and allows trespass rights for two other resident hunters who receive permits in the general drawing. Shortly after arriving in Salt Lake City, I had in my hands a coveted license and tag for a Shiras moose, scraps of paper I had become convinced I might never see.

With those documents in my pocket, David and I set out this morning in the predawn darkness for the twenty-mile drive to the Wapiti Ranch, a vast timbered highland where some of Utah's best Shiras moose live. The lower reaches are covered with sagebrush and are cut with numerous deep draws colored blood red with dwarf maples at this time of year. Higher up, stands of yellow quakies intersperse beautifully with healthy evergreen forests. As the sun rose higher above the eastern horizon, we sought in vain all morning for a bull moose of any kind. A lonesome cow materialized

Glassing hillsides aflame with color, looking for Shiras moose.

Main camp of my outfitter, nestled amid fall's splendor.

briefly in one of the high meadows, confirming at least that moose were around.

Despite a deficiency of bull sightings, the Cache Valley to our west is hypnotic, and one fairly basks in its beauty from the tops of these mountains. The valley likely received its name from mountain man and explorer Jim Bridger, who apparently hid a store of supplies somewhere in it. Shoshone Indians were the original inhabitants, and men such as Bridger maintained strong trading ties with them in those days. Later, Mormon settlers moved into the area, and the Leishmans are direct descendants of those pioneers.

While hunting on the ranch we will stay in a well-maintained assembly of campers and tents, with most meals prepared by Roland's talented wife, Ruth. David takes charge of making breakfast. I am comfortable here in every way and relish the grand view we have from the camp.

We spend the morning canvassing all the likely areas, concentrating on water holes because of the long drought. On accessible terrain we move by four-wheel-drive vehicle, covering as much ground as possible. As the day warms and the animals become inactive, we seek out their bedding and resting areas, trying to spot them where they have taken refuge from the heat.

The bull we are perusing at the moment has nice points all around but is obviously not fully mature. His mass is deficient; his spread 30 inches at most, and there is but a minimum of palmation. The uninitiated would swear he's a giant, but we elect to pass. David is certain we can find better. I ease closer to take pictures of the reclusive family before we move on through the forest.

Up ahead we spot a herd of elk, but the animals have already detected our presence and are moving rapidly away. Numerous game animals inhabit this land, a resounding tribute to the superb system of conservation and game management. There are only a minimum of cattle, a deliberate plan that allows wildlife to prosper.

As we traverse a long ridge, I am mesmerized by the riot of colors of the aspens. A plentiful purple variant grows here, contributing to the display. Flaming red gulches filled with maple and mountain mahogany move in and out of our view, making the mountains look like hulking creatures slashed in branching, dendritic fashion with a knife.

We have now covered all the range roads thoroughly, and we are tired from our series of lengthy walks. The moose have holed up somewhere to pass the heat of midday, and we return to camp for lunch and a much-needed nap. We will hunt the evening shift in a few hours. David doesn't seem worried, so I drift off peacefully in no time.

Upon arising I gather my gear and we move out once more. We locate two mediocre bulls but still can find no sign of the mature ones David has seen in the area. We finish our day watching a water hole until darkness sets in, then we make our way back to the truck by the light of the rising moon.

Roland Leishman spreads a marvelous meal on the dinner table. I have never eaten better in any camp. There are a couple of bow hunters with us, both of them seeking elk, and one is a real comedian. His rendition of seeing a big mountain lion at a water hole that evening is punctuated with hilarious gestures, and soon he has us all in stitches. The laughter conceals our recognition of the

potential for tragedy, but fortunately the cat had retreated before anything serious occurred.

The morning dawns overcast and unseasonably warm, even warmer than yesterday. Despite the fact that we are at 6,500 feet, I had to sleep on top of my sleeping bag for much of the night, highly unusual here, even in summer. Such unseasonable heat is cause for concern.

David has taken note of the higher temperatures as well and feels that a water hole holds the best chance. We spend much of the morning watching likely spots, and indeed a young bull comes to drink at one. He is even smaller than those we spotted yesterday, but watching him is entertaining, so we linger for a while before moving on to a more promising location.

There is a rutted range road up ahead. Deep cuts in the hardened surface pound us as we negotiate them, and I cradle my rifle like a baby. Four-wheel drive is necessary in places because of the steepness and loose dirt, but finally we top out in another of those garden spots that characterize

Moving our prize back to town for processing.

the high country of Utah. Aspens stretch ahead in a bewitching exhibition, looking like the colonnades of some magnificent building. The marble white trunks topped with yellow and purple foliage create a kaleidoscopic spectacle. I am thinking of reaching for my camera when David abruptly slams on the brakes.

"A big bull! Get out!" It's the first trace of excitement I have heard from this even-tempered young man. I strain my eyes trying to find the animal as I leap to the ground.

The bull is a hundred yards ahead. He is lying under a clump of scrubby willows near the road, quite simply the most impressive animal we have seen thus far. As we dismount he rises slowly and stands gazing at us, massive antlers swaying as he tries to determine whether to bolt or stay put. The animal has incredible front palms that extend far forward, but the upper palms are woefully deficient. Nevertheless, there are a lot of impressive points, and I wonder what to do.

"It's old Scoop Shovel, sure enough," David whispers as we try to blend in with the willows. "He's a good bull, but there are better. I'd kind of like to leave him another year and see how those tops develop, if we can find something else for you." I look at the surrounding cover and spot another white antler palm some thirty yards farther into the aspens.

"Another bull, David!" I whisper.

My guide squats for a better look. "Good tops, and nice and wide. That's the one!"

Frankly, old "Scoop Shovel" looks darn good to me, but I make it a practice not to interfere with selective harvesting, or the strong recommendations of my guide. The second bull rises as if inviting closer inspection, which he passes with no difficulty. I chamber a round and begin moving into position for the shot.

The old .30-06 roars, and the beast takes a few steps forward while looking at me as if nothing has happened. Again, again, and once more I shuck shells into the chamber and fire, aiming just behind the front shoulder. The bull hardly moves, and I am beginning to wonder if I am firing blanks. Finally, after what seems a full minute, the moose staggers forward a few steps and drops like a felled tree.

The four bullets all struck within a few inches, and all four are truly killing shots, proving that sometimes it takes an awful lot of energy to do the job. As has become my custom, I pay my respects to the animal and thank God for the success.

Admiring my trophy of a lifetime, I am again struck by how large is a bull moose. These grand creatures are amazing in many ways, and sheer size is not the least of their attributes. We spend quite a bit of time taking pictures before the real work begins. Fortunately, the bull's location is amenable to sliding it into the back of the truck after field dressing. We cart it to the ranch for professional butchering.

While driving back to the lowlands with David, I contemplate the privilege I have just enjoyed. I am now prohibited from ever again taking a Shiras moose in Utah, where the permit is once per lifetime and justly so. I could still draw a permit in Wyoming or Montana, but I don't think I'll apply. I can't stand any more rejection when it comes to moose. Besides, since I have my bull and the demand will almost certainly always exceed the number of available permits, I will leave them for others.

As I gaze out the pickup window at the extraordinary scenery, I reflect on the camaraderie, the great food and accommodations, the peace and serenity of the place, and I feel a deep desire to return here and hunt again. Not for moose, of course, but for something else, perhaps deer or elk. Or maybe to accompany a friend or loved one on a hunt for Shiras moose.

Roland recently had a European hunter who was so impressed that every morning he would step outside his tent, throw open his arms, and exclaim with a thick German accent, "Utah! My Utah!" I know how he felt.

Rocky Mountain elk. (Photo: courtesy of Eric J. Hansen)

ROCKY MOUNTAIN ELK

(Cervus elaphus nelsoni)

The size and appearance of the elk are imposing;
his air denotes confidence of great strength,
while his towering horns exhibit weapons capable of
doing much injury when offensively employed. The head is beautifully formed,
tapering to a narrow point; the ears are large and rapidly movable . . .
the head is sustained upon a neck at once slender, vigorous, and graceful.

—Dr. E. H. Smith, *Frank Forester's Field Sports,* 1849.

The American elk received its name from early settlers, who obviously didn't know that in Europe the term referred to moose. Be that as it may, no power on earth is now likely to change the common usage to "wapiti," which some biologists prefer. In fact, the term "wapiti" is falling ever more into disuse, even among scientists. And as Bill Quimby has observed, the hunter who returns to a Wyoming elk camp after a day afield and reports that he "saw a bull wapiti today" would probably be laughed out of the back country.

Elk once occupied virtually every suitable area of North America as far south as northern Mexico. The only mainland state of the United States to lack a native population may have been Florida, though there is some doubt as to whether they were present throughout all of New England. The Yukon and the Northwest Territories did not have any, nor did the major offshore islands such as Kodiak and Newfoundland.

Scientists recognize six subspecies, two of which are extinct today: the eastern elk (*Cervus elaphus canadensis*) and the plains elk (*Cervus elaphus merrami*). Early colonists invaded the range of the former and, with no restrictions on harvest, rapidly decimated them. The latter subspecies suffered much the same fate a century or so later. Another subspecies, the Manitoba elk, is today available only to residents of Canada, so I could not include it here.

The existence of a significant population of elk in open country, coupled with their seeming retreat to heavily timbered mountains, led to the common misconception that elk were originally plains creatures driven into less accessible terrain by hunting pressure and habitat changes. Ample evidence is now available to the contrary. There were indeed populations on the prairies, but others thrived equally well in high alpine zones at the time when Columbus arrived in the Americas. The plains animals were simply more accessible and more easily exploited, both for meat, an understandable necessity, and, in some areas, because their canine teeth held attraction as ornaments.

There were perhaps as many as ten million elk on the continent at the time of European contact. As with all native fauna, Native Americans had utilized them for millennia, employing primitive weapons along with driving techniques such as fire, natural obstructions, and low fences. At the low point of their population there were fewer than 100,000 elk in North America. Throughout their range today, however, the animals are increasing, and there are perhaps a million or more. Sportsmen and their organizations, particularly the Rocky Mountain Elk Foundation, have had a huge hand in that effort. The resurgence of elk has included restocking, closed seasons as needed, acquisitions of critical wintering habitat, and incentives for landowners.

Elk herds have been reestablished in several eastern states, including Michigan, Pennsylvania, Wisconsin, Kentucky, and Tennessee. Ongoing studies will decide whether it is feasible to reintroduce elk into Virginia and the Great Smoky Mountains of North Carolina and Tennessee. In Arkansas,

Rocky Mountain elk. Idaho, November 1985.

where the first transplants for the Buffalo River herd arrived in 1981, an elk season recently opened for the first time. Interest in the drawing for the few available permits has been phenomenal.

There is definitely a degree of competition between elk and livestock for forage, and that has required fine-tuning and negotiation to benefit both elk and landowners. The happy result is that many states and provinces now have more inhabited elk domain than at any time in the past two centuries. It bears stating again that the credit belongs to organized sportsmen and cooperating wildlife agencies and landowners. In many places imaginative strategies of range utilization have allowed elk and cattle to coexist and thrive by restricting cattle access to times of year when the elk are elsewhere.

The American elk is the second largest member of the deer family in North America, and the Rocky Mountain subspecies is by far the most widely distributed and abundant. A mature bull Rocky Mountain elk may weigh seven hundred pounds or more and stand five feet high at the shoulder, while a cow weighs perhaps five hundred pounds and is six inches shorter. The coat is light brown to tan, with older bulls being lighter and appearing almost tawny. The rump patch is quite yellow and distinctive. The Rocky Mountain subspecies is generally darker overall than other varieties of North American elk. The legs and neck are often darker than the main mass of the body. Bulls, with their more two-toned coat, appear lighter in the fall, and the dark mane contrasts sharply with the rearward aspect. The characteristic mane often identifies bulls even when their antlers have shed. Cows also have darker necks than bodies, but the contrast is less striking. In a hunting situation where visibility may be restricted, exercise great care in determining the animal's sex unless antlers are visible.

Elk dentition is similar to that of other cervids, except for their unique canine teeth, which are ivory. They are called ivories, tusks, buglers, or whistling teeth. My wife has earrings made from such a pair of teeth from one of my elk, and I have another "raw" pair, unaltered since extraction. It's possible to determine the age of elk, like deer, by looking at the annual rings on a tooth, usually one of the incisors, under the microscope.

Elk shed all their hair twice a year. The much thinner summer coat lasts only a scant two months or so. The cold-weather coat has some five times more insulating quality than the summer coat, sustaining the creatures well during the frigid months. This winter coat, in addition to being thicker, is also made of two different kinds of hair. The longer guard hairs contain thousands of tiny air pockets that trap body heat and protect the animal from freezing temperatures. The inner portion is a woolly undercoat, also extremely good at heat conservation. It is not uncommon to see elk with snow on their backs because the effectiveness of their coat is such that not enough body heat escapes to melt it. To conserve heat the animals can also make their hair stand on end, trapping more air.

Like buck deer, bull elk always grow and shed their antlers annually. Bulls that are in good condition and are more mature tend to shed the old antlers later than younger or undernourished animals. The antlers most often drop in March or April, and the pedicles heal and begin to produce a new set shortly thereafter, usually in May. They are covered with nurturing velvet that lays down specialized bone to produce the majestic headgear so prized and revered by hunters. Antler is the fastest-growing type of bone known, and one of the fastest-growing tissues of any kind. The rich velvet is highly vascular, and it accumulates nutrients for antler growth in amazing fashion. Even after the velvet sheds one can see the remnants of the sustaining blood vessels in the regular longitudinal ridges and depressions. Elk antlers that are still in the velvet are highly prized in Oriental cultures for medicines of various sorts, and that has given rise to game ranching of elk to provide that commodity in commercial quantities. There have also been regrettable incidences of poaching for the same purpose.

The antlers of Rocky Mountain elk are relatively thin for their size and widely spread, and mature bulls most often have a "six point" configuration per antler, including the tip of the main beam. Typical tines are relatively straight, and all have specific names. The first point above the burr is called the brow tine, the second the bez (pronounced *bay*), the third the trez (pronounced *tray*), the fourth (and often the largest and most prominent) the dagger tine, and the back two (including the tip of the main beam) are the terminal fork. Any tine that comes off the main beam in a different direction from what's usual (top or front in symmetrical fashion), or off the burr, or arises from any other tine, is atypical. The antlers of a mature bull elk may weigh forty pounds or more when fully formed.

Although elk are highly gregarious animals, mature bulls spend much of the year alone or in the companionship of a few other bachelor bulls. Cows and calves form loosely attached companies that may number forty animals, an arrangement that facilitates watching for predators. A cow will reliably stay with her own calf, but otherwise the composition of such a band of elk can vary considerably from day to day.

Elk, like all ruminants, have a series of four stomachs capable of digesting tough fibrous plant material by breaking it down into its component carbohydrates. The animals may consume up to fifteen pounds of plant material daily, with little chewing, allowing them to eat quickly and return to their sanctuary. They then regurgitate the material and chew it thoroughly while in hiding, chewing their cud exactly like domestic cattle. The succession of stomachs produces usable nutrient molecules that the animal can absorb to meet its considerable energy needs.

Elk consume an amazing variety of plants. One study documented 159 kinds of forbs, 59 kinds of grasses, and 95 kinds of shrubs. In winter grasses and shrubs predominate in their diet, with a gradual shift mainly to grasses in springtime. Annual forbs become more predominant as summer comes on. As fall and winter again roll around, elk gradually switch back to woody browse and grasses.

After a cold ride in the Selway-Bitterroot Wilderness.

Breeding of cows begins in September in most locations, triggered by the photoperiod, or the amount of daylight. There are two to four estrus cycles twenty-one days apart if the cow is not bred the first time she is ready. Gestation lasts about eight and a half months, and most calves are born from mid-May to mid-June. At birth they weigh around thirty-five pounds and have cream camouflage spots and very little odor, natural defense mechanisms. Nevertheless, the youngsters are susceptible to a wide variety of predators, including mountain lions (the major predator of adult elk as well), bears, coyotes, and, where present, wolves. The period when the calves are most vulnerable is sometimes referred to as "the hiding period;" it lasts about three weeks. It's particularly important that areas of dense cover be available during that critical time, interspersed with open areas so the cows can feed.

The calves rapidly grow and soon are as able as adult elk to escape predators. Elk calves grow as much as two to three pounds per day for the first few weeks, then level out at a lesser rate. By late fall, a calf that weighed only thirty-five pounds at birth may be up to 175 pounds, well able to tolerate the rigors of a harsh upcoming winter.

As with many game species, the animals are most susceptible to hunting when the rut is in full swing. That occurs for Rocky Mountain elk in September throughout most of its range. Bulls emit a haunting bugling sound during the rut, a noise seemingly intended to both attract cows and intimidate rivals. Rutting bulls spar with other males, construct and utilize wallows, and thrash trees with their massive headgear in displays of aggression and emotional intensity. Among Rocky Mountain elk, a battle to the death is a most uncommon occurrence, though such do occasionally occur. Dominant bulls accumulate a harem of cows that they tend and breed as each comes into estrus and becomes receptive. Mature but nondominant bulls breed but accumulate fewer cows. Even very young bulls are capable of breeding and doubtless do. Breeding bands may move around within a fairly broad piece of real estate, and active bulls generally lose weight during this intense period. Bulls usually do not defend a definable territory, though territorial behavior has been observed in some locations.

Bugling for elk is a highly effective method of hunting them, as subordinate bulls will frequently come to such a call. The most dominant bulls, those that have accumulated a harem, are not as susceptible, having little to gain by leaving their band to engage a challenger. The biggest bulls show up in November, after the rut is over and the snows have pushed them down out of the high country.

Elk migrate between habitat types. They survive best where there is good brushy forage and grass, making good winter range critical. The animals move down from subalpine meadows and other high-elevation habitats with the onset of winter snows, and they may move long distances to a wintering area that suits their needs. If the snow becomes too deep for them to reach nutritious grasses, elk will browse various shrubs. Bulls and cows typically winter apart, with the cows generally choosing areas at lower elevation and the bulls more likely to settle into mid-alpine shrub areas. Elk can be major competition for deer during harsh winters; they may subsist on browse instead of grass and can reach much higher to feed.

Management regimens for Rocky Mountain elk vary widely from state to state in the United States and from province to province in Canada. At the extremes are Colorado, where all elk licenses are sold over the counter and the herd is managed for maximum sustained yield, and Wyoming, where all tags are on a drawing basis and the take of bulls is severely limited. Some states allow private land permits, as do some Indian reservations, though the prices are high.

Most areas conduct elk surveys annually. In the Selway-Bitterroot Wilderness, aircraft are used to count the animals and to estimate the bull-to-cow and the cow-to-calf ratios. The latest figures show about 3,200 elk in that area, with a bull-to-cow ratio of 17 to 100 and a low percentage of calves. Hunters harvested some 185 bull elk there last year, and over one-third were mature six-pointers. The Selway is still a great place to have a chance at a mature bull elk, and it remains one of the few areas where you can use a rifle during the bugling season.

Late in the season, spot-and-stalk is the usual hunting method for Rocky Mountain elk. The later the better, most would say, as the bulls are hungry after the rut, generally have moved onto more

Bull elk polish their antlers in early fall.

accessible winter range, and are easier to spot in the snow. Weather is always a major factor, and warm weather can devastate a hunt. Bugling that was echoing in every canyon the day before can cease abruptly when a heat wave begins.

Most places with an elk season also extend the opportunity to bow hunt during the bugling season. It is during the rut that the bow hunter can approach closely for a killing shot. There are some quality late-season bow hunts, as well, in places like Washington State.

An elk is a big animal that can absorb a lot of energy, so go well prepared. I used 180-grain Nosler Partition bullets to take my Rocky Mountain elk, and the animal died quickly. The smallest caliber I recommend is the .270, though certainly a well-placed shot from a smaller bore weapon will do the job. Check the minimums in the state or province in which you will hunt, because a particular size weapon or foot poundage of energy may be required.

Elk hunting can be a cold, wet, windy experience, but mostly it is sunny and warm, with a backdrop of autumn colors. Elk can be as spooky as whitetails, so wear wool or a comparable synthetic to help you move quietly through the brush. Rain gear and, on later hunts, a down parka are mandatory. If you are hunting with no guide, be sure to take along fire-starting materials and survival gear, because the tall timber of elk country is disorienting; you may find yourself wondering which way will take you back to camp. Better yet, take along one of the newer GPS units. That way you'll be in camp for supper, with or without an elk. And getting back to your kill site will be a piece of cake.

Either way, a hunt for the Rocky Mountain elk is certain to be in your future if you pursue the hunting avocation seriously. Every well-rounded hunter must give it a try. There's nothing in North America to compare with the thrill of that massive rack viewed through the tall timber, or innumerable long tines towering above a stand of willows.

CHALLENGE OF THE SELWAY-BITTERROOT WILDERNESS

Falling snow and plunging temperatures greet my arrival at Moose Creek Ranger Station, where I am about to embark on my fourth elk hunt with a well-known local outfitter. I killed an elk the last time I hunted this remote region, but I return now to try to take a grand giant on a late-November hunt. My thin Southern blood recoils somewhat from the frigid air, but I will endure. I pull my parka a little more tightly around my face and snuggle my damp hands up the sleeves, hoping to keep my wool gloves dry during the horseback ride to camp. At the end of the trail the vast Selway-Bitterroot Wilderness beckons once more.

Elk hunting is perhaps the epitome of adventure to many. To the vast majority of hunters from the East, such a quest is a kind of holy grail, pursuit of a creature whose dimensions dramatically overshadow those of our usual quarry, the white-tailed deer. Someday, I had always promised myself, I would seek and harvest one of the magnificent stags with antlers beyond imagination.

And I would do so in the wilderness, not on a private ranch or other exclusive hunting area. My desire to come to the Selway springs from a passion for a wilderness elk experience, complete with classic creaking saddle leather, remote spike camps, and vast stands of virgin timber. I love a horseback hunt, but I will use my own two feet to enter those domains beyond the reach of our mounts.

I chose the Selway-Bitterroot Wilderness of Idaho after considerable research. The immaculate Selway is the second largest wilderness in the Lower Forty-eight, uncut by roads of any kind in most places. It has never experienced the lumberman's harvest to any significant degree, and the steep mountains retain their mantle of virgin evergreens. Cedar groves of thousand-year-old giants abound, as do Douglas fir, ponderosa pine, and thickets of lodgepole pine so dense one can hardly penetrate them. Interspersed here and there are open hillsides of willow, the nemesis of the hunter because of its treacherous interlocking growth and the uncooperative footing. These ominous obstacles for the human hunter, however, are for the Rocky Mountain elk a secure sanctuary. I hope to find my trophy bull here. The effort required makes my quarry a worthy adversary, and creates a truly memorable addition to my lifetime of hunting experiences.

There are distinct advantages to a rifle hunt in the Selway. It is one of the few areas in the

When the snows come the elk are easier to spot from a high vantage point.

United States where one may hunt the heart of the rut utilizing a modern firearm, rather than a bow or muzzleloader. I tried this approach on my first trip, a September affair, and the thrill of an elk answering the guide's practiced bugle is something every hunter should experience. Indian summer heat shut down the bugling that year, so I never had a decent opportunity.

Another advantage of the Selway is that a mixed-bag hunt is typical at virtually all times during elk season. I harvested a very nice black bear that first time out, and my partner took his first decent mulie buck. So the lack of elk didn't mean we went home empty-handed.

This pristine wilderness boasts abundant wildlife of all types as well as absolutely unspoiled terrain. Shiras moose abound, along with lesser creatures beyond counting. The fishing for native cutthroat trout is phenomenal, even in the smallest tributaries.

For my second trip here I booked a November hunt. As fate would have it, the snows didn't come on schedule. Instead, a cold rain fell for the whole week. Trickles of icy rainwater ran down my collar and seeped into my pants

via the wet saddle. My old .30-06 was repeatedly soaked, the only thing saving it from ruin being its innate toughness and the careful cleanings I gave it each evening. I collected a wonderful rutting mule deer buck that trip but saw only a few lonely cow elk. The silent monarchs of those mountains—the wilderness bull elk with the massive, high racks—remained unattainable in their secure mountain hideaways.

A couple of years later, I returned to hunt in October. At that time, between the warmth of September and the snows of November, the country is at its rich and colorful best. The evergreens don't change, of course, other than the occasional frosting of early snow. But the brushy hillsides flame with a dizzying array of autumn colors, the bright hues of yellow, gold, red, and even purple providing an unequaled visual feast. The sky is almost invariably deep blue, the mornings are crisp and cold, and the edges of the creeks are rimmed with ice for the first time. Drinking delicious wilderness water from the crystal-clear streams only adds to the experience. The elk hunting, however, is the toughest in October. But by napping at midday and spending long hours glassing early and late, one does see elk.

By the third trip here, I was four full years into my trophy wilderness elk strategy, and as that hunt neared its inevitable end I resolved to harvest the first decent branch-antlered bull I encountered. For the entire trip I had endured the shame, the embarrassment, the remorse of having missed an easy opportunity the very first day out of base camp. Even now I tell the story only with considerable consternation.

We had been riding out to our spike camp, a grueling six-hour jaunt on our reliable mountain horses, when a bull elk heard our noisy footfall, apparently mistaking us for a herd of cows. We dismounted and hastily set up to call this late-rutting animal to us. After an hour of bugle exchanges it suddenly appeared right in front of us, as if from nowhere, its massive rack dominating my field of view. I raised my rifle, but he was so close I couldn't find him. He disappeared as rapidly as he had appeared, leaving a dismayed hunter and a highly irritated guide to wonder why there had been no shot. To my eternal chagrin, my scope was set on the highest power, an oversight I determined never to allow again if I could help it. I determined at that point to forever check and recheck my scope setting with a zeal that only another similarly victimized hunter can appreciate.

On the last day I harvested my first wilderness Rocky Mountain elk, a modest three by four, no trophy by most standards. To me, however, the animal represented the pinnacle of success, so I elected to have a shoulder mount done despite the marginal size. After all, it had been four years in coming and met every reasonable criterion as a trophy, size notwithstanding. Now as we ride toward camp in the falling snow, I recall how majestic that young bull looks over my fireplace, and I smile a little despite the chill.

My thinking is entirely different on this trip. I am here for the last hunt again, and the weather is promising. There is deep snow along the rutted trail, good conditions for elk hunting. The mercury

Flying into the Selway is the only practical approach in many areas.

was near zero as our bush plane touched down at Moose Creek Ranger Station. I shiver as I settle into the cold, wet saddle for the long ride to the base camp near the first fork of Moose Creek. By the time we cross the rustic bridge over the tumbling rivulet, I am more than ready to be out of the cold. Dick Norris, my friend and frequent outfitter, greets me with a hot mug of coffee and an infectious enthusiasm and invites me into the spacious cook tent. I stow my rifle in the coolest corner of the tent and renew old acquaintances.

Dick's son Darryl, my usual guide, will join me this trip as before. Finally, after three previous hunts with marginal to terrible weather, conditions are ideal. A couple of nice bulls have been gamboling in the horse meadow near camp this very morning. There is six feet of snow up top, and elk are everywhere in the creek bottoms. I will settle for nothing less than the six-by-six I have always dreamed of harvesting. I express that thought to my hosts and steel my mind against anything that might tempt me to waver in my determination.

Despite my optimism, it will not be easy. The temperature continues to plunge. It is the earliest severe cold snap anyone can remember in Idaho, and nighttime temperatures are forecast to reach 20 below zero. Whiskey becomes syrup at such extremes, prompting jokes from some about using it on the morning pancakes. As I snuggle into my sleeping bag, I pray that I will be able to endure the cold and the brutal snow, and that I will persist and take advantage of this opportunity to take the bull I am seeking.

Everything in camp is frozen solid as I emerge from my bag, and the kerosene heater in the corner struggles to subdue the awful cold. A hot breakfast in the cook tent is most welcome, though sitting with my back toward the outer wall of the tent chills my rear. As we ride out, plumes of condensation billow from the horses' nostrils, and my own breath creates a frosty rim on my parka. Staying warm is a simple matter of dismounting and walking for a mile or so, by which time I'm sweating and ready to remount.

We ascend a high ridge that looks down on the main camp, where frosty evergreens frame the peaceful valley like a Christmas postcard. We spot a bull similar to the one I harvested last trip,

Elk in a distant meadow overshadowed by fall colors.

cruising the deep snow with a band of cows, but nothing worth taking. I return to camp cold but encouraged, and I am gratified to hear that several other hunters have also seen elk.

There is nightly snowfall with daily clearing, and the sun reflects off the snow creating blindingly bright days. It is a beautiful sight, the crystal-blue sky and a wealth of withered clouds clinging to the peaks of the Bitterroot Range. There are more elk about than I have seen on all my previous elk hunts combined, but we seem to be unable to locate a real monster. Darryl is aware of my lofty six-by-six standard, so we simply look and enjoy, admiring these youngsters for their potential as well as for their sleek, youthful beauty. Cows are also abundant, most of them presumably carrying next spring's calves, and we hope the severe weather will not stretch into a disastrous winter, threatening next year's elk crop before it is born.

As we ride toward camp late in the evening of our third day, we hear a most unusual sound, the clashing of antler against antler, accompanied by the grunts of struggling bull elk. We top a ridge overlooking a snow-covered creek bottom and strain through binoculars to locate the source of the sounds.

"I've got them," Darryl reports, without lowering his glasses. "Straight ahead, at the edge of that clearing."

I peer into the fading light and am treated to a sight many hunters never see. Two bulls, both fairly youthful, are engaged in a dominance ritual of ancient origins, pushing and shoving, swapping ends and reengaging, neither able to gain the advantage. My guide advises that neither is the animal we are seeking, so we simply enjoy the display, feeling privileged to witness such a spectacle. As we watch, a spike bull almost walks over us, nearly doing a back flip when he realizes what kind of menace he has unwittingly discovered. The commotion breaks up our two gladiators and ends the fracas. No matter, the light is almost gone, and there are many frosty miles to go before we sleep.

A week of elk hunting always passes faster than a Manhattan minute, and this week is certainly no exception. Before I can turn around, my fourth day of hunting is upon me. We have spent the last two days combing the evergreen flats along the untarnished creek, but we can't find what we're seeking. It is time to get up out of the bottom to hunt, because the big bulls obviously are not down from the high country despite the recent snow and subzero temperatures. We will take a snowy trail up Bailey Mountain toward the old fire tower and see what we can see. Finger-numbing cold makes me wonder if I can shoot in 20 below temperatures—indeed, whether my .30-06 is capable of functioning properly. I have never operated it in such extreme conditions, so I test fire it before we leave camp. All seems well.

Up, up we go, noting the change from cedar and fir to pine, breaking out into lush, snow-laden willow on stairstep ridges as we near the summit. A half-dozen elk are in the near valley, two of them bulls. One is a massive five by five, the best elk I have seen since my scope debacle of a couple of years ago. We glass the bull extensively, not even needing the spotting scope, since it is just a few hundred yards downslope, oblivious to our presence.

"A beauty. It'd look great on your wall," comments Darryl as he wipes the fog from his binoculars. "What do you think?"

I recall my meeting with my mind, my determination to settle such questions ahead of time. Nevertheless, I am enticed by this bull. I am a trophy hunter at this point in my career only in the most marginal sense, having never had the opportunity to turn down such a magnificent creature. This decision marks a radically new course for me, one that both attracts and repels me. To make matters worse, the extreme cold is taking its toll on me, and the apparent absence of elk larger than the one we are perusing makes my resolve even more flimsy. I grow immeasurably as a hunter in those moments of uncertainty. After looking for a few more moments, I swallow hard.

"Darryl, I've set a six-by-six standard for this hunt. I already have a smaller elk. I'll go home very happy with either a six-by-six or with no elk at all. Let's move on."

"Fine. It's your hunt and your choice. I think we can do better, too, but you never know."

Glassing brushy hillsides in the Selway is a prime hunting method.

I am by no means certain that my decision is the right one, but at least I am being true to myself. I have faith that I will eventually be glad for it. I hope someday to be able to conduct all my hunts in accordance with true trophy hunter's values, for the sake of conservation and for the sake of the younger animals I will pass up. For the moment I am satisfied to have transcended the temptation to compromise.

The beautiful five-by-five bull and its companions watch, with only a touch of wariness, as we mount up to ride to the next ridgeline. There is a nice overlook there covering a huge piece of real estate, and we will have our lunch there.

Lunch is frozen solid. The apple in my paper sack is as hard as a billiard ball. The meat and the lettuce—and even the bread—crunch loudly as I chew. A lone cow elk is visible a mile away, but glassing reveals no accompanying bull. My eyes pan back and forth as I eat, and, as I turn far to the right and look uphill, I almost choke. I whip my binoculars up to the spot and immediately my eyes are met by massive antlers with ivory-tipped tines, prominent and gleaming in the sunlight. The animal is a mere quarter-mile distant, with only the head, antlers, and the top of the back visible in the deep willows.

"Darryl, there's what we're looking for!" I whisper excitedly.

"Yeah, I see," he replies without emotion, swinging his binoculars to the animal. "A six-by-six—maybe seven on one side. Nice bull."

Darryl has been in this position before, spotting a big trophy bull elk with only a successful stalk between him and the celebration. I am excited, eager, determined not to make another mistake. He is cool and calculating, realizing that the presence of a respectable bull in no way ensures that we will be fortunate enough to take him. Snowdrifts are up to six feet deep, almost to the tops of the willows in most places. It is uphill to the animal with no approach but a frontal route, much of it on open willow hillside. Fortunately the bull is feeding, and there is a distinct crosswind drift to the breeze.

We plot a course on foot for a blackened snag near the animal and set out. The snow is as light as fine powder in the extreme cold, so its depth is not nearly as hindering as it might be otherwise. It also muffles our thrashing through the brush. We have no problem staying low: hidden willow branches under the snow continually entangle our feet, throwing me headlong more than once. I am doubly glad I have covered my rifle muzzle with a piece of tape to keep out moisture. I repeatedly check the weapon to be sure that nothing preventable will foil my chances this time, remembering again vividly the scope full of blurred hair two years ago. I have it cranked all the way back to lowest power.

"Can you hit him from here?" Darryl asks as we reach a small swell in the terrain.

It looks like a long shot, and I raise my rifle to confirm the impression. "He looks pretty darn small in my scope," I observe in a whisper. "Can't we get any closer?"

"We can sure try. I'd say we're about 350 yards now. The snag we spotted is just above him and to the right. If we can make it there, we'll be right on top of him."

Beads of perspiration form on my forehead as we climb, and rivulets of sweat stream down my back. As we approach the burned stump that is our marker, my eyes strain to spot our quarry.

I know it will be an offhand shot, because a rest in the spindly willows is out of the question.

"There he is. Shoot!" says Darryl in a whisper, finally showing emotion in his voice. He repeats the command as he squats down out of the way. "Shoot!"

The bull is on his feet now, checking out these two floundering, snow-covered bipeds. He won't stay long, I know from experience, so as Darryl squats my rifle goes up. It looks like maybe seventy-five yards, and at a target nearly as big as one of our horses. I place the cross hairs on the heart-lung area of his broadside presentation and squeeze the trigger.

The sweet sensation of recoil and the loud report confirm that the cold has not damaged my weapon. The bull lurches forward a few steps as I bolt another cartridge. I fire twice more in rapid succession before the huge animal goes down in a spray of snow.

The cold, the long days without success, the many previous disappointments—I forget them all as we admire this magnificent animal. My numb fingers struggle to operate the camera as we document this most momentous of hunts. Joy fills my mind and my heart is choked with thanksgiving to the great God who gives such experiences. Next week is Thanksgiving, and I will not forget to say special thanks.

A wilderness Rocky Mountain elk, a big bull from the remote back country, is arguably one of the finest and most difficult trophies to obtain in all the world. Every time I look at my Selway-Bitterroot trophy, my fingers recall numbing cold and my toes tingle. But I want to do it again.

Roosevelt elk. (Photo: courtesy of Erwin and Peggy Bauer)

ROOSEVELT ELK
(Cervus elaphus roosevelti)

To me still hunting elk in the mountains, when they are calling,
is one of the most attractive of sports,
not only because of the size and stately beauty of the quarry and the
grand nature of the trophy, but because of the magnificence of the scenery,
and the stirring, manly, exciting nature of the chase itself. . . .
The wapiti is not only the most stately and beautiful of American game—
but is also the noblest of the stag kind throughout the world.

—Theodore Roosevelt, *The Wilderness Hunter,* 1891.

In 1897, scientist C. Merriam Hart carried out extensive studies on the elk of the Olympic Peninsula of Washington. He noted the physical differences between these animals and the elk in the east, and named the new subspecies in honor of his friend and fellow hunter, Teddy Roosevelt.

Roosevelt was probably describing the Rocky Mountain elk when he wrote the above passage, but it applies equally well to the subspecies that bears the president's name. These elk are also known as Olympic elk, and they inhabit the coastal areas of extreme northwestern California, Oregon, Washington, and Vancouver Island of British Columbia. There are transplanted herds as well in several locations, most notably Afognak, Raspberry, and Kodiak Islands of Alaska and Santa Rosa Island off the California coast. The animals may live at or near sea level but are also found high in the alpine areas of such places as the Olympic Mountains of Washington State and the Cascades of Oregon. Nobody who has hunted these elk doubts that they live in some of the thickest and most inhospitable terrain in North America, where wet, cold winters and rainy, foggy summers are the norm. Unlike the elk to the east, there is no record of the Roosevelt elk's inhabiting anything except heavily timbered coastlines and mountain ranges.

The Roosevelt subspecies can easily claim the title of heavyweight in the elk clan. A big bull will sometimes top 1,000 pounds, a size almost never attained by Rocky Mountain elk or any other member of the red deer family. Cows are bigger than tule elk bulls, reaching 600 pounds at times. No reason is apparent for the size difference, except possibly the simple genetic separation of animals with propensity to grow to larger size. The forage quality of Roosevelt elk habitat is not particularly good, as abundant rainfall heavily leaches nutrients from the soils. The pregnancy rate for Roosevelt elk is considerably lower than that of the Rocky Mountain subspecies, however, and the nutrition factor may account for that difference.

The pelage is striking in these animals, mainly because of the extraordinary contrast between their very light bodies and extremely dark legs and necks. The coat lightens in winter, making the disparity even more obvious. As with other elk, the hair sheds twice annually, with the thick winter coat providing ample protection against the cold and wet of winter.

Besides coloration and size, the major distinguishing feature is the configuration and mass of the antlers. "Massive" is the word that describes the headgear of a mature Roosevelt bull, though seldom is the beam length of a Rocky Mountain elk attained. Like tule elk, there is more of a tendency to form palmation and crown points as well, and sometimes the dagger tine will fork to create an extra point. Generally, Rocky Mountain elk score much better than Roosevelt elk. One must keep in mind, though, that hunters take far fewer Roosevelt elk than the Rocky Mountain variety.

Lewis and Clark, on their expedition to explore the Louisiana Purchase, recorded that their party took 146 of these elk over a three-month period during the winter of 1805–1806. They not only consumed the meat but also made clothing and shoes from the skins. They even fashioned crude candles from the tallow. Without this magnificent resource, the expedition might well have failed. Thus, these elk had an important place in the exploration of our American West.

Roosevelt elk were originally an extremely abundant animal in the Pacific Northwest. Unfortunately, their very abundance made them a target for exploitation, and they were almost wiped out in many areas by market hunting. Sometimes they were killed just for their "ivories," the pair of canine teeth that were irresistible to many. Because of the increasing scarcity of elk, the Oregon legislature in 1872 passed a law protecting elk for part of the year, but unfortunately they appropriated no money to enforce the law. In 1899, with the elk almost extinct except in the most remote areas, a total ban on hunting went into effect. In 1905, Oregon instituted a total ban on the sale of wild meat and wildlife parts of all kinds.

Hunting resumed in 1938 in Oregon, with a season that allowed anyone who bought a license to take one bull elk. Under proper management the population has gradually expanded, so that in 1997 there were an estimated 66,000 Roosevelt elk in Oregon, 31,500 in Washington, 33,000 on Vancouver Island, and 4,000 in Humboldt and Del Norte Counties of California. Approximately 5,000 Roosevelt elk live in nearly pristine conditions in Olympic National Park. Under protective measures, Roosevelt elk are secure throughout their range, although some management challenges remain.

Roosevelt elk are not as prolific as the Rocky Mountain subspecies. Studies show that for all age classes of cows, the pregnancy rate is below that of comparable Rocky Mountain elk herds. One significant problem is the very low bull-to-cow ratio in most areas, with young bulls doing most of the breeding unless firm regulations restrict the take of bulls. Calving success is 96 percent for dry cows when the sire is a bull three or more years old. That figure falls off drastically if the cows are nursing a calf, but remains at 57 percent when older bulls are doing the breeding. When spikes are pressed into service for lack of mature breeding bulls, they succeed only 36 percent of the time when breeding dry cows and seldom successfully breed a nursing cow.

Additionally, spikes usually breed the cows a month later than mature bulls, producing a late calf that may not be hardy enough to survive the following winter.

The velvet of mature bulls sheds in July, but spikes may keep their velvet until September. Bull elk are infertile until antler growth is complete, so the spikes may not be able to breed when the cows first cycle. That could explain the late breeding behavior observed when yearling bulls service most of the cows. These findings have obvious management implications. In 1947 the ratio in Oregon was thirty-five bulls to every hundred cows. Today in some units the figure has slipped as low as one to two bulls per hundred cows during some years. Several units average only three to five bulls year after year. All evidence points to the fact that a minimum of three to ten mature bulls per one hundred cows is necessary to ensure maximum reproductive potential. Limited entry permits have been the solution for five of the fourteen coastal units to ensure adequate mature breeding bulls.

Mature bulls have three separate periods of behavior: rut, post-rut seclusion, and antler growth. The rut kicks off with declining light, referred to as decreasing photoperiod. That triggers the hormonal activity that brings the bulls into the rut. Bulls may wander as much as thirty miles per day seeking cows, though most often they stay within a couple of miles of their core home range. The rut occurs at basically the same time as that of the Rocky Mountain elk, usually September, and the haunting bugles of rutting bulls echo throughout Roosevelt elk country. Each time the bull bugles, it ejects urine along the underbelly and neck, and it trickles down the legs as well. The animal may also urinate in a wallow and roll in the fragrant perfume. Adult bulls have fully polished out their antlers by this time, and males clash in fights for dominance. When temperatures are low and humidity is high, the elk rut almost continually. If daytime temperatures reach 80 degrees Fahrenheit, however, the rut shuts down until the weather changes.

Bulls emerge from the rut weakened and tired, and enter a period of seclusion to regain strength for the coming winter. Mature male elk are often solitary, reclusive animals at this time, and they can be virtually impossible for the hunter to locate. In

Fresh snow blankets the vast Sky Lakes Wilderness.

the heavily timbered terrain of the Pacific Northwest, that can be an insurmountable challenge. The animals may gather in winter in herds composed of mature bulls only, cow-calf and yearling bull herds, or groups of medium-size bulls only. When the antlers begin to grow in late winter, solitary mature bull elk may once more associate with other bulls. For some animals it is less a social instinct than a chance gathering near a mineral lick, where they acquire the nutrients necessary for antler growth.

Cows, in contrast, are herd animals, with each herd having a dominant lead cow. Cows in good condition enter estrus spontaneously and are bred by a mature rutting bull when one is available. If the cows have been weakened by poor-quality forage in the summer, or even a stressful previous winter, they may not come into season in a timely fashion. Even the stress created by encroachment of humans or vehicular traffic can affect this vital function. Milk production for existing calves also leads to decreased fertility.

Calves are normally born in the last two weeks of May and are slightly larger than those of Rocky Mountain elk, a distinct advantage in the cold, wet habitat. Few predators are present in much of today's Roosevelt elk range, so poor nutrition and weather create the most stress. However, some Roosevelt elk units have increasing cougar populations, a fact that is becoming important.

The cow develops a strong bond with the calf, an attachment that grows daily for the first week of the calf's life. The cow will vigorously defend the calf against interlopers. The pair stay together most of the time until fall, when the bond gradually weakens. By September the two may be in separate herds, miles apart, and the calf can easily survive without the cow's milk from that point onward.

Roosevelt elk generally inhabit a fairly small home range that averages one to two miles in diameter in rough country such as the Cascades, and perhaps two to five miles in less vertical coastal terrain. In foraging, the elk seldom travel more than 1,200 yards during cool weather and 500 to 800 yards in July and August. Most movement occurs near sunrise and sunset, and elk normally feed sparingly at night. They work a circular route within their home range, perhaps nature's way of preventing overgrazing and habitat degradation. Most coastal Roosevelt elk herds do not migrate, but those of the Olympic and Cascade Ranges do, in the manner characteristic of their Rocky Mountain cousins.

Like other elk, the Roosevelt subspecies eats a wide variety of grasses, forbs, and browse: ninety-three different plants from four different habitats, in one study. The trailing blackberry is the preferred plant, amounting to 16 percent of the year-round diet. Grasses and sedges are also important, contributing 13 percent of the total annual diet. Another important plant species is the false dandelion, which contributes 8 to 10 percent. Consumption of those three species varies little with season. Several shrubs, primarily the vine maple, account for 30 percent of the spring and summer diet, but because the elk eat them very little in fall and winter, total annual contribution to the diet is only 7 percent.

Clear-cuts provide the best forage, five to seven years after logging. That habitat produces an incredible 5,500 pounds of green browse and forage per acre. When elk utilize such clear-cuts, its production goes up by almost 1,000 pounds per acre, an indication of the value of the pruning. Production of food useful to elk in clear-cuts begins to fall off a decade or so after logging. There is also a relationship between the amount of edge present and the use of clear-cuts by elk, because cover is an absolute necessity. If forage is a distance from adequate cover, elk simply won't venture out. The implication is that clear-cuts should be small, with interspersed areas of growing timber of varying ages.

These elk have few diseases. Brucellosis is not a factor, and other bacterial diseases are not generally a problem, except in isolated instances. Several viruses occur sporadically and can inflict casualties, including various bovine viruses and the virulent parainfluenza-3, which can decimate bighorn sheep but is not as dangerous to elk. Roosevelt elk have antibodies to several of these viruses, indicating high resistance. Parasites similar to the lungworms that infect domestic stock sometimes occur in elk, but they seldom cause death. Liver flukes are fairly common, as are intestinal roundworms and tapeworms. None of those are usually fatal, however, and edibility of elk meat is not affected in most cases.

The best time to hunt Roosevelt elk in the early to middle fall is when the temperature is low, the humidity is high, and the barometer is rising. In times of extreme winter cold, however, elk are more active when the temperature warms a bit. Falling barometric pressure causes elk to become extremely nervous, to move around a lot under cover of thick timber, and to maintain a high level of vigilance. Deep snow makes hunting easier in mountainous regions, as elk then move to more

Packtrain transportation into and out of the wilderness.

accessible areas. Tracking them is also easier in fresh snow.

There is much controversy in Roosevelt elk country (and elsewhere in the West) about access via U.S. Forest Service roads on public lands. Many of these roads have been closed in recent years to limit harvesting and other disturbances of elk. Research has revealed a direct relationship between road closings and adequate bull escapement. Poaching is also much less common in areas without usable roads. Many people would like to see full access by both road vehicles and ATVs, but who can argue with such facts? Judicious closing of some roads is an absolute necessity in certain parts of the range of the Roosevelt elk.

I have a friend who regularly hunts the Olympic Peninsula near Forks, Washington, for these animals, and he occasionally tags a real monster. Olympic National Park dominates that region, and the park serves as a reservoir of mature animals. Don't hunt this country as a novice, though, unless you are willing to risk having your hunting experience turn into a survival test. The mature forests there are as dense as anywhere on the planet, and the possibility of getting lost is very real. If you are going to attempt such an excursion, be sure you have a good GPS unit, not only for getting back to camp each day but also to make certain you don't wander across the park boundary and into big trouble.

The highest success rates for Roosevelt elk are not on the Olympic Peninsula, however. Your best bet, if finances allow, is to go with a good outfitter on Vancouver Island, where the Boone and Crockett Club and Safari Club International will both recognize your trophy as a genuine Roosevelt elk. Both organizations also recognize the introduced populations of Afognak and Raspberry Islands. If you hunt any introduced herd except those two, expect the trophy to be eligible for the SCI book but not the B&C. So far no bull from an introduced population has qualified for the B&C book. All have come from the native coastal and mountain herds of the Pacific Northwest, including Vancouver Island. The line for both B&C and SCI is Interstate 5 in Washington and Oregon, taking in Del Norte and Humboldt Counties of California. This demarcation is at odds with biologists of the Oregon Department of Fish and Wildlife, who unequivocally classify all elk in the Cascade Mountains of Oregon as the Roosevelt subspecies. The reason for these elk not being recognized by SCI and B&C is that a number of Rocky Mountain elk were released in a few places in the Cascades early in the century, and localized interbreeding may have occurred. An obscure fact is that a few Rocky Mountain elk were also introduced into other Roosevelt elk range early this century, some of it in the very core of it, yet that has not led to a change in record-book boundaries. It isn't imperative that the books recognize the same areas the biologists do, though ideally that would be the case. For the organizations, they have to draw a line somewhere, even if the boundary doesn't perfectly reflect biological reality.

Hunting success rates in most places are in the 10 percent range. The bull harvest consists of about 70 percent yearlings, 17 percent two-year-olds, and 14 percent three- to five-year-olds. Fewer than 2 percent of animals taken are over five years old. The latter category, naturally, is the one of which dreams are made. A Roosevelt elk in that age class will carry a set of antlers so imposing and heavy that they look like something out of a hunter's imagination.

The best in rain gear is necessary anytime one hunts Roosevelt elk. For this hunt, more so perhaps than for any other cervid in North America, be sure to carry enough gear in your pack to enable you to spend a night outdoors in rain and freezing temperatures. It's a good idea to line the bottom of your day pack with a lightweight plastic tube tent, and a space blanket sleeping bag can come in mighty handy. Fire-starting materials are absolutely mandatory. A flashlight with extra batteries is a good idea. The type of boots you'll need depends on whether you're hunting mountains, coastal lowlands, or snow-covered back country. Whether you choose pac boots, leather boots, or insulated rubber boots, be sure to carry an extra pair of socks. Your feet will get wet from sweat no matter what, and if they become cold the best way to warm them is to change socks and liners.

Take no less than a .30-caliber weapon to hunt these big-bodied animals. I used 165-grain Noslers to take my Roosevelt elk, but I'd recommend something slightly heavier. I hit the animal well, but better penetration with a heavier bullet might have saved having to fire again.

Any way you cut it, hunting these animals is truly an adventure of the first order. Be ready for anything when you go, but don't miss it. You may not connect on the first trip, but it will get in your blood and you'll keep coming back for more. I can almost guarantee it.

ROGUE RIVER GAMBLER

Weaving between towering forest giants, massive Douglas fir trees nearly ten feet in diameter, we follow the bull's fresh track. Six inches of early snow fell two days ago, and now the sun has made it soggy and the footing is treacherous. I welcome the snow, but with it comes pervasive moisture—both underfoot and dripping from the vegetation. With daytime melting, I can also expect noisy, crunchy walking after the inevitable overnight freeze.

The bull we are following has already covered some five miles without bedding, and he is feeding only sporadically. We know he is a bull by the occasional telltale urine pattern in the unspoiled snow and the track, which indicates an animal of respectable size. One thing about this animal—he is healthy, or he couldn't have walked these five miles uphill. We finally lose the track in a maze of other fresh elk sign as we top out on the Pacific Crest Trail that winds through this remote country.

I am in the pristine Sky Lakes Wilderness Area of the Rogue River National Forest, an area just south of fabulously beautiful Crater Lake National Park. Ron Adams, my friend, guide, and outfitter, conducts hunts in these heavily timbered mountains. The terrain is exactly as I had imagined when I contemplated hunting these elk of the rain forest, and I marvel at the deep, scenic woods we are traversing. I will be here for a week, the entire rifle season, so I should see plenty of this unblemished world.

Riding to camp on the day before the season opened, I found myself in a steady snowfall, the tiny crystals melting into my clothing. It was necessary to dismount repeatedly at intervals and walk a half-mile or more to warm up. The smell of sweating horses and wet saddle leather had conjured up pleasant memories of hunts long past. As we approached Ron's base camp, we heard the first elk bugle. I had relaxed into the complacency that sets in on a long trail ride, enduring the weather somewhat stoically and letting my mind drift into a state of semi-alertness. Suddenly there it was, a lengthy call from the dark timber above us. I snapped fully alert at the sound and peered into the dense forest in the fading light, hoping to catch sight of the animal. Again he bugled, chasing all thoughts of cold and wet from my head and rousing my hunter's blood. The season would open the next morning, and I had hoped against hope that the great bull would sound another revealing bugle in the light of dawn.

I had arrived amazingly dry, considering. Ron had assembled a fine camp in the vast wilderness, and I claimed my space in the corner of the spacious tent and unpacked my gear. The warmth from the wood stove and a delicious hot meal were good preparation for a night's sleep. The soft fall of snow on the canopy of the tent imparted a pleasant anticipation of the perfect conditions we could expect in the morning.

Now, as we climb the mountain behind camp, my lungs are protesting the thin, cold air. Newly fallen snow is perfect for quiet walking, and I am soon amid gigantic fir and hemlock, all heavily weighted by a mantle of white. As we move through the forest, I quickly understand why this rugged back country receives such light hunting. The terrain is alarmingly disorienting, with one giant tree looking much like the next. The day is overcast, with low clouds and patchy fog, and there are virtually no distinguishing landmarks. I am thankful for my knowledgeable guide and for my compass.

The new snow dislodges easily from the evergreen thickets, adding a frosty natural camouflage to my woolens. Despite the dampness, hunting conditions are ideal—except for the lack of elk or fresh tracks. I arrive back in camp weary to the bone from our trek but ever hopeful that tomorrow will be different.

Several more days of unproductive hunting come and go as we comb the countryside. There seem to be no elk in the vicinity, an eventuality no one could have anticipated. Sitting on a high rock outcropping chasing away the midmorning chill with a pleasant fire, we contemplate our shrinking

Roosevelt elk. Oregon, October 1994.

Down, down we go into lush meadows bordered by mature timber. The ground here is covered with fresh elk droppings and tracks, a welcome change. With the melting the walking is now less noisy, but there remain spots untouched by the sun where footfalls seem louder than ever. Ron suggests we stop for lunch on a sun-washed bench.

"Sure is a problem, having to crunch through that stuff," I comment as I unbutton my coat in the warm sun and recline against a fragrant evergreen bush.

"Let's try a different tactic," Ron suggests between bites on a granola bar. "I'll go down below the next few meadows and see if I can't move some elk up past you. Sitting here you may have a better chance than moving around."

"You'll probably see a big bull if I'm not with you," I groan, "but let's give it a try."

Engulfed with pleasant warmth as Ron departs, I have to move around some to stay alert. I amuse myself by observing a ground squirrel among the rocks that seems to be enjoying the sunshine as much as I. The fresh elk sign today is encouraging, I reflect, even if the droppings and tracks have not yet translated into a good bull, or even a sighting.

Ron estimated that he'd be gone thirty minutes, but an hour has already passed. The view through the heavy timber is no more than a hundred yards or so in any direction, and I fight sleepiness as I watch.

Suddenly an unmistakable sound pierces the silence—an elk bugle from somewhere below. I sit bolt upright, the drowsiness suddenly gone. The haunting sound recurs again and again with absolute clarity. Completely attentive now, I scan the openings in the trees for movement. *Where the heck is Ron? Is he playing games with me on his elk call?*

The next sound I hear is even more arresting—a dog barking! And it isn't just a

alternatives. As I had feared, daytime melting has glazed the entire forest floor with a crunchy layer of ice. Every step is a warning cry to any elk we might chance to approach. Since there is no hope of stealth, we park ourselves in hopeful anticipation of some serious melting.

The sun becomes pleasantly warm, and almost imperceptibly the temperature rises to a comfortable level. I am quite snug now, and it is enjoyable to watch a golden eagle floating amid the clouds, searching for a meal. A group of ravens harasses a northern spotted owl, apparently indifferent to the respect due an endangered species. We douse the fire and prepare to move on.

lackadaisical bark, it is a raucous, enthusiastic, hot-on-the-trail canine howl, coming from somewhere behind and below me, near the ridgeline we left earlier today. *What in the world is going on?*

The first flickering of movement comes from far down the slope, just a slight change in the quality of light between two gigantic trees. Is it Ron? I'll give him a piece of my mind if he is having a bit of fun with me. Barking dogs indeed.

A second movement convinces me it can't be Ron. Elk! And heading directly toward me. As the animals materialize, I quickly see that both are cows. Whatever Ron is doing, he's generating enough action to keep me fully awake now. I ease a shell into the chamber of my rifle and wait.

The glade below me is quickly filling with elk, at least a dozen. I scan for antlers, but all are cows and calves. I remain motionless, enjoying the proximity of so many beautiful creatures. I keep my .30-06 at ready as I peer into the dense woods beyond the herd. The elk are less than thirty yards below me, completely oblivious to my presence. They seem to be concentrating on some perceived danger far below and out of my sight.

Fresh tracks of a nice bull traverse a snowy draw.

There is now a subtle movement among the massive Douglas fir trees, perhaps a hundred yards away. Silently a creature strolls across a small opening. My heart races as a glint of sunlight catches the flash of antler. Any bull is indeed a trophy in this remote wilderness, but I will not shoot unless he is at least a respectable branch-antlered bull. He stops dead in his tracks some hundred yards away, where the chest is visible but the antlers are in the vegetation. I can unmistakably see several upthrust points, so I raise my rifle and squeeze off a shot at the vitals.

The bull lunges ahead directly toward the herd of cows and calves just below me, obviously unaware of my location. The other elk begin a nervous milling, and I quickly shuck another cartridge into the firing chamber. I scope in on the straight-on brisket presentation and fire again. As the thunder of the rifle echoes, the entire bunch takes flight and disappears.

I hurriedly gather my belongings, stuff my gear into my pack, and run down the hill to where I last saw the bull, my eyes searching for sign of a hit. No blood. I can't believe I could have missed such an easy shot. I peer into the dark forest, moving in the direction in which the animals fled, praying that my aim was true and that the animal is humanely finished.

The ethical hunter prizes a clean, certain kill, the culmination of the hunt that is painless, quick, and final. Even after meticulous practice, though, that doesn't always happen. I spot my bull in the

Packing the kill out through dark timber.

woods ahead, lying wounded and looking back at me from a hundred yards off.

I frantically seek a rest from which to dispatch the bull. The animal rises to his feet and starts walking away, moving down the mountain toward impenetrable young evergreens that will hide him from my view. A panicky thought seizes my mind, the horrifying prospect of losing a wounded animal. The thought weighs on my mind like the heavy snow on the burdened evergreen limbs.

I will have to make a hurried shot through thick timber at a moving elk. With a steady hand I touch off the Nosler handload, and I say an inaudible prayer of thanks as the bull tumbles.

The sound of my racing heart subsides only slightly as I approach the dead animal. I have already chambered another round, and I begin climbing over an intervening tangle of deadfalls. The woods seem tranquil now, the predator having triumphed and my quarry lying silent in a heavenly shaft of sunlight. There is no need for the ready bullet. As I come close enough to be sure, I ease the cartridge from the rifle and slip it quietly into my pocket.

Ron arrives, out of breath and panting, full of gladness and heartfelt congratulations. Kneeling beside the fallen monarch, we give thanks to God

for the superb elk, a gorgeous four-by-four that exceeds my expectations. My head, however, still spins with questions. Ron relates with a broad grin that he had descended a few meadows, as we planned, and had encountered the elusive herd, our bull among them. He had watched them for quite a while, almost kicking himself for leaving his hunter behind.

Since bringing me to the elk seemed impossible, he formulated a plan to bring the herd to me. The trouble was that the herd had tried to escape in the wrong direction, moving away from me after the exchange of bugles. There is a heavily timbered ridgeline to our west, and the animals could easily have entered the dense terrain and disappeared forever. Ron had lit out at a dead run and cut them off before they got there, imitating a pack of dogs with his ferocious barking. I reflect on Ron's quick wits with a high degree of appreciation.

Every hunt teaches something unique in a manner that the nonhunter could never fathom. I learned on this hunt that sometimes success can come suddenly and unexpectedly. Once in a great while, the unconventional works in a challenging situation. Ron's impromptu imitation of a Labrador retriever is a case in point.

Tule elk. (Photo: from the author's collection)

TULE ELK
(Cervus elaphus nannodes)

Nothing that is shall perish utterly,
But perish only to revive again

—Henry Wadsworth Longfellow (1807–1882), *Michael Angelo*

The tule elk has not perished, though it came precariously close during the nineteenth century. In its pristine condition, the state of California probably had a population of about half a million. Only six cows and two bulls survived the intensive slaughter that fed elk meat to the gold rush of 1849–1851. One authority states that there were only five elk left, while another claims twenty-eight. Whichever the case, these pitifully few were captured and held by a benevolent rancher named Henry Miller. The animals have recovered beyond anyone's wildest dreams. Modern biologists will tell you that the genetics of individual tule elk are so similar that they are virtually clones of one another. It is amazing that such a small gene pool could have led to a viable and varied population of closely kin animals.

In 1943 a hunt for the animals was instituted in the Owens Valley, with the harvest carefully controlled for removal only of excess animals. That practice continued until 1963, when the first stirrings of the antihunting movement in California led to the hunt's being shut down. Actually, that may have been a rare instance in which such a move was advantageous, because as a result the state had to seek alternative places for the surplus elk. Today numerous herds are present on public and private land, and the search goes on for new transplant sites. A hunt was reinstituted when elk numbers peaked over 2,000 animals. There are now tule elk in twenty-three separate locales, a January 1998 release of twenty elk into Kern County establishing the newest herd as of this writing.

These feisty little elk have always been found only in California. Except for a very few subspecies confined to the enormous Northwest Territories of Canada, tule elk are the only big-game animal in North America found in only a single state or province. The animal derives its name from the rushlike plants that populate the low country of interior California, territory from which they are now mostly excluded by gigantic farming operations crisscrossed by a maze of broad highways. Their propensity for such open country made them ideal for market hunters, and a number of fortunes were made in bringing them to table, which was an honored occupation in its time. From an estimated half-million animals in 1849, today there are fewer than 4,000 tule elk. Still, their remarkable recovery from the brink of oblivion is one of the greatest success stories in modern game management.

Habitat loss is the main reason there aren't hundreds of thousands of tule elk today. Vegetable growers occupy most suitable tule elk territory (animal rights devotees take note), limiting the numbers of tule elk far more than any present-day meat-eating hunter ever could do. The tule elk is confined to a few locations that will support self-sustaining herds, and many of the prime areas are on private ranch land. Public land in Owens Valley (Inyo County), Cache Creek (Lake, Colusa, and Yolo Counties), Lapanza (San Luis Obispo, Kern, and Santa Barbara Counties), and Grizzly Island are the prime sites where a hunter might draw a highly sought tule elk tag. Over half the public drawing tags, however, are for cow elk or spikes, not the massive-racked bulls that have made tule elk famous.

Encouragement of landowners to allow elk to inhabit suitable land has given rise to an innovative program that allocates a certain number of permits to private landowners, who may then sell them to an outfitter or directly to a hunter. That provides incentive to share valuable grazing land with the elk and much-needed removal of some of the highly aggressive bulls as they reach and pass their prime of life. To take a truly magnificent tule elk bull it is usually necessary to seek such a private land permit, as I did.

Tule elk. California, August 1994.

As I observed while conducting my own tule elk hunt, these animals are truly creatures of open country. I was amazed to see nine mature bull elk bedded in open grassland, with no brush or timber within many yards. Only one was mature enough to harvest and it had a broken antler, so I passed and had to come back the following year. The animal I ultimately harvested never bedded on open grassland while I was watching, but it was crossing such habitat on its way to higher ground with a harem of cows when I took it. No Rocky Mountain or Roosevelt elk would be caught in such a situation so far from heavy cover.

The tule elk weighs considerably less than other members of the elk family in North America, with a big bull seldom topping five hundred pounds. A cow tule elk will usually weigh no more than four hundred pounds. Exceptional animals may weigh considerably more. The color of these

elk is somewhat lighter than that of other elk, but the pelage is otherwise comparable.

The antlers are distinctive among the American varieties of elk and tend to have crown points and palmated tops, more like those of red stags than American elk. The beams tend to be more light and spreading, like the antlers of Rocky Mountain elk, though the tines may tend to be more arched rather than straight. Naturally, the antlers do not score as high on average as do those of Rocky Mountain or Roosevelt elk, but the racks can still be awesome adornments on such a diminutive animal.

Another distinguishing characteristic is the skull configuration, which is not only shorter but also broader in proportion than those of other North American elk. Somewhat surprisingly, the tooth rows of tule elk are longer, an adaptation that may be related to their specialized diet. Such differences are of interest mainly to taxonomists, but they can also provide practical tools to game agencies when questions arise regarding the origin of a particular elk.

The tule elk is probably the most aggressive of the elk family when it comes to rutting behavior. Fights can and fairly often do lead to fatal wounds, and I myself have observed a tule elk after the rut with one main beam broken just above the brow tine. The amount of force necessary to fracture a thick elk antler there would have to be immense. Another hunter in the area where I took my bull watched an impressive rutting battle and afterward harvested the vanquished bull. It had six inches of gut protruding through an abdominal puncture, a wound that would have certainly led to a fatal infection within days.

The susceptibility to fractured antlers may not be entirely due to the feisty nature of tule elk, however. Much of their prime habitat today is known to be calcium deficient, and antler integrity may suffer as a result. In the Owens Valley, up to 50 percent of tule bulls have broken tines after the rut.

The rut occurs a bit earlier than in other subspecies, beginning in July, and August is the peak bugling period. To me the tule bull sounds no different from the other varieties, though the experts may differ about this. Conception, gestation, and birth follow the pattern of other elk, except that the peak month of calving is earlier, from mid-April to early May.

Predators are not a major problem in most of tule elk range today, though coyotes and bears

Easing along quietly seeking tule elk.

take some calves, as do mountain lions, which also kill adult elk from time to time.

Tule elk of the old days migrated from the oak ridges to the fertile tule grasslands in summer, then returned to the oaks in the fall to feed on acorns and other late-maturing mast. Those grasslands of the San Joaquin and Napa Valleys are now completely domesticated, but the elk survive in isolated pockets. They love to forage on greenery, and ranches with alfalfa fields are a favorite. Their migrations may be much shorter now, and sometimes the pattern repeats daily. I have observed tule elk in an alfalfa field at dawn, and watched them later standing erect on their hind legs nibbling acorns in the California woods.

Hunting tule elk is a most civilized proposition, although the preferred hunting time, during the rut, features long days and the likelihood of significant daytime heat. The main

bugling occurs very early in the morning and just before dark. Five or six hours of sleep a night is the norm when you are pursuing these creatures, but it is quite feasible to take an extended midday nap. The elk are mostly inactive during the heat of the day, and they may not manifest a tendency to bed in the open under the hot California sun.

Many private lands inhabited by tule elk are patchworks of open and closed hunting areas. This means that hunting can become a game of property lines and fences, a situation that can be maddening. One landowner even hired a helicopter to drive elk onto his land for a client, a tactic that violated several state and federal laws. His approach naturally led to conflict with a neighboring rancher, who also had a client hunting tule elk at the time.

No special equipment is needed, and most any big-game caliber is more than adequate. I still

Tule elk tend to rest in the open more than other elk subspecies.

Mist-shrouded California oak ridges are prime tule elk habitat.

have some "hitchhikers" in the laces of my boots from that hunt, and I recommend you wear pants that shed prickly seeds easily. While mornings in tule elk country can be cool, a jacket is necessary only until sunrise, after which you can strip down to walking-weight clothes. Tule elk are usually easy to spot, but a good pair of binoculars is a must for judging trophy quality. You won't want to settle for just any bull when you go on this hunt.

Don't think this hunt is a gimme just because it typically occurs on private ranch land. The elk are by no means confined, and they will escape to thicker cover if they become suspicious you are hunting them. Equally likely, they may slip over a fence onto closed property, as they seem to know instinctively where they are off limits.

This hunt is different from anything else I have experienced in North America. It has all the challenge that accompanies any elk hunt, but with a more gentle and civilized twist. Taking a tule elk is likely to be a once-in-a-lifetime event, and it is a worthwhile and intriguing adventure. It also offers a unique perspective on rural California, truly a contrast to the average person's impression of that highly urbanized state.

TRULY TULE

Somewhere in the dark, far down in the valley, we hear him bugle in the impending dawn. The long, deep refrain is punctuated by several throaty terminal grunts, the distinctive sounds of a dominant bull. It appears that today the restless monarch is in our hunting territory.

I shake the sleep from my eyes, the long days and short nights having taken their toll. The predawn air is cold. On this hunt my wife and I have discovered that California's northern valleys can be oppressively hot during the daytime in August, but surprising cold develops overnight as the clear air yields up its heat. Each day we have been arising at a brutal 3:45 A.M. and retiring at 10:00 P.M., a schedule that results in so much lost sleep that even a midday nap is inadequate to atone for it.

Listening to the haunting bugle, I reflect on my unsuccessful tule elk hunt of last December. Hardly anyone who knows about tule elk can believe that my week-long effort was futile; indeed, I saw numerous bulls on that hunt. But I stuck with my plan and went home empty-handed rather than harvest an immature animal. I am beyond having to kill something on every hunt. The experience was well worth the effort, the final outcome aside.

Once more the bull's call echoes from the depths of Potter Valley, and our eyes strain in the slowly improving light to make out details in the alfalfa meadow far below. Several bulls across the valley answer the masculine challenge, but none make any move to contest the king.

We have been hunting this ridge every morning, and each day the bulls have greeted us with their eerie chorus. The biggest problem we have encountered is that of property lines. Some of the bulls have been on our ranch, but all the mature herd bulls have been holed up on adjacent properties on which we are forbidden to trespass. The lesser bulls are not even as good as the half-dozen I passed up last year. I can't help but begin to wonder on this last day of the hunt if perhaps my expectations have been too high for this particular subspecies.

This time I have booked additional days for this diminutive elk. Never before has Jeff Davis, my outfitter and guide, failed to help his hunter take a tule elk on a week-long hunt. Being now in my ninth day of hunting, I feel some degree of frustration, the kind that oppresses the spirit. I know that it will pass, however, so I rest in the assurance that better times are coming. The repeated messages from the giant tule bull down in the valley give me hope, a confident expectation that this may be the day I harvest one of these historic and beautiful creatures.

The game of chess comes to mind as I contemplate the bugling bull. Ours has been a challenging game of property lines, and so far the elk have won every match. The bull we seek is a master at making the right moves, but today he may have made a mistake.

Time, though, is still on the side of my opponent. If he can move out of our territory to the refuge of the adjacent ranch before shooting light, he may still elude us, despite our long hours of pursuit. The big ones always seem to thrive on challenges, on close calls, on near misses. They possess that magical mixture of luck and experience that defies even the best efforts to master them, more often than not. These maddening qualities are what make the hunt for such an animal all the more special, and all the more fulfilling when one brings the pursuit to a successful conclusion.

Right now, however, I am not thinking so much about a successful termination as I am of the frustrations I have faced. We glass intently toward the repeated sounds, ignoring the answers from lesser bulls. There are more bugles here than I have ever heard at one time before.

This gorgeous valley is a contemporary Garden of Eden, fertile to the very tops of its low mountains. It is a place of lush vineyards reminiscent of the valley of Eschol in Exodus, a land flowing with milk and honey—or at least with grapes and alfalfa. The gently rolling terrain is lush with green grass from the plentiful summer rains. The hills stairstep to elevations approaching several thousand feet, where dwarf oaks hang full of succulent acorns. The elk will retire shortly from their nighttime stay in the alfalfa patches to dine on the mast of the higher terrain and to find shade for refuge from the midday heat.

Forms approach us from the direction of the siren calls we have been hearing. Three in number, they are a half-mile distant now and in the growing light we are able with difficulty to determine that all are immature bulls. The assessment is confirmed as once more the stately call of the dominant bull emanates from the lowermost portion of the valley, and a dissonance of lesser bulls answers.

"He's got cows with him. He won't move out until they do," Jeff muses quietly. "We need to be sure exactly where he is and watch which direction they try to go, then we'll make our move."

"Sounds good to me. Can you see him yet?"

"Nope. Still too dark. There's a bunch of trees around that alfalfa field. They're probably under some of them."

Dawn is creeping in rapidly now, the glow of the rising sun not far below the mountains to our east. The sky is cloudless, and the pink horizon shows not a streak of overcast. I shiver from the morning cold and from excitement, giving rise to the uncomfortable realization that I could miss this bull, even if I get a chance to shoot, the way I'm shaking. I feel a little foolish donning a down parka in California in August, but I can't afford to be unsteady. The warmth of it feels incredibly good, and I begin settling down.

Jeff and I scan the noisy dark bottom for any sign of our quarry, and I also go through my usual preliminary check of my old Remington 700 .30-06. I learned long ago to leave nothing to chance, and I make sure the magazine has the normal complement of four Nosler 165-grain handloads and that the scope is cranked back to 4X. I stow the scope covers in case a quick shot is needed, being careful to place the rubber safety strap so that it doesn't interfere with working the bolt. All seems to be in order, so I return to glassing for elk.

The bugling is less frequent now, but the light is good enough to pinpoint the exact grove of elms from which the sounds are originating. I still can see nothing but tall grass and fence posts, but Jeff motions that he has the elk pegged. He points to the left of the largest tree in the grove.

"I see elk," he whispers. "In fact, I see our bull. He's a real dinger, too."

"Where? Where?" I ask excitedly, hoping to get my first view of a trophy tule elk. I scan the

Glassing scenic country for tule elk.

area, but I can't see the band. With a little help from Jeff, I finally discern what he has spotted. My heart leaps at the sight.

"He's a six-by-seven, nice crown points on at least one side," says Jeff. "The other side looks darn well palmated to me from here. Should be a keeper, to say the least. They aren't moving right now, just milling about and feeding. When the cows move, the big guy will follow, you can bet."

"Should we move up? They must be over a half-mile away."

"Wait for now. They could go right or left instead of coming up this way. Left, and they're over the fence and onto closed property."

"Don't they usually come up this way?"

"Usually. But you know how that goes."

Indeed. It seems that lately it always goes in favor of the animal. I am in a string of six defeats in my last seven hunts. Maybe today the tide will turn. "Hope springs eternal," goes the saying.

We wait. And wait some more. I smile ambivalently at Linda. She has been here before, too. She has seen me defeated more often than she has seen me win at this thing called hunting. She knows that losing this morning means that we go home without a tule bull, just like last time, despite long hours of toil and short nights of sleep. I can tell that she is praying fervently, as we have prayed together earlier. I am confident because I have an uncommon amount of resolve to make defeat a temporary condition, and because I trust God even when situations don't develop according to my personal plans. After all, I serve a trustworthy God and know that this game I play is not as important as I sometimes think.

The wait continues even as I converse silently with my Maker, finding a certain peace. I will taste victory today, whether or not the elk escapes. Finally, Jeff decides we should move closer. We will initiate a stalk to the present position of the elk, since they show a decided lack of intention in their movements. If the light gets much better we will be highly visible when we descend the ridge, in which case we might spook them and never get a shot.

We leave Linda in her high ringside seat to watch and we descend, staying as low as possible while monitoring the herd, which has now begun to move. We angle down to the fence bordering

closed property and begin a frontal approach, closing the distance to perhaps a quarter-mile.

A couple of hundred yards farther is a grove of giant oaks, cover for us in the open terrain. Crawling on hands and knees, we momentarily lose sight of our quarry in the deep grass. When we reach the trees, we hide behind one of the big trunks and immediately spy our objective. The entire herd is moving toward us, as if drawn by a magnet. I note with gratitude the welcome breeze in my face. There is no chance of our scent giving us away. For the elk to escape now it will take a monumental mistake on my part or a chance crossing of the fence out of range.

I rest my rifle in the crotch of the ancient oak and follow the big bull through my scope as he approaches. The cows are calling their timeless refrain, sounding for all the world like a flock of birds chirping. Several spike bulls are in the herd, youngsters of great potential. I have seldom seen a sight as inspiring or beautiful as the approach of this awesome group of animals, perhaps twenty in number, their gleaming coats resplendent in the growing light. Jeff laments that he neglected to bring his video camera, an instrument he had faithfully packed with him until this very moment in the hunt.

Every hunter knows that animals have an uncanny ability to sense danger, and tule elk are no different. Approximately one hundred yards away the whole herd stops, some primal sense having alerted them. They cannot see or smell us, but they discern something disquieting about the grove of trees ahead. A sleek cow interposes herself between the bull and me, so a shot is not possible.

The cows move forward nervously, and the bull moves up behind them. Just as I am beginning to fear that the creatures may shield my quarry until they are all out of range, the cows jaunt ahead and the bull is in the clear, a perfect broadside presentation. Placing the cross hairs just behind the shoulder, I squeeze off the shot.

The animal runs forward as I feel the recoil. Elk can absorb a lot of energy, so I work the bolt and place two more shots in the bull before he collapses into a lifeless heap. The remainder of the herd is off and running like oversize

Columbia black-tailed deer share tule elk habitat practically everywhere.

pronghorns, disappearing almost before we have time to notice.

The sun still has not peeped over the horizon as I approach the fallen monarch. I drop to my knees and thank God for the belated success, feeling a genuine gratitude at finally completing my quest to take one of these fine and unusual elk.

The old bull has numerous scars, in various stages of healing, on his face and neck, from fighting this year and in seasons past. These battle blemishes indelibly mark the creature as "truly tule," a typical example of the aggressive and tough subspecies. Jeff believes that this particular animal is "Old Broken Horn," the same bull I passed up on my first hunt because he had a broken antler. This year he is scarred but carries regal antlers that are undamaged, and the right one has gorgeous crown points whereas the left one is wonderfully palmated.

Linda arrives and helps with the picture session. Jim Guntley, a member of the family that owns the land on which we are hunting, helps us load our prize into his pickup. We drive down the serene valley toward the main ranch house where the animal will be processed, and a pervading joy fills me. Success is always sweet, but coming on the heels of failure it is particularly delicious.

Potter Valley is home to a harvest of blessings that people in many areas of our nation would envy. Plentiful agriculture provides for the needs of the ranching families as it has for a couple of centuries. I hope that the resident herd of tule elk have found a niche as well, supplying an aesthetic quality that would be missing without them. Wise use of this resource makes it valuable to the ranchers and returns to them a portion of their investment.

I am glad the tule elk has recovered sufficiently to allow hunters to experience the unique hunt these animals offer. Beautiful is this land, and beautiful is this animal. I am deeply thankful for being allowed to participate in the celebration of the tule elk's recovery.

Barren ground caribou. (Photo: courtesy of James L. Davis)

BARREN GROUND CARIBOU
(Rangifer tarandus granti)

The strong life that never knows harness;
The wilds where the caribou call;
The freshness, the freedom, the farness—
O God! how I'm stuck on it all.

—Robert W. Service (1874–1958), *The Spell of the Yukon*

The country of the caribou is a boundless land of varied faces, but most often it is covered with obscuring snow and forbids trespass to all but the most hardy. The barren ground caribou thrives in this environment, migrating in vast herds between the treeless tundra in summer and the boreal forest known as the taiga in the winter. Myriad distinct herds of this unique and beautiful cervid inhabit the north country, often with little mixing between populations despite marathon mass movements within their own territories. These migrations are so spectacular in scope that no other large North American mammal can match them, although doubtless the plains bison of old far outnumbered them at one time.

These creatures of the far north are circumpolar in distribution, being found across Scandinavia and the Russian Arctic as either wild or semidomesticated reindeer that for millennia have provided humans with an important source of food and clothing. In North America the animals are known as caribou, of which there are seven subspecies from a biologist's perspective: barren ground (*Rangifer tarandus granti*), central Canada barren ground (*groenlandicus*), woodland (*caribou*), Newfoundland (*terraenovae*), Peary (*pearyi*), the extinct Queen Charlotte Islands caribou (*dawsoni*), and the probably extinct east Greenland caribou (*eogroenlandicus*).

Hunters generally recognize six types, those found in the six caribou chapters of this book, which are subdivided by geographical location, body and antler size and type, hunting experience, and habitat preferences. Biological classification may be secondary to the hunter, and often our terminology doesn't exactly fit the scientific categories. The barren ground caribou of Alaska and the Yukon are larger than the more easterly central Canada barren ground subspecies of the Northwest Territories, and that is the major difference, both biologically and from a record-keeping perspective.

The Queen Charlotte Islands caribou deserves mention, at least by way of obituary, because it died out about 1910 for reasons that are not quite clear. Confined to the islands that bear that name, the animals were of body type and habits that apparently fitted the woodland caribou phenotype more closely than any other. Hunting pressure was not likely the total, or perhaps even a contributory, cause of their demise; habitat deterioration, change in climate, and loss of genetic diversity because of isolation may have been more important.

Caribou of all subspecies are uniquely adapted to life in a harsh landscape. Perhaps no other cervid tolerates such a diversity of terrain as the barren ground caribou. They are equally acclimated to windswept tundra and boreal forest, most of them in fact moving back and forth between the two in the course of their annual migrations. Many have said that these migrations are no more predictable than the cold Arctic wind, yet catching the migration has always been critical for the human inhabitants of the higher latitudes. Plentiful caribou ensured a time of abundance, whereas lack of caribou often meant starvation.

The caribou's pelage consists of hollow hairs packed tightly together for insulation, and it has always been prized as winter clothing and bedding. The insulating properties of the caribou's coat are far superior even to those of the spectacular hair on muskox hide. The caribou's hoofs are large, for walking on and digging in snow. They become harder and more concave in winter, and hair fills in between the hoofs as extra protection. On their forested winter range the animals dig extensively in the snow for lichens and winter greenery, that incessant and indispensable activity actually giving them their name. In the Micmac Indian tongue, the term *xalibu* means "the pawer." In the three similar tongues of the Inuit, Inuvialuit, and Inupiat, the term for caribou is about the same, being more or less *tuktu.*

The animals seem to prefer snowy conditions, and I have seen them stand for hours on an isolated patch of snow in summer. There the ceaseless wind and the temporary disconnection from vegetation gives some relief from the relentless insect assault they must bear during the brief warm season. The same warm coat that protects them in winter also traps summertime heat, so they often seek snow patches simply to cool off.

Caribou are so besieged by the incessant onslaught of mosquitoes and flies in summer that they can literally seem mad at times, running in vast herds in search of the wind or water that will provide respite. Their wanderings in summer consequently cover quite a bit more territory than fall and spring migrations.

After the long winter, one of the first plants to emerge in abundance on the tundra is the cottongrass (*eriophorum*), and its flowers are the most important food for caribou at that time of year. As the willows begin to green, the animals go on a feeding frenzy, devouring the tender young leaves, even in places where the only willow present is the ground-hugging Arctic variety. Diet in summer varies after that initial feast, with nutritious high-protein forbs of all types added to willow and dwarf birch leaves.

It is in winter that the metabolism of the caribou really shows its mettle. The animals are able to digest lichens, those curious, pale-colored plants that populate inhospitable terrain the world over. They wring from lichens a cascade of energy-rich carbohydrates that are indigestible by all other cervids and almost all other species. In areas of good winter range the animals actually gain weight on the strength of that extraordinary ability, though sufficient protein-bearing plants are also necessary.

Two big bounces and a stop on a makeshift landing strip.

Astounding Brooks Range country with lots of caribou.

There is a near absence of protein in lichens, meaning that the animals would rapidly become deficient in amino acids if they hadn't another special adaptation—the ability to recycle their waste urea, which is normally excreted. As far as I am aware, no other big-game animal is capable of that, except hibernating bears. It is the ability to utilize lichens, perhaps even more than their other physical adaptations, that makes the caribou uniquely suited for the harsh Arctic winter. Lichens are widely scattered on the tundra and the boreal forest where the animals often winter, allowing them a vast winter range much larger than their normal summer range—a situation opposite that of most other members of the deer family.

Most barren ground caribou bulls weigh three hundred to four hundred pounds when fully mature, with the cows averaging perhaps 25 percent smaller. In prime range in Alaska's interior, though, some bulls grow to gigantic size, reaching even seven hundred pounds, with antlers to match. On the Alaska Peninsula, the headgear grows equally huge, though body sizes there and in the Arctic regions are much smaller on average. During summer the massive antlers grow rapidly, often reaching mind-boggling proportions, the largest of any antlered animal in relation to body size.

Cow caribou are the only females of the deer family that routinely grow antlers. As fall and the annual rut approach, blood flow to the soft, nourishing velvet ceases, causing it to dry and begin to shed. Both bulls and cows may devour the strands of dehydrated flesh as they are rubbed away on the sparse vegetation, perhaps to preserve the hard-earned nourishment therein. Cows are usually bred for the first time at age three and a half years, but where conditions are ideal they may breed as early as one and a half years. Some 80 percent of cows are bred during the rut, and gestation is about 230 days. Cow caribou keep their antlers throughout the winter, allowing them weapons for competing with their own kind for the best feeding areas during the crucial period of embryo development, as well as providing a defense of last resort against predators. Cows generally shed their antlers in the spring, at calving time.

Bull caribou probably put more energy into their mating activity than any other member of

The August tundra is aflame with color.

the deer family. Some of that intensity is related to the attenuated nature of the rut, which lasts only a brief ten days on average. It peaks in southern Alaska on 1 October and in the Arctic on about 25 October. Sparring between dominant bulls often leads to fatal wounds. Commonly, the hard-working successful breeders enter the winter in a regrettably weakened state, making them vulnerable to marauding wolves prevalent in virtually all barren ground caribou range. Many of the older bulls may not survive to sire again the following year, since they may lose as much as a quarter of their body weight in the furious pursuit of cows. Like white-tailed deer, the animals' necks swell with the rut, and they may cease to eat altogether, so overwhelming is the impulse to mate.

Most barren ground caribou finish winter below the tree line, after which they migrate en masse back to the calving grounds on the treeless tundra. The pregnant cows lead the way, usually starting the trek in the growing light of April,

crossing treacherous icy rivers and a landscape still covered with snow. By early June they are ready to give birth, and almost all calves are born during a ten-day period. The average barren ground caribou calf weighs approximately fifteen pounds, although weights vary depending on the quality of forage the mother has consumed. Calves are highly vulnerable to predators such as wolves, grizzlies, and even golden eagles immediately after birth and for a few days thereafter. The short interval during which all birthing occurs is nature's common way of ensuring that the majority will survive, since the predators rapidly become gorged. Calves can walk within an hour of birth and run with the herd in a day or two, making them much more of a challenge for predators. Despite that, more than half of the calves succumb to predators during their first year. Those that survive increase in size by some 800 percent during the first half-year of life, entering winter weighing well over a hundred pounds. Youngsters who survive the first year have a life expectancy of up to seventeen years.

Alaska has some one million barren ground caribou at present, although some herds are shared with Canada. Thirty-three distinct Alaskan populations are recognized by biologists, ranging in size from a minuscule 73 animals to nearly a half-million. Two major herds lap over into the Yukon—the Fortymile herd (26,000 animals) and the Porcupine herd (152,000 animals). The Fortymile herd, despite robust numbers today, at one time wintered as far south as Whitehorse and became known as "the gold rush herd" because it was heavily exploited to feed the miners of the Klondike from 1897 into the early 1900s. It was once the largest herd in Alaska and the Yukon (a half-million animals in the 1920s), but overhunting, resulting from the encroachment of roads combined with heavy wolf predation, has caused the herd's numbers to remain low. The largest herd in Alaska today is the Western Arctic herd, a massive accumulation of 463,000 animals that, at this writing, is considered stable. Another important herd is the Mulchatna herd (220,000 animals), which has been rapidly increasing in numbers.

People have hunted the barren ground caribou for millennia, and the ancients harvested them with primitive snares and weapons. A common method was to construct a fence astride a migration route, drive the animals into a corral or a snare, and kill them. Today the modern rifle and the ubiquitous snowmobile have reduced the challenge to subsistence hunters, but finding the right bull and the right concentration of animals is still a formidable task for the sport hunter.

Judging trophy quality when looking at bull caribou is not easy, especially if there are large numbers of animals. In addition to the usual spread and mass, one must look individually at three separate aspects of the animal's antlers: shovel, bez points, and top points. The shovel is the broad, flat plate of antler that grows off one (or both) of the main beams just above the nose and is always oriented vertically between the nose and the bez, or front, points. Ideally, it should cover most of that area with a wide and unbroken expanse when viewed from the side. The most desirable trophies have double shovels nearly complete on both antlers, but most often the largest shovels are single and are accompanied by only a single slender point, or occasionally no point at all, on the opposite

antler. The bez point is almost always a single shaft off each main beam that extends forward up to two feet and broadens into a flat palmation near its terminus above the shovel, where there may be a highly variable number of points. The bez should have good palmation and numerous points, as well as length that extends at least as far forward as the shovel. Top points should be numerous and long, and the best antlers find them sitting magnificently atop a heavy and expansive set of main beams. Minor considerations are the back points and, in rare cases, extra front points that come off the main beams between the bez and top points. Almost never does a caribou bull have everything, and invariably some aspect of the spectrum is deficient or missing altogether. When one finds that extremely unusual animal with everything, it is the happy combination that makes for an extraordinary trophy, perhaps even a new world record. Most hunters will pay any price in physical exertion to harvest such a bull.

The key to that remarkable creature is to find where the most caribou are traveling—"catching the migration." That elusive trick is often frustrating, and rare is the experienced hunter who has never "missed the migration." Endless bare tundra awaits, with only a stray cow, or nothing at all, as payment for weeks of planning and long days of grueling effort. If everything is right, however, bulls will be everywhere, and one passes up animals that would be unbelievable trophies to hunters elsewhere. Don't pass up too many, though, because even the most concentrated migrations eventually end. Being too choosy can mean coming back next year for the bull of your dreams, a smarter and perhaps a trifle less discriminating hunter. If one wants a grand representative bull, that shouldn't happen. But if you are looking only for a top-ten bull, be prepared to return again and again and to inspect thousands of animals before finally finding one with everything.

Hunting caribou is still, for the most part, carried out on foot, although horseback and snowmobile hunts are the norm for some subspecies. In Alaska, the hunter and his gear are typically dropped off in good caribou country for a week or more of intensive hunting, a guide being optional there. I have always used a guide wherever practical, because I prefer to have the advantage of an experienced pair of eyes, a knowledge of the terrain, and an extra pair of hands after the kill. In the Yukon use of a guide is mandated by law for nonresident big-game hunters.

Once you spot the appropriate animal, it becomes a matter of getting into position to make the shot. That can involve hours of hiking, or it may be as simple as waiting at a strategic crossing until your quarry arrives. In like fashion, the distance one must shoot can vary tremendously, depending on whether one is trying to catch up to a moving animal or to take one that is resting, feeding, or approaching. Most of my caribou kills have been fairly short shots of a hundred yards or less. Making a stalk on a caribou to a reasonably close distance in most tundra is not difficult if circumstances are right.

Lean on the guide or outfitter for advice when choosing equipment. I recommend at a minimum sixteen-inch-high rubber boots for the soggy tundra, and, if you anticipate numerous fordings (as is usual in Alaska), wear hip boots. Good rain gear is a necessity, though a knee-length raincoat will suffice with hip boots. I have seldom hunted caribou in the north country when it didn't rain, although the occasional bluebird day turns up. Any rifle of caliber .270 or better is more than adequate. Binoculars are absolutely necessary for judging trophy quality, and a spotting scope is useful for finding a particularly special animal.

The land where the barren ground caribou calls is enchanting and addicting. I never cease to relish the prospect of one more hunting trip there. I look forward to the riot of color on miniature tundra plants, the varied fall hues that paint the landscape in late August and early September in most parts of the animal's range. Hunting caribou, unlike most other North American big game, is an ideal outing for a group of compatible hunters. It is an experience that no hunter should miss, and if you haven't tried it, I recommend you begin planning now.

SUPER CUB SAFARI

As a pilot, my mind is functioning at maximum capacity as we descend into unknown territory somewhere north of the Arctic Circle. The pilot of the vintage Boeing 727 is doubtless riveted to his instruments, the dense fog over Kotzebue, Alaska,

demanding his utmost attention. I wonder whether the airport has a modern instrument landing system, or if we are doing an old-fashioned nondirectional beacon approach. I abhor the thought of plowing a long, hot furrow in the permafrost of the Arctic my first time here, so I wish the pilot well and pray for divine assistance. I mention none of these thoughts to my hunting partner, Eddie Smith. He is the quintessential nonflier, and with a glance I can see that his level of terror is already off the scale.

The runway suddenly breaks into view, almost simultaneous with touchdown, and the giant bird lumbers to a halt with a deafening roar of its reverse thrusters, with only yards to spare. Before we can celebrate, we are deplaning, descending treacherous wet steps to the tarmac. The excitement of being here soon drives the apprehension of the approach to this Arctic airport from our minds.

This is my first foray into the far north country. I have flown the polar route a couple of times to Europe and to a duty station in Vietnam many years ago, but never have I touched this remote world of long and dark winters, brief summers, exotic Eskimos, and endless tundra. As I enter Kotzebue's tiny terminal building, I review the things I have read. I recall television documentaries as well, most of them romanticizing the invincible Arctic, so hostile and forbidding to man. I have a suspicion of such fantasies and can't wait to experience the region for myself.

Life in this land is reputed to be vibrant and robust, bright and colorful; on the other hand, the land itself appears dark, colorless, and seemingly lifeless, except for the winter aurora borealis in the sky overhead. Plentiful life and abundant death—the contrast is nowhere more clear than here in the high north. Even the ground is a medium of contrast, the green facade of late summer giving little indication of the permanently frozen soil only inches below. The surface loam supports all the living creatures here by giving life to edible plants, the bottom of the food chain. When the earth freezes it is an obstacle to life, even man, who exists here only with difficulty. Even modern structures slowly sink into an icy tomb unless special construction techniques are used.

We are here to hunt the majestic Brooks Range, a region of low mountains worn bald by freezing and thawing on ground bereft of vegetation. Barren ground caribou are plentiful in the Brooks Range, but finding a truly big bull can be a challenge of the first order.

Bush pilot Rick Herscher will drop us off in a mountain valley an hour from town by Super Cub. The weather is problematic, but a break is in the forecast for tomorrow. The days of August are still more than twenty hours long, so flying until almost midnight is an option, if necessary.

Kotzebue is well known for its polar bear hunting via Super Cub, which flourished from the 1950s until 1972, when Alaska shut down the industry entirely before the Marine Mammal Protection Act came into being. I am no fan of airplane hunting, but many of the stories are filled with the excitement and danger of flying small, ill-equipped aircraft over endless pack ice, then landing to make the final stalk. I am aware that in 1955 alone, two planes, complete with pilot and hunter, were lost forever on the ice, and I have to wonder about the dangers to modern Super Cub hunters seeking caribou. I pose the question to my host, and his answer is unnervingly inconclusive. If the weather breaks tomorrow, we will find out.

A cloudless new day dawns, with beams of sunlight dancing off the cold Chukchi Sea at our doorstep. I believe that I can see the white line of the pack ice to our northwest, though Eddie and the others are convinced it is only a mirage, a *novaya zemleya,* common in these latitudes, caused by the prismatic effect of the atmosphere and the angle of the light. Perhaps. While Rick motors into town by ATV to prepare the Super Cub, we watch native fishermen reaping a bounty

Caribou moss, the animal's staple food, abounds.

Barren ground caribou, Alaska, August 1984.

from the northernmost run of salmon in the world, filling their boat almost to sinking. We nevertheless chafe at the wait and climb the tundra hill behind camp to take pictures and satisfy the urge to explore.

At the sound of the plane's engine, we scramble back down the grade, ready to load our gear. The big red craft alights on the sand and coasts to a stop, its enormous tundra tires giving it the appearance of a hound dog pup that needs to grow into its feet. The engine dies with a final cough, and the canopy springs open. Rick beckons us to load up.

Eddie will fly first, to a location to our north and east near the mysterious spine of the Brooks Range, where we will spend a week out of touch with civilization. The takeoff is spectacular and I watch in awe, the flying sand stinging my skin, as the airplane gains altitude and disappears. Within two hours the machine returns, and now it is my turn. The touchdown is complicated, however, by a treacherous crosswind, and as the pilot wheels the aircraft around it unexpectedly noses over in the sand, the prop and engine both halting with sickening suddenness.

Rick leaps from the plane, hacksaw in hand, and rights the craft. He then inspects the bent prop tips, both of which are bowed backward about six inches. He begins to hack away at the bent metal but midway through recalls that a friend in Kotzebue has a spare propeller, the only one around. We remove the prop while Rick sends a man to purchase the spare. Soon the engine is purring again, and, gear loaded, we are off. I cradle my .30-06 Remington in my hands as we fly.

There are caribou here, all right. Rick flies low over a herd only a few miles from where he parked Eddie, and I note that most are still in velvet, although one huge bull has freshly scraped it away, leaving blood-tinged antlers shining prominently against the dark green tundra. We may hike this way tomorrow, and I note a prominent landmark for future reference. *Foolish,* I think, *these nomads could be anywhere within a hundred miles by tomorrow.*

Only now do I learn that Rick lost his tail wheel when he landed with my friend, and he replaced it in makeshift fashion to complete his runs. A pile of boulders marks the safe touchdown zone, and I experience my first tundra tire landing, three big bounces and a sudden stop. There is no damage this time, though Eddie is here to greet me and the terror in his eyes shows it was a hairy landing, at least in appearance.

Camp is a scant hundred yards from our improvised landing strip. Rick advises that we should minimize our work by hunting close to camp. The wandering animals roam endlessly, and one is bound to come by eventually. We agree, and off he roars, leaping from the ridgetop like a daredevil, the tiny craft suspended momentarily in the stiff breeze, then slowly gaining altitude and speed. Suddenly he is gone, leaving us amid vast grandeur and absolute silence.

After setting up, we ascend the ridge to do some glassing. A huge bull moose stands nearby, so photos are naturally in order. Dall rams adorn a lofty peak two miles distant, quarry for a later time. Caribou are abundant, but no good bulls are in evidence. We rejoice in the beauty and plan no hunting for today. The hour is already too late, even though same-day airborne hunting for caribou is permissible. We have plenty of time on our hands, and we slow down to revel in the thrilling beauty of the Brooks Range.

As we cook our freeze-dried supper, hydrated with water from a stream deep in the valley, we marvel at the lushness of the tundra. Arctic willow is particularly successful here, especially in the lowest elevations, and the leaves have already turned autumn gold. More astonishing are the variety of low plants—caribou moss, lichens, and liverworts—that are as plentiful and colorful as a hardwood canopy in October far to the south.

Dark is a relative term, and tonight barely achieves that status at all. I am a light sleeper under the best of circumstances, but particularly so in unaccustomed surroundings. There is an interlude of partial darkness, but not enough for me to achieve sound sleep. I arise early and begin preparing breakfast.

In good weather and visibility, getting lost in this mountain range is virtually impossible. We will separate for the day, Eddie opting to walk a pristine valley that trails off to our north; I plan to hike along the ridge to our west. We will not shoot a caribou today unless it is close to camp, but we want to explore and get the lay of the land. Wanderlust overwhelms our patience and we set out, pack and rifle on our backs.

The wind is picking up but the sky remains deep blue. The gray mountains around me are steep, their tops rounded in typical Brooks Range fashion. The moose we spotted earlier has disappeared, and for a half-mile I see no large animals of any kind. Walking is good on the rocky areas, but inevitably I must traverse low, flat places that are extremely wet and dotted with tundra tussocks. The deceitful weeds appear to offer firm footing, but I quickly discover that it's an illusion. The treacherous globular plants rotate just enough to throw one into the muck, no matter how you place your foot. Deep willows abound and scratch noisily against my pack as I pass. I wonder if the absence of game is a result of my amateurish ambling.

Without warning a small caribou bull bolts from the deep brush, rising effortlessly to the top of a small knoll not forty yards away. After recovering from the start, I pause to watch. The antlers appear at first enormous, but I have learned enough about judging caribou trophies to know better. The covering of copious velvet gives the illusion of mass. The few small top points, the short bez points, and the rudimentary shovel give away the fact that he is a youngster. Nevertheless the creature is beautiful as he stares at me with cowlike eyes, rightly considering me no threat. I continue walking while the bull stays just ahead, as if leading me onward, for a mile or more.

Breaking out of the willows and marsh, I find firm footing on the higher rocky ridge. I marvel at the flat rock which, peeling away from the mountain in layers over the centuries, has formed gigantic heaps reminiscent of a glacial moraine. Amid the jumble a solid spire rises, and in a sheltering crevice I find sunny refuge from the wind. From here I can see for miles, so I elect to wait, watch, and lunch.

I am tired from lack of sleep, and the warm sunshine draws me irresistibly into a nap. When I awake, the sun seems hardly to have moved, but I am aware that the temperature is dropping. I resume my glassing and marvel again at how such a vast land can have so few visible specimens of animal life. But I know that the lack of life may be an illusion, so I redouble my glassing.

Far off to the west, beside a rushing stream, I catch sight of a telltale movement. Keeping my glasses glued to the spot, I bring the scene into sharp focus. A grizzly. The first one I have ever spotted in the wild, in fact. Before long I have spotted three tiny cubs. *Triplets must be rare, especially in these extreme climes.* The mother is lying on her back, rolling in the sunny meadow less than a mile away, while the cubs frolic around her. For at least an hour I watch, completely enthralled.

The return to camp is inauspicious, and I see no game except the ever-present Dall sheep on the mountain across the way. Eddie has had his own encounter with a grizzly, also a sow, accompanied by a pair of half-grown cubs. After wading the rushing stream barefoot to preserve his boots, he had walked a couple of miles upstream. A very agitated female bear had faked a charge, roaring and carrying on like a mad bull before disappearing in the willows. Eddie had hastily chambered a round,

but luckily no shot had been necessary. Decent caribou bulls, however, were noticeably absent.

We are out of water, so one of us must make the long descent to the creek. I volunteer to do the honors while my partner handles camp duties. This time I will do more than fill canteens; I will bring back enough to last a few days. Shouldering my rifle, lest I encounter a bear, I head downhill with a collapsible plastic jug.

On reaching the creek and stooping to fill my container, I am startled out of my wits by a resounding snort from across the stream. My first thought is of a charging bear. Relief floods my mind as I spot the source of the commotion, a huge caribou bull that has caught my scent as he ascends the ridge across the creek. Sizing up the animal I am almost paralyzed by the sheer mass of the velvet-covered antlers—tall, wide, absolutely incredible. I could never find another so grand, I instantly decide, and even though this is only the

Arctic ground squirrels are constant camp companions.

second day, I will take this one. I chamber a round and make an offhand shot of forty yards. The giant bull goes down almost without another step.

My partner descends the hill in record time, sure that a bear has eaten me, rifle and all. He arrives shouting and out of breath. Both of us stand in respectful admiration of a superb trophy, the velvet virtually unbroken, towering tops, great bez points, and a magnificent shovel. I am satisfied with everything about the kill except the fact that it comes so early in the hunt.

Supper can wait while we get a few pictures and do the necessary caping and quartering. It will be quite a bit of work moving the meat and antlers, but the fresh meat is a welcome addition to our kitchen. We hope fervently that a grizzly will not attempt to claim our portion, though we would relish the opportunity to see one dine on the unusable carcass that remains.

Hunting is finished for the next several days, as high winds, rain, and occasional sleet dominate the weather. Frustration builds in my hunting partner with the passing of the days inside the tent. We spend time reminiscing about past hunts, dreaming about future ones, and gratefully drinking our hot chocolate to the last drop. There is ample time to rest and relax, and I must remind myself that I am here to do exactly that. Still, the hours begin to drag as inactivity takes a toll. The constant patter of rain against the tent becomes almost maddening.

While we are half asleep in our bags, there comes another of those unexpected snorts, like that of a rottweiler encountered while jogging, a little surprise mixed with unmistakable threat. This is at least the third time I have been so rudely jolted, but now it sounds like the real thing. We tumble from the tent, chambering rounds as we emerge into the rain, and in amazement we find ourselves face to face with a huge sow grizzly, right in the middle of our camp. Two half-grown cubs, perhaps the same ones Eddie saw a few days ago, are snorting like ponies, sounding anything but cuddly. We shout,

and the trio beat a hasty exit while we keep our rifles at ready. Soon they disappear up the steep slope to our south, and we return to our tent. Luckily, the bears apparently failed to smell the caribou meat, which was downwind in the stiff breeze.

Eddie finally gets his opportunity at a great caribou. Like mine, his wanders right into the vicinity of camp, a very nice bull much like mine. We have seen few acceptable bulls, but we got the two best, and both very near camp. There's nothing like following the advice of someone as experienced as Rick Herscher.

By now I am beginning to worry that our retrieval might be impossible for a while. The high wind refuses to die, and the showers seem endless. The expected day of our pilot's return comes, and still there seems precious little hope. Late in the day, however, we finally hear the drone of the long-awaited engine. Suddenly, two planes come into sight and touch down on the ridgetop.

Rick has recruited help from the Kotzebue friend who sold him the propeller. The break in the weather is too brief to retrieve the camp in only one airplane, so we will leave together. We are ecstatic as we load our gear and trophies.

In the back country of Alaska, big antlers are hauled out roped onto the wing struts. I have never seen anything like it, and it looks downright dangerous. But it's the only way, I'm told, so we pitch in and help secure everything.

The familiar landscape looks so peaceful and beautiful as I view it from the small craft. This perspective is far different from the one I have known for the past week. I have become accustomed to viewing the world in its microcosmic sense, so this panoramic view astounds me. The farthest point to which I walked from camp passes underneath us seconds after liftoff. I can't escape the thought that we have lost something with our efficiency and ingenuity, something that has left us woefully out of touch with an important aspect of ourselves. Thank you, Lord, for that reminder.

Mountain caribou. (Photo: courtesy of James L. Davis)

MOUNTAIN CARIBOU
(Rangifer tarandus caribou)

Hunting such top-of-the-world country as the ranges of the Mountain Caribou
is a fine place for any man to find out just how good he is. . . .
Such hunting entails hard hiking, all uphill or downhill.
It necessitates breathing rarefied air, to which the lungs at lower elevations are not
accustomed. It involves sudden and violent changes of temperatures,
long distances, and hours far longer than those accustomed to. . . .

—Clyde Ormond, *Hunting Our Biggest Game,* 1956

Mountain caribou are the largest of the family, with big bulls frequently topping 400 pounds, and animals as large as 600 pounds recorded in the Yukon. Their antlers are much more massive but of less overall length than those of the barren ground varieties, though exceptional trophies may exceed in size the largest of barren ground caribou. Perhaps because hunters take fewer mountain caribou, the latest Safari Club International record book shows that only one mountain caribou scores over 500, that being the top animal at 512 and some change. In the barren ground category, the first eleven animals score over 500 points. Hunting mountain caribou can be akin to hunting mountain sheep, as Clyde Ormond has observed. The habitat is what makes the difference in the animal's behavior and in the hunting.

The record-book classification of mountain caribou is nowhere found in current scientific literature, which instead designates the subspecies by the confusing term "woodland caribou." The term "woodland" is the common name for *Rangifer tarandus caribou,* found throughout the subarctic regions of North America. They are actually one cosmopolitan species to the scientist. To the hunter, this latter nomenclature conjures up visions of the abundant caribou of Newfoundland and the endangered animals of the Selkirk Range of Idaho and adjacent Canada. In actuality, hunting organizations use the designation "mountain" to separate the animals geographically. For our purposes "mountain caribou" includes the "woodland" animals of the Yukon, the Mackenzie Mountains of the Northwest Territories, as well as those of northern British Columbia. There is some undeniable artificiality and no doubt a degree of indisputable overlap in both camps, but there is also much to set apart the habitat in which these huge caribou live. Some of their habits are remarkably different from those of the barren ground subspecies, and the hunting is a different experience. One typically uses horses to hunt these creatures, and to my knowledge mountain caribou are the only members of their race widely sought in that fashion.

There is some roll to the terrain in most caribou country, but where mountain caribou dwell the vertical nature of the topography can be daunting, with elevations ranging between 3,000 and 7,000 feet. Don't expect to ride a mountain horse up the steep incline, either, once you spot the bull caribou you want. Much of the ground is too precipitous, and the final stalk will be by means of the hunter's own two feet.

Antler configuration also distinguishes the mountain caribou in the eyes of record-keeping organizations. Under the SCI system, the southern Yukon caribou are classified as the mountain subspecies south of the Stewart and Yukon Rivers, south of latitude 66 degrees, and west of the Mackenzie River, the Great Slave Lake, and the Slave River. All caribou from British Columbia, and all those in Alberta except the northeast corner, are mountain caribou. By the Boone and Crockett system, the boundaries are more complicated, but there is little practical difference. The animals may unavoidably overlap with barren ground caribou in certain localities, such as the Hart River and Bonnet Plume herds. At the boundary with the larger Porcupine herd of barren ground caribou, though, the dividing line is much more effective at separating the subspecies.

In the Yukon, the mountain caribou occurs in twenty-three separate herds, classified mainly on the basis of their traditional wintering grounds. All of those herds now seem to be secure. Four of the herds lap over into the Northwest Territories, and four are shared with British Columbia; ever-improving management cooperation exists between the respective game agencies. There are a total of about 35,000 mountain caribou in these herds, which range in size from 200 to 10,000 animals. The largest is the Redstone herd, which is one of the populations the Yukon shares with the Northwest Territories, and hunting is mainly from that side of the border.

My own mountain caribou came from the Nahanni population, another of the herds that sit astride the Yukon/Northwest Territories border. This vigorous herd consists of some 2,000 animals that at times range back and forth across the border.

For management purposes, the number of available animals may seem paramount, but herd composition is also of utmost importance in determining how many may be harvested from a given location. A healthy herd will have a minimum of 30 bulls (and preferably 40 to 50) and 30 calves per 100 cows. Male caribou suffer a higher mortality than females, including a somewhat puzzling higher mortality for male calves. Highly stressful adult male rut activity, followed by poor health after the rut, contributes to heavier predation on bull caribou, both by wolves and grizzly bears. In an average year, resident and nonresident sport hunters together kill fewer than 300 caribou out of a herd of over 30,000 in the Yukon, a minuscule figure when compared with mortality from predators and less selective native subsistence hunters. Nevertheless, hunting can have a detrimental effect on some herds, and from time to time closing the hunt for certain herds is necessary. Usually that comes about because of a skewed sex ratio, which can make selective hunting of bulls not sustainable.

Predators other than grizzlies and wolves can take a toll. These include black bear, lynx, and wolverine, particularly during the calving period in spring. Moose provide an alternative source of food for major predators and can take pressure off the caribou; in addition, moose do not compete with caribou for the same foods.

Mountain caribou live in high alpine and subalpine areas from spring calving in May until the rut in October. There they pass much of their time on windswept ridges and open snowfields, mainly to avoid insects and the heat. Summer is doubtless the time of greatest stress for caribou. These cooler summer areas are often irregular plateaus that harbor stands of subalpine willow and shrubs, as well as higher areas with sedges and tussocks. The October rut is the end of the season in the summer range, and the calving season in May marks the springtime return to that type of high habitat.

To pass the winter, mountain caribou migrate to forested valleys, mainly of white and black spruce with a moss and shrub understory. Unlike the barren ground caribou, their migration is thus altitudinal rather than long distance. Mountain caribou are quite faithful to a home range, and cows tend to return to the same calving area year after year. Radio collar tracking studies have demonstrated range fidelity, which is now also confirmed by DNA fingerprinting technology. This technique may eventually give insight into historical distribution patterns and herd identity, and may help determine the minimum size of viable populations.

As it does for most ungulates, winter may determine the strength and numbers in a herd, although caribou tolerate extreme cold better than summer drought or a late spring. Mountain caribou instinctively seek out those areas of least snow accumulation for their winter range. When snow collects to depths much greater than two feet, the animals may run a negative calorie balance when forced to dig for ground lichens, which constitute more than three-fourths of their winter diet. Winter evergreen shrubs make up 10 to 15 percent of the diet. Only a small fraction of their food consists of grasses and sedges, but that small proportion is extremely important as an irreplaceable source of protein. Moss in the diet indicates habitat deterioration, as it is less nutritious, and under normal circumstances caribou seldom eat much of it. Mountain caribou generally occur at much lower levels than the carrying capacity of the habitat, due to both natural factors and human

Mountain caribou. Yukon Territory, October 1989.

predation. Natural mortality is several times that caused by hunters.

Management options vary with the relative abundance of the animals and the composition of the herd, and managers consider all factors in setting the harvest. The target percentage for the allowable harvest is 2 to 3 percent of the adult caribou in the herd. Many herds are remote, however, and there is seldom a harvest at all. Those near roads are harvested more heavily. In the Yukon, restrictions on subsistence hunters are voluntary, but the natives generally cooperate with biologists when herd populations are clearly declining.

Wolf control can also be of great value when judiciously applied. Preserving critical winter habitat and restricting access to those areas are extremely important in certain areas. Logging is not incompatible with good caribou numbers but can be disastrous when roads traverse areas the animals use heavily in winter, or when the sheltering overstory is removed completely or indiscriminately.

The best hunting for mountain caribou is during the rut in October, when you can sometimes spot the animals from miles away in the high basins above timberline where they tend cows. The largest animals invariably show up during these cold, late hunts, which can take place in considerable wind and deep snow. It is a time for your best woolens and rain gear, since long hours in the saddle may be necessary to find an acceptable bull. For horseback hunts I like rubberized rain pants of the bib type, the only arrangement I've found that will keep the rear end dry on a wet day. A waterproof parka of Gore-Tex or similar material is good for the October hunts. Early in the season be sure to take a good rubberized raincoat.

Rubber boots are standard for hunting in Canada and are adequate even on late hunts. Wear two pairs of wool socks over polypropylene or silk liners, and you will be able to climb most any mountain almost as well as when wearing leather boots. Your feet will get wet from perspiration and condensation, but wet and warm is better than wet and cold. Take along extra socks and change them when you stop at midday for tea. And if your feet start getting cold, get off your horse and walk a couple of miles. If that doesn't work, change socks again.

Despite the mountain caribou's larger size, the same rifle setup required for other caribou is perfectly adequate. I used 165-grain Nosler partition bullets in my .30-06. I like a bipod attachment, a setup that has repeatedly worked well for me.

A frustrated hunter after a missed opportunity.

The land of the mountain caribou is breathtaking, with snowcapped mountains in every direction. To hunt there is indescribably pleasurable, a privilege we take for granted at great peril. To awaken on a crisp, frosty morning and gaze off into the distance at a band of these matchless monarchs in a high mountain basin is pure joy. Nobody should miss the experience.

TOUGH HORSES TAME THE YUKON

The numbing October cold of the Yukon penetrates my damp clothing like a thousand needles, driven relentlessly by the ceaseless wind. Snow falls horizontally, and a thick, icy fog rolls over the mountaintop like a chamois blanket, cutting visibility to mere yards. I button my flannel shirt to the top, blocking some of the stabbing cold, as I comment to my partner, Bob Walker, that we might freeze if our guide doesn't arrive soon with the horses and our cold-weather gear.

Today's long climb after a trophy caribou bull is over, ended by a bad shot, a complete miss that is one of the low points of my long hunting career. I feel chilled to the bone now, both physically and spiritually. This is only the first day of a backcountry excursion that should have me feeling like soaring above the clouds. It is hard to believe that I could have shot so poorly.

One day ago, I nailed the bull's-eye neatly from the bench at our base camp cabin while test firing my old Remington 700 .30-06. Today I might as well have been shooting a basketball at my quarry. I reflect on author Frank Forester's assessment of American shooting abilities in the past century, now a part of classic literature and hauntingly accurate for my current state of affairs. In Georgia, we seldom kill anything that we don't have plenty of time to appraise, to size up, to evaluate. We don't fire a shot without a solid rest from a tree stand, except in rare instances. Forester said of my part of the world: "The nature of the country precludes the possibility of long shots, since an animal can rarely be seen sixty yards off in the dense forests. . . . The same dense covert gives facility for stealing on game, and shooting it at rest . . . in that form which is best suited to a very sure, deliberate aim."

Maybe that quotation puts a 150-year-old finger on the reason that this hunter sometimes has insurmountable difficulty shooting offhand. Forester's description sums up the way things go back home, although we do most often "steal" on game from a tree stand nowadays. Even though I've taken dozens of mountain and plains animals over the years, I'm never comfortable without a good rest, and I'm dissatisfied if the animal is on the move. If he's on the run my chances decline to roughly one in a hundred, and worse the farther away he is.

The gigantic trophy mountain caribou bull I missed only a few minutes ago was perhaps a hundred yards off, a gimme shot for me with a good rest. But the varmint had been galloping around like some animal in a rodeo, chasing cows all over the snow-covered high country. There had been no possibility of a rest on the barren and treeless mountaintop we had climbed. Even the few rocks were buried in snow. I had also been trying to catch my breath and maintain my composure. I have some excuses, but none of them change the fact that I missed.

A shooting blunder is impossible to hide. The whole herd is off to the races, and this time there is no second chance. Bob gazes silently down the slope, perhaps wondering if he is hunting with a total incompetent. I sense the scrutiny, but I feel no condemnation from him. Rather I sense a certain measure of understanding and sympathy.

There is a smoking-hot assemblage of caribou tracks plummeting straight away from us down the mountain, disappearing into the thick fog. Our guide, Ted Neufeld, arrives breathless with the trio of tough mountain horses we had left tethered a thousand feet below, hurrying because of the intense cold he knows we face. His beard is caked with ice born of condensation from his breath and perhaps perspiration, but he is beautiful to behold as he materializes out of the fog. In the creeping chill I had envisioned his losing us and eventually having to pack our frozen carcasses back to camp. We rummage for gloves and parkas, then plunge down the mountain after the retreating herd, hopeful that the trail might lead to another opportunity at the monarch of the band, a giant bull with towering tines and a double shovel.

An hour passes, and then reality sets in. The herd is gone. Their tracks lead steadfastly toward the nearby border of the Northwest Territories, where we cannot legally follow, and we must

A spot of tea after a morning of cold and snow.

A reward after the day's hunt will be enjoying a fish supper thanks to Bob Walker's catch of fresh grayling.

abandon the chase. That grand bull will likely die of old age not many weeks hence, his energy sapped by rutting activity. He will not be immortalized by the taxidermist; rather, the king will wind up as carrion or easy prey for wolves. That thought arrives like a bearer of bad news, and it seems that the three of us come to the same dismal conclusion at virtually the same instant.

A tight grove of snow-covered balsam firs beckons with a promise of shelter and rest. Here we can start a fire, rest the tired horses, and brew a pot of tea while preparing ourselves for the day we must complete. Here there is shelter from the falling snow and refuge from the cold wind. We will survive this adversity, by God's grace, and emerge victorious as well, I hope. With full stomachs and a short nap behind us, we continue on through the high country.

We are hunting prime mountain caribou habitat, the Nahanni Range that splits the border between the Yukon and the Northwest Territories of Canada. The base camp for this late-season hunt consists of a comfortable cabin on Hyland Lake, where Bob and I are quartered in a heated wall tent adjacent to the main building. As the day draws to a close, we ride back into camp to the smell of savory stew. Terry Wilkinson, outfitter in this area, is also guiding and is our cook as well this night.

Terry tries to anticipate the needs of his hunters, and I have mentioned that I like salads. This is the only remote camp I can remember that nightly serves up garden fresh greens and firm, plump tomatoes. The food in fact can't be better. I eat in silence, my contemplative mood probably a result of simple embarrassment. I find myself toying with various excuses for my poor marksmanship. None seem to fit, so I decide to put the episode out of mind and concentrate on tomorrow. Instead of a first-day bull I'll have to prepare for more hard work and more cold days in the saddle. I can't help but think that what could have been an easy hunt may now turn out to be an ordeal.

We awake after a good night's sleep to a clear, blue sky. The pervasive clouds of the past couple of days have dissipated, leaving the Yukon atmosphere crisp and clean, a fitting complement to the elegant snowcapped peaks. Today we will ride south along the headwaters of the Hyland River, beginning where it leaves the big lake at our door. We bask in the warm sun, though the cold still refuses to yield more than a few degrees to its rays. Ten miles of walking and riding reveal only one band of caribou, tucked away in a high mountain basin to our north. The dominant bull displays less mass and length than we are seeking.

I am weary as we reach camp once more, and not a little bit discouraged. It gets dark early in October, and we ride back into camp under the cast of the northern lights, the apparition weaving and bobbing high overhead like some celestial fireworks show. It is no comfort to learn that the other hunter in camp, Roger Tyler, has also missed a caribou, giving me some depressed company. But Roger is a bow hunter, and to me the miss is entirely excusable, though he doesn't see it that way. The positive news is that no damage has been done to the animals, and there are still plenty out there.

There is a well-known weather phenomenon called radiational cooling that occurs on clear nights, the absence of an insulating blanket of clouds causing the earth to yield up much of its daytime heat. Though the temperature in the tent declines drastically when the fire in the stove dies, we are warm in our bags. Morning finds me reluctant to leave my cocoon, but Terry mercifully starts a roaring fire in the shepherd's stove. Soon the warmth drives me from my bag for another day of hunting in the frigid wilderness.

Terry's breakfasts are as hearty and filling as his suppers, and with stomachs full of Canadian bacon and pancakes we depart in yet another direction, northwest along the upstream bank of the lake. An icy mist hangs low over the lake, and open water is shrinking daily. We will spend three more days seeking caribou here before moving the entire camp to the road, where Terry has another base of operations. I want to take my bull here if at all possible, so we will hunt hard.

As we ride out, we spot a band of caribou high on a mountainside, one of them a decent bull, though Ted is unsure he's a taker. We elect to leave them and continue up the cavernous valley. We check a band undoubtedly out of our reach in the Northwest Territories and naturally find the best bull we have seen just across the border. We spend much time climbing to a remote basin that seems

Darkness looms as we pack the kill out of snowy country.

promising, but there is nothing of interest within. It's now getting late, so we retrace our tracks back toward camp.

Up ahead in the river bottom is a respectable caribou bull, perhaps the one we saw first thing this morning. He is weaving in and out among the balsam trees with an impressive entourage of cows. The herd is pawing and digging as they move along, partaking of the abundant lichen. I join Ted in sizing up the opportunity, and we decide in the failing light to try to take him. We make perhaps three separate stalks as the bull moves away from us, but before we can make our move the animal disappears with resounding finality into the dark timber on the lower slope of the mountain. We are defeated once more.

Disappointed, we return to camp in darkness. Another great meal awaits, and the fellowship in the cozy cabin is sweet. Sleep is good that night, and the next day finds us engaged in more of the same. The days pass rapidly, and before I can believe the time we are down to just a few days left. The caribou are not present in appreciable numbers now, and we must make some hard choices.

Bob and I have little input in the decision. We will do whatever our professionals decide. The judgment is that we should move to the other location, a prepared camp along the Tungsten Road where Terry has more supplies and an ATV. It is a grueling twenty-eight-mile trek across nearly trackless terrain, but we already knew the journey was a part of the bargain on this late-season hunt. I had hoped to be filled out with a giant mountain caribou, though, before undertaking the trip.

I watch as Ted and Terry make the necessary preparations. The two are obviously experts at packing and moving horses, and each beast is laden with two form-fitted wooden boxes for the long walk. The containers on each side must weigh exactly the same or a gradual shift can lead to disaster along the way. Bulky items such as large duffel bags go on top between the boxes.

The sight of the packtrain is splendid to behold. Terry leads off down the trail and Ted follows up the rear. The most experienced horses stay to the front of the string, the younger ones behind. A fledgling colt, carrying nothing except a full stomach of its mother's milk, trails along beside the mare, romping as a youngster is supposed to romp. By next year it will carry a burden of its own, if all goes well, with hoofs and legs toughened by another year in this brutal country.

There is no effort to string the ragtag train together, all of the animals rather making their own way down the long, winding trail. A soft snow is falling, dusting the animals and the gear they carry like a Christmas montage. Although the appearance is more suggestive of the disarray of a retreating army, the practical effect is enormously efficient. There is no attempt by any of the animals to tarry or wander. The beasts understand that this is the first leg of the long journey home to lush wintering grounds to the south, and they transport their burdens without any hint of reluctance.

There are mountain caribou high in an alpine basin to our north, probably in the Northwest Territories. I cannot resist the temptation to look, so I dismount for a steadier round of glassing. The remainder of the group are focused more on the move than the inaccessible caribou, so by the time I am finished the rest of the train is almost out of sight. As I engage my foot into the stirrup to swing myself up, without warning the saddle shifts treacherously, the result of a badly loosened belly cinch. Before I can do anything, the leather contraption spins 180 degrees, winding up with the seat under the belly of my horse.

Our whole helter-skelter caravan has by now disappeared through the low willows up ahead and has dropped over the next ridge, and I kick myself for putting myself in such a bad situation. I am no horseman, but over the years I have watched saddles being installed on horses, so maybe I can get myself out of this predicament.

I first wisely remove my precious rifle from its scabbard and stow it securely against a nearby bush. Struggling with the cinch rings and the

Twenty-eight miles to go before dark.

reluctant wet leather, I think I know what to do to tighten the contraption. The horse, however, seems to sense that its peers are rapidly leaving it behind and starts to move forward as I work. A firm shout of "whoa" is ineffective, and only incites the beast. A louder cry has an even more dramatic effect, and shortly the animal is running and I am shouting frantically and loudly. To make matters worse, the horse discovers quickly that the saddle is uncomfortably positioned. As it breaks into a gallop it reacts to the saddle as a rodeo bronco does to an unwelcome rider, bucking and heaving and lunging skyward with each leap. In abject amazement I behold leather attachments flying in all directions as the animal runs, and with that I concede total defeat. I am glad only that I am not still aboard, and that neither is my rifle. Whether the creature will fracture a leg before it catches up with the train I do not know.

There reverberates a frantic cacophony of sounds as the horse disappears over the hill and encounters the trailing edge of the group, led by colorful words from Ted that thankfully I can't discern at this distance. After an eternity my guide finally shows up with the wayward horse, and though I am relatively blameless I can't hide my chagrin. I will have a long and arduous task living down this display of horsemanship.

The new campsite places us in some of the most lavish mountain caribou habitat on the continent. From here we can glass several high alpine basins that herd bulls prefer in their relentless pursuit of estrous cows. Such "rutting bowls" are always above timberline, relatively free of brush, but contain adequate grazing and browse in the bottom of acute draws. There is already deep snow in all these bowls, but despite all the habitat, no animals are visible.

Morning breaks once more cold and snowy. A thick fog rolls in, obscuring all but the adjacent peaks. The restricted visibility will make our task more daunting than ever. Bob decides to go fishing today, seeking Dolly Varden trout and grayling in the nearby East Fork of the Hyland River. In the misery of the cold and falling snow, I almost envy him the opportunity to stay close to the warmth of camp. No matter, this is hunting, and I am here both to enjoy the experience and to endure whatever misery the elements dish up. I will persist to the end, caribou or not.

The ride is tolerable despite a wet saddle and a trail full of deep snow. We cross the lazy river, following a worn track that leads westward to a favorite caribou area where Ted has hunted in years gone by. We spot innumerable ravens and a few ptarmigan, but the only mammal we find is a lone bull moose moving with amazing stealth through snow-shrouded willows a half-mile away. We see the tracks of a good-size herd of caribou near the top of the pass, some five miles from camp, but no animals. The low scud that obscures the mountaintops all around is a monumental handicap, greatly reducing our chances.

A merry fire in the center of a broad valley offers a welcome recess from the trying conditions. We retrieve our lunch from the saddlebags and wash it down with hot tea. Then we move on, edging in the direction of camp. This day begins to look more and more like a complete washout.

Ted points up a steep intersecting valley at one juncture and relates how a few years ago he took a nice bull in a rutting bowl on top. He poses the question offhand whether we should take one more challenging climb to check it out, then rejects the idea. We move on down the valley.

We are approaching the end of another day. We have ridden and walked for perhaps ten miles, most of it without the aid of a trail. Ted gazes once more up the valley to our north, the location of his previous success, looking with a pensive expression at the forbidding mountain covered with chest-deep willows. A small valley intersects our own large valley, draining a high basin far above with a rushing rivulet of icy water. He looks thoughtfully at his watch.

"Four-thirty. Feel like making another little climb?"

"Sure. If you think it's worth it," I reply with resignation, dreading the sweat and exertion that are certain to follow.

"You never know. It's a good place."

"Let's go, then."

The climb isn't as bad as I had expected, once we leave behind the initial vertical portion and the ruthless alders. The higher mountainside is more open and less resistant to our steps. In one hour we are topping out, and Ted eases behind a clump of high alpine balsam trees for a better look at the broad basin. He raises his binoculars, then lowers them without a word. He turns toward me and flashes a broad grin that says far more than a thousand words. Caribou!

An inspection with the spotting scope reveals a real monarch, a grand old bull sporting wide, heavy beams, a huge shovel, and plenty of good top points. He is exactly what I want. The stalk is anticlimactic. In the rapidly fading light we quickly plot a course that takes us to about two hundred yards from the herd, and I humanely dispatch the grand old bull with a single shot from a sure, deliberate rest. I thank God immediately for my success, and also for the life of this ancient creature.

The long trek back to camp is uneventful, except for the small complication of our getting lost in the swampy terrain along the river we had negotiated so easily in the daylight. Yukon rivers frequently flow in a flat of marsh, with a deep main channel meandering randomly through the maze. To get to camp, we must cross somewhere. One can approach the main channel safely in only a few places because of the thick surrounding muck, deep soggy sludge that has been known to swallow both horses and riders. After a tense hour of searching, and no small amount of prayer on my part, we finally locate a secure approach and a shallow crossing. We arrive in camp to the smell of frying grayling, the aroma wafting on the welcome breeze as evidence that Bob has also been successful.

It is amusing how crazy the world can be at times. I have found a positive in the negative, a plus in the minus, and good in the bad. A blown opportunity on the first day of the hunt has broadened my experience and expanded my adventure to fill the full extent of my allotted time. The positive, the plus, and the good have come to me from writer Frank Forester, and I can more easily understand myself in light of his observation. I am able to discern how I came to be the way I am in my shooting, and I have been able to apply a bit of correction. My next hunting trip will find me much more practiced at offhand, odd position, and running shots. Or so, at least, I resolve.

Deep appreciation fills my mind as I drift off to sleep for the last time in the back country. The last night until next time, that is, in this grand place called the Yukon.

Central Canada barren ground caribou. (Photo: from the author's collection)

The Bathurst herd is perhaps the most classic example of a herd that summers on the tundra and winters below the tree line. Some of them summer close to the Arctic coast, using its cooling breezes and waters to help ward off insects. Most of the animals stay farther inland, however, and likely find relief from the insects by choosing bare ground or elevated glacial eskers where breezes provide a respite. In September and October they migrate south to the timber to pass the winter, using frozen lakes as resting areas, probably so they can spot marauding wolves at sufficient distance to escape. They feed among the timber and along the shores of the lakes, where they seek the sedges that grow abundantly there. They sometimes become a bandit of sorts during the winter, kicking open pushups made by muskrats to dine on the sedges stored within. Another important winter food is the abundant lichens of the boreal forest.

Central Canada barren ground caribou. Northwest Territories, September 1995.

seen the Bathurst herd firsthand, though, on several occasions. On one of my early trips to Yellowknife, Bill Tait of Adventures Northwest offered me a free ride on a midwinter caribou-viewing excursion by charter plane. I landed on a frozen lake and saw hundreds of wintering caribou deep in the boreal forest northeast of Yellowknife.

In spring the cows lead the migration to the calving grounds, leaving the wintering grounds in March or early April. In the 1950s most of the Bathurst herd calved west of Bathurst Inlet, but then for several decades they preferred a site to the east of there. In recent springs, they have reverted to the older site to the west; caribou habits are not

CENTRAL CANADA BARREN GROUND CARIBOU

(Rangifer tarandus groenlandicus)

It is colder in Meta Incognita than it is . . . 70 degrees north.
The reason for this difference may be that Meta Incognita is frequented
and vexed with eastern and northeastern winds, which are intolerably cold
because of the sea and the ice. This may also explain why the strait
was so jammed with ice this year.

—George Best, *A True Discourse of the Late Voyages of Discoverie,*
for the Finding of a Passage to Cathay, 1578

This caribou is native to Frobisher's Meta Incognita, so it is familiar with the cold and wind, as are all caribou. I hunted the exact spot to which Frobisher in all likelihood referred, the southern end of Baffin Island near the town of Lake Harbour, on the peninsula that still bears Frobisher's designation. The "unknown land" is one of the most scenic and interesting places I have visited in the north. It is not truly Arctic in the sense that it lies north of the Arctic Circle, however; in fact, it lies well to the south. Nevertheless, the habitat, terrain, weather, and animals are essentially the same.

The *groenlandicus* subspecies squares remarkably well in distribution with the hunter's central Canada barren ground caribou. As with most caribou, there is still some frustrating variance between the maps in the record books and the maps in biological reference works. Suffice it for our purposes to state that any caribou from the Northwest Territories that is from east of the Mackenzie River but not from any Arctic island except Baffin is a central Canada barren ground caribou under the Safari Club International system. Those from the Arctic islands are also included in this classification under the Boone and Crockett system. Both systems classify caribou from Baffin Island and from Southampton Island, which is south of the Arctic Circle, and all other islands south of the true geographical Arctic in the Northwest Territories, as central Canada barren ground in type.

These organizations split this type off into a separate category primarily to recognize that, under the old system of lumping all the tundra caribou west of Quebec into one barren ground category, large areas were excluded from eligibility for the record book: these animals are smaller than their Alaska and Yukon cousins. One added reason, already mentioned, is that the biologists actually do give them a different subspecies name with similar boundaries of distribution. I agree with the split and heartily endorse the reasoning on both counts. What's more, the hunting experience can be entirely different, and that is often one of my personal criteria for wanting to hunt a particular subspecies.

The largest caribou herd in the Northwest Territories is the 350,000-strong Bathurst herd. That herd ranges over a vast area extending from the Arctic coast west of Kugluktuk (formerly Coppermine) to well east of Bathurst Inlet and south to the Great Slave Lake. These caribou cross and recross the Arctic Circle in their annual migrations between wintering and summering ranges. The Bathurst herd is the most important herd in the Northwest Territories in terms of meeting the subsistence needs of native people, because it is accessible from more than a half-dozen aboriginal communities. It also receives considerable resident and nonresident hunting pressure due to its being so close to the territorial capital of Yellowknife. It is large enough and spread over enough terrain that it seems to be holding up well.

I have not hunted this herd, choosing instead to seek this subspecies on Baffin Island, where the experience is radically different and the chances of a record-book animal are considerably lower. I have carved in stone. After calving, they move with their newborns toward the coast for the summer.

This herd of caribou is of interest also because of the new diamond mine sitting astride their migration route, as well as other mining operations of various kinds. There is intense interest on the part of biologists, local people, and company officials in ensuring minimal disruption to the herd. Counts have been going on to determine how many caribou might be affected by the diamond mine. In one recent year, about 5,000 caribou moved through that region, and company officials were trying to decide which areas were most critical to the herd's health. The next year 30,000 caribou moved through the area, a variation that is no surprise to caribou biologists, given the fickle habits of the creatures.

As with all caribou, the rut is in October and involves battles between mature bulls for breeding rights. The bulls may enter the winter in poor condition, making them susceptible to predators or winterkill. In spring the cows lead the way back to the calving grounds, and most calves drop within a short period of time so that predators have easy pickings only for a brief interval.

One can hunt central Canada barren ground caribou in a variety of terrains and conditions that is unmatched by any other subspecies, except perhaps the Alaska-Yukon barren ground caribou. Even when hunting that latter subspecies, though, it is not possible to see polar bears, icebergs, and forty-foot tides. The Bathurst herd offers hunting similar to that in Alaska and the Yukon but lacking the diversity of terrain. The boreal forest and the tundra north of the Great Slave Lake have an interesting sameness about them, though from time to time there are highly unique formations to entertain visitors. Hunting the areas farther east offers opportunities to visit isolated communities and see historic sights. On south Baffin, though, one may sight a polar bear, narwhal, or walrus, and seals swim among the icebergs.

Many aspects of the Lake Harbour hunt are unique. Be certain you have Canadian funds to purchase your licenses when you get to Lake Harbour, because there is nowhere there to change money. Be prepared to don your hunting gear in the wildlife office in Lake Harbour for the boat trip to camp. By hunting gear, I mean get into rubber boots and rain gear, even if there isn't a cloud in the sky, because the salt spray will have you drenched and cold in minutes if you don't. Your gear will likely be in the enclosed cabin of the boat, where it should stay dry, but it's a good idea to have a padded soft case for your rifle and to sack up your duffel in plastic trash can liners just to be sure. You are in for a most interesting two- to four-hour boat ride, with the likelihood of interesting sightings around every turn of the coastline. The caribou here are abundant. They remain year-round, and there are some very nice bulls, though few are of record-book size. I found a wolf kill that was almost of record-book dimensions under the Boone and Crockett system, though, so the possibility is there.

The upside to hunting smaller-size animals is that there are fewer hunters and that the cost is a bit lower than hunting closer to Yellowknife. Air travel expenses may partially offset that savings, though. One gets to travel through the Nunavut capital of Iqaluit, rather than the Northwest Territories capital of Yellowknife, and an overnight stay may be required in one or both directions. Landing at Lake Harbour is not for the faint-hearted, either, as the airstrip is short and has a sharp drop-off at one end and a small mountain at the other. The pilots land here several times a week, although I bet they don't relish the approach, which is by visual reference only.

Expect two guides in the boat, as well as two hunters, when hunting south Baffin. You will hunt with two hunters per guide when walking, though, because one of the guides must stay with the boat lest you be stranded until the next tide comes in. The shallows at high tide can be a half-mile from the low-tide mark, and it is a full-time job just to keep the craft in the water while you hunt.

One other unique feature of this hunt is that one can hunt seals after finishing the caribou hunt. Purchase a license before leaving town. Don't expect to take any part of the seal home with you to the United States, though, since the Marine Mammal Protection Act strictly forbids importation. Make arrangements for the animal to be utilized locally before you take one.

Those interested in hunting record-book central Canada barren ground caribou might want to consider the Yellowknife locale. Charter aircraft can take you from the highly civilized

Caribou camp on the Hudson Straits, south Baffin Island.

environs of the capital city directly to the tundra camp. If you want to hunt from a native community, those hunts are available as well, with the advantage being a tradeoff of travel convenience for a closer look at local culture and perhaps a more remote location. Either way the caribou are abundant, the success rate high, and the camps and guides generally excellent.

This hunt was one of my favorites. If you can't do any other caribou hunt, do this one. The others are more expensive, more uncertain, more strenuous, or much colder. If there's another caribou hunt that is as economical, as interesting, and as certain to produce positive results, I don't know what it is.

ICEBERGS, BEARS, BULLS, AND BAFFIN ISLAND

The icy wind assaults my face, and a mixture of rain and ocean spray pours over my rain gear. The heave of the whitecaps exceeds six feet, and my natural inclination toward seasickness is threatening to manifest itself. In truth, the water in my face is a blessing because it has a soothing

effect on my stomach. I turn windward periodically to drink in the frigid air.

We are riding to caribou camp on south Baffin Island, and apart from the misgivings of my innards, the experience is starting out in breathtaking fashion. We have hardly departed the tiny Inuit hamlet of Lake Harbour when I spot my first iceberg, floating sedately in the open waters of Hudson Strait to our south. By shifting my gaze just a little, I see another through the fog a short distance beyond. As we proceed ever closer to the open sea, scores of icy floating mountains litter the strait. Noble and majestic, the translucent crystal castles silently guard our path, but we keep a respectable distance. The Inuit have a legend that the bergs are alive in the summer and, in the manner of all living things, must eat. They hungrily await their next meal. Doubtless the sleeping giants have occasionally devoured the unwary by spontaneously rolling, as they do, into a new position.

We hug the rocky shore for many miles, the twin motors of our launch propelling us toward camp, some two hours off. The barren coast conjures up the specter of desperate men coping with life where no wood grows, not even a twig as far as I can see. Englishmen and Frenchmen came here in search of riches and elusive passages to the Orient but most often found themselves struggling simply to stay alive. No one will ever subdue this harsh land, but some have learned to endure it. The Inuit survive and prosper here, by myriad specialized techniques, but the land resists taming by those who fail to heed their age-old knowledge.

This stretch of Baffin Island is its extreme southern extent, but even here the habitat is Arctic, even though we are two hundred miles south of the Arctic Circle. Rocks form such a prominent aspect of the terrain that in places nothing is visible but steel-gray buttresses where the land meets the sea, the pounding surf of a million ebb tides having worn smooth the serrated interfaces.

Few things in life are so welcome as warmth and comfort after the rigors of cold and dampness, and I eagerly await the appearance of the camp. As we motor behind an offshore island, the guide draws our attention to a spouting narwhal in the water near shore and then points straight ahead as the creature disappears into the depths. In the distance I can see our destination, an assemblage of windblown tents with the flag of Canada popping vigorously on its staff.

One obstacle remains between this reluctant sailor and my home away from home: a steep, stony embankment covered with a kelplike plant that makes the terra firma slick as petroleum jelly. Our Inuit hosts caution in their best English to "stay off the green," meaning avoid the vegetation. One ignores that advice at peril to life and limb. Above the high-tide mark, though, walking is secure.

Camp consists of a small group of heavily anchored round tents, bermed with sand and rock against the constant wind. Inside each hums a merry kerosene heater, which the camp foreman ignited as soon as we came into view. I shed my dripping rain gear to bask in the glow.

Unfortunately for a landlubber like me, hunting here is primarily by the aid of the ubiquitous Inuit boats. Days of tossing and rolling are ahead for me, with the constant threat of nausea. I gaze out the door of the dining tent at the thundering surf, visible through the fog, and wonder if I have made the right decision. The rain continues its slow drizzle, and a hovering mist alternately shrouds and exposes a small island across a narrow strait.

"Don't be in any hurry to get up in the morning, Doc," counsels outfitter Jerome Knap.

Lake Harbour is famous for caribou hunting.

"The weather is so lousy, and visibility so low, we won't be able to do anything until it lifts. But don't worry, there's plenty of time."

I am eager to hunt, of course, but the trip from Georgia has been tiring, so I appreciate a little extra rest. All night the pattering rain on the tent serenades me, and a comfortable foamy cradles me in my warm sleeping bag.

A late breakfast leaves all the hunters wanting to get going, but nobody is suggesting taking off in this kind of weather. During the few breaks we sight in our rifles and get to know one another. There are three U.S. citizens and five Mexicans, including the well-known Jesus Yuren. I speak pretty good Spanish, and I enjoy immensely conversing with the Mexicans. The Inuit are fascinated and perhaps even intimidated by this development. Of course, their Inuktitut is equally incomprehensible to us, so it is a standoff. I am to hunt with one of the Mexicans, and we find it convenient to be able to discuss certain things in a language our hosts cannot understand. I point out to my new Mexican friends that they outnumber us gringos by a margin of five to three. To this assertion they happily correct me, saying it is six to two, courteously shifting me into their column since I speak their language.

About lunchtime the weather begins to improve, and everyone hurriedly rechecks his equipment. Layers of fog still linger, but the clarity of the atmosphere at ground level is improving immeasurably. The wind has subsided, and one can now glass many of the surrounding hills. We all gravitate toward the boats, which must be retrieved from the deeper waters where they have been anchored against the huge swings of the tides. Soon we are all aboard and glassing for caribou, and I am very grateful for the smooth waters.

The caribou are still lying low, and we have difficulty finding any for the first couple of hours. I am beginning to wonder if these critters are an endangered species. Frustration shows visibly in my Inuk guide, Eliyah Padlug. Eliyah speaks no English and is unable to communicate with us without the help of his son Napatchee, but it's clear what he's thinking. Hunters want to see animals, and the caribou are not cooperating. Through the lips of his son, he assures us that we will find what we are seeking.

Magnificent icebergs in Hudson Strait on the way to caribou camp.

Another view of caribou camp.

We leave the boat for a while and climb one of the low hills that dot the island coast. There are many safe harbors among the rocks along the coastline, but their appearance is deceptive. If the tide goes out while you're gone, you can easily be stranded for the better part of a day. One of the guides will stay with the boat and move it as necessary.

One aspect of the scene that constantly amazes me is that the hills and mountains are uniformly less severe than they appear from a distance. In sheep country it is always the opposite. I don't ever recall having scaled a sheep mountain and then turned around to say, "Gee, that wasn't as bad as I thought it would be." But here, the mixture of ocean and bare rocks and fog and sky inexplicably combine to make the terrain look more formidable than it actually is.

There are caribou here all right. Two burst from their beds beneath the rocks ahead of us, apparently having been taking a rare rest break. One looks immense to me, but Napa (the nickname used by Napatchee) shakes his head in disdain. This is not a taker.

I have my heart set on a caribou in velvet and have even brought along needles, syringes, and a quart of formalin for preserving it. I naturally would take a monster bull without good velvet, but I am prepared to harvest a lesser one if it has velvet intact. The next caribou we see has no discernible breaks in the silky covering of his antlers, but the creature is too small to collect. I ask my hunting partner, Karel, to stay with Napa while I make a stalk to get close-up pictures; favorable wind and terrain enable me to move right in. Only when I begin clicking my camera does the animal become suspicious, and then he is so curious he comes toward me. The ungulate is within spitting distance before he decides that, whatever the strange clicking might be, he wants no part of it. He retreats precipitately, almost running over Napa and my Mexican companion in the process.

Several more such treks across the barren landscape reveal more caribou, but none with the towering tines we seek. My young Mexican friend and hunting companion turns out to be more picky than I where trophy quality is concerned. He has hunted much less, so I give him the short course in judging trophy caribou as we motor on. He seems grateful, and the set of his jaw shows that he is determined to harvest a good animal.

We return to camp amid constantly improving weather, although more than once we find ourselves deep within a fog bank. Almost uncannily, we always emerge unscathed and on the right course. I never see the Inuit consult any equipment, but they always know exactly where we are.

Nighttime finds hunters gathered in the cozy cook tent to exchange tales about the first day of hunting, and it is apparent that caribou are abundant in all quadrants around our camp. The two Americans and their guides have called on the radio to let us know that they have already filled out their caribou tags and have spent several hours transporting and loading meat, antlers, and capes. While all that was taking place, the tide went out and left them stranded. It will be well after midnight before the incoming tide rescues them so they can return.

Pancakes, complete with Canadian maple syrup and crisp bacon, greet me as I enter the cook tent. I have slept so well that I am beginning to wonder if I have picked up some strange Inuit sleeping sickness; usually I am a light and finicky sleeper. Following the hearty meal, we again board the boats for a long day of hunting.

There is fog again now, but no drizzle. The feel in the air is that of clearing skies, and the breeze gusts briskly from the northwest. Sure enough, before we reach our first stopping place, patches of blue appear overhead, the persistent mist over the water notwithstanding. I stow my rain gear, confident I will not need it again today.

The plan is to cruise into whatever bays the Inuit select, as the heads of the inlets are usually the lowest point of land. Often the caribou frequent these areas because of the quality forage there. The first place we stop there is a lone bull visible, but nothing special from a trophy standpoint. We leave Eliyah with the boat and climb a windblown hill that protrudes from the tidal basin. The structure is a unique formation that resembles a misplaced bit of South Dakota Badlands. It is, true to form, lower than it looks, but from its ignoble summit another half-dozen bulls can be seen, the farthest a couple of miles away. None are dandies, and, much to my vexation, I note that one is completely out of the velvet. The possibility of collecting a fully velveted specimen seems ever more unlikely. We make another practice stalk on the nearest animal, again getting

close enough to get good pictures, but neither my partner nor I am ready to harvest this one.

Caribou are everywhere today. Near the shore the animals are visible from the boat, and from the top of every promontory there are still more. The population here is absolutely incredible. I become concerned that our conscientious Inuit guides might get discouraged as we repeatedly evaluate and reject them all. We even have one of our secret discussions in Spanish about the possibility. I ask Napa, and he does not seem in the least perturbed.

Wolves inhabit Baffin Island in great abundance, and the evidence is everywhere in the form of caribou carcasses. Karel expresses a desire to pick up a good pair of antlers to take to a friend, so I help him look. We even carry a couple of pairs back to the boat, small caribou of no particular significance. We spot one antler near the water's edge as we motor by, the long tines beckoning us to take a closer look, but Eliyah has little patience with crazy hunters looking for dead caribou. He declines to stop by indicating that he doesn't understand our request. I mentally mark the spot, hoping perhaps that we can convince him to turn in there on the way back.

Even as we enter another bay, two hours from camp, I sense that this must be the place. A very good bull greets us at the entrance to the narrow neck of sea. The animal is lying near the high-water mark, basking in the sun, displaying velvet-covered antlers that would make almost any hunter proud. Despite our proximity, he only shakes his head and shows the whites of his eyes to indicate his displeasure at our intrusion. What abject disrespect, I can't help but think. The creature's supple coat glistens in the sunlight, and the roll of ample fat is evident. Velvet-covered antlers beckon me, but the top points are a bit deficient, so both Karel and I decline again.

The head of the basin we are entering has two deep forks, and both terminate in relatively flat terrain that dumps a rushing stream of icy water into the sea. We can see numerous bulls in the right branch, so we motor as quietly as possible toward them. Eliyah cuts the engine to little more than an idle, and the creatures move almost unconcernedly up the gentle slope and out of sight.

One of them looks good through the binoculars, and I say so as we disembark.

Twenty or more bulls are visible as we ease up to the crest of the first high promontory. I inquire of Napa where all the cows are; we have seen only one cow and more than fifty bulls thus far. He informs me that they stay farther inland with their calves, the higher and more irregular terrain offering some protection from wolves. This sport caribou hunt would be a lot more difficult if the situation were reversed.

I spot a bull that meets my expectations almost immediately and point him out to the others. I have told Karel that he can shoot first, so I ask if he wants him. The size is not so impressive, and the bez points are quite deficient, but he has six long points up top and a decent shovel. More to my liking, the velvet looks as virgin as can be. When Karel declines, I move up another hundred yards and position for what should be an easy shot. I

hope to put a clean lung shot on the animal. Ideally, he will just lie down and die gently, without falling and ripping that fragile velvet. I always feel a twinge of excitement as I prepare to harvest an animal, and this time is different only in that there is absolutely no hurry. My biggest challenge is to be sure I shoot the right caribou. I pick him up easily after my short stalk, and I wait for my heartbeat to subside before touching off the 165-grain Nosler from my .30-06.

The bull stumbles at the report, obviously hit hard. He doesn't go down immediately, and I chamber another round and actually consider making another shot. He is going to pass out of my view with a few more steps, but I am convinced he is dead and decide not to squeeze the trigger again.

As so often happens, a truly great opportunity to get wildlife pictures comes after the shot. This seems to occur most often when one is hunting animals that run in herds or bands. The inquisitive

Lining up for the shot on a nice Central Canada caribou bull.

bulls that remain all look perplexedly toward my bull, tipping me off immediately that he is probably down, although out of my view. The curious animals then walk almost directly toward me, and I have my telephoto lens connected in a flash to take advantage of the stately parade. They linger a full five minutes before the possibility of danger dawns on them, and then the whole group ambles away and out of sight.

My bull is indeed down, and much to my disappointment the tenuous covering on one antler ripped badly when he fell. The velvet is, in fact, already quite loose, and it becomes apparent right away that I must strip it off, rendering useless all the trouble I took to bring preservative with me. Oh, well, I will leave it here for next year's hunters.

After packing everything back to the boat, we continue on our quest for a caribou for Karel. It isn't to be this day, but I have the feeling that his time will come. He is patient and very cool. I think he is going to be one of the very best of hunters, and certainly he will be among the best of the elite Mexican hunting fraternity.

On the way back to camp my bladder dictates a stop, so I convince Eliyah to pull in where we spotted the caribou antler earlier. Karel retrieves the pair, and we are amazed at their size and perfection. They are the remains of yet another wolf kill, but this one an animal of definite record-book proportions, with eight long top points, an incredible pair of bez points, and a pair of big double shovels. Karel first wants to keep them for his friend but later insists that I take them, despite my protests, since he feels I might appreciate them more. Perhaps he is right, but I accept them reluctantly and make him a standing offer that he may have them back if ever he wants them.

My hunt is over, and as we search for another bull for my friend, we are treated to two appearances by *nanook*, the polar bear. The first sighting is in the head of another long tongue of seawater extending inland, where Eliyah sights a nine to nine-and-a-half-foot bear sitting among the rocks on a hillside just above the water level. He motors the boat to within a hundred yards, whereupon the bear rises to its feet and saunters

The scenic village of Lake Harbour.

Where else but Baffin Island can one see polar bears while caribou hunting?

away from us in no hurry whatsoever, providing ample opportunity for a great telephoto session. Five miles away and only a couple of hours later, we spot a second polar bear walking along a high ridgetop, this time a truly large bear of ten feet or more. Jerome Knap's boat pulls up abeam of us in time for him and his hunters to see this second bear, providing a great thrill for all of us. Although the spectacle is spellbinding, it is not unique. The hunters in our camp have thus far spotted a total of eight polar bears.

After a few days of enjoying the back country of Baffin, I am finally on the way back to Lake Harbour, salt spray and rain gear once more dominating the voyage. The pilot of the boat offers to take us out to view one of those "live" icebergs at close range. Knowing their man-eating reputation and my lack of sea legs, I am more than a little apprehensive. In the heaving sea, the monstrous frozen behemoths appear especially dangerous. We shoot the rest of our film, knowing full well that no picture can truly do justice to the spectacle.

The components of this particular hunt are not possible on any other North American caribou hunt, as far as I am aware. I top off my experience by staying with Eliyah's family in Lake Harbour, just to "go native" and learn a little more about this people called Inuit, a people whom I have learned to respect and admire in a very special way. A hunt for *tuktu*, as caribou are known in Inuktitut, is truly a great encounter with a radically different way of life, and with a beautiful, barren island named Baffin.

Quebec-Labrador caribou. (Photo: from the author's collection)

QUEBEC-LABRADOR CARIBOU
(Rangifer tarandus caribou)

Fog hangs low and heavy over rock-girdled Labrador.
Angry waves, paled with rage, exhaust themselves to encroach up her stern shores,
and, baffled, sink back howling into the depths.
Winds shriek as they course from crag to crag in a mad career,
and the humble mosses that clothe the rocks crouch lower still in fear.

—Elliot Coues (1842–1899), quoted in Pierre Berton's
The Mysterious North,

Such a description applies aptly to the land of the Quebec-Labrador caribou. The descriptive power of Elliot Coues still strikes alarm in me as I review some of my adventures seeking this noble and elusive animal. The furious waves of Lake Kakiattukallak, a large and unpredictable body of water near Bobby's Caribou Camp, have similarly terrorized me on every occasion I have hunted there. The powerful and incessant wind, unhindered in its path from the prairie provinces and the Northwest Territories, picks up momentum and dreadful cold as it blasts over the width of frigid Hudson Bay. Its full icy fury descends on northern Quebec and Labrador, where this subspecies lives and prospers despite the extremes meted out by nature.

It is the land and its people that make hunting the Quebec-Labrador caribou special. The Inuit natives are important outfitters in this vast, unspoiled area, where rivers, lakes, and magnificent abundance prevail during certain times of the year. Approximately 8,000 natives live in the area of northern Quebec, which has been designated by Canada as Nunavik, the companion to Nunavut of the Northwest Territories. Both entities have come about as part of recent land-claim settlements between natives and the Canadian and provincial governments. Other native groups include the Naskapi and Cree Indians farther south in Quebec, and the Montagnais people of Labrador. Like the Laplanders of Eurasia, all these Native Americans have in common a long and intimate history of living with and depending upon the caribou. Becoming for a short time a part of their culture and traditions, their land ethic, and their hunting techniques is what makes for a memorable caribou expedition here.

The word *ungava* in Inuktitut, the language of the Inuit, roughly means "faraway place." From that word comes the name of the big bay on the northern coast of Quebec and the associated broad peninsula. To the native peoples it is not at all faraway, but to the rest of us it certainly is. Nevertheless, modern air travel makes the journey much less arduous than in the old days, and the flights are well attuned to the needs of the modern sport hunter. Most outfitters expertly prepare both antlers and meat for travel, conforming unerringly to the standards set by the commercial air carrier. The airlines charge an extra $100 to fly a pair of exceptional antlers back with the skull plate intact, since they are normally split to fit into the aircraft more easily. The extra expense is worth it only when the trophy is truly a giant, and if the hunter may be inclined to list the animal in the record book. Excellent cold storage facilities are available in Montreal to protect the carefully boxed meat from spoilage.

The population dynamics of the Quebec-Labrador subspecies of woodland caribou are puzzling. In the 1800s the animals were abundant, sufficiently meeting the needs of both the natives and invading white explorers. Between 1890 and 1958, for unknown reasons, the herd was in constant decline to a low point of a mere 15,000 animals. That resulted in many deaths among the natives as famine set in; government disaster assistance was not the norm in those days.

Quebec-Labrador caribou. Quebec, September 1998.

By 1970 the herd began to expand once more, and it continues to do so today. In the two major herds, there are now probably more than one million animals. The larger population, the George River herd, is believed to contain at least 800,000, making it the largest single grouping of caribou (and one of the largest aggregations of any large mammal) in the world. The Leaf River herd to the west contains around 260,000 animals. This latter herd was identified as separate from the George River herd more recently because of a separate calving ground and a distinctive summer range. These population figures may be even higher today, since the former is the result of a survey done in 1993, and the latter is from data gathered in 1991. All evidence suggests that the herds continue to expand and are underharvested to an astonishing degree.

The third group of caribou in the region is the Torngat herd, a more or less obscure group that exists mainly in the mountains of the extreme northern Ungava Peninsula. Little is known about these animals, and no dependable surveys have been done. Scientists have collared some of the caribou and studied their movements, but there is neither an identified calving ground nor much information about summer ranges and winter retreats. The harvest is fairly small, and the numbers of animals come nowhere near those of the vast George River and Leaf River herds.

These groupings of animals are unavoidably artificial, and there is some documented mixing between the groups, but they appear to remain mostly distinct during the calving season in spring and during the summer. There is some fidelity to calving grounds, though the occasional animal will join another herd. On a number of occasions, collared animals have completely altered their normal pattern and joined other groupings.

It is perhaps the calving grounds that most accurately distinguish the herds. The Leaf River caribou calve in a large area to the east of the settlement of Puvirnituq and to the north of the river for which the herd is named. Sometimes they approach close to the shores of the Hudson Straits. The George River herd calves in the Pyramid Hills section of the mountains dividing Quebec from Labrador. Especially in that latter area, the habitat is so overused that there is little forage available, and the cows have expanded the calving area to both sides of the George River, encompassing most of their traditional summer range. In all likelihood they originally selected this region because the open tundra has few suitable sites for wolf denning. Since the wolves are having their young at the same time, farther south, they are absent from the calving grounds. Thus the newborns are safe from all predators but eagles, which do take quite a few soon after they are born. This limited region was once the principal summer range of the George River herd, but the caribou have now expanded that range because of the poor forage.

The vast numbers of these caribou have taken a toll on the habitat, and fall calf recruitment is at a very low level. Average weights of newborns in the George River calving grounds have also fallen considerably, as has the average size of adult cows. There has even been a decline in head size, as manifest by a shrinking of the length of the lower jaw by almost an inch over the past several years. No one knows if these changes portend an imminent disaster and a crash in population numbers, but the possibility is a concern of both biologists and native people alike.

Bull caribou in the past shared the summer range with the cows, but the poor quality of forage has caused the cows to vacate much of the overgrazed area as soon as the calves are able to travel. The bulls tend to avoid the bare calving grounds altogether. It is not known for certain where the main company of bulls spends the summer, but some data indicate that they are west of the George River in mixed tundra and transition taiga at that time of year.

Migration is a complex phenomenon in these caribou, perhaps more so than for any other North American cervid. From the calving grounds and summer range, the cows and calves may cover as much as 6,000 miles annually, the bulls even more. It is no great feat for either sex to walk over ten miles in a single day. These marathon migrations by hundreds of thousands of caribou wear deep trails in the fragile terrain and use up the animals' precious energy reserves.

A single calf is born to each pregnant cow in early April, and all the cows deliver within a two-week period. Twins are extremely rare. The youngsters are wobbly and unsure at first, but within hours they are up and walking. Within four or five days they can outrun a wolf with a little luck. During the first several days the cow and calf try to keep to themselves as much as possible, as that critical period is essential for the all-important bonding between mother and calf. By following the mother, the calf learns the migration routes that have characterized the lives of these creatures for countless generations. Much of the movement in summer occurs in herds that may contain 100,000 animals, massive conglomerations that minimize the overall onslaught of mosquitoes and other bloodsuckers. A caribou can lose up to two pints of blood a week during the height of the insect season, another critical energy loss.

The notorious warble fly is another source of torment for the Quebec-Labrador caribou. This large, hairy insect resembles a bumblebee, and it lays its eggs among the hairs of the caribou. They hatch to create larvae that burrow under the skin and spend the winter feeding on caribou flesh before emerging to start the cycle over again. The lesions caused by these larvae can cause considerable pain and can be debilitating enough to cause death.

Caribou are the best swimmers among the cervids of the world. Their thick, hollow hair not only has the best insulating qualities but also imparts extraordinary buoyancy. One-third of the caribou's body floats above the water as it swims,

Rainbow over Bobby Lake.

Bobby's caribou camp.

diminishing the possibility of accidental drowning. Also, the oversized hoofs, so well adapted to travel over snow-covered or boggy terrain, serve admirably as paddles. The Inuit have always taken advantage of the high-riding caribou, which is exceptionally vulnerable to a well-placed lance thrown from a kayak at a stream crossing. The caribou combat this by being tremendous swimmers. They can rapidly exit the water when danger is imminent, paddling quickly to shore.

Quebec-Labrador caribou move southward each fall as winter approaches and ultimately arrive in the wooded taiga, where they spend the winter. The rut takes place on their journey, and eligible cows are bred by the prime, dominant bulls. They prefer to rest in winter on open areas such as frozen lakes, which afford some advance warning of wolf attacks. Consequently the animals have taken to the vast reservoirs of the La Grande hydroelectric project, located in and near their traditional taiga wintering grounds. These frozen havens offer the open terrain the animals desire, and the surrounding lakeshore is rich in lichens, their main winter forage. The caribou from both the George River and Leaf River herds intermingle in the black spruce boreal forest in winter. They congregate in a sweeping band that stretches from the taiga coast of Labrador to the Hudson Bay, with the western portion being much broader from north to south than the eastern.

In winter, the caribou subsist mainly on the lichens of the northland. These plants are abundant, except on the overgrazed calving grounds of the George River herd. I have seen abundant "caribou moss" that extended to the horizon in all directions, with no caribou in sight for days at a time. In light of this, it seems incredible that there are places where little of the plant exists. The fact of hundreds of thousands of caribou clustered in a small area makes such shortages inevitable, though, as lichens grow only a couple of millimeters a year. Abundant lichen means that the caribou are grazing it exceedingly lightly. It takes thirty to forty years for a carpet of lichen to grow to maturity at this latitude, and in some of the places I have hunted it is literally six inches deep in spots. It is hard to believe that there are sections in which overgrazing

has virtually eliminated it, but such is the case in the Pyramid Hills calving grounds.

Like most caribou, the Quebec-Labrador subspecies also eat willow browse in summer. It is a highly nutritious food that, unlike lichens, is rich in protein. In winter, caribou may have to dig through deep snow to obtain carbohydrate-laden lichen. An aggressive and hungry caribou may dig as many as one hundred holes in the snow in a single day. During especially harsh winters caribou may feed incessantly, but even then the animals often lose 10 percent of their body weight.

Caribou cows with the largest antlers tend to dominate other cows in their domain. Antlered cows even drive off males, whose highly sought headgear has already shed by early winter. The cows with the biggest antlers may be able to confiscate the best feeding grounds for themselves and their calves, propagating the most hardy of the species.

It takes at least two months for the wintering caribou to return to their traditional calving grounds as they wander over northern Quebec and Labrador. The cows leave several weeks ahead of the bulls, journeying with their calves of the previous year. There are many rivers and lakes to cross, and many dangers. By the first of April they are back on the highlands, east or west of Ungava Bay.

Much about this subspecies remains a mystery. Upcoming research proposes to focus on the number of caribou in each herd, with plans to survey the George River and Torngat herds in 1999 and the Leaf River herd in 2005. The herds are showing several signs of stress from rapidly increasing numbers, with total population figures that almost numb the mind. Not only are there high numbers of caribou, there is also evidence that the average fall calf recruitment is down, and the average birth weight of newborn calves is declining. There should be at least 39 healthy calves per 100 cows, and the figure has fallen below that. Since cows can produce a calf annually until ten to twelve years of age, it may be some time before this translates into an actual decline in caribou numbers. On the other hand, the Leaf River herd shows encouraging signs of resilience, and calf abundance there may be better than in the eastern herds.

In Quebec, annual take by sport hunters amounts to some 16,500 animals per year and is

Back out onto the big water after the kill.

growing. The licenses purchased by nonresident hunters garner over $1.4 million for the government of Quebec, or about $85 per caribou. That is apart from such incidentals as air fare, outfitter fees, hotel and motel expenses, food while not in camp, gratuities, souvenirs, and the like. The resident take of caribou brings the government only about $400,000 per year, or about $44 per animal. Most residents spend very little on the above-mentioned extras, so the multiplier effect isn't nearly as great. Suffice to say that without caribou hunting by nonresidents, the whine of snowmobiles would be much more rare a sound in the subarctic regions of Quebec. Native and resident take of caribou in Labrador far outstrips that of nonresident sport hunters (11,000 by residents and natives, 2,000 by nonresidents).

There is also a winter hunt in which a sport hunter may participate, a grueling snowmobile affair that few hunters from outside the area participate in. It is legal to hunt the reservoirs in winter with a guide, and there are some extraordinary experiences to be had. The bulls may have already discarded their grand antlers, though, making the prospect of enduring subzero temperatures much less appealing to me.

Management of caribou in Quebec and Labrador is a modern affair. I know of no other caribou program that uses as much radio telemetry and satellite tracking data from collared animals. Movements are constantly monitored and data relayed to outfitters, many of whom are awaiting any indication that a herd may be moving in their direction. Biologists have also developed techniques to infer population data from the number of collared animals in a herd. The harvest is carefully tallied and analyzed toward the formulation of recommended management steps. As a top concern at present is the extreme degradation of habitat in the calving areas, a much greater harvest seems imperative.

This brings up perhaps the most salient feature of caribou hunting in Quebec. The hunt here is feast or famine. If the caribou are not present in huge numbers, one must travel many miles by foot to find one. I connected for the first time on my third hunt, but only after putting in ten miles on foot and another ten miles back to camp.

Just once I'd like to see the awesome migration of thousands of giant bulls that some have encountered. If you are in a camp where the caribou haven't yet arrived, or have just passed, don't blame the outfitter, the government, the caribou, or the hunters who were in camp the week before. It just happens that way in Quebec. In Labrador, there is an experimental hunt wherein hunters position themselves in front of the migration, pretty much ensuring an abundance of bulls. That kind of innovative plan is slowly developing in Quebec as well.

Of all the equipment needed to hunt these caribou, a quality pair of ankle-fit rubber boots are perhaps most important. The tundra is wet, even when there has been little rain, and rubber boots are indispensable. Good rain gear is a necessity. Rain pants that zip all the way up one side of the leg allows you to put them on and take them off without completely undressing or removing your boots, a tremendous advantage. I like a full-length raincoat, because then the quality of the pants isn't so crucial. Remember, you're hunting the land of the rainbows and are likely to break out the rain gear and take it off repeatedly, sometimes six to ten times a day.

The Inuit often rely on the hunter to provide the knife for skinning, so take along a good one with a sharpener. Plastic bags prevent your pack from becoming soaked with blood from hauling out the meat. A simple day pack will suffice for this type of hunt, as the guide will usually have along a packframe for carrying the heavier loads. I nevertheless recommend one with a generous amount of room inside, so you can help out more effectively.

Any centerfire rifle will do for caribou. I used 165-grain Noslers for all my caribou. Shots are usually not that long, so take your time and place yours well.

Every outfitter in Quebec and Labrador claims a 90 percent success rate, and maybe many do. But I went with a really good camp for three years in a row and had only one opportunity. Migration patterns are changing, the herd is poised for a change in dynamics of major proportions, and who knows how to predict the future? Nobody can guarantee anything in fair-chase hunting except to put you in good country where the caribou might show up.

Go and enjoy the rainbows anyway. The grand march of hundreds of trophy bulls could be on its way, just over the next ridge. The scenery, the company of other hunters, colorful ptarmigan and regal snowy owls, boisterous flights of Canada geese, the aurora borealis, the gentle wafting of the Inuktitut language in camp in the evenings—all these combine to make every hunt for these caribou a memorable experience. It's a must for every serious hunter.

NO COW, NO BULL

The air is smooth as we motor along in the vintage Otter between the town of Kuujjuaq and remote Bobby's Caribou Camp. I scan the endless tundra for signs of our quarry, and it looks uncannily as it did last year. Interlacing caribou trails converge at every isthmus between the myriad lakes, but none of the animals are in evidence. On an August hunt a year ago I saw but four caribou: two cows and two bulls. I have an uncomfortable, ominous feeling that I can't shake— no caribou again. Oh well, you simply trust God and hope for the best. It is certainly easy to miss the wandering journeys of the vast Quebec herds of caribou, but this is mid-September and I should be right on target. I try to console myself that it is sometimes hard to spot animals from the air.

The rumbling airplane finally covers the 128 miles and begins its descent. The familiar outline of Bobby's Lake comes into view, and soon we are touching down and taxiing to the dock. Ten smiling hunters greet us as we emerge, and I see immediately that the glowing reports we have heard are true. Antlers are piled high on the beach, and meat boxes are plentiful as well. All ten hunters limited out in just three days. Some of them took really nice bulls, too, and they tell tantalizing anecdotes about seeing the real giants after filling their tags. One French-speaking couple with a charming accent say that we should be sure not to shoot the first one we see, because they are simply everywhere. I can see that this ought to be a whole different story from last year's.

Camp owner Bobby Snowball (obviously not his Inuit name) has graciously agreed to let me return free of charge this year. I suffered the distinction of being his first client to have had no chance to get a caribou since he moved the camp to this distant location in 1991. Four other hunters took two reasonable bulls apiece. The only two bulls I saw, which appeared on the last day of the hunt, required a ten-mile walk around the big lake to reach.

When we finally arrived on the ridge where we had seen them, we found that another hunter from our camp had already killed them both. I was certainly ready to leave for home then, after a week of fruitless exertion and endless spitting rain.

This year will be different. I have taken the precaution of scheduling Bobby to guide me personally, and to do so in one-on-one fashion, a departure from the norm. I am inwardly certain I will score, and I automatically take to heart the advice to be patient and wait for a really good one. But a pinch of doubt still remains.

The guides have the day off, but now there are twenty more tags in camp to fill out. The quick success of the last hunt has them fairly well rested, so three of them agree to take the eager new hunters out for a short foray. My tent-mates are Ron Scott and Dan McVey of Yuba City, California, two of the nicest guys you could ever hope to meet in a hunting camp. We pile into one of the canoes with John, Bobby Snowball's son, and take off with rifles at ready.

Only one mile from camp the young man parks the boat. We won't be going far this day, it appears. Three hunters together is a bit much, but I'm in no hurry on this one, anyway. I'll let one of the others shoot if we see caribou. We traverse a boggy marsh and make our way up a low hill toward a pair of massive boulders. I pull out my Zeiss minis and begin to scan the surrounding tundra. It is good to be back in caribou country.

"I see a bull. No, two. And another behind them," John comments softly after less than five minutes. We all train our glasses to the spot, and I immediately see the first animal, a wide, heavy-antlered mature bull with double shovels. His antlers gleam redly in the sunlight, indicating that he has already shed his velvet. The other two still wear massive and unblemished coverings of the soft, dark material. Their slight potbellies and flowing white manes speak of prime trophies. There is a slight sway to their walk, perhaps the motion offsetting the imbalance created by their towering antlers.

As we watch, the trio feed slowly. They will likely move to the opposite shore of a small lake. John inquires if any of us would like to try for one of them, and despite my earlier decision I hesitate. These are excellent animals, but I really am not eager to end my hunt so quickly. All three seem to have some noticeable deficiency in the top points, and I remember that some better ones just left on the plane. Surely with this many caribou around I'd be smart to wait. While I mull, Ron pipes up that he'd like to try. That's fine with Dan and me. I get out my telephoto lens and decide to be the official cameraman.

We start around the lake to intercept them, but as we do they change course and seem to be heading right toward our first location. We double back and come up on the ridge near the two boulders. Ron lies down behind one and gets ready. I move behind him like a movie director, searching for exactly the right angle. I want to get him and the caribou in the picture at the same time, if possible.

When it looks almost right, but before I am perfectly set, he fires, and the biggest of the three falls immediately to the ground. Ron looks back to see if one of us is waiting to take a bull, and seeing nobody ready he makes a snap decision. His .338 booms once more, and another caribou tumbles. Both his tags are filled before he has spent a single night in camp.

Both are extremely nice bulls with double shovels. We do a brief picture session, marveling at Ron's "double-double."

"I guess two is my lucky number," he comments through his broad smile.

"Then why didn't you wait until the second day?" comes the reply.

After more pictures and handshakes, we bend our backs to the task of caping and quartering. While we do, Dan climbs back up to the big rocks to do more glassing. I am taking out one of the loins on the second caribou, about an hour after the double play, when Dan calls that he is going after a big bull.

"Wait here and he'll probably come by," John advises in a voice that is almost pleading. I don't blame him. He has his hands full with these two caribou, and to take another one a mile away will certainly prolong the evening. What's more, this is his day off.

"Don't worry, I'll help you pack it out," Dan calls as he heads out. I quickly rinse my hands in the lake and decide to go along, hoping to get some more pictures. I grab my pack and rifle, hurrying to catch up.

"This guy is bigger than the two Ron shot. Lots bigger. And he's traveling that ridge behind the hill," Dan tells me as we walk. "I don't think he'll come this way."

Shortly we part company, and I try to cover one of the possible routes the bull might take, still not certain I would shoot at anything less than gigantic. It isn't long after Dan disappears that I hear a loud rifle report from his direction, followed by a succession of several more. A quartet of cows pass in front of me at a dead run, disappearing before I can head toward the sound of the gunfire.

Dan has shot a very nice bull indeed, bigger than either of Ron's and with a huge body to match. I feel a twinge of envy for the first time. For the next couple of hours hard labor stifles such thoughts, and by the time we have the capes and antlers in the boat it is almost dark and a quarter-moon is rising in the clear sky. As we dock back at camp the northern lights are dancing overhead, and a curious flock of hunters and camp personnel come down to see what we have brought in.

Everyone, we learn, has seen caribou, a total of at least twenty bulls having been spotted during the afternoon. This should definitely be different from last year, no question about it.

Bobby's Caribou Camp is one of the most comfortable remote hunting outposts I have ever encountered in North America. Wooden beds with thick foam cushions, diesel fuel heaters, hot water always on the stove, daily maid service, and outstanding meals characterize this little slice of wilderness. If I can just get on a good bull, the experience will be complete.

A good night's rest leaves me eager to hunt. Bobby and his crew are ready, and swift motorized canoes fan out from the dock. Bobby has selected a high ridge about two miles down the lake for us. We see two small bulls swimming in the lake, their reddish pink antlers held high. I watch as they emerge, shake away the moisture, and head over the ridge to our west.

Soon I relish the familiar sensation of laboring along behind a guide. There is a high overcast, and

Nice caribou bull about to be taken by Ron Scott.

a brisk wind is in our faces. The interminable tundra spreads before us, painted with splotches of every conceivable color. We see no caribou from the first promontory, though a noisy gaggle of greater Canada geese take off as we watch. Far to the north we see another group of hunters, and a mile beyond them a second group. Our camp is deployed across the migration route like a skirmish line. Nobody seems to be observing anything, by all appearances.

We walk to the next promontory, a common tactic when few caribou are about. When a migration is in full swing, there is no need to move much; one can simply wait at a likely crossing. Today we must walk, an activity I don't mind but that nevertheless gives me an uneasy feeling. Have we seen only the tail end of the big herd? Have I missed the migration again? Questions fill my mind as we make our way across the rocks and spongy earth toward the next high point. An overcast dominates, and the clouds seem to match my mood of pessimism as one valley after another proves devoid of caribou.

After a prolonged glassing session, Bobby looks at me and searches for words. He speaks English like a Sioux warrior from an old Western movie: "No cow, no bull." It is a litany I hear several times as the day progresses.

I was here in August of last year trying to take a caribou in the velvet so I could add one to my collection. The weather was horrible the whole time. Today the sun finally peeks through the clouds, and warm sunshine pervades the subarctic prairie. We retreat to the boat by midday and motor down the lake to join two other groups of hunters for lunch. On a sun-washed lakeshore, sheltered by a grove of dwarf spruce, we have sandwiches and hot tea. Nobody has seen much, but one hunter has captured a good bull on video. He replays the tape for me. In view of how few animals we are seeing, the bull looks enticing to me now.

"We go big lake," Bobby tells me as we climb aboard the boat, referring to Lake Kakiattukallak, a Tahoe-size body of water south of Bobby Lake and joined to it by a short section of rapids. Bobby usually keeps a boat there, but all his craft are on the smaller lake at present. He has been discussing the situation with the other guides in Inuktitut, and it will be a task to move the boat. Last year almost all of the eight caribou taken in our camp came from the shores of that big body of water, so maybe the move is best.

The only problem is getting there. We cannot motor the rapids. We have a long line attached to the boat, and by walking in the water from boulder to boulder and pulling on the rope we are able to muscle the craft the 250 yards into the big water. I am so exhausted and soaked with sweat by the time we motor onto the choppy lake that I don't think I can hunt today. Worse, I have stepped in over my boot tops repeatedly. I am grateful for the warm sunshine as we stop to dry out. I pour the ice water from my boots and squeeze a pint from each wool sock before replacing them on my feet. I have no dry socks with me, a mistake I won't make again if I can help it.

A short climb from the first bay we encounter on the lake puts us within eighty yards of a small bull. I quickly decide he isn't nearly good enough, even with the paucity of caribou. His presence is most welcome, though. He stands broadside, looking at us, then moves tentatively closer to see what this intruder might be. Eight cows and calves are close-by as well, and they buoy my hopes. Maybe the big lakeshore will produce for me.

We power around the next two bays before turning in to one of them. We can see caribou immediately, all fairly small and none nearly as large as those killed earlier by Ron Scott. We disembark and take a short walk to the first hilltop.

A herd of a half-dozen cows are feeding in the valley to our left. My feet are cold, and I still feel uncomfortably wet from the intense perspiration of our upriver voyage. We continue our vigil as the wind picks up, creating more threatening whitecaps on the dark blue lake. We must traverse that body of water to get back to camp. Our only alternative to that unappealing course is to shoot the rapids again, thus depriving ourselves of the opportunity to hunt here tomorrow. I pull my parka from my backpack as the sun sinks lower over the lake, reflecting on the disquieted waters like millions of diamonds and doing nothing to relieve my growing sense of apprehension.

A caribou is visible on the ridge perhaps a half-mile distant, another small bull. I catch a movement to his left that turns out to be a velvet-covered antler cresting the ridge. I am tempted by

Delicious berries abound in August in the bogs of northern Quebec.

this bull, but the top points are short and he is quite narrow. He is yet another three- to four-year-old, more than likely. Bobby looks at me inquisitively, but I show him a thumbs-down. He motions toward the boat, and we are shortly beginning the perilous trip home across the surging lake.

Bobby is expert at negotiating rough water in a small open canoe. He would have been dead long ago otherwise, a victim of the well-known truism that the Inuit cannot swim. I am intimidated to no end by the waves, but soon we are safe on the sandbar just across the ridge from camp. After a short walk to the top we can see the camp's maple leaf flag whipping in the breeze. Here we are surprised to see a friendly young bull perusing us, his rack and demeanor marking him unmistakably as the one that greeted us on the first ridge above the rapids. I get even closer this time and take a few more telephoto shots before he

beats a rapid retreat to the west, over the next hill and out of sight.

Nobody in camp has scored. Ten hunters, and the only animals so far are the three my own party took yesterday.

We witness a great show of northern lights before retiring, the slowly undulating streaks mesmerizing everybody in camp. As the moon rises, they become almost invisible. Sleep comes easily after a couple of aspirins to soothe my traumatized muscles. I can walk all day without suffering, but doing so with chilled leg muscles is something else. Also, getting the boat up those awful rapids required more exertion than I was prepared for. At least the job is behind us now, and tomorrow I get to hunt the big lake.

Morning dawns with a brisk east wind and low overcast. We make our way across the isthmus to the boat on Lake Kakiattukallak, and shortly we are under way. We make to the southeast, in the lee of higher terrain, the center of the lake boiling with countless whitecaps. Soon we are on a low ridge facing into a stiff breeze that bends the flaming dwarf willows low and whips the sedge grass violently. As I bundle up for our glassing session, a feeling of desolation creeps over me. There are no caribou visible anywhere.

Bobby directs us inland for a couple of miles, and we stop at each promontory to search. Nothing. At our last stop I catch a movement on a nearby ridge, and it turns out to be an antler. A mediocre bull, on the dead run, soon comes into view, white mane flowing magnificently and nostrils flaring from the hard run. What is he running from? He comes within four hundred yards and never breaks stride, disappearing from view a mile distant.

Another motion then materializes out of the distant wastes. A hunter. So that's why our caribou was running. The man has to be from another camp, according to Bobby, since none of his hunters could possibly be out there. Everybody must be ranging far and wide, looking for caribou.

Bobby and I top each ridge, carefully glassing every nook and cranny for the elusive bands of migratory caribou. My guide lowers his binoculars and looks at me with thinly disguised concern.

"No cow, no bull," he says, the phrase freezing the moment and defining the day. I repeat his words and nod, then we move on to the next ridge. Several times more Bobby verbalizes the same dread expression. This is hard to take, this specter of last year that has returned to haunt me.

It begins to spit rain in the afternoon, adding to the misery. I must walk in rain gear, soaked in perspiration. At least I'm warm until I stop, I remind myself. We keep on moving but see nothing.

The wind begins to shift as we descend to our launch. We must now face a more treacherous lake than we had this morning. I am wearing my life jacket and find myself praying I won't need it as my guide skillfully tickles the canoe across the water. He greets each swell by cutting engine power, turning the prow exactly right to engage the ensuing trough, and emerging with only inches of gunnel to spare. I am thinking that in the event of a capsize, hypothermia and loss of consciousness would set in long before we could reach shore, nearly a quarter-mile distant. Finally we attain the beach. A delicious hot meal awaits us in camp.

We truly are hunting the land of rainbows. Passing showers create these majestic wonders late in the day, and as we enter the assemblage of frame tents a gigantic double rainbow forms over Bobby Lake. Who could create such a phenomenon but an omnipotent God? I am reminded of this truth as I snap pictures of the other hunters returning by boat to the landing, my telephoto lens capturing a vivid multicolored backdrop.

I awaken with a start that night, visions of another unsuccessful caribou hunt taunting me. I walk outside and see the night sky pulsating with the glow of the Arctic aurora. Stars are everywhere, the North Star and the Big Dipper high above the horizon. Tomorrow I will dig a little in my New Testament and try to make some sense of this impending failure. I return to the warmth of my sleeping bag and finally get some needed rest.

Bobby is late getting us under way after breakfast, as other pressing duties have accumulated while he has been providing me personal guiding service. I remain in the tent after my roommates have departed, and I spend a few minutes in devotional. In 1 John the exact words I need to put my mind at ease spring forth: "Everything in the world—the cravings of sinful man, the lust of his eyes and the boasting of what he has and does—comes not from the Father but from the world. The world and its desires pass away, but the man who does the will of God lives forever." Refreshed in spirit, I emerge from my tent to face the day with a potent reminder of the eternal perspective and how truly insignificant, on a cosmic scale, is such a small thing as a caribou hunt.

Cosmic or not, temporal or eternal, all endeavors require effort. I face another uncertain day with only a couple more remaining. The last caribou bull I laid eyes on was the one running from the distant hunter early yesterday. We saw nothing thereafter except the endless barren tundra in its autumn splendor. Today the wind has picked up and changed direction. The flag now shows a stiff southwesterly wind, which will bring the full force of it across the giant lake onto the beach where our boat is parked.

As we crest the low ridge I am horrified at the angry look of the lake, so comparatively tranquil yesterday. White froth boils like some giant stew in the rolling, tumultuous water. I express my alarm to Bobby, and he delays a bit by doing some glassing and mumbling that the boat should be light with only two of us in it. I remain unconvinced, though, and buckle on my life jacket before climbing aboard. I also lash my rifle and pack to the bow so they won't be lost if we capsize. We have some difficulty coaxing the boat to leave the shore against the wind, and as we launch into the gale I say a silent prayer for our safety.

The fierce assault of the waters starts as soon as we are free of the shallows. Giant waves, much bigger even than they had appeared from lakeside, surround us so that at times we can hardly see the land. The agitated, foaming monster that has us in its grasp repeatedly washes over the bow. I hold onto the sides of the canoe and yell to Bobby to go back.

"No can. We go up ahead. More easy."

He literally can't go back. The enraged water won't permit such a turn, and if he goes with the wind we'll miss the beach and dash to pieces where the pounding surf meets boulders, sending a white spray thirty feet into the air. Only his considerable skill prevents our capsizing into the frigid lake. It seems longer than the few actual minutes, but soon we are in more shallow and tranquil waters, though far from the north shore we had intended to hunt. We beach in a shallow bay near the rapids we forded two days ago and cover ground we have already searched, to no avail.

At a prominent boulder, we spend several hours glassing nearly one hundred square miles of barren territory. Bobby turns and looks at me at least three times, uttering the unwelcome words: "No cow, no bull." I soon begin returning them, sometimes beating him to the punch.

We break about 11 A.M. for tea in a crevice out of the wind, and I entertain myself with blueberry picking. The berries are plentiful and tasty, and my interest in them triggers a lesson in Inuktitut from Bobby. The word is difficult to transliterate into English, but it sounds like "you-DINE-knock." He tells me that the delicious and unusual salmon-colored strawberries we picked last year, so numerous in the bogs then, have been almost absent this year. I wish out loud that the caribou had been as plentiful.

We have seen nothing by 3 P.M. We have walked only a couple of miles, an easy day in this part of the world, but it has been entirely without a sighting. I am suffering severe second thoughts about my decision that first day. At this point there have been only four caribou killed by the entire camp, the worst record ever in Bobby's Caribou Camp. I thought Ron Scott was crazy to shoot two bulls immediately, but he's sure looking like the smartest guy in camp now.

There are numerous passing showers as sunshine gives way to clouds, and we are treated to rainbows once more. We descend to the boat for lunch and tea, with the wind unrelenting and the small inland sea still boiling like a witch's brew. As I nurse my hot drink, I gaze at the innumerable rivulets of color coming down off the heights. The dwarf Arctic willows of the shallow draws, all glistening and wet, are tinted gold, orange, and red by the frost. The color and motion give the impression of living fire. I am distracted by the sight, though the necessity of launching once more into the awful lake is fast upon us. Turning once more to face that terrifying adversary, I convince myself that perhaps it is better than before. But perhaps not. I tape record a final message of love for my wife and family, just in case, and seal it in a Ziplock plastic bag in my pack.

It isn't better. We want to go to the north end of the lake for the afternoon, but it isn't to be. We are pounded as badly as previously and must seek the shelter of our original beach. Bobby drives the boat almost uncontrollably into the soft sand and the security of solid ground once more. As I leap from the canoe onto the bank I thank God for the safe arrival, and I turn to look at Bobby. He appears a picture of Inuit unconcern, but I notice he is wearing his own life vest for the first time.

We have nowhere to hunt now. We climb the only ridge available and spend another hour glassing the north shore, knowing full well that if we spot anything it won't be possible to get to it under these conditions. There is a wide fjord we can't cross just beyond the near ridge, so anything on the next ridge is unapproachable without using the canoe, and I'm not going to die for a caribou if I can help it. I mull over the turbulent little ocean crashing on the boulders below us and wonder if I've ever done anything more dangerous in all my hunting career than our two forays into those seething waters. Not goat hunting, not sheep hunting, none of the big bears—well, maybe the goat hunt.

"No cow, no bull," I say as hope fades to zero. We have seen not a single caribou today. Bobby smiles weakly.

"Maybe tomorrow make better. Animals hard to know."

I know what he means, even though his syntax is a little off. At least he can communicate in my language, which is more than I can do in his. And maybe he's right about tomorrow.

Nothing shows. Bobby plans to move the boat back to the other, less treacherous lake adjacent to camp for our final day of hunting. He doesn't want to chance missing my last day of hunting because of wind. He will return tonight at dusk, when the wind dies somewhat, and move

the craft back through the rapids with one of the other guides. We will hunt tomorrow to the west of Bobby Lake.

I return to my tent a little despondent but nevertheless upbeat, knowing that a second straight defeat on the Quebec-Labrador caribou will probably set some kind of record, a distinction I already hold for cougar and Sitka black-tailed deer. Both those species are gimme hunts for most people, but each one took me three trips.

I learned rather soon after I met Ron Scott that he is also a Christian, and he hands me one of his business cards as I enter the tent. Printed on the back of it is another verse from the Bible, Romans 5:3, which reads: "And we rejoice in the hope of the glory of God. Not only so, but we rejoice in our sufferings, because we know that suffering produces perseverance; perseverance, character; and character, hope."

I am familiar with the verse, but the reminder is precious. I feel like I've found another real brother, and my heart is glad. It is well with my

Shed antler on the colorful tundra.

soul whatever happens tomorrow. I sleep soundly in light of that certain encouragement.

Dawn is as still as death, and Bobby wishes he had left the boat on the big lake. The rain is gone and the sky blue. But the absence of caribou is ominous, oppressive, and real. We motor several miles down the lake, park the boat, and start walking. The brisk pace Bobby sets soon has me sweating in my woolens, and I strip off my shirt and strap it onto my pack. Black flies swarm in the motionless air, and I stop and put on my face netting, which I fortunately remembered for this trip. Nonetheless, the insect attack continues unabated. They continually find the chinks in my armor and bite through my thin polypropylene undershirt.

We stop only briefly at each intervening ridge, finding no sign of our prey. We walk relentlessly until I can see in the distance a prominent *inukshuk,* or rock-man, on a hilltop. I wonder if that marks the boundary of Bobby's guiding area, but I cannot communicate with him well enough to make my question clear. Here we can see for miles, though, and we pass the remainder of the day fighting black flies, drinking tea, and eating bannock and sandwiches.

The midday heat is highly unusual here at any time, but especially in September. I find my view obscured by the thermal waves created by radiant energy vibrating the air. Bobby asks, "How you say bad looking in English?"

I miss his point entirely at first, but quickly he makes his meaning clear. He wants to know the English word for heat wave, which we are experiencing while glassing. I tell him.

"That my name. In Inuktitut is 'Ulio Umialik.'"

"Heat wave? That's your name?"

"Right."

Interesting. I wonder why he received such a name. Maybe he was born when it was

unusually warm. Maybe his mother had hot flashes while pregnant with him. Clarifying isn't possible, though.

At one point I finish a sandwich and wad up the plastic bag in which it was wrapped. I half-heartedly toss it some ten feet toward the dying embers of our fire, and it lands exactly in the center. It expands suddenly in the heat, then rapidly withers, gradually becoming only a speck before disappearing altogether. I can't help but compare the sight to my expectations for this hunt—inflated, and now reduced to practically nothing.

As the sun edges toward the west, reflecting brilliantly off a large pond, I turn once more to my host and say curtly, "No cow, no bull."

He looks at me to try to discern my meaning, posing the unspoken question of my attitude in the face of another defeat. I grin sincerely at him, and he understands. I am at peace. I hold no animosity toward anyone, and I plan to hunt with Bobby next year. I plan to take two giant bulls then. Hope is magnificent.

"No cow, no bull," he says. "We go."

With our lengthening shadows falling on the vast land, I start the long journey home.

EPILOGUE

The following year I returned to Bobby's camp and took that Quebec-Labrador caribou. The specimen was no giant, the hunting was no easier, and once more I walked perhaps a hundred miles in six days. The real monsters never showed, and Bobby was facing replacement of a heart valve as soon as the season wound down. He hoped to get well soon enough to move the camp to a location that might offer better access to the migration. Apparently the pattern has shifted over the past few years, demonstrating once more the fickle nature of this animal.

Woodland caribou. (Photo: from the author's collection)

WOODLAND CARIBOU
(*Rangifer tarandus terraenovae*)

There is that about the island of Newfoundland which suggests caribou.
The rugged ground breaks in flinty billows everywhere,
yet leaves now and again a spot of oily calm, a level reach of yellow barren.
The woodlands are evergreens that picture snows and wintry winds
even on golden summer days; and everywhere grow tangles of wiry vines
and undergrowth, conquered here and there by the level, bushy tops of berry plants.
And beneath all is a soft carpet of gray moss, ankle deep and moist,
which the caribou so dearly love—moss, which to them is a luxury in summer,
a necessity in winter, a feast always.

—Clay Arthur Pierce, *Trail and Camp Fire*, 1897

The woodland caribou is the only native large ungulate on the island of Newfoundland, as the moose are an introduced species. Caribou in Newfoundland have always been extremely important to indigenous and immigrant peoples. Humans have inhabited the island for perhaps 5,000 years, and there is evidence that all these cultures extensively preyed on the caribou. The aboriginal inhabitants at the time of European contact were the Beothuck, and those Indian people moved inland from the coast every autumn to intercept caribou migrating southward for the winter. For the most part their hunting used rough fences that herded the animals into range of their bows and arrows. They also used the Inuit method of catching the animals swimming, where they could spear or ax them.

Today hunters may take woodland caribou only in Newfoundland, if one uses the hunter's definition of these deer of the tundra. The southerly woodland caribou is endangered in much of its range and thus is not hunted. The woodland caribou of Quebec and Labrador are known, somewhat naturally, as the Quebec-Labrador variety in the record books. Those of northern British Columbia, the Yukon, and the Mackenzie Mountains of the Northwest Territories are mountain caribou to the hunter. For biologists, however, these are all woodland caribou, and the discrepancy between them and the hunting fraternity is one of fundamental confusion. Hunters often split species and subspecies as much on terrain, hunting techniques, and differences in experience as on any physical differences between the animals. Biologists are purists, examining the animal for any distinguishing features that justify a separate listing.

For many years, the biological location of woodland caribou has included a broad and varied band of habitat stretching from foggy Newfoundland westward and southward across the vast and inhospitable barrens of Labrador and Quebec, the northern parts of Ontario and the prairie provinces, upward into the mountains of the Yukon and the Northwest Territories, southward to British Columbia, and a short distance into the Selkirk Range of Idaho. A more diverse and widely spread environment hardly exists anywhere.

There may be a pending partial resolution of this amicable disagreement between the record books and the science books. In his recent work *Deer of the World,* Dr. Valerius Geist formalizes the very obvious physical differences between the caribou of Newfoundland and those of other locations in North America. His arrangement would not disconnect the Quebec-Labrador caribou from the mountain caribou, as hunters are determined to do, but would recognize a new category of caribou known as the Newfoundland caribou (*Rangifer tarandus terraenovae*). The scientific name he proposes dates from 1896 but was subsequently discontinued to allow for the present inclusive woodland classification, *Rangifer tarandus caribou.* Geist very logically suggests resurrecting the old nomenclature for the

Newfoundland caribou. He believes that the long isolation of this subspecies from mainland animals has given rise to significant physical differences under the influence of environmental and genetic factors.

The distinctive features of the Newfoundland caribou (or the woodland caribou of Newfoundland, if you prefer) are abundant. The coat is lighter than that of other woodland caribou, and the dark fur on the back and sides is darker than the black fur of the legs. The white neck markings do not continue onto the withers, as is common in other types of caribou, but stop abruptly short. The belly and inside of the back legs have more white than other caribou, which generally have black hair there. White hair may extend into the area between the antlers and continue forward onto the forehead in a manner most uncharacteristic of other woodland caribou, whose forehead is most often covered in dark hair.

The stags of Newfoundland are known for having impressive white neck manes, and it turns out that hunters are not the only ones who have noticed. Biologists recognize the feature as a distinctive characteristic of these caribou. White rings around the eyes are present most of the time, while they are uniformly indistinct or absent on mainland caribou. Overall, the markings of Newfoundland caribou are more like those of the Peary caribou of the high Arctic than the woodland caribou of the mainland, although their body size is equal to that of mainland caribou.

Only in Newfoundland are male caribou "stags" and female caribou "does," but that designation is serious to Newfoundlanders and should be respected, as I do here.

Newfoundland caribou are distributed all over the island and on a half-dozen nearby smaller islands, making up thirty-seven separate herds. More than half of these herds have been introduced, including all of those on satellite islands, as part of an ongoing management and enhancement program. The herds are monitored by radio telemetry studies, periodic censuses, a herd composition survey, and observational data.

Woodland caribou. Newfoundland, October 1996.

The physical barrier of open ocean separates introduced herds on smaller islands from caribou on the main island. There are between 80,000 and 90,000 caribou in these herds, and currently very healthy stag-to-doe (40 to 60) and calf-to-doe ratios (35–65 to 100 in fall, 30 to 100 in spring). All herds are on the increase.

In keeping with the growth of the herds, the caribou harvest has become immensely more productive in recent years. In 1980 only 1,000 caribou were harvested by residents and nonresidents. In the most recent year with complete data, more than 4,000 animals were harvested.

Newfoundland residents are able to obtain either stag only or either sex caribou licenses, and 75 percent of the available licenses go to residents. Since 1980 all nonresident licenses have been for stags only. Data from the most recently tallied year shows that Newfoundland issued 5,940 caribou licenses, of which only 782 went to nonresidents, far below the allocated 25 percent. Obviously, Newfoundland wants to do everything possible to make certain there is no shortage of nonresident licenses. Nonresident hunters are a major economic factor, and that is underscored by the fact that all nonresidents must use the services of an outfitter to hunt caribou and moose. The success rate on caribou runs around 90 percent for outfitted nonresident hunters but is only about 64 percent for residents.

The general biology of these caribou differs little from that of other types. They tend to exist in much smaller groups than the mainland caribou, with single animals and groups of only a few encountered relatively frequently. The rut begins in September, and herd stags gather together and tend bands of does generally numbering ten to fifteen. Breeding peaks in early October, with the exact timing dependent to some extent on weather and temperature. Animals in most herds make an annual migratory move, traveling south for the winter and back north for the summer. Calves are born on the herd's summering ground, usually in May, after a gestation period of about 225 days.

Like all caribou, those of Newfoundland have a strong liking for lichens, which are extremely important to their year-round diet. During the summer growing season, graminoids (grasses), various herbs, and deciduous shrubs assume an important place in the diet, providing an essential source of protein that may be deficient in the winter diet. Preferred shrubs include dwarf birch, rhodora, blueberry, sweet gale, mountain holly, cracker berry, raspberry, and saxifrage. Among the most utilized grasses and sedges are deer grass, cotton grass, and reed grass.

No wolves inhabit Newfoundland today, having been eliminated early in the twentieth century. The only significant predator of caribou in Newfoundland is the black bear, which in one study accounted for an amazing 46 percent of all adult caribou deaths. Predation of newborn calves must be quite common, given the taste for caribou that Newfoundland black bears have nurtured for generations.

There is only one documented disease among caribou in Newfoundland, and that is brain worm. This parasite reached Newfoundland with imported reindeer early in the twentieth century, but it has not been nearly the problem it is in more southerly latitudes. In mainland North America the worm is carried by white-tailed deer and can be passed on to moose. In Newfoundland, the infestation is generally not communicable to moose and is usually not fatal. Perhaps the reason that these worms have not devastated Newfoundland moose is that the preferred diet and habitat of the moose overlap only marginally with those of the caribou. The disease was first discovered in the caribou of Newfoundland in the 1970s. It causes disorientation, voluntary isolation from other caribou, the loss of the natural aversion to humans, and problems with gait and balance.

Hunting caribou in Newfoundland is almost always a wet, boggy experience. The open bogs attract the animals like magnets, and they often can be located by sitting on a hill and glassing the surrounding brown open areas. Once the hunter has located the right animal, he can usually approach within range by staying downwind and out of sight. I got some good pictures by walking behind my guide while he held up his arms to simulate caribou antlers. The animals eventually saw through our deception, but we were able to move in rather close.

Rubber boots and topnotch rain gear are among the most important items for hunting Newfoundland caribou. You will be constantly crossing miry, tundralike terrain characterized by

Beauty in Newfoundland is everywhere.

a deep layer of sphagnum moss that guards a virtual lake underneath. Intermittent high, rocky ground, however, offers firm footing and vantage points. Extensive walking (ten or more miles per day) is a part of most hunts, but in some areas guides may use vehicles to find a place to start. Be prepared for heavy hauling when the animal is down, and take a good pack and plastic bags to help keep blood off yourself and your gear. Most outfitters supply lunch and snacks, and there is little in the world of hunting more refreshing than hot tea and sandwiches beside a sparkling lake with a deep blue Newfoundland sky overhead. Of course, it rains often and unpredictably, so you might find yourself looking at more gray tones than blue ones.

Snow and extreme cold are the exception rather than the rule for Newfoundland in September and October. I recommend that you take woolen clothes, but you are more likely to want cotton while walking. It has been unseasonably warm when I've hunted Newfoundland, but going without warm clothing is a sure way to ensure an early freeze-up. A down parka for sitting in the wind while

glassing is always a comfort. To keep a dry rear, take a piece of foamy pad to place on the ground.

Any rifle adequate for deer-size game is appropriate for caribou. My .30-06 was loaded with 165-grain Nosler Partition bullets, and the combination was most effective. A .270 or .280 would be ideal. One of the weatherproof setups might set your mind at ease in rainy weather.

The outfitting business in Newfoundland is still respected by the people and the government. It is highly reliable and usually offers excellent service to clients. Your guides will be local Newfoundlanders who are knowledgeable and dedicated hunters. Enjoy yourself and be confident that you are in good hands. With luck, you will come home with a magnificent animal.

STAGS OF THE SPHAGNUM EARTH

A crimson sunset streaked with dark bands of cloud greets me as the bush plane approaches Deer Pond in the heart of Newfoundland. The wind buffets us and makes the ride as miserable as can be, but the scenery is stunning beyond description. The low angle of the sun imparts an unusually regal glow to the golden birch thickets below. In the approaching twilight broad yellow bands seem to climb upward on the deep green spruce ridges. I am en route to Pine Ridge Lodge, where I will hunt woodland caribou in the midst of this unspoiled splendor.

The rough air creates an unpleasant queasiness in me as we near touchdown. The pilot of the Helio Courier drops the flaps and slows for a landing on the boiling waters. I can hardly believe the contrast I feel between the magnificent view and the profound sensation of impending danger. I say a prayer to the Creator of all this beauty that perhaps He will allow us a safe landing on the restless lake. Pilot Dave Holloway greases the plane onto Deer Pond without incident, kicking up white froth with the plane's floats.

Dave is the brother of outfitter Wayne Holloway, who will guide us on our hunt. Wayne has a lodge with all the amenities on the shore of the lake, and I am looking forward to this experience with uncommon anticipation. He has an excellent reputation on this island province.

As we glide to a stop on the choppy water, we can see people awaiting our arrival at the dock. Emerald evergreens stretch around the lake as far as the eye can see, and bare hills are visible in the distance. This certainly looks like caribou country. We taxi to the dock, where several efficient camp personnel secure the plane and begin unloading.

Wayne has been outfitting hunts for woodland caribou, moose, and black bear for many years, and his success rate is outstanding. The facility is superb, and a weathered American flag flaps in the brisk wind beside the Canadian maple leaf, welcoming us Yankees. I am tired and hungry. The halibut in Halifax was outstanding during our forced respite there, but otherwise my diet has suffered in the past forty-eight hours. Wayne's full-time chef, Les Normore, treats us to our first outstanding feast, reminiscent of a Thanksgiving dinner down home.

Around the supper table we have an enlightening discussion about the local region, our prospects, and the nuances of local nomenclature. All discussion aside, it is simply good to be here. We have had a harrowing journey. We endured an engine failure before takeoff from Atlanta, a miscue that delayed us an hour and made us late for every subsequent leg of the journey. When we came through customs in Toronto, the immigration officer made all five of us Georgians open our gun cases, despite the fact that our schedule was tighter than a piano wire. As a result, we missed our second plane and had to overnight in Halifax, Nova Scotia, instead of Gander, Newfoundland. We are here now, however, and we will hunt tomorrow.

My sleep is almost always fitful for a night or two when I leave home. That, combined with the unusual Newfoundland Standard Time, which is at least thirty minutes ahead of the rest of the world, keeps my mind at full alert when I am supposed to be asleep. My friend and hunting partner, Jack Grabenstein, grabs me by the toe and awakens me only a few hours after I finally drift off. It is time to hunt. It is 4:30 A.M., Newfoundland time.

After a creative breakfast by Les, we depart on an easterly heading as the sky assumes an indescribable pink tone—pastel seems too bland a word for such color. We slog along the spongy trail toward Buck's Knob, where our hunt will begin in earnest. There are caribou here, no doubt, and we see several does right away. Doubtless this will be a day to remember. Jack is as excited as I, perhaps more so since he has drawn the privilege of first shot.

The uninitiated have little conception of how hard it is to walk on the unsteady ground of Newfoundland. The flat lowlands contain a type of moss known as sphagnum, and traversing it requires at least as much effort as climbing a mountain. Without the water-retaining abilities of sphagnum, Newfoundland and much of the north country would swing wildly between desert and flood. The sphagnum gathers moisture and releases it slowly, keeping the streams and rivulets flowing happily through all seasons.

There is a brisk breeze at our backs, wafting our scent toward the rising sun. Our plan is to walk an hour or so before making a lateral move to take advantage of the wind. Our hope is that one of the splendid caribou stags we are seeking will make a mistake and gain a degree of immortality as a trophy on the wall of my house or Jack's.

As we walk, Wayne demonstrates his knowledge of local flora and fauna; he can identify even the most obscure of plants. Many of my guides in the past wouldn't know a laurel from a lollipop, but Wayne knows almost all the common plants here, and he is glad to share his knowledge.

The unsteady trail takes its toll, and my legs feel a creeping tiredness as we negotiate the spongy surface. The pack I carry presses into my shoulders, making me wonder if I will be able to fulfill my commitment to the long day. I steel my mind with determination born of necessity and long experience. Nothing will hinder my chances at success if I can help it.

A rushing stream greets us near the lowest point of the trail, and the walking remains sloppy everywhere; I am glad I followed the advice to bring rubber footwear. Thick forest of ancient dwarf spruce predominates on all sides. This caribou trail we are following has been worn by countless hoofs over the millennia, and I feel privileged to share the ground.

We finally leave the muddy trail and ascend until we break into an open sedge meadow, the morning light increasing as we proceed. We are confident we will escape detection in the stiff breeze, since we have finally achieved the wind advantage with our long walk.

There are now caribou ahead, including the first stag I have ever seen of the woodland subspecies. A small stag to our left is accompanied by a pair of does and a calf. Another doe and calf spook in front of us, and I snap several telephoto shots.

Finally we spot several grand stags along the far edge of the bog, again accompanied by does. Wayne comments that the rut is now well under way, so the good ones are starting to show. Also, the cool wind and low temperatures have the animals on the move. One of the stags is almost a taker, though we feel that his tops are deficient. Both Jack and I decline to shoot, and we move on.

We cautiously cross trembling sedge marshes fringed with struggling tamarack trees, their bright yellow needles beginning their annual shedding. There are spots devoid of vegetation and deep sinkholes that can trap the unwary foot. We negotiate this perilous terrain for hours. A spruce grouse springs from a timbered edge, startling us with the thunder of frenzied wing beats. Interspersed in the sedge meadows that overlie the bogs are stands of wild cranberry and colorful pitcher plants, the only

carnivorous plant in Newfoundland and the official symbol of the province.

A terrific stag now presents just ahead, part of a small herd, and his rack looks Boone and Crockett to me. Wayne says he is only average and that we shouldn't shoot such an animal on the first day. Jack and I play with the stag for a half-hour, taking color slides and video of the marvelous creature. I put a simulated stalk on him and enjoy the thrill of being a motion-picture star, after which we bid the animal and his female companions good-bye.

The wear and tear of the miles is taking a toll on my legs, and I am glad to take a water break beside a shimmering lake. Caribou up ahead are moving toward us, so we wait until they pass, taking more pictures. The bounty of this country is ever apparent.

We spot several caribou on a rocky outcropping ahead, the animals bearing the same dusky gray color as the protruding stones. Several are bedded and no stag is immediately visible. We each consume a canteen of fresh water from the lake while we assess our options. There is no shortage of drinkable water in the back country of Newfoundland, because the sphagnum bogs continually leach-purify the waters they trap.

The herd indeed contains an exceptionally fine stag. He moves from doe to doe, lowering his head and curling his upper lip while checking to see if they are ready to stand for breeding. We stalk undetected to within 250 yards, seeking shelter from the favoring wind behind a grove of dwarf spruce. From here we can assess the quality of the stag. I see little deficiency, but Jack has first shot today and decides to stalk closer before making a decision. We can't make out whether the animal has a double shovel, but he is enormously palmated and has good top points.

After a stalk of some thirty minutes, prolonged by a suddenly variable wind, we finally approach to within seventy-five yards. Jack is uncertain, but finally he decides that the excellent mass and spread of the antlers are too good to pass up. His first shot is sufficient, although he follows up with a second to be certain.

What a splendid stag! I am envious of Jack's success, but now it is my turn. Pictures, caping, and quartering will consume a good portion of the afternoon, so we stop for lunch beside a nearby lake. While we eat I inspect the myriad low-growing plants, partridgeberries, pitcher plants turned crimson by daily frosts, and innumerable sweet wild cranberries. Mosses and ferns of every description create a virtual living carpet. A merry campfire at the edge of a succulent sedge meadow provides hot tea to wash down our stew and sandwiches. As the sun begins to sink, we shoulder heavy packs and begin our five-mile retreat to the lodge. We will hunt our way back as we labor home with our burdens.

We spot a huge stag as we start out, and Wayne and I leave Jack with the packs and make a quick two-mile trek to see how good he might be. But for one top that is deficient, I would shoot this stag without hesitation. We watch the creature exercise dominance over a lesser stag in a jovial sparring match before resuming his insistent checking of the does. He has a double shovel, mass as great as that of the animal Jack harvested, and impressive bez points. I turn him down only because one top lacks points, although the other is well palmated and has several. I have a nagging feeling that I could regret my decision later, but that's hunting.

Under another majestic, rose-colored sunset we trek the long, soggy trail back to the lodge. Jack demonstrates amazing strength and stamina as he carries the antlers and cape, as well as his loaded pack, the entire five miles, stopping only briefly for a rest. By the time we arrive at the lodge, my respect for my friend's endurance has grown considerably. My own clothes are soaked with perspiration, my shoulders ache, and my legs protest the hours of abuse. A hot shower and good meal go a long way, and I know that exhaustion will soon put me to sleep.

Departure at early light is accompanied by a 180-degree shift in the wind, putting the gentle breeze in our faces. We go rapidly into hunting mode, our senses tuned and our minds fully awake. A red squirrel scolds us from high on a dead spruce tree, the crimson highlights on the creature's back and the top of its tail gleaming in the sunlight.

It is not very long before we recognize that there are fewer caribou out and about today. The wind has almost died and the temperature is a dozen degrees warmer, so the animals are

A hunter scoping in on a nice woodland caribou stag.

Lichens hug the rocks all over Newfoundland.

undoubtedly hidden in the cool shade of the trees. We spot a small stag on our way up Buck's Knob, but he is only a youngster, staring inquisitively at us from a dense spruce thicket. We are fully five miles from the lodge before we see any appreciable number of caribou, and the only herd stag we locate is not what we want. Despite his relatively small size, this stag is herding does as if he were king of the bog. We get great pictures once more, and Jack lets the video roll while the entire entourage comes within yards of us.

Far to the east, deeper into the wilderness than Wayne has ever ventured in his ten years of guiding, we spot caribou. No antlers are visible, but this time of year a dominant stag usually accompanies a concentration of females. Maneuvering a mile over the treacherous sedge bogs, we make our way toward the rocky outcrop. It is already near noon, and we are seven miles from the lodge; I feel as if I am wearing anvils for boots. I hope fervently that I can take my animal

today, for I am not certain I can walk this far for a third day.

Only a lone doe is crossing the bog by the time we get to the ridge. We circle all the likely hiding places, but still we are unable to locate the herd. Perhaps they are lying in some shaded nook out of sight. I wipe my brow and gaze up at the unrelenting sun. My shirt is soaked with sweat and my underclothes are clammy. We climb a prominent hill to peruse several miles of unbroken sedge meadow, the far fringes invaded by spruce and tamarack trees. There are no caribou.

I continue glassing and spot in the sea of tan a family of greater Canada geese, foraging for berries. We greatly need to rest before hunting our way back toward the lodge, so we build another fire on a rocky hilltop to heat water for tea, eat our lunch, and take a brief nap. Wayne soon rousts us, and we resume our quest.

Before we turn westward toward home, we traverse the marsh to check another possible hiding place. A doe with two calves rests on a ridge along the way; so perhaps the other animals are on the other side of that last rocky outcrop ahead. As we pass, the animals rise and spook off into the timber. Out of the corner of my eye I catch a fleeting movement, and I quickly swing my binoculars around. It is a resplendent red fox, so colorful it appears aflame. We watch for several minutes as it stops and gazes at us before retreating for parts unknown.

There are no more caribou here, as far as we can determine. Disappointed, we begin our laborious retreat toward the lodge. There's a lot of country between here and there, so perhaps we can still find a good stag today. My hope is at low ebb, however, and the changing weather does not bode well. No matter, I can hunt in the rain; I only hope it won't be necessary.

On the way back we come across the same stag we saw earlier. He looks no larger than before, so we simply watch. Another small young stag passes by with a doe. We pause at the same lake where we stopped yesterday, and again we drink our fill. It will be a laborious task getting home from here, but I can make it. I take in a full pint of the cold water to fortify myself for the trip. It looks more and more as if we will be out walking again tomorrow.

I am struggling across another of the endless sedge bogs, trying to place my feet so as to avoid sinking in, when Wayne drops to his knees and swings his binoculars to the left. I see the giant stag immediately and grope for my own glasses. The animal has a good retinue of does, so he is of breeding quality, at least. The mass and number of points are instantly impressive, and the reddish main beams are the longest we have seen by far. The bez and shovel are of highest quality—long, substantial, and imposing by any standards. He has excellent spread and visible back points. The only glaring deficiency is the absence of good top points.

The long hike back after a successful day afield.

My thoughts race. The animal I passed up yesterday was probably better. Do I want to finish the mission now? I weigh all the factors, and consider the threescore miles I have walked as well. I slip in my earplugs and continue to ponder as I move forward, chambering a round just in case.

The stag looks even better through the riflescope. The distance is a little over a hundred yards, and the creature is beginning to mill nervously, so I must decide quickly. We have seen precious little today, and bad weather is coming. I make my decision and squeeze off the round, the solid whack of the 165-grain Nosler Partition bullet confirming that I have made a good hit. The stag stands for a moment, then starts moving away through the spruce forest that borders the bog. There is no time for another shot, but the nearness of the target and the solid impact imply that a followup won't be necessary.

I move forward cautiously, a chambered round locked and ready. Numerous does stand looking confused, so I feel certain the stag is down. The females spook off as we approach, their lord and master nowhere to be seen.

Easing onto solid ground, I walk directly to where the animal vanished from view. To my great surprise, he is standing behind a grove of evergreens. His head is down, yet he refuses to fall, despite a fatal wound. I feel certain that I have struck a killing blow, but to be sure we don't lose a wounded animal I put an assurance shot through the vitals.

The stag is a beauty, with a lush coat and an elongated white neck mane. The positive aspects of the antlers far outweigh the lack of good top points, and I am more than satisfied. He is 45 inches wide with incredible beam length, and will proudly grace my collection as a wonderful representative of the Newfoundland subspecies.

Following a picture session, we do the necessary chores and set out for the trip home. Jack Grabenstein again demonstrates his outstanding physical stamina by packing the antlers and cape back to the lodge, and I snap pictures to document the feat. Another scarlet sunset

Newfoundland is the only place where female caribou are called "does."

Woodland bulls carry impressive manes and headgear.

silhouettes our toiling figures as we complete the difficult journey.

Sitting in the lodge the next day as an unseasonably warm rain falls, I reflect with deep satisfaction on a hunt well done. The Newfoundland wilderness has gained another enthusiastic devotee. The boggy walking, the tenacity required for success, the soreness in my legs—all these fade in my memory as we relive the high points of the adventure.

Before long I will be back home, and the memories will fade still more. I thank God for the success, and I hope I can retain enough to relate the tale accurately. It has been too good to forget.

Peary caribou. (Photo: from the author's collection)

PEARY CARIBOU
(Rangifer tarandus pearyi)

Away, away in the Northland,
Where the hours of the day are few,
And the nights are so long in winter
That they cannot sleep them through.

—Phoebe Cary (1824–1871), *A Legend of the Northland*

Peary caribou live in the land of endless nights in winter, farther north than any other member of the deer family. They range from the offshore islands of the Canadian Arctic as far northward as land exists, and this harsh environment has resulted in some remarkable physical adaptations.

The Peary caribou is the smallest of the North American reindeer, both in terms of body size and population. It is no longer hunted where it occurs in the form most adapted to climatic extremes— that is, in the extreme north. In Resolute Bay, for example, most caribou meat is imported for the locals from far to the south, though residents do complain that local meat is far superior. The only sport hunts for the creature occur on Victoria Island, where resides a slightly less adapted caribou, from a morphological standpoint. This hunt gives the sportsman an opportunity to taste what hunting high Arctic Peary caribou would be like.

Peary caribou were designated as threatened in 1979, and in 1991 they were classified as endangered on Banks Island and in the Queen Elizabeth Islands. Caribou on all other Arctic islands, and on the Boothia Peninsula, were classified as threatened. Their numbers have declined drastically, and hunting opportunities are severely limited, even for the Inuit. There may be fewer than 2,000 Peary caribou north of latitude 74 degrees north today, whereas in 1962 there were over 25,000. About half the total population died off in a single winter in 1973–74. The animals have virtually disappeared from several islands, including Somerset and Prince of Wales. Increasing muskox populations are a possible contributing cause, but in many areas there has been no associated growth in the muskox herd. Severe winters are more likely the culprit, weakening the animals and leaving them malnourished.

Today only two communities have active sport-hunting programs for the Arctic island subspecies, making it a limited specialty hunt and probably the most expensive caribou hunt in the world. An extensive effort, both by the native peoples and their governments, is under way to conserve the subspecies. No other caribou hunting is quite like it, and in my opinion no caribou collection is complete without one.

Boone and Crockett does not recognize the Peary caribou as a separate subspecies, but Safari Club International has come up with a simple but ingenious way both to list them in the record book and to recognize their unique status, wherever they occur. Any caribou from any North American Arctic island, except the giant island of Baffin, is considered "Arctic islands caribou." These beautiful and unusual animals are commonly referred to by hunters as Peary caribou, even though they intergrade with the central Canada barren ground caribou to the south, and scientists do not classify any caribou as a Peary caribou unless it lives north of 74 degrees latitude (about the location of Lancaster Sound). On Baffin Island, the caribou are distinctively different from the Peary subspecies and are of the central Canada barren ground subspecies. Biologists are still conducting studies on the classification of the caribou of the Arctic archipelago, but for now at least they refer to caribou south of 74 degrees but north of the mainland (but including the Boothia Peninsula) as Arctic islands caribou, squaring well with the Safari Club International system.

In the high Arctic and Greenland, the caribou move freely across the ice from island to island, giving rise to a genetically homogeneous population. Adaptation to life in such a harsh environment has led to a high degree of specialization, and a number of features distinguish the Peary caribou from its more southerly kin. These adaptations make it highly desirable to preserve and augment Peary caribou populations, because to lose this particular genetic pool would leave a gap in the Arctic ecology that other caribou could likely not close, even if introduced. So far from the tree line, other subspecies would almost certainly die out in Peary caribou habitat.

Both Peary caribou and the more southerly Arctic islands caribou are almost completely white, with perhaps only a few gray hairs on the muzzle and the top of the back. However, caribou on the Arctic islands vary considerably in appearance and size from one location to another and demonstrate a remarkable adaptation to local conditions. A mature bull will seldom weigh more than 230 pounds. Their ears, tail, and legs are shorter, their white hair thicker, and their hoofs correspondingly larger than those of other caribou. The heavily furred muzzle is also short, to minimize heat loss. Other features recognized by biologists include a short, broad skull, hoofs that are broader relative to body size, lighter gray antler velvet, and the absence of a pronounced flank stripe. These features become more prominent the farther north and west the creatures are found.

These animals live in the harshest environment of any cervid, and the Peary variety is the only subspecies that lives permanently north of the tree line. The little white caribou seldom masses in great hordes like other caribou, congregating instead in groups of fifteen to twenty at most, with the norm being one to three.

Their diet is lower in lichens than that of other caribou because such plants are much less prevalent on the Arctic islands. The main items of their diet include mosses, grasses and sedges, forbs, and willows. The diet of Peary caribou overlaps

Encountering our first caribou after leaving Cambridge Bay.

only somewhat with that of muskoxen, and it remains a question how well the two animals coexist. Most authorities agree that the habitat of the two species is different enough to minimize but not to eliminate competition. Muskoxen prefer moist grazing areas where larger sedges are packed closer together, allowing high intake of plant material. Caribou, on the other hand, prefer more elevated areas where there are fewer plants. This difference seems to be much more pronounced here than on the mainland. When animal densities are high or when foraging is difficult, because of deep snow or hard ground ice, the relationship of muskoxen and Peary caribou may change, to the detriment of one or both. Suffice to say that the relationship between muskoxen and caribou is more complex than simple competition for food.

It appears that the major effect of weather on Peary caribou is actually the effect on availability of critical forage rather than the temperatures themselves. Deep snow or hard ice stresses the animals and takes an inevitable toll; more moderate conditions make foraging easier and preserve the population.

Climate and weather are the prime forces shaping caribou ecology on the Arctic islands. Climate is the major factor in determining plant distribution and abundance; weather affects annual plant productivity; and snow and ice determine forage availability, which in turn determines the animals' survival rate and the ability to produce calves. Severe winters have resulted in the loss of up to 90 percent of the caribou on some islands. The 1990s were especially hard on these caribou, as three consecutive winters produced some of the heaviest snowfalls on record. Winter survival also depends on how much quality forage was available the previous summer, for summer forage creates fat reserves.

Other types of caribou may live to be eighteen to twenty years of age, but a Peary caribou of sixteen years is considered ancient. Cows are often bred during their second season of life. The rut occurs in October, as with other caribou, and calving is likewise usually in June. Bulls reach sexual maturity the first year of life, though under normal circumstances they do not breed until they are several years old. Winter severity can lead to malnutrition in pregnant cows, resulting in stunted calves that have a poor chance of surviving.

On the Arctic islands, calving is more variable than elsewhere and may occur as late as early July. Like other caribou, the cows give birth to a single calf after seven and a half to eight months of gestation. Calves are particularly vulnerable to predators at birth and shortly thereafter, and nature's way of dealing with the problem is the common one: the calves are all born within several days, and wolves become quickly gorged. An hour after birth the calves can walk, and very shortly thereafter they can run.

Besides the obvious toll taken by scarcity of food and the harsh environment, wolf predation and human hunting are significant in certain areas. All Arctic communities participate in an ongoing and diligent effort to help caribou numbers recover. Victoria Island holds a healthy herd and no hunting ban is anticipated, although that remains a possibility if further population decline occurs.

As with most of its endangered major species, Canada funds and empowers a Peary Caribou National Recovery Team. In each Inuit community, the Hunter-Trapper Association (HTA) surveys the available caribou and decides, in conjunction with government biologists, upon a quota. Two members of each HTA sit on a regional wildlife management board, so there is plenty of local input. Only a few communities have quotas high enough even to consider a sport hunt, and subsistence needs always take priority over sport hunts. Commercial harvesting of Peary caribou has been halted by local authorities for the foreseeable future.

The recovery plan seeks to enhance the populations of caribou on the Arctic islands and avoid local extinctions. Since supplemental feeding is impractical, declining numbers resulting from poor forage are simply a fact of life. The first step in protecting a given population is to restrict hunting; caribou meat from other sources is supplied to the local community. If the population continues to decline, and if wolf predation is implicated, a wolf control plan may be inaugurated. If muskox competition is a major factor, accelerated muskox harvesting takes place. In the worst case, in which all variables are under as much control as possible yet populations continue to drop, biologists would consider a rescue operation for eventual restocking.

Management makes use of periodic counts, although such methods are expensive and require continued funding by the government. A harvest study conducted by the Nunavut Wildlife Management Board encourages all communities to do a count of harvested caribou, and interviews with native hunters reveal the number of animals spotted or taken.

One can expect to hunt these caribou on southern Victoria Island during early to mid-October, when the animals mass on the shore of Coronation Gulf and Dolphin and Union Strait, separated by thirty miles of water from the mainland. To me it seemed brutally cold, and the days were alarmingly short. I took all my best winter clothing with me, but my down parka failed to meet the standards of my hosts, the Ekaluktutiak HTA of Cambridge Bay. Fortunately, they loan heavily insulated Arctic parkas to hunters, so I was extremely comfortable. Temperatures were below zero most of the time, and the weather was good except for some low clouds.

All hunts start and finish at the local Renewable Resources Office, where one purchases the requisite tag and receives a briefing on the hunt and local conditions. On returning, one must obtain an export permit from that same office. I found the personnel there most helpful and hospitable.

If you are disinclined to invest in a true Arctic parka, at least purchase down pants and down underwear, available from most mail-order hunting supply houses. Long hours of relative inactivity in a *qamutik* (sled) make them indispensable. Underneath I wore regular cotton underwear, a layer of polypropylene long johns, wool socks, and liners. I also wore Sorel pac boots with thick felt liners. This arrangement made the hunt one of the most comfortable I have ever experienced. On the caribou-skin floor of the covered sled I actually found myself pleasantly drowsy as we bounced along. The Inuk guide has a much more difficult chore, facing the wind on the open snowmobile, and I didn't envy him his task.

Rifle care on late fall or early spring Arctic hunts requires special attention. I completely degreased the weapon before leaving home, this time doing it myself with Coleman lantern fuel. I put the whole bolt in a pan of the fluid for several hours, completely covering the metal and occasionally swishing it about to ensure deep penetration. I didn't have anything special done to the trigger mechanism, but it had been degreased shortly before. The weapon performed flawlessly.

Expect bitter cold, although the actual hunt was otherwise one of the easiest and most relaxed I can remember. The caribou were close-by the town of Cambridge Bay, so we stayed at the local co-op hotel, which was quite comfortable. The downside is that one misses the backcountry adventure, and there is considerable additional expense to this arrangement.

I do hope the Peary caribou of the true high Arctic one day will recover in numbers sufficient to allow a sport hunt, perhaps in the remote Queen Elizabeth Islands. To hunt Peary caribou north of 74 degrees latitude would be to relive the experiences of William Edward Parry, James Clark Ross, and other early explorers—to climb to the top of the world and seek this most unique of the cervids.

RETURN TO THE ARCTIC

The harsh Arctic wind seems alive, attacking me from all directions. I gaze at the barren landscape with the awe that all visitors must feel, no matter how often they see it. Without the Arctic clothing lent me by the Ekaluktutiak Hunter-Trapper Association (HTA), I would be truly suffering. But in my high-tech cocoon I am safe and snug—as much so as any native of the gentle temperate zones can be in these environs.

Today I am hunting Peary caribou with my Inuk guide, George Angohiatok. He is a native of Cambridge Bay, a hamlet nestled on a hill overlooking a cozy inlet on southern Victoria Island. George is a direct descendant of the Copper Eskimos, which Captain Richard Collinson and his crew of the HMS *Enterprise* first encountered while wintering here in 1852-53 while searching for the lost Franklin expedition. This distinct band of Native Americans already had implements of copper from local outcroppings, and hence the designation. Their Victoria Island cousins were later distinguished by the persistence and ingenuity with which they utilized the vast cache of goods left by Collinson's cohort Captain Robert McClure. McClure, participating in the same search, had to abandon his ship, the HMS *Investigator,* after more

Sled dogs are ubiquitous in the Arctic, and Cambridge Bay has its share.

than two years of being frozen into the ice at Mercy Bay on the north shore of adjacent Banks Island.

The temperature remains close to minus 10 degrees Fahrenheit, with a brisk breeze making it feel considerably cooler. It is late October, and winter here is already well under way. The daylight period is shrinking noticeably each day, as the sun sinks lower on the southern horizon. Of course, I have not actually seen the sun, because it is shrouded in low clouds, but its presence is evidenced by the soft light and the slight warming at midday. Within a month, the winter darkness will yield only to a noontime twilight. When winter gets serious in these parts, the hope of returning light is distant indeed. For now, we have about seven hours a day in which to hunt, but the low angle of the sun gives the landscape a foreboding aura that must have been terrifying to those early European explorers. Certainly the passing of summer is no cause for rejoicing, even among the Inuit, who have lived here for centuries.

For safety, we hunt in pairs. A damaged snowmobile could spell disaster for the lone hunter faced with a thirty-mile walk home. The other guide is George's father, Sam, leading a hunter named Vern Mattie from Illinois. Vern is hunting both muskox and caribou; I seek only the diminutive *tuktu* of the Arctic islands. On this particular day, and in the direction we are hunting, muskoxen are more abundant than caribou, and before long we spot a lone bull that looks like a taker. I join the stalk for the picture opportunity, so we leave George with the snowmobiles and the sleds.

The snow underfoot is as soft as cotton, and our approach is almost noiseless; the temperature seldom rises enough to form any kind of crust. It is like walking on confectioner's sugar. Here and there a tentative Arctic willow grows, the ground-hugging plant revealing that the snow covering is light. The illusion of deep snow results from the sheer vastness of the white land. We keep hidden behind a boulder, and the muskox doesn't sense our approach. My companion's shot is quick and secure.

My hands are freezing, and I wait eagerly for George's arrival with the snowmobile and sled, where I left my caribou-skin mittens. I take more photos of the animal and the happy guide and hunter. It is impossible to miss the deep reverence the Inuit have toward the creatures that share their land. To them, hunting is a spiritual experience of the first order, a return to their roots. The butchering and skinning are soon complete, and nothing useful goes to waste. The head and cape go to the hunter; the meat and remaining hide go to the people of Cambridge Bay, minus a small sampling the hunter wants to take home.

There is a herd of caribou up ahead, and after securing everything aboard we mount up. I am looking for a respectable Peary caribou, but not necessarily a specimen for the record book. I would rather have a representative animal with more white in the coat than particularly large antlers, although I would settle for a slightly darker animal if the antlers are exceptional. George and I have talked at length, and I have confidence he understands what I want.

The beauty of the country enthralls me. Beyond the milling herd of caribou, there is a dark bank of clouds that reminds me of a Georgia

The local Hunter-Trapper Association outfits all hunts in Cambridge Bay.

squall line, threatening to bring bad weather. I feel only a slight breeze now, so there is no such change coming, by all other appearances. I am looking to the south, and I realize that the darkness is the result of the ebony open water out in the Queen Maud Gulf. The phenomenon demonstrates that the sea is not yet completely frozen; its blackness absorbs light from an otherwise white sky. To my north the sky is noticeably brighter, the higher country and more consistent snow cover revealing itself by its effect on the nebulous atmosphere. By such subtle signs the Inuit have guided themselves unerringly for centuries. If I can see these things, and know thereby our approximate direction of travel, of what secrets are my hosts aware? I strain hard to see the *sastrugi*, the sometimes faint vertical ridges of snow that cover the land, etched by the prevailing wind. The Inuit use these to guide their way, but I cannot find them in the fresh, powdery snow. The effect is more prominent later in the season, when the hunt is for polar bear and seal.

Inspection of one caribou herd after another reveals beauty beyond compare. The animals are difficult to spot until one has accustomed the eyes to look for the delicate outlines against the distant snowy hills. Their coats are the color of the moon. There are bulls in each herd, all of them in constant motion chasing cows in a rutting frenzy that is apparently near its apex. Smaller bulls hang along the periphery of each herd, and any approach to the harem is met with a vigorous charge from the commander of the group.

None of the dominant bulls are particularly outstanding, all falling short in some way. This is the most common problem in hunting these animals, whatever the subspecies, since the one with the great top points so often lacks a shovel, and the one with massive bez points has only nubbins up top. Onward we go, enjoying the sight of so many animals massed in such a small strip on the south shore of Victoria Island. We are seldom out of sight of caribou. If happiness and satisfaction to the Inuit are synonymous with abundant game animals, as I have often read, my companions should be contented indeed.

The muskoxen on this part of the island are so numerous and so visible that one sees more of them than caribou in places. It is not uncommon to have two or three small herds of eight or ten animals in view at once, assuming their characteristic defensive positions at our approach. We already have our muskox, however, so they have nothing to fear from this party.

My guide skillfully puts the snowmobile and its trailing load, which includes me, into a wide arc to the left, perceivable only by the changing position of the dark sky to our south. In failing light, we finally give up the quest. At a fishing hole chipped out on a frozen lake, George demonstrates how one fishes for Arctic char through a hole in the ice, using a hand line to jig, as the rest of us consume solidly frozen sandwiches. There are no takers today among the char in this lake.

Our original plans were to motor to the northwest for fifty miles by snowmobile and hunt from a cabin on Wellington Bay. The hunting party that preceded us, however, encountered few caribou there, most of the animals having already congregated along the shore of the island both east and west of the town of Cambridge Bay. So we luxuriate in the comfort of the Ekaluktutiak Cooperative Hotel. Here I can thaw out my frozen cameras, take a hot shower, and sleep in a real bed. As an added bonus that evening, I am privileged to watch via satellite as the Atlanta Braves claim the world championship by taking the sixth, and final, game of the World Series from the Cleveland Indians. There are five other hunters in the hotel and four are from Ohio, so I celebrate quietly. I am completely unaccustomed to such luxury while hunting. I gaze out the window into the still blackness, the temperature pegged near 20 below zero, and thank God for His good grace.

Next morning dawns unchanged, the distant Arctic hills shrouded in a low, icy haze. We head west, where there are reportedly more caribou and fewer muskox. Several of the hunters need a muskox, and the report of our numerous sightings sends them off to where we were yesterday.

Soon I am in my down cocoon bouncing along behind George across the icy countryside. The engine of his snow machine is the only sound to shatter the quiet of the silent landscape. I marvel at the inventiveness of the Inuit as I lean over and gaze at the runners of the *qamutik*, gliding soundlessly and smoothly over the snow. Steering is accomplished by a rope attached to the snowmobile, with a knot some eight or ten feet in front of the sled, where the rope makes a Y, with a strand from the knot to each of the two front runners. When we turn, the rope on the outside of the turn tightens, while the one on the inside becomes slack. By such skill the Inuit have survived, even thrived, in conditions that brought nothing but despair to other men. I am hunting with the best. Today we will find the right caribou.

The *qamutik* in which I ride is a marvel. Unlike the dogsled I rode in while hunting polar bear, and another in which I hunted muskox in the high Arctic, this one has a plywood shield that protects the rider from the icy wind. Our speed is perhaps twenty miles per hour at full tilt, and the chill factor quite significant, even on a still day. Installed in the front of the boxlike shield is a Plexiglas pane that allows me to see forward.

As we clear the edge of the settlement, we begin to see caribou. I climb onto a sturdy ice chest to get a better look, leaning over the plywood frame and occasionally burying my head in the hood of my Arctic parka for a needed warmup. From this position I can instantly see anything of interest that comes our way.

Time after time we stop to check herds of caribou, which casually move aside as we pass, spooking only a short distance from us. The opportunity for pictures is fantastic, but my best camera, a venerable old Pentax I purchased while in Vietnam, fails in the dreadful cold, leaving me only with "idiot proof" models. I worry a bit about my rifle, whether it will fire properly when the opportunity arrives. After all, it is almost as old as the camera, and so is the scope.

Crossing a frozen lake, we spot a small band of muskox. The hulking creatures round up on a small hillock, a frozen island in the middle of the lake, as we glide by. On the other side of the lake are still more caribou, and a massive set of antlers is visible just over the hilltop. As we near the herd, the bull stands up in all his splendor, the best we have seen by far. George stops the snowmobile, and we hold a short conference as we look the animal over.

"Nice mass and spread, and a good shovel. Not much up top. Can we do better?" I question him carefully. Hunting Peary caribou is a new experience for me, and I really don't know how much we can expect. He replies that we must be patient, for there are really good ones out there, and besides, this one has short top points and little in the way of back points. I defer to my hunting sidekick, who has graciously offered me the first shot, since he took the muskox, and he confers with his guide.

"If you don't want him, I'll try for him," Vern asserts. I inquire if I can go along again, and of course it's no problem. More good pictures, I hope.

Animals in the Arctic have a resolute quality in their demeanor, and seem to accept the inevitability of death more readily than, say, a white-tailed deer. I don't believe that caribou are any more stupid than animals at lower latitudes, but they seem to possess a lot less instinctive aloofness, the quality that hunters commonly refer to as spookiness. Their main defense against predators is the vast country, their superior ability to reproduce, and fleetness of foot when pursued. Conserving energy for the harsh winter is primary, and they are not nearly as concerned about the approach of danger. We simply march up within range of the rutting bull, and my partner brings him down with a well-placed shot.

Vern's bull is nothing short of fantastic. As the downed creature reclines in the snow, I marvel at the long guard hair on the face, and the incredibly thick winter coat. The antlers curve gracefully, dark and massive against the contrasting white background. I almost can't believe I have passed up the opportunity to harvest such a magnificent specimen. As we take pictures, then watch the Inuit wield flashing blades to skin and quarter it, I wonder whether George was wise in his advice to me.

The expertise of our Inuit companions shines through again, the task of preparing the caribou for sled travel taking only minutes. The remainder of the herd has retreated only far enough to feel no immediate threat. They resume feeding on the tundra grasses, pawing and scraping in the snow. We leave them in a roar of snowmobile engines, and they hardly look up as we surge past.

Finding a good bull for me is now the goal. We motor onward, the miles slipping by, the cold wind in my face reminding me how stout my guide must be, exposed constantly as he is to the driving wind. We are roughly paralleling the shore of Queen Maud Gulf as we travel westward away from town, dark clouds to our south again indicating open water. The ramparts of a seaside cliff, so steep and so typically Arctic, loom in the distance, heralding a clearing trend with improving visibility.

There are still plenty of caribou, but the special bull I want continues to elude us. We climb a series of higher hills, spotting perhaps a hundred more of the animals on and around the margins of a large body of fresh water with a rigidly frozen surface. This is Kitiga Lake. As we near the shore we see a medium-size bull lying in the snow, twitching as if dying. George motors in a circle and stops a scant twenty yards from the creature. I scramble out of the *qamutik* in hope of discovering the reason for such strange behavior. The bull lies there and continues to twitch, his

Several herds are visible, the largest near a small island in the lake. We motor over for a look, and finding nothing of interest we move toward a rocky outcropping in the smooth icy surface. I don't see anything grand and striking anywhere, only mediocre bulls. Again I wonder about my earlier decision to pass up the animal Vern has taken.

As we approach the small island, the caribou begin to move aside in their casual fashion, allowing us to move to within a couple of hundred yards before they depart. Abruptly, from behind the hillock on the islet there bursts another band, and the bull is bristling with antler points. He is so impressive I'm almost speechless; George is equally moved. He immediately kills the engine as the animal trots rapidly away across the snow-covered ice, the immense rack dominating the scene. I can't believe there is a bull with that many points anywhere.

"What a brute!" George exclaims. "Good enough?"

I shuck a cartridge into the firing chamber and flip off the scope covers and the safety. As always in this type of hunting, finding the creature is the hardest part. My first shot flies wide of the fleeing animal, but the second is right on target. The huge bull is dead in the snow, another victim of my ancient Remington 700 in .30-06 caliber combined with a handloaded 165-grain Nosler. The range was about 150 yards.

The points up top and overall beam length are less than ideal, but those are the only deficiencies of this monster. The shovel is double, with not just a small second shovel but two truly huge, well-formed pieces that guard the nose. Most impressive are the massive bez points, so large my

Peary caribou. Northwest Territories, October 1995.

eyes closed and head moving to and fro with no apparent pattern.

"Don't get close," George cautions. "He's probably just asleep. Sometimes they do that. He might wake up with a start and hurt somebody."

I'm skeptical; surely the animal is sick or injured. Suddenly the animal sleepily raises his head, then jumps quickly to his feet, befuddled by the strange contraption parked only feet away. Other than being a little wobbly, he trots off down the slope with no apparent disability, heading for the frozen lake.

hand can't possibly span one of them. There are not only nice back points but also three highly unusual front points where I have never seen spikes on any other caribou. Truly the exceptional bull I had hoped to find, and more so. I admire again the special cold-weather adaptation of the nearly white coat. What a trophy! George is almost as impressed as I with the creature, and we have a joyful session taking pictures. This bull is unquestionably special. I silently thank my God for giving me far more than I requested.

Caping and quartering consume less time than it takes for the other hunter and me to down a glass of tea and some frozen bannock. As the meat is being secured, I can't resist the temptation to count all those points. Fifty in all! This will be a hunt to remember for all of us. I can now appreciate the fact that these Inuit really do look upon such an animal as a gift from the bountiful land to those who persist in its pursuit. The death was only incidental to the giving of the gift by the land, a necessary part of the drama of the ebb and flow of life on the tundra.

As I am leaving the hotel the next morning to walk the length of the main street to the Renewable Resources Office, where I will get my export permit, I turn to see the sun rising in the southeast for the first time on this trip, the thick clouds having temporarily fled. The sun is still hidden by the hotel, but on either side of the building are two *parahelions*, or "sun dogs," gleaming just above the horizon. These unusual images of the sun result from refraction in the atmosphere caused by the low angle of the sun. The real sun backlights the hotel with a splendor that is breathtaking. Rising like a rainbow from each of the sun dogs is a partial arc rising upward, such that in the mind one can visualize a full circle joining the images.

Cold lunchtime beside a qamutik *on a frozen lake.*

Early morning departure from Cambridge Bay is a scenic experience.

That moment summarizes my trip. Later that day, I walk from the tiny Cambridge Bay air terminal toward the aircraft that will take me away from the wonder and beauty of the barren white land. The sun backlights the gleaming craft as it illuminated the hotel earlier. Ice crystals streaming off the wings in the light wind remind me of angel hair on a crystal Christmas decoration. The sun, however, is now high enough that the sun dogs are gone.

All this I file away in my mind as I trek to the aircraft, the incredible cold tempering my regret at departing. But the memories will always be mine, and my hope is that I will return again to hunt another day.

Cougar. (Photo: courtesy of Lon Lauber)

COUGAR

(Felis concolor)

There he was, a long-tailed, tawny, bewhiskered lion. . . .
The cat balanced himself with downhanging tail like any alley pussy brought to bay. . . .
But this cat was a lion, a real American lion with all of the power and
latent ferocity of his species. He was a male with powerful shoulders
and round paws as big as a man's outstretched hand.

—Frank C. Hibben, *Hunting American Lions,* 1948

Of all the creatures that inhabit contemporary North America, few are so storied in the hunting community, and perhaps none are as mystical, as the cougar. From boyhood I have sat wide-eyed around many a campfire listening to tales of great and dangerous cats in the Georgia back country. The veracity of these accounts is a bit dubious, since in actuality no naturally occurring wild cougar has been documented there for more than a century. But it is that legendary status, in my opinion, that has propelled the animal-rights coalition to several recent state ballot initiative victories that have eliminated or severely curtailed cougar hunting in some places.

Besides the more common names cougar and mountain lion, the animal has been variously referred to as the catamount, American lion, panther, puma, and painter (this latter term is simply a local corruption of the word "panther"). In Latin America the animal is called the puma. The scientific name means "cat of one color," in contradistinction to the other New World cats, all of which bear spots. The cougar has a pattern of dark spots and a ringed tail when born, but those markings disappear by the end of the first year of life.

Cougars are, for reasons not apparent, confined to the Western Hemisphere. There are a total of thirteen subspecies of cougar, but the differences among them are minimal. These amazing predators have spread wherever there were sufficient populations of mule and white-tailed deer, their principal prey. At one time the big cats were in all of the temperate forested terrain in North and South America, but they have been extirpated from most places east of the Rocky Mountains. In the East the cougar occurs naturally now only in Florida, where the local subspecies is highly endangered. There have been repeated sightings in many places in the eastern United States in recent years, but the origin of those cats remains obscure. They may be released animals, either imported from elsewhere or perhaps pets that have escaped or been set free. It is also possible that at least some are from remnant indigenous populations, or have traveled long distances in dispersing from existing populations.

The cougar is by no means threatened or endangered. Conservative estimates from western states of the United States and Canadian provinces reveal that there are between 36,000 and 42,000 of the big cats in North America, figures that do not count the considerable populations in Mexico, Central America, and South America. About 2,500 are taken by sport hunters annually, and some 520 are removed by authorities, mainly because of threatening behavior or killing livestock. The interesting aspect of the statistics is that the locations with the lowest sport harvest (such as California, with zero) have the highest depredation kill (120), while the principalities with the highest sport kill (such as Idaho, where 350 cats are taken by sport hunters) have the lowest depredation rates (three cats per year in Idaho). It is self-evident that in more enlightened locations like Idaho the sport hunter is paying hard cash for the privilege of doing the job of culling aggressive and accessible cougars, whereas in California and Oregon the public is commissioning salaried professionals to do the same work at taxpayer expense.

Cougar guide and his dogs take a break in the sunshine.

Cougars establish and use a home territory, with a smaller core area for resting and a larger domain in which they hunt. Male lions utilize a more extensive area, up to one hundred square miles or more, while females maintain a smaller area, especially when accompanied by kittens. The females keep the young scrupulously apart from the toms, because killing of kittens by adult males is common if the opportunity presents. The ranges of male cougars have long been known to overlap, but the ranges of females were generally believed not to coincide to a great degree. More recent studies, however, have shown that significant parts of female lion ranges often are shared. Resident lions, especially males, mark their territory with scrapes or scratches on which they may deposit urine or feces. Transient lions may also leave their marks there, perhaps simply recording their passing.

A mature male cougar may weigh up to 150 pounds, and larger ones have been occasionally encountered. Adult females weigh around 70 to 100 pounds. From the nose to the end of the tail a large cat may be eight feet long, with almost half that length being tail. After the animals reach one year of age, they lose their kitten fur and assume a color that is most often tan but can vary to grayish or reddish. The underbelly is covered with white hair. The tail is round and of approximately the same diameter throughout its length, and usually is tipped with dark brown or black hair. The backs of the ears are generally that same darker color.

Cougars are longer and slimmer than the jaguar and most other large cats, and the head is relatively small. They possess excellent facility in all the primary senses. Due to several complicated adaptations of the eyes, their vision is best at night, when the pupils dilate widely. In daytime the pupils assume the characteristic feline vertical slits that protect the sensitive eyes from bright light. Their eyes have excellent stereoscopic function, contributing to their efficiency and precision as a predator.

Despite their great size, cougars are considered one of the "lesser cats" because they are incapable of roaring. They are normally silent, though a variety of vocalizations are sometimes heard, the most impressive of which is the "scream" that can be emitted by estrous females.

Cougars are sexually mature at two and a half years, and they most often breed every other year, though sometimes an individual may produce litters in successive years. They will breed at any time of the year, but mating usually occurs in late winter or early spring, and cubs are born in late spring or summer. When male lions simultaneously encounter a female in heat, they may engage in battle. Gestation is about 92 days, and when the time comes for birth the female seeks out a hidden, inaccessible location to den. These dens may be in dense vegetation or on a cliff face, depending on the type of habitat. Contrary to what one might think, no bones or other kill debris are usually found near the site, an instinct designed no doubt to protect the cubs from predators.

Most often three or four cubs are born, although one or two more or less than that number occur. They are woolly, blind, and weigh about a pound. Cubs are nursed for up to three months and become capable of independent living at fifteen months. After weaning, youngsters may remain with the mother up to two years of age, learning by experience and exposure the art of successful hunting and survival. Life expectancy in the wild is a maximum of twelve years, but captive lions have lived several years longer.

The primary prey of cougars is deer, which in one study in the Rocky Mountain West composed 81 percent of the diet. Another study showed that a typical cat consumes an average of fifty-eight small mammals and forty-eight large ones in the course of a year. It takes nearly three days for an adult to consume a deer-size animal; other mammals they will eat include porcupine and elk. The cats sometimes consume domestic stock, but that accounts for less than 1 percent of the diet of most lions. In certain areas and under certain conditions, however, that figure can be much higher. Cougars will also graze sparingly on green grass at times.

A recent study documents the feeding behavior of cougars extremely well. The largest cats uniformly kill the largest animals, such as elk. Not surprisingly, it takes a big cougar to kill a big prey animal. In Yellowstone National Park, over 66 percent of the diet of cougars consists of elk, and the elk consumed are primarily juveniles. Mule deer constitute only 14 percent of the Yellowstone cougar's diet. They also consume bighorn sheep (2 percent) and moose (1 percent), and they take an occasional antelope as well. Prey biomass is 93 percent ungulates such as elk, deer, and sheep, though the total number of individual animals consumed is only 35 percent ungulate, reflecting the ungulates' larger size (one elk or moose, for example, equals several dozen porcupines). How well this Yellowstone study applies to regions where elk are not so plentiful is subject to debate, since most areas report deer as the primary prey. For the hunter, however, it means that to take a big cougar as a trophy, hunt where there are elk.

Cougars are a consummate predator. They are in constant intimate relationship with their prey, and are almost always either seeking, approaching, pursuing, consuming, or digesting. Besides hunger, prey movement probably is the most important stimulus to the attack, and some believe that has led to the common tendency of prey animals to freeze in position briefly when they sense a predator. Cougars are highly successful in killing what they attack, with the kill rate approximating or exceeding 80 percent (by comparison, the African lion's success rate is a mere 10 percent of animals charged). Cougars kill by firmly gripping the shoulders or neck with the sharp retractile claws, kicking at the prey with the hind legs, and applying a devastating bite to the back of the neck that often breaks the spinal cord. It is an incredible feat for a 150-pound cat to kill an 800-pound elk. The creatures are amazingly agile, and are able to jump an estimated eighteen feet vertically and thirty feet horizontally.

After the kill the cat may drag the prey for some distance before consuming a part of it, and then the carcass is covered with leaves and other debris to conceal it. Until the prey is consumed, the predator stays in the general vicinity unless it is disturbed.

Cougars almost invariably enter the chest cavity and devour the lungs and heart first. The big cats have been known to kill much more than they can reasonably eat, though that is undoubtedly rare. Such occurrences most often involve domestic stock, and the reasons for the aberrance may be related to the ongoing stimuli of abundant prey movement. Attacks on humans are rare, considering the numbers of lions and their proximity to people in places like California, but attacks are on the increase.

The cougar is a highly secretive animal that is mostly nocturnal and seldom is seen in the wild by the casual observer. Surprisingly, about a

Cougar. Idaho, January 1989.

hundred cougars are taken each year in Idaho by opportunistic deer and elk hunters, reflecting a tendency of the cats to be active when their prey is most active. Notwithstanding, most are taken with hounds, and to outlaw hunting them with dogs, as Oregon recently did by voter referendum, amounts to an unreasonable restriction. Yet the same people responsible for enforcing such illogical statutes are the ones compelled to call for an experienced houndsman to deal with a problem cat. What are they going to do when the radicals succeed in eliminating houndsmen altogether? Very probably there will be little alternative but to try to trap the creature, an effort in which a successful outcome becomes far more difficult and time-consuming. The only reasonable method of hunting cougars is to pursue them with a pack of dogs. A mountain lion can kill a dog easily, but fortunately the cats don't know that. An occasional rogue will learn to kill dogs, and thereafter it presents a dangerous situation for the houndsman.

Hunting of cougars is a wintertime activity wherever it is practiced. There are two basic types of hound hunting, one on snow-covered ground and the other bare ground. The former is perhaps the more formidable for the hunter, and the latter is more of a challenge to the hounds, since snow captures and maintains the scent tenaciously. Where feasible, such as in parts of Arizona and New Mexico, horses can be used to put the hunter in range of the quarry. On snow-covered ground pickup trucks or snowmobiles are typically used to find fresh cougar tracks. Depending on the prevailing terrain and the age of the track, the hounds may be released to attempt to tree the cat.

While the level of experience of the houndsman is paramount, in much of the cougar's northern range snowfall is another important factor. Often a hunter is defeated from the outset by adverse weather. My own story is a case study. In the southern Rockies, warm, dry weather can be just as difficult, as high temperatures contribute to the difficulty of following the track and the exhaustion of the dogs. In ideal conditions, a cougar will tree quickly because the pursuing hounds are fleet of foot and have far more stamina.

One piece of equipment deserves special mention. The snowshoes supplied on my hunt were nearly five feet long, and for an inexperienced snowshoer they were too challenging. The newer types with short aluminum frames are as light as a feather and are infinitely easier to maneuver. Perhaps had those been available, I would have been able to use the darn things. Ask your guide about snowshoes if you're going on a hunt in the northern Rockies, and make sure he has the best available.

Good cold-weather clothing is a must, but be prepared to strip down for walking and climbing. Take along a day pack, both for packing out your quarry and for carrying in necessities. A good flashlight is mandatory, since striking a trail late in the day can mean returning in the dark.

Hunting cougars demands the utmost in energy output once you strike the trail and the hounds are loosed. A high-energy food source, such as energy bars, comes in plenty handy after several hours of struggling uphill on snowshoes. Such travel is perhaps the most intense expenditure of calories in the entire world of hunting, as one is battling steep inclines, unaccustomed footwear, high altitude, and deep snow. It might be just two hundred yards to the ponderosa pine where your cougar is treed, snarling at a circling pack of dogs on the ground below. Or it might be miles of marathon struggle against the worst nature can throw at you. Be prepared for either.

Any caliber rifle, and most handguns and bows, will take a cougar, since the animals are easy to kill if the shot is true. I used 165-grain Nosler Partition handloads in my .30-06, and the bullet passed through the animal without expanding, making only a quarter-inch entrance and exit hole. I've seen far greater damage done with the lighter, higher velocity bullets of a .243 or .270.

If you're a bow hunter, don't assume this hunt is easy just because you're shooting a treed animal. The big cats have a way of finding the highest tree and putting plenty of branches between you and them. Be proficient with firearm or bow, too, because a wounded cat can kill or maim thousands of dollars' worth of prime hounds in a few seconds. An outfitter gets more nervous than a lion up a sapling if you can't reliably hit a practice target at thirty paces.

Go the full distance on your hunt. Don't have an outfitter find you a fresh track and call you to come out to hunt tomorrow. Most of the hunt may be already done at that point. Ride the back roads and trails by snowmobile or on horseback, or even walk them, until you discover a fresh cougar track. Then when you take your cat, you'll be proud that you've really been hunting.

RUN SILENT, RUN DEADLY

My legs ache as if I am pushing them up the final yards of a stalk on the world's biggest ram. I feel a deep burning in my calves and thighs that gets worse with each step. I am up to my waist in Idaho's powdery snow, hunting cougar with guide and outfitter Larry Jarrett. I didn't mean to be in this predicament, but circumstances have put me in a very uncomfortable and wearying situation. Despite my tiredness, I am energized by the wonderful sound of dogs. The ecstatic canines up ahead sound more excited than any squirrel dog or coon hound I can remember.

"Man, what beautiful music!" I find myself saying through labored breathing, a sentiment my determined guide echoes. He pushes back his weathered cap and wipes the steaming sweat from his brow, pausing only long enough to be sure his greenhorn cougar hunter is keeping up. I feel better as we near the treed cat. The unmistakable rhythmic baying of Larry's prize hound, Drifter, proves the dogs are looking our prey in the eye.

The pack of dogs we are using is a mixed-up group, consisting of a blue tick and several Walkers, along with a smattering of black-and-tan. Larry is most considerate of this efficient group and is always sure the cat can be corralled before he turns them loose. He is almost always right, because he knows his area so well. It has been frustrating for him to guide me in this quest. I have been here in Idaho with him on two previous hunts, and both times I was unable to take a lion because bad weather made it impossible to find a fresh track. This is some of the very best lion country anywhere, though, so I know we will eventually succeed. Time is ultimately on my side, but it is in short supply again this trip.

On my first visit here, snow had been present, though not abundant, but there was devastating daytime warming. The balmy days had combined with overnight freezes to make the crusty snow so hard even an elk couldn't show a decent track, much less our light-footed quarry. On the second trip, there had been no snow, so we spent the entire ten days looking for a track in the mud. It works in Arizona to hunt on bare ground, but here in Idaho, it is no soap. These dogs have never smelled a cougar track except on snow-covered ground, so asking them to perform in those conditions is asking the impossible.

This is trip three, and I have high hopes it will be the last, though confidence has faded to these last hours of my final day. After a solid week of hunting, I have already begun to conclude that there will have to be yet a fourth foray. No matter, I have already decided; I'll never quit, even if it takes a dozen hunts. I do, however, regret that my guide, with a sterling success rate, has to suffer along with his unfortunate client.

In truth, we did find a fine, fresh track on my first outing, but the cat had been heading into terrain that was impossible to hunt, with gigantic rocks that would have allowed the animal to "tree" in a cave or underneath a rocky overhang, or to cross frozen lakes where we couldn't follow. Larry is careful to make sure that any track is a possibility before he turns the pack loose. Ideally, he locates a track that is less than a day old.

Despite the difficulties and disappointments I have experienced with Larry, he is my type of lion hunter. I have always wanted to be involved in the process from the start, seeking a hot track with the guide. I wanted a guide who knows where one might encounter such a track, but I wanted to avoid being "on call" after a fresh track has already been located. The hunt has always been far more consequential than the actual kill, and on this cougar hunt I have been tested again as to the depth of my conviction. Additionally, like most people, I have a schedule to follow, and mine is set months in advance. This inherent inflexibility makes it difficult to drop everything and go at a moment's notice. So my views on how to hunt are somewhat tempered by these facts. Nevertheless, it has always been my desire to scour the winter wilderness for a fresh track.

Larry is a weathered man with an unruly beard and slightly thinning brown hair. He is approaching a somewhat gruff middle age, but generally he has been a well-organized and pleasant companion. He is a bit dismayed that the weather turns wicked every time I come in from Georgia, and I get the feeling that somehow he thinks I am responsible. And I can't help but wonder if he's right. All I can do is live with it, however, and make the best of the situation. Down deep, Larry knows that too, but he still seems to be getting more than a little impatient with the elements, and maybe with me.

The problem this trip is the exact opposite of the first two. For weeks before this January outing I have watched weather reports from the Northwest, and I noted with satisfaction the talk of record snowfall. Even Boise has a foot of snow, most unusual for a place of low altitude and moderate temperatures. Before I left home I spoke with Larry several times, and he was more optimistic than ever before. His only reservation was that when it came to hunting with me, he has learned to expect the worst.

On my arrival, Larry briefed me about conditions and his concerns about too much snow this time. He predicted it would be a very difficult hunt if we could find a fresh track, requiring snowshoes, contraptions with which I have no experience. Finding a fresh lion crossing might be tough, too, contrary to what I had been expecting from the snowy weather reports. In such conditions the cats tend to stay with a concentration of deer or elk and may move very little. A pocket of abundant food is a precious thing to a wild creature when the snow is ten feet deep, and the cougar is no different from other animals in that respect. Thus were dashed my expectations of ensured success, and I prepared myself for another long and difficult hunt. Optimism reigns supreme in the hunter, however, and only as this final day winds down is my faith on the wane.

Hounds don't like cougars and they say so loudly.

It is cold. I left temperatures more conducive to golf than to hunting, but Idaho is a powdery wonderland in the grip of single-digit temperatures. The night I arrived the high country received another foot of snow, as light as confectioner's sugar. I just knew that there would be a lion track in the first creek bottom. Larry assured me that if anything did move, we would be on it like a goose on a grasshopper. He expected we would experience improving odds daily until the next snowfall, assuming that the cold weather held, to keep the snow from crusting. The forecast has consistently indicated that a warming trend is the least expected of all possibilities.

We are hunting the South Fork country along the Boise River, a region of towering rock cliffs, high country ranch land, deep timbered draws, and a rich supply of feline predators and their prey. Larry regularly hunts the area to keep the cat numbers in check, an invaluable service to all who have an interest in maintaining a natural balance. On our previous trips there was ready access to all parts of the area, but this time I simply can't believe we are in the same place. Our usual direct route is completely closed by monstrous drifts, forcing us to drive an extra hour each day just to get to the river basin. Snow along the main road has been piled ten feet high by snowplows, so that it reaches well above the level of the cab of the truck. Even at the edge of the pristine river, perhaps a thousand feet below, snow is plentiful and treacherous.

In this setting, seeking cougar tracks is darn near impossible. Many of the likely crossings are accessible only by extreme effort, using the snowmobiles Larry has packed atop the vehicle. Making our job more difficult, hundreds of animals, mostly deer and elk, have been pushed by the snow to the very edge of the river in search of food, and their tracks are a maze to be negotiated and sorted. The big cats frequently step in such tracks, because the snow is packed more firmly there, and that conceals them from prying eyes.

Cat up a tree and looking back. (Photo: courtesy of Larry Jarrett)

My guide covers a huge amount of ground every day. He checks every potential cougar crossing every single day because skipping a day means a track might be two days old before he finds it, making it more difficult for the dogs to follow. With years of experience to guide him, Larry follows this procedure with little deviation, other than the occasional fit of intuition that surprises me with a quick side trip.

We have ridden and walked innumerable miles the first several days, encountering many interesting sights, but no cat track. We have snowmobiled for miles along snow-clogged roads and trails, and we have cut through creek bottom and over wintry mountain crests. Larry has repeatedly displayed the irritating habit of showing me every tree in which he has treed a cougar since World War II. "Here's where Drifter put that monster tom up back when . . ." *Where in the dickens is one for us now,* I just keep wondering.

Every day has been essentially the same, except that each has provided a little adventure of its own. I have come to a peace with myself long ago about tough hunts, and I have countered the frustration with a determination to enjoy the hunt to the fullest, whether I take an animal or not. After all, an unsuccessful hunt is simply an occasion to plan another. I have gradually come to realize that the odds of finding what I am seeking in these conditions are against me. I can and will find joy in the experience, by God's grace.

We have encountered a surprisingly large number of deer. They have provided endless diversion, and I have taken numerous photos. I have fantasized about what kind of monster racks the big bucks must have had before they cast their headgear. I have even kept my eyes open in case I might find a recently dropped rack, though the snow apparently holds all of them prisoner for the winter. On one occasion, I saw nearly a hundred mule deer on a single slope above the river; every deer in the river drainage has apparently been driven down onto the lowest terrain.

Yesterday a huge bull elk, still sporting his massive rack, blocked our road and refused to let us pass. He retreated for a mile or so but declined to turn off the beaten path into the deep snow. When he had run enough, he finally whirled to confront us, not realizing that we had no choice but to follow. When the bull had huffed loudly with lowered head, threatening to put a massive brow tine through the truck radiator, we had turned around and used the less vulnerable rear of the truck to force him to a turnoff point. The bull finally raged away in anger, probably thinking the truck was the most persistent pursuer he had ever encountered, and leaped into deep snow to escape.

Nighttime temperatures have dropped to below zero, and we have ceased to worry about the snow crusting over. The extreme cold and deep snow have begun to take a heavy toll on the deer, and we have counted perhaps fifty carcasses in our hunting area.

Breakfast on this last day was more than a bit somber, with Larry's frustration showing a little but my own well disguised. We planned around the breakfast table to make no major changes in tactics, and I have already tentatively checked my schedule to see when a lion hunt next year might be possible. We set out early this morning in darkness, as usual, stars blazing overhead and hot coffee mugs filled to the brim, and drove the sixty miles to our starting point along the South Fork.

By midday it became obvious that the usual spots were unchanged, with only deer and elk tracks. Over lunch we considered doing something different, something desperate and radical, to try to salvage the hunt. The old familiar "wait till next year" feeling has been setting in solidly, but I was more than willing to try something unconventional, if it held a glimmer of hope.

"I'm always afraid to send a hunter off alone to look, because they always find a large coyote track and rush back with a false report of a lion," Larry had counseled me between mouthfuls of ham sandwich. "It's always that way. One time I snowshoed five miles for a damn coyote track."

"I know a cougar track," I remember insisting, although there was no way I could be absolutely sure I could distinguish one from a big coyote track. I thought I could, at least, like all the other hunters before me.

"Well, I'm thinking we should split up for the last half-day. But let me draw a lion track for you." He had stooped down and created a typical lion print in the snow, emphasizing the more rounded pattern of the four toes, and particularly three small linear ridges present only on the back pad of the cougar. "Now don't come back with any report of something that doesn't match this description exactly."

"I won't," I had promised.

And I had realized that if one of us didn't find something quick, this hunt was over.

Larry had planned to go up one creek drainage, one so thick with brush that we couldn't check it by snowmobile, and I was assigned another. We would meet back at the road by 3 P.M. to compare notes. He had dropped me off at my creek, and as the truck roared down the road I set off.

I had traveled no more than a hundred yards when I saw it—the unmistakable tracks of a large lion! I had got down on trembling knees in the snow and inspected the prints carefully, confirming my initial impression. I had followed the tracks until one of the numerous coyote tracks intersected it, so I could do a direct comparison.

There could be no doubt. There on the ground before me was the culmination of nearly three weeks of cougar hunting. And my guide and his dogs were off down the road to who knows where, probably with one chance in Avogadro's number of finding a similar track. I had felt an overpowering compulsion to find Larry, and I had to do it soon if we were to have a chance to bay this cat.

Before heading out, I had followed the track for a few hundred yards but finally lost it in a confusing maze of deer trails. Then, miraculously, I had found another lion track, larger than the first, and looking even fresher.

Back to the road I had hustled, and set out in a brisk walk to find Larry and his pack of lion hounds. As I hurried along, I had mulled over the two big lion tracks, discovered so quickly and so close together. I had surmised that perhaps the cats were sticking tightly in pockets and moving very little, simply because they had the

A dead cougar up a tree—and determined to stay there.

deer where they wanted them, helpless and unable to move.

I had found Larry's truck a couple of miles up the road, and then I considered my options. I had fired a shot, hoping Larry would answer the signal. After thirty minutes he finally appeared, and I could immediately see that he too had found something. In fact, he had encountered perhaps the same two tracks, and had jumped a large lion off a recent kill. To my consternation, he had been dubious, even irritated, at my insistence that I, too, had found fresh tracks. Larry had examined my lion tracks closely and had concluded that they were indeed legitimate. We had then set off quickly to turn the hounds loose. Finally, I'm off on a lion chase!

I had never before been forced to strap on these most frustrating of gadgets, but snowshoes are a necessity in these conditions. I struggle mightily with them, while Larry gradually left me behind. I am in good shape, but walking with a barn door on each foot is tiring and irritating. The only alternative to my slow progress without them was no progress with them, and Larry had been too far ahead to advise. I finally took them off, stuck them up in the snow, and struggled on without them.

Larry had the pack on leash and had been waiting for me to catch up before he released them. As I approached, it was evident that he was incredulous that I had left the snowshoes behind. In frustration he had given me a pretty good tongue lashing, pointing out with unmistakable clarity that if the cat crossed the top I'd be in deep trouble in ten feet or more of snow.

The unquestioned leader of the pack is Drifter, a lion hound of considerable fame in these parts, highly sought-after as a sire. He weighs in at 90 pounds and has a razor-sharp nose and a real hatred for cougars that has been intensified over the years by his numerous close encounters. The dogs track silently until they are very close to their quarry, often until the cougar is up a tree. That makes them more difficult to follow, but it also allows them to surprise the cat and tree him quickly most of the time. I am hoping that this chase will be short and sweet, because we are truly out of time: the sun drops ever lower in the cold blue sky.

On release, all the dogs had disappeared in a fluid motion up the snowy mountainside, as if they had dropped off the face of the earth. For some fifteen minutes I had wondered if those dogs might not have found a deer carcass to chew on and decided to take the day off. Just when I had begun to wonder where they could be, Drifter had yelped loudly, as if he had just stuck his foot in a steel trap. Were they onto our cat? Was that sound an indication of pain?

Less than thirty seconds ticked by, and steady baying filled the valley with that sweet music houndsmen relish. With three fruitless hunts behind me now, it is truly a concert that the world's greatest orchestra cannot outperform.

I struggle onward and upward, stepping in Larry's big tracks. The cacophony of canine sounds is intense, emanating from a dark grove of aspen and spruce a half-mile above. Larry finally removes his snowshoes, as much out of sympathy as anything else, and both of us work along, sweat soaking our clothes despite the frigid air.

The place the lion has treed is beyond belief. As we approach, I get my first sight of a bayed mountain lion, but not up some sturdy monarch of a fir or pine tree. The animal has obviously had little time to study the situation, because he has climbed into the most spindly patch of overgrown willows one can imagine. There he clings for dear life to the fragile tops, clutching several of the small trunks for uneasy support. Nearby are large trees one would expect a lion to climb, so the dogs must have been a sudden surprise for the cat, leaving no time to be choosy.

We maneuver to get a better look at the treed lion. There is an ominous frozen waterfall just underneath the cat, creating a sheer drop of thirty feet or more below the base of the willows. We will have to be careful not to get an unwelcome toboggan ride down there. The lion looks ever more nervous as we near, twitching his tail rapidly and grappling to maintain his tenuous support on the tree trunks.

"He's gonna jump out for sure! If you can be sure and kill him, take him from here," Larry advises. I have no reservations that the old .30-06 is more than up to the task, so I chamber a round, center the vitals in the scope, and squeeze off the shot.

Most of the time, there is no hurry about shooting a cougar. The situation here is a very unlucky cat hunter with very little time to spare, combined with a nervous and precariously positioned cat. Usually the dogs are secured away from the base of the tree, so that a wounded animal won't kill a dog or two when he hits the ground.

Fortunately the shot is true, and the cat is dead. All four legs twitch involuntarily.

Now comes the most perilous part of this hunt. The animal, lodged tightly between the intertwined tops, cannot be extricated. Working at the top of a treacherous chute of ice that leads nowhere but down, we are slipping and sliding, trying to shake the critter loose. Just when I think we are going to have to return to the truck for a saw, down comes the great cat with a mighty thud. He continues right past us, rocketing bottomward along the ice chute and out of sight. The excited hounds, who have not yet ceased their barking, are on the dead cat in a flash, savoring the intimate contact with a creature they love so much to hate. They are allowed benign chews, licks, and sniffs, a joyful time to savor the sweet taste of success. For this hunter the pack has had endless hours of riding silently in the dog box on the back of the truck, and I am more than happy to share the moment with a deserving crew.

Following a hearty picture session, which includes the hounds, we skin the animal before beginning our descent. The gladness that fills me to overflowing with this last-day success is impossible to express in words. I think Larry's satisfaction is even greater, if his grin and the happy spring in his step are any indications. His demeanor is entirely uplifted by my success, and there is no question that he feels a great sense of relief. He shakes my hand and pounds me repeatedly on the back in congratulations. For my part, I am also thankful he has forgotten my snowshoe debacle, and even more thankful I had to pay only a very small price for my lack of forethought. I know I am forgiven when I retrieve the contraptions on the way back to the truck and he says not a word.

On the drive home we review the day's events and conclude that the initial loud yelp of pain was indeed from Drifter. The venerable hound has a slashed right ear and a scratch on the face. Apparently he surprised the cat at close range, drawing a slap from a razor-sharp claw before the creature scrambled up the nearest tree. Such is the lot of a silent running dog. It is hazardous duty, but no one can doubt how rapidly the animal treed. I'll take a hunt with that bunch anytime. It has been another sterling performance from a sterling group of canines. And a mountain lion is finally mine.

Jaguar. (Photo: from the author's collection)

JAGUAR
(Panthera onca)

The definitive proof of a jaguar's proximity is its own booming call,
echoing out over the swamp, a sound to thrill the heart of the hunter,
a sound that tells us there are still some wild places left on earth.

—Antonio de Almeida, *Jaguar Hunting in the Mato Grosso,* 1976

The jaguar is a true ghost, a presence most often sensed not at all by unsuspecting humans. It is only when the animal's activities conflict with man's, and most especially when that conflict involves livestock, that it becomes apparent that *el tigre* is about. Tony Rivera, who became famous as a poacher of jaguars, has spent more than thirty years pursuing the spotted cat all over Central and South America. Today he is playing a new role as a catcher of jaguars for biological researchers. In discussing the secretive nature of the animal, he tells me that he has only once in all his time in the jungles seen a jaguar that had not first been treed by dogs. Many others have spent longer in the jungles and seen fewer of the clandestine felines.

Getting a fleeting glimpse of a jaguar as it crosses a jungle road or bursts from hiding to fade quickly into the forest is akin to seeing a cougar, though far less common. To observe one of the great cats is not the objective of preserving and perpetuating them, contrary to the allegations of some misinformed environmentalists. To see them in the wild is the privilege of the hunter alone, for the most part. Jaguars deserve protection because they are a necessary and desirable part of the natural order, and are a fearless predator that fills a niche no other animal can occupy satisfactorily. A good pack of hounds is an absolute necessity for seeing one outside a cage, something researchers have only recently begun to appreciate adequately.

The jaguar is listed as endangered in the United States, a status that was made official on 21 August 1997, when the U.S. Fish and Wildlife Service published a final rule declaring any naturally occurring jaguar within the boundaries of the U.S. protected under the Endangered Species Act. The animal has been listed since 1973 in its current range, but reports of the animal north of the Mexican border brought to light the fact that it did not enjoy protected status within the borders of the United States. While there was no season on the creature anywhere in the country, and anyone taking one would have been subject to prosecution under various state statutes, the oversight meant that there was no federal protection for jaguars north of the Mexican border. This final rule emphatically corrected that deficiency.

There is reason to agree with the decision by the federal government. There have been a minimum of sixty-four jaguars killed in Arizona since 1900, admittedly most of them early in the century. The last one taken there was in 1986. In 1996, Warner Glenn of Douglas, Arizona, treed a jaguar with his pack of cougar hounds, the first such occurrence in his long career hunting Arizona's mountain lions. Warner did what the outdoorsman of today is supposed to do: he took plenty of pictures and reported the cat to the authorities. He also published a booklet on the experience entitled *Eyes of Fire.* In the old days, that cat likely would have been shot. A cat treed was a cat killed. Thanks to a conservation-minded hunter, that particular jaguar still roams free, as far as anybody knows.

Presence of the big spotted cats north of the Mexican border has been well documented over the past two centuries. Most of the sightings in the United States have been in Arizona, usually in the mountainous country south of the Grand Canyon. *El tigre* has been reported in southeastern California as well, especially between 1814 and 1860, the latter date confirmed through a well-documented report about an animal killed near Palm Springs. There are nine reports of jaguars in southwestern New Mexico, the last time in 1905 (that is, until the one treed by Warner Glenn crossed into the extreme southwest corner of that state in 1996). A jaguar was killed close to New River, Louisiana, in 1886, the farthest east the species has ever been reliably reported, and early biologists included the animal in the fauna of the Gulf coastal region. It probably persisted in the brush country of South Texas until fairly recent times, though no breeding population is believed to be present there now. The last confirmed jaguar sighting in Texas was in Kleburg County in 1948.

Mexico is the northerly beginning of viable breeding populations these days as one proceeds southward. A respectable number of jaguars may exist in both Sonora and Chihuahua, where plenty of remote areas and much favorable terrain with abundant prey species support them. Two jaguars were reportedly killed in Chihuahua in 1989. There are a few individuals there who keep reliable packs of good hounds with which to catch them. Wherever livestock conflicts are infrequent there may be remnant populations.

The Mexican province of Tamaulipas is the northernmost jaguar range currently known to contain a healthy breeding population. In all the remote and inaccessible jungle country from there south to northern Argentina, the cats are likely to be present, though pertinent data is spotty or absent.

Jaguars prefer warm tropical climates, usually live near water, and occur only occasionally in large arid regions such as the desert Southwest. They consistently prefer wet lowlands over mountain ranges but can survive in an amazing variety of terrain when necessary. They are one of the few cats that readily swim and even seem to enjoy doing so. Their documented prey species include at least eighty-five creatures, ranging from the larger animals such as deer, javelina, and capybara to the relatively small armadillo, immature crocodiles, various monkeys, birds, and coatimundis. They are efficient predators, and in fact the word "jaguar" is said to mean "carnivore that overcomes prey with a single bound," a tribute to their quick and deadly attack. They belong to the genus *Panthera,* which in the Latin carries the connotation "hunts for all," thus giving recognition to their wide variety of prey. The species designation is *onca,* which means

"hook" or "barb," a reference to the splendid sharp claws the animals possess.

The largest of the species are the forest jaguars of South America, which prey on large game. At least thirteen different subspecies have been described over the years, but there are no genetic studies to confirm that number. Information from other sources seems to justify a limited number of subspecies, although it remains to be seen if the old designations will hold up, as they so often do not. The issue was last addressed in 1939, so perhaps more studies will be forthcoming.

The physical features of the jaguar are similar to those of the leopard of Africa and Asia, although the jaguar is larger, stockier, and much more powerful of jaw. They are technically classified as the only roaring cat of the Americas, though a deep-throated rumble is a more accurate description of their vocalizations. I still remember the spine-chilling growl that greeted me as I approached my treed jaguar, a sound that would strike fear into anyone unaware of the animal's propensity to avoid human contact at any cost. Even knowing that, one has significant trepidation approaching a jaguar. Jack O'Connor saw only one of the animals in his hunting experience, but his description is vivid: "Suddenly a *tigre* walked out of the brush a few hundred yards away.... Even in the gray dawn he was bright orange, a wild, beautiful, terrible thing gliding along through the chill dusk of that lonely canyon.... I must have been afraid as well. I do know that cold sweat broke out on my forehead, and that when I remembered I had a rifle my hand was trembling.... If you think you're immune to thrills, just run across a *tigre* alone in the wilderness.... You may know he won't hurt you, but you won't believe it." I kept reminding myself that the animal seldom attacks people, but the agitated demeanor of the snarling feline seemed to deny it.

Jaguars weigh from 150 to 300 pounds, with the larger individuals coming from the Mato Grosso of Brazil and especially the great Pantanal floodplain that abuts the border of both Paraguay and Bolivia. There an exceptional male may top out at 350 pounds, by far the largest cat of the Americas and a true heavyweight when compared with the leopard, which seldom weighs even half that. It seems unclear if jaguars grow larger in those dense jungles because a single kill provides more meat

Jaguar. Campeche, Mexico, March 1998.

with less expenditure of energy, or if a genetically increased size allows them to kill larger prey more consistently. In the southwestern United States, it is likely that abundant deer and javelina were the primary prey, allowing for development of a larger cat. Like most big cats, the jaguar hunts mostly at night and may use a variety of techniques, including stalking, lying in wait, and simply outrunning prey over a short distance.

The jaguar's spots tend to be arranged in larger rosettes than are found on the leopard, and they are usually farther apart. More of the spots are completely enclosed than on leopards, and in my observation the confluence of elongated spots on the chest and underbelly gives rise to the frequent appearance of a tigerlike pelage, with actual stripes. There is a black color phase, though even in such melanotic individuals slightly darker spots usually can be discerned. Black and spotted cubs can occur in the same litter.

Throughout most of their range jaguars breed year-round, though there seems to be a slight tendency toward a spring breeding season at the northern and southern extremes, where there is more seasonal variation in temperature. A female is

sexually mature at the age of three years, and males at four years. Gestation is calculated at 93 to 110 days, with an average near 100. The female dens up in a cave to give birth, and usually two cubs are born, although any number from one to four is not uncommon. The newborns weigh about one-and-a-half to two pounds, and their eyes open after thirteen days. They remain with the mother for nearly two years before seeking their own territory.

Jaguars have been known to live for up to twenty-two years in captivity, though studies in the wild have documented few individuals older than eleven, a testament to the dangerous nature of their occupation. In the wild they roam over territories up to sixteen square miles, but on occasion they may wander for long distances for no apparent reason. One individual was tracked by means of a radio collar as it made a colossal move of more than five hundred miles. More typically they hunt a small area until prey becomes depleted, then move on within their established territory.

The current status of the jaguar is regrettably indistinct. Wendell Swank and Jim Teer did a comprehensive evaluation in 1987, but little new scientific data was available for their compilation.

The best jaguar dog in the Yucatan was eaten by a jaguar shortly after this photo.

the animal is bordering on extinction. The jaguar is crafty, secretive, and nocturnal, so extirpation of a population from prime habitat is difficult if not impossible. A cattleman who owns a good pack of hounds can do considerable damage, however, and it is here that a well-managed sport hunt for the species could be of great value in discouraging illegal kills, bringing in money to ranchers suffering livestock losses, and giving economic value to an animal that previously has had none. Chronic cattle killers that can't be successfully transplanted to an area with more abundant natural prey, or who return after such a move, are called in Spanish *cebados,* and their destruction by stockmen is inevitable. I foresee a fund established by scientific and hunting organizations to reimburse ranchers for livestock losses and to mount a determined effort to transplant offending jaguars to remote areas (a step almost always skipped by livestock owners). A companion program would permit repeat offenders to be hunted by sport hunters, with part of their license fees going to a depredation fund. One problem with this approach is the lack of reliable internal controls in many countries with viable jaguar populations, but there are places, such as Mexico and Venezuela, where a prototype program could be successful.

Several ongoing attempts are being made now in Mexico and Venezuela to obtain accurate information on jaguar populations, movements, and reproduction. It is suspected that in remote areas where there is minimal conflict with ranching, the jaguar thrives and is by no means endangered. It appears that the great cat may be a classic case of an animal classified as endangered by simple lack of credible information. Thankfully, world opinion on sale of the hides of all spotted cats has provided a measure of safety for these populations, however tenuous that may be.

There is no question that deforestation, cattle ranching, and illegal trade in jaguar skins have contributed to a contraction of range and population decline, but there is no evidence that

I am including the jaguar in this book despite the obvious and undeniable fact that it is the exception among the forty-two featured big-game animals. I took my jaguar with a dart in Mexico, and the animal I darted still roams free. I would strongly prefer to have a mounted mature male jaguar in my trophy room, but that is an impossible dream at this time, unless I can find a legally taken pre-1973 specimen for display. Even then, I would not have the satisfaction of knowing that I took it with my .30-06. Nevertheless, I still feel that this matchless animal deserves inclusion because it is uniquely American, it ranges into the United States even today, and it is majestic beyond belief.

The recent listing of the jaguar by the U.S. Fish and Wildlife Service as endangered in the

United States also created a Jaguar Conservation Team, currently chaired by the state of Arizona. Its goal is to further knowledge of the jaguar in the United States; to study Mexican jaguars, because they are the source of all cats that cross the border; and perhaps ultimately to establish a breeding population in Arizona and other border states. This appears to be a worthwhile project that deserves the support of sportsmen and sporting organizations, even though such areas historically have possessed only marginal jaguar habitat and the likelihood of a sport hunt in the United States is highly improbable. Nevertheless, just to know that the remarkable cats are there would be a triumph of major magnitude, and a rare instance where mainline conservationists (hunters and their allies) could probably agree with preservationists about total protection for them. Everyone involved would have to be content with the knowledge that opportunities to see a jaguar in the wild will almost certainly never occur, except perhaps for a lucky few cougar hunters. Once again, only hunters would

be privileged to view the creatures, as is so often the case. We are indeed a fortunate group.

Hunting jaguars in the jungles of Central and South America starts at the site of a fresh kill, either a live bait animal or a recently killed cow or other livestock. When such a hot track is available, jaguars are fairly easy to tree with a good pack of hounds, with the exception of the occasional large male jaguar, which sometimes learns to kill dogs. Once the dogs are loosed, it is a wild, straight-line chase through dense jungle until the cat tires and seeks refuge in a tree. If the dogs have far outdistanced their human companions, the creature may rest up and jump out for another dash when the much-feared humans approach. Most often the dogs will tree the cat once more, and all that is necessary is pictures of the treed animal, for which there is usually plenty of time, and then the shot. With a dart it is essential that placement be in a highly muscular area such as the thigh, since penetrating the viscera is almost invariably fatal, a slow and painful death that no hunter would knowingly inflict.

Jaguar hunting involves cruising jungle trails by ATV to check baits.

These spotted felines have awesome teeth.

It is also possible to attract a jaguar with a predator call, though I personally know of nobody who has done it successfully. When a fresh livestock kill is discovered, a tree blind can be productive if one waits patiently at dawn and dusk. This is the opposite of leopard hunting, where the hunter is in a ground blind and the bait is in the tree. In this method, the carcass must be secured so it can't be easily dragged into the thick underbrush. Since shooting a jaguar today is everywhere illegal, this tactic could be used to capture a rogue animal with a dart. Some jaguars learn that the hounds are no threat and will not tree, instead methodically killing the whole pack one dog at a time. In such a case one must use such creative but difficult methods as tree stands or live traps.

Caliber and load for jaguar hunting are not a matter of serious consideration at this time. Like cougars, jaguars can be easily killed with a .22 rimfire directed at exactly the right spot. Since there is no current legal sport hunt for the animals (and there hasn't been since Belize discontinued its habitual livestock-killer sport-hunting program several years ago), such a discussion is academic. The animals are not hard to kill and are not considered as dangerous to man as the aggressive leopard, despite their larger size and formidable musculature.

That is not to say there is no danger in hunting jaguars. I almost had heart failure while having dinner one evening on my first dart hunt when a tarantula emerged from a hole in the ground next to my chair and showed every intention of dining with me. Such spiders are not a menace, except perhaps from the standpoint of inducing cardiac arrest. The notorious barba amarilla, a highly venomous and common snake that frequents the jaguar jungles, must be avoided at all costs. The outfitter who took me dart hunting keeps a fresh snakebite kit with the party at all times, because unless treatment for a bite is begun immediately the victim almost invariably dies before medical help can be reached. The guides on my expedition were expert at spotting the snake, and we saw only one, a huge specimen perhaps seven to eight feet long.

Be sure to pack tick spray of the type found in the brand Permanone. Ticks in the Yucatan can be pervasive, and I sprayed my clothes copiously. This product is designed to be used only on clothing and is highly irritating when applied to the skin. Virtually none of the bloodsuckers will reach skin if you follow this preventive measure. Top-quality facial insect repellent is good to have along as well. I recommend a very light set of jungle clothes, cotton being the coolest. Make sure the pants are long enough, and your boots high enough, to tuck the legs into the tops of the boots as extra protection against ticks. I wore standard leather hunting boots and left behind the cumbersome and hot snake chaps, despite the unsavory local serpents. I'd rather keep my eyes open, trust my sharp-eyed guides, and stay cooler while dashing through the jungle behind a pack of baying hounds.

On a hunt of this type, camera and film are among the most important items, since the trophy is in the photos. I'm having a poster-size blowup made as a souvenir of a truly memorable hunt. And I'm keeping my eye out for a legal jaguar mount for sale, so the public in my area can better see what one of our American spotted cats looks like. It's the best I can do under the circumstances. But to tell you the truth, it's pretty darn good overall, and I feel an uncommon degree of satisfaction with the experience. I think I'm reaching a point of maturity in my hunting career where I can feel fulfilled without a trophy.

The jaguar is a special animal, and just seeing one in the wild is a thrill. I am glad I did.

GATO PINTADO DE CALAKMUL

Motoring down the road in the ancient army Jeep belonging to EcoSafaris, I have a distinct feeling of déjà vu. I was in this same location last year after spending a day in Chetumal, and we covered this same ground around this same time of day. The Hale-Bopp comet had been in full array then, and along this highway I can recall seeing its brilliant light dominating the western sky. No such spectacle is evident this night, but Orion the Hunter is high overhead in the crystal vault of heaven, boding well for my return visit, I hope. It seems that the hunter's constellation always brings the breaks my way.

I am returning here after an eminently unsuccessful experience on my previous trip. Failure is a relative term, but last year nothing seemed to go right. The only way to regularly catch the elusive jaguar is to put out baits of live sheep or goats, chase the predator with dogs, and hope it will tree close enough that one can capture it. That

is our plan, as it was last year, but at that time the bait had not been in place long enough, nor had enough tangled jungle roads been laboriously opened with thousands, perhaps millions, of machete swings. The result was an interesting but unproductive week. The closest I came to seeing a jaguar was a very fresh track in a cave, but, as we say back home, tracks make thin soup.

As it was last year, my old Remington 700 .30-06 is at home. I will be trying once more to get a true trophy photograph of a live jaguar. This hunt is to allow one to participate in, and thus help fund, a scientific study that, we can hope, will someday lead to a reopening of jaguar hunting.

My driver and host, Francisco Zavala Castillo, is better known as Pancho, and he works for Tony Rivera's EcoSafaris. It is his job to get me to camp and then go with me tomorrow to check the numerous baits. He has high hopes, even though the last two hunters were unsuccessful in darting any spotted cats. One of them left early, but the other was able to tranquilize a puma after it had been run up a tree by the hounds. The experience of a Yucatan hunt had to leave an indelible impression on him.

Pancho relates some bad news. A jaguar has killed two of Tony's best dogs just a few weeks ago, attacking them while they were tied up near camp. The team is left with only three trained hounds, plus a couple of promising pups. One of the experienced canines is young, too, but they performed well on the puma they treed last week. Nevertheless, the loss leaves me with a sharp feeling of uneasiness about the pack's ability to bring one of the extraordinary spotted cats to bay.

Very few people have seen at close hand this memorable slice of the Yucatan I will be visiting. In the land of the Maya, there are several unique species of larger animals, although few besides the jaguar top a hundred pounds. The white-lipped peccary, the brocket deer, the tropical white-tailed deer, and the tapir are all found here. In the centuries since the Spanish conquistadors, all of the virgin jungle has been stripped; the regrowth is distinctly different in character but nevertheless highly fascinating.

In a tiny pueblo along the main highway west out of Chetumal, we stop at a roadside stand and purchase an item I have specifically requested. On my annual mission trips to Honduras, I always get a bunch of *datiles*, a tiny, sweet banana unavailable in the United States. The vendor has plenty of them, and they cost only a couple of dollars for a full stalk. I break off a couple and carefully peel them, taking care not to touch the edible portion after handling the skin, since there is no way of knowing what kind of awful bacterium might be on it. The taste is sweet and familiar. The deal consummated, we motor onward. There is nothing better after a day of jaguar hunting than to sit in the shade and munch these tiny, rare, and inexpensive delicacies.

As we approach the *ejido* (town) of Narciso Mendoza, the last few miles of the journey are smooth and regular, a welcome change from the battered pavement we have been on. The tiny village has changed not at all since a year ago, with only one exception: there is electricity now. I am visiting the jungle a month earlier this year, and the temperature is noticeably cooler. April was hot, muggy, and uncomfortable, so the chilly wind of early March is a welcome sensation. As we motor along, the road changes radically to four-wheel-drive country, and Pancho deftly switches gears in the venerable truck.

The Yucatan is full of surprises. A bird that looks akin to a southern whippoorwill is sitting on the road. As our vehicle approaches, its red eyes gleam in the headlights, the reflective tapetum reversing the light to create a gleaming jewel of effervescent scarlet. Finally the resting bird flies with muted wing beat out of sight. Then it reappears, sitting farther down the road. As we once more come within an eyelash of running over it, the bird flutters off into the darkness. In a minute or less, it appears again as the headlights illuminate a new section of road. This sequence repeats dozens of times.

"What is that bird, Pancho?" I ask in Spanish.

"*Un tapacamino. Siempre en la carretera.*"

So that's another unique feature of the Yucatan: birds that refuse to leave the road. I'm not surprised. It seems that everything here is a little unusual. I file away the information even as the bird's red eye becomes visible once more ahead. Perhaps

five miles of such nonsense ensues before the bird finally disappears for good.

Camp is a dream, individual tents spread widely apart so that nobody has to listen to his neighbor's snoring. Over each tent is an artistic roof, or *pecho*, skillfully made of *pencas*, a giant palmetto that grows in profusion in the nearby jungle. The leaves must be cut on the quarter moon, I'm told, when the moisture content is perfect, or the thatch will rot away quickly. I don't know how much truth there is to the tale, but the camp hands adhere to it religiously, and their *pechos* seem to last a long time. The giant *tinto*, a tree with irregular interlacing ridges that looks like a mass of tangled alders grown together, stands guard at the door of one tent, a silent sentinel I remember from last year. I am told that there is very good

Milk from the chicocepote *tree is harvested to make useful* chicle.

wood in the center, despite the anomalous appearance of the surface.

There is good news from the camp personnel, who have been out checking the baits and administering the tethered sheep food and water. A jaguar killed one of the sheep last night. They are certain it is one of the great spotted cats because the carcass was consumed starting at the brisket, and a puma always eats the internal organs first. If we had been here a day earlier, we would have been in great shape, but now the trail will be cold. Sometimes a jaguar returns for another easy meal, but sometimes they move on. I must hope that this one will return.

The meals are fit for any gringo's stomach, prepared by a lady hired by camp manager Javier Dias Narrbaez. Happily, even the salads are safe for consumption here. Around a meal of delicious quesadillas we discuss the upcoming project. Biologist Cuauhtemoc Chavez is also at the table, and we cover the scientific aspects of the program as we eat. Part of my mission here is to help appraise the overall program, and I am satisfied that the study seems to be well grounded. Six jaguars and several pumas have been captured and collared thus far, and the only item separating the study from complete credibility seems to be money, which is in desperate need.

Temoc, as the biologist is fondly nicknamed, is a graduate student of respected Mexican biologist Gerardo Ceballos of the University of Mexico. The young man is doing this study to complete his thesis to earn a master's degree in biology, and he hopes to extend it to cover his doctorate as well. He plans to attend every darting hunt. He not only supervises the treatment of each cat that is caught but he will also take samples of blood, hair, fecal material, and ectoparasites (usually a tick). He conducts a complete physical exam, which includes checking length, girth, footpads, vital signs, and palpating the stomach.

The need they are facing is funding to put up four towers to monitor the movements of the collared cats. Plans are afoot to put up a surveillance airplane from time to time as well. The towers will be capable of watching the activity of all collared jaguars twenty-four hours a day.

My sleep this night is fitful beyond imagination. The pack of dogs we will use seems

suspect to me, and two hunters just left without seeing a jaguar. Besides, I'm cold. I dig in my bag for my rain gear and spread it over me. In the wee hours I finally fall asleep, and it is only a short time until Arias, husband of our cook, wakes me.

After coffee, cookies, and juice, we board the Jeep. The whole scene feels uncomfortably familiar, and I even seat myself on the right side of the truck bed, where I sat every time we went out last year. My pack is full of cameras and film, and I have high hopes as we bounce down the narrow trail. We are surrounded by a tangle of jungle vegetation, and I duck my head at intervals to avoid vines and low limbs. At various locations are small *riochuelos,* or little riverbeds, dry this time of year. There is little water with which to concern myself, but all the ravines have steep banks that we must negotiate with caution. Spectacular limestone formations are common along their courses, much of it eroded into sharp, jewellike splinters.

The first few sheep are unmolested and seem content, despite the peril they unknowingly face. The fourth one, however, has been hit by a jaguar. We all dismount to inspect the kill. The carcass is already stiff, but the pattern of consumption confirms it to be the work of one of the big spotted cats, not a puma. I question the men about it as they unload the dogs. This is the same location where a sheep was killed the night before I arrived, and they think it is a big male jaguar already wearing a collar. The only reason to give chase is to inspect him visually and check his health, but we won't dart the cat unless he has no collar. Shortly the hounds and the houndsmen are quartering nearby, and several loud cries from the dogs indicate they have caught a scent. Nowhere is a trackable trail evident, however. The animal has apparently left the scene.

As we move back to the truck and reload the dogs, disappointment rests heavily on me. We quickly move out, because eight more sheep wait to be checked and already dawn is approaching. If we don't make good time to the last bait the temperature will be too warm, and any trail will be cold. Soon we are jostling along the narrow road once more, the chill of night still encompassing us as we move through the abundant vegetation.

The forest through which we are traveling is a vast, unbroken wilderness punctuated by small settlements and an occasional rough road. The Calakmul Biospheric Reserve is along the border of both Guatemala and Belize, and the population of jaguars here is thought to be excellent. There is little livestock ranching in this region, so ranchers—the biggest threat to the jaguar—are scarce as well.

The most prevalent large tree here is the rough-barked *chicocepote*, all of which have a row of chevronlike machete cuts running from near the base all the way up to the major branches, thirty to forty feet off the ground. The *campesinos,* or locals, cut the trees so as to elicit a flow of white resin from them. This sap is collected in leather pouches and sold as chicle, an important gum base that has been used as a major ingredient in chewing gum. All the gum trees bear an edible round fruit, but it is so high up in the canopy that I can't get to it to sample a bite.

The light is now excellent, and I am once more filled with wonder at the spectacle of the dense forest at dawn. Birds are visible everywhere, including an occasional chachalaca, an edible species that flies much like any game bird, bursting from the edge of the road in a rush of grayish-black feathers. We pass a huge colony of coatimundis, raccoonlike creatures that move through the trees more like monkeys, swinging from limb to limb, their long tails waving. Pancho tells me that they never occur alone, but almost always inhabit the giant *amates*, a huge tree with smooth bark that grows along the banks and gullies of the *riochuelas.* Monkeys of various kinds, including the spider monkey and the larger *saraguate*, or roaring monkey, also prefer this habitat. I attempt to photograph the coatimundis, but the darkness under the canopy and their continual movement make that impossible. Two tiny black birds with red heads also elude my efforts, though Pancho identifies them as beautiful *cardenales*—very different from our solid red cardinals back home.

We are nearing the seventh sheep, and incredibly, it, too, has been killed, this time by a puma. There are distinctive puma tracks in the sand among the leaves, and Pancho and Javier consult at some length. We will check the other baits before trying to run this cat. The kill is fresh enough that we should make it to the other baits and back before it is too old, and they strongly prefer that we chase a jaguar. They are certain that two uncollared jaguars are in this stretch of jungle, and they want to capture them. Pumas are included in their study, but mainly to determine their effect on jaguar populations. I want to chase a jaguar very much for my own purposes, too, since the local puma is essentially the same animal that is so common in the American West. If there is no hit by a jaguar, we will return here and loose the dogs.

The next sheep is also dead, eaten internal organs first, a dependable but not invariable sign of a puma kill. I descend from the truck and place my hand on the dead sheep. The carcass is still warm, and the limbs are quite limber.

We have several more baits to check, but this cat might have been on the sheep carcass as we arrived. If so it should be easy to tree. Pancho tells me all about it, and I hastily agree. Treeing and darting a puma will be fun, but I can't help being disappointed. Still, there are kills all over the place, so we've got a lot of cats working.

"Es possible que este puma tiene pintitas," Pancho comments as we loose the dogs. Could be a jaguar, he says in so many words, a "puma with spots." Has he seen something in the tracks that has escaped me? There is no question, though, that this cat ate the entrails first. It has to be a puma.

This time the dogs react immediately as they hit the ground. Full cries emanate from all three as their nostrils fill with hot cat scent, and they are off like so many bullets into the jungle. We are close behind, the metallic clanging of the machetes leading the way. We go hurriedly but in single file, the most experienced man in front to watch for the deadly barba amarilla. I keep a sharp eye out as well as we move behind the baying hounds, putting perhaps a kilometer of jungle quickly behind us. It is difficult to concentrate on the ground, however, amidst the distractions of the jungle. *Comahen,* the giant, dark-brown nests of a termite, are suspended high in the branches all around us, and there are *epifitas*, a type of bromeliad, or air plant, at eye level and above almost everywhere.

Suddenly the dogs lead us off to the right. I am more and more certain the animal must be a puma, since that species runs in circles whereas the jaguar flees in a straight line, and for a longer distance. One of our number, the fleet-footed Javier,

Various interesting critters share our camp—including this tarantula.

has outrun the rest, and he intercepts our party as we divert in the new direction. He is running hard as he passes us, and points to a warm bed of flattened vegetation underneath a big, smooth-barked *amate* tree.

"*Es un tigre! Lo vi!*"

He has seen the animal, and it is a jaguar! We have not run the animal from the carcass as we had supposed, but rather the animal was lying here in the shadows digesting its meal, which gave me the false impression of a circular chase. We hurry after the barking. The temperature has risen, and I am sweating profusely. I wonder out loud whether the dogs can tree the animal when it is so warm. Pancho isn't worried, and he gives me a look of pure confidence. But these dogs are inexperienced; how can he be so sure?

My heart pounds with excitement and exertion. Over fallen *chicocepote* trees, through thick stands of red-barked mulato trees, and around impossible deadfalls we go, the music of dancing machete blades accompanying our every step. In the distance we can hear the dogs fading away, their course as straight as an arrow's flight.

Finally, after a half-hour of frantic chase, there is a sudden change in the cacophony of the dogs, the rhythmic baying that signifies a treed animal. I run harder than ever, all thoughts of a barba amarilla completely purged from my mind. The regular cadence of the dogs leads us to our prey,

and the nearer I get the more my mind races with excitement. We can now see the hounds, literally trying to climb a tree ahead. Javier is already with them, and all eyes are trained on the pute tree, a large specimen with highly irregular bark.

As we come closer, my eyes strain to see what all this effort is about. For the first time in my life, I lay eyes on what I have come to the Yucatan to pursue. A mature jaguar, the grand cat with a tawny coat covered by gorgeous black spots, sits a scant fifty feet up at the second branching of the tree, teeth bared. As we approach, the beast lets out a mighty roar such as one might expect from an African lion or leopard. At the savage sound the hair on the back of my neck stands up, and I am certain my eyes go wide with amazement.

"*Es una hembra. No hay collar,*" says Javier to Pancho as we catch our breath.

An uncollared female. The two set about preparing the dart gun while I hastily get my cameras ready. I wouldn't miss these pictures for anything. Arias and his helper clear away some of the brush so we can take photographs and shoot the gun without obstruction.

There is no hurry now. The cat is breathing hard after running perhaps two miles, an acute and prolonged exertion the animals are ill accustomed to. It will do the pretty lady no harm, though, and we should have plenty of time to complete our task. I use up two rolls of film before I am ready to dart the gorgeous creature.

The missile must go true. A perforation of the abdominal wall or the lungs would be fatal. I position myself so the dart will go nowhere near those vital areas, using the tree trunk to shield them. My dart is right on target, striking the back leg about midthigh. We wait a full ten minutes, and the cat shows only minimal grogginess. Another dart is necessary, so the biologist loads the gun with more tranquilizer.

My second dart lands within an inch of the first. While Pancho and the crew safely secure the dogs a dozen yards from the tree, Javier climbs to a position adjacent our prize, carrying with him a rope and a long stick. The cat roars another warning at the approach, but her head sways lazily. Using the forked stick, Javier deftly places a loop of rope around one of the drunken feline's rear feet, a tactic that by now she resists only minimally. A sharp tug and the line is firmly attached.

At the tug, the animal lunges slightly and loses her grip. Javier is ready, and as the cat slides out of the tree he braces himself, slowly playing out the line and letting our trophy gently and unharmed to the ground. The spectacle of the regal dappled

feline suspended between heaven and earth is one I shall never forget. Soon the animal is safe, laid out on her side with Temoc attending her like a patient in intensive care.

The scientific work comes before any posing and pictures for me. I am shooting all the time as they work, though. Temoc first makes certain the cat is sufficiently asleep, then places his bandanna over the animal's eyes, both to shield her from the sight of hated humans and to protect the corneas from drying and foreign objects. Next he does a complete physical exam, including listening to the heart and lungs with a stethoscope, checking the teeth and jaws, and palpating the abdomen. From this latter examination he determines that our jaguar is carrying cubs, which should deliver in a couple of months. He then does the needed measurements, starting with the length (167 centimeters), the weight (47 kilograms), the measurements of the paws and girth, and the size of the head. He deftly plucks a tick from the haunch, takes a few hairs from underneath the belly, probes the rectum for a small sample of feces, and draws blood from the jugular vein. Then he attaches the radio collar. Last, he applies a long-lasting sterilizing solution and antibiotic to the small dart wounds to prevent infection.

The scientific part done, I can now get my pictures. First the bandanna comes off that beautiful face, and I burn up two more rolls of film in short order. One handles a live jaguar discreetly at first, because the sensation of touching such a deadly creature with impunity takes some time to sink in. Soon I am holding the head behind the jaws, and my companions are flashing picture after picture.

We can be in no hurry to leave; we must be certain our painted lady is safely awake. She is recovering nicely, and defiance is returning to those blank

Epifitas, or air plants, are common in the jungle.

eyes. We back off, and the helpers move the dogs farther away as the tranquilizer wears off. The front legs come alive first, followed shortly by the back ones. The jaguar tries to get up, then with a surge she is off, covering ten yards before stopping and lying down again. The head is up and those fierce eyes are blazing as she regains her majestic composure. Soon she is up and away. Farewell, my friend. Maybe we'll meet again someday.

Seven jaguars are now collared in the Calakmul Biospheric Reserve. We have done a good day's work already, and it is early afternoon. But we must first check the remaining sheep, and feed and water them. To our amazement, the last one is dead and buried under a pile of leaves and brush. We have found three sheep killed today! This last one is so typically puma that we decide to return tomorrow to try to collar it. Jaguars never cover their prey in such a manner. Suddenly we have more active cats than we have time to pursue.

That is not the end of the cat kills, even though we have checked all the sheep. As we return past the sheep, one of the first ones we checked has been killed since we passed this morning. Even Pancho is incredulous as we examine the half-consumed carcass. It is stiff now, the kill having been apparently accomplished just after we passed. Pancho wields his machete and cuts the rope to free the carcass. He feels that the cat will return and drag the meat to a more secure location nearby; perhaps we will be able to pursue it tomorrow.

As we return to camp, the African call of "*Simba! Simba!*" comes to mind. The Masai chant the words after a successful lion hunt, and the chant seems appropriate here. The thrill of victory is a grand sensation.

After a nap, I head for the dining area as darkness gathers. A disquieting roar shakes me, a sound that could be a big cat very nearby. Tony has arrived, and he and Pancho are at the table. I ask them about the roars from down the *riochuela,* and they smile. The sound is from the *saraguate,* the roaring monkey. A different call emanates from the opposite direction, an odd metallic and musical note they easily identify as the chachalaca bird. The

creatures make the loud cries as they fly up to roost and are most vocal when a weather change is in the offing.

Sleep is better tonight. We arise at 4 A.M. once more and are off after breakfast. This time we have a definite plan. We will first try the jaguar that killed the sheep early yesterday. If the carcass is gone, we will know the cat is likely nearby. If it is undisturbed, we will move on. High hopes buoy my confidence, and I know I am in for another treat.

The body of the sheep killed yesterday is gone. We pile out of the truck, unleash the dogs in the semidarkness, and barking fills the air once more. They jump the cat, the excited yelping signifying a close encounter, and they are off with us in hot pursuit, ringing machetes in the air. Soon I am perspiring heavily again.

The dogs move completely out of earshot, and we follow on faith. Not uncommonly it is necessary to fan out to find them, since the jungle absorbs sound so well. After two hours we locate the treed cat in a small *chechen* tree, a species with a corrosive sap that will badly burn human skin. It is a male jaguar, already collared, so only visual inspection is necessary. He apparently is doing extremely well, tolerating the approach of man only reluctantly. The rested animal jumps deftly from the tree, and but for the restraining chains already attached to the dogs, we would be off once more.

It is a long walk back to the truck, and now I have time to look at the jungle floor. Everywhere there are droppings and scrapes of the tiny brocket deer, a favorite prey of the jaguar. We never see the creatures, but they are obviously abundant. Cold drinks and sandwiches await us at the truck, a welcome refreshment after hours of exertion.

I hope fervently that this program will succeed. It has many strong points, and the experience is most rare. The jaguar of the Calakmul deserves more attention than it has been receiving, and I am proud to have participated. Maybe others will join me and we can accomplish some good.

Now that I have seen them, I know that the spotted cat of the Americas is unique and unforgettable. No hunting career is entirely complete without seeing one of them in the wild.

Black Bear. (Photo: courtesy of Jeanne Drake)

BLACK BEAR
(Ursus americanus)

Up from his stony playground—down from his well-digged lair—
Out on the naked ridges ran Adam-zad the bear.
Groaning, grunting, and roaring, heavy with stolen meals,
Two long marches to northward, and I was at his heels.

—Rudyard Kipling (1865–1936), *The Truce of the Bear*

The American black bear is the only species of bear that makes its home only in North America. The reasons why are not clear, but the fact is that the animal is not found in the Old World. The spectacled bear of South America is closely related but distinct. Black bears are extremely abundant, the estimated population of 500,000 making its numbers greater than all the other bears of the world combined. In its original range, it occurred in every state of the United States except Hawaii and every Canadian province and territory. It also ranged well into Mexico, inhabiting Sonora, Chihuahua, Coahuila, and probably several other states. It has disappeared from some Eastern and Midwestern states, though most retain a remnant population that seems to be generally increasing.

In the west and north, including all of the Canadian provinces and territories, the population is stable or increasing. In Mexico, the state of Coahuila has the best bear range, and the species has recovered remarkably from historical lows. The ranch in that state on which I hunted Carmen Mountains white-tailed deer loses several score cattle to bears each year. Some of the hunters accompanying me actually saw bears, although I was not so fortunate. The noteworthy aspect is that black bears are now plentiful there, whereas a few years ago there were virtually none. A hunt began in Mexico in 1997, with a few permits given to landowners. The continuing success of black bear conservation in Mexico depends on making their presence economically valuable, so such permits are a step in the right direction.

Some sixteen subspecies of *Ursus americanus* have been recognized, though taxonomists readily admit that physical differences between them are virtually nonexistent and consist mainly of color phases. The bluish gray "glacier bear" of southeastern Alaska is one of the rarest. The lightest colored bears are found a little farther south on islands off British Columbia, and those so-called Kermode bears are protected by law. Some of these very lightly colored bears are also present in low numbers on the northwestern mainland of British Columbia. Black seems almost universal in the eastern part of the continent, with more brown phase animals in the west. The most common color everywhere is black with a brown tint to the muzzle, and quite a few animals have a white blaze on the chest. One particularly striking such mark is on a specimen taken in 1997 by Robert Shelton in Maine. It consists of a perfect round white spot a foot across, in the center of which is a remarkable black spot a couple of inches wide, creating a natural bull's-eye on the chest.

The likeness among the subspecies is far more striking than any dissimilarities. Body sizes vary widely, with the largest black bears coming from eastern North America, where winters are shorter and food may be available more consistently. A large male black bear may weigh upward of 300 pounds, although in my home state of Georgia the record is over 600 pounds live weight. Such monsters are rare, but they do exist. Females seldom attain more than 250 pounds. Mature males average 30 inches high at the shoulder, with females somewhat less. Skull size as an average is probably the largest on the islands at the extreme ends of the bear's range, Newfoundland in the east and the Queen Charlotte Islands in the west. All black bears have an outstanding sense of smell, very good hearing, but only average vision. The eyes of all black bears are brown.

Black bear. British Columbia, May 1992.

Black bears are often confused with grizzly bears, although the distinction is usually not that difficult to make, even when the black bear is cinnamon or brown. The ears are the most reliable clue, since on blacks they are prominent and large compared with the head; on grizzlies the opposite is true. A humped back is said to identify the bear as a grizzly, but the absence of a hump cannot be trusted, since from some angles a grizzly's hump may not be visible. The facial features of the black bear are distinctive, with a more elongated and pointed muzzle than the typical "dished" appearance of the grizzly. The black bear's claws are much shorter and less prominent, enabling the adults to climb trees, which grizzlies cannot do. Most competent guides can tell a black from a grizzly at a glance, but it is advisable to observe as long as necessary to be certain. It is far better to pass up a shot than to make a mistake.

Distinguishing between black bear tracks and grizzly tracks is even easier than telling the animals apart. Black bear tracks show claw marks that are small and often indistinct, though all five of the toes are usually visible. The front pad makes a flat depression like that of a grizzly, but the heel mark

sets the grizzly track apart: that feature is absent in black bear tracks. So in distinguishing the two, go front and rear. Presence of prominent claw marks and a well-defined heel print mean a grizzly.

Female black bears are sexually mature at three and a half years, although those in the southeastern United States more often breed a year earlier. Males are capable of breeding at that age as well, though they grow until about eight years, and the larger, older males do most of the mating. Females are receptive in June and July, and copulation stimulates ovulation. The embryo floats free in the uterus for several months, the delay in implantation being characteristic of most bear species. Insemination to birth takes six to seven months, but embryo implantation to birth is only about two months. Since growth and maturation of the fetal bears requires production of glucose from her protein stores, the mother bear loses muscle and other body protein until they are born. After birth, the mother's fat stores are then burned by the cubs' drinking her milk.

Two or three cubs are commonly born in the winter den, although up to six have been reported. At birth they weigh only a half-pound and are hairless, with eyes and ears closed. In the southern portions of the black bear's range, only the females enter dens, and then only to give birth. Bear cubs grow rapidly, and by the time they leave the den they may weigh several pounds. They are also covered with hair, and their eyes and ears are functioning. The mother stays with them for a year and a half and dens with them (except in the Deep South, where they do not enter a den at all) until they are one year old. The female thus is bred only in alternate years, the onset of estrus apparently inhibited hormonally by milk production. An average of 65 percent of female bears breed each year, though, the excess over the expected 50 percent reflecting cub mortality and various reproductive failures. Bears live only about ten years in the wild, but in captivity they may reach the age of thirty.

All black bears in cold climates den up for the winter. The hibernation phase is remarkable, because they do not eat, drink, urinate, or defecate during the entire time. Body temperature declines by several degrees and overall metabolism slows by some 50 to 60 percent. Their weight naturally decreases during this phase, and they may emerge from the den weighing 25 percent less than when they entered. Recycling of nitrogen from urea (which allows them to skip urination) may even result in a gain in lean body mass during hibernation. This process involves a biochemical conversion of urea with the chemical glycerol (produced from body fat) to make alanine, an amino acid that is a building block of protein. Perhaps more remarkable is that they lose no bony mass despite the inactivity. By contrast, if a human being ceases to be mobile, he rapidly deteriorates, losing calcium from the bones and experiencing shortening of tendons and ligaments and contracture of muscles.

Den selection depends on locale. In northern areas, dens are constructed to allow snowfall to cover the entrance, providing warmth and security. In more temperate southern areas, bears may select cavities in large trees, or they may simply find a dense thicket with heavy overstory and prepare a crude ground nest in which to give birth.

Black bears eat a highly omnivorous diet, convenience perhaps being the defining consideration. They have short, simple digestive tracts that require highly digestible food, so most browse-type plants are too woody. In the southeastern United States a favorite food is squaw root, a parasite of red oaks that resembles an ear of corn growing from the ground. Other foods include blueberries, raspberries, serviceberries, blackberries, cherries, small mammals and insects, and larger mammals as the opportunity presents. Black bears readily take to most any form of carrion, and human garbage is especially tempting. In spring they concentrate on succulent new vegetation and overwintered mast; in summer they

In soft sand one can sometimes see the claw marks of a black bear.

eat squaw root and newly ripened berries; in fall they turn to acorns, hickory nuts, grapes, greenbrier, and beech nuts. They can be a nuisance, liberally partaking of such crops as corn and apples. Where food is plentiful, it is not uncommon for black bears to gain over two pounds a day in the fall in preparation for hibernation.

Black bears are efficient predators of white-tailed deer, especially fawns. In fact, mature boars are significant predators of most neonatal ungulates, and where bears are abundant they can be a limiting factor on prey populations. Mountain sheep and goats are relatively immune to this pressure because of their birthing sites. In grizzly range, the larger, more aggressive ursids largely displace black bears from that role, as all age groups of grizzlies participate in predation.

Like all North American bears, mature males are opportunistic cannibals who will readily eat cubs and even adult females. One study from Ontario shows that black bears in populations hunted by man are one-tenth as likely to be involved in cannibalism as bears from areas where sport hunting is not allowed. That is likely because sport hunting concentrates on removing large males, thus reducing contact between them and family groups.

Black bears roam over a large range, males covering twenty-five or more square miles and females ten to twelve. Naturally, there is a core zone where cover, food availability, and other habitat needs are more conducive to survival, so a bear may spend most of its time in that smaller area. A dependable food source and areas of inaccessible terrain are always necessary. Because of fluctuations in food sources, home range also varies with the season of the year. Males tolerate encroachment by other individuals into their home range more readily than females, who may vigorously defend their right to a particular zone.

Males may mark the boundaries of their home range by biting or clawing trees several feet above the ground, usually in an open area such as an old road or trail. These marks can be a dependable measure of body size, since male bears often reach as high as they can from a standing position to bite chunks of bark from the tree. Since most such marks are refreshed frequently during the summer breeding season, they probably have some

Glassing for bears high in the Purcell Wilderness.

relationship to sexual activity. There also may be social factors, such as identifying dominance order to other bears.

While the bear described in Kipling's quotation is probably not demonstrating usual behavior, bears do exhibit a variety of well-known vocalizations and aggressive posturing. They may emit a low moan or growl when threatened and actually roar when fighting with other bears. Black bears are far less likely to attack humans than are browns or grizzlies, but the sheer numbers and much wider distribution of the black bear results in hundreds of incidents of threatening behavior across North America each year. Most of these occur where bears are protected and interact freely with tourists, but even there only a small percentage result in mauling or other contact. Conversely, in areas of low human encroachment and no hunting, mature boars that hunt neonatal ungulates may transfer that behavior to human beings who enter the forest during the birthing season (usually June and July, but varying with altitude and latitude). These bears have learned to rush anything that moves and is too slow to escape. Maulings and deaths occur each year as a result.

This species is subject to at least twenty-five kinds of endoparasites (mainly worms of various types), and about half that many species of ectoparasites (ticks, fleas, mites, and the like). These afflictions are much more common in the southern range, where temperature and humidity are more conducive to the survival of parasite vectors and transmission. They are seldom a significant mortality factor in healthy populations. Other diseases are less common and usually not a serious problem, although trichina worm infestation is very widespread. Consumption of bear flesh by humans can result in trichinosis, a painful and debilitating disease. Thorough cooking of any animal flesh, especially bear meat, is recommended.

Sport hunting offers the only cost-effective management tool for controlling black bear populations. About 25,000 to 30,000 black bears are taken in sport hunts across North America annually, the harvest amounting to approximately 5 percent of the adult population. Since the reproductive potential of black bears is excellent, and man-caused mortality is the major factor for adult bears, this harvest is certainly sustainable.

Poaching has potential for becoming more of a problem, and special programs to detect and deter it may be a focus of future management efforts. But bear hunting involves hard work in inaccessible areas. It requires a great deal of time for relatively little gain, and there is no ready market for bear parts, such as exists in Asia. Law enforcement in North America is also much more effective and has greater backing by both legal hunters and the population in general. Some unethical people doubtless take black bears for their gall bladders to treat stomach and digestive ailments, but better remedies are available at any corner drugstore for less effort and lower cost.

Problem bears surface frequently, usually because people think it is fun to feed them, thus habituating them to handouts and human presence. Feeding almost inevitably leads to the death of the bear, hence the public information sign: "A Fed Bear Is A Dead Bear." Such bears engage in threatening behavior and must either be destroyed or moved to a remote area in the hope that they will fend for themselves again. Although the feeding of bears is the cause of much trouble, however, it is naive to think that simply ending it would eliminate conflicts between bears and humans. The animals are extremely attracted to any exotic scent, and eliminating scents in the environment is impossible.

Transplanted problem bears frequently encounter resident bears in whose territory they are unwelcome, so they get pushed from place to place seeking food and a home range in an unfamiliar area. Usually, such a bear eventually encounters human habitation and continues its delinquent ways until ultimately it is destroyed. A friend who guides in northern British Columbia had a very bold black bear enter his remote hunting camp more than sixty miles from the nearest road. It proceeded to terrify hunters, guides, and horses and destroy pack boxes and tents. It became necessary to shoot the bear when loud noises, warning shots, and other nonlethal means failed to drive it away. My friend duly reported the kill to the authorities, explained the circumstances, and turned over the hide. It was never confirmed, but one would suspect that the animal had been transported to the wilderness to remove it from contact with humans. The tactic obviously didn't work.

A good trophy black bear is a mature male with a full, unrubbed coat. Early spring is the best time to hunt because the large males emerge from the den first and the coats are pristine until warm weather induces rubbing of the winter hair. The later in the fall it is, the better the coat will be and the more chance that the females will be denned up, lessening the chance of shooting one by mistake. A single male can breed several females in the spring, so taking males makes sense from several perspectives, including reducing cannibalism.

A black bear with a 22-inch skull (combining length and width) is a rarity. On a recent hunt in Coahuila, Mexico, I saw the skull of a bear taken on the ranch where I was hunting deer. It looked as big as a gallon milk jug, one of the largest I have ever examined, but it measured only a fraction over nineteen inches. Such measurements are impossible until after the kill, of course, so one must learn to judge a living bear's trophy potential. A mature male with unrubbed coat should be the minimum standard.

Equipment needs will vary with where you are hunting. In the far north, be prepared for snow and cold, both spring and fall, so take waterproof footwear and woolen outer garments. In the south, cotton or synthetic clothing is adequate either camouflage or colorful. If the terrain is swampy, ankle-fit rubber boots or hip boots may be necessary, the latter almost always when hunting Alaska. A light day pack is usually all that is necessary, and in it should be rain gear and a down parka, as well as fire-starting materials, a flashlight, survival food such as chocolate bars, and a large plastic bag in which to carry your bearskin to camp.

Any modern centerfire rifle will kill a black bear, but I recommend the largest-grain bullet available in the caliber. Bullet placement is always the most important factor, so take your time when shooting and don't fire until you're sure of the identity (grizzly or black), sex (if at all possible), whether or not the animal is alone, and how big it is. Remember, too, that more people are mauled by black bears than by grizzly bears each year, so don't saunter up after the shot, assuming your quarry has either gone down or has fled like a white-tailed deer. It just might pounce on you if you aren't ready for a follow-up shot.

Hunting black bears is a privilege in jeopardy as the antihunting movement tries to turn public opinion against it. We hunters must counter their mendacity with truth and a lofty and demanding code of ethics. If we don't, we could ultimately see all bear hunting halted, to the detriment of the species and, by loss of revenue and attendant increased poaching, all wildlife. Bear hunting is eminently defensible and should never be allowed to fall into disrepute. If we get our facts straight and insist on sound scientific management, it never will. Resolve to do your part.

CONSOLATION PRIZE

Grizzly range often overlaps black bear range, especially in the southern zones of Canada. On this hunt I have my sights set on a mountain grizzly, one of the classic silvertips, and I have chosen southern British Columbia to search for the ancient veteran I want. Coincidentally, this is terrific black bear habitat. Some hunters in this area have harvested both varieties on the same trip, and naturally I hope to be among the lucky few.

The outfitter for this trip into the back country is Lloyd Harvey of Toby Creek Outfitters. Most of his operation centers on the virginal Purcell Wilderness near Cranbrook, British Columbia. Lloyd and his guides hunt the high alpine snow slides in the spring, vertical terrain where the snow melts earlier on the lower parts of the exposed ground. In these areas recurrent avalanches wipe away willow and other larger woody plants, and the green grasses that bears love emerge sweet and succulent as the snow line retreats up the mountain. Bears of all sizes and varieties congregate to feed on the tender shoots, driven by hunger after a long winter nap.

Lloyd has a twelve-year string of successes with his grizzly clients, even though he has only one such permit per year, and I certainly don't want to be the one to break it. This is my fourth grizzly hunt, and I will stop at nothing that is legal and ethical to get a big, mature male bear. And maybe pick up another blackie, as well, along the way.

The problem this year is an impossibly early spring, with the vegetation in mid-May looking like a month or more later. The sky is blue, and a cool breeze ripples the vast stretches of grass we

A beautiful day to pack into the back country.

encounter on our ride up Toby Creek to the base camp. With all the slides completely melted off in the usual hot spots, and the bears dispersed to the four winds, we will be at a distinct disadvantage. I greet this news with resignation; it seems that the whole year has seen similarly unusual hunting weather. It has been a terrible year for me: I have encountered shutouts on bighorn sheep, Sitka black-tailed deer, and even tule elk, all at least partially because of adverse weather.

Lloyd's area includes over 1,100 square miles of the Purcell Mountains, encompassing the whole of the Purcell Wilderness Conservatory. Despite the area's inaccessibility, substantial development has sprung up on the periphery, and the edges of bear country are under the pressure of human encroachment. Once one leaves the roads, however, one could be far back in the Yukon or Alaska, and I sense true wilderness as we ride in amid the snowcapped grandeur of the Canadian Rockies.

Accommodations in the main camp far up Toby Creek are superb, and there are spectacular peaks and high alpine basins on all sides. After a three-hour trail ride, we emerge into a small

meadow just across the creek from several of the famous "bear slides." The cabins are wood heated, and all have propane lights and comfortable bunk beds. The cookhouse has a propane stove and refrigerator. Towering spruce surround the site, and wildlife visitors to the glade are many. A spruce grouse greets us with a springtime mating ritual, and magpies call noisily from the thicket nearby. I notice a well-used salt lick within spitting distance of the main cabin, with ungulate hoofprints abounding. Grizzly scat is all over the yard, as are the prints of a seven-foot bear, though all of the droppings and tracks are old. I am in the right place, it seems.

My guide, Joe McDonald, looks more Indian than his Scotch name would imply. With his colorful bandanna, buckskins, and wide-brimmed hat he looks for all the world like a transplant from a previous century. He is extremely competent, fit, and determined, and his age, fifty-four, is no handicap.

South Fork Camp will be our home for what we hope will be two fun-filled weeks. My wife, Linda, is accompanying me on a real backcountry hunt for the first time, and having my best friend along is an added treat. The packtrain into camp through beautiful weather leaves us both exhilarated, with temperatures and sunshine more what one would expect back home in Georgia this time of year. The unusual weather is somewhat ominous for bear hunting, though, and I even sense a bit of trepidation in my guide. Surely these bears will be doing all they can to shed those lush winter coats as soon as possible.

Sometime after the camp closed last winter, a large grizzly raided the horse feed cache, ripping into it with powerful claws. It is his scat that is all over the meadow, brimming with oats. Moose and mule deer visit the cabin yard daily, but the offending grizzly has vanished. I remark to Linda how I wish he would return for another bite.

Certainly there are bears about. The problem is, they show little of the usual tendency to concentrate on the slides. And none of them are the grizzly we want. Before I look at blackies I want to give a grizzly every chance to materialize. In fact, any black bear we see will have to be excellent or I won't shoot him. We glass and reject a number of decent blackies. Most are as yet unrubbed, fueling our optimism that we might be able to find bears with good pelts despite the warmth. If this weather

continues, though, every hide in the Purcell Range is in imminent risk of ruin.

Superb weather continues for the first three days of the hunt. Surefooted mountain horses carry us over rocky trails, many of which are still blocked by winter deadfalls, necessitating that we pack a chain saw along each day. Unlike our wilderness areas in the United States, there is no prohibition against them in the Purcell Range.

One of the biggest treats to any trip into the back country is the abundance of wildlife. The excitement is augmented by the daily visits of many animals to the cabin yard in search of salt. Beautiful spruce grouse, referred to by our Canadian friends simply as "chickens," strut daily at the edge of the clearing, seemingly unconcerned about our presence. To the ostentatious rooster, we are just part of an unending parade of large animals entering and leaving the meadow.

We see a couple of black bears a day, but according to Joe there are usually many more. The scarcity of blackies, and the complete absence of grizzlies, confirms our suspicions that our situation is not ideal. Cooler, wetter weather moves in finally, and we begin to see a few more blackies. As we arrive back at the cabin near dusk one evening,

Our wilderness home for two weeks of spring bear hunting.

Flowers emerge as the snow retreats down the mountainsides.

there is a very acceptable mature bear on the avalanche chute across the creek from camp. Careful glassing in the fading light reveals that he is unrubbed, with prime fur that is long and black. We decide to make a fast stalk.

We use the horses to cross the creek, and within minutes we are crawling up to the bottom of the avalanche chute. We move in as close as possible and finally spot our animal in a brushy draw that bisects the slide. He is moving toward the open area, so I hurriedly set up to shoot, and chamber a round in my old Remington .30-06.

At the report of the rifle, the bruin leaps high in the air and cartwheels into the darkness of the nearby spruce forest.

"Sure looks like you tagged him good," Joe comments as the animal disappears.

"I sure hope so," I answer, having no reason to doubt his observation. The trigger squeeze and recoil felt good, so I am confident I have a dead bear a short ways into the dark woods.

It doesn't matter how good a shot feels if it didn't cut a single hair. That is regrettably the case, as best we can tell. I can almost always tell when I pull a shot off, but this time there is no evidence of a hit, despite my confidence. It wasn't even a long shot, no more than a hundred yards. It was acutely uphill, however, so likely I shot over the bear. Since

I'm not supposed to miss, and thought I hadn't, we search long after the pungent woods are inky black, combing the steep terrain for any sign. We have fortunately brought our flashlights, but the search is fruitless. Hours later we backtrack to the horses and make the short ride to camp, my heart heavy. Linda has stayed in camp all day, and the wonderful meal she has prepared on the wood stove comforts me.

The first order of business the next day is a thorough search of the area we inspected last night. Nothing. Even after four hours of looking everywhere possible that the creature might have gone if wounded, we come up empty-handed. We give up by noon. I can hardly believe I blew such an easy shot, and my humility level climbs considerably. I resolutely determine not to mention good shots I have made in the past, and to avoid the subject of marksmanship altogether.

My son-in-law, Michael Price, is with us on this hunt, seeking black bear out of another camp. He rides in with his guide, Eddie, the next day to visit and spend the night. The new companions add considerably to the social life, and we receive them joyfully after their long ride in the rain. Near evening the rain lets up, so Michael and I don our jackets and head to a prime glassing spot near camp, where we can observe three of the best slides in the area.

As dark begins to close in we have seen nothing unusual, except for the absence of the commonly observed elk and mule deer. There's nothing really peculiar about that, though—animals eat and move about at odd times, especially when the weather is miserable. But then there is something moving in the brush on the center slide. A bear! Is that why the ungulates are hiding?

I put the spotting scope on the bear, hoping to see if he's the one I missed. To my utter amazement, the creature is incredibly large, and the broad head and humped back confirm that this is not a black bear at all. This is what I am here for! The grizzly stands in the open for only a few seconds in all his glory, but I can see an infinity of silver-tipped splendor as his lush pelt ripples in the breeze. Oh, if only there were another fifteen minutes of light! I hope against hope that the bear will still be nearby when morning breaks.

I awake early and spend the first thirty minutes of daylight searching for the supreme bruin. Joe stands by with the horses saddled and ready, just in case. There can be no such luck for

me today. A very nice black bear does come out, however, one slide over from where ol' Bonzo had been earlier. He is about six feet, by Joe's estimate, and unrubbed, with a pelt that has hair not quite as long as that on the bear I missed. We mark his location as a possibility for another day, but for now we will try to find that grizzly. We spend the day searching and return late to camp once more, exhausted by the effort.

As the hunt progresses, frustration builds for both my guide and me. Linda graciously takes over most of the cooking chores, giving us more time to hunt. It is great to come in late and have a hot supper on the table. A happy sidelight to the trip is her obvious enjoyment of the frontierlike lifestyle.

Despite many hours of trail riding each day and many more hours of glassing slides and basins, the only grizzlies we spot are a single sow and a year-old cub. By day eight we have decided to try again for the black bear I spotted a few days ago.

We find him again as we ride into camp from a quick check on a likely grizzly slide. The day is still

Guide ties tails together for the packtrain.

young, so we decide to take the bear only when conditions are ideal. We have to abort two stalks, once when our bruin disappears and again because of unfavorable wind. We retrace our steps and plot a different approach, putting us downwind.

This time the bear is straight across the slope, and a little belly crawling places me in position. If only he will move a little to clear a small intervening hump in the terrain. Oh well, if he won't move, I will. I crawl uphill another ten yards, watching carefully that the bear has his head down. When everything looks right, I slowly squeeze the trigger of the old .30-06 with real finger concentration, my earlier debacle vivid in my memory.

Fortunately, the 165-grain Nosler flies perfectly to its mark, taking out both lungs and blowing the animal backward into the bushes. We approach the downed creature cautiously, nevertheless. Joe reminds me that more people are mauled each year by wounded blackies than by any other animal in North America. Our bear, however, is very dead.

This animal is truly a magnificent specimen, nearly six feet from nose to tail with longer hair than we had estimated and a pelt marvelously intact. He might even be the same bear I missed last week. We set up for stunning pictures, the day being bright and sunny with only an occasional fluffy cloud. We position our prize to capitalize on the breathtaking contrast between green mountains with their high mantles of snow and the divine blue of the sky.

Now fast upon us comes one of the strangest episodes I have ever encountered in my hunting career. People sometimes appear in the most amazing places, and we look up now to see two guys on mountain bikes moving out of the dark forest toward us as we complete our pictures. They aren't antihunters, but they eye our prize warily as

we begin the skinning. One of them relates the tale of their ascent today to one of the peaks along the trail they have been on. They had left bikes and helmets unattended for several hours, and when they returned one of the helmets had been crushed by two pairs of massive teeth. These bikers from the city naively think that the helmet has been gnawed by little "forest creatures," as they say. When Joe demonstrates what really happened by using his fingers to simulate the incisors of the great bear, their mouths drop open in disbelief. There can be no doubt. The big, old sow grizzly, probably the one we saw up that same trail with her yearling cub, has tried this invader's hat on for size.

I don't think those unarmed guys have the slightest idea how perilously they have been living, nor how close they have come to an encounter of the worst kind. After more discussion, they go off happily down the trail toward the trailhead, some three hours off by horseback. Partly riding, but mostly carrying, those unwieldy and misplaced bikes over the rocky terrain, they are obviously in terrific shape though a little short on judgment.

Despite several more days of intense effort, the grizzly we are seeking never shows. I am disappointed, but at least I have my consolation prize, a beautiful and mature male black bear. Though a worthy game animal in its own right, the blackie must be North America's most common substitute for the primary game animal. I have encountered the animals while hunting all the North American sheep (except the desert bighorn), and while hunting elk, mountain goat, Coues deer, mule deer, black-tailed deer, moose, and, of course, grizzly.

I have taken several black bears, but I have never hunted specifically for them. When a guy comes home with such a terrific consolation prize, how can he complain?

Alaska brown bear. (Photo: courtesy of James L. Davis)

ALASKA BROWN BEAR
(Ursus arctos middendorffi)

For those who have hunted these giant carnivores,
the reasons for feeling compelled to chase them are far deeper than
what is found in a magazine story or a rug.
It is the respect and admiration for a creature that almost defies description. . . .
They are the most unpredictable animals we hunt in North America.

—J. Wayne Fears, *Hunting North America's Big Bear,* 1989

I must confess to similar sentiments when I went on my brown bear hunt. "Apprehensive" is a word I would add to clarify my feelings as the wilds of the Alaska Peninsula lay before me. Only in the most rudimentary sense did I realize how much a part of brown bear management the hunt plays. It provides irreplaceable information for the biologists responsible for monitoring and managing the brown bear population.

Seldom have I read anything about brown bears that didn't begin with the reasons for distinguishing the subspecies from the interior grizzly, and for good reason. Many people, even some hunters, have only the foggiest idea about the differences and similarities. As detailed almost everywhere, the two bears are one and the same: the habitat accounts for their variances in appearance and behavior.

Thus the major record-keeping organizations have devised artificial boundaries to delineate the two "kinds" for purposes of book entries. That is a practical matter, and not at all unprecedented—they do the same for caribou, moose, black-tailed deer, and a number of other species. The morphological differences between the animals in different regions play the major part in establishing such man-made borders, to be sure, though sometimes the hunting experience and differences in terrain are a factor.

Brown bears occur everywhere in coastal Alaska except the islands south of Frederick Sound in the southeastern part of the state, and in the Aleutian chain of islands south of Unimak, as well as some of the Bering Sea islands. They are referred to by records organizations as grizzlies when outside the recognized but artificial delineation of Alaska brown bear range. The designation *Ursus arctos middendorffi* is currently recognized by taxonomists to apply only to the brown bears of the Kodiak Island group, based on genetic testing of that geographically isolated subgroup. According to biologist Dick Sellers of Alaska, "The lumpers have prevailed. . . . DNA analysis . . . shows that brown bears of southeast Alaska are more closely related to polar bears than to other populations of brown bears." He attributes the genetic differences between bears on Kodiak and adjacent islands to many centuries of isolation from the mainland. Nevertheless, they are all brown bears from the hunter's perspective, once more showing that scientists and hunters have a distinctly different way of viewing animals, even though their efforts and ours are always complementary.

Safari Club International recognizes any bear from Alaska's Management Units 1 through 10 and 14 through 18 as being an Alaska brown bear. In other units of the state these bears are considered grizzlies for record-book purposes. Boone and Crockett uses a similar line, but it may be more difficult for the hunter to certify the qualification of the animal because a major portion of the boundary is the 62nd latitude parallel on the western end. Carry a GPS receiver to be certain.

The bottom line is that some distinction needs to be made, for the simple reason that the coastal bears are much bigger, on average, than their inland cousins. Additionally, the density of coastal bears is much higher, making the experience and the challenge one of greatly different scope. On the coast one might see many bears and be forced to exercise extreme discretion in finding a true trophy, avoiding small bears and lone females at all cost (females with cubs are illegal, naturally). Inland you may spot but few, although the same measure of discretion must apply; the temptation may be to take a bear of any size because it's the only one you have seen. Either way, the hunter must display a great deal of discipline to be certain to contribute positively to management of the bear population. Taking mature male bears is the key.

Coastal bears attain greater size because the bounty of the sea is available to them, principally in the form of salmon runs but also various types of seaside carrion and live creatures. A huge brown bear holding a flapping salmon in its mighty jaws is a familiar sight on television documentaries, and no matter how often one sees the spectacle it never seems to lose its raw fascination. The bears gorge on the fish when they are plentiful, thereby assimilating protein that an inland bear seldom encounters in such abundance. In addition to the resources of the sea, brown bears will eat almost anything else: various items of plant matter, mammals from mice to moose, and even on occasion smaller members of their own species. The foraging season on the Alaska coast is significantly longer than it is in the interior, further contributing to growth of coastal bears.

The debate over the potential size of Alaska brown bears may never be over, but one can safely say that they are the largest purely land-dwelling carnivore in the world. The polar bear attains similar (some say larger) size but spends little time ashore. The largest specimen of a coastal brown bear ever recorded and accurately measured, as far as I can determine, tipped the scales at slightly over 1,700 pounds and measured about nine-and-a-half feet from nose to tail. Such an immense creature's hide would almost certainly square between twelve and thirteen feet, as we hunters measure them. The potential for producing such a monster is still there in the genes, and as with the Chadwick ram of Stone sheep fame, a lucky hunter may someday bump into a new world record.

Unlike the inland grizzly of North America, the coastal brown bears of Alaska still inhabit most of their historical range, where human encroachment has not rendered it unfit. In Alaska the percentage of lost habitat is much less than in North America as a whole. Populations are healthy over much of that range, but there is deep concern about human impact on the brown bear in the future, particularly in locations such as Kodiak Island, where cabins seem to be sprouting in every inlet. Recent land swaps engineered by interested parties may be of benefit in preserving historical brown bear habitat there and elsewhere.

Like all the *Ursus arctos* group, Alaska brown bears have the characteristic brown or buff hair, but usually without the silver tips more characteristic of interior bears. The face is often

Evidence of our quarry's presence.

described as dish-shaped, which means that it appears round when viewed from the front and concave when viewed from the side. The hump is prominent, the eyes and ears relatively small, and the overall appearance of the animal is blocky. The shuffling gait and deliberate mannerisms of such a bear might deceive one into believing these animals are slow, but they can move with incredible quickness for short distances, achieving speeds of thirty miles per hour for short bursts. At a more relaxed pace they are capable of long-distance movements in short order, demonstrating considerable endurance. The skull of the Alaska brown bear is naturally larger than that of the interior grizzly, and biologists recognize some differences in skull shape as well.

Mating occurs in the spring, when the large males that are the hunter's dream are most vulnerable. The time the female is available for mating varies greatly among individual bears. A male may stay with a female for several days, or the female may wander away and mate with a different male during her fertile period. The fertilized ovum, delayed in its implantation, begins developing in the fall. Usually two or three cubs are born in January or February and weigh two and a half pounds or less. Although most litters are weaned at two and a half years of age, intervals between successful breeding of adult females averages five years. In a recent study on Unit 9, where I hunted, the average litter size was 2.54, and average survival of cubs approximated two per reproducing female.

That same report reveals an encouraging increase in numbers of bears in that population, both in percentage of adult males and in total numbers. The percentage of the population harvested today is approximately half that of the early 1970s (8.4 percent then, as compared with 4.8 percent in the study), and mean ages of adults captured were higher, facts that speak well of today's management techniques and should ensure the future of Alaska's brown bear resource. Estimates are that the population can sustain a harvest of 2 to 6 percent, depending on the productivity of breeding females and cub survival. Unit 9 of the Alaska Peninsula was estimated to have 5,680 brown bears in areas open to hunting at the time of the study's conclusion in 1994. An

additional 2,000 to 2,500 bears resided in national parks and other areas closed to hunting within Unit 9. The Peninsula bear population has greatly benefited from a staggered open season schedule, which allows spring hunts in even-numbered years and fall hunts in odd-numbered years. That innovative management tool was instituted in 1977 after emergency closures of bear season on the Alaska Peninsula two years in a row because of unusually high harvest rates. The staggered season was used instead of a draw system, which would have inevitably limited hunting opportunities to those lucky enough to draw a permit.

Brown bear densities are astounding in the best management units, especially when compared with interior grizzly habitat. Between 50 and 140 bears per hundred square miles is not uncommon along some stretches of prime coastal regions. Conversely, in the more harsh interior, grizzly densities may be as low as one bear per hundred square miles or more. No wonder hunters usually see more brown bears on a single hunt than they do grizzlies on several. My experience certainly confirms that impression.

Recent harvest figures for brown bears are hard to obtain because Alaska doesn't separate the statistics into brown bear and grizzly, and indeed it can't under the Boone and Crockett system because of the differences between management unit boundaries and record-keeping boundaries. Under the SCI system it is a simple task of adding up the bears taken in units counted as brown bears. The average yearly harvest of 1993–94 and 1995–96 was 730 for the brown bear units mentioned above.

Brown bears may live to be thirty years old, though the average is considerably less. The biggest ones come from Kodiak Island, where the skulls tend to average slightly larger and thus dominate the record books, and from the Alaska Peninsula. My bear was an honest ten-footer but failed to make B&C because it was about an eighth of an inch short. Any ten-foot brown bear ought to be a B&C bear, but some have small heads, particularly those from the Peninsula. To the east and west of these big bear areas, body and skull size gradually decreases toward the extremes of the range in either direction. Obviously, prime hunting areas are where the biggest bears are located, but very

The paws that made the prints.

respectable bears often come from less prestigious areas, and usually those areas cost less to hunt.

Hunters play a very important role in brown bear management. Alaska bear biologist Dick Sellers has stated, "Conflicts with economic interests . . . and irrational fear—not hunting—led to the demise of the grizzly on the American frontier. Ultimately here in Alaska *Ursus arctos* will be pressured more from these same factors than by carefully regulated sport hunting." The hunter, moreover, is a friend of the brown bear. Sellers emphasizes that cooperation between managers and hunters is the key to successful and stable bear populations. That means that we as hunters must seriously seek to make our hunting experience a positive contribution to brown bear management.

All brown bear skulls must be sealed after harvest, at which time the age, sex, and location of the harvest are recorded. Such data are important in determining future harvest quotas, current population size and trends, makeup of the population by age and sex, and the like. Many complicated components are factored in, most of which are in the domain of the biologist and not

the hunter, but the result is a sustainable and huntable population. As with all bear hunting, the hunter should hold himself rigidly to the standard of taking a mature male. Harvesting a female bear is sometimes unavoidable, but if there is any indication that a bear is female the hunter should exercise restraint, no matter how large the bear may be. It goes without saying, but I'll say it anyway, that anyone shooting a female with visible cubs should be prosecuted to the full extent of the law, assuming there was no threat to a person's life from the bear. Shooting a female with cubs usually condemns the cubs to death as well, as they have little chance of survival without their mother. The percentage of females in the harvest is important in determining the level of harvest the population is able to sustain.

All hunts of which I am aware are essentially spot-and-stalk. Mature male bears emerge earliest from the winter den, and where temperatures and snow conditions are not extreme they may remain active all winter. One may spend his hunt glassing treeless snow slides for early emerging boars in springtime and walking willow bottoms while buds on the impenetrable brush hover near bursting in the long daylight. In fall you will spend your time stalking salmon streams teeming with the fall's run, watching for a mature bear as it fishes.

Simply put, a good trophy is a mature male. One time-honored rule of thumb when evaluating tracks is to measure the width of the front paw pad in inches and add one for the average square of the bear's hide in feet. For brown bears in the Kodiak Island and Alaska Peninsula areas, I recommend a standard of at least eight feet (a seven-inch paw print) as the minimum. Evaluate a harvestable bear carefully, if time and circumstance permit, to be certain it isn't so badly rubbed that areas of bare skin make it unsuitable as a trophy. As to skull size, I wouldn't give it a thought. A big, mature male is a trophy brown bear, no matter the skull numbers.

Brown bear hunting can be some of the most comfortable in the world if one hunts from a luxury boat in southeast Alaska. It also can be some of the most grueling, even miserable, if one is backpacking the Peninsula in spring, when wet snow or rain may fall every day. Good rain gear, hip boots, layered clothing, and a warm sleeping bag are essential on such excursions. If you take your bear in an area remote from the beach, expect a long and exhausting backpack, carrying the heaviest load of your life. Exceptional conditioning is required for such a hunt.

I wore wool pants and a wool shirt over polypropylene underwear most of the time on my brown bear hunt. Binoculars are essential, but I don't believe a spotting scope added much to our armamentarium. Big bears look big to the naked eye, or they are on the move and unattainable anyway, though occasionally one might intercept a bear spotted far off. You will have to help with the skinning if you are successful, so don't go if you aren't willing to get your hands greasy. A single guide can't do much with a thousand pounds of

Wildlife abounds on the Alaska Peninsula. Here, a molting ptarmigan.

bear unless he is an Olympic weightlifter. Carry a good knife and a sharpening stone, and pray you get to use them.

For brown bear and polar bear I used 200-grain Nosler Partition bullets, handloaded as always. In both cases the combination was highly effective.

Have a good time. Wherever you go in coastal Alaska to hunt the giant brown bear, it is the experience of a lifetime. I wouldn't settle for less than the trophy of a lifetime, even if I had to return repeatedly.

THE EMPEROR OF AMBER BAY

Sometimes in hunting one encounters an individual with a story bigger than life. At times, the account of an impossible adventure becomes so bizarre that it reaches the unbelievable. Such a tale is being spun for me at this moment as I stand in the dining room of Painter Creek Lodge, bleary-eyed and haggard. I am hunting Alaska brown bear with Marlin Grasser's outfit on the Alaska Peninsula. Few men will ever have such an adventure as this burly man has experienced; even fewer will live to relate it. I gaze in awe at the huge bear rug enshrined on the wall of the lodge. Despite my travel fatigue, the story accompanying the beast that wore it comes through sharply.

Marlin was following the hot track of an eleven-foot brown bear when it turned the tables and charged him at close range. He had managed to get off one shot, striking the monster in the neck and knocking the creature down momentarily. Shucking another shell into the chamber, he was absolutely horrified when the next shot failed to fire. As the bear struggled to his feet and rushed upon him once again, he ripped two more shells through the mechanism in quick succession with the same terrifying results—nothing. Before he knew it, he found himself dangling upside down and being flung about, firmly clamped in the beast's jaws.

Obviously, the story ended happily. Probably because of the severity of the neck wound, the critter had dropped him in the snow and ambled off. Fearing the giant might be watching him for movement, and unaware of the bear's location, Marlin lay quietly for thirty minutes before he dared so much as twitch an eyebrow. Then he had risked moving just enough to determine that his adversary had departed. He quickly disassembled his rifle

and discovered a tag-alder seed in the sear mechanism, preventing it from cocking the firing pin. He blew away the obstruction, then tracked down the bear and killed him. His own blood had mingled gruesomely with that of his prey on the fresh snow as he skinned out the monster.

No, I think to myself, *I don't want quite that much adventure.* I will be as cautious as can be, because I value my own hide more than I do that of a bear. This is my first attempt to take dangerous game with my old .30-06, so I find myself tentative about the weapon's ability to do the job. I have read that it will, but I have never tested it with live creatures weighing a thousand pounds or more.

Marlin is supremely confident that my rifle is plenty sufficient, if I place the shot well. Nevertheless, I can't help but notice the cannon he is using as backup. Despite his unblinking assurances to me, his close call has changed his own outlook. He always does the tongue-in-cheek "Grasser test" for caliber adequacy in his backup weapon. A rifle passes the test only when the whole hand will go down the barrel, fingers spread, without any of them touching the inside of the bore.

For this part of my quest, I have obtained 200-grain Nosler Partition bullets handloaded to perfection. I am satisfied that I can place the shot accurately, given the right situation. I have resolutely determined not to attempt a shot farther than two hundred yards, and then only if I have a good rest and an open field. I have practiced like never before for this trip, and I can shoot a good group with the handcrafted loads. However, the harder recoil caused me to develop an irksome flinch at one point, so I went back to plinking with a .22 rimfire to cure the problem.

I have lain awake nights, even weeks before the trip, imagining the final stalk, and by the time I arrive and begin looking over the terrain I have pretty well exhausted my imagination. The reality of the imminent hunt starts me dreaming again, however, and I wonder if perhaps hunting big bear might not be the most difficult kind of hunting psychologically. The excitement that accompanies the quest is a natural high of the most virile sort. The same sensation must have been well known to ancient man as he prepared to tackle dangerous animals with primitive weapons. I think at length about King David in the Bible, who tackled the

Eurasian bear with his bare hands and emerged victorious. Surely I can prevail with a .30-06, and most certainly if the Lord is with me as with David.

My hunt begins at the base camp, where I enjoy the company of several other incoming hunters. The short season on the Alaska Peninsula means that everyone who has a brown bear hunt will be here at once. I delight in comparing notes on calibers and loads, and I note with a bit of masochistic satisfaction, and a trace of trepidation, that I am the only hunter in camp armed so lightly.

Everyone uses Marlin's tale as a takeoff point for some similar, or much more tragic, story they have heard. Like kids in camp telling ghost stories around the campfire, we revel for hours in trying to scare the pants off each other with yarns of horror and human carnage in bear country. One guy sits by the fireplace with a somber expression and reads *Alaska Bear Tales,* a collection of truly horrifying narratives. The guides are quite reserved, perhaps more than a little amused, having heard these same conversations from every new crew of bear hunters.

Resting on an upthrust snag for the shot of a lifetime as my bear approaches.

My planes have kept getting smaller, all the way to Alaska, starting with a jumbo jet in Atlanta. Now I am down to the workhorse of the tundra, a Piper Super Cub with standard 30-inch tires so it can land on otherwise hopeless terrain with ease. My guide, Jerry Lancaster of Tok, Alaska, has preceded me to our austere spike camp in the back

country several miles up the creek from Marlin's encampment near Amber Bay. He waves as we touch down on the gravel bar and seems to be straining to get a look at this weirdo who wants to kill a brown bear with a .30-06. I dutifully reminded my outfitter months ago that he should warn the guide about my choice of rifles so that there will be no last-minute surprises.

We must ford the rushing river to reach our campsite. I don my hip waders and almost capsize in the stiff current, under the burden of my heavy duffel. By the time I emerge on the alder-choked bank, Jerry is having trouble restraining his laughter at my antics. After a second trip for the rest of my gear, we relax inside the ample tent.

I like Jerry from the start. He is almost exactly my age, older than the majority of my previous guides. Most of the brown bear guides I have met are either in our age range, or, like Marlin, are ageless. Absent in them is the brashness I frequently encounter in sheep, moose, and elk guides. It seems that serious outfitters prefer a more mature individual when lives may hang in the balance, and they try to avoid the invincibility syndrome of youth. I don't mean to imply that there aren't some excellent young brown bear guides; there just aren't any in the Painter Creek group. Jerry epitomizes maturity and stability. He is a family man like myself, married for twenty-five years to the same lady, and shares many of the core

values I hold closely. He will be a great companion for what could prove to be a trying hunt.

The plan is to spend the bulk of our time glassing and waiting. Spring bear hunting is like many other types of hunting in that it requires a huge measure of patience and persistent watching. The bears are just emerging from the den, and mating season will soon be in full swing. That has already been demonstrated by two mating bears on a gravel bar that I saw from the Super Cub. Boars will be chasing sows, and both sexes will be shaking off the winter sleep, revving up the digestive system, and getting reproductive duties accomplished. Brown bears resurrect from the den to new life each spring, when their activity increases to its greatest of the year. The most uncertain factor is likely to be weather, since cold, wet, and windy periods can cause the bears to hole up for days. They sometimes even return to the winter den when temperatures turn colder, I'm told.

Opening day of the short season on the Alaska Peninsula dawns ominously. Flowers are

Threading our way up and down streams in waders is part of the plan.

blooming and birds are singing back in Georgia, and as I peek out the tent door at the falling sleet, I can't help but think wistfully of comforts and home. Low clouds obscure all the surrounding high terrain. We pull our best rain gear over our wools and set out for a nearby ridge where open boulders provide a resting place. We hope either to spot a bear above us on the alder-choked slopes, or perhaps catch one passing by unawares in the broad creek bottom. One can never tell when an unexpected break may make a hunt an instant success.

Despite the miserable conditions, it is good to be hunting again after the winter layoff. The prospect of encountering the big brownie I want seems good, as we have a full two weeks to accomplish the task. Several prominent bear tracks dot the snow of the higher terrain, evidence that at least some of our local residents have emerged. In places we can trace the track back to where it ends, all the way to the den itself, where a dirty streak in the snow marks the spot. I am amazed at how high the creatures climbed before checking in for a winter's sleep. We find some medium-size bear tracks in the sand along the creek, but not the nine-inch-wide prints I am looking for. Nor are the tracks very fresh.

By noon we have seen no bears, but other inhabitants that share their domain are greatly in evidence. The famous Alaska Peninsula caribou herd is spread across the hills and wading across the creek, and I get some good closeups. An ostentatious male ptarmigan, strutting in his flamboyant courting plumage, entertains us, clearly demonstrating his anxiety to find a mate.

The extraordinary scenery is typically Alaskan, with whitecapped mountains all around. But even the commanding presence of the snowy ladies is overshadowed by the glory of the active volcano to our north. The map identifies it as Mount Chiginagak, a snow-rimmed caldron visible only when we have climbed the mountainside a considerable distance. Every time I see it the cost of the long climb is worth the price.

The weather worsens, and we are soon drenched. We return to camp to dry out, a nearly impossible task with only a propane cook stove for heat. There's no fuel in this high country, anyway, so we don't even have a wood stove. Thankfully the rain ends that evening, though the

foreboding sky seems to indicate the respite will not last. Jerry does the cooking as I continue to glass, an activity that can still be done easily as midnight approaches. I have no problem getting to sleep after this long day, despite the fact that darkness lasts only about three hours. My first day ends with the bears leading, one to zero.

Breakfast is Jerry's strong suit, and after a hearty meal we set out in the rain again. It's pure rain, this time, with none of that solid stuff mixed in. Either way, we are still wretchedly wet and miserable. We climb another nearby ridge to glass a different basin and look for fresh tracks, all the while maintaining our vigil. Old tracks traverse the melting snow near the distant tops, but again no luck on a live bear, and no other fresh sign of bear activity.

After two days of unproductive hunting, my optimism begins to wane. I relate a Winston Churchill speech to Jerry, something about never giving up. I am actually recommitting myself to this quest more than I am attempting to inspire my unflappable guide.

We awaken to the same patter of intermittent rain against the tent wall, a cacophony that only rarely ceases completely in this part of the world. It seems prudent, in view of the absence of recent activity in our sector, to hunt down the creek toward Marlin's camp and see if they are having any more success than we. The intervening five miles hold some excellent bear habitat, and we certainly have as good a chance downriver as anywhere.

We set off down the rushing stream in our ever-present hip waders with our sleeping bags stuffed in our packs, just in case we are invited to spend the night. The necessity of tall rubber boots in this country is repeatedly underscored as we cross and recross the stream to avoid thick brush and stay on open terrain. The hunting is again unproductive, we discover no bear tracks, and toiling through the streamside alders is no fun. We arrive by noon soaked, cold, and tired, and with a raging appetite.

Marlin's wisdom is simple: It will take improved weather conditions to bring out the brown bears. His hunter has already filled out with an eight-footer on opening day, and we admire the flawless chocolate brown hide as the older man does the fleshing. This is one man who obviously knows his bear hunting, so on his advice we stay the night and head back to our higher camp the following morning.

The weather is indeed better as we finish breakfast and embark back upstream after a relatively comfortable night. Visibility has improved all the way to the tops of the mountains, and we are assaulted by only the occasional spitting shower. We spend the morning on a higher ridge near their camp, glassing fresh terrain where several bears were observed two days before the season opened. Nothing shows, however, so we head back to our own camp without further delay.

We navigate the gravel bars for several hours, zigzagging back and forth as before while periodically glassing the surrounding mountainsides. Patches of sand adjacent the gravel bars run smooth, free of bear tracks. After arriving in our cold and lonely camp, we spend the remainder of the day combing the now-familiar slopes for signs of activity.

I am beginning to wonder if there are any live brown bears on the Alaska Peninsula. There are the two I saw flying in, to be sure, but they were several basins over. To encourage myself, I review the statistics on brown bear hunting and am reminded that we are hunting in the heart of habitat rivaled only by legendary Kodiak Island. The average hunter sees eight bears during the season, and guided hunters in this area have enjoyed approximately 90 percent success over the years. Perhaps the rotten weather is indeed the problem. We resolve to do more climbing on the morrow and look at our area from a different perspective.

The next day we awaken to more rain. Visibility is better, however, and we travel four or five miles up the creek until the wandering gravel bar gives way to vertical sod walls crowned by alder flats. We climb to the top and spend most of the day glassing the snowy basins. One cannot miss several suspicious holes in the high country snow, possibly still-occupied winter dens, but there are no tracks or other signs of activity.

As we descend the steep terrain near day's end, disaster strikes. I step on loose gravel at the stream bank and it caves off into the creek, throwing me atop my rifle and jamming my elbow. My concern is for the rifle, however, as I know

how critical accuracy will be if my moment of truth arrives. Jerry inspects the weapon and suggests that we go ahead and chance a test firing right now, letting the considerable crash of a nearby waterfall and the walls of the steep canyon absorb the noise. To my great relief, the rifle is still perfectly on target.

As I pocket the spent cartridge and slip a fresh one into the magazine, I catch a fluid movement in my peripheral vision. A brown bear is walking warily up an alder-covered hillside some four hundred yards away!!

"Jerry, look!" I exclaim in disbelief.

Both of us immediately hide behind an intervening bank while the bear ambles slowly and watchfully up the slope, stopping at intervals to try to determine the source of the disturbance.

"He's not sure what the noise was all about. And he hasn't seen us, I don't believe," Jerry whispers loudly over the noise of the stream. "But he's a relatively small bear—seven and a half feet and probably an immature boar. You want to try for him?"

"Seven and a half? You already know my answer, Jerry," I reply.

We have made a firm commitment to a mature boar, eight-and-a-half feet or better, and I'm not about to violate it, even for the first bear we have lain eyes on in five days. We watch as the majestic young animal tops the ridge and disappears.

"Well, that is encouraging," I observe as we walk back toward camp.

"Sure is," Jerry answers. "I guess that guy was bedded there in the brush, and your shot disturbed him. Maybe we should just walk the creek bottom and fire the rifle every few hundred yards."

I don't have to ask if he is joking. I know that even one such shot is risky, as the larger boars would likely leave the basin if they were troubled by gunfire. We hope that this fluke occurrence will at least break the ice for us, and it has already provided a wonderful thrill.

There is no letup in the weather as another day dawns. Driving wind and incessant rain force us drenched from the field. Now there is nothing intermittent about this brutal siege of weather, and for the next three days we are confined to the tent, the adjacent mountainside obscured in fog and rain. We are suckered out briefly by a pause in the precipitation on the third day but are soon almost blown off the mountain by blinding snow and sleet. We long for the warmth of the wood stove at the lower camp. All my clothes are damp, and the only way to dry them is to wear them to bed and let body heat remove the moisture. I pray repeatedly for improved weather.

The river is beginning to rise. Not only is it raining but the temperature is warming, causing massive snowmelt on the higher terrain. We awake in the middle of the night to find the torrent licking at the very edges of our tent. A small rivulet that enters the main stream just above our camp is swelling as well, threatening to engulf our tent. We dread the thought of moving all our gear, as well as the tent, in the driving, soaking rain. With shovel and ax we make like beavers to divert the small stream back into the main creek.

My prayers are answered overnight, for morning brings the sun, creating a majestic display of cheery shafts between the clouds for as far as the eye can see. The brightness soon dissipates and the rains return, but at least we had an opportunity to dry out a few items. Fortunately, the downpour soon subsides and the temperature drops, and the threatening stream abates. I lift a prayer of thanksgiving and whisper another of my unending petitions for success.

We are glassing near camp when a spot on a high meadow catches my attention, a microscopic brown dot I don't remember seeing before. My breath sticks in my throat as the tiny object is joined by another, even smaller one. Bears!

"Jerry, come here!" I yell. "I see two bears!"

I have glassed nearly a hundred hours now, and the joy of connecting feels great. The pair are about two miles away, about to disappear behind a crest of ground. Jerry gets only a brief look before they are hidden from view, and there is no time to set up the spotting scope.

A pair of bears is precisely what we are looking for on a spring hunt. Two bears together in May can mean a female and a boar, in which case we are in business. But it can also mean a sow and a nearly grown cub, in which case we are observers only. All we know is that one bear is larger than the other, and we won't see them again without climbing the intervening mountain.

It takes a couple of hours of trucking but we find the pair, still carousing on the high terrain. However, the larger animal turns out to be a gigantic female with a nearly grown cub. Nevertheless, the excitement fuels my enthusiasm, and we watch the mom and overgrown baby with great interest. Despite the disappointment, the effort definitely has been worthwhile. The cub puts on an acrobatic demonstration on a snow patch, sliding down and rolling playfully like the youngster it is, then standing upright and looking toward Mom as if for approval. The sighting is a definite occasion for hope.

We return to camp, and another day of intensive glassing and waiting proves futile, despite relatively good weather. That night, as we dine on Jerry's "rainbow stew," a concoction of whatever is available mixed together in a pot, we plot our next move.

"I think we ought to go back closer to the coast. There is more activity there, and apparently these high-country bears are going to sleep until July. Let's call on Marlin again tomorrow," Jerry suggests.

I agree, and we set our mind to do it. We hope the other hunters are filled out and gone, as two out of four had already scored when we visited a week ago. It has been eleven days since we last saw an airplane, and we are afraid Marlin's food supply might be even lower than our own.

We hunt down the creek to the other camp the next day, and again we see no bears. Neither of the remaining hunters has scored, either. Moreover, the weather has made it impossible for the airplane to pick up the two hunters who have taken a bear, and the poor guys have been waiting nine days. Camp is crowded, and food is tight.

Despite the conditions, only one hunter is hunting, and Marlin suggests we try the canyon where his hunter scored on opening day. It has produced bears in other years, and no one has been back in there, so it might be just the place to look. There is adequate food to afford us a couple nights before heading back up the creek to pack for the trip home. We are more than happy to share the warmth of the wood stove, so we jump at Marlin's offer.

We follow a well-worn caribou trail separating one of the coastal mountains from the seaside marsh. Today is surely the best weather we have seen so far. The sun breaks through the persistent clouds over the Shelikoff Straits and begins to warm my

Alaska brown bear. Alaska, May 1990.

back as we walk. It is truly a treat. I had almost forgotten the sensation.

Stopping sharply in midstride, Jerry raises his binoculars to the mountain. He immediately comments softly and without emotion, "I see a bear."

The words have been all too rare up to this point, but surely this could be a harbinger of better things. As predicted by Marlin, the sun has come out, and we see a bear.

High on the mountainside are not one but three bears, a female and two rollicking yearling cubs. We watch briefly as they feed and then move on. With this weather, sightseeing must be kept to a minimum.

The rugged coastal mountains are resplendent, with white crowns shining like jewels in the intermittent sunshine. Long tongues of snow descend almost to the coastal marshes in places, and the alders are beginning to show traces of pale green. Blue sky is laced with fluffy white clouds— a welcome change indeed. I feel joyous as we leave the foraging bear family, a heart full of hope beating in my breast and a ready rifle on my shoulder. It is good to be hunting.

Another hour passes pleasantly but uneventfully. I look back up the mountain where we had left the sow and two cubs. I immediately spot a lone bear a bit farther along on the same mountain.

"Jerry, has that sow left her cubs?" I ask, puzzled.

"No, she wouldn't do that. Let's look through the spotting scope. You don't see the cubs?"

I can't find the cubs because this is a lone boar. Jerry's assessment is that the varmint would get stretch marks trying to make eight feet, and moreover he is obviously young. I get that old swallow hard feeling, but I tell him I will pass again. I am probably crazy to hold back this late in the hunt, but I won't kill an immature bear. I will return to hunt again if we can't find the mature male I want. It is eight and a half feet or nothing.

"We're finally seeing bears, so let's keep looking. We haven't even reached Marlin's canyon yet," I reason.

Jerry agrees, and we move on, enjoying the sights and the sunshine. Our hopes are buoyed by the wave of sightings. The sun drives away most of the clouds, and I marvel at the beautiful colors. We are in the midst of a very rare bluebird day on the Alaska Peninsula. Even so, an occasional passing cloud reminds us of recent tempests by spitting new snow at us as we walk.

As we near our destination, a terrified caribou cow goes past us, plunging downhill at a fearsome clip. At her side is a tiny newborn calf, the first we have seen, and it is running valiantly, trying to keep up.

"What the dickens scared them?" Jerry questions. "It couldn't have been us. She's upwind. Maybe there is something going on in that ravine."

We cross the stream flowing from Marlin's canyon, opting for an observation point on one shoulder of the narrow entrance to take better advantage of the wind. Numerous birds are feeding on the carcass of the previous hunter's bear, including three beautiful bald eagles. Bears are cannibalistic, and we hope that a large cannibal might be here.

We glass the steep walls and the intervening alder thickets to no avail for some forty minutes, however, and I feel hope slipping away again. It has been a long and difficult hunt, but we have tried hard. Just when I am beginning to think of looking elsewhere, Jerry comments in a matter-of-fact tone, "There's your bear."

What? There's your bear? What's he saying? No scrambling for the spotting scope? No indecision?

He points to a ridge a quarter-mile away, and I see what he means with my naked eye. A huge boar is walking—no, waddling—behind a slightly smaller female, obviously bent on propagating the species.

Excitement boils over, and hope becomes reality. We watch them for a few minutes as they disappear into a branch canyon with terrifically steep walls. It seems unlikely they would climb those walls without good reason, so we recheck the wind and plot our stalk.

"Let's go," commands Jerry in his quiet voice. We will descend to the creek bottom and climb a promontory just the other side of their location and hope to get a shot when they emerge. We sidehill from our perch to intersect a rushing rivulet, reaching it in only a handful of minutes. We have to cross the branch leading into their side canyon to climb to the next ridge.

As we approach the small stream, Jerry suddenly whispers and motions at the same time: "Get down!"

The pair have reversed direction and are back near where we first spotted them, almost directly above us. They are so close they could easily see us if they looked our way. Fortunately they do not, nor does our favorable wind change. We crouch low and half-walk, half-crawl up a small gulch on the opposite side of the canyon. We emerge into the clear and can see the alder slope well, but the bears have disappeared into a thick tangle of vegetation. I know they will reappear at any moment, so I search desperately for a rest. The distance looks about 125 yards, plenty close, but I need something solid to be absolutely confident about my shot.

I try lying down and using my bipod, but it is no good. On this steep slope only a sitting shot seems possible. My mind races backward to all the constructed scenarios that have haunted me for so long, and this definitely isn't one of them. Searching anxiously, I try a spindly alder snag, blackened by some long forgotten fire, and find it

surprisingly steady. I chamber a cartridge, and I'm ready for business.

The animals cooperate perfectly, as if by divine intervention. As soon as I am ready, I see movement in the tangle of alders on the opposite slope. The lead animal materializes through the brush, and my spine tingles. I quietly remind myself of the importance of a steady shot and a good trigger squeeze, and I fight off the inclination to tremble.

"The sow is first. Just wait for the boar," advises Jerry quietly, his positive tone adding to my confidence. As I watch the female through my scope, she breaks into a shuffling run, apparently trying to shake her brawny suitor.

The boar is next, and I follow his movements through the brush, watching for the point at which he will be in the open. I pay extreme attention to trigger finger control, remembering that a wounded bear can deal out terrible retribution. When the creature is unobstructed by vegetation, I place the cross hairs on the massive shoulder and touch off the shot.

The sweet sensation of recoil and the solid sound of a hit are my reward. My impression that

Barren ground caribou are calving during brown bear season on the Alaska Peninsula.

I have done well is confirmed when the giant bruin immediately begins to roll downhill. His rapid disappearance into a small alder-choked ravine makes accurate follow-up shots impossible, although I fire again before he is out of sight.

"Looks good, looks very good," Jerry offers, assessing the situation. "Just don't assume he's dead. Be ready to shoot again if he comes out."

The bear cannot get out of the gulch without coming into my field of fire, the best I can tell. We see where he has disappeared and where the gully empties into the stream. The ground along the whole length of the other side is visible through the alders. As we contemplate options and possible approaches, the tops of the tall alders in the small ravine begin to shake, the movement progressing toward the nearby mouth. The bear is coming out.

I have already instinctively reloaded. I wait expectantly but more nervously than with my first shot. My heartbeat accelerates and my temples are pounding. The bear will appear not forty yards off, if he continues on the course he has set, but we won't see him until then. *Settle down, don't blow it now,* I keep telling myself. *Now is the time to prove that you are a hunter.*

Finally, the bear's head appears, wagging slowly from side to side as I watch him through my scope. He is bleeding from the mouth, so I feel certain we have him. To be sure, I put two more shots into his neck. The bear is dead.

We approach with great caution, with rifles at ready. The bleeding hulk has stained the bubbling stream in the small ditch a deep red. The downed bear is on terrain so steep we cannot keep our rifles at ready as we climb, so we alternate climbing and standing guard.

The hardest part of most any hunt comes after the kill. The anxiety born of many days of deprivation is finally lifted, but the physical task is arduous. First we must roll a 1,000-pound bear to level ground, and then skin it. The work consumes several hours and requires considerable ingenuity.

The bear squares less than an inch short of ten feet. The full body mount will amaze anyone who sees it, and will be one of my most cherished trophies. Truly the taking of a magnificent brown bear is a treat no hunter should be denied.

There is a sign over the fireplace at Painter Creek Lodge that states, "The charm of fishing is that it is the pursuit of that which is elusive, but attainable; a perpetual series of occasions for hope," the saying attributed to someone named John Buchan.

I believe the same can be said about hunting, as my thrilling adventure amply proves. I thank God for rewarding our patience and persistence with one of the most extraordinary trophies in the world. It is my expectation that my experience may inspire another hunter somewhere, when hope seems dim, to pray and never give up. Maybe in an hour of discouragement that hunter will remember how well the combination worked for me in another time and another place. That is my fervent hope.

Barren ground grizzly. (Photo: courtesy of James L. Davis)

BARREN GROUND GRIZZLY BEAR

(Ursus arctos richardsoni)

While living among the Netschilluk Eskimo . . .
I remember their telling me a story of a very strange animal. . . .
They described it as a black monster, as large and heavy as a muskox,
with a face like that of a man and feet like those of a bear.
They report them to be very ferocious. . . .
I think it can be no other than the grizzly bear of North America,
which is thus shown to occasionally extend its limits
as far north as the Arctic Ocean.

—Frederick Schwatka, *Nimrod in the North*, 1885

Spanning east across the mainland of Canada's Northwest Territories, all the way to the Hudson Bay and up the Boothia Peninsula, and all across the vast treeless terrain that rims the coast of North America's mainland, there does indeed occur a subspecies of the grizzly bear. The barren ground grizzly is slightly smaller than its cousins from more temperate climes, but it has the same dished face, the same humped back, and the long, terrible claws that have forever inspired fear among the natives and deep respect from the invading whites. This subspecies has escaped the devastation wrought on other populations, such as the plains grizzly, by fearful humans and modern firearms. This bear has been spared because it lives in some of the most inhospitable and inaccessible lands on the planet. They are present east of the Back River but seem to decrease in number as one moves eastward toward the Hudson Bay.

The barren ground grizzly is recognized as a separate entity only by Safari Club International's record book. Animals from the Northwest Territories east of the Mackenzie River are counted as belonging to this subspecies. The Northwest Territories has an estimated 5,050 grizzly bears at the time of this writing, and it is the only place that has the barren ground variety by record-book definition. Some of these bears are doubtless interior grizzlies of the Mackenzie Mountains and adjacent riparian habitat, but the approximately 2,860 that live on the Arctic Coastal Plain are unquestionably barren ground grizzlies. No doubt the bears of the short northern coast of the Yukon, as well as those of the North Slope of Alaska, fit this type quite well morphologically and by habitat type and activity patterns. Bears I have observed on the North Slope seem to have more silver-tipped hair than those of the Northwest Territories, but otherwise they appear very similar. The Mackenzie River Delta intervenes with a completely different habitat and may have isolated these two populations from one another to some degree.

All permits for sport hunting of barren ground grizzlies are allocated, like polar bear and muskox permits, to the native Hunter-Trapper Associations (HTAs) of several Arctic communities. Tuktoyaktuk has five tags east of the Anderson River, all of which are usually sold as guided sport hunts, while their seven tags west of that river are most often used for subsistence purposes. Kugluktuk (formerly Coppermine) has five tags total, and three of those are used for sport hunts. Bathurst Inlet shares a quota of five permits with the village of Bay Chimo, and these villages sell all five as sport hunts. Paulatuk has a quota of seven permits but currently offers no sport hunts, though it has done so in the past. While these hunts are expensive, they are often highly successful affairs and offer a quality wilderness experience by snowmobile over awesome and unbelievably remote lands. These twenty-nine permits, of which thirteen are sold to sport hunters, are a small percentage of the total population and should represent a sustainable take.

My experience with the barren ground grizzly is relatively limited, but observation leads me to believe that their coats are considerably longer and perhaps more dense than those of other grizzlies. The hair on my own specimen is fully six inches thick, a coat that gives the animal the look of a bear a foot bigger in hide size. The skull too is large for a bear of modest dimensions, making me wonder if these bears, like those of Kodiak Island, don't generally have slightly larger skulls. These observations are true of my own barren ground grizzly as well as others of which I have knowledge. Few barren ground grizzlies have ever qualified for the Boone and Crockett record book, and Safari Club International's separate listing is limited in number so far.

A mature male grizzly of the barren ground subspecies will seldom weigh more than 500 pounds, though specimens much larger have been recorded. About 5 percent of male animals weigh 600 pounds in spring, while some 10 percent achieve that size in late summer, when weights peak. Females are considerably smaller. If the hide of such an animal squares seven feet, it is an exceptional specimen.

The claws of these creatures are often large for their body size. I harvested my bear on 30 April, just after it emerged from the winter den. There was absolutely no wear on the claws, which are fully five inches long. Polar bear claws and those of other grizzlies seldom reach such a length. One is tempted to think that the long period in the den, which may be up to six months for even the shorter-denning males, contributes to this phenomenal claw size, although experts claim that growth ceases during denning; many a bear hunter might disagree.

Male barren ground grizzlies have the largest home ranges of any of their family in North America. A mature male may range over 4,000 square miles of territory. Females inhabit about 1,200 square miles, still a fairly large piece of real estate. The low productivity of the barren lands on which they live almost certainly accounts for this movement. Female home areas tend to vary with the season and the presence and age of any accompanying cubs. Males cover their home areas throughout their time out of the den, moving farther and faster in spring when seeking food and mates. Younger males (like all young grizzlies) wander extensively, seeking their own home range. Females expand and contract their ranges much more dramatically as food supplies wax and wane, staying in the same area in times of abundance.

Just after emergence from the winter den, males tend to frequent eskers, those long, low hills of gravel that are the residue of glacial activity throughout the Arctic. These areas tend to undergo the earliest snowmelt, exposing berries from the previous year. Perhaps because males head for these eskers, the later-emerging females tend to avoid them, both for their own safety and that of any cubs.

Studies have suggested that eskers are valuable denning sites for barren ground grizzlies, but that has not been borne out by recent satellite tracking. Because these formations are key feeding areas early in the spring, however, they are still important to barren ground grizzlies. This has implications in using the esker gravel for roadbed construction, fill, and concrete. Caution is in order as man continues to penetrate the Arctic.

These bears readily scavenge caribou carcasses, but the barren ground grizzly is also an extremely efficient predator of caribou and small mammals. Analysis of bear scat has shown that over 60 percent of their springtime food volume consists of caribou, with another 8 percent coming from Arctic ground squirrels. This tendency to utilize so much animal protein is a distinctive feature of these bears. Biologists believe that the low productivity of the tundra has forced these grizzlies to become more aggressive predators. The amount of mammalian protein falls off dramatically in early summer, when plant species such as horsetail, various sedges, and Arctic cotton become more important.

In summer, all the bears leave the eskers and concentrate activity on heath tundra and tall shrub habitat, both for escape cover and for relief from heat and insects. Tall is a relative term on the tundra, as such areas usually have dwarf willow and dwarf birch less than two feet high. Here are also horsetail, willow buds, and certain tender sedges, often found growing in association with heath and shrubs. Leftover berries may be available as well, perhaps an important food source until the new crop begins to ripen. This is a time of relative stress for the bears, since the caribou have departed

Barren ground grizzly. Northwest Territories, April 1996.

for the calving grounds and the new berries are not edible. In late summer the caribou return, the blueberries, cranberries, and crowberries are mature, and it is time to put away a layer of fat for the upcoming winter. Barren ground grizzlies consume more berries at this time of year than all other seasons combined.

There is no preferred habitat type in late summer, presumably because of the abundance of food. In fall the bears return to the tall shrubs and begin to search for a den site, which is almost invariably associated with such plants. The bears never den in lower, damper areas of the tundra, but always on well-drained heath tundra slopes with tall shrubs whose roots will support the roof of the den. Before settling in the grizzly gathers nesting material, creating a mat made almost exclusively of crowberry vegetation. Barren ground grizzlies spend more time in dens than any other North American bear.

As with all denning bears, metabolism slows and the bear's body undergoes physical changes that allow it to oxidize stored fat. The exception to this is the developing embryo, which requires glucose (a kind of sugar) for energy and is unable to use the mother's stored fat. Glucose is available to the embryo after the bear enters the den only from the mother's protein, usually from her muscle tissue. Losing protein to the developing embryo would be a major threat to her survival except that the gestation period is short after the delayed implantation of the fertilized egg. Since cubs begin to breathe air at birth, oxygenation allows them to at once exploit fat from the mother's rich milk, which is produced from stored fat, so her protein loss stops. Newborn cubs weigh between one and two pounds.

Perhaps related to the harshness of their environment, barren ground grizzly bears exhibit a flexible reproduction strategy that often involves the females' mating with multiple males. Twin cubs are born most often, and they may be sired by different boars even though born to the same mother. That no doubt contributes to the diversity of the gene pool. Females give birth only every three years on average, since it takes two and a half years to bring cubs to independence. Barren ground grizzlies have the lowest reproductive rate of any grizzlies, making them fragile in terms of conservation.

An interesting fact is the extreme likelihood that the polar bear is a direct descendant of the barren ground grizzly. Not only are the two species in uninterrupted contact along the seacoast portion of their ranges, but the polar bear has been demonstrated to crossbreed with grizzlies to produce fertile offspring, irrefutable evidence of close kinship. On numerous occasions barren ground grizzlies have been observed on sea ice hunting seals exactly as do polar bears, lying in wait by a seal hole. It isn't hard to see how lighter colored bears would naturally be better at such activities. My own barren ground specimen engaged in just such seal-hunting behavior.

Management of these unique bears of the barrens is accomplished by scientists using helicopters and fixed-wing aircraft, satellite technology, and tracking collars. Population and other studies have been ongoing since 1987. The objective is to mark 10 to 15 percent of the population and then use recapture techniques to derive useful data. A tooth is extracted for aging, an ear tag or an internal lip tattoo is placed, and on some bears either satellite or VHF collars are affixed.

The future of the barren ground grizzly seems secure, given the amount of attention focused on it by the governments involved. Development in the Arctic by commercial ventures seems to be the main area of uncertainty, but corporations also appear interested in protecting the bears. Many have, in fact, supplied funds to help study the animals. The barren ground grizzly is probably even more vulnerable to human encroachment than its interior cousins, so such precautionary measures are highly prudent. There is much less cover on the barrens where these animals live and reproduce, making them more susceptible to the impact of humans from longer distances. The mere presence of a development might alter their movement patterns, perhaps to their detriment. Road building, increased access to bear country by humans, and human/bear conflict are other potential problem areas. Barren ground grizzlies require enormous amounts of uninterrupted wild terrain to thrive. They occur at very low densities, and replenishment from adjacent populations can occur only on a limited basis.

Almost certainly, any hunt for the barren ground grizzly will involve snowmobiles. The icy wind in your face for hours on end can be vicious, and the temperature will be below freezing much of the time, even during the long daylight hours. A

It's only April in the Arctic, but the big male grizzlies are out and about.

Snowmobiles are essential for hunting the barrens.

high-quality Arctic parka with a fur-rimmed hood, wool shirt and vest, bib down pants, down underwear, and caribou or wolf-skin gloves are recommended. I used all of these on my hunt, and the cold was not a problem. Caribou-skin clothes are not necessary, however, since those outfits are uncomfortable when the temperature is above zero Fahrenheit, as it usually is on the barrens in late April and May.

The feet are always an area of special concern, so bring along the best cold-weather boots you can afford. Leave plenty of room for the toes to move around while wearing two pairs of wool outer socks and an inner polypropylene or silk liner. Tight fit constricts the circulation and contributes to cold feet, and in extreme circumstances it can encourage frostbite. Be sure to take sunscreen for the face and tinted ski goggles to protect the eyes. Lip balm is another necessity, as is a balaclava. Some of these needs moderate somewhat later in the season, but the best bears are taken early, in late April or the first week of May.

I used a 165-grain Nosler Partition bullet in my .30-06 to take my barren ground grizzly. These bears are not ranked as one of the really big bruins, but adequate firepower and good shot placement are nonetheless essential, both for safety and a humane kill. Any rifle in the .30-caliber class is adequate, and even a .270 is probably sufficient, though I would tend upward in power rather than downward.

The vastness of the country they inhabit, the minimal impact of the hand of man, and the difficulty of reaching the area add to the charm of hunting the barren ground grizzly. To do so will always be the province of a lucky few, and I am fortunate to have been so blessed. Mine is a vivid memory of hardship and challenge I will carry with me for the rest of my days.

ARCTIC SILVERTIP

Yes, there are indeed grizzlies here. I dismount my snowmobile for a close inspection of the huge tracks in the April snow. My native guide judges the impressions to be at least a week old: much too long ago to attempt following. Besides, the track is heading north toward a place where an Inuvialuit hunter took a bear of this size several days before, so we might overtake only a kill site.

In two days of travel in the Horton River country with my guide, James Pokiak of Tuktoyaktuk, we have encountered no other evidence of bears. We heard this morning via radio, however, that an airplane pilot spotted a large grizzly just yesterday out on the Amundsen Gulf ice pack, a few miles north of the mouth of the Horton. That news, plus these old tracks, gives rise to increasing hope. The barren ground grizzly often makes forays onto the sea ice in search of seals.

Grizzly camp on the snow-covered barrens at 10 degrees below zero.

This is my seventh hunt for grizzly bear, but my first for the barren ground variety. I have never had a legitimate opportunity to harvest a grizzly, but my confidence is high. James has only one permit per year for the tundra bear but has excellent success. My expectation is to take a mature male bear—a very old one, I hope. Time will tell.

The bears are definitely out and about, bitter wind and deep snow notwithstanding. We motor up the creek seeking a safe place to cross a treacherous ice chute. Visibility is so poor that James dismounts in several places to walk ahead for an inspection of the lower terrain. There are pitfalls for the unwary here, and I am glad he is careful. Despite his caution we founder briefly in one place and my snowmobile turns over harmlessly in another. Finally upright and moving we motor onward, but no living creatures appear except the ever-present ptarmigan and the occasional Arctic fox.

Perched at the edge of a breathtaking precipice, we break out lunch and enjoy the view, limited as it is by the haze and low fog that is now boiling up from the sea. The hot tea is welcome. We fry canned meat for sandwiches and eat it with bannock. I munch dried beluga whale flesh, dipped tentatively in thick whale oil, a delicacy I have tasted before but still have difficulty appreciating. The high-fat lunch warms me, and soon I am ready to move onward.

The barren lands along the Arctic coast have always fascinated men. One can cover hundreds of square miles and see absolutely no large mammals this time of year, although muskox, caribou, and grizzlies are plentiful. There is simply such an awesome expanse of territory in which to hide that their numbers seem small. Caribou migrate for the winter to the taiga, far to the south.

Intermittently we can see unfamiliar cliffs along the Amundsen Gulf in the distance, the highest one holding a cluster of buildings that constitutes the Horton River DEW Line station. From there we will be able to inspect a hundred square miles of the frozen gulf when visibility improves. We will wait until a better day to make the lengthy trip, however.

The day proves entirely fruitless, not unexpectedly, in view of the white haze. It is tempting to camp out in the open near the windy gulf, but it is too cold and the gale too brisk to remain in view of the sea for very long. We choose instead to spend the night on a sheltered plain out of sight of the DEW Line station but in an area commanding a good view nonetheless. There is always a chance a bear could amble by. As the semidaylight night settles in, we feast on fried pork chops and bannock. I notice once again my Inuvialuit guide's aversion to plant food other than bread, a characteristic I have observed of virtually all the Arctic natives with whom I have hunted. James is not as rigid as some in this respect, and he helps me consume a can of English peas, opened at my request. I get the impression he relishes the peas about as much as I do *muktuk,* frozen whale skin.

The caribou skins on the floor of the tent are welcome insulation. Awake but warm in my sleeping bag, I review my long quest for my first grizzly bear. I bought my first grizzly permit some ten years ago, and I have hunted interior grizzly three times in British Columbia and three times in the Yukon. I will still want an interior bear, even if I am successful on this hunt, but any grizzly will be a major victory. I have hunted with one other outfitter who had a near-perfect record, and I ruined it for him by having no opportunity. Could I be so unfortunate again? Lord, let me take that bear I want so badly, I pray selfishly as I snuggle into my cozy bag.

Better visibility greets us in the morning, and the air is noticeably warmer. The water bucket in the tent has but a thin glaze of ice. Perhaps our bear will be foraging actively in the warming air. James decides we should wait until tomorrow to begin our journey up the Horton River and instead use this day to search for the bear seen out on the ice. Leaving camp unattended and intact, we take the lighter sled, just in case we need it.

Motoring north along the coast, we cover ten to fifteen miles of coast, scanning the ice for the telltale brown spot. We do see an occasional seal, but otherwise large mammals are disappointingly rare. Among the jumbles of old ice from previous winters one could easily miss a grizzly, but James seems satisfied. I trust the intuition of an experienced guide, so I cruise along behind, drinking in the beauty of the fascinating landscape.

This coastline is truly worthy of the designation "barren ground." It was apparently christened such by Sir John Franklin (who years later commanded the "lost Franklin expedition" seeking the Northwest Passage) in the early nineteenth century while he was conducting explorations up the MacKenzie River for the British Royal Navy. No trees grow for many miles to the south, where the stunted evergreens of the taiga begin to appear in but scattered fashion. The only sizable vegetation is the invincible Arctic willow, which attains a height of only a foot or two in most locations. The tundra itself, however, is lush with

low-growing plant life, viewed readily in the few melted areas. The abundant rocks found in the eastern Arctic of Canada seem to be much less in evidence here. It is apparent how such a verdant covering of vegetation could support teeming animal life during the short summer season. No wonder the caribou come here later for the summer feasting.

As we proceed on our snowmobiles along the top of a high ridge adjacent the Amundsen Gulf, a slope inclined sharply toward the sea greets us. Here we see one of the most peculiar sights I have ever encountered in nature—a field of snowballs rolled uphill by the prevailing wind. The warmer weather has created wet snow at the surface that is ideal for making snowballs, apparently. Starting as pebbles of snow, the balls are pushed along by the stiff, cold breeze until their weight overcomes their momentum. Some have amazingly attained a diameter of six inches or more. James has seen almost everything the Arctic has to offer, but this is evidently new to him as well. He dismounts his machine and crushes several of the spheres as if seeking the invisible mechanism that has propelled them up the hill. He then shrugs, smiles, and remounts to move onward. The Arctic never ceases to surprise.

Following lunch, we ascend to the Horton DEW Line station for a long-range view of the whole adjacent stretch of sea. We reach the summit by motoring up a snowy draw, the steep sides demanding constant uphill leaning to keep our machines upright. Finally pulling up to the station and shutting off our motors, we hear the deep-throated churning of a diesel generator. I don't know why that is a surprise to me—of course such installations require electric power. It is obvious that the massive upright fuel tanks feed the engines and keep them running with only occasional maintenance. Vital information is fed via satellite to a distant central facility. Inside the complex is off limits, but we can walk freely about the grounds under the watchful eye of remote cameras. I can imagine that some technician somewhere is taking note of our every move.

We descend below the station in a forty-knot wind to glass the icy sea far below, an expanse that stretches beyond the horizon toward distant Banks and Victoria islands. Roald Amundsen passed this very spot in 1905, victorious in being the first to navigate the elusive Northwest Passage. I snug my parka tightly against the frigid gale, hardly able to tolerate exposing my face long enough to use binoculars. We won't be able to stay here long, but all I can see from my cursory glassing is several ringed seals. No bears, either grizzly or polar, are in evidence. James cautions me to be careful on the glasslike snow, since slipping on the sheer incline could be a disaster. It looks more than a thousand vertical feet to the snowy beach.

Satisfied that the bear is no longer where it was reported a few days ago, we charge off again. I am feeling ever more comfortable on the snowmobile, but the ride back down the ravine is faster and wilder than the ascent. I am glad I got to see a remote DEW Line station up close, but I'm also glad when we reach more horizontal real estate.

We spend the remainder of the day searching every pocket near the mouth of the Horton River. James saw a big grizzly here last summer while conducting one of his guided float trips on the Horton, and he is certain the bear will show eventually. In the back of my mind I hope that bear is not the one killed earlier by the native hunter. The absence of tracks, other than the old set we saw earlier, has me concerned. That's my

usual state of mind on grizzly hunts, however, so perhaps it's just normal for me.

As the eerie twilight descends once again, we return to camp to dine and rest. Tonight's treat is lake trout, caught by James's daughter Rebecca. Fried golden brown in melted butter, it is my idea of great eating, though I shun consuming the skin, as my guide does without hesitation. He also saves the nearly boneless tail section for later consumption raw, another favorite of the Inuvialuit. Sleep comes readily, outside my sleeping bag tonight, because it is so warm, perhaps only slightly below freezing. We have six more days to hunt, and we haven't yet traveled any distance up our target river.

We break camp next morning in sunshine, the first full appearance of the sun on this trip. The brightness of the stark white landscape is astounding, and it is apparent that the Arctic spring is fast upon us. The ptarmigan walk into our disassembled camp, scratching in the softening snow for morsels from the tundra. *Siksiks* become visible all over the hillside, a good sign, according to my guide. The squirrels are a favorite grizzly food, and their appearance may herald active feeding by the bears. Sleds loaded, we motor due south with plans to go as far up the Horton as we can. The famous smoking hills are visible due east,

The Arctic village of Tuktoyaktuk, home of my guide and his family.

sulfur-laden mounds that have burned mysteriously for centuries. We won't be able to visit them, most likely, because the ice on the river may be getting too thin to cross safely.

Even with tinted goggles I can hardly see in the blinding light. James leads the way as always, and shortly we are cruising the endless tundra west of the Horton. Without apparent reason he coasts to a stop and signals me alongside him, motioning for my binoculars. I gladly pass them over, amazed he would ask for them. He can see without magnification better than I can see with it.

"A bear! A big one!" he exclaims, passing the glasses back to me and pointing. Try as I might I can't see the animal until I put the binoculars to my eyes, and even then it is but a faint spot. It appears to be alone, and James comments that it is digging in the tundra for a squirrel.

"Get your rifle! And extra shells! Hurry!"

I scramble back to the sled and remove the rifle from its padded case, checking it to be sure all is intact. I pocket a whole box of 165-grain Nosler handloads, sling the rifle over my shoulder, and remount my machine. James has already disconnected the sleds, and we are off.

The bear spots us as we approach and takes off, the magnificent fur rippling as he runs. If he can reach the river he may escape us in the rough terrain or on the thin ice. We hurry to cut him off. The chase is on, and the cold slipstream whips my bare face and the bumps pound me. I struggle mightily to avoid a disastrous wreck at this critical juncture, and I come perilously close on several occasions.

I pull alongside James as the bear doubles back, heading for a ravine that leads to the river. I shout at him, "Is he good enough?"

"He's a really good bear for this area. Take him if you can!" he returns without hesitation.

Finally, after negotiating several deep gullies and covering myself with snow in the process, I believe I am close enough to make the shot. I chamber a round, rest as best I can, and try to lead the galloping bruin. At the shot he spins a full circle, obviously hit too far back, then continues in the same direction, only faster. I lead a bit more on the second shot, and he stops dead in his tracks, but still standing. On the third shot he goes down hard.

My approach is cautious, rifle ready. The magnificent creature is dead, however. The last two shots struck the chest less than six inches apart. I have my grizzly!

For the longest moment, I stand and admire my Arctic prize. Then I kneel conspicuously before the bear in full view of James and I thank God aloud for letting me have such a grand animal as a trophy. The bear is truly special, truly wonderful, truly worthy of my deepest respect and admiration. He will have a degree of immortality that a natural death would disallow, and I am glad for that as well. I stroke the long fur, tousle the famous hump on the back, admire the ferocious teeth, and run my fingers along the five-inch claws. The splendid coat has thick, chocolate brown hair and classic silvertip tones. Awesome is a pitifully insufficient adjective for such a creature. My quest for a barren ground grizzly is over, but the exhilaration of the experience will never leave.

As we return to Tuktoyaktuk, we cut the fresh trail of another large grizzly, only hours old by all appearances. The track follows a meandering creek bed and rambles in and out through deep patches of snow that look as if a bulldozer has been here. I am glad to see the tracks and that the animals are managed well. I have shared in the harvest, contributed to the economy, and removed an old male as a valuable trophy. Nothing could be better.

Interior grizzly bear. (Photo: courtesy of James L. Davis)

INTERIOR GRIZZLY BEAR
(Ursus arctos horribilis)

The grizzly, king of the forests and mountains, a magnificent creature,
perfect specimen of rugged strength, the heavy-weight champion par excellence,
when prime carrying a beautiful pelage, particularly the 'silver tip.'
How well he often justifies his name—Ursus horribilis.

—Major Neville A.D. Armstrong, *After Big Game in the Upper Yukon*, 1937

The first grizzly bear I ever saw in the wild was in the Brooks Range of Alaska. Amazing and terrifying are the two words that come immediately to mind as I contemplate that 1984 experience; amazing because of the wildness of the land, and terrifying because of several close encounters our party had with the beasts. We saw thirteen grizzlies on that trip, one a huge female with half-grown cubs that walked right through our camp as we waited out a week of drizzle. Fortunately the trio weren't in a mood to challenge us for our supplies, so we watched in awe as they retreated over a distant mountain in less time than it takes to compose this paragraph.

The Brooks Range and the North Slope are the far northern extent of interior grizzly bear range in Alaska, and the lowest densities of the animal in the state are there. All across the Northland, including Alaska, the Yukon, and the Northwest Territories, as well as northern British Columbia and the Rocky Mountains of Alberta, there are probably as many grizzly bears as ever in history. The barren ground grizzly differs from the interior grizzly mainly in its habitat adaptations and the techniques used for hunting it, so one can truly say that the grizzly lives all the way to the Arctic coast. The animal still is relatively plentiful (compared with prehistoric times) in only a small percentage of its original range, though, when one includes the Lower Forty-eight: it has been extirpated from most of its former range in the south.

When the American Indian, with his primitive weapons, encountered the grizzly bear, he was most often inclined to avoid a fight. When the necessity of confronting one of the great bears was thrust upon him, he swallowed hard, girded himself with all the courage he could muster, and quite often prevailed. The modern rifle has tipped the balance of power decidedly.

Before the advent of the white man and his high-velocity arms, the grizzly bear ranged over most of North America. I just recently met a man whose grandfather early in this century reputedly killed the last grizzly bear in Old Mexico, in the state of Coahuila. In fact, the earliest record I have found of grizzly bears in North America was in Mexico near the present site of the city of Monterrey, where a man named Sebastian Vizcaina observed bears feeding on a whale carcass on a Gulf of Mexico beach in 1602. From his description, many biologists believe the animals almost certainly had to be grizzlies. Skulls have been found in southern Ontario and in Labrador, where live grizzlies have never been recorded. Actual historical presence of the great bears has been documented as far east as Ohio and Kentucky.

Today the big silvertip bruins are gone from all of North America east of the Rockies and south of Yellowstone Park. The grizzlies of Yellowstone are isolated from the robust populations that extend from northern Montana up into Canada and Alaska, though that might change if a healthy and expanding population were established along other strategic mountain ranges, such as the Selway-Bitterroot Range between Idaho and Montana, or other similar pieces of prime habitat. These corridors could perhaps provide a natural interaction between the northern populations and the remnant to the south. Many are proposing and promoting a "Yukon to Yellowstone" chain of such habitats to reconnect these southerly populations with their long-lost cousins.

The grizzly bear was little known in the East, except for sporadic and widely scattered encounters, until the Lewis and Clark Expedition of 1804–1806. President Thomas Jefferson commissioned that journey to explore the Louisiana Purchase, following the two great rivers of the Northwest—the Missouri and the Columbia—then returning along a slight variation of the same route. In the process the explorers encountered numerous grizzly bears and recorded killing an incredible forty-three, a figure difficult to comprehend today. It could be that the bears they met were more aggressive, since they had not been exposed to modern firearms, and that a "shoot on sight" mentality naturally developed in those early explorers. Equally likely, in the days when the endless wilderness was often seen as an enemy to be subdued, such carnage was perceived a victory.

Male grizzlies travel and subsist over individual home ranges of perhaps 1,000 square miles, a vast stretch of land in which a dominant individual rules in a form of social hierarchy. The animals will accommodate to the presence of man, but they respond poorly to alteration of habitat. Ancient bear trails are worn deep in grizzly country. Often a dominant male, perhaps following his father and grandfather before him, will wear "stomping trails," strutting a dozen yards to a strategic scratching post, the paws hitting the same spots on the ground every time the animal approaches. I have seen numerous examples, complete with fresh bear tracks in the regularly spaced depressions in the soil and recently shed hair on the rubbing post.

When they are mature enough to leave their mother, young bears may wander long distances before establishing home ranges, males usually moving about twice as far as females. A dominant male will tolerate subordinate bears to a point, especially where there are concentrations of food such as salmon streams, but the youngsters know when to beat a hasty retreat. Home ranges of males often overlap, there being no exclusivity to the range of a grizzly. Females with cubs will not tolerate proximity of an adult male, as cannibalism is common if a dominant boar has opportunity to make an easy meal of the youngsters.

A full-grown male grizzly can weigh up to 1,200 pounds, specimens on the Great Plains having reportedly attained that unbelievable size before the species was eliminated there. More typically, interior grizzly bears weigh far less, and a 600-pound animal is a big one. Females weigh a little more than half as much. They consume huge quantities of food in the fall and may weigh as much as 30 percent more than when they emerge from the winter den. The creatures are stocky, show the classic humped back, and sport a pelage that can vary from light tan to chocolate brown or even black. They may or may not have the classic silver tips on the individual hairs, a characteristic more common in the southern reaches of their range.

Grizzlies vary enough in coloration that it can be easy for the novice hunter to confuse them with the smaller and darker black bear. Distinguishing the two is often extremely important, since in many black bear hunting areas the season on grizzlies is short or closed completely; conversely, a hunter may be disappointed to find that his "grizzly" is simply a lighter-colored black bear. One should look at considerably more than coloration. The head of a black bear is always much more pointed and lacks the flat, "dished" appearance of the grizzly's face. The ears of black bears are much larger in proportion to the head and are more pointed as well. Young grizzlies, however, have proportionally larger ears relative to body size, and regrettably they are sometimes killed by hunters who mistake them for black bears. Study your target carefully before pulling the trigger.

The presence or absence of a hump is truly a definitive sign, since grizzlies almost always have one while black bears never do. It must be pointed out, however, that a black bear may seem to have a hump owing to body position or viewing angle, but when the animal moves it's gone. Once more, study carefully before deciding that a hump is present.

The claws of the front paws are very different on the grizzly, being longer and more prominent than on black bears. For the hunter such an evaluation can usually be made only after a kill. The major practical observation related to the claws, however, and one that can be seen before the animal is on the ground, is the appearance of the creature's tracks. Bears cannot retract their claws, so the tracks usually show claw marks in front of the toe impressions. Grizzly tracks, unlike those of the black bear, always show the imprint of claws if the ground is soft enough to reveal footprints.

The range of the interior grizzly includes all the area inhabited by the bear outside Alaska and north of the lines in Alaska established by the record-keeping organizations for purposes of delineating Alaska brown bear range. The only exception is the case of the barren ground grizzly of the Northwest Territories, so designated east of the Mackenzie River Delta and north of the tree line there. The Boone and Crockett Club does not recognize this latter designation as distinctive, but Safari Club International does. Additionally, there is some difference in the boundaries between Alaska brown bears and interior grizzly bears for record-book purposes. The Boone and Crockett Club uses a more complicated system based on mountain ranges and geographic meridians, while Safari Club International recognizes any Alaskan *Ursus arctos* specimen from outside Game Management Units 1 through 10 and 14 through 18 as an interior grizzly bear. That sounds simpler, and I think it is, but it should be pointed out that the Game Management Unit boundaries can sometimes be as confusing to the

hunter as the well-defined Boone and Crockett line. Rely heavily on your GPS or, better yet, on a competent guide. All grizzly bears from the Yukon, Alberta, British Columbia, the Lower Forty-eight, and the Northwest Territories west of the Mackenzie Delta and south of the tree line are also considered interior grizzlies.

Populations of grizzly bears are difficult and expensive to estimate. In Alaska there are between 32,000 and 43,000 brown bears/grizzlies, though exact breakdown is all but impossible. In Canada there are about 25,000 grizzly bears, and the official breakdown is as follows: Alberta has about 1,000, British Columbia 13,000, the Yukon 6,300, and the Northwest Territories 5,050. The latter figure includes a preponderance of barren ground grizzly (*Ursus arctos richardsoni*), however.

There are five separate small populations of grizzly bears in the Lower Forty-eight, all of which are listed under the U.S. Endangered Species Act. All five combined have fewer than 1,000 grizzlies. The areas are the Yellowstone ecosystem, the northern Continental Divide ecosystem of Glacier National Park in north-central Montana, the Cabinet/Yaak ecosystem in northwestern Montana

Interior grizzly bear. Yukon Territory, May 1996.

Seven inches wide—this one's full grown!

and northeastern Idaho, the northern Cascades ecosystem of Washington State, and the Bitterroot ecosystem of Idaho. The latter three generally harbor fewer than twenty grizzlies each, and there may be no permanent resident grizzlies at all in the Bitterroots. There is no legal hunting of these bears, and their long-term outlook is not bright. Except for the northern Continental Divide bears, the lack of continuity between them and robust grizzly populations seriously limits viability and genetic diversity.

No significant biological difference exists between the brown bears and the grizzlies, and diet seems to be the defining factor. Biologists do recognize the Kodiak subspecies (*Ursus arctos middendorffi*) and the barren ground subspecies (*Ursus arctos richardsoni*) as being sufficiently distinct to qualify for a separate subspecies name. In fact, "splitters" (people who maximize the differences between similar animals for naming purposes) recognize nine subspecies of brown bear/grizzly. There is a very real size difference between the above three major varieties, however, which can be summarized in a phrase: available protein. Interior grizzlies (as well as barren ground

grizzlies) have to scrap for any appreciable and consistent source of rich animal protein, but coastal bears of southern Alaska can rely upon salmon streams. An interior grizzly is usually limited to smaller prey that is more widely scattered and harder to catch, or to the occasional bonanza of a large animal carcass left by winterkill, human or animal hunters, or other natural causes. The bears are sometimes able to kill larger animals, though not nearly as efficiently or consistently as wolves.

Like brown bears of all types, the interior grizzly breeds in the springtime. After emerging from the den as early as March, they soon begin seeking females and generally mate in June. The bears feed sparingly at this time of year and spend their time searching for mating opportunities. Spring is the prime time for hunting because this mobility makes the animals more vulnerable to hunters, and the claws and hides are in much better condition after a winter in the den.

The female enters a den around November, depending on the latitude and the amount of snowfall, and gives birth to two or three tiny but well-furred cubs in midwinter. Dens are usually on the leeward side of a steep mountain slope near or above timberline where snow accumulates to cover the site. The bears usually dig their dens on talus slopes rather than using natural caves.

While bears are in the den, they do not develop the "hypothermic torpor" characteristic of smaller mammals; they can be aroused fairly easily from their winter's sleep. Body temperature drops no more than 5 degrees or so, and the animals gradually lose weight as they burn stored fat. Smaller mammals enter a deeper state of sleep but periodically arise to perform vital bodily functions such as urination, while bears normally do not feed, drink, urinate, or defecate while hibernating. Grizzlies, along with other bears, are able to recirculate urea in the body instead of excreting it, and to utilize the water produced by burning fat reserves. They theoretically could stay asleep for the entire period they are denned, though females with newborns periodically awaken, and males may occasionally arise and change positions.

Females breed for the first time around five years of age, and they may have cubs every three years or so until about age twenty-five. After mating, the embryo floats freely for some months before implanting in the fall, usually in September. Gestation averages about 245 days but can vary considerably because it includes the period prior to implantation. The cubs weigh only one to one and a half pounds at birth. They grow rapidly on rich mother's milk, reaching several pounds by the time they emerge from the den with full coats of hair. The adorable creatures are fondly referred to as "hairball cubs" by delighted hunters when they observe them. The little critters seem to roll along behind the mother, the movement of the tiny legs hardly apparent. Female grizzly bears and their cubs are of course strictly off limits to hunters, a legal requirement easy to meet. I know of no ethical hunter who could be induced to kill such a family group, the only exception being a life-threatening attack by the mother bear, a tragedy that sometimes occurs.

Foods the bears enjoy are extraordinarily varied. As naturalist and hunter John Muir

Courting male and female willow ptarmigan in molting spring plumage—part of the visual feast of grizzly hunting.

observed of the grizzly, "To him, almost everything is food except granite." That is not quite true, but the bears do consume a vast variety of foods, though they have a decided preference for high-protein animal matter, whether ripening carrion or a fresh kill. They often build huge mounds of leaves and dirt over carcasses of larger animals, and can consume up to ninety pounds of meat per day until it is gone. They have no aversion to eating a broad variety of plant material as well, which constitutes almost half the average bear's diet. Some of the bears are persistent hunters of small game, and they can sometimes be seen digging for ground squirrels or other small mammals. They expend huge amounts of energy dislodging and chasing these animals, and one would think they might run a negative calorie balance as a result. Actually, the energy content of a fat, two-pound Arctic ground squirrel is considerable, so they likely do well at this activity. A favorite spring food is the fresh grass that emerges along the retreating snow line at the bottom of natural avalanche slides, places where springtime hunters often seek them.

A good trophy is a mature male grizzly with an unrubbed (or minimally rubbed) coat. One can selectively harvest males by hunting early in the spring or late in the fall, because the females den up earlier and emerge later. Also, most fertile females will have cubs in tow in the spring. Judging bear size can be difficult for the neophyte, but as one wise guide advised, "Big bears look big." I have taken several fine bears of all types in North America and have never had to look twice to know when to shoot.

Valuable information can be ascertained from head size, since, in general, the smaller the head in proportion to the body, the larger the bear. Lack of ear definition also usually means it is a big one. If one has opportunity to check the tracks beforehand (a relatively rare circumstance, I'd wager), the rule of thumb for brown bears and polar bears also applies to grizzlies—front pad width in inches plus one equals the square of the bear's hide in feet. If the pad is at least six inches wide and no smaller prints accompany the tracks, most likely you are dealing with a mature boar that will make a fine trophy.

Techniques of seeking grizzlies vary with the area hunted: I have hunted grizzlies on foot, by backpacking, from horseback, from snowmobiles, over large animal carcasses, and by floating a river in a boat. Hunting is typically in early morning or late evening, because bears tolerate heat quite poorly and move during the coolest times of the day.

Fall hunting is often impractical except when using a natural carcass as bait. In most places where grizzlies are hunted it is legal to check a carcass that has died naturally or has been killed by animals or hunters. Usually it is illegal to move the bait, sweeten the site with other meat, or for a hunter to fail to utilize edible meat from a game animal to attract a bear. In some places, such as the Yukon, it is legal to bait for wolves, and sometimes grizzly bears could be taken at such sites, though that would be illegal. Hunts that include moose or caribou are popular in the fall, and

Cast elk antler adds to the Yukon spring scenery.

one should hunt as late as possible because often one can utilize kills by previous weeks' hunters as well as your own, in hopes that a male grizzly might show up. The best aspect of hunting over legal bait is that it allows a high level of selectivity for mature males, because often there is unlimited observation time. Having taken part in such a hunt on several occasions, I have discovered another truth: Grizzlies never show up at a carcass I'm watching (in the same way that elk and moose don't come to my calls, and deer ignore my antler rattling).

I took all five of the bears in this book on spring hunts, a time of year when bait is generally unavailable and one finds a bear by simply looking for it. The days then are long in the north country, the bears are more active in the evenings, and one can sleep all morning with a good conscience. You may need to sleep until midday, too, because you should plan on late evenings, and you might be up half the night skinning and packing if you take a bear near dark, as was the case with my Yukon interior grizzly.

If there is any hunt where the hunter needs to be in excellent shape, a spring bear hunt is it. In a spot-and-stalk situation, be prepared for the mad dash of your life. The bear may be on top of a mountain above an alder jungle just across a roaring river, but you're off and running. Nature creates few obstacles that will keep a dedicated hunter and guide from trying for the prize of a lifetime, except perhaps darkness. Some grizzlies come easy, but mighty darn few, in my recollection.

"Use enough gun" certainly applies when one hunts the interior grizzly or any other large bear. I used 165-grain Nosler Partition bullets to take my interior bruin, but many would recommend more firepower. This hunt was the only occasion in my bear-hunting career when I had to go into the brush and fire again. In such a situation most would find it a comfort to have a bigger caliber, at least as a backup. If you find yourself in such a situation, it is best to stay uphill of the bear and remove your riflescope if possible, or at least crank it back to minimum power.

Have a warm parka in your backpack, good rain gear handy, and rubber boots when hunting the north country for grizzly. In Alaska, hip boots and knee-length raincoat are the gear of choice. It still gets very cold on a May night in the Yukon, so

plan on a warm sleeping bag and a roll-out foamy pad. A sharp skinning knife and sharpener are essential for the extensive work that follows a kill. Don't expect your guide to do it alone. Not everyone likes skinning, but nevertheless do all you can to help—even if it's only to hold the legs while your guide does the work.

Finally, there comes to mind another quotation, a statement I think all grizzly hunters can agree is timeless. It comes from Clyde Ormond's book *Hunting Our Biggest Game*: "There is something highly personal and elemental about a man's killing a grizzly. No matter how much experience he has had with other species of big game, the question of how he will react to a grizzly encounter persists until he has actually contacted his first [one]."

That sums up the questions I had about taking my first of the big bears. There aren't enough left for every man to take as many of them as he wants, so I may very well never take aim at another. But the fact that I have done so makes me a little bit more aware of who I really am. And that's an important part of what hunting is about.

YUKON: PERSISTENCE, PATIENCE, AND PRAYER

Rain mercilessly batters our tent beside the Nordenskiold River. A vicious wind whips the overhanging rain fly, and the sound is like that of Old Glory at full mast in a March tempest. I can't help but wonder if our pitiful synthetic cocoon can hold up to it. We are many miles from any other shelter, deep in the wilderness.

It is a precarious low point on a very difficult hunt for an interior grizzly bear. This is my seventh such quest, all the previous ones having been unsuccessful. We are now ten days into the hunt, and I have only two days more before I must depart for Whitehorse and a long plane ride home. Thoughts of an eighth grizzly hunt surface occasionally in my mind.

This is the time on any hunt when I naturally sag in spirit, so I must call on hidden wells of strength to sustain me. I spend time conversing with my Maker, praying I will keep an exemplary attitude to the end and never give up. I also petition divine providence to finally deliver the mature male interior grizzly that has been the

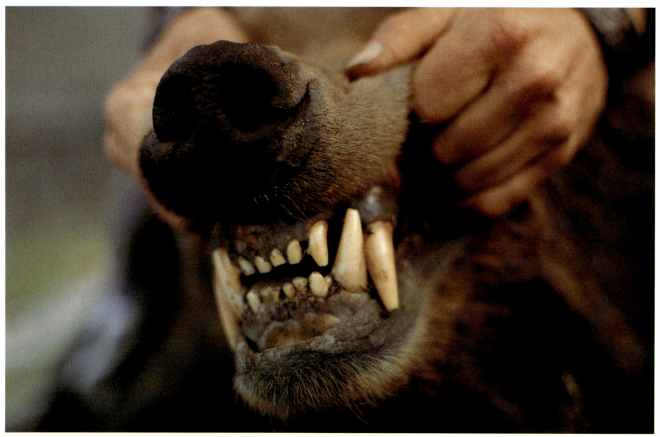

An eight-foot male bear has big teeth.

desire of my heart for more than a decade. My guide, Allan Jones, acquiesces without protest to what seems to him strange habits. His blue eyes are piercing and full of questions, but they are friendly and warm. He seems to recognize that we certainly need a miracle if we are to succeed at this late date.

Reflection sets in as I consider the first ten days we have spent together traversing this remote country. Outfitter Rod Hardie has arranged for us to hunt some of the most pristine wilderness in North America, and his method is to keep us in a prime grizzly location. Rod takes six hunters per year for spring grizzly, and he has an enviable success rate of 80 percent or better. Three hunters, to my wicked mind none as deserving as I, have come and gone with mature boars already. One man was seventy-four years old and already has several grizzlies to his credit. Another couldn't walk more than a few hundred yards at a time. The third hunter was engaged in only his second big-game hunt, and amazingly killed his bear by dismounting and shooting from the horse trail.

There will be no such breaks for me. Rod has us backpacking, except for a brief three days of horseback hunting. We have already climbed about half of the highest mountains in his area, it seems. There can be no question who has worked the hardest, waited the longest, and agonized the most. I silently seek forgiveness for my envious thoughts, and I resolve grudgingly to compare myself to others no more. I will just do the best I can and I will do it as many times as necessary to achieve my goal, God willing.

It isn't really necessary to remind myself that the experience so far has been a blast, the rigors and lack of a bear aside. We have seen five grizzlies, the most impressive a huge sow with a pair of inquisitive 250-pound cubs, their commanding presence so near that one could almost feel their power. On the first day of the hunt we witnessed a departing mature boar a mile away, his razor-sharp sense of smell having apparently detected our terrifying aroma. We never saw him again despite several days of searching.

Springtime in the high country of the Yukon is particularly splendid, and we have been blessed with mostly crystalline days, the hurricane flailing our tent notwithstanding. Flowers are blooming everywhere, the most ostentatious being the glorious mountain bluebells in the high meadows. Beautiful creations bask in the sunshine, nourished by the warming temperatures and the recent snowmelt. The poplars, as Canadians refer to quaking aspen trees, are swelling with new buds near bursting. The river bottoms are already greening, and daily the annual process creeps higher up the slopes.

Animals also have been much in evidence, the most numerous being the regal Dall sheep. Jack O'Connor hunted them here in the early 1950s and wrote a story about taking a great ram on a mountain visible from our present location. We have seen perhaps two hundred of the snow-white animals, most of them mature rams. Several have been a hunter's dream, heavy and awesome with long, curving horns and upshot tips. Allan guides for such sheep in the fall and dutifully notes for Rod the location of the largest rams.

More entertaining are the scattered groups of ewes with the inevitable retinue of prancing newborn lambs. The tiny creatures scamper about like rabbits, moving as a fluid unit amidst the older sheep.

Hungry golden eagles, sporting wings of six feet or more that gleam like silver in the sunlight, soar incessantly over the lambs, hoping to catch an easy meal. The youngsters rapidly grow too large and agile for the birds, so the birthing season is the eagles' only opportunity. We have observed the drama for hours but have seen no lambs carried off. The birds soar periodically to a high rock cliff, perhaps a nesting site. They powerfully yet gracefully ride thermals to elevations higher than the surrounding peaks, then nonchalantly fold their wings and plunge 1,000 feet or more. As the ground approaches their wings open and they ascend majestically again.

Wood bison and Rocky Mountain elk are recent additions to the Kluane region where we are hunting, and we have seen both in abundance. Moose, mountain caribou, black bear, mountain goat, and, of course, grizzly bear round out the list of big-game sightings. Waterfowl abound in the lakes, the most impressive of which are the stately trumpeter swans. The kingly white birds sail

Claws are prime and sharp on my bear.

grandly over placid waters, trumpeting noisily at any intrusion. Mallards, pintails, teal, and countless other species would challenge any waterfowler's identification capabilities. I have been lost amid a swirl of color and mating activities.

But I have not found my bear. Like any ethical grizzly hunter, I am insistent on harvesting a male if at all possible. I am a hunter, and by definition I am a committed conservationist. Too many large, old grizzly boars rapidly become a detriment to healthy population dynamics, and some must be removed regularly to ensure the health of those that remain. I will take one of the beasts gladly if my opportunity ever comes, and the species will be better off for my efforts.

Placing my rain gear against the undulating tent wall, I attempt to create a barricade as I stow my belongings next to my mattress. My dry clothes and other vulnerable items are secure in plastic bags, and my old .30-06 rifle rests on top of the pile. It's hard to sleep in the noise of the storm, and I insert earplugs to see if they will help. In the Yukon there is no true darkness in May, and that too makes sleep hard to find.

The new day begins without rain, and the wind has shifted from easterly to westerly. Skies are clearing, a harbinger of rising barometric pressure and falling temperatures. The only apparent damage to our gear involves our sleeping bags, which are soaked at the foot because of contact with the tent wall.

We will trek downriver today. This valley is part of the domain of a huge boar grizzly of exactly the size and age class I want. His stomp lines and rub trees are visible at regular intervals along the faint horse trail we are following. The tracks were as fresh as they were gigantic when we dropped into the river bottom several days ago, so we will finish out the hunt here in fading hopes that "big ugly" will show himself. If not, I have to ponder some intense negotiations with my wife, my accountant, my banker, and my outfitter—to the ultimate end of planning an eighth hunt for interior grizzly.

There are numerous ways to hunt the grizzly of North America's mountains, the most common being the use of a chance carcass for bait, usually on fall moose hunts. True spot-and-stalk hunting is the purest form, however, and such a springtime hunt is the epitome of fair chase. Not that I am opposed to taking a grizzly in other ways, since I have already tried to find one on carcasses of moose, caribou, black bear, wolf, horses, and, on this trip, the corpse of a grizzly taken by another hunter. But in the spring it is easier to be sure the bear is a male, and the coats and claws are in better shape as well. I have spotted grizzlies on other hunts, but I have never had the opportunity to conduct a stalk for one I wanted to harvest.

Leaving our camp intact, we shoulder pack and rifle once again and head downriver. The stiff breeze is almost at our backs, not good for surprising a bear. We hope the crosswind will carry our scent in the direction of the surging river and away. We could hardly hope to ford that swollen torrent anyway, so icy and wide it is.

Four miles later we are on a high promontory glassing sidehills, steep ravines, and willow-shrouded river bottom. On this trek we spot two magnificent shed elk antlers, but not a single living large mammal of any kind. Dejected, we shuffle back upriver to camp for a brief lunch courtesy of Mountain House and discuss over spicy chili the limited options for our final day and a half.

The massive mountain to our south is the most accessible high terrain, and by all indications it is the most likely to produce our bear. We discovered and chased a huge black bear near the top of that peak the day we arrived, but we couldn't climb as fast as the bear could walk. There are lambing ewes all over the mountain, and numerous elk cows are calving nearby. All of these are tempting targets for a marauding grizzly that may have learned to hunt such readily available protein. Perhaps our resident old boar will show. Beyond doubt the imposing vertical slopes of the 3,000-foot massif are our best bet. We have already established a glassing base in a meadow near the river, a broad swampy field of tundra tussocks that offers an unobstructed view over several miles of promising grizzly domain.

Before walking to our chosen location, we collapse onto our sleeping bags for a couple of hours of sleep. My aging legs are as weary as they have ever been. When I look at my watch, it is 5:30 P.M., time for bears to walk. I awaken Allan and we hastily prepare to depart. The glassing meadow is a short thirty-minute journey away, and we plan to spend at least four hours there. We are rapidly approaching our last chance on this hunt, and we must make the best of the time.

Intervals spent glassing are never wasted. We count more than thirty rams on the more distant of the two major slopes, and a group of eighteen ewes with ten new lambs inhabit the adjacent mountain. Two elk cows and a moose cow with a new calf are also visible. We can see a pair of wood bison, black against the tawny lower slopes, two miles farther upriver, their humped backs reminiscent of grizzly. The day is resplendent, with a sparkling azure sky studded with the occasional cloud. Animals are abundant and seem glad of the warming temperature. The wind is still westerly and stiff, and serves man and beast well in keeping the emerging mosquitoes at bay.

The time creeps by, and 8 P.M. comes and goes. Allan is checking a promising ram with the spotting scope even as visibility starts to wane. My eye sockets are sore from the pressure of the Zeiss minis, but I persist. Allan returns to his binoculars and we both continue our vigil.

"Bears!" we exclaim in unison.

Any grizzly sighting is special and heralds the possibility of action. We both note immediately, with some disappointment, that the immense sow we have spotted is moving rapidly. She is just above where the black bear passed a couple of days ago and is obviously bent on leaving the country as hastily as he did. Moreover, she is being followed by this year's healthy hair-ball cub, just emerged from the den for the first time. The sow stops every quarter-mile to check the dainty pursuer, and when satisfied the tike is motoring along well she takes off again.

"What the heck is the big hurry?" I ask, admiring the sow's blond and black coat as it ruffles in the breeze.

"Something spooked her. Don't know what. Maybe our scent swirled in," responds Allan, as transfixed as I as he watches the pair cross the sheer face. "Could be she's running from big ugly, too. She should have two cubs. Maybe he got one."

"Are big boars the biggest threat to these cubs?"

"No question about that. Would you try to get that hair ball away from her? Only another grizzly, a big one, could do it."

The pair are in obvious flight. If the sow smelled us, that would explain it, but the blast of wind in our faces makes that unlikely. I lower my binoculars as the two disappear and gaze in dread at the vertical distance that separates us from the path the pair are following. Could my weary legs climb the loose shale on that face? In the back of my mind I hope it won't be necessary, even for a mature male grizzly, but I immediately reject the thought and steel myself for the possibility.

We originally had planned to glass here the last morning, so perhaps we will stay here tomorrow evening as well. After all, we have seen three bears in this remote valley, and all of them took the same path across the face. To boot, each seemed to be running from some unseen terror. What could it be? Whatever the answer, glassing until almost midnight produces no more sightings.

Everything in the tent is dry as we arrive home, and we are able to spend a comfortable though regrettably short night. We arise at 5 A.M. for the early glassing session, finishing the last of our oatmeal before departing for the meadow. I now vacillate between two options: should we try downriver in the afternoon, or should we spend it glassing nearby "bear mountain"?

The morning passes quietly. As on most days, we sight no more bruins. As the sun climbs, we hear the drone of a Super Cub engine. Allan takes out his radio, our only lifeline to the outside world.

"Hey, Rod, do you read me?"

"Yeah, Allan, where are you?"

"Down in the meadow ahead of you. Everything's fine here. Spotted a sow and a cub up on this mountain yesterday."

"Big cub?" Rod inquires, knowing that sows with older cubs come into estrus and attract male bears.

"Naw. Just a fuzz ball."

"Too bad. I'd still stick to glassing the walls of the valley. Big boar in there somewhere. Good luck. See you."

Rod signs off and continues his never-ending supply and maintenance runs to camps all over his area. He is prohibited by Yukon law from communicating by radio any information on the whereabouts of wildlife to any hunter or guide on the ground. I am gratified to observe that he adheres scrupulously to the letter of the law. He seems to do so in all regards, even having his guides remove all litter from their campsites, including old trash they didn't bring in. Their tireless efforts have made for one of the cleanest areas I have ever hunted.

Back to camp for lunch and a midday nap, we resolve to return for a final evening of glassing. I try to sleep, the long walks, steep climbs, and short nights having worn on me. Unable to become drowsy, I arise for a short devotional period. I remind the Lord that I want a mature male grizzly, a fact of which He is no doubt already aware. I also mention that I will willingly accept defeat if it is His will, and more especially if there is some higher purpose for my failure. The outcome aside, I find a deep peace I cannot fully comprehend.

I emerge from the tent, stuff my gear in my backpack, and prepare to return early to the glassing place, a mile or so from camp. As an afterthought I awaken my sleeping guide and advise him of my intentions, fearful he might be distressed to arise and find me gone. He reluctantly and drowsily agrees as I amble off down the trail.

The afternoon and evening promise to be long and arduous: eight hours or more of watching. For better visibility and to pass the time, I break off deadfall snags and tenacious willows and make myself as comfortable as possible for the prolonged final watch. In less than

Backpacking is part of the plan when hunting Yukon grizzly in springtime.

an hour Allan joins me, fresh from camp chores, and we settle in.

It is a time of rich conversation. We are both philosophical about our imminent disappointment, though we are obviously not ready to concede just yet. Allan has been guiding sheep hunters for seven years and has never failed to get his hunter a ram, an outstanding accomplishment. He got his first grizzly hunter a bear just before I arrived. He is facing almost certain defeat for the first time, but I am an old hand at it. I recount for him the tale of fourteen unsuccessful guided hunts of one sort or another over the years, perhaps a North American, if not a world, record. I remind my young friend that disappointments are a part of life, something to appreciate because of what they teach us about ourselves and our faith. I share with my guide many of my innermost feelings as the hours slip by and our quarry fails to appear.

The wind picks up as the sun edges toward the west, its scattering rays obscuring the farthest reaches of the valley walls and contracting the reach of our binoculars. The massive face adjacent our meadow, where we saw the bears before, remains less affected by the phenomenon because it is positioned directly to our south. The chill breeze drives me once more to my vest and coat, which I pull from my nearby pack. I am finally tiring of Dall sheep, eagles, elk, and birds. I am near to throwing in the towel. As 7 P.M. passes we discuss the freeze-dried stroganoff we will consume for dinner, and a gnawing hunger beckons me toward camp, away from this place of impending defeat. Allan and I agree we will tough it out until 9:30, then call it a hunt.

Huddled against the creeping cold of late afternoon, I persist in glassing, hoping to finish well. I strain to see the distant slopes through the glare of the sinking sun. We are intent in our searching, and my sideways glance at my guide finds him engrossed in his work. Inspired by his diligence, I return to my own glassing.

Without warning, Allan jumps excitedly to his feet and exclaims, "Get your clothes off!"

"What?"

"Get your clothes off and stuff them in your pack! Look!"

He points up the adjacent mountain and as I follow his finger I see the dark spot immediately. A monstrous grizzly has just topped the ridge, almost exactly where we saw the sow and cub. I rip off my coat and vest, shoving them into the internal frame pack. There will be gallons of sweat if I have to climb the massive wall atop which strides the prize of a lifetime!

"Let's watch him a minute. He's on the sow's trail. He may pass by so fast we don't have a chance," Allan mulls, watching the beast's every move.

As the animal moves tentatively across the meadow, we keep the bear in constant view. We follow his fluid motion, oscillating hair flowing in the stiff wind, massive shoulders and haunches propelling him in casual fashion. The animal ambles with no apparent sense of urgency.

"He might come down one of those guts if we go up," cautions Allan, referring to the innumerable deep ravines that crease the vertical face. "He'll be out of sight if we climb."

"He's hesitating, Allan. We've got to stay downwind and go to him. We can always glass down and find him if he descends." My own words

fill me with dread, since I know I am committing to climbing the mountain.

"That sow couldn't be in heat. No doubt he smells her. Maybe he won't follow, though. He'd still like to eat that cub, probably. Man, what to do?"

Glassing the massive animal again, we note a reluctance to move, a tentativeness that speaks of equivocation. The necessary action on our part crystallizes in my mind. We must move with resolve, and we must do it now.

"We've got to go to him, Allan," I insist this time. "The climb may kill me, but we've got to. It's our best chance."

I look upward and gulp, noting again with foreboding the incredible vertical real estate that separates me from what I have sought for many years. But finally, after seven hunts, I have an opportunity to put a stalk on a truly grand old boar of a grizzly. I will indeed reach him or die trying. Lord, be with us and please give me some extra energy, I pray silently and fervently.

Breathing is easy at first, but inevitably the terrain steepens. My chest is heaving with each step as up, up we go, into the thick spruce, then into shorter but more resistant willow thickets. The beast rapidly disappears behind the vaulted incline we are ascending, our closeness to the mountain hiding him completely. The timbered ridges edge away slowly below us, stairsteps of dense vegetation we have conquered. We are then on open sandy slopes, where high alpine vegetation clings tenaciously, unsteady places where the footing is treacherous. Between these exposed ridges are deep gullies choked with malignant tangles of willow and dwarf poplar, noisy and nearly impossible to traverse. I push myself mercilessly, urging my body to do the unimaginable, climbing relentlessly as my chest pounds and my lungs grope for oxygen. Allan looks back after we have climbed a couple thousand feet, wondering if the old man can make it. Somehow I manage a thumbs-up, despite my pain, and he flashes a welcome smile. More up awaits us—*siempre arriba*, as my Spanish-speaking friends say.

Finally the higher terrain spreads before us, and we begin seeking intently. The bear is nowhere in sight. Has he already crossed? Did he escape down a deep draw out of our view? Will we ever see him again?

Allan pauses to glass periodically, causing me to wonder if he really expects to see something, or if he is giving me time to catch up without appearing to wait. The wind is flawlessly favorable to our position, blowing steadily from the west. The animal may escape, but not because of our scent. Not this time. Thank you, dear Keeper of the Wind.

Suddenly Allan drops to his knees, simultaneously motioning me down and raising his binoculars. The animal is still there. Now I also see the bear, and the sight is without doubt one of the mightiest and most moving spectacles in all of nature. The creature stands poised at the edge of a rocky rim, exactly where we saw the sow and cub pass. Sniffing the air, the beast is still patently undecided whether to chase after them. The female with the tiny cub can't be in season, but this male knows her sex and perhaps holds dim hopes, either amorous or culinary, possibly both. One can almost feel the animal's wavering and the implications for our stalk. If he takes off after the sow, my only option is an unwise shot of almost five hundred yards.

Tentatively and without resolve, the creature slowly turns and lopes back whence he came, away from the sow's trail, sniffing the ground for more likely nourishment. He actually looks disappointed, but Allan and I rejoice with exchanged glances. At the edge of another rocky precipice, five hundred feet above, we should be able to see the bear within range.

Gazing again at our objective, I urge my failing legs upward. The rocks are much closer now, but the ascent is nearly vertical. We have eaten nothing in over eight hours and my reserves are near empty. *Oh Lord, give me strength to make that rock pile!* Adrenaline flows and I manage to place one foot above the other, the heavy pack and rifle pulling against me without pity. Allan is already removing his pack and readying his rifle for possible backup duty. The bear must be in range from his higher perspective, but I will know for certain in a very few minutes. He motions me encouragement without communicating any particular urgency, and I gasp the last yards to his side.

"Take off your pack and leave it here. Let's get out your rifle!"

Complying, I stand semierect and I can now at last see the grizzly some 250 yards away on the other side of a broad, flat ravine choked with willows. The bear is digging on an open slope, oblivious to us. I crawl to a small pile of rocks ten yards closer to the bear and prepare to shoot. Chambering a round, I wait for my heaving chest and racing heart to settle down. There is no hurry now. I glance at my watch, a little embarrassed that something as mundane as the time of day would appear important now. It is 8:23 P.M. We should be proud that we climbed that monster of a mountain in only fifty-five minutes.

The shot is long, but I manage to put a bullet in the animal. Confused by the sudden sting, the creature charges downhill, not knowing from which direction he is being attacked. The bear immediately disappears into the willows as I hastily discharge another round ineffectively. Groping for more ammo, I reload the chamber and magazine and wait, assuming a stable sitting position. The bear must now cross an open face 150 yards away to continue downhill. When he emerges I will be ready.

"There he is!" I exclaim quietly as he appears. The big bruin is now cautious and sniffing the air, apparently wounded fairly lightly and motoring as if unimpeded. Centering the scope on the massive and intimidating shoulder, I squeeze off another shot, and the beast crumples.

"Good shot! Now we've got him!" shouts Allan triumphantly. "Uh-oh, he's gonna tumble! What a roll!"

The bear indeed rolls. Like an immense, fuzzy beach ball he assumes a fetal position and plummets off the rocky cliff out of sight, thumping and crashing in the rocks and brush below.

"Ought to be dead. You tagged him good that last shot. But we've still got to be careful," advises Allan wisely. We edge down and around, my rifle reloaded as we traverse a dense field of dwarf poplars and alders, peering into the thick ravine where our prize has disappeared. What's that snapping, cracking sound?

"He's thrashing around. Be careful, he may charge when he smells us. Stay uphill," counsels my young guide as we move across the slope. The wind is blowing directly from us toward the bear, but there is no other approach.

"Ease ahead, but stay in the poplars. He may come at you fast, so be ready. Scope on lowest power. He's bound to have our wind now."

The breeze is cooling the back of my neck, a perilous sensation all hunters recognize as an unmistakable warning to prey in front of them. As I edge forward, the ominous cracking is still emanating from the draw below. It is delightfully terrorizing, and despite the cold sweat on my brow I realize that this is what I have always gleefully dreaded, almost sadistically. A wounded grizzly is immediately before me, and I have to finish him or die trying. My sandpaper mouth refuses to moisten, and my mind whirls.

"No hurry," says Allan. "I'll cover you from here. Don't go down there where he is unless I say so, but ease on around above him and see if you can spot him." Ten yards, twenty yards, now thirty I move. The threatening noises from the impenetrable thicket are now less than forty yards from me. I scan the tangle of vegetation with binoculars, but still I see no movement. Warily progressing across the dwarf poplar grove, I finally observe a patch of mahogany, much darker than the surrounding vegetation. It's the bear's head and shoulders. He is facing away from me, chewing in rage on a dead snag, though I can hardly see well enough to shoot. Needing better visibility, I step clear of the poplars into the opening that spans much of the slope between me and the animal.

"Don't go down there! Dammit, stay back!" I hear Allan yelling at me, obviously fearing for my safety.

"Don't worry. I see him!" I return in a somewhat muted call, hoping not to stimulate a charge. The bear is now clearly visible and is undulating back and forth, thankfully in no condition to attack. I place the cross hairs on the massive neck and fire once, then once again. As the explosion echoes across the valley and the noise dies, all becomes still.

"Got him! He's dead! He's dead!"

"Be careful," cautions Allan, unable to see from my perspective. "Don't assume anything. Wait until I get there before you go in!"

As the two of us approach the beast, I throw a stick and strike the still, massive form. No reaction. Flipping off my safety with another round chambered, I ease up to the bruin and touch him with the extended barrel, my finger caressing the hair trigger of the .30-06. There is again no response from the very dead bear.

The grizzly is immense. The span between the ears is nearly a foot, the first characteristic I note. I turn to face my jubilant guide, whose bearded face sports a toothy grin from ear to ear, his hand extended in a firm handshake. Whooping for joy, I admire my magnificent prize with euphoria.

Before our picture session, I engage in a ceremony that has become standard. I drop to my knees beside my fallen prey, my hand on his enormous head, and I thank God aloud for hearing my prayers, for protecting and preserving me and my guide, for energizing me during my climb, for a great guide like Allan, and for giving me this incredible bear, one of His unique creations.

The bear's front paw measures seven inches across, almost certainly an eight-foot bear, rare in these parts. He is quite old and grizzled, and has a small rub between the ears, a minor distraction that is easily repaired. The skull is record class, truly a magnificent trophy.

As Canadian flight number 588 lifts off from Whitehorse, the captain reminds passengers of the beautiful Yukon scenery below. I gaze for a moment in deep thought at the panorama of snowcapped mountains, frozen high-country lakes, cascading streams, and meandering glaciers. I wonder if anyone else on the flight has experienced the glory of it all so closely, walked over it until their legs were too tired for another step, sunk in spirit to depths too low to be fathomed, and subsequently been lifted to lofty planes few can understand.

I lower the shade by my window seat. My heart glows with inestimable satisfaction, and my thoughts turn toward Georgia and home.

Polar bear. (Photo: courtesy of James L. Davis)

POLAR BEAR
(Ursus maritimus)

The bear, a huge, powerful and almost invisible animal,
perfectly designed for non-skid travel over all kinds of ice. . . .
He was a wraith, in a place that belonged on another planet, and the silent,
liquid rhythm of his movement as he flowed across the rough going of
his special world was something that might be captured in motion pictures,
but not by my stumbling prose.

—Grancel Fitz, *North American Head Hunting,* 1956

The polar bear is perhaps one of few species to have retained its most ancient scientific identification. The name *Ursus maritimus* was attached to the animal by C. J. Phipps in 1774, and that nomenclature is still in use today, although over the years the animal has held other designations. The creature should perhaps be classified as *Ursus arctos maritimus;* the great white bear is closely related to grizzly and brown bears and interbreeds with them to produce fertile offspring. Its distinctive physical characteristics and unique habits, however, are sufficient for scientists to allow the polar bear to keep its unencumbered species identification. Nevertheless, the word *arctos* means "north country," and it seems a shame to omit the designation from an animal that is, according to Canadian biologist Ian Stirling, "the Arctic incarnate." They are excellent swimmers and can paddle at six miles per hour, however, so the word *maritimus* undoubtedly fits well.

Polar bears inhabit the Arctic wherever sea ice is a seasonal or permanent feature, but like brown bears they are absent from the Southern Hemisphere. They are most numerous on ice pack within a few score miles of land but have been reported as far north as 88 degrees, incredibly close to the North Pole. Scientific data indicate that there are perhaps 25,000 polar bears in the world, a figure that is conservative. Fourteen fairly discrete populations exist in Canada, one of which is shared with the United States and four with Greenland. They occur as far south as the James Bay between Quebec and Ontario, an area almost as low in latitude as Calgary, Alberta, with the harsh winters of the frozen Hudson Bay providing an icy highway that allows this highly temperate excursion. They hunt efficiently for seals wherever there is sea ice, and suffer want of prey in its absence. Summer is a time of relative fasting for polar bears, and the white bruins wait patiently on shore for the return of firm sea ice.

A large male polar bear may weigh as much as 2,200 pounds, though such a massive animal is no doubt uncommon. More typically, an animal of 1,000 to 1,200 pounds is considered big enough by most hunters, and the raw hide of such a bear should square in excess of ten feet. Females average much less, usually between 350 and 500 pounds. The body of a polar bear is more elongated and agile in appearance than that of the brown bear. The hair is hollow and appears pure white after the late-summer molt, though seal fat and blood may stain the new coat over time to a slightly yellowish color that makes them easier to spot in their white habitat. The eyes, nose, and footpads are black, as is the skin itself underneath all that obscuring white hair.

The animals may live to be thirty years old, although exact aging with dental annuli (teeth rings) is sometimes difficult, perhaps because all polar bears do not den each winter (only females bearing cubs will predictably enter a den). Once a polar bear is fully mature it has few enemies, though on rare occasions a killer whale may take a swimming polar bear. Some die of old age, but many are harvested by Arctic natives. Natural mortality is about 4 to 5 percent of the adult population per year, and the sustainable harvest by humans is about 1.5 percent of the adult females and 3 percent of the adult males.

Polar bear. Northwest Territories, May 1993.

Like all North American bears, polar bears breed in the spring, with mature males roaming the ice seeking receptive mates. Female polar bears are bred for the first time at age four or five, although that varies according to the location, and they are more generally bred at four years in the highly productive eastern Canadian Arctic. The fertilized ovum is delayed in implantation, and gestation is 195 to 265 days. Pregnant females enter a den in October or November, with most maternal dens being on land. Such dens are usually situated on the lee side of a steep bank that covers early with drifting snow. Females seldom move inland very far to establish dens, which mostly occur within thirty miles of the nearest salt water but have been reported as far as a hundred miles inland. Some polar bears of both sexes construct summer dens to escape heat, insects, and other hungry bears. Adult males normally roam the winter ice without denning at all. Females bearing young do not use the same den again, but they are more or less faithful to the area for subsequent dens. Major denning areas are known in several locations, notably Wrangell Island off Siberia and Cape Churchill on the Hudson Bay of Canada.

Cubs are usually twins or single. Triplet births occur, but the extra cub is usually a runt that will not survive. The tiny creatures weigh about one and a half pounds at birth, their eyes and ears are closed, they are nearly hairless, and they are completely helpless. On rich mother's milk they grow and change rapidly so that by the time they leave the den in March or April they gaze at their new world with wide, dark eyes, looking like white balls of hair. They usually remain close to the den for a week or two while becoming acclimatized. They are vulnerable to predation by male polar bears for their first few months, and they face a host of other obstacles as well, including stress by icy water and subzero temperatures. About 50 percent of cubs are lost during their first three years of life, the majority during the first year.

The main prey of polar bears is the ringed seal, which is most available when out on the ice for molting in May, June, and July. Additionally, polar bears capture numerous baby seals during the pupping season in April. At that time the youngsters are cached by their mothers in snow-covered dens above a breathing hole, and the bears' excellent sense of smell locates them. The baby seals are a nutrition bonanza for the bears; they may weigh more than thirty pounds, with plump bodies that contain 50 percent fat. The bears eat only the fat and leave the rest of the carcass for a host of scavengers that follow in their wake, including Arctic foxes, ravens, and gulls.

When prey is less abundant, the bears may wait for hours at a breathing hole for a seal to surface. Seals have developed ingenious methods to detect the presence of their archenemy and will often send up a spray of bubbles before surfacing, hoping any ambushing bear will reveal itself prematurely. Experienced bears know to hold their place patiently until the seal's ploy has been played out, and when it actually surfaces they lunge and grab the unlucky animal by the head with their powerful jaws and pull it onto the ice. Such is the strength of a mature polar bear that lifting a thrashing seal weighing several hundred pounds is usually no major task. The bears also stalk seals, a method that is occasionally successful. Inuit legend has it that polar bears use a paw to cover their revealing black noses during stalks, though that bit of traditional knowledge has never been proven.

Polar bears also eat other types of seals (principally bearded, harp, and hooded seals) as well as other animals such as young walruses when the opportunity presents. Polar bear cubs are doubtless not a major food item, but there have been documented incidences of cubs, and even their defending mother, being eaten by large male polar bears. Scientists feel that in healthy polar bear populations very few young are lost to cannibalism. The bears are strongly attracted to carrion and will seek it out when it is available. They also eat plant material from time to time, though they are surely the purest carnivore among the bears of the world.

The polar bear is managed in Canada's Northwest Territories, where all sport hunts occur at the time of this writing, in a way that is probably the most intensive and effective of any game animal on earth. Expensive surveys are done by helicopter, a method that has been adopted exclusively to preclude the inherent bias in ground-based sampling by snowmobile—some bears live in rough ice and are missed by the latter technique. Captured bears may receive satellite tracking collars and a lip tattoo or ear tag. Scientists also take appropriate scientific samples, such as a nonessential tooth from the lower jaw for aging purposes. The various populations of Canada are surveyed on a rotating basis, with fieldwork occurring mainly in the spring but also in the fall. It is one of the most dangerous wildlife-related management activities anywhere, but it results in superb monitoring and sustainable management. Ongoing work should eventually open all Canadian populations where there is a sport-hunting program to importation into the United States, though that process is likely to be slow at best.

Apart from the pure science of determining populations, the heart of the Canadian management system is the Flexible Quota Option, which has been implemented by most major sport-hunting communities. The percentage of females in the harvest is extremely important in determining the

Camping out on the Arctic ice pack—it's actually quite comfortable.

rate at which polar bears can be removed by hunters. In fact, the fraction of females in the harvest serves as the denominator in the classic equation used to calculate the allowable take from a given population. There has been some problem in implementing sex-selective harvesting in the past, so the Flexible Quota Option was developed to allow adjustments to the quota when a community takes too many females. Credits are allowed for past underharvest of a quota, but if no credits are available any overharvest can be compensated for by future quota reductions. The system seems to be working extremely well.

All polar bear hunts in Canada require use of a native guide (Inuit in the east and Inuvialuit in the west), and dogsled transportation is mandatory on all sport hunts by nonnatives. The experience is one of the most challenging in all the world of

Fresh polar bear tracks abound as we sled along.

hunting, with the uncertainties of an exotic means of transportation, the bleak and brutal ice pack, the hazards of fickle weather and shifting sea ice, and the dangerous nature of the prey combining to make for an electrifying experience. The majority of hunts require considerable travel on the dogsled from the host community to reach good polar bear habitat, but in some places you may see bears right away.

Several types of dog team arrangements are used in the Canadian Arctic. Most first-time hunters visualize an arrangement whereby the dogs are hitched side by side like horses pulling a stagecoach, and that is the system most often used in the western Arctic. The advantage is that direction can be controlled more effectively by a well-trained lead dog, narrow passages can be negotiated, and there is less tangling of the traces.

The disadvantage is that each dog must be fitted with a harness and then placed in line, a time-consuming and laborious process. In the east, the dogs are placed on individual lines with no tandem rigging to hold them together. The longest of the leashes belongs to the lead dog, and the running team appears akin to a fleeing pack of wolves in its race across the ice. The advantage is that little training is required to start young dogs, which naturally adapt to this way of running, and the hookup is quick and efficient. The downside is that the constant intermingling of the dogs causes monstrous tangling of the traces that requires periodic stops. I have ridden on dogsleds using both methods, and either way the powerful canines will move you along at a brisk pace.

Hunting techniques vary from one community to another, but in most places the hunter cruises until spotting a satisfactory bear, sometimes from an iceberg or other high point, and then a stalk is planned. It usually requires considerable maneuvering by the hunters to stay downwind until they are close enough to release a few dogs to bay the bear. The dogs will likely start to howl and strain at the traces when they catch the bear's scent. Considerable skill and experience are required on the part of the guides to determine exactly when to release the dogs. The bear may escape into rough ice if it suspects hunters are approaching, so it is possible to wait until one is too close, yet releasing the dogs too soon may result in a long, arduous trek from where the sled must be left behind. If too much time elapses, dogs could be lost to the bear before the hunters catch up.

In the old days, such determinations were even more critical. In a recollection from the days before the natives had firearms, Inuk elder George Kappianaq of Igloolik recounted in a 1990 interview about hunting polar bears with primitive weapons: "When the dogs are keeping the polar bear at bay and occupied, I should get close to it and start to stoop low and I should not stop until I get right up to the polar bear. . . . When the polar bear goes after a dog away from your direction, you should rush at the polar bear and cast your harpoon to the place where the elbow is situated. . . . If you only wound it, you are going to be faced with danger."

It is hard to imagine what it must have been like to experience such a heart-pounding encounter. One's life was literally up for grabs. When you go on that dogsled ride after the white giants of the polar ice pack and are fortunate enough to be successful, stuff a little of your misplaced pride and remember how it used to be done. Even if you're using a modern bow and arrow you will always have a firearm backup, and that's a luxury that was unavailable to courageous Inuit hunters in millennia past.

Probably the average hunter spends more time agonizing over what equipment to pack for a polar bear hunt than for any other excursion. The list of items that are different from the average hunting trip is fairly short, but special mention needs to be made of a few.

High-tech, cold-weather clothing is adequate and more comfortable to wear and easier to don than caribou skins. Moreover, making the skin clothes is a dying art in the North, and they may not be an option for most future polar bear hunters. You may not have a choice in the matter, but my advice is to use them if they're offered, even if it costs extra. They're incredibly warm and functional, they make for great pictures, and you

might be among the last hunters to be privileged to wear them.

The same can be said of footwear. The double skin mukluks fashioned by the Inuit women are without equal as protection against frostbite. You can get by nicely with high-tech clothes, but why spend big bucks for something that isn't nearly as quaint and that you may use only a time or two? Whichever you choose, be sure to have available icebreaker-type boot blankets for riding on the sled in the biting wind. People have lost toes without them on such outings.

Skin gloves come with the caribou outfits, and are usually also fashioned from caribou skin. Wolf fur is equally good, in my experience, for this part of the costume. Skin gloves are preferable in my opinion because with wool gloves underneath your fingers stay warm and ready to shoot when you slip off the outers. The latest synthetics boast of that as well, but I've never worn a pair that did as well as wolf or caribou skin.

For quick trips outside when camped, take a pair of down pants and a parka. Down underwear isn't necessary but is good insurance against a truly brutal turn of the weather. Polypropylene against the skin will keep it dry even if you have to make a long, sweaty trek for your bear. If you don't like to sleep in polypropylene, take along a cotton jogging suit and avoid a clammy feeling in the sleeping bag.

Your hat should have flaps that allow one to button it securely over the ears and to pull the parka hood tightly over the head. The best ones are lined with animal fur, since even rabbit hair is better insulation than most wool or synthetics. A balaclava is extremely useful, and one shouldn't venture into the Arctic without one. The cold wind will freeze exposed skin if the temperature really drops. For the same reason, and to protect the corneas from wind burn and sunburn, take along a good set of ski goggles and a pair of sunglasses. The last thing you need is a case of snow blindness, which, like frostbite, is guaranteed to ruin the hunt.

Most guides heat the tent as necessary to keep you warm, but a good Arctic sleeping bag is desirable. I used a large layered bag and lined it with a down bag. One could sleep outside in a snowbank with that arrangement.

Dog sled transportation is mandated for all sport polar bear hunts.

Bring along binoculars and a good skinning knife. Your rifle should be thoroughly degreased and ride on top of the sled in your view in a padded, soft case. When camping, the case, with rifle inside, should be outside the tent but near the door so you can get to it easily. Being outside prevents condensation from fouling it and causing a disastrous failure at the wrong time. Don't worry about a polar bear crashing your tent; that happens only when the dogs aren't along, except in the rarest of instances. The dogs will be staked downwind of your position, most likely, and any approaching bear will give rise to a blood-curdling dissonance of howling. You'll have plenty of time to get your rifle.

Polar bear hunting is an experience most of us will have only once, at most. Put away any anxiety, and enjoy it to the fullest. The dogs will take you where the ice seems endless, the land utterly barren, and the call of the wild ever near. Go, trust your guides, relax, and enjoy. You probably won't pass that way again, so make the most of it.

THE ULTIMATE ARCTIC ADVENTURE

The only sound is the soft whoosh of sled runners on snow, punctuated by an occasional crunch as we traverse a chunk of embedded ice. From time to time, my guide, Aleeasuk, cries softly to the dogs, *Ooiee* or *Iee,* meaning "Turn left" or "Turn right," to which the dogs obediently respond.

The new ice that has formed over the long, dark winter is as smooth as glass and holds only a superficial frosting of powdery snow. In areas devoid of old ice, it is clear sailing and steady sledding. The term "old ice" refers to the impassable jumbles of fragmented sea ice from winters past, manifest in the brief summer as floating aggregates of ice chunks that never completely melted. On refreezing after the short open-water season, jagged points and razor-sharp edges are everywhere thrust skyward in all directions. This can indeed be formidable terrain to navigate.

Such obstacles are everywhere, and we constantly adjust our route to get around the crystal ramparts. The positive aspect of hunting in such a domain is that the polar bears we are seeking love the rough ice, because the seal hunting here is usually good. Additionally, the big white bears seem to head instinctively into the impenetrable maze when they encounter hunters.

There is something about the pure whiteness of the polar bear that is frightening. I remember sensing this as I stood in Jonas Brothers Taxidermy in Seattle in 1975, gazing at a giant mounted polar bear killed years before by Arthur Dubs hunting out of Kotzebue, Alaska. Only in Herman Melville's *Moby Dick* have I read an accurate articulation of my feelings that day, feelings that drove me to return repeatedly and stare in awe at that specimen. "Witness the white bear of the poles," wrote Melville. "What but their smooth, flaky whiteness makes them the transcendent horrors they are? That ghastly whiteness it is which imparts such an abhorrent mildness, even more loathsome than terrific, to the dumb gloating of their aspect. So that not the fierce-fanged tiger in his heraldic coat can so stagger courage as the white-shrouded bear."

White they are, these bears, and formidable. "Dumb," as Melville indicates—I don't think so. I ponder the passage as we sled eastward, gliding on icy runners toward an encounter with one of the "transcendent horrors," and I hope my courage will not stagger if I am presented an opportunity to display it.

We are hunting out of Resolute Bay, NWT, Canada, on the last hunt of the season. It is the middle of May, when the lower part of Canada is blooming, but here in the high Arctic we are still two months or more from breakup of the sea ice. Six hundred miles north of the Arctic Circle, spring comes late and summer leaves early. The old cliché about the North Country is more true here than anywhere else in the world—the two seasons are indeed winter and July, literally. But for a polar bear hunt, the country just doesn't get any better.

The Canadian law stating that all sport hunts for polar bears be conducted by dogsled helps preserve a vanishing element of Inuit culture. For the most part, only in those communities with an active sport-hunting program are there any traditional dog teams at all, most Inuit having readily adapted to mechanized transportation. Maintaining a dog team requires tremendous effort, for the owner is committed to year-round seal hunting and fishing to feed a ravenous corps of canines. Ready-made dog food cannot supply enough energy to allow the animals to survive in these climes, and fresh meat is absolutely necessary to their health and vitality. For the average dog team, one ringed seal every other day is sufficient. For an Inuk (singular of Inuit) to keep dogs, there must be a darn good reason, or the commitment isn't worth it. Polar bear sport hunts provide a profitable reason to go to the trouble, and thus an important aspect of Inuit history is preserved.

Two dog teams are involved in this trip, since I have a Swedish television representative filming the hunt for a documentary, which he wants to conduct from the sled. From the start, this causes some problems I have failed to foresee. There is ongoing and explosive friction between the two dog teams, for example, and more than a few canine entanglements, both in error and in anger. Despite that, we finally get lined out and I am experiencing my first dogsled ride, with the cold May wind in my face as constant reminder of just how far north I have ventured.

We also have a snowmobile and *qamutik* (sled) accompanying us to carry the heavier supplies, such as the generator the cameraman needs to recharge his batteries. The wildlife officer from Resolute Bay, Eric Doig, also is along on his powerful machine. He is obviously enjoying the outdoor adventure after days of relative boredom in the local office. The snow machine either precedes us or trails us by enough distance that one can seldom hear the engine. Thus the quiet of the dogsled is not compromised, to my relief.

There is something a bit disquieting about being out on a frozen ocean miles from land. Can we really trust that four-foot-thick layer of ice? We occasionally encounter seal holes that readily confirm that there is indeed dark water, sinister and mysterious, surrounding us for miles. The Inuit take it all in stride, as would anyone accustomed to ice fishing or snowmobiling. But for this Georgia boy, it is unnerving, and it takes a while before I begin to feel everything is all right.

It is our first day, and we left Resolute Bay about 6 P.M. We plan to travel exclusively at "night," though daylight is never gone this time of year. Because the sun does sink lower toward the horizon during what we normally call night, however, the temperature drops ten to twenty degrees. That makes the "night" preferable for travel because the cold keeps the dogs from overheating, and the firmer snow conditions are more conducive to sledding. The dogs (and we) can rest just as well while the temperature is higher.

It would be a serious omission to fail to discuss the attributes of my guide and assistant guide on this expedition. The head guide is the only female guide I have ever been assigned, Aleeasuk Eckalook (first name pronounced ah-LEE-sook.) She is as rare as can be in her vocation, although there is at least one more lady polar bear guide in another Inuit community. Aleeasuk was born in the Arctic back country of nearby Somerset Island, where her parents lived the nomadic life of their ancestors, raising ten children in the process. She left the bush only to attend school at age nine. She is at least as comfortable out on the sea ice as she is in town, she does her own seal hunting and fishing for her dogs, and she appears to be intimidated by nothing in this hostile land. Despite her unusual vocation, she lives a more or less settled life nowadays, as do most Inuit, with her husband and three children. Her parents never left the land, and the death of her father in 1992 is said to have ended four thousand years of nomadic Inuit history, as he was the last Inuk to live solely off the land and its bounty.

The assistant guide also merits some attention, because he is interesting as well. He exhibits a classic example of crisis in modern Inuit society and the effects of the white man on that culture. Ekaksak (pronounced ee-KACK-sak) has lived an up-and-down life, mostly hunting and trapping, and he claims to have killed more than a hundred polar bears before the current quota system was established. With the decline in the fur trade, he had trouble finding employment, a common problem here. His inactivity led to some bad habits, and he got into trouble with alcohol and even spent time in jail. His marriage dissolved long ago, and he never sees his children. He craves self-esteem, most any psychiatrist would discover quickly, and has sought it in the solace of the Arctic, where his only heritage lies.

Ekaksak signed on for not one but two expeditions to the North Pole, both quests by snowmobile. On one of the excursions, he was retrieved from the Pole with his Japanese partners by airplane; on the other, with Norwegian companions, he traveled all the way across the ice pack, finally being rescued while adrift on an Atlantic iceberg near the Norwegian territory of Svalbard. This piddling polar bear hunt must be just a source of some cash to him. Despite his experience he does his best to make this Arctic novice welcome, entertaining me with electrifying tales of his adventures.

About halfway to our first-day destination, we encounter a returning polar bear hunter who has taken a nice eight-and-a-half-foot bear and reports numerous others spotted. His dog team is obviously tired, and the animals stand in their traces with tongues hanging long and plumes of breath lingering in the icy air. They whine intolerantly at our own dogs, though, indicating that they have weathered ten days on the ice as well as their race can expect. A bellyful of fresh polar bear meat is

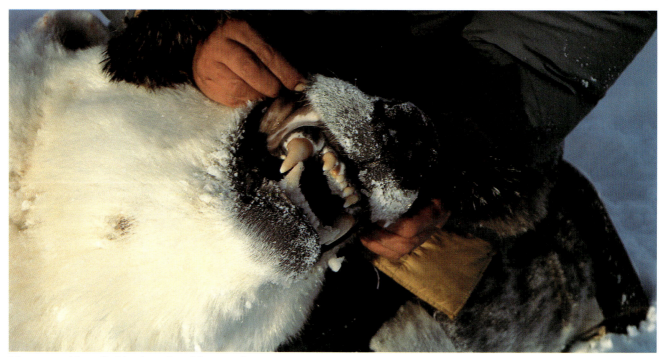

Many a seal has died in the grip of these teeth.

the fuel of the day, and the energy has rejuvenated them, no doubt. We leave the satisfied hunter and journey onward, constantly on the alert for a bear. We don't encounter one this day, but I revel in the smooth, quiet ride and the bewitching seascape with its stark beauty. The high, black bluffs along the coast loom grimly to our north, and there is no visible sign of life apart from our party.

We have mushed some forty miles from Resolute Bay along the south side of Cornwallis Island, and we establish camp at its southeastern cape. A large iceberg is marooned firmly against the imposing shoreline, and it provides a beautiful backdrop for our tents. We stake the dogs out in the fashion of the Arctic, separated from one another to prevent fighting. The shorefast berg is "blue ice," made of fresh water of glacial origin, perhaps from nearby Devon Island or even Greenland. Since it is fresh, we can use it for camp water instead of the usual snow. Unless one is cooking something, the fresh pack ice is unusable because of its salt content, though the salt leaches from multiyear ice, leaving it quite fresh. The ice from the berg has a taste when melted that is entirely untainted, reminding one of mountain spring water.

Our plan is to rest all "day" and resume our travel toward evening, to maximize the stamina of the dogs. About travel time, however, all thought of breaking camp evaporates as an immense weather system slams into us with the ferocity of a Georgia tornado. The wind howls relentlessly and soon tops fifty miles an hour. Huge drifts of snow, unusual in such immense quantities in the Arctic, pile up against the tent. The dogs, who can't eat until we kill something, curl up and allow the snowdrifts simply to cover them.

For some sixty hours we endure constant tent flapping, the tempest seemingly determined to rip our flimsy dwelling to shreds. The horizontally driven snow makes any trip outside a survival experience, and relieving one's natural inclinations has never before been so uncomfortable. Aleeasuk and Ekaksak are unperturbed, their quiet confidence providing a reservoir of assurance for me. They repeatedly point out that we are warm, dry, and comfortable, and we have plentiful supplies, fuel for our stove and kerosene heater, and ample food. In addition, we have the marooned glacial ice just outside the tent as a source of fresh

water. What more might a polar bear hunter want? I gradually become accustomed to the constant wind and snow, and finally I settle into a calm reading of Berton's *The Mysterious North.*

I have to check my wristwatch to know what time and day it is, because the blizzard does even more damage to my circadian rhythm than the constant light. We sleep when we feel like, and arise to eat or read in our sleeping bags whenever slumber becomes impossible. By the time the storm breaks, induction into the Arctic is complete. Time has come to matter very little, except that we must travel when it is coolest for the sake of the dogs.

The storm finally subsides, and the wind and snow ebb and cease. The weather has cost us about three days all told, and grave doubts have begun to creep in as to whether I will have time to find a quality bear. Nevertheless, I prepare my equipment, test-fire my rifle, and make sure everything is still in order. I am now mentally ready for what I hope will be a thrilling and productive encounter with a large male polar bear.

As we prepare to depart, I check on a newborn puppy, the offspring of one of the sled dogs, which has been brought along because its mom has essential work to do. The little tike reached one week of age exactly when the storm broke three days ago. I had expressed to Aleeasuk my grave doubts that it would survive outside in such a brutal nursery, but survive and thrive it has. My inclination had been to bring the pup into the warm tent, but I rapidly discovered that the Inuit think differently. To help it survive would be to weaken the species. Here in the Arctic, perhaps as nowhere else on earth, the law of survival demands a price for any weakness or deficiency, and that often means death. The strong somehow survive, be they domestic dog, wild beast, or man. The result of the natural culling process is a stronger line, more hardy and more enduring. The pup's eyes will be open before we return to Resolute Bay, and its first view of the world will be appropriately stark white. I christen the pup Blizzard, in honor of his surviving the storm.

Our plan is to head east along the south coast of Devon Island, seeking a monster bear. Along the way we pass near Beechy Island, a high and barren islet that features a swampy spit of land connecting it to enormous Devon. This bleak location is where the doomed Franklin expedition of Arctic explorers spent their first winter in 1845-46. Six men died that brutal winter, and their graves are still there. All of the expedition, 134 men, disappeared into the Arctic wastes, all dying of scurvy, starvation, and exposure. I try to get a mental picture of the way they must have felt, the desperation and the hopelessness. The desolate landscape would surely have been all too familiar to those poor souls. A historic site of tragedy unfolds before me, an echo from the past that sobers my mood and gives me great cause for rejoicing that we are so well provisioned and in touch with civilization by radio. Let me have no delusions about identifying more than superficially with those brave souls simply because I am here.

Having to wait out a storm usually doesn't bother me, because the hunting after the weather lifts is usually the best. Every animal I have ever hunted, including the polar bear, is inactive during any terrible disturbance in the elements. Sure enough, we begin to see polar bears and fresh tracks as soon as we leave our campsite. No doubt, this is some of the best polar bear habitat on Earth. We pass on an eight-foot male, electing to observe him from afar, the dogs howling as they catch his scent from a mile or more away. Surely there is a bigger bear out there somewhere, one to match a gigantic set of tracks we have spied. Aleeasuk estimates that the beast will go at least nine feet, perhaps more, so we carefully maneuver the dog team downwind of the area to which we presume he has traveled.

From the top of a small iceberg, my guide shows me our prey with the spotting scope. What a sight! The polar bear has a slight yellowish hue to the white hair, making it stand out against the stunning whiteness of the frozen Parry Channel waters. We watch for an hour, trying to determine the best way to approach so we can release the hungry dogs for the chase. We have traveled perhaps forty to fifty miles already today, and it is near midnight. In anticipation of a long chase and stalk, the Inuit deliberately break out the stove and prepare a late-night snack as the sun finally peeks through the clouds low on the northern horizon. I can't believe they can think of eating at a time like this, but they know that taking care of the body comes first in these latitudes. I force myself to down a few mouthfuls of dry bannock, and I wash it down with hot tea.

I am really concerned about the dogs. Their labor is constant, except for the rest breaks when we stop to climb an iceberg or to eat. The new snow from the recent storm makes the old phrase "tough sledding" take on more significance. The new stuff is much heavier and wetter, the temperature having risen from 20 below zero Fahrenheit to 0 degrees, and it edges upward as the sun slowly begins to climb in the sky. As we work our way to the bear, the dogs' tongues are virtually dragging on the ground.

The idea is to get as close as possible to the bear before the animal senses our presence, staying downwind if possible. The Arctic ice is as nearly odorless as any environment on earth, so the slightest scent easily reaches a sensitive nose. When a bear takes off, several dogs are cut free, and they quickly overtake it. The same heat conservation factors that protect the bear from extreme cold make him unable to run long distances without overheating. The dogs labor under no such constraints, and the biggest polar bear is remarkably vulnerable to a pack of sled dogs in the right ice conditions.

We spot the bear again at the edge of impossibly rough ice, luckily before he is aware of our presence. As we mush closer, the animal looks our way, then turns and heads in the other direction, ambling along at an incredible speed without any obvious effort. Aleeasuk halts the sled and cuts free the three most experienced dogs, and they immediately surge after the bear, their senses primed from several hours of maneuvering downwind. When the sled stalls in rough ice, she cuts the rest loose and we proceed on foot, taking only the essentials with us. Within a quarter-mile I am soaked with sweat, struggling over irregular ice chunks as big as cars while wearing the heavy caribou-skin clothing. I shuck the immense outer coat, leaving it for retrieval on our way back, and keep my legs churning through the impossible terrain.

Sled dogs have a reputation for being vicious, and these are ravenously hungry as well. To see such savage beasts bay an equally ferocious bear is an unforgettable sight. A good bear dog is a prize indeed, and Aleeasuk cautions me once more to be certain of my shot as we struggle toward the primal

Traditional Arctic caribou-skin clothing of the Inuit.

conflict ahead. I see now why the sled dog was instrumental in the survival of these Inuit people, with the inborn canine hatred of the polar bear, and the bear's instinctive respect for the dogs. Without such dogs, it is quite possible that all the Inuit people might well have succumbed to predation by polar bears long before the arrival of Europeans.

The big bruin is sitting on a Cadillac-size ice block as we move closer, and the commotion dies down a bit and assumes the appearance of an uneasy standoff. Whenever one of the canines ventures too close, or makes a frenzied charge to nip at a white flank, the creature swats with lightning swiftness. The dogs are quicker, however, at least this time, and manage to avoid harm. In the meantime, I move in to about seventy-five yards and choose a relatively flat ice block from which to shoot.

My breathing is heavy from laboring over the icy chaos, but also from sheer excitement. I position myself and prepare to shoot, chambering a round only when all is ready. A wary calm settles over me, as it often does at the moment of truth, and I patiently wait until the dogs clear. When the time seems exactly right, I touch off the shot with a simple and gentle squeeze on the hair trigger of the .30-06.

One can tell instantly from the bear's reaction that the shot has found its mark. On the big bears, I usually just keep shooting, but this time I hesitate. I secretly have been hoping for a one-shot kill, but I quickly think better of it as the fatally wounded bruin begins attacking the dogs in a frenzy. I put in another shot behind the shoulder, carefully avoiding Aleeasuk's prize dogs, which are swarming around the bear.

I feel as if everything has slowed to a crawl as the giant collapses on the ice, obviously finished. My legs feel like lead in the heavy caribou-skin trousers as we move up cautiously, keeping the rifle at ready. The dogs know it is over, and after moving in to nip gingerly at the creature, they respectfully back off while Aleeasuk and I assume command of the bear. I carefully circle the animal, watching for any sign of life before gently touching an ear, then an upper eyelid, watching for any response. The bear is dead.

He is a creature of awesome beauty. All the fur is intact and virtually unscarred from previous fights, and he measures a good nine feet plus some change. Ekaksak arrives shortly and estimates the

bear's age at fifteen years, judging from his size and tooth wear. I expend several rolls of film, taking full advantage of the sun. The time of the kill is about four in the morning, and we accomplish the necessary duties in the bright sunlight.

We camp on the spot to rest and savor our triumph. The sled dogs shortly enjoy a much-welcomed meal of fresh polar bear meat, which they wolf down before it freezes solid, a rare treat indeed. Between the two dog teams, all but one forequarter of the bear is consumed in one orgy of feeding. Aleeasuk and Ekaksak display the legendary Inuit skill with a knife, skinning the bear and caring for the hide.

Gratitude permeates my meditations as I reflect on the experience, and I thank God for it all. No setting could be better for such ponderings than the profound quiet of an Arctic night, sledding in near silence by the light of the midnight sun. According to poet Robert Service, it is "the quiet that bludgeons you dumb," and I'm saying very little as we sled toward home.

My musings drift off in the direction whence we came, one hundred miles to the west to Resolute Bay. I think of the Inuit people who inhabit this stark, brutal land, and their heritage, so embodied in these two guides. Their lot, and that of their kin, has been made much harder in the past by well-intended but misguided policies of my own government, as we presumptuously impose restrictions on their meager resources. Despite our imperialism, our impetuosity, and our persistent interference, they hold no grudges and treat Americans with respect. The game they hunt is plentiful and well managed, and they and their people have been quick to respond positively to scientific game management. They understand that what is good for the bear, the walrus, the seal, or the other renewable resources in their land is also good for the Inuit.

They cannot, however, understand the forces far away, so foreign to their way of thinking, that would deprive them of the right to utilize these resources on which their people have depended for millennia. Preservationists of various stripes (as opposed to true conservationists) conspire to limit the value of their sport hunts by prohibiting importation, to eliminate their right to hunt and utilize the plentiful seals, and to abolish their fur

Long guard hairs surround the black footpads of polar bears.

trade by emotional condemnation of the practice of trapping. It is my studied observation that the Inuit and their way of life are far more endangered, and receive far less sympathy from the world, than any of the animals they hunt and trap. None of their game creatures are even remotely endangered, except perhaps the Peary caribou.

The name Resolute Bay comes from a British warship (HMS *Resolute*) that was abandoned in 1854, imprisoned in the ice near where the village stands today. It was one of several ships lost by England while searching for the missing Franklin expedition. The ship melted free the next summer and was found floating unmanned in Baffin Bay by whalers sixteen months later. It was purchased by the U.S. government, refurbished at great cost, and presented to England as a gift. When it was

decommissioned and destroyed after twenty-five years of service, some of its main timbers were used to build a gigantic desk, which was then presented as a gift by England to the United States. The "Resolute Desk" has been used in the Oval Office by virtually every American president since Rutherford B. Hayes.

I will always wonder if President Bill Clinton signed the 1994 changes to the Marine Mammal Protection Act on the Resolute Desk, and if he knew the history and implications of the amendments he was putting into law. The people of modern Resolute Bay, and their counterparts all over the Arctic, deserve better than we are giving them under the terms of that act, even as it is currently constituted. Nevertheless, the 1994 amendments were a step in the right direction.

Gray wolf. (Photo: courtesy of James L. Davis)

GRAY WOLF
(Canis lupus)

Alone in my tent that night, tired after my 28-miles' journey,
I sat and listened to the eerie howling of many wolves.
One seldom sees these animals in day time, but at night—
especially in winter when they are hungry—they roam about and come close to camp,
often in bands as many as forty strong.

—Major Neville A.D. Armstrong, *After Big Game in the Upper Yukon*, 1937

Back in 1984 I received in the mail a most interesting flyer from Alaska, offering me the opportunity to hunt the elusive gray wolf of the tundra by ski-equipped light aircraft. The hunt would be conducted in the meager daylight of February and early March, and expected temperatures would be well below zero. The outfitter stated in his brochure that the plan was to pair up the airplanes for safety against freezing to death should something go wrong. If conversely everything went right, we would land and shoot the animals after we had coasted to a stop in the frozen wilderness. Each night we would return to a comfortable base of operations, hoping the sparse twilight of winter would not catch us too far from sanctuary.

Although I never experienced such a hunt, I must confess to a fascination with the concept, partly because I am a pilot and such a demonstration of piloting skills is always beautiful to watch. In addition, the wolf holds a power to absorb one's emotions in a way that every hunter feels. On a gorgeous Yukon night when we had found a crispy fresh wolf track on a Hyland River sandbar, outfitter Terry Wilkinson howled exactly like a wolf, and we received an immediate, close, and spine-tingling answer. More calls were greeted by nothing but silence, and we never saw the animal. Such is the mysterious and elusive wolf. Although I have seen hundreds of fresh wolf tracks in a half-dozen states and provinces, I have actually seen a wolf only twice in some sixty guided hunts in North America.

Taking a wolf from the wild is one of the ultimate accomplishments for most hunters, rivaling the grizzly bear in the stubbornness of the back country to yield its prize. I didn't take up the offer on the flyer, and I have never been wolf hunting, though I aspire someday to do exactly that. Today the use of aircraft in the manner described is illegal in Alaska and elsewhere, so more conventional means such as snowmobiles, watching a bait carcass, and the like are the usual method. I took my wolf incidentally, as perhaps 95 percent of sport harvested wolves are taken, while I was after a grizzly bear.

The wolf is said to have inhabited almost every corner of North America when the white man arrived. In fact, the animal occupied practically all lands north of the tropics in both the Old and the New Worlds. Despite its absence from the Southern Hemisphere, the wolf is said to have been the most widely distributed land mammal prior to civilization.

Genetically, the gray wolf is the same animal wherever it occurs. The distinction between subspecies in various parts of the world is perhaps nowhere more blurred than in the case of the wolf. To complicate matters, there is virtually no difference between the chromosomes of the wolf, the coyote, and the domestic dog of whatever breed. It appears that all the canids of those three types are, in essence, variations of a single genotype that has become distinct with the passage of time.

The male wolf grows to enormous size, much larger than a German shepherd dog, a fact that continually amazes visitors to my trophy room. A large adult male can reach 150 pounds. A big female can weigh in at 120 pounds, although the average for both sexes is considerably less. The wolf has a huge foot, much larger than that of the dog and well adapted to walking long distances over snow in

Gray wolf. Yukon Territory, September 1995.

search of prey. Color variation is practically legendary, with pure white and pure black animals sometimes found in the same pack in North America (in Eurasia there are no purely black wolves). The animals are typically gray or tan with a white underbelly, but there is also a reddish intermediate phase. One color phase may predominate in a particular region. I have seen a taxidermy display of a trophy caribou bull beset by two large wolves, one black and the other a dirty white. Each measured a full eight feet from nose to tail, and they appeared to have had a combined live weight almost equal that of the beleaguered caribou.

Wolves can live up to sixteen years in captivity, although in the wild a wolf of ten years is ancient. Injuries from the flying hoofs and slashing headgear of desperate caribou, moose, and sheep pose a significant mortality factor, and studies have shown that most adult wolves have suffered broken ribs from such encounters. Despite that, the majority of wolf deaths are still caused by humans. Rabies is a major disease of wolves in the Arctic, and possibly is on the increase as the animals recover from historically low numbers. This viral illness can infect any mammal, but canids such as foxes and wolves are especially susceptible, and it appears to be a significant limiting factor in their population growth in some years.

Normally only one female in a pack is bred, no matter how many adult females are present. That runs counter to my considerable experience with domestic dogs, which are in a near-hysterical mass breeding mood at the mere smell of a female in heat. The breeding female of the pack is impregnated by the dominant male in the early spring, when most wolves are in top condition after the feasting of winter. Following a gestation of sixty-three days, the female enters a den to give birth, usually about mid-May. Like dogs, the pups are blind at birth. The dominant pair are responsible for bringing meat to the growing pups; they disgorge food on demand from their full stomachs. As among all predators, reproduction rates decline with lack of prey.

It is a good thing that fundamental factors prevent unchecked multiplication of wolves, because the creatures are capable of reproducing at a phenomenal rate. Internal competition for breeding rights in the pack keeps subordinate animals in check. Wolves that attempt to gain the dominant breeding position and fail are usually driven from the pack, and they may unite with another receptive wolf and form another pack after being pushed out. Such natural dispersion is another aspect of wolf population mechanics, and wolves that are ejected from a pack may travel several hundred miles in search of company.

Wolves have adapted to high natural mortality rates and can lose up to 35 percent of their population before numbers decline the next year. Larger packs may be more affected by a high mortality rate than smaller ones, as long as the breeding pair are not killed, since a single litter will make up for significant losses and may completely replenish a small pack.

The major factor in wolf population dynamics is found in the complex social structure of the wolf pack, which is among the most intricate of the entire animal kingdom. Packs may consist of family members from pups up to age five or six years. An average pack consists of seven to nine wolves, although as many as fifty or more have been observed together; such large accumulations usually occur in the spring, when related wolves may congregate for a short time. Wolves are philopatric, which means that they like to live near where they were born. Thus neighboring packs are usually close kin.

Today the range of the wolf has shrunk drastically northward, so that major concentrations are found only in the circumpolar regions of Canada, Alaska, and Russia. Healthy populations exist farther south in Minnesota and northern Michigan, and the range has expanded as humans have learned to accept wolves as a part of the natural diversity. In addition to the much-discussed reintroduction of wolves into the Yellowstone ecosystem, there is also a natural influx reaching down the Rocky Mountain chain. That is thought to be the most significant change in wolf range in North America since about 1940, when the amount of land appropriated for livestock ranching reached the limits of economic feasibility.

There is no question that coexistence of livestock with a healthy wolf population is problematic, and that conflict has been the main factor in the shrinking wolf range. There are about 12,000 wolves in Alaska, and the Yukon (where I took my wolf) has about 4,500. The total for North America is in the range of 65,000, so the wolf is not endangered as a species, and overall it never has been. Like virtually all predators, though, it is listed under CITES as Appendix II and is on the U.S. Endangered Species List in the Lower Forty-eight, where it is in fact endangered or extinct in most of its historical range.

In the North, a pack may range over several thousand square miles. The winter range is huge but varies with availability of prey. In summer the range of the dominant pair is greatly restricted because of denning activities. Subadults may range widely at this time of year, because territorial defense is more relaxed during the denning period.

Wolves are efficient killers. Each wolf consumes an average of twelve pounds of meat, most of it from ungulates, each day, or the equivalent of fifteen to twenty caribou-size animals per year. In Alaska, wolves take 6 to 7 percent of the caribou each year, and 11 to 14 percent of the moose, where available.

The creatures swallow big chunks of meat with little chewing and may eat much more than the average daily poundage at a single meal. A pack usually stays with a deer or caribou kill only a day or so, or about three days if the animal is a moose. Conversely, they may go without food for long periods, especially in summer, when prey are highly

mobile, traction is good, and young ungulates have become fleet of foot. In good times for the wolves, such as deep winter, there have been reports of multiple kills inflicted on a herd or family group of prey species during a single attack, though that is not the normal pattern. The preferred prey is often caribou, and the kill success on adult caribou is extremely high. Moose are much more likely to escape, by backing into thick brush and slashing at the wolves with the front hoofs, or by entering the water, where their long legs give them the advantage. Studies in the Yukon have shown a definite preference for moose, though, despite their more formidable defensive capabilities.

Northern native peoples have always hunted the wolf for its skin. Certain tribal groups of American Indians hold the wolf in high esteem, and the Athabascan peoples have even divided themselves into two "clans," one being the wolf and the other the raven. With the advent of the modern rifle and the snowmobile, hunting the wolf has obviously become more efficient, but it is still grueling, subzero work.

Since most wolf kills are incidental to a hunt for some other species, I will touch only briefly on the subject of rifles and loads. I killed my wolf with my selected grizzly load, a 200-grain Nosler Partition bullet fired from my .30-06, but most hunters use the rifle they happen to be holding. When I plan a wolf hunt, I will probably

Landing at Hyland Lake in the Yukon for a fall hunting trip.

take a flatter shooting rifle with a lighter bullet, such as my .270 or .243, since a great deal of punch isn't required.

The best times to hunt wolves are the coldest times. Snowmobile excursions and hunts over bait are available in some places and are conducted most often in the dead of winter. Wolves thrive that time of year and may weigh ten pounds more than in summer, because their prey is relatively immobile. Additionally, their coat is in prime condition then, making for a better trophy. Because temperatures in wolf country can drop to well below zero, the very best winter duds are needed, such as one would wear hunting polar bear or on a late-season deer stand in northern Alberta. Pay special attention to the feet, which can get very cold on long snowmobile rides.

On the subject of snowmobile hunting for wolves, a word of caution is in order. You can almost always rely on your outfitter to keep you legal, but be advised that in some places, such as the Yukon, it is unlawful to pursue or harass wolves from snowmobiles.

Judging trophy quality may not be possible, unfortunately, until after the shot. The best trophies are the biggest wolves wearing prime pelts, so if several animals present it's a good bet to shoot at the biggest. That can be tough if the creatures are on a dead run, as is often the case. Wolves can appear about the same size, since pups of the past spring are almost adult size by midwinter. One can often tell the pups by their behavior, however, and by the fact that their pelts look less full. On the other hand, any wolf taken in fair chase is a trophy.

This is one hunt I still have to make. I've killed a wolf, certainly, with the old .30-06, but a hunt dedicated to the task would cover the subject more completely. The wolf is a fascinating animal and is, like the grizzly, one of the symbols of true wilderness. The animal has many friends and perhaps even more enemies, and that dichotomy is part of the mystique that surrounds it.

Someday in the chill of a Yukon winter, or perhaps in Alaska, I hope to be loading a sled for a week in the back country with a top wolf guide. Winter is the most demanding season in which to hunt. It is the season when the tundra and the taiga and the boreal forests belong to *Canis lupus*. I want to be there to experience it.

PHANTOMS OF THE WILDERNESS

We ride silently back into camp with black mountains looming all around, dominating the skyline around Hyland Lake, where our base camp is located. The sun slipped below the western horizon only a short while ago, leaving us bathed in an eerie twilight. The red afterglow reflects, firelike, in the strand of the Hyland River beyond where it empties into the lake, and we can make out the snowcapped pinnacles of stately high ground across the lake. The horses plod steadfastly toward oats and hay and rest, indifferent to the scenery we behold breathlessly.

It has been a long day for my guide, Lowell Davis, and for my wife, Linda, and me. Hours spent glassing have been nearly fruitless, save the sighting of several beautiful moose and caribou. We have seen no grizzly bears, nor even so much as an old track. I am accustomed to it, however, this being my sixth grizzly hunt. Still, there is immense joy in the splendor of the Yukon, where the quiet, the clean water, stunning vistas in all directions, and the impenetrable wilderness produce an experience beyond compare. It is mainly hunters who are privileged to appreciate this place, because for the most part only hunters will go to the trouble and expense to get this far from the rest of mankind.

This is a fall hunt for grizzly, and the main method of hunting is to check the recently felled carcasses of both moose and caribou. Other hunters have already come and gone, and the remains of their kills have been stripped of all meat fit for human consumption, leaving us with legal bait for a bear. I had planned to take a moose for the freezer, too, if I could find one in the right place early in the hunt. I have already seen numerous moose, but none have been appropriate. It is almost too late in the hunt now to take an incidental moose, so I will probably pass now on any that present.

One particular pile of leftovers from a previous hunt provides me with the most likely location to encounter a bear. High in a wooded basin above our camp are the remains of a huge moose, and the whole scene can be viewed a half-mile distant from the trail. We will dutifully ascend the steep incline again tomorrow and do what we have already done twice, checking that stinking,

Another in a series of gorgeous Yukon sunsets.

reeking residuum for a bruin. This is a strange practice, but in the fall it is the only type of grizzly hunting with any realistic chance of success. Wandering around hoping to bump into a bear in this thick country is impossible, absent pure dumb luck, a little of which I have often yearned for while hunting grizzly. I feel compelled to tell you that despite these feelings I don't believe a whit in the concept of luck, since I am certain that all details are controlled by an omnipotent God.

Our evenings have been spent in the company of two other hunters and their guides, but this morning they left on a journey to a remote location known as South Camp to search for moose. This quiet evening is yet another special experience, with the happy glow of the cabin stove chasing away the nighttime chill and the rustic table set with sumptuous backwoods fare, all of it illuminated by a pair of flaming candles. Often the meal has consisted of fresh Arctic grayling direct from the lake at our front door. That wonderful fish has virtually no fishy odor and tastes like the finest any restaurant could offer. Tonight the three of us constitute the whole camp, and the food is different. I savor the aroma of sizzling caribou steaks and frying onions as I recline against a pile of gear in the corner.

Don Wilkinson, brother of outfitter Terry Wilkinson and the boss of this part of the territory

of Caesar Lake Outfitters, worried aloud last night that our prime moose carcass might be history. He discovered the tracks of a big pack of wolves coursing the muddy horse trail that ascends the ravine. A bear takes several days to consume such a bounty, but a hungry pack of wolves can accomplish the task in a few hours. I contemplate Don's words as we eat, and I voice my apprehension to Lowell.

"Don't be too concerned. We've got other carcasses. Anyhow, you just might get a chance at the rarest of trophies. Not many people ever get to see a wolf. If they're on our carcass, or even still in the area, we might get to throw some lead at them."

In scores of hunts in the back country of the far north, I have seen only one wolf, and that was a scraggly, mangy critter in northern British Columbia a few years ago. The varmint had been on a moose carcass, but I had not purchased a tag and couldn't take it, much to the consternation of my guide. We had managed to get within forty or fifty yards of it, though, and I got some great pictures. I had previously believed that wolves were so wary and wily that one could never perform a successful stalk on them. That episode had demonstrated beyond doubt that my impression had been wrong. If they get on my moose carcass, I will most certainly try to get a shot at one, since Yukon law allows one to take a wolf and purchase the tag after the fact. Besides, how dare the cagey canines eat up my best, perhaps my only, chance at a grizzly?

Linda and I are in a comfortable tent near the cabin, and I step into the night to start a fire in our shepherd's stove. A million stars wink overhead, and the thick wedge of white known as the Milky Way stands out clearly like a gigantic arch. The northern lights are running wild along the horizon, making crazy zigzag patterns and waving at me with ghostly fingers. I think about wolves again, realizing that in this setting I can realistically expect to hear their plaintive howls, calling a mate or seeking their kind. I hesitate briefly and catch the long downward arc of a meteor entering earth's atmosphere and burning out in a brilliant flash of glory. No wolf howls, but I am awed by the strangeness and the beauty, the wildness and the unpredictability of the back country.

We awake to the usual bells, those the horses wear to make them more retrievable after their night of foraging. Lowell always comes shortly thereafter to rekindle the fire in our stove, so we can arise in luxurious warmth. Today we plan to check that moose carcass again, and maybe, just maybe, we'll catch a ravenous monster bear. After eating, gathering our gear, and preparing the horses, we depart for the now-familiar valley. True to Don's word, the trail is littered with fresh wolf tracks of all sizes, tracks that are in the prints made by Don's horses, so the wolves were not simply passing through. It takes almost two hours to get to our ridge, a high rampart that faces the distant blue horizon that is in the Northwest Territories, the rambling, serrated border of which we must avoid to stay hunting legally.

All our days are much the same, fortunately or unfortunately, depending on your perspective. Bright sunshine, cloudless skies, and warm temperatures in late September are unusual in the Yukon. This is great weather for glassing and sunning, ideal for comfortable napping, and perfect for reading a book or having a picnic. For hunting grizzly, though, it's a disaster. All those heavily furred creatures remain inactive until almost dark. As we make our way back to camp, we witness another spectacular sunset fashioned by the infinite hand of the Almighty, and I wish for less beautiful weather—a most unusual wish, it must be admitted.

It is time for more fish for supper, so I arise early and make my way to the "fishing rock" a quarter-mile from camp. The grayling are as cooperative as ever, and I retrieve enough for another fine supper of boneless fillets. After I clean my catch, I enjoy another of Lowell's now-famous breakfasts and then assist Linda with tidying up while our young guide prepares the horses. Lowell and I will go back to the head of Hyland Lake today to check an overripe caribou carcass. Linda takes a day off to enjoy the splendid weather and read another book. There are no wolf tracks in this direction, but near dark we encounter a huge bull moose on a river sandbar, exactly where I had longed to see such a creature early in the hunt. It is fun to simply stalk as close as possible and take pictures. The snapping shutter puts the bull on alert, and he spooks back up the river toward the safety of more remote terrain.

After another night's rest it is back to our valley moose carcass. Linda has had enough of tarrying alone at the cabin and accompanies us today. The temperature soars so high it feels almost like summertime in Georgia, giving rise to the faint hope that a bear might be able to smell our pungent baits for many miles. On the downside, the thought occurs that a heavily clad bear would be very reluctant to move more than a few yards in such heat. Whatever the case, there is no bear, but once again the trail is littered with fresh wolf tracks.

We enjoy another long, gorgeous day perched on our glassing ridge. Lowell, a reverent young man in his early twenties, points out that his formula is four hours of glassing for every hour of horseback travel, one we are holding to pretty well. I begin Peretti's novel *The Oath*, a book that both Linda and Lowell have finished earlier in the hunt. As the shadow of the opposite mountain lengthens and the evening approaches, I reach a most exciting portion of my reading; I have just about quit glassing. No matter, the other two are doing plenty.

It comes as suddenly and unexpectedly as a summer storm, and elicits an accompanying chill that courses through my backbone. It starts with a low moan, and increases to fill the valley below with an incredible howl. A wolf! We all look at each other in amazement. I forget the book and start searching the facing mountainside. Why is that darn wolf howling like that in broad daylight? Three more times as we search, the creature lets loose with its mournful cry.

"I've got it!" I cry softly. There, on a small, willow-covered hillock across from us, a ghostlike form sits with nose pointed skyward. It lowers its head and begins drifting silently, like a spirit, among the willows and balsam trees. I keep my binoculars on it while I direct the others to the place. As they prepare for a hasty departure, I monitor the creature, which rapidly begins a smooth, gradual descent to the valley floor. We will have to hurry to have any chance of intercepting the animal. We mount up and take off after the wolf, which is wandering in the direction of our camp.

Fresh, feisty grayling for breakfast, caught right from camp.

It is a wild ride, punctuated only by a couple of pauses to check the progress of the wolf. If the animal keeps moving, I might get a long shot at it just above our moose carcass. If it disappears when we aren't able to mark the spot, all might be lost, since we would have no option but to wait and watch, hoping against hope that it reappears. The horses carry us to a spot just above a small lake, perhaps a half-mile from where we last saw the creature. We can't help but wonder about the unusual daytime activity, especially in such warm weather, and why the wolf is alone.

All eyes comb the marshy areas and brushy hillsides around the still water. There it is! In the middle of a small meadow, exactly where we had seen it last, the animal has found something to hold its attention. It is standing, then lying down, then standing again. The open terrain appears to make a close approach difficult. I hold the supposition to myself only briefly before whispering the thought aloud to Lowell, who just shrugs.

"Get your stuff. Leave your pack, and Linda; you stay here and keep tabs on the wolf. If it moves, try to keep track of it," he orders as he secures the horses to several lanky willows. With Linda perched to watch the action, we set out down a draw toward our objective, running because we don't know how long the animal will stay in that spot. We will be out of sight and unable to tell. Of course Linda will know, but she has no way of communicating with us.

I had been getting thirsty for some time before the wolf howled, but being engrossed in my reading I had neglected to drink. My tongue is now cleaving to the roof of my mouth, either from dehydration or excitement, probably both. We move quickly toward the small open meadow, which we are able to see only intermittently because of groves of intervening balsam trees. As we get closer, I try to convince Lowell to let me set up in one of those groves for a long shot, but he steadfastly refuses. The first one is at least four hundred yards from the animal, and the last a mere two hundred. I much prefer a longer shot from a rest at a standing target, rather than a shorter shot at spooked game from an offhand position. I almost plead with Lowell to set up in the final place I can get a decent rest.

"Nah, it doesn't get fun until you're under fifty yards," he retorts softly with a grin. "We'll get you closer, then it gets interesting."

Despite his calmness, I don't like the sound of it. Wolves are crafty, and down deep I am sure we will be forced into an inconclusive running shot. I back the scope off to 2X, check and recheck the rifle, and inform Lowell that I have chambered a round as we near the edge of the last willow cover. I am extremely thankful for the cool breeze quartering from our left, carrying our ample scent well away from the wolf. With only fifty yards to go to the naked meadow, we can't even be sure the canine hasn't already departed. I briefly wonder if Linda is sitting on the high ground, chuckling as we conduct a full stalk on an empty meadow.

Now it is a military-style belly crawl to get into final position. The field is really an extension of the lake just below and is as marshy as can be. I feel like I am crawling in ice water, which is exactly what I am doing. The cold liquid quickly soaks to the skin, chilling me with a suddenness that is a resounding shock, to say the least. Finally we reach the end of the willows, and there is nothing but grass between us and where we last saw the wolf, a hundred yards out in the meadow.

"Get out in front of that willow and shoot from a sitting position," Lowell commands gently, and I extend my crawl a short distance past him in compliance. Now it is time for my rear end to feel the icy fingers of the alpine swamp. I sight in on a lone willow in the center of the meadow where I think the animal is, and I wait. Is the wolf still there? How can we get it to stand, if it is? Can I hit it from this unaccustomed shooting position? Questions pop in and out of my head like bees to a hive, perhaps all to be answered in just a few seconds.

Eeeeeeeeeeeee! Eeeeee! Eeeeee! comes the sound from Lowell's lips, mimicking a dying snowshoe hare, a frequent prey species for the wolf. The wolf stands up immediately at the sound, already centered in my waiting riflescope, fiery eyes looking right at us. I softly and with unexpected confidence squeeze the trigger.

The explosion of the cartridge is followed immediately by the resounding thump of the bullet, and the creature disappears from sight as quickly as it appeared. No matter, I know instinctively, I have won this round. I have come to recognize the feel and sound of a good shot. I have my wolf.

I can't believe all that has happened. We whoop and shout and wave to Linda in jubilation as we approach the fallen animal. For the moment, I even forget the cold and damp. We have triumphed in convincing fashion, and against odds that had seemed impossible only a few minutes before. I drop to my wet knees and thank God for the success.

The big wolf is a female measuring over six and a half feet. We cautiously watch her last dying twitches and note that the bullet has hardly damaged the coat. I comment that the 200-grain Nosler Partition bullet, custom loaded for my Remington 700 .30-06 and intended to take a much larger animal, probably has gone on through without expanding, accounting for the lack of blood. We confirm this as we skin the animal.

While Lowell retrieves Linda, the horses, and the rest of our gear, I note the object of the wolf's interest in this particular patch of real estate. She had cached a caribou leg, apparently that of a healthy calf by its size, and was enjoying a meal.

A joyful picture session follows, and then the skinning chores. Darkness is fast upon us as we thread our way back to the horse trail and begin our long, treacherous descent to camp. The return trip is once more illuminated by the aurora borealis, and I have to bundle up to keep from freezing, the chill of my wet clothing having returned to haunt me. I can't even walk to keep warm, since the dark trail has many unpredictable obstacles that only the horses can see in the low light. Nevertheless, it is a happy ride because of the sweet taste of success.

Taking a wolf is not easily planned. But when the opportunity presents, it helps to be ready and to have a good advisor and companion like Lowell. I am blessed to have had these, and as a result I now have a beautiful wolf. The experience is one I'm unlikely to be privileged to repeat. It is as unique as the trophy it produced, and I've filed it away in my lifetime of unforgettable memories.

Walrus. (Photo: from the author's collection)

WALRUS
(Odobenus rosmarus)

When he got there he starts to listen....
It was a clear evening with no winds....
The walrus were making sound far out on the water...
the sound of bellowing,
he saw then there were plenty of walrus.

—Noah Piugaattuk, Inuk elder, Igloolik, Northwest Territories, circa 1900

The walrus is a vocal animal, capable of a wide variety of sounds. Their sounds have been described as sounding like chimes of different types, outright whistles, and intimidating bellows. Undoubtedly each has its meaning in walrus social circles. The Inuit have been aware of walrus noises for many centuries, taking advantage of the quiet of the Arctic to locate this important source of food and materials.

Recent scientific studies have revealed interesting facts about the language of the walrus, much of which takes place underwater. Some 80 percent of the sounds are specific to the individual animal, and studies are now ongoing to try to find out what the singing means. Underwater the mature male walrus at times emits a virtually continuous song that can go on for many hours.

Two types of walrus inhabit the offshore waters and rocky coastal edges of North America: the Atlantic (*Odobenus rosmarus rosmarus*) and Pacific (*Odobenus rosmarus divergens*) walrus. The Atlantic variety is available to the sport hunter in several locations in Canada, principally in Foxe Basin and the northern part of Hudson Bay. A sport hunt for these animals was made available for the first time at Igloolik in 1996, at which time I became the first non-Canadian to participate. The Pacific walrus is also available to sport hunters in Siberia. The native peoples of Alaska hunt it with regularity, but at this time there is no nonnative hunt for that subspecies in North America.

From neither Canada nor Siberia can the animal or any part of it be imported into the United States, the Marine Mammal Protection Act standing solidly in the way. That makes hunting walrus unattractive to most hunters. For me, the experience alone was adequate repayment for the costs I incurred, which were considerable. I simply had a fiberglass replica of my Atlantic walrus made for my trophy room by taxidermist Joe Martin of Hamilton, Ontario, and I donated the shoulder mount he did of my walrus to the visitor's center in Iqaluit, where the awesome creature is on permanent public display.

Of all the animals considered part of the classic North American big-game collection, the walrus is probably the ugly stepchild. It is the only true marine mammal on the list, the polar bear's status under our U.S. law notwithstanding. It is the only one that has ivory as a major part of the trophy (though certain cervids, such as the elk, have a form of ivory in one pair of teeth). It is unquestionably the least studied and the least understood animal considered to be big game, probably because its aquatic Arctic environment, subsurface lifestyle, and body morphology make it hard to count or track and difficult to mark and recapture. It is the only big-game animal outweighed by another animal of the same general type (the elephant seal), but despite that the other animal isn't considered big game. The walrus is the largest of the classic North American big game by far, outweighing the heaviest purely land animal—the bison—almost by twice.

The genus name *Odobenus* means "those that walk with their teeth." Apparently someone observed a walrus using its tusks to hoist itself upon an ice floe or onto land and applied the term. While these giants do use the impressive ivory instruments in this fashion, that is not their primary purpose, which is probably dominance displays and fighting. They will not hesitate to use them, however, for more utilitarian tasks such as hacking away ice that has trapped their calf or moving along the bottom while feeding. The tusks are not used to dig for food on the bottom, though, as one might suppose.

Researchers have recently found a valuable research approach using large males. A satellite telemetry apparatus can be attached to one tusk to track the animal's wanderings. Though not as long lasting as telemetry devices fitted on land animals, the method has yielded valuable and reliable information on walrus movements for the first time. Invariably the cold and the corrosive effects of salt water ruin the device after a year or so, and it eventually falls off.

The tusks of the Pacific walrus are far more massive and curved than those of the Atlantic variety, but on average the body size of the latter may be slightly larger, especially in Foxe Basin where I hunted. A big male Pacific walrus may have tusks that are more than three feet long and weigh as much as twelve pounds each, while those of the Atlantic walrus never approach such dimensions. Body size of a mature male of either subspecies may reach 4,000 pounds and twelve feet in length, while an adult female may weigh 2,000 pounds and be nine feet in length. Up to one-third of total body weight is blubber, a fact that regrettably made the animals a fine substitute for whales when that population became depleted by whalers in search of high-quality oil.

These remarkable animals spend their entire lives in water that is freezing or below, and even when they haul out onto ice floes or land they tolerate brutal winds and frigid air temperatures. In winter they frequent the open-water areas (polynya) in the otherwise frozen seas of the north, or they may maintain a breathing hole in fast ice, never emerging on the surface. The fat content of their bodies is extraordinary in itself, since they subsist on a clam diet that is virtually fat-free and thus low in energy.

The Pacific walrus ranges back and forth between the Bering and Chukchi Seas, most of them wintering southward as ice forms. Both these bodies of water are shallow and offer fine feeding on bottom dwellers for the walrus. During summer in the Chukchi Sea, most of them stay on the Russian side. There are believed to be an incredible 250,000 walrus in that ecosystem. From that vast population only fifty to sixty were removed by sport hunters per year until passage of the Marine Mammal Protection Act. Had hunters realized the permanence of the legislation and the near impossibility of any alteration, we perhaps would have been more aggressive in defending our interests. Had we in place today's pro-hunting element in Washington, we could have sought and perhaps been granted an exemption for sport-hunting trophies. Had only the Congressional Sportsmen's Caucus, Safari Club International, the Wildlife Legislative Fund of America, Wildlife Forever, and other advocacy groups been in existence, perhaps this could have been accomplished. Little did we know.

The Atlantic walrus is much less migratory and much less numerous, and its range is significantly smaller than in the past. The creatures were once recorded as far south as New York, but overexploitation by commercial interests depleted them everywhere except the most inaccessible areas. Today they are still found in all the Canadian eastern Arctic, where most populations seem stable or increasing. Highest numbers are in Foxe Basin, where as many as 5,500 may live. They are present in waters around Greenland, but unlimited take by native subsistence hunters has their Baffin Bay population in a state of perpetual decline. The east coast of Greenland is thought to have a stable or increasing number of walrus. Svalbard and Franz Josef Land have sizable and mostly unhunted populations that are slowly recovering from commercial overharvest.

Walrus eat mostly bottom-dwelling invertebrates, typically clams. They may consume up to 3,000 clams in a single day, sucking them up with their vacuum cleaner mouths. A walrus mouth is constructed to do the job, having a high roof, thick lips and lateral walls, and a tongue made like a sledgehammer to provide the needed suction. They ingest mainly the siphons and feet of clams, those parts that protrude from the ocean floor, though they may in the process also take in bits of shell and rock, which are excreted. They also eat snails, crabs, worms, shrimp, fish, and occasionally a walrus develops a taste for seals. Such a rogue is usually a big bull that has learned to capture the smaller pinnipeds, and often these bulls can be distinguished by their darkly stained tusks, the effect of blood and fat. Such an animal would have a higher level of environmental contaminants, since walrus normally leave out many intermediate prey species with their usual diet.

Walrus can have up to a hundred pounds of food in their stomach at once, a huge amount that is paradoxically considered a small meal relative to their body size. They usually feed in water less than three hundred feet deep, severely limiting their ability to subsist in deep ocean. It is not known how deep they can dive, but the deepest a monitored animal has ever gone is just over four hundred feet.

The body of a walrus resembles that of a seal but is far blockier and, out of the water at least, much less streamlined. The flexible back flippers can rotate forward for locomotion both in water and on land. The neck is massively thick, and the muzzle is broad and adorned with heavy, light-colored bristles. Their skin looks loose and wrinkled around the flippers when they are out of the water, though it flattens when the animals are stretched out swimming. Skin color is white while a walrus is swimming, but due to dilation of surface blood vessels they may become pink or light tan while exposed to the air. The skin is the thickest of any North American big-game animal, and it gets more so with age. Around the neck of a mature bull it may be fully two and a half inches thick. The hide there may have prominent coarse tubercles in adult males, a secondary male sexual characteristic like a hairy chest in men. Walrus have scant reddish brown hair when born, but

Walrus. Northwest Territories, August 1996.

older animals, particularly males, lose most of it. Older males tend to be lighter in color.

Cows are bred for the first time at age six or seven, and probably every third year thereafter, though some may conceive every two years. Vicious and sometimes deadly battles may occur between males for breeding rights, but that is uncommon. More often the cows are tended by a breeding bull for five to six days, then the bull moves off peacefully and another joins the herd. Inactive breeding bulls and younger nondominant bulls stay on the periphery, away from the main herd. Mating is in February or March in most areas. After successful breeding, there is a delay in implantation, or "embryonic diapause," similar to that in bears, until about June. Calves are born almost a year later, either in May or June, making the gestation thirteen to fourteen months from impregnation to birth, though the fetus is actually in process of growing less than a year.

Births are almost always a single calf. At birth the youngsters weigh between 85 and 140 pounds. Male and female calves weigh about the same at birth, but recent studies have shown that the males grow faster, and for a longer time as well. There is a strong immediate bond between mother and calf that is somewhat exceptional in the animal world, and the two stay together for at least two and often three years before the youngster becomes independent. Recent studies have preliminarily shown that calves of ages up to three years may still nurse substantially, though the older the calf the more bottom creatures it tends to eat in a natural progression toward autonomy.

Walrus may live up to forty years, though it is difficult to be certain in the wild. Studies of dental annuli (teeth rings) become unreliable due to wear of the outer layers in walrus that have stopped growing, which occurs at nine to ten years in females and fifteen to twenty years in males. But the fact that they live considerably longer than that is well known, and forty seems a good bet. That makes them not only the largest North American big-game animal, and the strangest, but also the longest-living mammal. Only the American alligator, a reptile, is a big-game species that can claim greater longevity.

Walrus hunting is done only when the wind is perfectly calm, mainly for safety among the heaving ice floes but also for ease of detecting and approaching the creatures. In the early days it was the most hazardous of occupations for the Inuit hunters equipped only with spears tipped with whalebone, ringed seal-skin floats, ropes made from bearded seal skin, and exceedingly brave hearts as they skipped among moving ice floes to

Leaving summer camping site near Igloolik, heading for a walrus hunt.

Herd of walrus backlit by the Arctic twilight.

find and capture their prey. Today the task is accomplished much more safely with modern power boats and high-powered rifles. Still, a day with stiff wind and lurching icebergs on the open water can sink the participants to an icy grave. I wore a flotation survival suit on my hunt, an indispensable unit supplied on most sport walrus hunts for a small fee. Even my Inuit guides wore similar suits, a tribute to both the danger of the hunt and the safety margin provided by technology, something to which the native hunters have always been quick to adapt.

Approaching a walrus is usually not difficult, since they are normally not intimidated by man. Rather, they are likely to try to dissuade you, using bellows and displays of aggressiveness. Some of the walrus we approached slipped quietly into the water, but more frequently they refused to budge. The hardest task is selecting a big bull, which should be light in color and large of body and tusk. The problem is that unless another bull is close at hand for comparison, it may be difficult to judge size. All sport hunts are guided by experienced Inuit guides, though, and these accomplished hunters possess the uncanny ability to determine accurately which bull is the oldest and most mature. Tell them your expectations and trust their judgment.

No special equipment is required for the hunter who uses a flotation survival suit. You can hunt in your coat and tie and Gucci shoes with this arrangement over it. I highly recommend the suit I wore, made by Mustang Survival of British Columbia. It is a blaze orange miracle that shut out the cold wind like the best parka and would keep you warm and floating for much longer than anything else available. I am only glad that wind and water conditions did not force me to test it.

Honestly, I'd leave the Guccis at home, though. I wore my rubber boots over sock liners and woollies. The boots are the same LaCrosse sixteen-inch-high ones I use all over Canada in the fall and spring. They are mighty handy when the deck is slick from walrus fat and blood, or when standing or climbing on an ice floe that demands good traction.

For armament, I fired my maximum .30-06 load to dispatch my walrus, a 200-grain Nosler Partition bullet propelled to top velocity by 59 grains of IMR 4350 powder. If I had not pulled the shot slightly low, the creature would have died without ever knowing I had fired. As it was, I was an inch or so off and had to fire a second time. There is no excuse for failing to make a one-shot kill on a walrus, except for the rocking of the boat and the movement of the animal. I claim both.

You must forget the implications of not having the incredible skin-ivory trophy in your home if you are to experience the infinite richness of a walrus hunt. The sight of gigantic bodies, looking almost black against the stark white of shifting sea ice, causes a shudder to course the spine and gives one a sense of kinship with the Inuit of old. The cold air and the quiet easily transmit the cacophony of distant walrus sounds. The human hunter as a predator faces a daunting task, mere steel and lead looking pitifully impotent against the might of a big bull walrus. We may never defeat the protectionist forces that keep the desirability of the hunt and the value of the walrus resource so low. I recommend it anyway. It's a matchless adventure.

As one Web site puts it, the *aivik* is a paradoxical animal, one that is "relaxed yet irksome, graceful yet clumsy, gentle yet ferocious." Just to be out there with them makes the experience well worth it.

A HISTORIC FIRST IN IGLOOLIK

Even as we coast to a stop at the terminal building in this remote village, the stark landscape reminds me that I am back in the Arctic. The faint green of late summer on the tundra is the only vegetation, and endless gray gravel is painted with occasional swirls of residual snow as far as the eye can see. I marvel all over again how people and animals can survive in a habitat so severe and unforgiving. The ancient FirstAir twin turbine disgorges us at the terminal building, and I am here on this most unique quest.

As I step from the plane, I sense the chill in the air. I have just spent time in Iqaluit, new capital of the Inuit entity of Nunavut, and I am somewhat acclimatized already. The difference between south Baffin Island and the geographical Arctic is only a matter of a few hundred miles, but here there are ice floes all over the sea and the air is many degrees cooler.

Igloolik means "place of more than one house," indicating that the native people have found this small island attractive since long before contact with the white man. One reason is the nearby availability of the king of North America's pinnipeds, the Atlantic walrus, a mainstay of Inuit diet and a source of natural materials. Not too far away, too, are abundant caribou on the mainland and on Baffin Island, as well as some of the most prolific runs of Arctic char in the entire world. Small wonder this giant gravel bar has been host to the Inuit for millennia.

Brad Parker of the Northwest Territories Department of Renewable Resources meets me in the terminal building and arranges transportation to the ice-choked waterfront in town. He will use his own boat to transport me to camp, some seven miles east of the hamlet of Igloolik. While Brad is the wildlife officer and would ordinarily have no hands-on involvement in native hunting enterprises, the Inuit of the local Hunter-Trapper Association are new to sport hunting and need some guidance.

Brad assumes an uncommon amount of responsibility for my hunt, which is the first organized walrus sport hunt for a foreigner. Whereas on most hunts the renewable resources officer sells you your license, gives you verbal and written information, and bids you good luck, this time Brad is much more. He is not only my transportation but he and his wife, Tam, are also my hosts, my cooks, and my primary contacts. In the future he hopes that the guides of the HTA will take over such duties, but the initial hunt is important enough that he wants to maintain a close presence to ensure that I am well treated and that the experience is positive for all concerned. I am deeply grateful for the depth of commitment he and his family are devoting to the project.

Also there to greet me is Mr. Kim Seto, senior officer representing the Canadian Department of Fisheries and Oceans in Nunavut. His presence is another indication of the historic nature of this hunt. I discuss with him the overall situation related to walrus hunting, and he is optimistic that beneficial arrangements are in process. Many communities are establishing, by means of voluntary actions of the local HTAs, the essential quota system that will ensure that the resource is used in a sustainable fashion. Igloolik is only one of several communities in various stages of starting a sport hunt, and the Department of Fisheries and Oceans is involved in fielding and taking action on all such requests.

Canada North Outfitting, whose owner, Jerome Knap, was instrumental in arranging this hunt, has provided a high-tech marvel for me to wear on this expedition. Before I board Brad's craft I am required to don a survival suit designed to prolong consciousness in the event one falls into the icy and treacherous sea. I read the accompanying flyer with great interest, noting especially the section that graphs expected survival time in the water for various temperatures and body sizes. I am skinny and fairly small, so I would last less than two hours suited. Absent the flotation suit, it's a matter of minutes. The lapel features a prominent monogram declaring "Nunavut Tourism," making me look more like a whale watcher than a hunter. The orange color and the smart cut of the synthetic fabric impart a feel that is ostentatious, perhaps even feisty.

Camp is on a point of land some distance nearer the walrus floes than is the hamlet of Igloolik. Many Inuit families move out onto the beach in summer, not only for the renewed feel of the land that such camping conveys but also to place themselves nearer the good seal and walrus hunting. I tour the string of dwellings and meet some of the interesting inhabitants, many of whom speak not a word of my language, nor I any appreciable amount of theirs. Nevertheless, we communicate crudely with hand gestures and smiles and pats on the back. The Inuit penchant for friendliness has been their hallmark since whalers and explorers first penetrated their forbidding land. They are most intrigued as to why a white man would venture here for the sole reason of hunting their walrus. Curiosity aside, all seem to grasp the potential value of my presence, and that of future hunters, to their community. I am a

fellow hunter, and on that basis I am freely and warmly accepted.

Walking the endless gravel bar behind my seaside tent, I am struck once more by the vastness and the utter endlessness of the Arctic. The first white men in this area sailed past where we will hunt walrus, proceeded by Igloolik, and entered Foxe Basin to our north. The quest for the Northwest Passage in this area was thwarted by the eternal ice of Fury and Hecla Strait, a shallow passage that seldom thaws in summer and is guarded at the eastern end by obstructive Amerson Island. Near here it was eventually realized that a passage to the west would have to be sought elsewhere.

This sandy point on which my comfortable tent and several others are situated has been inhabited seasonally for thousands of years. I stroll inland for a short distance to explore, noting that the gravel here has been colored red, perhaps by a species of algae. Picking up a piece of rock, my inspection reveals that the coating rubs off. Peculiar, but not unexpected in the Arctic. I walk onward to the second natural berm beyond a small

Elderly Inuk recalls many walrus hunts from the old days—but I need a translation from his native Inuktitut.

Spectacular Arctic sunset.

lake, where the Inuit have several dog teams staked so they can water at their leisure.

Old campsites abound, and strewn about the ground is an astounding quantity of dry walrus bones, some perhaps hundreds of years old, and most coated with the same red algae. Sprouting among the bones and the old rings of rock that constitute ancient tent sites, purple saxifrage and Arctic poppies bloom in abundance. The tundra is more alive than I have ever seen it, though one must look closely to appreciate the variety of flowering plants that flourish here. The Arctic is host to more than two hundred species of flowers, and I find several dozen on this single, gravel-strewn spur.

Walrus hunting is done nowadays with modern weapons and boats, and the danger is relatively minimal. There is a bit of apprehension about the field of ice we will be required to motor through on our journey south, but it can't be anything like the terror that must have accompanied such treks when men used skin boats, harpoons tipped with bone and ivory, and raw courage to take the *aivik,* as the walrus is called in Inuktitut. Perhaps even more hazardous than hunting them from kayaks were the late-spring treks on foot over moving ice, harpooning them after pretending to be basking walruses, crawling slowly to within range, then battling a 4,000-pound titan on a sealskin cord until it was dead. Such hunts were carried out by groups of several Inuit, and the work had just begun when the animal was

killed. Hauling it onto a moving ice floe and butchering it without becoming fatally dipped in the freezing water was challenging, to say the least. Moving the giant creatures back to land was accomplished by first shaping the large blocks of meat and allowing them to freeze, then skidding them by manpower to camp over miles of incredible ice jumbles and melting floes. Many an Inuk never returned from such a hunt, and today we can scarcely imagine the difficulty and danger.

Even in the modern era the Inuit bury their walrus meat for several months to allow it to cure or ferment (I hesitate to say rot, but that's essentially what it does). Several large mounds are near my tent, heaps of gravel hiding a cache of gestating walrus meat. They eat it fresh as well, but they strongly prefer that it stay in the ground for at least five or six months. We age our beef and ferment our wine, so who are we to criticize the ways of the Inuit?

My guides will be middle-aged Cain Iqaqsaq and his twenty-year-old son Kailapi. Both are among the most experienced walrus hunters in the world, especially the older man. Cain speaks no English, and all my communication with him is through his bilingual son. Both men are excited to be the guides on this inaugural sport hunt, and perhaps earn a small place in Inuit history by so doing.

Since neither of my hosts has ever guided a sport hunter, I spend a good deal of time in conversation with them about what I want to accomplish. I explain to them that the head and shoulders, as well as the tusks, will be donated as a mounted specimen to the Nunavut Visitor's Center, a repository of Inuit culture in Iqaluit. I want to take a very mature bull walrus for that reason, though the experience of the hunt is by far the most important aspect to me.

The wind howls like a tempest across the unobstructed barrens in these parts, and the Inuit know that one never tempts the freezing sea in such conditions, not even with modern boats. All walrus hunting is done in the glassy calm, and we are prepared to wait for such conditions, no matter how long it takes.

I have soon exhausted all the local attractions and talked with everyone willing to converse, as well as having taken pictures of every Inuk who will hold still. Waiting now in my tent, the merry kerosene heater blazing, I get caught up on some reading. Perhaps tomorrow the wind will cease. I soon drift off to sleep.

The insistent flapping of the tent walls awakens me and tells me we are not going anywhere today, either. The offshore ice is heaving and bucking, and whitecaps froth angrily in all directions as I emerge for a look. The icy wind stabs me before I can retreat to don my parka. I spend the morning watching and photographing glaucus gulls and Arctic terns along the small lake behind camp, hoping the wind will die. The days are almost continuous in August here in the Arctic, and a prolonged twilight lasts until the next day dawns. We can leave whenever conditions will allow.

About 3 P.M. I am engrossed in a monograph from the U.S. Fish and Wildlife Service proposing cooperative polar bear conservation between the United States and Russia. Brad Parker interrupts my reading by hailing me through the tent door. The wind is dying, and I should prepare for a possible hunt if conditions continue to improve. My gear is already waiting in logical and organized fashion, so it will not take me long to comply. It might be days before another opportunity presents, so I am all set in a few minutes. When all is ready, I resume reading. Before a half-hour passes, Brad returns with a thumbs-up. Here we go!

My rifle is stowed safely in a padded case underneath the sheltered foredeck area of Cain's boat. After enrobing myself in the vivid survival suit, I join a host of others who will accompany me on this adventure. Brad will bring along his assistant, Adam, and a freelance photographer from Yellowknife named Paul Micklen. Kim Seto will ride in a separate boat with the head of the local Hunter-Trapper Association. Our boat will lead the way, and when we spot walrus we will leave the others a mile or so behind so we don't crowd the animals. The mosquitoes are terrible on the beach as we await final word to depart, attacking us with a determined vengeance now that the wind has subsided. I raise the hood of my survival suit to fend off this new menace.

Examining the essential gear for walrus hunting, I note the traditional rope made from long strips of bearded sealskin, the toughest rope-making material available to the Inuit in the past and still the preferred material for securing a float to a walrus with a harpoon. The shaft of each harpoon is stiff steel about a half-inch in diameter, and the tip is as sharp as a scalpel. For safety, the lethal point is detached from the shaft when not in use, but remains tied to it with a thong of sealskin. When the points are attached to the lance, the sharply honed edges gleam like the teeth of some deadly predator. From the spike attachment a length of sealskin rope secures the arrangement to a bright orange float. In millennia past the whole skin of a ringed seal was inflated and used as the float, but the Inuit have quickly adapted to high-tech ways, though they cling charmingly to certain things, such as the sealskin fetter that is used by everyone in preference to modern ropes. None of this arrangement will be used on my hunt until the animal has been dispatched with my rifle; the float is then attached to prevent losing the prize.

Motors fire up, and we push off from camp. The extraordinarily clear air is almost balmy now that the wind has died, and I am tremendously comfortable in my blaze orange uniform. Sunlight dances like millions of stars on the water and floating ice, and I retrieve my sunglasses, mindful of the need to protect my eyes. To our west lies the mainland of Melville Peninsula, but much sea ice separates us from that barren shore.

As we move out, what appears to be a solid sheet of offshore white turns out to be a shifting, broken zone of melting ice pack, some of it with the characteristic blue color of multiyear or glacial ice. All of it is seriously undercut by the restless sea, with the extensive submerged part of each individual berg showing in the calm water well beneath the surface. In each case a thin and treacherous shelf extends several feet away from the main body. I can only imagine how easy it would be to take a bath in the ocean if one walked about carelessly on such a place. Each chunk of ice is finely sculpted, the water, the wind, and the waves producing a unique marvel of architecture, a process that continues even as we watch. Some portions of each berg are solid and secure in appearance, but slush marks the softer areas, with the occasional precarious floe capsizing as we pass. We are cruising through a sweep of awesome ice carvings.

Maneuvering between the floating glacial chunks, we gradually work our way to more open water where we motor unhindered for a few miles. At intervals we proceed with extreme caution between leviathan icebergs, ever mindful that shifting ice has crushed many an unsuspecting boat. At one point Kailapi jumps off onto a small flotilla of ice and helps shove the boat through unharmed, though an ominous grating sound accompanies his efforts. We spot both bearded seals and harp seals lounging among the floes, in addition to the more plentiful and smaller ringed seals that are the favorite food of the polar bear. At our approach the pennipeds slip off into the water, but not before my telephoto lens catches images of several. Each marine creature has its special place in the Inuit survival repertoire, and each provided a specific necessity the lack of which could have spelled death to the Inuit of old.

Off to our southwest lies the town of Hall Beach, its oil storage tanks visible and curiously out of place on the horizon. To the north and south a striking mirage forms, a *novaya zemlya* that one would swear to be a massive cliff of ice towering from the water's edge. I know from previous experience that this is a peculiar Arctic phenomenon caused by the diffraction of light, but it is always disquieting. Even through binoculars it cannot be distinguished from a real cliff. At one point the illusion has us practically surrounded, giving one the sensation of being trapped at the bottom of a basin ringed with walls no human could climb.

My Magellan GPS indicates that we are thirty-five miles from camp. Looming just ahead is a gigantic iceberg, and Cain noses the boat gently into the snowcapped giant. A short hike to the top for glassing is what he has in mind. While they are looking in one direction I instinctively glass in another, and to my surprise countless dark forms fill my field. Tapping Cain on the shoulder, I point in the direction of my find.

"*Aivik!*" he exclaims, confirming my impression. Kailapi sees the walrus as well, and we soon are loading back into the boat.

"Good news. Lots of walrus," confirms Kailapi. We leave the rest of the party at the iceberg to climb and watch from a distance, and we motor slowly toward the hulking shapes resting on floating rafts of ice.

Within ten minutes we spot two bulls on the ice immediately in front of us, their heads raised inquisitively. Bull walrus are not very spooky and in fact may be downright defiant. These two are average size, and we have no intention of taking either; watching the creatures through my binoculars, however, is intriguing. While we are still more than a hundred yards away, both slip into the water and disappear in a swirl of ice and frothy liquid.

"I thought they wouldn't be afraid," I comment to Kailapi, envisioning a risky, two-hundred-yard shot at a six-inch target from a bobbing boat.

"Not all of them do that. Wait and see."

I'm not convinced. We motor past several smaller animals, all of which slither into the sea like the first, by all appearances acting like the numerous seals that disappear so readily at our approach. Paranoia begins to creep into my thinking. I'm beginning to wonder if all animals act atypically when I am the hunter.

Finally, we spot two huge, dominant bulls on a block of floating ice. They raise their heads and roar, displaying their tusks menacingly, swaying back and forth and shifting uneasily at our advance. Despite their threatening posture and obvious agitation, they show no tendency to plunge into the water and disappear, preferring instead to confront us head-on. The ice on which they rest is large enough that I am hopeful I can kill the larger and have him lodge, so it won't be necessary to retrieve him from the water. The bigger one is well

Harp seal resting on an ice floe.

above average, according to my limited knowledge. Kailapi rapidly confirms my impression.

"Do you want to shoot?" he asks, as we come to within thirty to forty yards, the clicking of my camera being the only shots fired thus far. Suddenly I remember that I am here to kill a walrus. Stashing the camera in my pack, I unzip the padded rifle case and retrieve the old .30-06. I already have cartridges in the magazine, so I work the bolt and chamber a round.

Killing a walrus is not the challenge I had supposed, though it is certainly imposing to be so close to such an immense creature in his natural habitat. Armed with a modern rifle propelling 200-grain Nosler handloads, the kill at such close quarters should prove easy. I have already decided on a head shot to maximize chances the animal will remain on the ice, but hitting the tiny kill zone offhand in a rocking boat is not as easy as one might think. My first shot is slightly off the mark, though the walrus is obviously dazed. The next shot, a little more toward the eye, finds the deadly spot. The beast collapses resoundingly into a lifeless heap, and both tusks jam solidly into the ice floe as he topples.

The most vexing problem in hunting walrus is the possibility of losing the beast if he slips into the water before a harpoon can be driven in. When we move in closer, Kailapi immediately strikes the bull with the harpoon, and the implement appears to sink into the flesh sufficiently to hold him. As soon as the harpoon hits, the animal slides gradually and relentlessly into the water, but the attached sealskin line gives me a confident feeling. To my horror, though, when he applies pressure to the line, the harpoon comes up empty. I feel a sinking sensation in my stomach that more than matches the drift of my walrus.

Desperately, I grab an oar and row feverishly toward the spot just off the berg on which the animal had rested moments before. To my relief the walrus is still visible, three or four feet deep in the water. Cain uses the other harpoon to drill him in the side, his aim true and secure. As the walrus is brought to the surface I wipe nervous sweat from my brow, a sense of deep relief in my heart. The guides then attach more secure lines to the back flippers so we can't lose the animal again.

Another boat motor breaks the silence as our trailing party motors up. We rig up a double pulley system and call on all hands to help haul the walrus onto a larger ice floe. Cain digs a hole in the opposite side of the iceberg and attaches the boat anchor, and the pulleys are arranged between the anchor and the walrus. A slippery chute is prepared by chipping away any ice that might hang on the carcass as it is extracted from the sea. Sheer manpower then accomplishes the delivery of the giant onto the ice.

I am amazed at the size of the creature as I crouch beside him. I know the species is huge, but this monster is even bigger than I had imagined. To my disappointment, the animal landed on his tusks in the fall after the shot, breaking the left one badly, though it is still attached sufficiently for good pictures. Kailapi returns to the original floe and retrieves several small fragments so the taxidermist can fully reconstruct the tusk.

After we take several rolls of film of the animal, guides, and the happy hunter, I am privileged to examine firsthand the amazing structures that makes these unique mammals so well suited for their habitat. The back flippers are reversible so that locomotion on land or ice is possible, though their real strength lies in the powerful swimming strokes they can make.

Butchering must be done differently from usual, since the cape must be prepared for a shoulder mount, a concept that is difficult for these Inuit to grasp at first. My explanation of what I want is sufficient, however, and soon sharp blades are flashing and huge chunks of walrus meat are being dragged to all sides of the ice floe to cool. It appears strange to see steam rising from the carcass, but this is indeed a warm-blooded animal, despite the almost fishlike appearance. Each large piece of meat is left attached to overlying skin, in which it will be wrapped for its long period of curing in the ground. The edges of the cut skin are incised so a sealskin rope can lash them together for protection of the delicacy. The cape is lightened by skinning out and removing the muscle and bone in the front flippers, and by removing as much flesh from the skull as possible.

Soon we are enjoying fresh walrus ribs boiled in seawater on a Coleman stove brought from the boat, as well as tea made from freshwater blue ice. I try a bite of the boiled liver and find it more to my liking than venison liver. While the men butcher the walrus I photograph the aboriginal scene, trying to imagine Inuit men in centuries past accomplishing the same task with far more primitive tools.

The sun sinks low, and the prolonged Arctic twilight is shortly upon us. A huge bull walrus on a floe a hundred yards away gives us a demonstration of a giant's back-rubbing technique as he sticks all four flippers into the air and bellows as he gyrates in wild glee. Then he disappears into the water, only to resurface with an alarming blast of breath just beside our floe. I scramble to ready my camera, but the beast is gone.

The larger boat will carry all the walrus meat, and shortly all are loading the heavy pieces into the craft. The usable portion includes the intestines, a delicacy I am loath to try, though I am told that when boiled it tastes like scallops or shrimp. The entire length of the bowel is stripped

Evidence of past walrus hunts from Igloolik rests among summer's flowers.

of its contents, looped upon itself to make it more compact, and then loaded on board. The favorite walrus treat to the Inuit is the stomach contents, which often consists of a treasure trove of freshly devoured mussels, clams, and other bottom-dwelling shellfish. This particular animal has a disappointingly empty stomach, however.

Motoring back through the placid waters is an idyllic experience, the sharp images of drifting ice on all sides reflecting crisply in the calm sea. We encounter hundreds of walrus, and two huge bulls put on a show of defiance that is positively savage. At one moment one of our companion boats is practically surrounded by a surging herd of walrus, leaping like porpoises in and out of the icy water.

Twilight in the Arctic lasts many hours in August, and we witness a changing panorama as the sun finally drops below the horizon near 11 P.M. It never becomes truly dark, and there is an eternal crepuscule as the sun journeys beneath the northern horizon on its voyage back toward sunrise. We arrive at camp near 1 A.M. for a quick supper, then I collapse on my bed to sleep.

The next day we motor northward for whale watching, finding a pod of impressive bowheads just to the north of Igloolik. Reaching them requires negotiating very shallow water surrounding a series of barren islands, marooned icebergs marking the limits of the deep. Sighting the whales is a reward for navigating the treacherous straits, a feat that skilled boatman Brad Parker accomplishes with little trepidation. We are shortly surrounded by the behemoths, spouting frothy blasts of white breath and bringing to life the ancient whaler's cry of "Thar she blows!"

Distinct noises emanate from a surfacing whale, a kind of explosive exhalation. The creatures inhale deeply just before diving, making another unmistakable sound as air is sucked deeply into boat-size lungs to allow them to stay underwater for twenty minutes or more. The gigantic heads rise briefly out of the water, and following the sucking inspiration of air each disappears with a thunderous dive and a flap of the enormous tail. I feel a deep sense of gratitude to God for allowing me to be so close to this largest of His creatures.

Our goal on today's excursion is south Baffin Island, where a small stream has a spectacular run of Arctic char. Kim Seto fished here last year, and his description of catching a twenty-pound fish on every cast intrigues me. I have never seen fishing like that, but such an experience might inflame my marginal passion for the sport. Our guide is Brad's Inuk wife, Tam, and we are soon doing exactly what Seto had predicted. I catch my limit, each of the giant char taking fifteen to twenty minutes to land. My shoulders and arms ache with the struggle.

Departing and leaving behind new friends is always painful, but now I feel once again the beckoning call of home. The airport is full of happy Inuit faces, children and parents, old people and young, the healthy and the crippled. I have come to love this simple people. Their culture is actually quite profound, their psyche complicated, and their history and roots inscrutable. I think back to the magnificent walrus I took, and I remember the special relationship these people and their forebears enjoyed with the huge creatures. I have in mind a quotation from Barry Lopez, in his book *Arctic Dreams:* "It was the gift [of the animal] rather than the death that was preeminent in the Eskimo view of hunting."

As my plane lifts off from the barren gravel strip, I see the floating, shifting ice sheet stretching to the horizon, the place of the walrus. I am grateful for the gift of another of God's priceless creatures, and as a fellow hunter I am one with my Inuit brethren.

American alligator. (Photo: from the author's collection)

AMERICAN ALLIGATOR
(Alligator mississippiensis)

Away to the Dismal Swamp he speeds
His path was rugged and sore
Through tangled juniper, beds of reeds,
. . . where the serpent feeds,
And man never trod before.

—Thomas Moore (1779–1852), *The Lake of the Dismal Swamp*

The American alligator has only recently been classified as a big-game animal for the purposes of the sport hunter, earning listing under certain circumstances in the Safari Club International record book in 1998. It was hunted to near extinction in much of its range, the demise driven by the demand for quality hides in an environment of inadequate harvest controls. It is estimated that between 1870 and 1960 perhaps ten million gators were killed. Loss of habitat and senseless killing also decimated the species.

The alligator was one of the animals afforded protection by the Endangered Species Act in 1973. Its recovery has been remarkable, and in four short years it was downlisted to threatened status. In 1984 it was removed from the threatened classification. Florida still classifies the animal as "a species of special concern." The resilient reptile now once more numbers in the hundreds of thousands across its original range of nine states (Florida, Louisiana, Texas, Mississippi, Alabama, Arkansas, Georgia, and the Carolinas) and is by no means endangered except in certain areas, particularly where cold temperatures limit the northern extent of its range.

As a general type, there are many species of crocodilians in the world, but only two of them are classified as the genus *Alligator.* Besides our familiar North American version there is only the Chinese alligator, which has been extirpated from much of its original Asian range and is still truly endangered. That species is much smaller than the American alligator, though similar in appearance.

Alligators belong to the reptile class, which also includes snakes, turtles, and lizards. All crocodilians are cold blooded, air breathing, egg laying animals, as are most reptiles. The crocodilian types such as the alligator are distinguished from other reptiles by their size and by the fact that they alone possess four-chambered hearts, like mammals and birds. That makes their metabolism far more efficient, since blood from the lungs is not mixed with venous blood before being redistributed to the body. Their heads are perfectly designed for living in water, the eyes and nostrils riding high so that they can be above the water while the rest of the animal remains submerged. By manipulating the air volume in their lungs, they control perfectly how high the body rides in the water. The animals can remain completely submerged for ten to twenty minutes at a time, and longer when the temperature is cold and their metabolism is slow.

An adult alligator is dark in color, almost black on top, with lighter splotches on the sides that give way to a light yellow underbelly. They have a mouthful of seventy to eighty sharp, conical teeth set in bony sockets in the jaws. These fixtures are designed for grasping and ripping, but there are no chewing teeth, as the creatures gulp their prey whole or in large chunks. Powerful mandibular muscles forcefully close the mouth, but the counter muscles that open it are weak, allowing fairly puny restraints to neutralize the viselike jaws by preventing their opening.

Alligators swim primarily by means of the motion of their powerful tail. The relatively rudimentary feet are used for land locomotion, tiptoeing along the bottom of lakes and streams, and paddling duty to maneuver and maintain the desired depth in the water. The feet are partially webbed, and each bears three toes with long, sharp nails. Special valves cover the trachea to keep water out of the lungs when the animals feed underwater, and likewise the eyes, ears, and nostrils are covered by valves to protect them from water.

Alligators have good senses of smell and hearing. They also have good eyesight, though it is most effective at dusk and dawn. Their size can often be distinguished by the reflection the eyes return to a light shined on them, with larger animals reflecting a brighter red color, and females and smaller animals often showing a dimmer green. Experienced gator hunters usually have some sense of what kind of alligator they are seeing by the light of the lantern, although obstruction of the eye by intervening vegetation can sometimes yield misleading conclusions.

The animals are creatures of fresh water, though they have no hesitation about entering brackish water as well. They may be confused with the endangered saltwater crocodile, which shares the southern portion of their range in Florida and is similar in size and body configuration. However, the crocodile has a much narrower, more pointed snout, and the fourth tooth is always visible when the mouth is closed.

American alligator. Florida, July 1997.

The largest American alligator ever recorded was an unbelievable 19 feet, 2 inches and reputedly weighed 1,400 pounds. Many doubt the veracity of that measurement. More typically, a big one today will be between ten and twelve feet long and weigh 500 pounds. Most authorities feel that the maximum length for these creatures is more on the order of fourteen feet. They live for many decades, perhaps even reaching the century mark in rare cases, and have the distinction of being the longest-living of the North American big-game animals.

Alligators are sexually mature when they attain six feet in length, at which time they may be ten years old. Males are highly territorial and will fight viciously with other gators to defend their domain. Fights also break out with regularity during courtship, often resulting in the loss of limbs and tail, a common blemish among large alligators in the trophy class.

Courtship and mating take place from March through May, and during that time the swamps may resonate with the haunting call of the bellowing or roaring of both sexes. These calls serve to announce their presence and draw other gators.

The animals vibrate the body as they rise on the legs as high as possible, then gradually sink back to the resting position as the call ends. During the mating season the males also emit a strong scent, which may play a role in attracting females. The dominant males usually stick to deep, open water. This contrasts with the females, who prefer swampy areas with shallow water and plenty of plant life, also prime areas for nesting.

After mating, the female constructs a raised nest by scraping and mounding up vegetation with the mouth and tail. This structure may be elevated some two to four feet above the surrounding swamp terrain and may be seven or eight feet in diameter. The female digs a hole in the center for a cache of eggs. She may lay some twenty to seventy eggs at a time, which she then covers with dirt and vegetation. The female then stays in the immediate area, awaiting the hatching of the eggs as the sun warms and incubates them. Her presence serves as a deterrent to raccoons, which are the major cause of egg depredation.

The hatchlings emit a chirping or squeaking sound when they begin to emerge, and the female comes to their aid by uncovering them, an essential task if drought has hardened the mud covering of the nest. For two or more years, the mother gator may stay close-by and act as a guardian for the youngsters. The tiny animals make a noise that signals danger and brings their formidable bodyguard on the run to their defense.

The newly hatched gators weigh about one to one and a half ounces and are about six to eight inches in length. They are quite susceptible to predation by a variety of hungry raiders such as hawks, herons, raccoons, snakes, and bobcats. The entire hatch will not survive, with about 80 percent perishing during the first year, but they tend to stay together at least through their first winter of life. Those that persist may stay together for two or three years before dispersing to take up the solitary life characteristic of the species.

From the time of hatching, baby gators, like other reptiles, are quite independent; other than her guardian role, there is no nurturing or feeding behavior from the mother. The youngsters begin foraging immediately for small water creatures such as tadpoles, minnows, crayfish, and snails, and also for aquatic and terrestrial insects. They grow rapidly at first and may be about eighteen inches

Airboat transportation is the norm in the shallow waters of south Florida.

long and weigh approximately eight ounces by the end of the first year. By the time they are four feet in length, they have few enemies other than man and larger alligators.

Adult alligators feed on a wide variety of smaller animals, including almost anything that shares their domain. Muskrats, raccoons, beavers, snakes, fish, and waterfowl are common prey, most of which are swallowed whole. They may also attack larger animals or consume carrion, ripping off chunks of flesh.

In winter alligators do not truly hibernate when it becomes cold, but rather enter a state that could be described as suspended animation. They retreat to a place where they can be insulated from the cold, such as a hole or cave in a stream bank, and there they undergo a dramatic slowdown of metabolism. Their body temperature decreases, the heartbeat slows, and the respiration becomes difficult to detect. When the warmth of spring arrives, the increasing temperature ignites the body processes once more. In their range in southern Florida, this phase may not occur at all because cold temperatures seldom occur.

The gator is a foundation species upon which many other animals depend. When their population became severely depressed, fish, birds, and mammals alike suffered because the "gator holes" of retained water were absent in the swamps. These wallows served as reservoirs that were dependably wet, even if the rest of the swamp dried up completely. This interdependence was not apparent until the gator holes were gone.

There are two methods of taking a trophy alligator, both of which are perfectly legitimate and exciting. In all areas except Florida, a line must be attached to the gator before it is killed, usually accomplished by baiting a line and hooking the gator much as one would a fish. For a price, the sport hunter can accompany a licensed alligator hunter and select a large specimen from the night's catch. With the fair-chase method, the hunter evaluates and selects a trophy animal visually, stalks it or awaits it at a likely location, and shoots before any line is attached. This latter method is legal only in Florida as of this writing, and it is the only means of taking that qualifies an alligator for entry into Safari Club International's record book. A line may be attached after the initial hit is made to be certain

a fine animal isn't lost. The line is usually a harpoon attached by a rope to a large float. The alligator leaves a trail of bubbles as it moves along the bottom, giving away its position and making possible a harpoon thrust to secure it.

Killing an alligator with one shot is highly unlikely, so precautions such as harpoons are prudent. The kill zone is perilously small, being the "soft spot" that runs behind the eyes and around the back of the head at water level. Since trophy gators are seldom observed to leave the water, your shot will most likely be at that tiny target. In addition you will be trying to hit a moving animal from a rocking boat. If you can accomplish the task, my hearty congratulations.

Alligator hunting in Florida is an activity of summer through early fall, when temperatures are at an oppressive level and the mosquitoes beyond numbering. Wear your coolest duds, take plenty of insect repellent, and muster a lot of patience. In most cases the guide will have a potential trophy located for you, but it may be a number of days before you take your shot. Airboats are used extensively and guarantee safe transport through otherwise impenetrable terrain.

The land of the American alligator is as spellbinding as Alaska or the Rockies, as fascinating as Newfoundland or the Yukon, as mesmerizing as a crisp fall sunrise viewed from a deer stand. It is truly different from any other North American hunting experience, with a whole new texture and a completely different cast of characters. From the birds to the plants to the animals, it is unique.

SWAT TEAM STRIKE IN BREVARD COUNTY

Bad weather is building as I cruise down Interstate 95. The metroplex of Jacksonville, Florida, looms like the city of Oz in the distance, a gleaming assemblage of modern skyscrapers that looks like anything but big-game country. I can see a rainbow towering over the city against a backdrop of ominous inky clouds farther south. The silver canvas of the St. Johns River stretches to my west from the I-95 bridge toward the setting sun, shining like precious metal in the declining light.

This is my first venture into Florida for big game. The creature I will be seeking is a giant alligator that my host, Don Hampton of H&H Guide

Spectacular wading birds abound near the headwaters of the St. Johns River.

Cypress trees stand in quiet water in alligator country.

Service, has found and has primed me to harvest. I met Don at the Safari Club Convention six months ago, when I booked this hunt. I hadn't planned to include the American alligator in my North American experience until I examined the awesome specimen Don brought to the convention, and I decided on the spot to hunt one. After I saw that mount, it seemed to me that a big-game collection that doesn't include the alligator is not complete. And all the more so for me, since the creatures are native to my home state.

Despite this, it still feels strange motoring along in my car to a big-game hunt. I always start out such adventures with an airplane ride. To be journeying down a busy interstate not too far from home, my old .30-06 stowed safely in the trunk and no nagging concerns about whether it will arrive with my other baggage, makes for a refreshing change. To boot, the animal I will be hunting is one of the most intriguing creatures in all of North America, if not on the face of the planet.

The sky becomes progressively darker as I motor southward, and an intense storm looms ahead. A gigantic tongue of fire leaps far out to sea, traverses the horizon, and ends with a crackling, whipping

bolt of flame. Directly in front of me it divides into a multiple bolt that creates a complete circle of light, the ferocity and nearness terrifying. Another streak travels the same path to terminate in an explosion of fiery rivulets like a Fourth of July exhibition. A massive downpour follows, slowing my progress, but soon the tempest subsides.

As I drive, familiar names crop up every few minutes: St. Augustine, Daytona Beach, Disney World, Canaveral, and Cocoa Beach. Well before midnight I arrive at my destination, and soon I am resting comfortably in my motel room, visions of giant alligators dancing in my head.

On his trophy hunts, Don guarantees the client a chance at a nine-foot gator or better. I have high hopes of doing considerably better than that. My rifle is sighted in with 200-grain Nosler handloads to be dead on at 50 yards, a more or less typical distance. Aiming at the kill zone is like shooting at a peanut, because the reptilian brain is so small. In addition, the head and back are covered with armor plates that make bullet penetration and effectiveness highly unpredictable if the shot is off by even an inch. That, combined with the offhand nature of most shots, makes for a challenging task for the hunter. I have studied the creature's anatomy, and I will place my shot in the soft spot that is just behind and below the eye, an anatomical feature that extends around the back of the head to join the same structure on the other side. A shot there from the side or the back should have a chance of killing the gator instantly. Maybe I will accomplish the first one-shot kill Don has had in several dozen trophy hunts. I feel confident that the old rifle is up to the job if the situation is right and my hand is steady.

The phone rings at 4:45, and Don's familiar voice rouses me from deep sleep. I arise and splash my face with tap water, apply a thick coat of sunscreen to my face and neck, and don cool camouflage clothing. I gently tuck the rifle into its padded case after checking to see that my small pack is well stocked for a full day of hunting.

Don arrives in his white pickup, pulling the airboat that will propel us into the heart of the gator's swampy habitat. I have seen such boats before but have never ridden in one, so this should be some experience, the hunting aside. His assistant today is Steve Smith, and we are soon motoring toward the nearby farm lake where we will hunt. It is adjacent the headwaters of the same

St. Johns River I crossed two hundred miles to the north at Jacksonville, where it empties into the sea. The waterway is a unique ecosystem that flows almost due north, parallel to Florida's east coast. It sometimes runs within a few miles of the beach and in the process supplies fresh water to much of the booming sunny coast. All along its course is prime alligator habitat, and this particular farm pond is the benefactor of a continual influx of gators from the river that must only cross an intervening levee to be in new domain.

At the launch site we are joined by another pair of gentlemen, affable chaps like the first two. Keith and Kevin Cowart are big men, burly brothers deep of voice and easy of manner, and each extends a brawny hand in friendly greeting. All of my hosts are discussing a recent bank robbery that has captured their attention. Only through further conversation do I discover that their interest is vocational. All four are members of local SWAT teams in the police departments in Melbourne and Palm Bay. Maybe hunting alligators for fun is natural for guys with such dangerous occupations. Steve will ride with us while Keith and Kevin walk the long levee and act as spotters. In the event of a kill they will assist us with their own airboat.

A beautiful sunset over Lake Washington in Brevard County. Dainty water hyacinths are pretty but choke many waterways in Florida.

The drone of thousands of mosquitoes fills the air as we prepare our gear, and my exposed skin is a tempting target. I bathe myself in insect repellent and the assault wanes. I stow the can in my pack, certain I will need it again.

Don has prepared me for a long and difficult hunt. Several hunters have gone until the very last day before taking their gator this year. I am hunting a particular gator, and we have already discussed the need to wait for just the right shot. If it doesn't develop today, perhaps it will before week's end. I have four days to hunt, and I am ready to invest it all to take a really good animal.

Putting the boat into the water in the dark is short work, and I receive a pair of earmuffs to protect my hearing. The aircraft engine just behind me is almost frightening as it surges at full power, propelling us over a massive tangle of water hyacinths that separate us from the open water ahead. These nonnative plants are a scourge in many parts of Florida, choking waterways and crowding out native plants. They grudgingly give way to the Lycoming engine and powerful propeller. Soon the last of them is behind us and we are free.

Don illuminates an intense spotlight to show me some alligators while we traverse the big lake. Dozens of pairs of eyes are visible, most near the shore. Red reflections reveal their locations, but most submerge shortly after the light falls upon them. It is against the law to hunt gators with a firearm using the aid of a spotlight, so this is only for the enjoyment of viewing the creatures.

The light of dawn is increasingly upon us, and before me is a wild scene. A group of anhingas, water turkeys, are roosting in the bare branches of a dead tree to the east, the birds and stark branches silhouetted against the quickening sky. A great blue heron sails across in front of us, and the white bodies of egrets and ibises cruise to the west, their brilliant plumage reflecting the coming sun. Soon we are near the south shore and Don guns the engine to drive us up and over another bed of hyacinths, then he deftly kicks in rudder to maneuver us into a position facing the open water. I remove my earmuffs as the engine dies with a groan, and the silence of the marsh is upon us.

"That old big boy has been hanging around this south shore. I saw him just last week. But he's smart, so we'll be patient. He was out there to the right when I last saw him." Don is setting up a camera tripod and attaching a sandbag for me to use as a shooting rest. The arrangement feels eminently workable. It should be like shooting off a bench.

While glassing, I see movement along the opposite bank, well out of range. It is an alligator, no doubt about it. I point it out to Don, but it is a small one, perhaps a female. The minutes tick by and the sun edges toward the eastern horizon, but there are no big reptiles.

The radio crackles to life. It is Keith. There is a hint of irritation in his voice.

"You guys ever turn on your radio? The big boy is between us and you. You can't see him for those willows."

"How far? Which way's he moving?" "Toward you. Couple of smaller ones nearby moving away from you. Just wait where you are."

My heart leaps as I get ready. The adrenaline pumps and I review all I have learned. Shoot good and steady. Shoot at the waterline, just under and behind the eye. Don taps me on the back before I insert my earplugs and tells me to shoot exactly under the eye if a side shot presents. He is afraid I may hit the armor plating if the shot is off, and he thinks I'll have a better chance at inflicting a fatal wound if I'm a little forward rather than a little back. I adjust my thinking and get ready. Can it really be this easy?

Minutes pass as the hot sun edges into view, washing us in a rapidly warming caldron of sunshine. I peer through the vegetation, hoping to see the slow movement of a huge gator. Beads of perspiration pop out all over me as I wait, and I mop my brow with my hand to keep the trickle out of my eyes. Nothing shows.

"Keith, where is he? Can you see him?" whispers Don into the radio.

"He's stopped at the edge of the hyacinths. Don't see him right now."

We wait. The heat is intensifying, and I adjust my cap to shield my eyes from the sun. A pair of mottled ducks wing their way over the sparkling lake, and an osprey circles lazily overhead. But there is no sign of our gator. We scan in all directions with our binoculars, but the big reptiles are becoming ever less obvious with the climbing sun.

"I think we'll move, Keith," calls Don into the radio. "Where was he when you last saw him?"

"Back this way. I'd move toward the palm tree. Just to the left of it from your position."

Soon the mighty drone of powerful pistons breaks the silence, and we move into the dark water and away from our hyacinth hideaway. We burst free amid the clamor of birds rising raucously from the shoreline.

Ahead an alligator moves silently to our right near the shore, the ripple of its movement breaking the glassy surface. I turn and look at Don, but he shakes his head. It isn't our animal. A couple more cut the water nearby, but none are any bigger than the first, so I continue to scan the lake. I can now see the other two men stealing quietly along the levee, but they appear not to see any more than we do. I mark their position to avoid sending any lead in their direction, should our quarry appear. Doubt is clouding my mind with the rapidly rising temperature, and I can't help but wonder if that smart old gator hasn't holed up under the shoreline vegetation to pass the day in the shade, out of sight and out of danger. Maybe this evening or tomorrow morning, I muse silently.

To steady the boat, Don lodges it up on the floating vegetation with a mighty surge of power. This raft is more unsteady than the first, though, and the boat rocks ever so slightly.

More waiting follows, and Keith and Kevin radio that they are moving out of sight so they won't be in the line of fire. My rest is useless in this new spot, because the position of the boat dictates a shot to my left, away from the tripod, if the beast comes up. I cradle the old rifle in my arms, most hope of action today having been stowed. At Don's instruction I already have a round in the chamber, and I remind myself of the need to eject it as soon as we declare the hunt over.

All is dead still and only the occasional drone of an insect or the call of a bird intrudes on the quiet. Without warning, a monstrous head breaks the surface twenty yards in front of the boat, a massive alligator that causes the boat to rock in his wake. The huge jowls are obviously those of a mature bull gator, and Don makes his decision immediately.

"It's him! Shoot!"

I place the cross hairs at the base of the gigantic head, so big it fills my Redfield scope despite my having cranked the magnification back to a mere 2X. I snap off the shot, and the animal disappears in a swirl of foaming turbulence as I rapidly work the bolt.

I shot offhand and very quickly, but I was so close it is unthinkable that I could have missed. As Don begins to start the engine, he stops abruptly as the creature's head once more appears, this time some sixty to seventy yards out in the lake and moving away. I center the scope once more on the tiny kill zone and squeeze the trigger. The recoil jars me and a distinct smack indicates I must have connected, but not to the elusive fatal spot I have practiced hitting in my mind for weeks. The animal once more boils the surface as he shoots a spray of mist into the scorching air and disappears.

The engine now roars to life and we are off toward the vanishing ripple. A trail of bubbles has risen to the surface indicating where he has gone, bubbles that rise in a gator's wake as his feet hit the bottom of a shallow body of water like this one. He has moved fifty yards and stopped.

"He's hit well, I'm certain. Let's put a harpoon in him so he doesn't get into the hyacinths," Don counsels.

"I can't believe he isn't dead."

"I told you they're hard to kill. Most guys say the same thing."

"Well, get a line in him if you can. We can't chance losing him." I had hoped to leave him floating dead in the water with a well-placed first shot, but it isn't to be. Don's words on how hard the creatures are to kill haunt me as I scan the lake. I have already chambered another cartridge, and I will obviously have to shoot again.

It isn't easy to harpoon an alligator one can't see. The lances have points that are attached to a long pole and secured to a fifty-foot rope, the opposite end of which is tied to a float. When the point sinks into a gator, barbs prevent it from pulling out. A number of attempts are unsuccessful, after each of which the gator moves without surfacing. Steve finally hits home at the end of a vanishing bubble trail, and the waiting game starts to see how long the gator can hold his breath and deprive me of another chance.

Twice the reptile breaks the water for a quick gulp of air, disappearing in a sudden swirl before I can place another shot. However, I finally hammer the beast a killing blow in the white of the neck

A giant gator with gaping jaws is about to be hauled aboard the airboat.

just behind the head as he rises, a dim premonition telling me to be ready and waiting where the fading bubble trail ended. I didn't plan it that way—I just shoot at what I am able to see in this game of pop-up target. Finally, we use the harpoon line to pull in our quarry, which has given up at last. He is completely still in the water as we bring him to the surface.

"Don't assume he's dead. They can look that way and still take your arm off," Steve says as we draw the animal toward the bow of the boat. I am awed by the size of the beast. As we prepare to bring him alongside, we place a shot directly downward into the brain area, just to be certain there are no accidents. Don then uses tough electrician's tape to make several loops around the beast's mouth, a security measure that seems unnecessary to me, but with a monster gator like this he isn't going to take any chances.

With the arrival of the rest of the crew, we gather around to admire this fantastic prize. With considerable effort we manhandle five hundred pounds of alligator into Don's airboat, and Steve uses his razor-sharp knife to enter the animal's dorsal soft spot just behind the eyes, where the spinal cord is accessible to the long blade. I am impressed at the care they take to ensure that there will be no unexpected and potentially tragic resurrection of this giant.

The only disappointment is that the big gator, though a trophy by any standard, is regrettably not the immense one we had set our hearts on. Happily, though, he has all his feet and legs, some of which are often missing in a gator of this age and size. Perhaps a foot of his tail is missing, for he measures only 10 feet, 6 inches in actual length. His girth and weight are those of an eleven-and-a-half-foot animal, though, and he is a true trophy. I am happy with the outcome, and I put my hand on the creature's head and thank God for delivering this creation into my undeserving hand.

The picture session is the most trying one I can remember. Subzero temperatures in the Arctic are nothing compared with the blazing south Florida sun in July, and before we finish my mandatory five rolls of film I am soaked with sweat. After we struggle to deposit the creature in the back of Don's pickup, he attaches the alligator harvest tag to the end of the tail. My guide will spend the rest of the day transporting my prize to a licensed processing facility, where the meat and skin will be prepared and the hide validated as a legal harvest.

I bask in the cooling flow of air as we gratefully climb into the air-conditioned cab of the truck, and my wet clothes cause me to chill quickly. Don is pensive, wondering how disappointed I might be that we didn't take a gator a foot or more longer.

"Shortest hunt I've had all year. Most guys have gone at least a couple of days, several to the last afternoon. You're lucky in a way, not so lucky in another. Sorry. I thought sure he was the big guy when he popped up in the right place with that massive head and big old jowls."

"Don't worry about it," I assure him. "I'm happy. You can't get the biggest fish in the pond every time. I've got a good gator. I've got some time to see some sights now."

"Yeah. How about an airboat ride up the St. Johns this afternoon? Should get some good pictures. You can go in and take a nap while I get this guy skinned and processed."

"Sounds good to me. What time?"

"About 5:30. Keith and Kevin might go, too."

Sleep comes easily after a bite of lunch. Before I know it, there is a knock at the door. My host has returned, and I am refreshed. Don looks tired after a long day.

"Sure you want to do this?" I ask.

"No problem. I'm used to it. The gator is in the cooler, and you're about to have a great ride on a fabulous river."

As we drive to Lake Washington, one of a string of lakes that are the pearls on the necklace of the St. Johns River, we talk about airboats, alligators, and local ecology. The lake we are visiting is the fresh water source for the city of Melbourne, and the importance of the St. Johns system to man's well-being in eastern Florida becomes even more clear to me.

Airboats have always fascinated me. Several are being unloaded as we arrive at the lake. They are unceremoniously dumped onto the grass or sand, the big aircraft engine is ignited, and they are literally driven into the water. Loading them is just the opposite—the driver simply taxis across the parking lot, sliding the boat on its belly and up onto the waiting trailer. Simple as can be, and a tribute to the power of an aircraft engine.

Airboat trails cut every part of the big swamp around the crystal-clear lake, and once more I am thrilled by the animal and plant life. We follow the silver ribbons cut through the watery wilderness, catching sight of wild hogs, deer, innumerable birds, and plants of varieties seldom seen elsewhere. One of the most impressive items is a type of pigweed that lines the airboat trails and grows to a diameter of eight inches or so at the base, the biggest weed I have ever seen. We return to the docking area under threat of a thunderstorm moving in from the north, but the downpour never reaches us. Instead we are treated to a fiery red sunset over Lake Washington, the swaying marsh grass silhouetted against a panorama that dominates the western horizon.

I am happy. Tomorrow I will drive home to Georgia, rested and satisfied. I got my gator and I made new friends. And I was part of a SWAT team strike, too.

Rocky Mountain mule deer. (Photo: courtesy of James L. Davis)

ROCKY MOUNTAIN MULE DEER

(Odocoileus hemionus hemionus)

On a small plateau stood a big buck. . . .
His head was slightly turned toward me,
his nostrils were quivering and distended,
and he looked as if prepared to bound away. . . .
He seemed utterly oblivious to my presence;
and there was a look of proud defiance in his eye
that gave him a most noble, majestic appearance. . . .

—Roger D. Williams, *American Big Game Hunting*, 1875

The Rocky Mountain mule deer is perhaps the second most sought-after big-game animal in North America, after its cousin the white-tailed deer. I have observed mule deer in most Western states and provinces where they occur, and I have taken Rocky Mountain bucks in Wyoming and Idaho. I have had a high-country mulie doe eat out of my hand in Montana while on a sheep hunt, and I have been fascinated by close encounters with nice bucks in New Mexico, Colorado, Alberta, British Columbia, and South Dakota. The massive racks of years gone by are extremely hard to find nowadays, but they are still out there for the hunter willing to go the extra mile off the beaten path.

Mule deer have been abundant in certain areas since early explorers first penetrated the region. Estimates of how many were present prior to European contact run as high as ten million, though most authorities now believe that figure to be excessive. George Bird Grinnell, one of the founders of the Boone and Crockett Club, accompanied the Custer expedition to the Black Hills in 1874, where he reported the animals common among the bluffs and tall buttes and commented on their utility in providing fresh meat for the soldiers.

The range of the Rocky Mountain mule deer is extensive in the western part of North America south of the Yukon and Northwest Territories borders, extending well into California, Arizona, Texas, and New Mexico, where they intergrade with the desert mule deer in the extreme southern part of all four states. Boone and Crockett Club listings lump all these mule deer into one category, but Safari Club International divides them along principal east-west highways and county lines to recognize the desert subspecies to the south. The deer cease to exist on the plains east of central Kansas, Nebraska, and the Dakotas, and east of the northwest corners of Texas and Oklahoma, although they were probably more extensively distributed in earlier centuries. They are rarely present in southwest Manitoba but are abundant from central Saskatchewan westward. On the western border of their range they intergrade with the Columbia black-tailed deer in British Columbia, Washington, Oregon, and California, but are for the most part isolated from the Sitka subspecies in the northwestern part of their range.

Mule deer crop up occasionally where they aren't supposed to be. Iowa, Minnesota, and Missouri, as well as the Yukon, have reported them from time to time. They never extended farther east, probably because of their genetics as well as their requirements for food and escape cover. They are adapted to brushy, shrub-filled habitats, and they are at a competitive disadvantage when in proximity to white-tailed deer. Mule deer have never naturally occurred east of the Mississippi River.

The lines drawn to separate mule deer, desert mule deer, and the two black-tailed subspecies are certainly defensible biologically and from the hunter's perspective, but overlap is undeniable. As O. C. Wallmo has observed, "Subspecies are not totally distinct entities with ranges enclosed by lines on which all taxonomists agree for all time." We just have to do the best we can by drawing lines in the most logical places, and I believe that has been done to the best of human ability in most cases.

The Rocky Mountain subspecies is the largest in body size of all the various black-tailed deer. They average about 200 pounds for a buck and about 150 pounds for does. Bucks in some areas frequently weigh 300 pounds or better, with rare individuals weighing 400 pounds. A mature buck stands about forty inches high at the shoulder.

The coat sheds twice annually, and color varies from reddish gray in summer to dark gray in winter, when it is much thicker. The tail is short and white with a black tip, this small speck of black hair giving

an entire species its name. There are expanses of pure white on the underbelly, inner parts of the legs, and the rump, and almost invariably there is a white throat patch. Some white hair usually occurs on the muzzle, which contrasts handsomely with the black forehead patch.

Mule deer have a bouncing gait, called "stotting," that helps them escape predators in the shrubby terrain. They may cover up to fifteen feet with a single bound, and may leap upward two or more feet while running. Top speed is about twenty-five miles per hour over short distances. Major predators include the cougar in much of their range, as well as wolves in the northern reaches. Fawns are sometimes susceptible to predation by golden

Rocky Mountain mule deer. Wyoming, October 1987.

eagles, and when stressed even adult mule deer can fall victim to coyotes and feral dogs.

Like most widely distributed large mammals, these creatures tolerate a broad range of temperatures. In the northern Rockies in winter, severe cold spells of minus 70 degrees Fahrenheit can occur. In the desert Southwest, summer temperatures can reach 120 degrees. The deer have special mechanisms to both preserve and dispel heat, allowing them to persevere and even thrive under such conditions if the extremes do not last too long. It appears that deep snow is far more detrimental to these animals than low temperatures. On an Idaho cougar hunt one January I counted more than two hundred mule deer carcasses in a single drainage of the Boise River, a terrible winterkill that apparently struck mostly fawns. The snow that year was as high as the cab of a pickup truck.

The antlers hold strong allure for most hunters. When I first saw a set of gigantic antlers from a mature mulie buck, I stood with my mouth open for a full minute, I'm sure, my previous contact with deer having been limited to modest whitetail specimens from the Southeast. A big mulie buck is truly majestic. The antlers of all the blacktails are distinguished from those of whitetails by the "dichotomous" pattern—repeated forking rather than branching off one main beam. Once you notice that difference, which is not apparent at first glance, it's fun to demonstrate your skill at differentiating uncannily between mule deer and whitetail antlers at every opportunity.

As among other cervids, antler growth is almost totally dependent on genetics, nutrition, and age. Growth begins from pedicles indistinguishable from those on whitetails, and the truly bony growth is nourished by highly vascular modified skin—the velvet. The width of the pedicles increases year by year, making age a necessary ingredient for massive antlers. Special cells in the pedicles lay down a cartilaginous matrix that is later mineralized into calcium-rich bone. Apparently as a response to increasing levels of testosterone in the fall, the thick walls of the blood vessels in the velvet contract at the appropriate time in late summer, depriving it of the nourishing flow of blood. That causes it to dry, fragment, and shed.

Bucks use their antlers during the rut for fighting and for dominance displays. A battle between dominant bucks can be as innocuous as a staring contest, or it may involve a few seconds to a half-hour of serious combat. These fights can be fatal, but most often are not. The peak of the rut is usually in November. Unlike whitetails, mule deer does do not flee the buck, instead simply making him wait until they are ready. Does are receptive for up to thirty-six hours, and if not bred they cycle again within three to four weeks.

The rutting behavior of mule deer puts them at a reproductive disadvantage when their range overlaps that of whitetails, especially where there are insufficient mature mule deer bucks. A mature whitetail buck will displace immature mulie bucks and breed mule deer does when no older, mature bucks are present to make the whitetails keep their distance. The "mule-tail" hybrid of such unions is inferior genetically and thus contributes nothing productive to the survival of either species. Since no whitetail does are bred by mule deer bucks, that leads to a relative reduction in the numbers of mule deer where such crossbreeding occurs.

Does are normally bred around age one-and-a-half, and almost all of the healthy ones become impregnated. Bucks are capable of breeding as yearlings, but seldom do they have the opportunity when older bucks are in the vicinity. Gestation is around 203 days. Twin fawns are the rule (60 percent in one study), while single fawns are less common, and triplets rare (1 percent). Newborn mule deer fawns usually weigh about eight to ten pounds. By the time the snow flies in fall, the youngsters are up to seventy pounds. Up to 25 percent of the fawns are lost to predators during their first few weeks of life, mostly coyotes but with a smattering of kills by bobcats and golden eagles. Some 75 percent are lost by the end of their first winter. Doe fawns have reached full maturity by age two-and-a-half, while bucks continue to gain weight up to age seven. A natural seasonal variation in weight occurs with changes in the availability of food, and mule deer may lose about 20 percent of their body weight over the winter. In captivity, the animals may live up to twenty years, but in the wild a ten-year-old is ancient.

After the rut the antlers shed anytime from November to March, though most shed earlier rather

Glassing brushy draws for a good mulie buck.

than later, often in January. This dropping of the antlers is caused by bony erosion probably related to a decline in testosterone levels, and it occurs sooner in mature bucks than in younger ones. As with antler growth, the time of shedding can be influenced by diet, disease, and injury, with afflicted bucks tending to lose their antlers sooner. The pedicle bleeds a bit when the antler falls off, but within a few weeks it has scabbed over and healed. In a healthy buck a new antler soon begins to grow.

A mature mulie buck is not hard to judge for trophy quality. The mass and length of the tines mark it instantly. If the antlers are not visible for a considerable distance with the naked eye, it likely isn't a monster. Ideally, the antlers should be nearly twice as wide as the ears, though that utopian dream comes true only rarely. I just know when I see one whether it is big or not, and so will you.

Be sure the massiveness is there, because the trophy is in the age, and antler mass is a function of the deer's age more than anything else.

Major differences exist between the antlers of the Rocky Mountain mule deer and the smaller blacktails, but there are no real or important distinctions from desert mule deer. The mule deer have more symmetrical antlers on average than the blacktails, and there is more propensity toward brow tines, which are usually short compared with those of whitetails and quite often are absent on mulies.

Rocky Mountain mule deer eat an immense variety of plants. They live in warm and moist terrain in summer, places that are rich in nutritious forbs of various types. In winter they browse heavily on woody plants, especially sagebrush, juniper, piñon, bitterbrush, serviceberry, mountain mahogany, and various oaks, especially the Gambel species. One study listed 788 species they consume, more than I had imagined to exist in their range. They seem to have the ability to utilize whatever is at hand.

The habitat mule deer prefer is the brushy draw, a feature common to rough terrain all over the West. They shun grasslands as permanent living quarters, though it is common to see them feeding in the many open areas, particularly in fields of alfalfa and other crops. The brushy draw has at its high end a relatively flat swale, which is often home to a mule deer favorite—the western snowberry, which thrives in relatively dry upper terrain. Lower down in the draw increased moisture sustains a proliferation of plants used by mule deer, including silvery buffaloberry, common chokeberry, common snowberry, golden currant, and various species of wild rose. At the bottom of the draw there are ash, elm, box elder, and hackberry, also favorites of the mule deer. Where the draw flattens into a narrow stream floodplain, cottonwoods grow in considerable quantities and are used by the deer for food and cover. The deer also browse juniper, fir, and pine on the northern slopes, though these are more useful as cover during times of heavy snow.

The social structure of mule deer consists of a family group of does and fawns. Dominant bucks are often solitary, though they may form small bachelor groups except during the rut. These deer concentrate in severe weather and deep snow in the lowest areas available, on south-facing slopes, or where it is sheltered with evergreen cover.

Hunting mule deer is possible throughout its range, with some of the hot spots for big Rocky Mountain bucks being the Kaibab Plateau of Arizona, the Jicarilla Apache Reservation of New Mexico, and virtually any of the magnificent draw regions of Nevada, though getting a tag there can be a chore. Classically, most people seem to hunt mule deer in Montana initially, where the famous Missouri Breaks have produced good mulies for decades, or in Wyoming, where some of the best hunting is with outfitters who have leased private ranch land.

Gear for hunting mulies varies so widely that it is impossible to capsulize it. If you're going with an outfitter, follow his recommendations. You will be walking a lot, so good boots are essential. Pac boots or insulated rubber boots are exceptionally good in snowy terrain. Fleece or wool is ideal for moving quietly through the brush, but in many cases an early season hunt in low country is warm, so I recommend light cotton. Take a jacket for cool mornings. Be prepared for brutal cold even in the early season, including snow, throughout most mule deer range. Rain is likewise a possibility, so take good rain gear. Be in good shape for most mule deer hunting, though one need not be in "sheep shape" unless you want to be totally relaxed walking the hills and draws of mulie land. Carry a daypack with all the essentials, especially plenty of drinking water.

A flat shooting rifle like a .270 or .280 is probably preferable to the .30-06 when you start talking long shots. I have killed mule deer at 300 yards with my old .30-06, but such a long shot usually involves some divine guidance for the bullet trajectory. I've mostly hunted mule deer with handloaded 165-grain Nosler Partition bullets, but I killed my first one using factory-loaded 180-grain bullets.

Hunting Rocky Mountain mule deer can be an experience as varied as the foods these animals eat, and some people are absolutely nuts about this species, choosing to hunt little else. I, too, could easily become engrossed in the richness of the varying habitats, the different fall and winter seasons, and the various states and provinces in which one can hunt for mulies.

The mule deer is a fascinating animal, and a big buck is an opponent more than worthy. He is more than likely to leave you empty-handed. But he is obtainable, and with persistence he can be yours. I'll probably be out there with you, trying to get a bigger and better one, or taking a grandson on a hunt. Everybody who hunts ought to at least try a mule deer hunt. You won't come back the same, I can assure you, and you'll probably have a craving for more.

DEER OF THE WIDE-OPEN SPACES

This is so different from the last time I hunted Wyoming. I have seen every conceivable type of October weather in the Equality State, and this trip is showing me yet another face. I hunted antelope here for the first time a dozen years ago, and I have returned often. Last time, I flew my own single-engine airplane into Newcastle, where we hunted in snow and cold on the fringes of the Black Hills,

Rocky Mountain sunsets are a part of mule deer hunting.

with imposing Devil's Tower looming like a gigantic tombstone on the horizon.

Mostly I have experienced the cool of the fall, a time of year when the brushy draws where the mule deer hide turn blood red and the aspens become yellow and quake with anticipation of the coming bad weather. But not this time. There is hardly a hint of autumn in the air, and there has been no rain for months. The prairie grasses are crackly dry and appear to emerge from hard-baked mud. The roads on the ranch are choked with dust that permeates every pore as we ride.

The morning was a most hopeful beginning to this hunt, and opening day was almost closing day for me. As dawn broke over the magnificent ranch country, we saw perhaps a hundred deer, including a couple of fair bucks, not quite good enough to take. We walked four or five miles

down an eroded valley, relishing the start of another hunting season. In the process, I almost had the opportunity to take a real monster mulie before the sun had cleared the eastern horizon. I had waited for almost an hour for him to appear from the secluded draw into which he had disappeared. Somehow he had beaten me, as the real giants so often do, and the last view I had was the disappearance of the huge rack over the top of the ridge as he retreated from danger. Just over the top his luck ran out: a pair of poachers downed him just inside the property we are hunting.

The landowner caught the two rogues after they had dragged the buck across the fence, the blood trail showing clearly what they had done. The last I heard about it, the game warden was on his way to investigate. Those guys had permission to hunt on an adjacent twenty-acre tract but assumed that anything within range was fair game.

I am already tired of eating dust. I need an attitude adjustment, this morning's incident having taken some of the glitter off my hunting prospects. Snapping back will come, but for now I'm just bouncing. Bouncing along the range roads is a time-honored tradition in Wyoming, whether one is seeking a lost cow, checking a water hole, putting out salt blocks or hay, or just hunting. When the weather is wet, the two-track ruts run deep and the dirt turns to sucking, sticky mud. In the throat-parching heat, I wonder if the dry, cracked ground will ever feel the kiss of heavenly moisture again. I remove my sweat-soaked hat and wipe my brow with my shirtsleeve, all the while searching every ridge and draw for my quarry.

I reflect silently on other mule deer hunts as we ride. I remember a hunt on a ranch near here where I took my first mule deer many years ago. I spent lots of time then riding the irregular range roads and saw lots of game. I recall the pungent smell of sagebrush, the numerous barbed-wire gates, and the steepness of the hillsides, which mandate four-wheel drive even in dry weather. The meat shed was hanging full of fat deer that year, as well as pronghorn antelope, ready for processing. My first real trophy mulie came a few years later on that same ranch, a nice four-by-four that I had mounted then donated to a special cause when I later took a better one.

Then there is the Selway-Bitterroot Wilderness, that undefiled area in Idaho, where I have hunted elk so many times. The mule deer are in rut there in November, as they are almost everywhere, and the hunting can be very good. More than once I failed to get the elk I was seeking, but the mature mountain buck I took instead on one such hunt still graces one wall of my house, stately and tall in antler and massive in chest and body. When I look at the animal it evokes memories of a grand hunt.

My mind returns to the business at hand. My nephew and partner, Reed Matthias, brakes the truck to a halt, and we disembark for a look from the conspicuous brow of a sagebrush promontory. The blue sky has only an occasional wisp of thin clouds, and there is no breeze. Everything that moves, except for a meandering golden eagle riding the thermals in the distance, is seeking protection

from the scorching sun. Prospects for spotting the fantasy buck I have in mind seem remote, and ever more so as the heat of the October afternoon climbs to record levels.

On the treeless plains of Wyoming there is no hiding from the relentless, fiery sun when the weather is clear. We try to find shelter, nevertheless, sitting in the shade of the truck, glassing every brushy draw and every shadowy spot. We find nothing but a lone doe resting under a rocky outcrop. Hope fades as midday heat drives away the wispy, tentative clouds high overhead. We might as well take it easy until evening. At least we can observe the antelope, which seem to tolerate the direct sunlight better than most other creatures.

It is time to rest and relax, taking a cue from the animals. We break out bologna and cheese sandwiches and wash them down with cold sodas from the ice chest. A prairie dog town across the broad plain provides some diversion, the inhabitants popping up and down in their daily chores. After a brief siesta we move on, trying to cover more territory before evening. The ranch is prime deer country and the owner strictly controls access, so we know the bucks are here. Reed has already taken his antelope, and he has no deer tag, so his job now is to help me get my deer.

Evening brings us to the top of another of the endless series of sagebrush ridges. The mule deer have sought out the shade of the ubiquitous evergreens atop the highest ridges, and several deer are resting within our view. We now see a buck, the first one that merits a close look since that unhappy episode this morning.

Through the spotting scope the animal appears to be a four-by-four, but he is deep in the shade so it's hard to be sure. The approach is difficult, but to backtrack would take an hour or more of driving and walking. We drop to our right onto a bare slope out of sight of the buck and sidehill for perhaps a mile over the irregular terrain. When we arrive at the end of the ridge the buck occupies, we ascend to a point above and wait to see if he will appear. A doe that accompanies him suspects something and stands inquisitively to look in our direction. Another appears, and finally a forkhorn buck shows himself. I chamber a round, just in case.

Finally the wind shifts and carries our sweaty scent directly toward the mulies. Suddenly the whole group spooks and is off at a dead run. As so often happens, the mature buck leaves by a different direction than the lesser deer, and we spot the animal only when he springs free of brush a hundred yards away. We make a quick judgment that he is not what we seek, although I am uncertain. The open terrain provides ample opportunity to second-guess myself through the spotting scope, however, and I decide with satisfaction that the judgment was correct: narrow and somewhat spindly, no better than a number of other bucks I have already taken.

Motel accommodations in Sheridan are crowded during the short deer season, but we made reservations well in advance and are treated to meals with our rooms. I eat and rest well that night, and I hope against hope that the poached buck is not the best my host has to offer.

Morning light reveals another bluebird day as we arrive at a perfect valley on another part of the vast ranch. Crossing a cattle gate we enter a range slightly less brushy, slightly lower in elevation, and more heavily grazed. Cattle wander in every draw, and I question whether the deer will frequent an area where the cows are so numerous. Nevertheless, I have been told that there are several nice bucks in this section.

Down to our left in the deep draw we spot a telltale movement, a shadow that at first appears to be yet another of the numerous cows. A quick check through binoculars reveals it's a buck! And there is another of approximately equal quality nearby, both of them feeding away from us, completely unconcerned. We scramble out of the vehicle and shoulder our gear for the task of trying to overtake the moving animals.

Another promontory looms in the dawn light, and we rapidly ascend for a better look. Crawling to the top we stay as low as possible and begin glassing. They are now topping out on the next ridge, already almost a mile away. We'll never catch them, I moan out loud, as I watch the white rumps fading away into the thick sagebrush.

We are after them as rapidly as possible, and in some twenty minutes we've spotted them again. They have covered another half-mile and are now acting as if they might bed shortly to escape the warming sun. Naturally, they have chosen the thickest patch of brush in this section of Wyoming,

and as we watch they settle in and disappear completely, like a couple of apparitions. We carefully mark the spot and make our stalk to within a hundred yards.

I have never been able to make running shots consistently. In my native Georgia virtually all my hunting is from tree stands, so such shots are not only impractical, they are near folly even under the best circumstances. The distances I am accustomed to shooting are generally short, the underbrush is dense, and the escape cover is like the hair on a Saint Bernard. I have always told my guides that if they will give me a standing shot, I have a chance; if I must shoot at something on the dead run, I am down to sheer luck.

Something goes wrong with the stalk. Perhaps a capricious breeze carries our scent to the creatures, or a twig snaps in the dry brush. Whatever the cause, before we can settle in for a wait the two are off and running like a couple of kangaroos, bouncing and weaving, bobbing and dancing, hopelessly outmaneuvering my .30-06 bullets. I let fly several at the larger of the two, but the attempt is futile.

The long walk back to the truck is the epitome of dejection. *Nope,* I remind myself, *you're no Jack O'Connor, not by a long shot.* Certainly not when it comes to running shots, a feat the old master handled generally successfully, at least according to his writings. Reed is kind and says nothing.

Combing several sections in the afternoon is as unproductive as yesterday. In this heat it will be purely accidental to see anything alive after 8 A.M. Since my time is limited on this five-day hunt, I must keep moving and looking, or at least remain perched on a good glassing area. Despite a good effort, we see no more bucks this day.

The Wyoming Department of Fish and Game is doubtless one of the best such organizations in the world. I have never been checked in the field by a game warden anywhere other than in my native state and in Wyoming. As we exit by the cattle guard where we entered, the game warden is waiting to check our licenses. On a dozen trips to Wyoming, I recall being asked for my license at least four times. Tales of these wardens showing up far back in sheep country, backpacks and all, abound in every hunting camp. One must commend them for their diligence. The legal hunter has nothing to fear from such checks and should lend them every kind of assistance.

My mind will not rest tonight, as I have seen a trophy buck both days of the hunt thus far. Circumstances simply refuse to gel for me. Perhaps tomorrow will be my day, and on that optimistic note I drift off to sleep.

The morning dawns woefully bright and clear—yet another summerlike day. One can see it coming even as we mount the truck in the dark, with stars stretching from horizon to horizon. The glow in the east soon promises the sun, and its

return to the dry prairie brings the familiar deep blue to the sky. Dust boils from the range road once more as we motor along, raising a column that must look like a buffalo stampede from a distance. We continue to stop at likely locations for short walks into good deer country, but the breaks are maddeningly slow in coming.

The air is again unseasonably warm by midmorning, and we see several sidewinder rattlesnakes as we walk. The persistent summer has obviously extended their period of activity. Nothing is going right. Rattlesnakes in October in

Wide-open country with plentiful brushy draws is a good place to find success on mule deer.

Wyoming, for goodness sakes! And this particular morning I can't even find a deer, much less the buck I am hoping for. Perhaps we have already seen all the good bucks that one trip will allow. Maybe I will experience my first Wyoming shutout, an eventuality every hunter must be prepared to face without complaint.

Lunch is a delight in the shadow of a pleasant pine tree with a fine view. Days are long and nights are short during the October hunting seasons in Wyoming, so a midday siesta is almost a requirement. The weather hardly permits anything else, so I curl up under the edge of the vehicle for a snooze.

Midafternoon arrives, and we climb aboard the truck. I always feel a little guilty hunting from a vehicle, but today Reed and I will let our legs rest a little. There are but two days of hunting after today, so we must be prepared to go the extra mile.

Down a long valley we ride, and a glimmering water hole materializes in the distance behind one of the oft-encountered earthen dams. Both native and domestic creatures benefit from such water holes, and perhaps we can find the dominant buck in this section of the ranch. It is still much too early to see deer moving about, so we casually drive along, scanning the green hillsides.

A shining spot glimmers high on a hillside. We stop to investigate and immediately realize that the unusual gleam is the top of an antler! We scramble from the truck and break out the binoculars. Again I have great difficulty judging how good the animal is. The deer is just under the brow of a high hill, resting in the shade of high bushes. I spot the white throat patch and one of the antlers, and after a fair amount of pondering I decide to try for him. He appears to be quite heavy and wide, but a precise judgment is impossible. To make matters worse, there is no way to get any closer because of the sweep of the terrain, unless I want to circle a couple of miles behind and come up ten yards above him. The inevitability of another

After a few days of acclimatizing to us, this high-country Rocky Mountain doe eats out of my hand.

chancy running shot faces me if I choose that course of action. The buck is a good four hundred yards away, a very doubtful shot with my .30-06, but I will always take my chances with a long shot over a running one.

Rock-solid concentration is the key to any shot, and the importance of it grows with each added yard. At four hundred yards, another important element—luck—comes into play. Someday I may decide that such a shot is better left untried, the animal better saved for a more opportune day, but in the foolishness of youth I am still learning about such things.

The white neck patch should be about a foot above the chest cavity, I surmise. I will hold just at the top of the patch and hope for a straight drop with no windage error. I squeeze off the shot carefully, noting with satisfaction the sharp report and the light kick of the departing 150-grain Nosler handload. The buck leaps to his feet at the crack of the rifle but is unable to stand! Down he goes, out of sight except for legs thrashing in the air!

Climbing the steep hill takes a good fifteen minutes, and the truck recedes to the size of a toy as we ascend. The buck is dead. He is an excellent trophy, a five-by-five that measures twenty-eight inches in spread. We admire the beautiful animal and note that the shot dropped about fourteen inches, just about what I had anticipated. I feel extremely fortunate as I receive Reed's heartfelt congratulations.

I have proved to myself that I must know my limitations and choose to act where I can take fullest advantage of my strengths, avoiding having to expose my weaknesses. This hunt has revealed both sides of that spectrum, and I have learned a valuable lesson.

Returning to Sheridan with my prize, we again encounter the game warden, who duly checks my trophy. There is joy in the successful culmination of the chase, and this is such an occasion. I congratulate the warden on the good job he and his colleagues are doing managing the wild creatures of Wyoming.

As we prepare to depart the Sheridan airport, there is finally more than a hint of fall in the air. A cold wind whips the open airport and a frigid rain has begun to fall. An occasional wet snowflake drifts by, the first of many to come. The hunting this second week should truly be superb. I wistfully ponder how much more pleasant it could have been if this weather had moved in a week earlier.

But one should never complain. Such is hunting, dealing with the elements and doing one's best whatever the circumstances. Most shutouts I have endured were mainly because the weather refused to cooperate. This time I tagged my buck in spite of it. I couldn't be happier, unless the critter had turned out to be of record-book proportions. But he is respectable, and I rejoice in that fact.

Sheridan lies off the right wing as we ascend, and the gorgeous snowcapped Bighorn Mountains just to the west beckon. For now I will relish the memory of a hunt on the Great Plains and look forward to my next trip to Wyoming with gusto. It probably gets much better than this, but for the moment the thought is hard to entertain. Happiness settles in to accompany me on the trip home.

Desert mule deer. (Photo: courtesy of Eric J. Hansen)

DESERT MULE DEER
(Odocoileus hemionus crooki)

For some reason all the game on the deserts of Sonora grows good heads,
and the buros are no exception.
Some of the finest mule-deer heads I have ever seen
have come from animals that never experienced freezing temperatures
and never took a drink of water in their lives.

—Jack O'Connor, *Game in the Desert*, 1934

The desert mule deer inhabits the southern parts of Arizona, New Mexico, and California, as well as a slice of west Texas and the northern part of Mexico, including the states of Sonora, Coahuila, and Chihuahua. Separate subspecies are present in Southern California and in Baja California, as well as on Tiburon Island and Cedros Island. For record-book purposes, Safari Club International lumps all of these together into the desert mule deer classification. That organization considers the mule deer of northern Mexico desert mule deer. Those west of the Pecos River in Texas, and south of a complicated line of highways roughly dividing Arizona and New Mexico into a southern third and a northern two-thirds, and those in the four southernmost counties of California, count as desert mule deer for that organization. Boone and Crockett lumps all of these animals into one classification with the Rocky Mountain mule deer.

The Mexican situation is a continuing series of developments. The mule deer of Sonora have become legendary in recent years, and the writings of such men as Jack O'Connor are being pulled out, dusted off, and rewritten in a hundred different ways to tell of the monsters taken there recently. My own desert mule deer from Sonora was a world record in the nontypical category when taken, truly the trophy of a lifetime, and one I did little to deserve other than by being there at the right time.

Another success story for desert mule deer is in the state of Coahuila, where progressive private landowners have reestablished the animal. There is now an active and ongoing hunting program for them in that Mexican state, a little-known fact in the world of hunting. Most of the deer, if not all, are on private land, so you must have permission and use a guide and outfitter. Just be sure you're clear on the name the Mexicans use for the desert mule deer. They're known as *buro* deer. Whitetails are known as *venado*, so don't use that term when referring to mule deer. It is perfectly acceptable to say specifically *venado cola blanca* for whitetails and *venado buro* for desert mule deer, if you prefer.

The desert mule deer is identical to the Rocky Mountain subspecies, with few exceptions. They grow antlers as big as their northerly cousins, but their body size seldom will top 200 pounds. My world-record buck, before field dressing, weighed only 180 pounds, a fact that I read off the scale in disbelief. The antlers alone must weigh 25 pounds, leaving the body at a scant 155 or so. With such outlandish headgear available, it's no wonder that U.S. hunters with mule deer fever invade Sonora every year.

One major difference between the mule deer to the south and those in the Rocky Mountain ecosystem is their adaptation to the desert environment. That makes them a widely scattered subspecies, and you should not expect to see more than a few during a week of hunting.

The few physical characteristics of note include a dark stripe running the length of the center of the tail. The desert mule deer also has a smaller black forehead patch and a smaller patch of white on the rump. Their coat tends to be slightly lighter than that of the Rocky Mountain subspecies, and they have slightly larger ears, probably helpful for dissipating heat. They rut later, meaning that the annual exodus of hunters to Sonora is in January rather than November. The desert deer also have a larger home range, with some bucks in west Texas roaming over as much as twenty-five square miles.

The Sonoran Desert, where many of these deer live, is dry and hot, and there the animals eat a completely different set of plant species. In the high mountain areas the vegetation types may be much the same as in more northerly regions, but there is much less rain and snow cover in winter, and the latter may be completely absent. Desert mulies seem to achieve their greatest antler size on the flat or rolling desert regions of northern Sonora, where they consume the desert plants. Wright's buckwheat is a year-round favorite, as are the leaves of the vicious *uña de gato,* or cat's claw bush. It is miracle enough that they can eat that notorious shredder of the hunter's gear, but it is at times among the least prickly portions of their diet.

Guides in Sonora seek out the areas of cholla specifically because the desert mule deer relishes those malicious cacti. The multiple spines are an inch long and sharper than a needle—and they are a favorite of these deer in the spring. Just walking through a patch of cholla is an experience in delicate maneuvering, yet the deer are somehow able to eat both fruit and plant without injury.

Equally miraculous is the way they delve with impunity into barrel cacti, prickly pear, and other dangerous plants. The desert mule deer I killed showed no evidence of damage to lips, tongue, or mouth. Less ominous plants consumed by desert mule deer include wait-a-minute, fairy duster, wild grape, and indigobush. As with the Rocky Mountain subspecies, almost any bush, sedge, or forb is food to the desert mule deer.

Naturally, in a land where water is at a premium, prolonged dry spells can dramatically affect the reproduction rates of does and the antler growth in bucks. The year after I harvested my marvelous book buck, a severe drought impaired the harvest. Try to hunt desert mule deer after a wet summer, if at all possible. Months without rain in their world is significant and sometimes devastating.

The basic and general biology of the desert mule deer is essentially the same as that of the Rocky Mountain mule deer. Of most significance to the hunter is the late rut. There are probably fewer major predators, such as cougars, in the Sonoran portion of the range, but I am unaware of

Desert mule deer. Sonora, Mexico, January 1996.

Dropped desert mule deer antler and prickly pear cactus.

any statistics suggesting that their fawn survival is any better than that farther north, possibly because of the abundance of coyotes. If fawn survival is no better, it could also be because the harsh environment has its own unique mortality factors, not the least of which might be learning to eat the many dangerous plants.

In hunting the desert mule deer, take along your best leather boots as defense against the awful cholla. But be sure to watch where you step anyway, because even the best combination of rubber and leather can't guarantee that those razor-sharp spines won't penetrate. Expect a tremendous amount of walking, possibly more than on any other flat-ground hunt in North America. Of course, you could get the perfect break and shoot a nice deer from the *sendero*, but don't count on it.

One can hunt in total disregard of the usual camouflage clothing and do perhaps as well. I killed my desert mulie wearing a bright blue chamois shirt and red suspenders, and I got more colorful pictures as a result. It's amazing how well one can take really good trophies by staying out of sight and motionless when necessary, and by being aware of the wind drift. Patagonia climbing pants are my favorite for many types of hunting, but especially in the desert, because they are tough

and durable, and the double seats and knees offer some protection against nasty plants.

As with all members of the deer family, a rifle in the .30-caliber range really isn't necessary; anything from .222 up will do fine if bullet placement is good. I used my all-purpose load, a 165-grain Nosler handload, to take my desert mule deer.

Getting a rifle into Mexico is unavoidably complex, but it's possible as long as you are willing to jump through all the hoops. A move is afoot to simplify the process, though, and as I write this I have been informed that the regular customs people, rather than the military, will now be checking the firearms. Commercial services can handle most of the details, a course I have chosen the last several times I hunted in Mexico.

Besides the rifle and scope and more basic gear, take your warmest sleeping bag if you'll be tenting or otherwise exposed, because ice sometimes forms in the drinking water overnight in Sonora in January, and farther north it isn't anything but colder. You probably won't need your rain gear unless you leave it at home: see what the day is offering, and then leave it behind unless threatening clouds are in view. Be sure to take a good skinning knife, because your Mexican guide, no matter how experienced, probably doesn't have one. Good binoculars are a must, so take your best.

The desert is a bewitching place to hunt, so filled with contrasts that it can confound the senses. To look at the desert in January, with freezing temperatures superimposed over the effects of heat and drought, one would be hard pressed to conclude that magnificent creatures could dwell there. But dwell they do, in relative abundance, and in proportions of antler that make even the most experienced hunter salivate.

EL BURO GRANDE DE SONORA

The rocky terrain spreads before me desolately, and the dry plants on all sides appear dead. The only visible life is the occasional *vaca,* or cow. Bare soil is everywhere, but the arid country supports a wealth of bristling plants, the most ostentatious of which have a profusion of spines. Stately organ pipe cactus adorn the landscape, as do ocotillo and cholla.

Ironwood and paloverde, the trees of the desert, are abundant in the lower terrain but become scattered as the elevation increases. These hardy plants maintain rich green leaves even in the winter, and they add diversity of color to the scene.

I am amazed that the fat cattle, late-coming foreigners to this strange land, can subsist so well on the sparse grass here.

I survey the land from a rocky promontory, a rare feature among the rolling hills and sandy arroyos. The meandering creek beds are one of our principal routes by which to navigate this treacherous landscape. I spotted a doe desert mule deer, or *bura,* as we approached from the nearby Jeep, but no *buros,* or male mule deer, are in evidence. I am suffering in the heat of midday, and it seems that every animal must be resting underneath one of the shading plants, out of sight and unapproachable.

The desert here is a place of remarkable contrasts and beauty. The bare dirt is so thoroughly dry that one wonders how plants survive at all. The steep-banked washes we have been negotiating are one clue, since moving water was obviously a factor in sculpting this land. We are hunting in early January, when daytime temperatures of 85 degrees Fahrenheit are not uncommon, creating a major disparity with nighttime readings that are often below freezing. There can be some spotty rain this time of year, I am told, though this season has not been so blessed. As we survey the land, the twelve inches of rain

An old .30-06 rests against its prey.

the region receives are long forgotten, except as a legacy in the plants. The hillsides have several varieties of tan grasses that adorn the open areas, and the sticker bushes and brush of all varieties could not have grown so robust without nourishing rain. Cacti, many of which serve as watery reservoirs for the animals that subsist here, are everywhere. These villainous desert residents are a necessary part of the ecology. Any rain brings a burst of intense photosynthetic activity in Sonora any month of the year, but we seem destined for unending clear skies.

The hunting site is Rancho Rosa Crisanto, some sixty miles north of Hermosillo, Sonora, Mexico. Desert Sun Safaris, the brainchild of Ivan Romo of Hermosillo, has leased thousands of acres of private ranch land on which to conduct hunts for desert mule deer and several other species.

Yesterday I walked twelve miles with my guide, Quirino Sandoval, and we saw quite a few does. The big boys, who are supposed to be heavily in rut now, were nowhere in evidence. We struck several fresh *buro* tracks but lost all of them in the maze of footprints that fill each arroyo; so much for the myth that you stay with a track until you spot your quarry. That tactic no doubt works best when a recent rain has erased all the confusing competition.

It is indeed a pleasure to soak up the warm air as we wait and watch. The sky is so blue that it defies description, the kind of azure high-pressure expanse that readily discourages moisture. A tiny bird with a long, slender black bill, a head the color of an olive, and a gray body with dark highlights on the wings and tail forages for leaf larvae directly over my head, so close that my binoculars cannot focus on it. *God certainly does provide for his creatures,* I think quietly as the petite feathered fairy flits off. Also searching for food is a resplendent cardinal, a bird so common back home. The only difference I can see is its markedly frazzled crest, perhaps the result of dining amidst thorns.

We have already walked twelve miles or so again today, and as we eat our lunch I can't help but wonder how much walking is ahead of us this afternoon. My legs feel strong, but my hips are bothering me. It seems that the advancing years are always springing a surprise on me, and I hope that the persistent trauma won't slow me down. I am in good shape for my age, but the miles and the passage of many seasons are taking their toll.

There is a perfect rock against which I can recline, and another on which to prop my weary legs. I open an aluminum foil wrapper to find several tortillas, hand rolled to perfection. The first two are stuffed with the inescapable *frijoles,* refried beans that are eminently edible but not my favorite. I try to be thankful nevertheless. I wash them down with water, finding them a bit bland but not bad. Then I dig out another and discover to my delight that the last three are filled with meat and a delicious vegetable salsa. Pure joy and thank you, Lord!

By glassing we locate several dozen more cattle feeding in the distance, but no deer. Just as we are preparing to leave, Quirino motions me to be quiet and still. A young *buro* is approaching, inexplicably up and on the move in the heat. The wind is soft but steady, and in our direction, so he walks to within thirty yards, unaware of our presence. Inevitably, he crosses our fresh track and lingering scent, does a surprised double take, and then spooks like a rabbit. I am highly surprised at how *nervioso,* or shy, are these relatively unhunted mule deer. This is the first time the ranch has ever been hunted by paying *cazadores* like me, so they ought not to be so spooky; but even the does run at the first hint of our presence. Perhaps the *vaqueros,* the cowboy ranch hands, have hunted them, though the deer are now so valuable to the landowners that most ranchers strictly prohibit such activities.

As the young buck disappears in the desert vegetation, I am greatly encouraged to see antlers, even if the wearer is only a yearling. Up to this point I have seen only tracks, does, and a single small shed antler. We leave our perch with hopes rising and renewed vigor.

Quirino senses that I need a break from pushing through the endless creosote bushes, the alder of the desert whose drought-stricken branches seasonally give all the hillsides their brown tone. The most heavily vegetated places are full of them, and their stiff limbs scrape against my pants as we walk. My guide suggests we return to the Jeep and spend the late afternoon cruising some of the likely ranch roads instead of continuing to battle the brush.

Tales around the campfire in Sonora.

The sun retreats slightly from overhead before we descend the hillock and board our vehicle. We have gone only a mile or so when we encounter another hunter from our group. He hails our arrival thankfully, since his guide is unable to get their Jeep started. Theirs has been an aberration among Desert Sun vehicles, which have run reliably for the most part. A little tinkering and a push and they are mobile once more.

As we drive, Quirino tells me of his family, as well as his history of trekking for desert game. He and two of his brothers are well known in Sonora as the best *guias,* or guides, in the business, though he is charmingly modest about it. In the off season he is an active *vaquero,* working cattle on a big spread nearby. Most of his guiding has been for *borregos,* or desert bighorn sheep, but the last three seasons he has been unable to find such work in Sonora and has relied on guiding deer hunters. At first I am apprehensive: sheep hunting is far removed from deer hunting. But I am relieved to learn that his experience is vast and that he has guided successful hunters to many desert mule deer. At age fifty-five he may be past his prime physically, but he is as crafty and wise as any old

hunter. His eyes are yet undimmed by years in the merciless sun, and he spots animals easily. Quirino speaks no English, but thankfully my Spanish is more than sufficient. It is easy to see that he appreciates the rare opportunity to talk directly and extensively with a gringo hunter.

The afternoon crawls by as we move from one likely spot to another, stopping occasionally to search. A group of six javelinas crosses the weathered two-track, scurrying off in the subsiding heat to root for supper like the little pigs they are. We have seen many of their plowed areas, especially at the bases of the plentiful barrel cacti, which the swinelike herbivores often tear open and consume despite the guarding spines.

There are definitely desert mule deer here. A group of five does presents in the distance traversing the road, but still the *buro* we seek eludes us. As we enter higher terrain, a Coues deer buck with lowly spike antlers ambles across an open hillside in clear view. He disappears into a tangled draw, as the diminutive desert whitetails are prone to do.

Despite all the effort of two days of work, not one of the five hunters in our group has yet scored.

Around the sumptuous dinner table I am tantalized again with tales of the giant mule deer here. Everyone except me has viewed, and a couple of them have turned down, bucks in the 30-inch class! My friend George Hubbard got a brief look at a real monster just forty yards away, but he could get off only a single shot in the dense brush. He and his guide are certain that the shot went astray and didn't cut a hair.

I am a bit dejected, though I try mightily to hide it. The melancholy is soothed as I slice into a T-bone steak and listen attentively to the experiences of the others. I have little to add to their tales, however, except for a brief soliloquy about the beauty of the desert. The largest antler I have seen is an unimpressive shed I carried back with me; it is lying on the table, testimony to my lack of success.

Tall tales flare with the ironwood campfire, and everything from religion to politics comes under discussion. The rising full moon casts a light almost as bright as twilight, making the mountains to our east clearly visible. The Big Dipper is gorgeous and prominent, but the lower two stars of its handle are hidden by the northern horizon, an unusual sight to visitors from higher latitudes.

In our bonfire debate, I discover that my companions and I harbor major philosophical differences. One is a Christian who believes the Bible is not trustworthy; another is an agnostic; a third won't say, though "skepticism" is probably the defining word. I am an unashamed evangelical Christian. We cover most of the major areas of disagreement while downing a couple of six-packs of mineral water seasoned with fresh lime juice. It is easy to see that we will settle nothing by continuing, so we all amiably agree to disagree and call it a night.

As we retire to the warmth of our sleeping bags, my liberal Christian friend comments that we'll see who is right by who gets the biggest deer tomorrow. I shudder at the statement, which appeals to my deepest sense of self-centeredness, and silently pray that the divine will be done, not mine. Of course I would like to kill the biggest desert mule deer on the planet, but most often I am better served by settling for a lesser accomplishment and not having to struggle with the pride of being number one.

It gets very cold in the desert at night, even though the elevation and latitude would seem to dictate otherwise. We are at only 2,200 feet, and south of the Arizona border by about a hundred miles, but my light sleeping bag is inadequate. Somehow I missed the information on what to bring. That I brought a bag at all is lucky: my companion George spoke by phone to a returnee from the previous hunt and passed the tip on to me. There are still a few wrinkles in this operation that need to be ironed out, but I will survive, sleeping with all my extra clothes underneath my bag and my coat and vest on top.

My expectations for this hunt have been low ever since I booked it. I want only a representative desert mule deer, so I affirm to the others at breakfast that I plan to harvest one of the deer they have been passing up if I can just spot one of them. I gulp down my breakfast. I don't need a monster *buro,* just a respectable one, and if one presents I hope he will be mine.

Quirino is determined to change tactics today. We will take a road that has been thus far untraveled by the other hunters, and as we head down it I sense the *vaquero*'s determination. The pensive countenance and quiet answers to my questions indicate that he will accept nothing but success. We have to keep ourselves downwind of our quarry, because both of us are more than a little odoriferous after two days of hard hunting in the heat.

Quirino swings left down the untraveled road and puts the vehicle in four-wheel drive for ridge running. There is a high seat for the hunter, but I prefer being behind the windshield in the cold of the morning. Besides, I don't like to hunt from a vehicle, and we won't drive far before we do our daily ten or twelve miles on foot. A big *buro* has been seen near this area, and perhaps our fellow hunters have pushed him this way. Light is just breaking, the pink glow of the coming sun creating the early morning wonderland that every hunter knows intimately. It is as still as the moon now, and our Jeep shatters that stillness irreverently. I am eager to dismount and begin walking.

Suddenly, the Jeep lurches to a stop overlooking a broad arroyo, the other slope of which is adorned with copious cholla. Quirino points toward the area, raising his binoculars.

"Buros! Mire!" (Mule deer! Look!)

I see them, too. Before I can focus my binoculars, however, I am disappointed to hear my guide utter the word *chiquita,* a word used extensively for anything small.

I center on one of the animals and rotate the knob of my Zeiss glasses to clarify the image. My eyes almost bulge out of my head! I've seen a lot of mule deer, but never anything close to this. The beast rotates his head in our direction, and the massive rack spans twice the width of the ears! *Chiquita?*

"No, no! *Hay uno muy grande!"* Quirino corrects himself, apparently having glassed the accompanying doe first. I have already bailed out and ripped a round into the chamber.

The distance is perhaps too great for my .30-06, though I have killed quite a few animals at long range with it. The animal is now looking at us, and my only chance is to do it now. I estimate 300 yards, though Quirino optimistically says 250. Either way it is a fleeting opportunity, because the deer are appearing increasingly nervous. Pacing now and on full alert, they will bolt and run in a few seconds, for certain.

"Tire rapido, rapido!" advises my guide unnecessarily, meaning hurry up and shoot. As he speaks I am still struggling to achieve some semblance of a rest for a very long and unavoidably hasty shot. I place the cross hairs on the buck's shoulder and instinctively elevate just slightly above body center. My finger rests lightly on the hair trigger of the Remington 700, and I squeeze gently until the satisfying explosion and recoil jolt my senses. The echoing *whack* confirms that I have struck my target. The buck runs with a revealing limp, and a futile second shot chases the animal over the cactus-studded ridgetop.

The shot was a hit, no doubt about it. And what a beauty! The horrifying possibility of a nonlethal wound always enters one's head whenever an animal runs from view after the shot. One of the guides was bragging last night about how any hit was a sure kill, because they would find the animal. These guides are indeed legendary in their tracking, and I am confident. But I don't want to have to fall back on their remarkable talent. I say a brief, inaudible prayer as we scramble down the steep ridge.

I beat Quirino to the place I last saw the animal, and I immediately find the tracks of a running deer. To my immense disappointment there is no blood, not even a drop. In my heart I know the animal is hit, blood or no blood.

We search the area thoroughly but find no confirmation that the bullet connected. Quirino picks up the dry trail and we start down into a sandy flat, thick with paloverde and ironwood. Before we lose sight of the higher terrain ahead, we notice a doe standing and staring, with her eyes fixed on something in the thick brush that intervenes.

Quirino threads his way almost magically through the maze of rambling trails in the thicket. This time the track is absolutely fresh, with no confusing overlay of later disturbances. I discern only an occasional track, but he sees every one and moves us confidently and quietly along, pointing occasionally to his discoveries. My whole being is on alert, completely tuned to locating our quarry. The beat of my heart seems audible.

Finally, a full three hundred yards into the thicket and just below where the doe was standing, we find a single spot of blood. *Oh no!* I scream in my soul. The worst thing to happen would be to wound such a magnificent creature so lightly that he escapes completely, perhaps to live, perhaps to die. *Please God, let us find him!* Twenty yards farther is another spot of blood, and then no more. We follow the phantom tracks, while I keep my rifle at ready and my senses honed.

"Alli esta!" whispers my guide excitedly, pointing ahead with outstretched arm. Almost simultaneously I see the buck, lying down and looking back at us. As he rises to his feet I raise the rifle and fire quickly, instinctively, as if at a flushing covey of bobwhite quail back home. This time the impact almost bowls the animal over, but he succeeds in scurrying perhaps twenty yards more before surrendering forever.

This incredible *buro* is finally down! I approach the wonderful animal with my customary deep respect, but the size of the antlers practically overcomes me with awe. Such an animal is rare in any hunter's experience. I drop to my knees and thank my God for hearing my heartfelt pleas, and for all the good things I continually seem to experience. I am careful to

Mexican guide with ocotillo and cholla in foreground.

beseech God's blessing on my faithful guide in Spanish so he can more fully appreciate my feelings.

The majestic animal measures 41 inches outside spread, with two marvelous kicker points, short triple brow tines, and eight measurable points on each side. Body weight on the rancher's scales is a minuscule 82 kilograms, undressed, or about 180 pounds on the hoof, making the outsized antlers seem even larger. The buck has the biggest rack of any deer the outfitter has ever taken since he started his hunting business.

Am I lucky? Some might believe that to be the case, but, to my way of thinking, blessed is by far the more appropriate word. Appreciation permeates my thinking, humbling me with more thanksgiving than I can remember on any previous hunt.

Our group of four Georgia hunters ultimately takes three of the Sonora giants, all terrific bucks with spreads of better than thirty inches, but none of the others approach my dream buck in dimensions. Incredibly, we have seen perhaps ten takers, and even the unsuccessful hunter had a couple of opportunities that circumstances beyond his control undid. Wes Vining of The Trophy Connection, who booked this hunt, ought to be proud.

Flying back to Tucson on our way back home, I gaze down from 20,000 feet on the very ranch where we have hunted. The blazing red of the sunset reflecting off the Sea of Cortez partially obscures my view of the exact ridge where I found my monster buck. The experience has been remarkable, but it is dwarfed by the majesty of the Creator's masterpiece.

More immediately coming to mind, my wife's birthday is tomorrow, and I want to be there. We have been married for over thirty years, and I have seldom failed to be with her on that special day.

Taking such a deer as this hunt produced is a rarity to be sure, a chance of a lifetime, but even the best of hunts does not constitute the essence of my life. Now I am ready to go where my heart is. I am ready to go home.

Sitka black-tailed deer. (Photo: courtesy of Eric J. Hansen)

SITKA BLACK-TAILED DEER

(Odocoileus hemionus sitkensis)

*We spent the night tied to an abandoned cannery dock nestled at the base of
the tall Kodiak Island mountains. . . . It was a stunning evening.
Overhead hung a broad blue plate of studded sky, while all around us rose the sharply-defined
trim black silhouettes of the surrounding hills.
Bare of trees, these mountains towered several thousand feet above the sea below.
High overhead, their ridges flowed into one another.*

—Spike Walker, *Working on the Edge*, 1991

One never feels alone when hunting Kodiak Island. It might seem for brief periods that you are unaccompanied in the wide-open spaces, but boats ply the numerous fjords, aircraft buzz overhead, and cabins along the beaches threaten to civilize the wilderness in places. Paradoxically, the reason for all this furious activity is the quest for wildness that pulses in the breast of every man, a deep longing for untamed territory that Kodiak so nearly fulfills for many people. But that very desire to be alone in uncivilized country is overwhelming the site.

The Kodiak Island National Wildlife Refuge is getting help in protecting critical habitats, though. The Kodiak Brown Bear Trust funnels money into projects aimed at protecting the wildlife environment from encroaching development. *Exxon Valdez* oil spill settlement money has worked wonders buying and arranging swaps for private land to preserve what is special about Kodiak.

Beautiful Kodiak Island is 3,588 square miles of unparalleled scenery. It is the second largest island in the United States after Hawaii. Kodiak is 100 miles long and 40 miles wide, but no spot on the island is more than 15 miles from salt water, so irregular is the serrated coastline. Kodiak City was the first settlement in Russian America in the late eighteenth century, but the capital was kept in Sitka blacktail country when it was established at New Archangel, now Sitka, in 1899. Later, "Seward's Folly" was purchased in 1867 at two cents an acre, and the vast Alaskan wilderness became U.S. territory. For a paltry $7.2 million the vast resources of Alaska became ours, a deal rivaled only by the Louisiana Purchase. Much of the state is set aside as permanent preserve, with vast national parks and wildlife refuges comprising millions of acres. Today, two-thirds of Kodiak Island is included in the Kodiak National Wildlife Refuge, as are an additional 50,000 acres on Afognak Island.

The Sitka black-tailed deer is an island deer throughout much of its range, whether one hunts the transplanted herds of the Kodiak archipelago, the vast stretches of offshore islands in southeastern Alaska, where the animals are native, or the deer of British Columbia's Queen Charlotte Islands, where they have been introduced. Few of the deer inhabit Alaska's mainland, on account of the area's severe winters and snow conditions. Tlingit and Haida Indians of the island-dotted southeastern archipelago of Alaska have used the deer for centuries. The island of Kodiak had no deer in those prehistorical days, although there were plenty of brown bears and an estimated population of 20,000 Alutiiq people at the time of contact with the Russians in the early 1700s. These natives are not American Indians from an anthropological perspective but are more closely related linguistically and otherwise to the Yupik Eskimos of western Alaska and Siberia; they are more distant relatives of the Inuit and Inupiat of the Arctic. Their culture survives today on Kodiak, and they have come to view the black-tailed deer as a welcome addition to their homeland.

For hunters hooked on pursuing native species, Kodiak with its blacktails presents a minor problem. These deer are one of only two species in this book that I hunted in territory not occupied as historical range at the time when Columbus arrived in America (the other is the eastern Canada moose of Newfoundland). Having researched the situation, however, I have decided that the animal nevertheless fits the bill, as inhabiting native range, albeit through a somewhat minor technicality. Not only is the animal an original species of the mainland and of many other islands off both Alaska and northern British Columbia, but it actually reached Kodiak somewhat on its own.

Deer came to inhabit Kodiak Island by way of four separate transplants, the first in 1924. A paltry fourteen deer from Sitka, Alaska, were released on spruce-covered Long Island, three square miles in

Sitka black-tailed deer. Alaska, November 1995.

size and four miles east of Kodiak City. It is separated from Kodiak proper by a chain of rocky smaller pieces of land. The original animals were joined by a few more deer from Prince of Wales Island, released in 1930, and additional deer from Petersburg, released in 1934, for a total of thirty animals transplanted. That small number of deer had grown to about eighty by 1938. It is not documented in detail, as far as I am aware, but apparently the biologists who planned the introduction on Long Island never intended actually to stock deer on the main island of Kodiak. They probably hoped that the creatures would make their way along the chain of islands by swimming, something they do quite well, which required less than a mile in the water for each hop of the journey. Two bucks and three does were spotted on Kodiak as early as 1931, having done exactly that.

So while deer are not native to the island, I take great pleasure in the fact that they weren't helped all the way to Kodiak but had to swim to get there, just like the brown bears of eons ago. Had Kodiak been closer than its thirty miles from the mainland, they might have made it without a boost (though they don't inhabit the mainland closest to Kodiak). In any event, the cover on the northern part of Kodiak is ideal habitat for Sitka black-tailed deer, and the treeless southern portion is surprisingly productive for them as well. They rapidly spread out over the entire island in the 1950s, and they populated all the other islands in the Kodiak archipelago, including Afognak, Whale, Shuyak, and Raspberry. Today Sitka blacktails in these areas number in the thousands—so many that the annual limit has been five deer per hunter, though recent seasons have allowed only four.

In most of their range, the primary cover type is 75 percent Western hemlock, 20 percent Sitka spruce, and 5 percent cedar. It was originally thought that the absence of these sheltering evergreen trees would severely limit the deer herd's expansion. That has proven only slightly true, because all parts of Kodiak hold excellent populations of deer now, regardless of the predominant tree type. Dense stands of cottonwood, birch, and alders offer some protection from severe weather, but during the most severe winters lack of conifer shelter does produce significant mortality. The brushy habitat on the south part of the island seems to grow a more diverse and abundant food supply than spruce habitat, so those areas support more deer than the evergreen areas—until a severe winter comes along, as happened in 1968-69, 1970-71, and again in 1987-88.

The deer declined in numbers from that most recent severe winter, but since 1992 the population trend on Kodiak Island has been steadily upward. There are now between 350,000 and 400,000 Sitka black-tailed deer in Alaska, with approximately 100,000 of them in the Kodiak archipelago. Harvest figures for 1996 reveal that hunters took 8,844 deer from the archipelago, 79 percent of them bucks, and that 82 percent of the deer came from the main island of Kodiak, while the remaining 18 percent came from Afognak, Raspberry, and Shuyak Islands.

The Sitka blacktail is a stocky creature of the mule deer type, with a short face and a more reddish brown summer coloration than other blacktails. In winter the coat becomes quite gray. The tone of the face and chest is striking in the sharp delineation of colors, making for a pretty and well-defined coat. The dark spot on the forehead is generally smaller than in other mule deer.

An average buck weighs about 120 pounds, though on Kodiak they often attain 150. Does seldom weigh as much as 90 pounds. Antlers are often reddish in color, caused by rubbing against the prevalent alders. They are stouter, with much shorter beam length than those of other blacktails, with a typical configuration of three points on a side (including eye guards). When the normal dichotomous branching in the back tine is absent, the antlers appear much like a whitetail rack, especially when a brow tine is present. On Kodiak, bucks are better endowed and seem often to have this four-by-four whitetail-simulating arrangement

(again including eye guards). Hunters on Kodiak use the term "eye guards" instead of "brow tines" and do not count the eye guards as points. The ideal is thus a four-by-four with eye guards—the same as a five-pointer by Western count.

The superior antlers on this island could be a result of superior genetics, but biologists maintain that the cause is forage quality and the milder winters. To plead superior genetics with a stocking of only thirty original deer, and those from an area not known for producing big racks, does seem questionable.

Sitka blacktails rut in November, and a high percentage of estrous does are bred. Two fawns are usually born at six to eight pounds apiece, and they live about ten to twelve years under ideal circumstances.

During the summer on Kodiak, the deer feed on a wide variety of succulent plants, moving to high alpine and subalpine areas. They eat fireweed, red-berried elder, Nootka rose, salmonberry, reedgrass, and hairgrass, to name a few. Where conifers are a part of the landscape, the blacktails tend to move into them in winter for cover, but they browse evergreens sparingly because it is extremely poor forage. On Kodiak, and probably throughout much of their range elsewhere, these deer tend to move to lower elevations during periods of heavy snow cover, and they may even find forage on the seaweed-laden beaches, although the nutritional quality of such a diet is far from optimum.

I had always thought that clear-cutting of old-growth forests in Alaska resulted in an explosion of deer numbers, and that is partially correct. For some fifteen to twenty years the brushy regrowth provides abundant browse and healthy deer numbers. What I didn't know is that the second-growth spruce forest then kicks in and crowds out much of the necessary understory, resulting in a crash in deer numbers that may persist for more than a century. Another condition prevalent on even the youngest clear-cuts in much of the Sitka blacktail range is winter snow so deep that it renders open areas unavailable to the deer at the time of greatest need.

There are only two predators of these deer on Kodiak Island: man and the brown bear. On the mainland, wolves and black bears are also a factor. Winterkill due to nutritional stress, cold temperatures, and deep snow can result in significant losses. The main infirmity found in the deer is parasitic lungworm, which most often affects younger animals. As with most deer herds, hunting pressure has little effect on the population's viability.

When hunting mule deer in Wyoming in October, one uses much the same equipment as when hunting white-tailed deer in Georgia. But when hunting on Kodiak, and indeed on much of the Alaskan coast and the Queen Charlotte Islands of British Columbia, specialized equipment is in order.

It never stops raining on Kodiak, except when it snows. Spike Walker caught a rare evening, when he penned the opening quotation, because he could see the stars. Clear nights do happen in coastal Alaska, but on Kodiak they are particularly unusual in November, when most people hunt Sitka black-tailed deer. For that reason, bring excellent rain gear. As in most of Alaska, hip boots are necessary for two reasons. First, the lush vegetation is invariably coated with dew, frost, or snow that will soak your thighs in short order. Second, if you use hip boots you won't need rain pants;

It can get cold hunting Kodiak Island in November.

a knee-length raincoat will then be adequate during showers.

If you are hunting earlier than November, rubberized knee-length rain gear is highly preferable. From early November on, precipitation is usually in the form of snow, so a breathable synthetic rain jacket is adequate. While I have used synthetics in moderately wet conditions with good results, when the going gets truly liquid nothing can beat real rubber. Synthetics are acceptable in a snowstorm, however, and they are far more comfortable for climbing; also, they are a lot lighter, a consideration when backpacking. But be careful.

Early season backpack expeditions in Sitka blacktail country (especially Kodiak) may take one to places where no wood is available for a fire, a tight spot to be in if you become soaked.

Methods of hunting Sitka blacktails vary little from place to place on Kodiak. Indeed, the essence of Sitka blacktail hunting is simply this: climb. On the other hand, one may find a very nice buck on the beach if heavy snowfall has pushed the deer down the mountain. On my third hunt for the subspecies, we put in a good 2,000 feet of climbing each day and saw a great many deer. Everybody from Chuck Adams to Craig Boddington recommends getting high and glassing down, and even though it is heart-pounding hard work, it produces results whether you're hunting in August or November.

Glassing begins once you are up 1,000 or 2,000 feet. The deer may be near the beach or up higher, but you will see them, and lots of them. Sitka blacktails are wary little critters, more so than mountain sheep but not nearly as much as Coues whitetails. But don't expect to dawdle once you've spotted a good buck, and don't expect the diminutive creature to sit still while you make a stalk. The vegetation is just too thick for the usual approach, unless one is lucky enough to be well above the thickest vegetation and able to circle around to a good shooting location. That has never worked for me, and trying to get closer to a Sitka blacktail always leaves me wondering where he went.

A good tactic is to attain a high overlook and watch likely feeding areas early and late in the day. If one finds a good buck out of range, there is a hope that the animal will be back the next day, although the little critters can wander a lot during the November rut. Just keep in mind that the deer being on the move gives the hunter a distinct advantage.

Someday I want to hunt the southeastern part of the state, where native Sitka blacktails inhabit all the offshore islands as well as the mainland. The largest-bodied Sitka blacktails come from Prince of Wales Island. Wolves and black bears inhabit the southern half of this island chain, but brown bears are absent. For some reason the blacktails grow larger where wolves are present, presumably because their numbers are kept in check. In the northern half of the southeastern archipelago there are neither wolves nor black bears, although brown bears are numerous. Sitka blacktails are more abundant there, perhaps because the brownies are less efficient predators.

Mention of brown bears brings up one final point. Hunter conflicts with the bears are rare, even in the heart of their range, but prudence is in order. One should be ever aware of the possibility, especially when walking up salmon streams, transporting meat, or (heaven forbid) returning the next day to retrieve part of a carcass. It is by far better to pack out the entire animal at the time of the kill rather than chance a brownie's claiming your prize, or, worse yet, defending its meal when you least expect it. At least one friend has told me about the "dinner bell phenomenon"—a large brown bear's coming to the sound of his rifle shot and immediately taking possession of the free meal. That friend wisely chose to retreat and hunt somewhere else. Keep in mind the fact that every few years a deer hunter is fatally mauled.

As I said, I would like to hunt Sitka blacktail somewhere other than Kodiak Island someday. On a recent excursion to the Queen Charlotte Islands I saw numerous Sitka bucks, some in the yard of the fishing lodge where we were guests. All bucks there seem to be of the forkhorn configuration, so trophy quality is not the best. The Kodiak mystique is special, and the siren call of that resplendent paradise across the Shelikof Strait from mainland Alaska might lure me once more. I find myself dreaming of hunting there again.

KODIAK CONQUEST

The roar of a huge Steller's sea lion startles me as I stand at the end of the Kodiak dock, watching an approaching seaplane. A pride of the giant creatures lives amid the barnacle-encrusted pilings, and as they streak by their agile bodies remind me of a *Nimitz*-class nuclear submarine. They spend most of their time feasting on the refuse from the nearby seafood processing plant. I am amazed at the similarity to the sound of an African lion. Some things are named in extremely astute fashion.

I have been here twice before hunting Sitka black-tailed deer, yet I have never harvested one. I shut out that troublesome fact for the moment and concentrate on the plane as it glides onto the water just off the Kodiak waterfront, kicking up plumes of salty spray. The huge radial engine growls softly as the craft taxis forward to discharge its cargo.

I can't help experiencing a twinge of sorrow. I stood in this exact spot preparing to hunt the same quarry on both my previous outings. The regret is not that I hunted unsuccessfully but that nobody else seems to have suffered the same failure. I should have hunted harder or had better breaks, or something intangible; the problem remains elusive. All I can determine for certain is that for some reason I've been chosen to be the world's worst, or unluckiest, Sitka blacktail hunter. It is a burden that has plagued me since I was last here, and one I long to unload.

On my last trip the hunt was close to Kodiak City. I had been treated to some of the worst and some of the best weather that November has to offer. From our perch on the shores of Hidden Basin we watched the sea's surface freeze and thaw daily, and navigating daily the thin film of heaving, scraping ice in a thin-hulled boat had been adventure indeed. A spill into those frigid waters meant almost certain death. There in a beachside cabin, on days when one couldn't possibly venture out into the gale, my companions and I watched the powerful williwaw

wind rip the tops off heaving breakers, slinging the water downwind and adding a touch of saline to the downpour. There also had been a few days of sunshine, when the surrounding peaks gleamed like diamonds in the frosty air. Tanner crabs fresh from the water made many a memorable meal. And we had seen deer, too, plenty of them. Unfortunately, there had been few bucks of any kind, and most had been spikes or forkhorns.

Seahawk Air will take me to another place and another outfitter this trip. It is Seahawk's plane that is approaching even now, momentarily driving away the sea lions. The big DeHaviland Beaver slides into its mooring, the forty-eight-foot wing overshadowing the tiny dock, the beaming faces of hunters from the south part of the island showing through the windows.

My inadequacy is rampant as I learn that these four hunters were unguided, and took a whole passel of deer with bow and arrow. A couple of the racks they unload would look good on any hunter's wall. My discomfort intensifies, and I find myself doubting that I am really a good—or even a mediocre—hunter.

Finally, the cargo is discharged and our gear loaded. It will actually take two trips to get five hunters, plus two guides and a nonhunter, out to Munsey's Bear Camp. My apprehension about a third

Most access on Kodiak is via float plane.

One can see dozens of square miles of prime deer country from some places.

unsuccessful hunt is unabated by the optimism of the others, but I keep it to myself so as not to dampen their enthusiasm. Discouraging them is not too likely, anyway, because everyone who reads hunting magazines knows that Kodiak is a deer hunter's paradise. Soon the big Lycoming radial engine is rumbling again, and we are up and away.

The nonhunter who accompanies me thinks that perhaps he is my problem. Bob Walker, the mayor of our town of Dublin, Georgia, has fallen in love with Kodiak Island and has managed to find a way to join me on all my trips here. He comes for the change of pace, the beauty of the landscape, the companionship, and, not least of all, the seafood. He wonders whether he may be some kind of bad-luck charm. I don't believe in any such thing, of course, and neither does he. Still, I'm afraid that if defeat strikes again, he might insist that I come back alone next time.

Any ride by airplane low over Kodiak is a remarkable experience. Today there are a few low clouds and the occasional flurry, but the glistening snowcapped peaks are resplendent. Rocky fjords

serrate the coastline, and the ocean laps constantly at their worn ramparts. I strain to spot tracks, those of a deer or a bear, as we flow above the untouched snow of the high country. In the bottom land adjacent a river, far below, broken lines dot the white expanse where some creature has passed recently, and many more such tracks are in the snow nearby. The lodge at Munsey's comes suddenly into view, and our pilot swings the plane around and slides the pontoons onto the water. Docking with no wasted effort, we are at our home away from home.

Previously I hunted with a new outfitter in an area of considerable local and unguided hunting pressure. There were hundreds of does, but I could count the branch-antlered bucks of two trips on the fingers of one hand. All of them had acted as if they had already heard a box of shells fired at them. I hunted as hard as ever, but taking a buck proved impossible. I had blamed the weather the first time, but by the end of the second trip it had become obvious that the weather wasn't the only problem. In spite of it all, I became enamored of the Kodiak

Up top there are numerous blacktails—but finding that good buck isn't easy.

country. The seafood alone was worth the trip, but I wanted that buck, too. I am determined to take one this time.

Munsey's is one of the older operations on the island, founded by Park Munsey in 1956. He had promoted the place mainly as a destination for hunting Kodiak brown bear, but also as a fishing camp. Park died an untimely death in 1983 and is buried at his favorite location in all the world, the knoll behind the main house near the undefiled waters of Amook Pass. His son, Mike, continues the operation with his wife, Robin, and they outfit three or four hunts per year for Sitka black-tailed deer, which were uncommon on this part of the island forty years ago.

Smiling, blonde-haired Robin meets us at the dock, a very pretty hostess whose tanned face and fashionably windblown appearance are neatly at home here in the back country. Mike is more weathered, a little more rotund than his college marathoning pictures would suggest, and has a budding grizzled appearance that will obviously bloom into the seasoned maturity so typical of Alaska. I like both of them immediately.

Comfort is the word that enters my mind as I settle in. The camp has everything a guest could want, even radio and telephone. A diesel generator provides electricity, and running water in the house and the adjacent cabins comes from a reservoir on the crystal stream that enters the sea nearby. There are also hot showers and real beds. The lady of the house prepares the meals, and they are fine fare indeed. Transportation to and from hunting areas is by modern skiff, powered by Evinrude.

My sensation of comfort, however, is short-lived. Wake-up is two hours before daylight, and soon the cold salt spray is buffeting me as we motor toward an isolated stretch of beach to begin our first day's hunt. Our hot breakfast is soon just a pleasant memory as I shield my face against the icy mist. Bob Walker huddles beside me, wearing everything he owns. My guide and our boat pilot, Keith Globis, flew in just for this hunt, and just to guide me. He is vastly experienced as a hunter and a guide, and my unsuccessful hunts seem to intimidate him not in the least. We will work for it, but we will be successful, he asserts confidently. I'll have to wait and see. On some animals I've turned out to be a tough case.

With the cold wind surging from the bow, we maneuver eastward through Amook Pass, breaking into a larger body of water where the lights of an inactive cannery wink in the distance. The operation looks gigantic, but a caretaker is now the only inhabitant. Changing times have killed yet another business. We weave among boulder-size islands, and soon we catch the incoming current and negotiate our way toward the pristine beach, dead ahead.

The tides on Kodiak run as much as thirty feet, so parking a boat for a day of hunting can be tricky. The unwary might return to find themselves high and dry, with a cold night ahead. Keith expertly anchors our skiff in deep water, and the whole arrangement is tied firmly by a long line to the brush along the high-water mark.

I gaze up at the steep, alder-infested slope and quietly dread what's coming. I badly want to hunt these deer, but getting above those wicked bushes is always daunting. I remember bearing the brunt of those crisscrossed, intertwining trunks virtually every day I've hunted in Alaska. Keith senses my uneasiness and assures me that he knows the best, least obstructed way to the top. We start out stripped to shirtsleeves for work, despite a lightly falling snow, and soon we are damp within and without.

Two hours later we are indeed above the worst of the brush. We spot a doe, then another, standing like statues, watching three predatory apparitions move laboriously past. They ease off into the misty distance, disappearing in silence as we continue.

"We should start to see more deer now," Keith comments, mopping sweat from his brow with his arm. "They're staying high, and they aren't in full rut the way they should be. But we'll find them."

"Sounds like you're preparing an excuse already," I comment wryly.

Hardly have I spoken the words when we spot our first buck, a mature three-by-three with no eye guards. This creature is high in antler but not wide, so we pass him up. After all, the hunt is only a couple of hours old, and already I have seen as many bucks as I did on the entirety of one of my previous hunts. We move on after the animal glides off into the endless brush.

From the high ridgetop we can see Amook Island to our west, as well as the sheltered cove where the main camp is located. The boat is far below, a mere speck in the cold sea. Towering peaks behind us have deer, mostly does, scattered all along the line separating high brush from more

barren terrain. Majestic scenery all, and I am spellbound. We move to an especially inviting and sweeping vista, where we break out our lunch, washing the food down with cold water from a nearby tumbling stream.

We spend the rest of the day on the high ground, sighting perhaps a hundred deer, about ten of which are bucks, but all are immature except for the first. One stands on a ridgetop just ahead, focused on us, trying with all its faculties to figure out what we are. Three does accompany the buck, but rutting behavior is not apparent, and the group silently vanishes in gliding, unhurried blacktail fashion. Seeing so many deer gives me plenty of hope. At least this place shows no evidence of intensive meat hunting, or the deer would be more spooky and the bucks fewer. I begin to believe my guide is right. We will find the animal I seek.

On shaky legs after eight hours of climbing and descending, we return to the boat near dark. The plunge downward takes longer than we thought it would, so we find ourselves motoring back in rapidly failing light. As a result, we must take great care among the numerous rocky islands. We are glad to see the warm, welcoming lights of camp as we round the sheltering headland at Munsey Cove.

I am soaked to the skin, and I relish a hot shower and a change to dry clothes before settling in to enjoy Robin's delicious supper. My companion, Bob, is suffering leg cramps, so I dig in my bag for the muscle relaxant I brought with me. Sleep that night couldn't be better for either of us. Tomorrow will bring a deer for my collection, a real wall hanger, I am almost sure. Dreams of a big, mature buck recur with regularity.

Yesterday's light snowfall is gone when we awaken, our sleep interrupted by the rumble of the big diesel generator. Today will be brilliant and clear, an unusual day in November on Kodiak, but we are tentatively able to forecast it by the pale half-moon and the twinkling stars.

After breakfast we motor down the passage in the opposite direction, Amook Island on our left, and stop at a small beach several miles from camp. A tiny cabin there has occupants, as evidenced by bulging meat bags hanging high in several trees. A man emerges, protesting our arrival, before we can even secure the boat. He and several companions are not through hunting, and we are not welcome on their part of the island. We wisely elect to go elsewhere, though Keith is sure the place he had in mind is beyond the reach of most hunters who seek only the delectable flesh of the black-tailed deer. So much for solitude.

Solitude. Don't go to Kodiak for it. There are an incredible variety of attractions there, but one never feels alone. Airplanes dot the sky and boats navigate the strait below. Human figures meander at beach-side cabins where there were none last year. Gunshots ring out from many directions this time of year, and hunters of both deer and waterfowl abound. Go for the beauty, the seafood, the company, the blacktail hunting. But don't go expecting solitude. I determine not to let this interfere with my hunting. We will go to Amook Island for the day, and we will climb higher and farther than anyone else, and we will find the deer we seek.

The alders grow larger at the ascension site Keith selects, making navigation beneath them easier than yesterday. But the mountainside is also steeper. The toil takes its toll on Bob, and the going for me isn't all that easy, either. No deer are in evidence during the grueling two-hour climb, except for one lone doe. All that changes quickly as we top out, however, reaching the breathtaking view from the island's spine as a reward for our efforts. From here we can see the treacherous Shelikoff Straits to the west, but, more important, we see deer right away.

No fewer than six bucks are visible within the first twenty minutes. None are good enough, but their presence indicates that nobody has hunted here intensively. We slowly work our way along the backbone of the island, probing the thickets with our magic glasses, finding deer everywhere. Many, many does, and the occasional buck, ebb and flow amid the ideal cover, and finally we spot one worthy of a closer look.

With blacktails, a closer look is often more theory than practice. The little critters wind up looking straight at you every time you so much as blink. An effort to better our position causes our intended subject to melt away and disappear. One small ridge separates me from a complete view of the bowl in which we last saw him, however, so I convince Keith that I should creep closer. As quietly as my woolens allow, I ease toward a better vantage point.

As I move, I spy another buck, massive, high, and wide, obviously king of the island. He stands in an opening in the dense alders and stares at me as if made of stone, some 350 to 400 yards to my left. I don't need to examine this guy to know he is a real prize. He is positioned near the ridgeline and doesn't stay still for long. While I chamber a round and shuck my scope covers, he begins slowly making his way toward the safety of the other side of the mountain. I rest on my climbing stick and make a hasty decision to try to take him, even though the odds are unquestionably against me. As the buck turns broadside and is about to disappear over the crest, I touch off a round, aiming for the top of the back. Unable to adequately steady the rifle, I can't feel good about the attempt.

I miss. Plain and simple. My companions had also spotted this second buck but thought that I had perhaps shot at the original animal. We walk hastily to the last place I saw him and find no blood, just fluffy-fresh tracks in the snow. It appears certain that the buck suffered nothing more than a leisurely stroll out of harm's way. Now he's gone.

The remainder of the day is heavy with regret. Had I held a little higher, and probably a good deal more steadily, or perhaps not fired at all and hoped for a better opportunity, it might have turned out differently. Keith has had enough of my stewing, and he offers the welcome opinion that he would have done the same thing. I am slightly comforted. After all, a clean miss is clearly a just cause for rejoicing.

Around the table in camp, I am forced to relate the entire tale several times, and the buck, the best Sitka blacktail I have ever encountered, comes out the winner each time. By now, three of the other four hunters have success tales to tell. I feel waves of doubt about my prospects again, but Keith is unconcerned, even as I remind him what a hard luck case I am.

Mayor Bob is exhausted, as am I, from the unaccustomed workout. Nothing short of total disability will keep me home, but my friend can afford the luxury of taking the day off. Today Keith and I will start on a beach not far from camp, and we will walk back to the cabin after our hunt. Bob will spend the day reading and resting.

Today's terrain is supposed to be less steep, to give my weary legs a bit of rest. Theory and reality seldom meld, however, and we seem just as upward bound as before. We spot many deer, but just as high on the mountain, and all of them as

From base camp one generally travels some distance by boat before hunting.

elusive as ever. A young three-by-three with prominent eye guards, just a little too young to be of interest to us, uncharacteristically approaches us from above. I snap picture after picture as he comes within spitting distance. Give the animal one more year, and he will definitely have these upright creatures figured out.

We discover two sets of brown bear tracks in the crunchy snow, one a nine-footer and the other somewhat smaller. They are so fresh that we repeatedly glass ahead without success to see if we can spot the bears. I am amazed that these big predators can move through so much deer country without emptying it of all deer. But they appear undisturbed.

A bedded buck near a high ridgeline is heavy and mature, but unfortunately he has no eye guards and only a forked horn on one side. A good stalk would put us in position to take him, and I fret aloud about not being able to find a good one in a vulnerable spot like that.

Lunch on a high perch is always special, and today we are truly high. As we overlook the broad plain of Kodiak's Uyak River to our right, enjoy the blue sky arching overhead, and peruse the salty waters of Amook Pass, I can't think of a more beautiful setting. While we enjoy sandwiches and granola bars, several deer appear in ghostlike fashion below. One is another mediocre buck, and he beds in plain sight a mere three hundred yards distant. He is in range, but I am not even tempted, given the immature antlers and the prospect of something much better. He spots us as we assemble our gear to move on, and retreats.

As we sidehill along, I am treated to a rare sight—a silver fox, looking plump in its long winter coat. I have never before seen such short legs on a fox, and together with the long, bushy tail, the creature's motion is more like that of a giant woolly worm than a fur-bearing mammal. It pauses at the top of the ridge on a rare crest of exposed rock and looks back at these strangers as if in protest. I scramble to get out my telephoto lens, and as I aim the camera and set the light meter, the fox slips coyly over the top and out of view. Disappointed, I stow the camera back in the pack, only to have the fox reappear, as if to taunt me. I know better than to scramble again for the camera, and in another instant our friend disappears for good.

There is no wind whatsoever now. This is highly unusual for the windward side of the island, and its absence makes the world one of unaccustomed quiet. Every touch of fabric against brush, every step of boot on snow, resounds. The sleeping elderberry bushes rattle like wind chimes as we pass, and the dry grasses and wild celery crackle like crushed paper. Keith pauses to assess the situation.

"We're making so much noise that I think our only hope until something changes is to find a good overlook and hope that something shows up."

We move on for another thirty minutes, finally selecting a vista that includes Munsey's Bear Camp far below, the weathered red assemblage looking like a set of toy buildings. We find a strategic position, covering an expanse of brushy draws and grassy, snow-covered meadows, and seat ourselves for a couple of hours of quiet, patient glassing.

I see absolutely nothing. For the first time since we broke above the brush line, no deer are present anywhere, not even on distant Amook Island. I find myself doing the unthinkable, contemplating whether yet another hunt for these wily Sitka blacktails might be necessary. There are yet two more days of hunting before a defeat is official, but I can't banish the thought. I adjust my wool collar against the invading cold of late afternoon as the sun disappears behind the big island across the fjord.

Suddenly, the whisper of my guide jolts me from my daydream. I snap my gaze toward him, and he points downhill. He makes a sign with his hands: antlers, with the outspread fingers held over his head. A good one, he mouths silently. I glass frantically, but all I see is the empty brushland.

Keith motions for me to move over, his finger to his lips. I gather my belongings with a minimum of rustling, assuming from Keith's actions that the deer is quite close.

"A four point with eye guards. He was feeding in that little meadow," he says, pointing below and whispering almost inaudibly. "He fed into the brush toward us."

I briefly see the top of the buck's back, about a hundred yards below, then he is again invisible. There is no rest on the hillside, so I use my walking stick again, though the unsteadiness gives me little confidence as I sight into the brush.

"He's vacating. Look below!" says Keith, with a note of urgency. I scan the area but do not see him. Keith points to a thicket two hundred yards distant, and I instantly see the animal. The buck has apparently sensed something and is moving away in the unhurried but efficient blacktail fashion, melting into the endless Kodiak alder tangle.

"Go ahead and try a shot. Wait for him to cross an opening," Keith counsels. The shot is makable, but I wish I had a better rest. Help me, Lord, this is a good buck. The creature briefly presents broadside, and with great concentration I squeeze off the shot. The recoil jars me, and for a second I lose sight of him.

Now the buck is in more of a hurry but shows no sign of being injured. The distance has stretched to perhaps 250 yards. I elevate slightly and touch off another round, and he jumps high and kicks his back legs, an indication of a hit. I shoot once more as he shows briefly in another opening.

"Gather your stuff. I'll head on down. We don't have much light. I couldn't tell if he's hit," Keith calls to me as he departs in a jog. "Hope you got him. Don't want to make you feel bad, but he was a darn good four-by-four, good eye guards."

I get the distinct feeling that my guide doesn't have any confidence in my shooting. I would not have bet on the shot, either, but I know how a tagged animal reacts, and I could see better than Keith. As I hurriedly gather my gear and stuff my pack, doubt and hope mingle in my mind. I rush to catch up with my guide.

Before I reach the place I last saw the buck, I have the verdict. The shot was on target, at least one of them.

"I'll be darned! Here he is, dead as a hammer!" calls Keith from deep in the thicket, causing my heart to soar.

"Really?" I yell back, almost in disbelief. A tremendous sense of relief courses through my veins, chasing away the self-doubt and fear of failure that every hunter dreads. I hurry through the thick alders, bobbing and weaving to miss the worst of them, and gratefully approach the downed deer. In an act that has become a necessity for me, I kneel and thank God for the gift of this beautiful creature.

Two of the bullets hit the vitals within an inch of one another. There is no sign of a third, so apparently I missed completely with the last shot. But good enough, I got him, and it was a humane kill. Perfect!

Pictures and preparation take place by the failing light of the sun, which unexpectedly casts a pink glow over the scene, backdropped by the clear waters of Amook Pass. I finally have completed this difficult quest. My protracted experience perhaps imparts a greater than average appreciation for Kodiak's blacktails. Most hunters have no problems on their first hunt, then they leave, believing the hunt a foregone success story. For me, though, thankfulness runs deep.

As the float plane lifts off the water, I look back with admiration at the rugged coastline surrounding Munsey's Bear Camp. With the baritone clamor of the big Beaver engine, Harlequin ducks take to the air flying in perfect formation—a symmetry like that of the rack of my black-tailed deer. Such a symmetry cannot come from chance but only from the design of the Great Designer. I appreciate this more fully with each passing day.

The challenge of Kodiak is still waiting. For the deer hunter, it is the promised land. Go, and take your most thankful spirit with you. May you gain more than mere hunting success. May your spirit be revived and your gratitude magnified, as mine has been.

Columbia black-tailed deer. (Photo: courtesy of Eric J. Hansen)

COLUMBIA BLACK-TAILED DEER

(Odocoileus hemionus columbianus)

The big trophies almost never come easily,
but instead are the product of research and often long seasons of hard hunting.
A good buck is earned, and is awarded a place of honor in the hunter's den. . . .
Our deer are our most democratic game, favoring not the wealthy nor the influential—
only the dedicated, persistent, highly-skilled hunter.

—Craig Boddington, *Campfires and Game Trails,* 1989

Once on a hunt for Coues whitetails, I encountered a Californian who had already spent considerable time that season hunting his home area for Columbia black-tailed deer. I hadn't realized until then that hunting this subspecies takes so much stamina and determination. Before long it became obvious that there were distinct differences in conditioning required for hunting Georgia whitetails and Columbia blacktails. This man's endurance was far superior to my own. He could outwalk and outclimb me from the very start.

The land of the Columbia blacktail is steep and rugged, whether one pursues them in coastal Washington or Oregon, in relatively open (but still incredibly steep) chaparral country of coastal California, or on rugged Vancouver Island or coastal British Columbia. This animal lives in the densest stands of timber and brush imaginable, impenetrable tangles reluctant to yield to the hunter. To boot, one is frequently targeted by the capricious winds and rain that wash in from the mighty Pacific to wet and rearrange Columbia blacktail habitat. Get in shape and have some good rain gear with you for this hunt.

The dividing lines between the Columbia blacktail and its adjacent cousins, the mule deer and the Sitka blacktail, are only a bit different when comparing Safari Club International and Boone and Crockett systems. Roughly speaking, the coastal deer of Northern California west of Interstate 5 are Columbia blacktails. From there the line is the highest points of the Cascades in Oregon and Washington, and the highest points of the coastal ranges of British Columbia. Columbia blacktails are west of that line, including the Olympic Peninsula and Vancouver Island but not the Queen Charlotte Islands, where the species of deer is introduced Sitka blacktails. The end of the line for Columbia blacktails in British Columbia is a line roughly between Bella Coola and Bella Bella.

Some mixing occurs between this subspecies and the Sitka blacktail in the northernmost area, but the deer there are not abundant and the zone of intergradation is minimal. The blending with mule deer at the southerly extent of the animal's range, particularly the eastern edge of its range in California, has been considered more problematic. The obvious difficulty is that the larger mule deer from border areas might dominate the record books in this category if some control weren't maintained to ensure that submitted trophies are actually of the Columbia subspecies. Safari Club International recently required the hunter to submit photographs of the metatarsal glands for record-book entries in the Columbia black-tailed deer category. The hope is that this will authenticate the specimen's status by documenting the distinctive glands found on the hind legs. In the past, such photos had been required only for entries from places where serious intermingling occurs.

I should point out that there is a significant difference between the scientific designation of Columbia blacktail range and the boundaries established by hunting organizations. Scientists consider the Columbia black-tailed deer to range all the way down the eastern side of the Sacramento Valley and almost to Lake Tahoe. The geography is radically different from that found in the record books, where the line is drawn much farther west. It appears that the boundaries established by Safari Club International and the Boone and Crockett Club are conservative and should result in few mule deer entries being included in the record books as Columbia blacktails.

These petite deer inhabit dense coniferous forests much of the year, though in areas where elevation is available they may summer high and winter down low. Typical range is Douglas fir type in the alpine areas, and oak woodlands interspersed with grassy areas at lower elevations. In both places there is usually an understory of various shrubs and ferns and scattered open areas of annual grasses and forbs. In areas of clear-cutting, deer numbers are higher because of the increased growth of edible plants, but the old-growth forests provide essential shelter during the deep snows of winter, when plants may be inaccessible.

Coastal blacktails eat a wide variety of plant species, and in California a favorite forb is the starflower. The deer compete to some degree with livestock, but since they are browsers they eat very little grass. They can eat certain plants that are toxic to domestic animals, such as horsetail and bleeding heart. They sometimes will consume plants in one area of their range that are disdained elsewhere by the same subspecies.

A buck seldom weighs 200 pounds, even in the areas of Washington and Oregon known to produce the heaviest blacktails. The animals average somewhat less in coastal British Columbia, on Vancouver Island, and in California, where mature bucks seldom achieve 150 pounds. In addition to size, several other physical traits distinguish these creatures from their cousins.

The color of the Columbia blacktail is generally the same as that of the mule deer, but in winter they assume a reddish color reminiscent of their close kin, the Sitka black-tailed deer. The tail is solid black on the dorsal side, except for a white fringe that contrasts with the mule deer's solid white tail with a black tip. The tail of blacktails is also much wider for their size than that of the mule deer, making it appear significantly larger. The tail lacks piloerectile facility, however, and is never used for signaling in the manner of whitetails and pronghorns. The metatarsal glands on the hind legs of a blacktail are about half the size of those on a mule deer and are located much nearer the hoof than in mule deer, about halfway down from the joint. The face is darker and much shorter, giving the blacktail a more pleasing profile and a more petite and handsome appearance, in my opinion. The ears are also a bit smaller in comparison to body size.

The antlers naturally are of the type carried by mule deer, being dichotomous (branching) instead of having points arising from a main beam. Antlers on Columbia black-tailed deer are mostly shorter and thicker than those of mule deer, a trait congenial to their densely forested habitat. In open country, such as chaparral areas of California, the rack may assume a broader and thinner appearance, more like that of mule deer. Columbia blacktail antlers are usually lacking brow tines throughout much of their range, though my Humboldt County blacktail was an exception. The back fork in a mature buck is often unbranched and very heavy, giving a look to the rack that is unmistakably blacktail.

The main predator of the Columbia blacktail is the coyote, which can easily kill fawns as they are born and for several weeks thereafter. In winter coyotes will frequently use snow conditions to their advantage and kill adult deer. Mountain lions are a major predator where they are abundant, and no doubt in certain areas golden eagles and black bears take some deer. In heavily populated California, as with white-tailed deer on the East Coast, the automobile is another factor. The availability of prime habitat, which is becoming problematic in certain places, is of major importance to black-tailed deer numbers. In California, some areas are experiencing significant declines in deer populations as a result of overgrazing and disturbance of the natural fire cycle.

The blacktail's dense habitat has resulted in a change in defensive response over time. Rocky Mountain mule deer and desert mule deer exhibit "stotting," the classic mule deer bounce, to flee danger. The blacktail behaves more like a whitetail and is far more likely to simply sneak off into the dense brush and disappear.

Perhaps three million deer occupied current Columbia blacktail habitat before the arrival of the white man, and historical lows were the norm early in the twentieth century. Today there are perhaps half as many as were in the primordial population, and further increases seem unlikely, given the

A happy hunter approaches his prize—a last-day success!

encroachment of civilization and the problems that can occur with overpopulation.

Up to 200,000 hunters seek deer in California each year, and many of them hunt the Columbia subspecies. Overall success rates run between 8 and 35 percent, with a good guess at the average hunter kill ratio being about 20 percent. That is surprisingly low for a state with so many deer, but the statistics are based on license sales and not hunter effort. I would imagine that the success rates are even lower in some parts of the range, particularly the rain forests close to the coast.

There are several options when considering such a hunt. One can elect to do a rain forest hunt in Washington or Oregon, mainly on public land where the odds of taking a truly great buck are remote, or one can hunt British Columbia, where outstanding bucks are indeed a rarity though the deer are abundant. An unattractive third choice is to hunt unguided on public land in California, which all but ensures a shutout for the out-of-state hunter who has little time to learn the terrain. For the best chance at an outstanding blacktail, one can hunt the central valleys of northern California just west of Interstate 5, where the intergrade with mule deer produces outlandish blacktails in very nontypical blacktail habitat.

Hunting these deer is either a spot-and-stalk event, as in the chaparral areas of California, or a quiet prowl through dense rain forest that is immensely challenging. Sometimes they will be in broad clear-cuts that necessitate very long shots, particularly in the Cascades of Washington and Oregon and on Vancouver Island. Where vegetation is recovering after a clear-cut, they can be hard to spot and harder to hit, so a highly accurate, flat-shooting, scoped rifle is best. In dense cover, open sights are adequate.

Waterproof leather hunting boots are a necessity. Rain gear is imperative, though rubberized gear is not. I used Gore-Tex gear with good results. Since you may be doing a lot of sneaking through deep brush and dense thickets, use soft camouflage clothing to stay quiet and unobtrusive. You may be hunting in a lot of coastal fog and overcast, and the country is impenetrable in many areas, so a compass or GPS is highly desirable, unless you have a knowledgeable guide. Along those same lines, be prepared to spend the night in the woods, particularly in the coastal areas of Washington and Oregon, even if plans call for returning to camp. A light day pack will hold survival supplies, a few chocolate bars, a space blanket sleeping bag, and fire-starting materials, in addition to such necessities as extra ammunition.

Depending on the area you hunt, some of this may be unnecessary. If you take your Columbia blacktail on a ranch in California, where I got my best animal, you'll likely stay in a comfortable ranch house with all amenities. If you're backpacking the northern Cascades, it's a whole different enterprise. The variety of experiences and challenges is part of the joy of hunting

PACIFIC COAST BUCKS OF RANCHES AND RAIN FORESTS

It must be a somewhat comical caravan, all of us crowded into the long cab of Jeff Davis's pickup, guides and hunters alike. We hunters have just arrived in California to partake of Jeff's specialty, the Columbia black-tailed deer. The drive over the mountains from Sacramento was scenic, but the ranch itself is the real treat. We are now driving among spreading oaks and high chaparral, prime habitat for our quarry. Dark is approaching, and tomorrow is opening day. Our host hopes to whet our appetite by showing us some of the bucks that range over the impressive coastal ranch we will be hunting.

The huge chunk of Humboldt County that is the Cottrell Ranch doubtless harbors some of the best black-tailed deer habitat in the world. The ranch has been in Graham Cottrell's family for more than a hundred years, and hunting pressure is held to a minimum to keep numbers and quality of deer high. The Cottrells run a cattle operation, but the cows too are kept relatively few in number to assist the native wildlife. The mainstay of their family operation has become timber, because the coastal forests are dense with massive Douglas fir and, on the higher slopes, ponderosa pine. Oak trees of all types abound, and this year's mast crop is one of the best in years, a good harbinger for creatures that thrive on the ranch.

For years I have anticipated taking an outstanding black-tailed deer. After deliberate consideration I have chosen what I believe to be the best of all available experiences. Here in

Glassing for Columbia blacktails in scenic California.

coastal Humboldt County there can be no argument about whether my quarry is a true black-tailed deer, and on private land there are some good bucks to be had. To boot, the terrain on the ranch varies from giant evergreen forest to open meadowlands, where the deer love to feed, giving me a chance to encounter a good number of animals.

There are bucks here, a fact that becomes quickly apparent. We spot a couple, neither being very large. Jeff remarks that the area we are approaching has a pair of potentially record-class animals, both of which he has seen within the past week or so. As an added encouragement, he tells me that my guide, Steve Cognata, and I will start my hunt tomorrow on the high meadow we are approaching. Before first light we will be covering this same stretch of the ranch, getting in position to hunt.

To our disappointment there are no deer anywhere on the tan grassy knob ahead. We motor over the top, chatting like unwary chickadees as we drive, noting the rich oak fringe that should hold numerous deer. Reaching the other side of the bare hill, we park the truck and disembark to look over a promontory into a deep ravine.

A small buck is feeding along the edge of the gorge and watches us as we look him over. A commotion just below causes us to startle, and we change our focus immediately.

"Look! A shooter!" exclaim Jeff and Steve simultaneously.

A beautiful four-by-four with prominent eye guards is standing now just forty yards below, staring intently at us. He reluctantly breaks away and plunges downward, reemerging on a ridge perhaps twice as far away. There he stands broadside and displays his supple body and wide rack, enticing and enchanting us at once. He then descends like a rolling wheel for the deep timber below, disappearing with the lesser companion close behind.

"Wow! Hope he shows tomorrow," says Jeff as he follows the buck in admiration. "That guy would score almost book, I'd bet."

"You're making my mouth water, Jeff," I reply, hoping we haven't made a monumental mistake coming here before the season opens and disturbing

such a wonderful animal. I wonder out loud if he isn't spooked out of the country.

"He'll be here. They're awfully territorial and aren't easily bumped out of their home range. And anyway, there's a better buck on the other side of this ridge."

I wish silently that I could share Jeff's optimism. It seems like a bad omen, if I believed in such things, that on the eve of opening day we've bumped a grand specimen from his bed.

The camp on the Cottrell Ranch is one of the most comfortable I have ever enjoyed on a hunt. The house has electricity, beds with clean linens, running water, hot showers, and one of the best cooks in Humboldt County in Gloria Cottrell, Graham's wife. The place looks to be about a hundred years old and is as quaint as a picture postcard. Flanked by dense evergreen forest and canopied by oak trees perhaps five hundred years old, it is truly a place of beauty.

My fellow hunters are experienced and amicable, U.S. citizens who have hunted Africa and other faraway lands that are still unknown to me. We spend the first night sampling delicious California wines and getting to know one another. I enjoy their company and am gratified when they express no objections to my saying grace over the sumptuous dinner. We then retire early in expectation of a predawn breakfast.

Long before first light, we embark with full stomachs and high hopes. Steve and I will approach the hill known as Bloody Run, the place where we saw the fine buck last evening. I caution Steve that I am often a hard case, and frequently I must hunt hard to achieve my objective. With characteristic guide bravado he assures me that all is well and that I will get my chance, despite my history.

It is too dark to see much when we first arrive, and we wait in the truck for the sky to lighten. I don my down vest against the chill of the cool wind off the nearby Pacific. As the light improves we move out, the familiar feel of pack and rifle filling me with nostalgic recollections of myriad similar forays. The thrill is that of not knowing what the day holds—what adventures, what hardships, what triumphs, what blunders. The beauty of the coming dawn and the clear sky fill my heart with joy.

We stay as close to the edge of the dark timber as practicable, hoping our elusive quarry will miss our intrusion. Up ahead are three does, and their sharp eyes already have us pegged. They stand for several minutes high above on the hilltop, then slowly retreat over the brow of the bluff. A pair of does in a ravine below never know we are here, and we edge quietly past to the next draw without alerting them.

A massive rock protrudes from the flank of our mountain, and it is here that Jeff has seen a buck of record-book proportions. Intensive glassing in the improving light fails to reveal him today, though. Up we go toward the top, nearing the area where the good buck fled a scant twelve hours ago. I can't imagine a smart old buck coming back out into the open, but it can't hurt to look. Suddenly, Steve drops to the ground and motions me to do the same.

Up ahead five does feed unawares, the wind being in our faces. They block our approach to the promontory we visited earlier. We back off and try to move around them, and immediately we bump into a small three-by-three buck with velvet still clinging to one antler in a streamer that flaps like a banner in the breeze. We don't want the animal, of course, but it is good to see antlers glistening in the sunlight.

Flanking all the animals and dropping off the backside of the hill, we move quietly to a vantage point. We sit in the dry grass underneath a massive oak tree and wait, looking across the basin toward where we were last night. I notice now for the first time the extraordinary bounty of acorns, large and succulent, on the ground. These deer should be as fat as corn-fed pigs, but they won't have to feed long to fill up.

The does move toward us, and a wise old one tops out a scant ten yards away. No movement on our part is necessary to cause her to do a reversal and head back up and over the hill, taking the others with her. The incident proves simply how well the doe knows her home territory and that she sensed something sinister about the two motionless apparitions.

At last the way is clear to approach the hot spot we have been trying to reach all morning. We move across the flat top of the knob, staying well back from the exposed brow, and no more deer block our path. We finally get there, but the big buck is nowhere to be found. The sun is rising, along with the temperature, so I shed my outer layers of clothing as we rest and survey our surroundings.

There is movement in the trees far below, a small spike buck as best we can tell. Soon we find several bucks, but all are young and certainly not trophies. Still, the sightings give hope of better things to come. The warm sun imparts a touch of sleepiness, and I recline against my pack between periods of glassing.

"I see another buck, down there under that oak tree," I comment to Steve as we wait and watch. "And another to his left."

"I see them. There's one over to their left, too. He looks bigger."

"I see him. Heavy, huh?"

"Looks like a good three-by-three, at least," mulls Steve, now peering through the spotting scope. "Really wide and tall. But no fourth point and no eye guards. Look at that potbelly, though. An old animal, I'd bet."

"Good enough?"

"Nope. Not the first morning of the hunt. But he'll score uncommonly good for a three-by-three, I can tell you that. That back point must be a foot long."

I take my turn at the spotting scope and marvel at the sight. I have my heart set on at least a three-by-three with eye guards, the configuration we call an eight-pointer back home. I have a nagging feeling I might be making a mistake turning down a mature animal, even if it is early in the hunt. But I'll stick to my practice of following the advice of a competent guide.

More deer materialize like ghosts out of the dark timbered edges, feeding on acorns and frolicking like children at play. By 10 A.M. we have seen eighteen bucks, but the oldster is by far the best. Steve believes he could be the dominant buck in these parts, and I again have the feeling I might be making a mistake. But the decision is irrevocable now, as the buck has faded into the thick timber.

At lunchtime we return to the ranch house and dine extravagantly once again. We admire the beautiful buck with a single prominent drop tine that one of the other hunters has harvested, a unique trophy with a feature seen only rarely in true coastal blacktails. I would take such a buck without hesitation, and I congratulate him on his magnificent trophy.

Afternoon nap time past, we return to our perch. Many deer are again visible, and two young bucks are sparring down in the oak flat, providing minutes of enjoyable entertainment. Only hunters get to watch such antics, for the most part, and as always I revel in the spectacle.

The big three-by-three again appears, this time with another smaller buck with a single brow tine. Still not good enough, according to Steve. There are deer all over the bottom beyond the two, feeding and resting.

For no immediately apparent reason, the deer abruptly scatter in all directions, several does and two small bucks charging up the steep hillside toward us as if in fear for their lives. The animals stop just below us and look back down the hill toward where the two larger bucks have been feeding, all eyes showing white and all senses trained to possible danger.

"A bear! A big bear!" I call quietly to Steve as I spot a huge black form ambling lazily through the trees.

"I see him! What the heck is he doing? Does he think he can catch those deer?"

"He's stopped now. And our two big bucks have disappeared into the timber, too."

The deer we can still see are within seventy-five yards of us, and one doe finally looks up the hill and spots us. The others continue to watch the bear as it gradually moves off into the fir thicket, but this old girl has us clinched. For a full ten minutes the doe is immobile, until she finally decides that we are a bigger threat than the bear. With a flick of her short black tail, she bounces down the hill into the forest and out of sight.

I am amazed at how these animals rebound. Not a half-hour after the bear passed by, the two larger antlered deer emerge from a buckbrush thicket and begin feeding once more. Why can't the trophy buck we saw last evening be that unconcerned? On the other hand, bruins are extremely common on the ranch, and the deer likely see more of them than they do people.

Our day ends with twenty-seven bucks spotted, an astonishing total even here in the heart of Humboldt County. Around a table filled with the best in grilled beefsteak, we swap tales and rejoice in this terrific ranch. We are privileged to enjoy 35,000 acres of the best coastal black-tailed deer habitat anywhere.

The aroma of brewing coffee arouses me at 4:30 A.M. Today we will do more walking and try to sneak through the dark timber if our prey is not visible in the open.

As the dawn light breaks, we move across the open hillside to our vantage point. The deep valley is filled with heavy fog that looks like a smooth layer of whipping cream applied with a spatula. As it lifts, we begin once more to spot deer in nearly every nook in the gigantic basin. The morning is a repeat of the previous, including another sparring match between the two immature bucks. Neither the big 3X3 we saw earlier nor the spooked buck of our first evening is visible, however, so we will have to go to Plan B.

I don't need to tell most people that I love to hunt and that I go to incredible lengths and make significant sacrifices to do so. Nevertheless, not all hunting is created equal, and some aspects of my favorite activity are more appealing to me than others. Sidehilling through impenetrable timber while clinging to the vegetation to keep upright is not what I like best. The ground is as dry as sawdust, and the dead leaves and grasses crunch underfoot. I am deeply appreciative when we intersect an old logging road and follow it to a point a half-mile below our original position on the hill. I am hot, thirsty, and a little frustrated. I remove all but my undershirt in the hot sun, and we intersect a road that will carry us back to the top and the waiting pickup.

Around the table back at camp we calculate that we walked some six miles through the dense forest and back via the logging road, and the only deer we saw were just below our original position. Jeff and Steve talk about our next move, since I am slowly but surely running out of time. Jeff has an idea where a big 3X4 with eye guards may be, and we make plans to look for him.

This time we cross a couple of locked gates and some cattle guards, drive a winding mountain road for several miles, and then turn up a rough range road where we park in a scenic glade beside a spring. Deer sign once more abounds, and I feel my hope rising. Despite my high and perhaps unreasonable expectations, however, nothing shows except a pair of young bucks and a sprinkling of does. The mature animal that reputedly rules this area is absent. I watch one side of the promontory while Steve inspects the back. On his return he reports in hopeful tones that he has found a very good buck one mile to our west on another ridge, but unfortunately the hour is so late we will have to try for him tomorrow.

As we wend our way back toward the truck, a touch of depression begins creeping into my mind. I am down to my last day. Once more, I will be forced to go to the wire if I am to return home successful. In the midst of such a deer haven I am not prepared to give up until the very last minute. But one can't help but have some down times when nothing seems to work.

The most positive aspect of our vigil this evening is the large buck that Steve spotted in the distance. Given my history on this hunt, I can't believe that we will find him tomorrow, but it seems our best bet for my last day. If we can't locate the buck in the morning, it's back to our original ridge for the afternoon.

Chain saws and falling timber surround us at our parking place in the deep timber the next morning. We seem to be far enough from the logging, but I can't help but wonder if the noise and the human presence might not have moved the animal Steve spotted last night to parts inaccessible. We have little choice but to try,

however. The mountain the buck was on is high, and we will have to climb in the building heat for two hours or more to reach his sanctuary. *Lord, help us,* I pray as we sweat and toil upward.

There are deer up ahead now, moving stealthily away from us in the improving light. One is a small buck, only a forkhorn; the others are does and young spotted fawns. They hesitate long enough that I could get off a shot if one was a large buck. They gradually fade into the timber and disappear.

Topping out, we leave the commotion of the logging operation behind and near the spot where Steve spotted the buck last night. We overshoot slightly and find ourselves well above the ridge that is our objective, an understandable error in the dense forest. We must descend perhaps 1,000 vertical feet to get below our quarry, since the wind will reveal our presence otherwise. We drop down a steep gulch, hating the thought of giving up the hard-earned elevation.

We have seen no deer since that first group, a puzzling development in such ideal habitat. The ground is littered with acorns, and another scenic spring gushes from the hillside, the lush green of the ferns creating a veritable garden in the wilderness. Where are all the deer? Has the

Columbia black-tailed buck watching us as we seek his grandfather.

distant noise of chain saws and falling trees spooked them? Steve is as deeply puzzled as I. We move down the small rivulet and then cross it; the buck's ridge and the meadow where he was feeding is just ahead.

Thankfully the wind is in our faces as we gaze upward. We reach a prominent rock on an open ridge, but still nothing alive is in evidence. We can continue on upward, but the thick timber would make a shot highly improbable, even if we kicked the buck from his place of repose. Steve is convinced that he is there, somewhere out of sight, and that if we play our hand right we can take him. I am dubious, but I listen carefully to his plan.

"I'm going to leave you here and circle way up to the left. That guy was in this very meadow, and maybe he'll come out if I go upwind and move downhill slowly. Don't go to sleep. Shoot anything decent that's wider than the ears."

"Don't you worry. The clock is ticking," I note wryly, looking at the rising sun and glancing at my watch. Nine o'clock.

"Should take twenty or thirty minutes. Look at the left ridge occasionally. Don't get fixated on any single spot. I'll wave my hat if you're to come to me. Just wait and watch if you don't see me." He shucks off his pack and plops it down beside me before disappearing over the ridge to our left.

This tactic almost never works for me. I mull the only time I can remember when it did, when I took a great wilderness Roosevelt elk a few years ago. The times it didn't work fill all the fingers on both hands. Nonetheless, if the guide is dedicated enough to climb an extra mountain, I will take advantage of the opportunity. I check over my rifle and arrange my gear so I have a solid rest no matter where a buck might appear. I lie in total readiness, scanning the dark forest and the scattered oak groves for any sign of movement. A creeping boredom sets in, but I refuse to give in to the inevitable drowsiness that follows hours of intense physical activity. Lord, I pray silently, if it could be Your will. . . .

One loses track of time in such circumstances, but an eternity seems to be dragging by in only a day. Without warning I spot a single deer two hundred yards above. The animal is a spike buck, and he is gazing intently up the

Columbia black-tailed deer. California, September 1996.

hill at some unseen object. For a full minute I look at the animal through my riflescope, and then I investigate the surrounding terrain with my binoculars to see if he has company. Nothing but birds and vegetation. The small buck begins to bounce in alarm down the hill directly toward me. I think about the camera in my pack, and even feel tentatively for it, but something tells me that I can't afford to be distracted. I retract my hand and remain at full vigilance.

Now there is another movement at the edge of the grove. It is another deer, and it has antlers I can easily see even at this distance through the scope of my rifle. There is obvious forking of the headgear into at least three or four points. A dark and mature body proceeds through the oak woods, then stops and turns the regal head uphill and away. Something unseen is holding the buck's attention. The antlers are definitely wider than the ears. No doubt about it. This is a dominant buck.

My rifle is a big question mark on a long shot like this, the barrel having recently been shortened two inches. I have no assurance that the animal will stop in the open, either. I see a grand opportunity coming, and at the same time doubt clouds my mind. The two conflicting thoughts clash like a battle of air masses along a storm front.

The buck trots a few steps and stops inexplicably in the only possible place where the shot is completely unobstructed. The antlers turn in kingly fashion as he stares once more up the hill, the wide rack mesmerizing in its splendor. I center the cross hairs automatically on the kill zone and squeeze the hair trigger lightly. The explosion rocks me backward as the animal shifts into high gear and disappears.

Working the bolt rapidly, I hurriedly move my aim to the next clearing, arriving on the spot just as the buck breaks into view. He is running low, in an uncharacteristic gait, indicating a probable hit. I can't be certain, though, so I lead him by a few feet and fire once more. The creature disappears completely. As the thunder of the firearm dissipates in the big woods, nothing remains but silence. My head spins with doubt.

"What happened?" calls a voice from high up the ravine and out of sight, the disturbance a welcome relief from the silence. Shortly Steve appears, and I wave a greeting.

"He went to your left," I call as he descends below where I last saw the deer. "Don't know if I hit him or not. I think so, though."

"Which one did you shoot at?" he questions in a dubious tone as he moves in the indicated direction. "Oh, my God, never mind. Here he is!"

"Did you find him?" I question loudly, but before the sound reaches Steve a resounding whoop of joy resonates across hill and dale, filling the air with the sunny noise of victory. It is very good news indeed.

"I don't often get excited about a blacktail, but wait till you see this one!" Steve calls back, reappearing and descending to help me with our packs.

"Is he a four-by-four?"

"I'm not saying anything else except that he's world class. World class! Just wait and see."

I approach the kill site with the apprehension of a teenager on a first date with the prom queen. The buck is piled up against a giant pine tree, a chest wound exactly where I had placed the cross hairs. My second shot hit home as well, breaking the back leg and halting his flight.

It is always the antlers that draw the hunter's attention first. These are awesome for a blacktail, tall and wide with four highly symmetrical points plus three-inch eye guards, a typical five-point configuration that is 19 inches wide and as large as many Wyoming mulies.

I bow before God, rest my hand on a magnificent antler tine, and say a heartfelt prayer of thanks for such a grand specimen. As always with such a victory, I am deeply happy and fulfilled.

Our outfitter, Jeff Davis, is as overjoyed as I when he sees the creature, which is truly a special animal. The whole experience has been absolutely extraordinary, and I continue to learn more with each hunt. The lesson this time is never give up. It is a model I must follow, and one all of us must diligently teach others.

Southern white-tailed deer. (Photo: courtesy of Jeanne Drake)

SOUTHERN WHITE-TAILED DEER
(Odocoileus virginianus virginianus and texanus)

A mature whitetail buck is the easiest animal on the face of the earth to underestimate.
He's capable of things the average hunter simply refuses to believe.
The more credit you give him for wiliness . . . and for wariness . . .
the closer you are to the truth—and to collecting his scalp.
And the less credit he gets, the better he likes it.
Like old Lucifer, he prospers best when nobody believes in him.

—John Wooters, *Petersen's Hunting,* April 1987

So much has been written about the white-tailed deer that it seems futile, and impossibly redundant, to try to consolidate even a small portion of it here. Even though I have more experience hunting the whitetail than any other creature, a statement shared by many North American hunters, I feel inadequate to the task. I couldn't agree more with Wooters's assessment, and that might be the appropriate place to start. Consider the trophy whitetail a worthy opponent in the age-old game of hide-and-seek, and you have at least a modest chance of bagging a real wall-hanger.

That statement applies even during the rut, when some bucks seem to lose their senses in the fanatical pursuit of does. The wily old master, though, who carries the massive rack of a five- to seven-year-old deer, most often is not nearly as susceptible as one might think. He may, in fact, be entirely nocturnal and impossible to take unless one exercises special techniques such as drives or rattling. A few years ago I twice saw a big buck on my farm in the headlights of my truck, but when I put a friend on a stand in perfect position he saw no trace of it in two long days of waiting. I finally put my patient hunter on stand a full ninety minutes before daylight with a misty rain falling. He killed that deer as it chased a doe in the early morning fog while the light was still dim enough that he couldn't be sure of the rack.

Deer most often live less than ten years in the wild, with average lifetimes being much shorter, especially among bucks in heavily hunted populations. Hunting mortality is a significant limiting factor, and thus does tend to live considerably longer on average. Whitetails can live twice as long in captivity, as is common with many kinds of animals.

There were perhaps forty million white-tailed deer in North America before European contact, although some authorities dispute that figure as far too high given the mature forest overstory that prevailed in those days: the lack of sunlight at ground level limited available browse. By 1908 there were a mere half a million or so, a dramatic and shameful decline that reflects the frontier mentality that natural resources were inexhaustible. In my home state of Georgia the creatures were, for practical purposes, extinct until well into the twentieth century. It is a tribute to hunters that restoration efforts have succeeded so well. In fact, in many areas overpopulation is the biggest threat to the animals.

A general description of the white-tailed deer is unnecessary, since there is hardly a hunter in the temperate zone of North America who does not pursue them. The coat undergoes a seasonal transition throughout the animal's range, with coloration being more reddish in summer and more gray-brown in winter. The long tail with its stark white underside is the animal's namesake and its most prominent feature, apart from antlers in males. The tail is used as a danger signal, and more than one frustrated hunter has been greeted by its good-bye wave.

White-tailed deer belong to the family known as cervids, or hoofed animals that regurgitate their food into the mouth for further chewing. Like resting cattle, deer and other ungulates chew for hours, preparing their food for passage into four successive stomach compartments. The term "ruminant" implies an animal that chews a cud, while "ungulate" has to do with the number, appearance, and use of the toes. There are an even number of toes in ungulates, the middle two being well developed into weight-bearing hoofs, while the other two are "dew claws" that don't touch the ground unless they are on a soft surface, such as sand or mud.

It is the antlers of the white-tailed deer that hold such fascination for most hunters, though I must say that I enjoy hunting and taking even antlerless deer, a task I must accomplish for management purposes and to put meat on the table. The cycle of antler growth, maturation, shedding of velvet, utilization of the antlers, casting the antlers, and then repeating the cycle parallels many interesting aspects of deer society. This timeline is useful as a kind of calendar of the annual pattern followed by all deer, regardless of sex.

Unlike black-tailed and mule deer, the antlers of whitetails consist of a main beam from which a variable number of points arise. A buck's first set of headgear may be simple spikes, although on excellent range a three-by-three or even a small four-by-four rack is not unusual. Spikes on well-managed land are often late fawns from the previous year, and it is not possible to judge their potential for producing trophy racks if the animal is obviously a yearling. For that reason I have ceased to cull spikes from my own land, and instead I concentrate on removing as many does as possible. I will sometimes take a buck with a deformed rack, one which has forks but lacks brow tines, or a "cowhorn" spike (long and heavy spikes) that is obviously past its prime.

The time of antler shedding, which is usually during February and March in Georgia, is also one of nutritional stress for most whitetails. The mast crop has for the most part been consumed, the new growth of spring is still weeks away, and stands of succulent cold-weather vegetation are at a premium. On my own land some forty acres of ladino clover is in its prime that time of year, if I

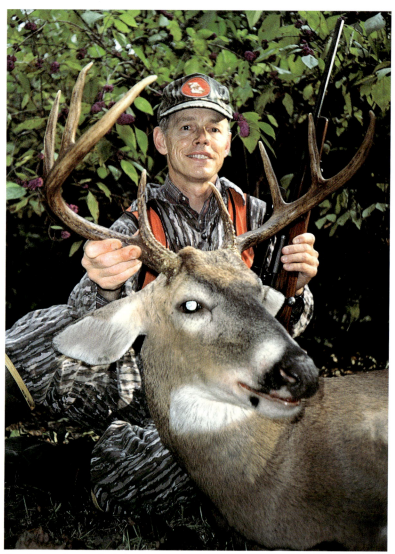

Southern white-tailed deer. Georgia, October 1996.

have successfully culled enough of the excess population to prevent overgrazing. This crop is the key to keeping many Georgia deer thriving, although winter wheat, oats, and abruzzi rye are also important winter agricultural supplements. Deer need approximately five to seven pounds of these high-protein foods daily, enough to provide 5,000 to 10,000 calories per day. They will also voraciously eat shelled corn and deer pellet supplements during this time of year. There are numerous Vidalia sweet onion farms in my area, and sometimes the critters will paw the ground to get at the tasty bulbs, as the sweet taste of the onions appeals to the deer as much as it does to people. Extensive deer damage is more common on summer crops such as soybeans.

On good range where the bucks are not overharvested, practically all the fertile does will be pregnant when the bucks drop their antlers. With healthy population dynamics, there probably will be no rutting activity at this time of year. If bucks are taken in excessive numbers, some does may not be bred during their first estrus cycle and will continue to come into heat about every twenty-eight days (up to a point, at least). I have observed scraping activity, a sign of rutting, as late as April on heavily hunted property near my home. If all the bucks eighteen months of age or older are killed before the available does are bred, the last resort is last spring's crop of male fawns, some of which are sexually mature by this time. Seldom does a button buck breed his mother, since does tend to drive them into territory remote from their own home areas. Fawns produced by such an unnatural union would be born very late and likely would still have spots when hunting season opens. In the South, due to a more forgiving climate, fawns are dropped over a longer spread of time than in the north, where harsh spring conditions can kill early fawns.

During the Georgia winter, when it is least available, the animals need the most food. It is then that the does are pregnant and the bucks are preparing for the growth of new antlers. If no supplemental feed is planted for them, or if a farmer's wheat field isn't handy, they must browse heavily, eating whatever is available. Whitetails consume dozens of plant types: anything that is high in protein, carbohydrates, or fats and that is nontoxic and palatable. Where the population is held in check by natural factors (under "natural" one must include the hunter; unnatural population control might include vehicular collisions, diseases brought on by overpopulation, and mass culling operations) there is little or no harm to local foliage. Where natural predators are absent, the deer almost invariably proliferate unchecked, and a "browse line" appears on the vegetation. In such areas, the woods (and sometimes lawns and private gardens) look as though they are frequented by a herd of cattle, everything edible being scoured up to the height a deer can reach.

When the antlers of a buck shed, there is a brief period of bleeding from the bared stump of the antler pedicle. This then scabs over, and soon it starts growing the next season's antler. In my area this normally occurs during April, and I have often observed bucks with bulbs of new growth while turkey hunting in the spring. One always tries to speculate whether a buck spotted at this time of year has trophy potential, but that is difficult until some length and branching occurs. In early spring, a better indicator is body size and configuration, a mature buck's potbelly, and a gray muzzle indicating age.

The special antler pedicles on the skull consist of true bone covered by vascular velvet. New antlers grow a half-inch per day, the fastest growth of any tissue in the animal kingdom. Apparently some special neural mechanism sensitizes bucks to the tenderness of their growing headgear, and

Sunrise from a Georgia deer stand.

they are very protective of the new antlers. While testosterone levels in bucks are high during the actual rut, they drop to extremely low levels during antler growth, which diminishes aggressive tendencies, providing additional protection for the growing antlers.

As the bucks are developing these new symbols of power and authority, the does are pregnant and the fetuses are growing rapidly. Gestation lasts about two hundred days, and in Georgia fawns are usually born in June. When conditions are ideal twins are the norm, though single births or triplets occasionally occur.

A pregnant doe establishes a fawning home territory of ten to twenty acres, and she defends that area against interloping does, although she will tolerate her own offspring in adjacent areas. If that adjacent area encroaches on the territory of another dominant female, however, the younger does may be forced to disperse. Such does have a much higher mortality rate among their newborns, since the places they must occupy usually are not the best. Also, the new mothers are unfamiliar with food sources, lurking dangers, and escape routes in the new territory. Such

competition for fawning range is a natural limiting factor in deer populations.

A doe chooses a secure location in which to give birth, and like many ungulates she eats the afterbirth, presumably to reduce the scent and to preserve precious protein. Newborns weigh between four and eight pounds, with heavier fawns being dramatically more likely to survive. For the first few weeks of life, twins bed in different areas, several hundred yards apart; they begin to bed together after three to four weeks. The doe goes to each in turn to nurse and clean it, providing an extra measure of protection from predators should they be discovered during this critical time.

In the Deep South, a significant number of fawns are lost to diseases such as salmonella and to tick infestation and debilitation in some years. Predators there take only fawns for the most part, with bobcats, coyotes, and feral dogs leading the list. Where they are present, bears, cougars, and wolves take adult deer and fawns alike. Mature deer may sometimes be killed by feral dogs, though in my experience deer generally outlast the dogs when it comes to a chase.

Hunting from elevated stands, permanent or otherwise, is typical.

478

Summer is a time of nurturing for Southern whitetails. The does nurture the fawns, and the bucks nurture their tender and rapidly growing antlers. Fawns keep the does busy feeding, since the rapidly growing youngsters consume about eight ounces of high-protein milk each time they suckle. After feeding, the fawn urinates and defecates, and revealing scent permeates the immediate area. The tiny creature instinctively scampers to a new hiding place right away, leaving behind its mother, whose relatively strong scent might give away the fawn's location if she is followed. Nobody is certain whether a doe knows her own fawn's vocalization, but she is virtually infallible in distinguishing her fawn's scent. To locate her offspring, the doe will return to the area where she left the fawn and softly call to it. Does never mistake the fawn of another for their own. It would seem logical, however, that does might at least confuse one fawn's bleat with another, which would explain why does often come running at the sound of a generic fawn distress call.

Fawns begin feeding on greenery within a few days of birth and wean by ten to twelve weeks of age. Even into the following January many does are still producing milk, however, and one occasionally witnesses fawns nursing in late fall, or attempting to do so, though the youngsters are two-thirds as large as their mothers. As the fawns become increasingly mobile, and as fall approaches, the doe may range over two hundred acres or more with her offspring.

Meanwhile, the bucks remain mostly invisible and nocturnal while their antlers mature. Their antlers reach maximum potential with good nutrition and age. An unexplained peculiarity of antler development is the tendency of an injury to one side of a buck's body to produce a deficient or malformed antler on the opposite side. This surely has to do with dysfunction related to the side of the brain affected by an injury. The arrangement of the spinal cord would cause a right-sided injury to be felt in the left side of the brain. The innervation of the head, however, is not crossed as is the rest of the body, since sensation comes directly from cranial nerves. Although that theory makes sense, I know of no study that has elucidated the exact mechanism by which this occurs.

For the most part, both sexes lie low until late summer, when the bucks begin to shed their velvet and climbing testosterone levels begin to trigger aggression. That is when they stake out their territories with "rubs" and assert their position in the social hierarchy with posturing, dominance displays, and sparring. All-out dominance fights await the onset of the rut, when the prize is the estrous doe, but by that time the dominance order has been well established and many fights avoided. The size of the deer's antlers and body often determines which animal is dominant, though there have been observations of lesser bucks (from a trophy standpoint) driving off bucks with bigger headgear.

Deer can suffer some degree of food scarcity in late summer, when many of the browse species have become unpalatable and the mast has yet to fall. Particularly in areas of overpopulation, the animals may weaken to the point that they become susceptible to disease and parasites. That is particularly true if a drought occurs at a critical time, as is common across the South. I try to make certain my food plots are in good condition at this time of year, and I make an effort to supplement with feed corn whenever appropriate.

Summer is also the time of greatest danger from epizootic hemorrhagic disease and "blue tongue," illnesses that tend to occur in sporadic epidemics. They are the most common deer diseases in the South, probably because they are mediated by bloodsucking insects common there. Deer also act as intermediate hosts for ticks that carry Lyme disease, which with the rise in deer populations in various parts of the country has become an increasing threat to humans. Since other hosts are also required, however, white-tailed deer are not entirely at fault.

Deer also may harbor a variety of worms, intestinal and otherwise, or fall victim to several common bacterial diseases. My friend Mike McCarn shot a younger buck one year that had horrible abscesses throughout the liver. It was so sick that the antlers fell off at the impact of the bullet.

Fall is the hunter's favorite time of year, and fortunately it is also the time of greatest deer activity. Does are feeding in anticipation of the winter, and bucks are preparing for the rut. The rut begins when the antler velvet sheds, and it lasts up to three or four months, though the peak in a healthy population with adequate numbers of bucks is only a couple of weeks. The rut for Georgia deer peaks in November, a reflection of the fact that the area was stocked with Wisconsin whitetails nearly a half-century ago. Where native southeastern whitetails are predominant, such as in areas of Alabama, the height of the rut is much later, usually in January.

It is a well-known fact that bucks are more susceptible to hunting immediately before, during, and after the rut. Before the rut, the bachelor bands of spring and summer break up. Most sparring before the onset of the rut is between younger, subordinate bucks, while the real king of the woods saves his energy for when it counts. When the pushing and shoving begin in earnest, an unsuccessful challenge by a subordinate buck may require that he leave the area. In their search for a new range, such bucks may fall to hunters' guns or to the other major modern predator of whitetails, the automobile.

Another change in the deer herd that occurs with the onset of the rut is dispersion of button bucks, which are driven away from the family group by the mother. The doe will tolerate female fawns even when in estrus, and often reunites with them after being bred. Male fawns must leave, though; these youngsters may move only a couple of miles, or they may wind up twenty miles or more from their original home. That apparently prevents a button buck from breeding his mother should a mature buck fail to appear. Nevertheless, I have killed several pregnant does in December and January that were still being accompanied by a button buck. Perhaps in some cases even a male youngster is allowed to rejoin the mother after the rut.

Many articles have dealt with buck rubs, the removal of bark from saplings and small trees by the rubbing of antlers against wood. Normally the rubs are not as much for removing velvet or for practice fights as simply to mark a signpost. Mature breeding bucks make them, apparently to advertise their claim on the local doe population. A specific glandular scent from tiny organs on the animal's forehead distinguishes the rub of one deer from that of any other. These chemical messengers are known as pheromones, and the deer can read them as well as we can read a printed sign.

This function of buck rubs aside, it should be noted that all antlered bucks make some rubs, regardless of dominance status. Partly they are simply following their nature and practicing for the time when they will be the dominant buck, and sometimes it is only a matter of removing the velvet, which is usually accomplished quickly. Seldom does one get to witness that phase.

Bucks rub almost any type of tree. I have noted most rubs to be on softwoods such as cedar and pine. In hardwood areas they select ironwood, willow, hickory, and maple. I see fewer rubs on oaks and cypress, though they do occur. Deer infrequently, if ever, rub the same trunk twice, doing all their damage in a single session, though the same tree is sometimes used in successive years if it survives the initial assault.

Scrapes have little relationship to rubs, except that they occur in the same woods and there may be some overlap in their function. A scrape in my area is a scooped-out three- to four-foot-wide depression in the leaves where the buck keeps the ground freshened and moistened with his urine, which he allows to run down his haunches and over the tarsal glands, producing a strong, musky odor. Does and subordinate bucks also utilize the scrape, but it is the estrous doe that really starts the breeding sequence when she deposits urine with hormone content that tells the buck she is receptive. There is always a "licking branch" overlying the scrape, and the tip of it is invariably dead or dying from molestation by the buck. The broken tips of this branch hold another scent from the nasal gland of the buck, further identifying him as the dominant male.

A receptive estrous doe will remain in that condition for only about twenty-four hours. If a buck finds such a doe, the buck will accompany her until she is no longer receptive, then move on to try to find another. If he finds one, the buck remains with her, again for twenty-four hours. I believe that may explain scrapes going inactive. The buck that encounters estrous does several days in succession may not be able to make his rounds back to all his scrapes.

Hunting over an active scrape has always been a favorite and indispensable tactic, because

A nice buck falls to an old .30-06.

successive generations of whitetails may use the scrapes year after year. I have noted with frustration that the bucks don't always show, though. And when they do return, their appearance can be ill-timed. Once I took off a week during the peak of the rut to hunt over a particular scrape and spent some forty hours tending it in a well-concealed stand. As soon as I went home, another hunter killed a gorgeous ten-pointer the second time he sat on my stand.

On my property on the Oconee River in Georgia, the bucks weigh a little more each year as a result of management improvements. Two ten-pointers we took last year weighed 165 pounds each, while an especially nice eight-pointer tipped the scales at 185 pounds on the hoof. Some areas of the state regularly produce 200-pounders, but in most areas few southeastern whitetails attain such a weight. In selected southwest Georgia locations some will go a little more than that, but the legendary 300-pounder just doesn't exist south of *Odocoileus virginianus borealis*—except in the rarest instances.

Trophy quality is a matter of opinion, unless you're considering record-book measurements. In Maine, 300 pounds of animal is a trophy. In Georgia, sixteen inches of spread with at least eight points is a trophy to the average hunter. For me to kill a buck these days, it must be a truly mature animal with mass, width, and height of tines.

Gear for hunting whitetails in the South is basic and needs little discussion. I always wear a head net, both to discourage mosquitoes and to reduce the chances of the deer spotting me. One should use camouflage clothing, including gloves, and wear the mandatory orange vest. Don't be afraid to wear insect repellent for fear of tipping off the deer—if it smells you, it's gone. None of the so-called scent blockers have earned my endorsement; positioning yourself and approaching your stand with a favorable wind is of utmost importance. Given the choice of wearing a Liberace coat on the stand or hunting with an unfavorable breeze, I'll take the glittery coat every time.

Personally, I like sneaky and quiet. I've tried antler rattling, grunt calling, fawn bleating, and other techniques, but with no appreciable success. In my experience, any noise you make in the vicinity of a mature buck is most likely to ensure he won't appear. I'm convinced that where the buck-to-doe ratio is high enough, antler rattling undoubtedly works, but few places in my area have that many bucks.

Finally, get comfortable for stand-hunting. It may not often be truly cold in the Georgia woods or in much of the southern part of the whitetail's range, but long hours on an uncomfortable tree stand are intolerable. I put seat backs that fit the contour of the spine in all my stands, and I have armrests on most of them. A four-inch foam seat is standard equipment. A buck will almost always beat an uncomfortable, antsy hunter. Get comfortable in a position with good visibility so you can be still. When a trophy buck shows, he will be yours.

A BUCK IN HIS BEDROOM

I like to hunt quail. I make no excuses for that indulgence, even though the tiny brown bird is no match for the Cape buffalo, bongo, giant rams of the high Altai, or other big game. As I am principally a hunter of big game, it might be easy to feel somewhat restrained when I relate my passion for explosive covey rises, graceful pointers, and briar britches. I was schooled differently, though, and in my part of the country the measure of the better hunter is still how well he handles a shotgun, not how well he stops the charge of a leopard.

This digression is necessary to preface how I came to be walking up the interstate highway in early morning darkness on opening day of deer season in Georgia. My destination is a tall pine tree in the middle of a clear-cut where a big buck has been hanging around. I spotted him while hunting quail there two seasons ago. My resplendent white pointer, the incomparable Hank, had just pointed, and I had dropped a couple of the speedy bobwhites when the deer broke from a brush pile scarcely thirty yards away. Single-minded Hank paid scant attention to the commotion as he retrieved the fallen birds, but I had watched with unrepentant awe as the buck departed with several gazellelike leaps through the tangle of briars and brush.

I considered trying to hunt that buck all last season, but I never sought permission from the landowner. All summer I have pondered that chance encounter. The buck had to be at least two-and-a-half years old when I saw him, with a wide eight-point rack. He had seemed a bit spindly, as young bucks often are, so he was a marginal trophy at best. But a couple of years can make a huge difference in antler size.

The tract of land of which I speak consists of only forty acres, half of which is planted in cotton. Deer do not feed on cotton, I have on good authority, so the animal's nutrition must come from elsewhere. One-fourth of the plot is in seven-year-old planted pines, as dense as an alder jungle in Alaska and ideal bedding habitat for whitetails. The remaining acreage is now ten feet deep in brush after being clear-cut four years ago. There is little to draw a deer into this small piece of land except world-class cover, since none of the three types of terrain provide a preferred winter food source, though the clear-cut offers good browse.

The adjoining large acreage has been the focus of my meditations of late. I used to rent the hunting rights to that land before it was purchased by a friend. I have plenty of other places to hunt deer, but this little field next to my old hunting lease has some interesting possibilities. The new owner next door never invites me to hunt because he and his numerous relatives and friends cover the place pretty well, and besides, I have a place of my own. But the small parcel of land I am approaching in the dark belongs to another friend who often accompanies me on hunts across North America. He doesn't hunt much, though, and I had a feeling he might let me put up a stand on the property.

I called that friend, Bob Walker, not a week before the opening of deer season, the burning in the back of my mind demanding that I do something to relieve my curiosity. Could I hunt on the land that corners with my home road and the interstate highway? He had given me permission without hesitation, asking only that I leave the stand there so his son-in-law could use it when he comes down for Thanksgiving.

My thinking had crystallized long before I approached Bob. The well-fed deer on the large adjacent tract have access to hundreds of acres of generous white oak trees heavy with acorns, cultivated food plots, and a huge creek to provide water. Most of the productive contiguous terrain is covered with mature or nearly mature timber, however, so the forest floor is open and offers little security to the reclusive whitetail. The tiny acreage I have spent so many hours analyzing offers that one commodity that is deficient on the larger property. Surely the resident deer spend a lot of time where the groceries are, but inevitably they must retire to safety to pass the daytime hours. It should be possible to intercept that buck.

Placement of a climbing stand had taken me hardly an hour. I had gone directly to where I jumped the buck two years ago and looked for a stately pine that the logging crews had missed. It seemed to be positioned perfectly so I could cover most of the approach routes to the deepest and thickest brush piles in the clear-cut, as well as the most direct path from the feeding grounds to the planted pine thicket. A preliminary trip up the pine confirmed that it would be quite easy to reach forty feet above the ground. The view had been absolutely breathtaking, all the intertwining deer trails easily visible from my lofty vantage point. As I had descended to let the spot rest until the opening day of deer season, I felt a twinge of excitement at the prospect of hunting there.

The only problem had been the weeds and brush. Local ticks and chiggers have a way of eating one alive, and I had been forced to walk in dog fennel and ragweed as deep as my neck to reach the pine tree. An old logging road crosses the property, one end starting at the dirt road on which I live and the other terminating at the fence paralleling the interstate highway. I didn't want to leave a trail of human scent when I came to hunt, so I decided to do some minor trimming along the logging road with my tractor. Soon the way to the stand was clear from both sides. It seemed unlikely that the deer would pay much attention to a tractor, given the constant roar of diesel engines on the interstate scarcely a hundred yards away, as well as the intensive farming operations nearby.

A check of the forecast the night before has told me all I need to know. A frontal system is approaching and the winds will be southeasterly, perfect for a silent and scentless walk from the interstate, at least from the perspective of a deer coming from the dining area to the bedroom. I

have parked my truck on one corner of the planted pines, scaled the wire fence, and now I am walking the quarter-mile down the busy four-lane highway, where I will climb back over.

An hour before first light I reach the second place I must get over the wire barrier. Placing my empty rifle on the other side, I grasp a small tree and stairstep up the fence, using my flashlight with impunity under cover of noise and headlights emanating from the road. Shouldering my weapon again, I start optimistically up the mowed trail, my rubber boots squeaking a bit in the dew-soaked grass. The moon is nearly full, so only in shaded areas is a light necessary. In the dark shadows in my part of the world a person never assumes all is well, because the local diamondbacks and timber rattlers crawl at night well into November. The date is 26 October.

I reach my stand with plenty of dark remaining, sweat beading on my forehead from the brisk walk, the heavy clothes on my back, and the unseasonably warm temperatures. I slip my boots into the appropriate straps for the climb and secure my rifle across my back. Forty feet later my whole body is sweaty from the exertion, but I am on top of the world. In the bright moonlight that flows from behind I can make out all the details of the recovering forest, and I can't help but wonder if perhaps one could kill a deer here by the light of a full moon. That would be illegal in my state, but I can't suppress the thought that it might be possible. I ease a round into my rifle, cringing at the inescapable metallic sound it makes.

The chances of seeing a deer good enough to kill are slim any day, because I've become mighty particular. Somehow, though, optimism has permeated my thinking ever since I first started to contemplate this big pine tree and the surrounding terrain. We shall see what daylight brings.

I settle in and lean back against the sturdy pine trunk, relaxing and letting my body cool while I wait for the dawn. I slip on my camouflage head net and my green military gloves, hoping to reduce the amount of exposed white skin. Equally important, this will also ward off the mosquitoes that are bound to find me in their search for an easy meal.

Quiet settles around my position, interrupted only by the growl of the nearby highway. Shortly I begin to feel like just another knot on the side of the big pine tree, the natural world oblivious to my presence. The words of John Madson come to me, some of my favorite prose as applied to deer hunting: "When you go into the woods, your presence makes a splash, and the ripples of your arrival spread like circles in water. Long after you have stopped moving, your presence widens in rings through the woods. After a while this fades, and the pool of silence is tranquil again. You are either forgotten or accepted—you are never sure which. Your presence has been absorbed into the pattern of things, you have begun to be part of it, and this is when the learning begins."

I am learning even as I sit in the darkness. There are many indications that this will not be a good opening day. The southeasterly breeze is fairly stiff, and the white blooms of the ever-present dog fennel wave back and forth in the clear-cut, sending fear into a white-tailed deer that interprets the motion as a sign of a predator waiting to pounce. Wind makes whitetails nervous because everything moves, blurring the important visual sense. It also carries away scent, and its rustle interferes with listening for danger.

Nor is the full moon a good sign, since deer feed at night and bed during the day this time of the month. It is also as warm as August, so the animals will be bedding early to avoid the heat. Nothing seems to bode well for my hunt, except that I am in a location with great potential that has not been hunted for deer since who knows when.

A streak of light finally appears on the distant horizon in front of me, at first competing with the streaming luminance of the moon. Gradually dawn prevails. There is a dark band of clouds silhouetted along the skyline, a harbinger of the approaching front, and a distinct red outline develops around its edges. It is still much too dark to judge a buck's antlers, though I could easily see a deer now. A waking bobwhite quail shouts its raucous covey call, the shrill sound carrying easily over the noise of the road. I silently mark the location for later reference.

In the improving light a grand panorama unfolds, the colors of early autumn materializing out of the gloom. A white mist coats the ground, thin and tentative, rapidly dissipating as the day begins. Yellow hickory trees and oaks still green dominate the horizon along the adjacent property, backlit by the brilliant red sunrise. A squirrel stirs in the leaves. Satisfied that the noise is not a deer, I continue to watch, deeply intrigued by the evolving spectacle. In the clear-cut itself flaming crimson dogwood trees abound, as do the deep oranges and golds of falling muscadine leaves. I will have only a short time to see my quarry,

A young Georgia deer hunter approaches his early morning prize.

because when the sun clears the band of clouds it will shine directly into my face.

Time always flies when one is thus occupied, and this comfortable day is no exception. I become consumed with watching a red-tailed hawk as it hunts for a meal. Sailing to and fro it sends the resident squirrel scurrying off to safety. Before long the grand raptor is sitting on a nearby limb, trying to figure out what this camouflaged apparition with the orange vest might be. My mammalian prey can't see the orange, but the bird can and is not fooled. It soon sails off to seek a less crowded location.

I glance at my watch. There has been adequate shooting light for some forty-five minutes, but I have heard not a single shot. I am probably sitting within earshot of a couple of dozen hunters on stand. It is 8 A.M., and within a few minutes I will feel the full force of the sun. I wonder if perhaps I should call a halt to this quest. I have neither seen nor heard a deer, so maybe I guessed wrong about this place. Perhaps all the deer simply retired to bed long before daylight. Or maybe I put the stand in the wrong place. Possibly that spot over there would have been better, on that other pine tree.

My mulling is short-circuited by a sudden rustle in the deep brush. At first I see nothing but the shaking of a wild cherry tree, a shower of leaves raining down. Is it another squirrel? Something is now walking in the thick underbrush, the crunch of leaves audible whenever there is a break in the traffic noise. It's a deer! No, two deer! And one has a towering set of antlers!

I try mightily to make myself invisible, but deer are seldom fooled when something unusual invades their home grounds. The buck follows the doe nonchalantly, but he has already spotted something and stares directly at me for a long while. I can't move a muscle until the buck averts his gaze or he will be off and running. The antlers are quite a bit wider than the ears. He is a heavy-beamed eight-pointer with long brow tines: exactly what I am looking for, about twenty inches wide and with good mass.

The doe has not even looked in my direction. As she eases away through the thick brush, the buck finally takes his eyes off me and takes several steps into an American beautyberry bush, partially obscuring himself. I use the opportunity to ease my rifle into position, thankful that I have taken pains to reduce my scope power to 3X, since the buck is only forty yards away. I can see him plainly through the scope despite the intervening vegetation, and it is quite apparent that the animal has me pegged. I decide to shoot through the spindly brush, since I can see his exposed chest. Flipping off the safety with a quivering thumb, I center the cross hairs and squeeze slowly. I am jarred backward as the old .30-06 thunders.

The buck is obviously hit hard. He leaps like a bronco coming out of a rodeo chute. As I hurriedly chamber another round, he runs with his tail low and heads to my right, then doubles back to the left and heads straight away from me. Puzzled, the doe stands just below me and watches the departing buck, wondering what has happened. I watch intently as the buck disappears from view in the thick cover, and I mark the spot carefully. Since the shot was obviously effective, I climb down immediately. At my first motion to remove my face mask and gloves, the doe snorts and is off for parts unknown, white tail flagging.

I carefully unload the rifle before I start down, then I turn and insert my feet into the straps. Soon I am safely on the ground, where I recover the spent casing. As I head toward where I last saw the buck, groping sawbriars claw at me from every direction, several finding my ears and face. I ready another round as I move forward.

There is no need to look for a blood trail. Just ahead, in a small clearing, lies the magnificent animal, the shot having taken out both lungs. He lies on one side, the last dying kicks of the legs telling me that a follow-up shot will not be necessary.

Admiring my tremendous prize, I reflect on what a privilege it is to have good friends who will let you hunt on their property, and how wonderful it feels to guess right for a change. The heavy antlers measure 20 inches in width, the usual standard of excellence in our area. Until this grand day, I have never killed a Georgia buck with such a spread. I thank my God out loud for the resounding success, giving Him full credit for creating such a marvelous creature, and for giving me such joy in its pursuit.

Northern white-tailed deer. (Photo: courtesy of Ian McMurchy)

NORTHERN WHITE-TAILED DEER
(Odocoileus virginianus borealis)

*I was clear above the surrounding underbrush and had
a fine view of the magnificent quarry.
His head was thrown high up and well back; his ears erect, nostrils distended. . . .
I imagined I could see the defiant gleam of his jet black eye.
His glossy coat glistened in the brilliant autumn sunlight,
and his spreading antlers and powerful muscular development
characterized him as a giant among his kind. . . .
I raised my rifle slowly to my shoulder . . .*

—George Oliver Shields, *Cruising in the Cascades and
Other Hunting Adventures,* 1889

My consultant on the northern white-tailed deer advises me that ongoing studies of DNA in deer reveal that the name "northern whitetail" is valid to indicate an animal from a particular type of habitat, but that the subspecies designation *borealis* should be dropped. The animal is the same as its cousins to the south, although it is well adapted to the lower temperatures and certain morphological features are evident in it. More for convenience and history than for scientific accuracy, then, I have left the older nomenclature, but the reader should realize that with whitetails, as with virtually all other North American animals under which several subspecies are listed, the genetics are almost uniformly identical wherever they occur.

Many a whitetail hunter has sought the northern variety of *Odocoileus virginianus* in a determined attempt to put himself in exactly the same position as Mr. Shields. Getting to that point can be a simple matter—witness my own hunt for this subspecies—or it can be a brutal, time-consuming, bone-chilling effort that saps a person's will and spirit. The pursuit of the southern whitetail is often a gentlemanly game of sitting on a comfortable stand with the mosquitoes buzzing outside your head net as the afternoon sun sinks lazily. In the north, it can be 40 degrees below zero with a strong wind and blowing snow, severe enough to make a thin-blooded Southerner wonder whether he will end the experience alive and with all his toes intact.

We go to such far-off places as Alberta, British Columbia, and Saskatchewan to seek the northern subspecies, not because the hunting is easier or more enjoyable, but for one reason: northern white-tailed deer are big. A mature buck may average almost twice as big as one from Texas or Georgia, and the massive rack of such an animal can be of record-book proportions. Huge antlers do come from the South, but it is the far North that dominates the books. For that reason, many airline flights from Dixie in November are loaded with whitetail enthusiasts headed north.

Body and antler size are only the beginning of the differences between the most northerly race of whitetails and their cousins to the south. These hardy creatures are well equipped to survive deep winters, although the margin of safety is perilously thin at times. They have been expanding northward for some time, but much of that is dependent on the hand of man. Should the land ever return to pristine conditions in those fringe areas, the whitetail might well disappear.

One factor in the changing whitetail map is their displacement of mule deer from traditional range by expanding westward. Where there are healthy populations of both species, that doesn't seem to occur. If there is a dearth of mature mule deer bucks from heavy hunting pressure, though, the whitetail buck may supplant the immature mule deer buck to breed the estrous mulie doe. That can result in a one-way hybridization producing inferior offspring that are unable to propagate. Another factor in this displacement of mule deer may be the aggressive pursuit methods of whitetail bucks in rut, and the counterbalancing tendency of whitetail does to run from the buck until ready to mate.

As agricultural practices have spread northward in Canada, the white-tailed deer has followed. In these subarctic regions, the deer take advantage of high-protein barley and wheat to help them survive. Clearing of virgin forest and conversion of open plains into aspen parklands have also made the habitat more hospitable for the whitetail. Their range has moved significantly northward this century, and they have now penetrated a short distance into the Northwest Territories and the Yukon in small numbers, reaching almost to the Arctic Circle along the Mackenzie River system. Even the maps of whitetail range produced fifteen to twenty years ago do not show a population

in the area where I took my own northern whitetail near Grande Prairie in Alberta. White-tailed deer now live in places the animals have never before inhabited. Almost every state in the contiguous United States has them, though they are rare in Utah, Nevada, and California. They have never been present in the offshore Canadian provinces of Prince Edward Island and Newfoundland, and none are likely to show up in Alaska.

In the poplar and spruce forests of the northern parts of the Canadian provinces, whitetails face a whole different set of circumstances. Fawning time, and the attendant weather, is critical. A late-spring storm can be a disaster for the newborn crop. Deep snow in winter can force a severe die-off of even the hardiest and most mature animals.

The general biology of whitetails in the northern part of their range is essentially the same as in the South, but many of their habits and survival techniques are different. Food types are divergent as well, but the white-tailed deer shows

Even noisy oil rigs don't bother whitetails that grew up with them.

This unoccupied century-old house guards the edge of a prime barley field.

the same ability to use a tremendous variety of food, both browse and otherwise. Coyotes are extremely efficient predators of whitetails, particularly fawns. Wolves and, in some areas, cougars become significant predators of both adults and fawns in these northern latitudes.

Weather has a much more marked effect on all phases of whitetail life in the North. One biological fact I observed on my Alberta buck was the incredibly thick hair, which is hollow and supplies excellent insulation. My buck had ice almost an inch deep encrusted on the muzzle, and the underbelly was likewise well glazed. Presumably that would melt off only when the temperature rose, though perhaps body heat alone would remove some of it over time. I was amazed that the active animal was so unencumbered by the layer of ice.

It is undoubtedly far more crucial for northern whitetails to prepare well for winter. They are indeed tremendously active feeders in the summer, laying up much-needed fat stores. Fawns in particular are susceptible to winterkill because they must reach much of their growth potential as

well as lay away a store of fat, a task that requires huge numbers of calories. Late or small fawns in the north country may not have time to accomplish that. Generally, the larger the fawn at birth, the better chance it has to make it through its first winter. Does must store enough fat for their own use as well as to allow a fetus to develop during a time of deprivation. Bucks face the rigors of the rut, and that frantic activity may consume as much as 20 percent of their total body weight (and all of their fat reserves) so that they enter the dead of winter dangerously lean. By December, rutting bucks have no body fat except for a small amount around the heart.

Populations of whitetails in the North are thus dramatically affected by the weather. Poor fall forage due to failure of the mast crop, an early snow that makes feeding difficult, or simply too many deer can dramatically reduce winter survival.

The rut is also a bit different for the whitetails of the North. Though rutting activity may last almost as long as elsewhere, most breeding takes place from 15 November to 10 December, since the timing of fawn births is tremendously important to their survival.

A revelation to me when I went hunting in the northland in November was the character of the scrapes. Rubs on trees were identical to what I had observed back home, but the scrapes were entirely different. Scrapes in the deep snow of an Alberta November were worked just as if the snow were loose soil, and urine was deposited in yellow streaks in exactly the manner it would be on bare ground. Apparently the energy expenditure to reach bare earth (which would be frozen solid anyway) simply isn't worth it, and the deer have adapted.

There is a fairly marked difference in the carrying capacity of the land in the North when it comes to number of whitetails. Although the deer are bigger, the harsh conditions of winter dictate a smaller population. On my land in Georgia, for example, it is estimated that there are about forty to fifty deer per square mile, and that fluctuates mainly because of legal harvest. In the northern extremes of the whitetail's range, that figure is dramatically lower. Even the northern part of the United States has a greater carrying capacity than does northern Alberta.

One technique deer use in any area of deep snow is to form "yards" in dense conifer stands that are near feed and most often have a south-facing slope or natural opening. They spend the winter there, finding shelter among the conifers. Absence of such shelter has been shown to reduce survival considerably. The yards are essentially a grand natural scheme for conserving energy, with numerous deer sharing the work necessary to keep open vital trails to feeding and resting areas.

Another behavior that enhances winter survival is migration, an activity all but absent from Southern herds. Whitetails will sometimes move many miles from their summer range to an area that allows them to wait out the winter. The moves are led most often by older does who apparently learned from their own mothers where to find the best shelter and food during winter. Family groups of older does, their adult daughters, and fawns frequently move together.

Hunting white-tailed deer in November varies in difficulty, principally by how cold it is. The wily whitetail isn't usually susceptible to spot-and-stalk hunting, though in some Western states and provinces the tactic is feasible in open country. The sharp eyes, noses, and ears of the whitetail make moving up on them in heavy cover all but impossible. That means that when you go to Canada to hunt them, you will most likely be doing the same thing you would be doing if you were in Alabama or Texas—sitting in a stand or blind. The difference in temperature can be 100 degrees Fahrenheit, though, so prepare to dress as if you were on a polar bear hunt. The technique is the same in most places. Laboring to the stand through deep snow in heavy clothes can produce a sweat even if it's 40 below zero, and the moisture comes back to haunt you as soon as you've cooled a little. In certain locations, such as Maine, whitetails are hunted by tracking them in the snow, and that exercise-intensive method requires that one dress accordingly.

For the waiting game, the best gear is down, both for outer clothes and underwear, if the temperature drops to really brutal. Wool clothes, especially the great camouflage wools currently popular, are inadequate in subzero temperatures unless one is moving constantly, though supplementing them with down underwear helps significantly. For sitting on a tree stand in Alberta or Saskatchewan in November, I'd wear something white or snow/tree colored and filled with down from my boots to my cap. I recommend top-quality pac boots, and I wouldn't leave home without a good foamy seat and a pair of Arctic boot blankets to slip on over my walking boots. The best gloves are ragg wool gloves, which can be slipped inside wolf skin or caribou-skin mitts, which have been tied together over your neck with a cord. One can shoot easily wearing the ragg wool gloves, and the skin covers can be quickly and silently shucked. The small amount of time required for that maneuver isn't likely to be nearly as much a disadvantage as being unable to feel the trigger.

Drives seem to work in the open country up north far better than they do in my part of the world, where the best one can hope for in most situations is a fleeting glimpse of the departing white flag. In the North a bedded buck can sometimes be flushed to a waiting gunner, who must decide in a flash if the animal is good enough. Rather than thrashing the brush and spooking the deer, it is much better to come in upwind so the animal can smell you, ease along slowly and quietly, and hope he tries to sneak out undetected. The waiting hunter has a far better chance, north or south, of getting a good shot using that approach.

So far, I haven't mentioned rattling or grunting, because I've never had success with either. That observation runs counter to conventional wisdom, and to countless magazine articles. I've tried both numerous times in Georgia, however, and I've never had any response except an occasional blank stare in my direction from a buck on a food plot. I don't claim to have done it exactly right or to have used it in the right place (such as Texas, where the deer apparently have a definite tendency to respond to it), but my advice is to leave such tactics to the guides unless you are a whitetail expert.

You're far better off, in most cases, to hunt where there is a well-managed population of deer. Find an active scrape line, get to your stand quietly and early, then sit very still and don't try anything fancy. Most good bucks are killed exactly like that, and I highly recommend the most unobtrusive technique possible. So will your guide, most likely. Best of luck, stay warm, and maybe a genuine monster, all points and mass with his thick hair matted with ice, will come by. It sometimes happens like that when you least expect it.

ONE-MINUTE HUNTING IN ALBERTA

Arriving in Edmonton, Alberta, on a snowy November night, I gaze down from the plane at the stark white landscape, a small shiver and a bit of dread permeating my bones. It is cold out there, and forecast to get colder. Unseasonably cold, even for this part of the world, which we in the Deep South perceive as the "Frozen North." A brisk snowfall shows in the landing lights on final approach, and the white snowplowed streets below give testimony to the ongoing battle against impending winter.

I am on my way to Grande Prairie, Alberta, to hunt white-tailed deer with my good friend Lowell Davis. This constitutes a rare opportunity to hunt Canada without the services of a licensed outfitter, the province having installed a special category of permit for friends and family of residents a few years ago. It originally applied only to Canadians, but this year it includes nonpaying aliens as well.

The flight to Grande Prairie is an early one tomorrow. I check into the motel near Edmonton International Airport and petition the clerk for a wake-up call in six hours. I can't help but do a rough calculation in my head of how much this

One keeps a good lookout into brushy edges and deeper timber when hunting the wily northern whitetail.

short night's sleep will cost, and it comes to nearly $20 an hour. Oh well, it's better than toughing it out at the airport on a plastic chair. I drift off to sleep after a refreshing hot shower.

I blast the sleep from my eyes with hot coffee and then wait for my ride back to the airport. In view of my fatigue and the short night's rest, I am glad it is Sunday. Lowell and I will not be hunting today, that peculiarity being the law and custom in much of Canada. It is as brutally cold as I had expected when I step from the motel into the waiting van. Check-in at the airport is routine. The snowfall has stopped for the time being, and the visibility looks wonderful in the predawn light that eerily pierces the waiting room windows. Snowplows are busy on the runways, either clearing or maybe grooming them like ski runs—it's unclear which. In any event, we should be rolling—or sliding—down one of them soon.

Grande Prairie is almost due northwest of Edmonton near the British Columbia border, a scant eighty miles from Dawson Creek, B.C., and the start of the Alaska Highway. My destination is the heart of the famed Peace River country, an area I have passed through many times, though I have never stayed long enough to get acquainted. These are the lower reaches of the great Mackenzie River system that drains the vast interior region of the North American continent into the Arctic Ocean, and I consider at length the implications. Water in our hunting area will flow for untold hundreds, perhaps even thousands, of miles before finally emptying into that icy sea. Chance may then lock some of it into the Arctic ice pack. People in ages past have made a similar journey—explorers, Native Americans, fur trappers and traders, missionaries, prospectors. I anticipate my own adventure, following in the footsteps of those who have gone before me, with equally high hopes for success.

Lowell guides for a Yukon outfitter in the late summer and early fall and does logging work as a part of the family business much of the rest of the year. He is a relentless hunter, living and breathing the activity. I am confident we will have a great time if I can count on my duffel full of high-tech gear to keep me warm enough to enjoy it. When last I talked to him, my host had been forced to rethink the camp setup he had planned. The ranch he had intended to hunt, a huge block

of lightly hunted private land, has had its population of whitetails decimated by last year's brutal winter. He has scouted the area intensively and found only the more hardy mulies in abundance. I want a northern whitetail, so the mule deer can rest easy. Consequently, Lowell has been searching closer to his home, but despite good deer numbers he still has not been able to locate the quality buck I want.

Landing at Grande Prairie, I note that the snow here is deeper than in Edmonton, and the wind blows ominously across the runway in intimidating swirls. Wheat and barley fields stretch toward the horizon, and arrow-straight survey lines surround each quarter-section of land in a precision patchwork of geometric squares. This country was settled by the white man *en bloc* in the early twentieth century, when the Canadian government sold the land to prospective settlers for pennies an acre. The surrounding countryside was duly surveyed and mapped in advance of the pioneers. It is thus a region with every appearance of checkerboard planning. What excites me is the intensity of the farming combined with large areas of undeveloped woodland, ideal habitat for the giant white-tailed deer for which the area is famous.

The terminal is as modern as any in the north country. My bags arrive undamaged and on time, and I say a prayer of thanks as they materialize on the conveyor belt. Lowell is supposed to meet me here, but he is nowhere in sight. He is absolutely dependable, but he has been known to underestimate the time needed to arrive at any given destination. I relax in the waiting area and watch the snow swirling outside.

Before I can get too cozy, there appears a bearded face sporting a boyish grin and sparkling blue eyes, a hand extended in warm greeting. Lowell is as handsome as ever, as rugged as the land he calls home, and as friendly as a new puppy. Indeed, after loading my gear into his Chevy 4X4, I am introduced to his new dog, Sue, eight weeks old and the model of enthusiasm. I fend off the little demon while she chews on one hand, cuddling her in my lap as my friend drives and we renew our long acquaintance. Of great interest to me is a grand buck he spotted near dark last night in a barley field south of town, and his description is tantalizing.

"I'll tell you one thing, we're going to hunt that field tomorrow. All I can say about the deer I saw is, Wow!"

"Really? What is he? An eight-pointer?"

"Maybe nine or ten. He didn't come out until almost dark, and he was chasing a doe. I've got a plan to take him, I hope."

We are hunting the heart of the rut, mid-November. We've got a good chance if we are patient and don't foul up, a distinct possibility with any mature whitetail buck. Lowell details another possible complicating factor—he saw a local outfitter parked at the other end of the same field just before the buck came out, but the man left without seeing the animal. The question is whether they might return to hunt there tomorrow.

First stop is to drop off my gear, including my ancient Remington 700 .30-06, at the home of my friend's parents, where we will be lodging. They have just constructed a new home on their own quarter section, and the driveway approach through a virgin spruce forest heavily laden with new-fallen snow is as picturesque as any Christmas card. We have just time for a short drive around town before attending the Alliance Church service with Lowell's family.

The service is truly a blessing. In addition to meeting many of Lowell's local hunting buddies and his family, I meet many other friendly people. There is a unity of spirit in this congregation identical to what I feel in my home church. There is a profound satisfaction in just being here.

The head of Lowell's clan is Del Davis, an accountant and a dedicated bow hunter who has imparted to his son a love for hunting and the outdoors. In the schooling he has given Lowell I see sound testimony to the philosophy of service above self and of family before personal pleasure, a set of values I admire and respect. But I somehow can't picture Lowell taking on such a confining vocation as his father's, and I wonder quietly where the young man's life is heading. Perhaps someday he will purchase an exclusive outfitter area and make the stewardship of that splendid asset his life's work.

A delicious home-cooked meal awaits the entire family after church, the artful creation of Lowell's mother, Phyllis. Afterward we check the accuracy of my old rifle, finding it shooting a bit lower than usual but grouping tightly at less than an inch at a hundred yards—as good as ever after I had to shorten and recrown the barrel. A couple of clicks up perhaps to compensate for the extremely dense, cold air, and I am shooting three inches high at a hundred yards, my normal setting.

We then take a tour of possible hunting spots, and our first stop is the field where my friend had planned to put me on a tree stand until he saw the buck last night. There are a number of does plying the edges, but no bucks are visible. A deer trail intersects the field every few dozen yards, the deep impressions in the snow testimony to intensive activity. In a couple of days we will try to install a tree stand at a promising location if we can't take our barley field buck.

The barley field is our next destination. The buck was near an oil-pumping station at the far entrance. He apparently lives in a muskeg and poplar thicket that constitutes the half-mile-long northern edge. There is ample evidence of deer activity here as well, and in the failing light we can see seven deer feeding. There is no way to enter the property from our position except to park on the road and walk in, and weather predictions call for wind out of the northeast, a forecast that would mean a long trek from here. We stand in the cold for a moment to test the brisk wind, and it is indeed northeasterly. We must plan accordingly.

Returning to church that evening, we break up into small groups for prayer. I pray for the Davis family and for my two friends, and Del Davis eloquently petitions the King of the Universe on my behalf, asking Him for a big deer for me. I am always asking for something for myself, being the selfish person that I am, but it is humbling somehow to hear such a request in my behalf by a man I have known only a short time. Perhaps God will hear his prayer and grant me favor in the upcoming hunt. And perhaps I am manifesting my own incurable selfishness by hoping that such will be the case.

The temperature as we return home is near minus 20 degrees, much too cold for my thin Southern blood. As we scurry into the warm house, I can't help but feel uneasy about Lowell's proposed plan. He is concerned that some other party will beat us to the field, so he plans to drop me off at the road and have me walk in my Pillsbury doughboy costume, white and all, for a half-mile up the edge of the barley. Meanwhile he will park on the road near the oil pumper, giving ample notice that someone is hunting. It will be difficult and time-consuming for me, but the prevailing wind allows no choice if I want a crack at this buck.

I am exhausted from the long day and the short night's sleep in Edmonton, yet I am late getting in bed once more because of stimulating conversation with the Davis family and an hour of preparation for the hunt. Lowell wants to be at the field an hour and a half before shooting light, to allow me time to get in position and to beat out any other hunters. Daylight and legal shooting time will arrive at exactly 7:55 A.M., so breakfast will be at 5:00 A.M.

The wind is much more calm as we embark in the morning. There are several inches of new snow, but thin, intermittent showers are the only precipitation now. We arrive at our jump-off point at 6:15, and I climb into a deep snowbank on the roadside, preparing my gear and my rifle. I have a folding camp seat that will allow me to sit comfortably, and I strap it to the back of my pack. When I am about ready to depart, Lowell stops me.

"Look. The drift of the exhaust is from the road toward the field now. It's changed completely."

"You're right. Wonder if it's swirling around or something?"

"Let's watch a minute before you take off."

The wind is steadily out of the west now. Satisfied, we elect to go to the other end of the field and wait for daylight. It appears that we can approach the parcel of ground where our buck resides by walking down a plowed and maintained road, at least for a part of the way, and be moving into the breeze.

Sitting in the dark, Lowell points to the line of trees where I would have been walking through darkness and deep snow. "There's an awesome line of scrapes up that tree line. And there's a busted bale of alfalfa they're feeding on about halfway to the other road," Lowell offers as we watch the minutes tick by on the digital clock on the dashboard. I can see ahead the security lights at the oil rig, and the pumping arm materializes in the gloom. It is perhaps three hundred yards off.

"Are we going to start down the right side in the trees or go to the oil rig?"

"We'll go to the pumper. He was chasing a doe just the other side of it. Maybe he'll show again."

Ten minutes to go until legal shooting light. The landscape begins to unfold before our eyes, and it is time to move out. We anticipate waiting at the pumper for a couple of hours, perhaps more, so I put on my full complement of clothing. White is the order of the day in this world of snow. I load my rifle with 165-grain Nosler handloads, best for deer-size game, and we set forth.

The drone of a diesel motor emanates from the pumping station, and I wonder: *Would a white-tailed deer become adequately habituated to such noise to move in as close as Lowell has said? To be sure he would.* The memory is still fresh of a recent Georgia buck I took less than two hundred yards from a roaring interstate highway.

Despite the ongoing commotion, we can see at least three does in the barley field, their forms now easily visible in the improving light. No antlers are visible, but the grader has pushed up a bank of snow that is perhaps a hundred feet in length, obscuring much of the field. Since there is already activity on the field, we crouch low and begin a slow, camouflaged approach to the berm of snow. We reach it undetected and begin to glass the edges of the field. We have already passed by a portion of the field, behind us and to our right, and momentarily neglected to scan it. I raise my binoculars, feeling awkward in my confining, bulky garb.

As I search for antlers on the does in the field, I feel Lowell's hand on my shoulder. He pushes me roughly to the ground, almost knocking me over. I drop immediately to a full crouch, one knee on the ground, and look at him. Excitement animates his countenance as he points toward the woodland to our right.

"There he is! Fifty yards! Oh, my goodness, he's close," he whispers, rising as slowly and deliberately as a human being can, looking without the aid of binoculars. "He hasn't seen us! Let me be sure it's him."

My heart is pounding to be this close to a possible trophy whitetail. Lowell nods again and motions me toward the inviting berm, a perfect snowy shooting bench if ever I saw one. I spot the

Northern white-tailed deer. Alberta, November 1996.

animal as soon as I top the heap of packed snow. The buck is slowly ambling away, now out seventy yards. To my dismay, all I can see is rear end and antlers. A disquieting thought enters my mind, and I take my eye from the scope and turn to Lowell.

"Is it legal shooting time?" I whisper, not wanting a technicality to deprive me of this prize but not wanting to transgress the law, either. He glances at his watch with a worried expression, and shoots a smile back at me.

"No sweat. OK by one minute."

Satisfied, I turn back to the marvelous animal, now some 125 yards out and still moving away in a steady but slow gait. I center the cross hairs on the creature, marveling at the width and height of the lofty antlers. He first turns slightly right, then slightly left, drifting farther and farther away, but never giving me a broadside presentation. He is now at 150 yards, reaching the limits of what I consider a reasonable shot. I make my decision. I have never before tried a Texas heart shot, but this is the ideal situation if ever there was one. I position the cross hairs squarely on the center of the tail and slowly squeeze the trigger.

Flame leaps from the muzzle in the subdued light, the flash temporarily blinding me. The explosion jars my senses but the unmistakable whack of a solid hit returns immediately. And now I can see that he is down! The shock has spun the buck sideways in the deep snow, and the upper half of the body is visible, lying broadside. I shuck in another cartridge and place the cross hairs on the shoulder. Another boom from the rifle and another solid thump returns, confirming one more good hit. The buck lies completely still.

Lowell's smile distorts his youthful beard as we whoop joyfully. He shakes my hand and slaps my back, gestures I readily return as we start toward the vanquished king of the barley field.

"I can't believe it! He was so close! What a setup! Can you believe it?" Phrases of like content pour from our lips as we approach the downed animal, massive antlers dominating the creature's still form.

The animal is a gigantic 8-pointer with a 24-inch spread and one double brow tine that I count as only one point. The buck rough-scores 150 points and has a body like a small elk, over three

Whitetail range has crossed the Cardinal Divide so that these deer now drink water that flows into the Arctic Ocean.

hundred pounds, exactly what I have been wanting. I am ecstatic at our instant success, one of the rarest of occurrences for me. I have experienced this kind of immediate success only one other time, and that was at least an hour after legal shooting light when I was hunting California bighorn sheep. Oh, I have had a rare first-day kill or two, but never one this easy.

I kneel before the buck and thank God for my victory, commenting to Lowell that I believe his father's prayer for me has been answered. I could have been laboring along, sweating and seeing nothing, while Lowell sat in the truck and watched the buck depart. But here the trophy lies, conquered in the snow.

Pictures, four rolls of them, follow as usual, though the bitter cold takes a toll on my cameras and both develop glitches before we're done. I may never take a better whitetail, so I document the event meticulously. Through it all I am overflowing with inexpressible joy, showing in my demeanor the deep emotion of the moment.

After the necessary hauling, butchering, and caping is behind us, we take an evening drive to the nearby property of Jack Barton, a man who owns land on which he feeds a hefty herd of wintering whitetails every year. With his permission, I conceal myself in his granary, a place around which the deer abound, and I try to photograph a buck in the same class as the one I killed. It is a privilege to be so close to a grand buck like that, but I am unable to get him into the open with sufficient light to take a good picture. After I dismount the little shed, a truly giant buck comes in as the light fades. Jack allows only bowhunting on his property. He feeds up to 250 deer each winter, significantly increasing the carrying capacity of all the adjacent land at great personal cost. He has a couple of dedicated bow hunters on his land at any given time, and the opportunity to hunt there is precious indeed. I feel blessed to view bucks that most people only dream about. We see some eight bucks this night, the granddaddy known as "Lucky" being the most spectacular of all. Someday, maybe one like that will appear for me. Miracles do happen, I'm convinced.

We spend the next day exploring the Rio Grande area, where the Wapiti River wends its way toward the mighty Peace River, and ultimately to the even more spectacular Mackenzie on its way to the Arctic Ocean. I see many moose and mule deer, as well as countless whitetails, including a dozen bucks. None are as magnificent as mine, and I am satisfied. We set up a stand on the well-traveled field I would have probably hunted today had I not been successful. Lowell has a friend from Michigan, John Searles, who will be in late tonight. He will most likely brave the subzero temperatures twenty feet above the ground, a prospect I am now glad is his instead of mine. I feel like one of the chosen few to have had such an easy hunt. I count it a privilege to help a fellow hunter, and I put my heart into choosing exactly the right location for the stand.

I will do whatever I can to help John Searles score, and I'll bet he will be successful. In fact, if Del Davis prays that he is, I'd almost stake my life on it.

Coues deer. (Photo: courtesy of Lon Lauber)

COUES DEER
(Odocoileus virginianus couesi)

Below he sees a lovely panorama of mauve and violet desert spotted
with silver tanks where cattle water, with brown threads of dry arroyos,
and with the distant purple upthrust of other desert ranges like the one that he is hunting.
When he pursues the little whitetails he becomes a creature of the upper air
like an eagle or a hawk; he almost ceases to be a terrestrial being. . . .
If I were to pick the game animal best fitted to survive unrestricted hunting,
I'd take the Arizona whitetail. His brains, his wariness,
the type of country in which he has learned to find refuge when hard pressed—
all combine to make him the most difficult of all deer to kill.

—Jack O'Connor, *Game of the Desert,* 1934

The white-tailed deer of the American Southwest are somewhat of an enigma. Whitetails are a species often associated with Eastern hardwood forests, lowland swamps, and bottom lands along river corridors. The desert terrain of Arizona, New Mexico, and adjacent parts of Mexico seems an unlikely place to encounter them. For many years the opinion held sway that the animal was an entirely separate type of deer. That has proved not to be the case, but still its adaptive modifications and habitat needs are distinctive enough that it holds a subspecies classification.

The earliest report of what was later called the Coues deer was probably that of James Ohio Pattie, a trapper who observed the animals in the San Francisco River area of Arizona in 1826. H. M. T. Powell later described numerous small deer at Guadalupe Pass on the Arizona/New Mexico border in 1849, as he journeyed to the California gold fields; the animals he described were most likely Coues deer. Commissioner Bartlett of Arizona's Santa Rita copper mine made the first detailed description of these animals one year later.

The man whose name is associated with the deer, Elliot Coues, first saw the animals when he served as surgeon at Arizona's Fort Whipple in 1864–65. Coues was only twenty-one years old, but he was already an accomplished naturalist and writer. He had a special interest in birds, but his enduring legacy is the animal that bears his name. Coues prepared the first scientific description of the tiny whitetail during his stay in Arizona, and he correctly surmised that the animal is a variant of the larger Eastern whitetail. His writings contain a detailed analysis of the differences between the white-tailed and black-tailed deer in the area. There is no evidence that Coues ever collected a specimen, however.

Apparently Coues pronounced his name *cows*, and that pronunciation persists in Arizona today. In national and international hunting circles, however, it is usually pronounced *coos*. The name was attached to the subspecies for the first time in 1874 by another army surgeon-naturalist, Dr. Joseph T. Rothrock. By the time W. W. Price conducted his scientific study of the Coues whitetail in 1895, when he collected seven specimens from the vicinity of the Huachuca Mountains of Arizona and adjacent Sonora, Mexico, the subspecies name *couesi* was firmly established.

Coues deer inhabit all of southern Arizona and are found south of the Mogollon Plateau and westward to Bill Williams Mountain. Coues is the only whitetail subspecies in Arizona. In New Mexico, Coues deer are found in the southwestern part of the state in habitat virtually identical to that in Arizona. The Mexican states of Sonora and Chihuahua have good populations, and some inhabit western Durango and some parts of the Mexican states of Zacatecas, Nayarit, and Jalisco.

A mature Coues buck in good condition reaches an average live weight of 120 pounds and a shoulder height of 31 to 32 inches. That is larger than the Carmen Mountains whitetail, according to the only complete study of the latter animal; a mature Carmen Mountains buck averages only slightly more than 100 pounds (at least in the population studied). Other scientific literature asserts that the Carmen Mountains subspecies is intermediate in size between Coues deer and the larger whitetail subspecies to the east, but the only study of Carmen deer with adequate sample sizes contradicts that. It's safe to say that the Coues deer is larger than the Carmen Mountains deer, according to the best scientific data currently available.

The antler configuration of mature bucks is typical of whitetails, with points arising from a main beam. Antlers of Coues bucks are typically smaller than those of other whitetails, however, including those of the Carmen Mountains whitetail. A Coues deer that scores over 100 points is a true trophy. In another study, the average antler spread was a mere 11.2 inches, the main beam length was 10.6 inches, and the average mature animal had an 8-point configuration, including brow tines, though atypical antlers are not uncommon.

The ears are probably slightly longer (6.4 inches) for body size on Coues deer than those of other whitetails, an adaptation that may allow dissipation of desert heat. The tail is approximately seven inches in length, slightly long for the body, and is distinctive because of its ruddy dorsal surface. The pelage is more the color of mule deer, with a strong presence of gray tones. The white neck patch just below the jaw in whitetails is present in only 25 percent of Coues deer. Albinism or partial albinism (piebald), fairly common in other whitetails, is extremely rare in Coues deer.

Coues deer will inhabit suitable terrain at elevations of more than 3,000 feet, although they are most often found between 4,000 and 8,000 feet. They prefer the habitat type known as the Upper Sonoran zone, also called the oak encinal belt, as well as the yellow pine transition zone. They occur in discontinuous pockets of suitable habitat that are like islands within certain mountain ranges and along certain waterways. Other favored habitats are riparian deciduous forests, mountain conifer forests, desert grasslands, some types of upland desert, and suitable chaparral/oak habitats. The home ranges of does are between one and two square miles in size, while bucks roam an area about twice as big.

Interaction with other species is inevitable, but certain factors minimize competition. In general these deer prefer gentler slopes than do desert bighorn sheep, so contact and competition between those two species is minimal. Desert mule deer tend to stay below 3,000 feet. One study reported 62 percent of mule deer sightings and only 1 percent of Coues deer sightings at elevations below 3,000 feet. Between 3,000 and 4,000 feet, 87 percent of the sightings were of whitetails and only 36 percent were mule deer, so that is the zone of transition. Above 4,000 feet most sightings were of Coues deer.

There is about a 50 percent overlap in preferred plant species for the two deer, a figure minimized by altitudinal separation and by the whitetails' preference for seasonal grasses and forbs. Desert bighorn sheep strongly prefer grasses to browse, so they compete little with Coues deer. Competition with domestic stock is minimal because Coues deer consume relatively small amounts of grass.

Desert mule deer and Coues deer can interbreed and produce a fertile offspring, a fact that underscores their close kinship. However, the result is an inferior animal that competes and survives poorly.

The rut occurs from December through January, and peaks in late January. Gestation lasts about two hundred days, and birthing occurs most frequently in July and August, the desert's wet season. Fawns are usually born along sheltered hillsides and ridges, most often in heavy cover, and within ten days they are active and visible. They weigh four to six pounds at birth and double in size within three months. Twins are quite common. Like all whitetails they have spots at birth, but they lose them within fifty days or so. Fawn survival is most intimately connected to water availability. Newborns nurse for two to three months.

Bucks shed their antlers by April or May, and they begin growing again almost immediately. By September they are mature, and in most cases the velvet disappears in October. A wet, rainy summer with good forage should make for better antlers,

Coues deer. New Mexico, November 1988.

though so far there is no scientific confirmation of that common impression.

The diet of the Coues whitetail varies with the season and the amount of rainfall. Longtime Arizona Game and Fish Department employee T. Knipe identified an amazing 610 plant species consumed by Coues deer, and he suspected there are an additional 434, for an astounding total of 1,044. It is a revelation to some that so many plant species grow in the Southwest; this desert region possesses a rich and dynamic diversity of flora.

The most critical season for drought is summer, which normally brings adequate rainfall to nourish the arid terrain. Coues deer flourish where annual rainfall is fifteen inches or more and tend to be absent where fewer than ten inches per year fall. Drought not only hinders the growth of important plants species; it also increases the competition between whitetails, other native species, and livestock.

During wet weather, Coues deer consume large quantities of fairyduster, kidneywood, ratany, mimosa, and desert honeysuckle. With a lack of rainfall, they turn to drought-resistant varieties such as fendlera, wire-lettuce, prickle-poppy, and mountain hackberry. They also consume oak browse of various kinds, especially Emory oak. They likewise dine on mountain mahogany, silktassel, ceanothus, false mesquite, and buckwheat, this latter plant being the favored shrub in many locations. In spring the deer consume freshly emerging grasses in small quantities, but forbs are of more importance. They also consume new twig and leaf growth with the onset of spring, and again as the summer season sparks a flurry of plant activity. In fall and as winter approaches, browse species become more important. The year-round diet is generally made up of 75 to 80 percent browse, 15 percent forbs, and minimal grass.

Surface water is probably necessary to maintain Coues deer, but they obtain some water from plants. A water source is absolutely essential when dry conditions or cold weather have reduced plant growth, however. An adult Coues deer needs about one to one-and-a-half quarts of water per hundred pounds of body weight in winter, and that may double when temperatures are high and may quadruple for lactating females. Fawn mortality is high when surface water is lacking.

Coues whitetails are afflicted with few diseases. Microfilaria, a nematode (worm), has been problematic in some cases and shows a predilection for attacking the ears of Coues deer. This parasite has been known to blind elk by attacking the eyes, but it has not affected deer in that way. A variety of other nematodes occur in Coues deer, but most are asymptomatic. Virus and bacterial diseases are rare.

Predators of this subspecies include cougars, which probably kill more Coues deer than all others combined. The big cats tend to select adult deer, and they demonstrate a predilection for bucks over of does. Coyotes and eagles are frequent predators of fawns. Doubtless black bears, bobcats, and feral dogs catch some Coues deer in certain parts of their range.

Management of Coues deer goes back into the nineteenth century. Despite Jack O'Connor's opinion that the little desert whitetail might be able to endure unlimited hunting pressure, Arizona and New Mexico have been protecting these animals for many decades. New Mexico set the first deer season in 1897, and two years later limited the take to one buck per season. Arizona started issuing deer tags in 1946, and today there is a drawing for them. There are approximately 32,000 Coues deer in Arizona and 7,000 in New Mexico. In the Mexican states of Sonora and Chihuahua, the deer are plentiful where they receive adequate protection from poaching. Considerable variation in deer density occurs on good range in Mexico, and no estimates are available on how many Coues deer are present. The largest take of whitetails in the history of the Arizona hunt occurred in 1984, when 7,119 Coues deer were harvested. More recently, 4,500 to 5,000 Coues deer have been harvested annually, and the overall hunter success rate has been between 20 and 25 percent.

Management of Coues deer is not problematic in most instances, but there have been some ups and downs. In the 1950s overpopulation caused significant habitat damage, resulting in a subsequent crash in deer numbers. Hunters were slow to realize that taking does and fawns is essential to controlling deer numbers, and in fact there was resistance to doing so. Our

Hunter and spotting scope in bright morning sunlight, with a wicked cholla plant in foreground.

understanding today is much better, but there remain people who do the deer no favor by passing up does where such take is legal and necessary.

Good, quiet camouflage clothing is of more utility in hunting these animals than any other in North America, with the possible exception of the closely related Carmen Mountains whitetail. Fine optics are also essential, both for spotting and accurate shooting. Leather boots are preferable, along with a day pack containing plenty of water, some chocolate bars, and other essentials. In Mexico, be sure you have a good, sharp knife and a sharpening device, as your guide may not.

Coues deer hunting is done differently in the United States and Mexico. To the north, the hunter normally climbs in the dark to a high promontory, glassing as the early morning light improves. The animals generally will feed for an hour or two in early morning, then bed. The hunter stalks within range of the bedding location, so as to take the animal when it reappears. On my first Coues deer hunt I was actually able to stalk the animal I took while it rested in its bed, but most often that is impossible. If one fails to see a desirable buck in the morning, glassing may continue all day. If you find a good buck too late in the day, mark his location for investigation the following morning; there is a good chance the deer will still be nearby.

In Mexico, walking and flushing is the method of choice on guided hunts. I'm not certain why, unless perhaps it has something to do with the language barrier and well-known gringo impatience. I have been able to convince my Mexican guide to hunt Coues deer "American style" on a couple of occasions, but it doesn't seem to work as well south of the border. The advantage of walking and jumping a deer is that you usually see a lot of game and you do not get bored. The disadvantage is that trophy judgment must be instantaneous, and your target is often a tiny kill zone receding rapidly and erratically into thick desert vegetation. Of course I never miss, but you might.

That last tongue-in-cheek statement aside, missing a Coues deer is not just possible, it is inevitable if you hunt them enough. They live in big, open country covered with heavy brush, and they are small, crafty, and constantly on the move.

A flat-shooting rifle of any centerfire caliber is adequate, but ideally I would tend toward the smaller bores, such as .243 or .223. I like a bipod attachment, but frankly I've seldom had time to set one up while hunting these deer.

Coues deer hunting is a special experience, no matter the technique you use or the locale. These elfin deer are true jewels set in the natural splendor of the high desert, and just being there is rewarding in itself. This is a hunt you will want to do repeatedly, as I have.

BRUSH BUCKS OF THE BLACK RANGE

It is nearing midnight as I arrive in camp deep in the Black Range Primitive Area of New Mexico. Ahead I can see the welcome light of a friendly campfire, signaling that our long and exhausting horseback ride is at an end. I am weary from traveling: first by air, then by pickup, and finally five miles of trail with packstring in tow. At last I will begin my quest for the tiny Coues deer of the Southwest.

The blackness of the trail becomes just a memory as I fill my stomach with the basic fare of a Ross Johnson camp. The man has a reputation for being hugely successful at finding trophy animals, but his camps can be decidedly Spartan. The saying is that if one wants big animals, it's Ross Johnson; if one wants great food and comfort, it's Howard Johnson. But tonight I am famished, so who cares? The meal is more than adequate.

I don't mind arriving in camp late, and I don't mind meals after midnight when the situation warrants. But I'm horrified to discover that wake-up is at 3 A.M. That leaves me two-and-a-half hours to sleep before my first Coues deer hunt. Who in the world could shoot straight in that condition? Almost before my eyes close, I am awakened by a light in my face. It's time for breakfast.

Coues deer territory is like sheep country in many respects, and horses are only for transport into and out of this remote wilderness. All hunting is on foot, and so for two hours we labor uphill, my flatland lungs groping for oxygen in the thinning air. The feeble beam of my puny flashlight hardly pierces the thick gloom as we walk. I am in good shape, but the miles of climbing finally begin to exact a toll. I am glad when we finally arrive on a high ridge far above our campsite, the eastern sky only beginning to brighten. Our elevation is approximately 7,000 feet, according to my guide, Perry Harden.

My underwear is soaked with sweat, and a chill begins to creep in. The predawn air is below freezing, and there is only a hint of the coming sun. I pull out my scratchy, noisy old down parka, a veteran of many high-country hunts, and wrap myself in it. Perry is displeased by the ruckus, but I am certain that without it I will freeze to death. I resolve to be as quiet as possible as I settle in to await the dawn.

Slowly the day creeps upon us, and distant ridges materialize. The sun creates a shining imminence below the horizon. This is my first hunt for big game in a desert region, and I am spellbound by the variety of prickly plant life. Vicious cholla cactus, pernicious prickly pear, stately ocotillo, and graceful yucca surround us, along with numerous nondescript thick and thorny bushes. I am warm enough now to enjoy the awakening of the desert, the clear atmosphere and unspoiled terrain unspeakably pristine.

The sunlight arrives, the welcome rays first striking the tops of the highest peaks to our south, then marching down the slope. As the shadows retreat into the valley, we glass in earnest. Perry has told me that we can expect to see Coues deer stand up to greet the early morning sunlight.

The rich texture of the desert mountains is bewitching as it unfolds before me. I visually comb the thick groves of mountain mahogany where supposedly there is a good buck living. Deer should be out foraging on the green leaves of that plant, or higher up in the bountiful dwarf live oaks, laden this time of year with succulent acorns. There are also juniper and piñon trees, the ripe fruit of which attracts the bantam ghosts of these highlands. But I don't see the tiny deer.

"It's time," whispers Perry, sitting close-by my side as we glass. "We should get some action soon." Most of the surrounding terrain is now bathed in effervescent sunlight, and the chill of the air is subsiding.

We plan to use the early morning to try to find a good buck, and then we will watch him until he lies down. The deer usually feed again around noon, so we will make a stalk to wherever he disappears and try to be in position to shoot when he reappears. Now if only a deer will show.

"I see one. A doe and a fawn. And over there is a spike."

"Where?" I plead, searching intently. All I can see is rich desert flora.

"Down in the mahogany. And there's another doe just above them in the open."

"I see her. Now where are the others?"

My unpracticed eye has a hard time seeing anything in these parts if it isn't as big as an elk. These gray ghosts are tough to spot. I finally find the others, but not without concentrated effort. I watch them all, trying to train my vision.

Now there are more deer. The small buck is near the top of the ridgeline. Numerous does and fawns feed among the prickly foliage, and there are mule deer farther down in the valley. A herd of elk appears in the distance, their tawny bodies supple in the morning light. But the trophy buck never appears.

"Let's move over to the other side of the hill. There's a lot of good country there that we can't see from here. And take off that noisy coat."

I pretend not to hear about the parka. A cold wind is still blowing, and I don't want to be shivering so hard I can't shoot straight. I move out with my companion, carefully trying to keep down the obtrusive scraping sound.

"Bucks! Down!" comes the whispered warning as we approach an ancient barbed wire fence. I see the pair of animals down the draw ahead of us, moving in our direction. If they keep coming, they'll move right in front of us!

"One of them is darn good. Get ready to shoot!" advises Perry as we park ourselves to await the animals. I chamber a round in my .30-06 as quietly as possible and move to the fence post ahead of me. As I ease up to it, my treacherous coat scrapes on an *uña de gato* bush, the curved thorns making a sound like fingernails on a convertible top. Did the deer hear?

They did indeed. Both of them stop in the edge of the brush on full alert and look directly at us. I try desperately to get in position to take a shot at the larger, but before I can ready myself I am making more noise, and both animals disappear into the thick brush. We move to a position with

Paloverde is one of many thorny plants in Coues deer country.

better visibility of the opposite hillside, but neither of the deer reappears.

A measure of dejection is natural when one makes a mistake. Sheep hunting gear is great for high, rocky terrain, but it isn't appropriate for these little Coues deer. I should have brought something quieter—much quieter. I wonder if I can score, given the clear choice of freezing to death or making an unacceptable racket. My skinny little frame can't take the cold unless I can either wrap it or keep it moving; neither seems an option with these animals. I look over my guide's gear as I stuff my noisy parka in my pack and only now notice how quietly Perry is dressed, all downy soft and noiseless. He even has chamois gaiters to cover the lower parts of his pants legs so he can drag silently through the worst brush.

We spend much of the remaining day lounging in the warming sun, napping between glassing sessions and enjoying the plentiful wildlife and desert scenery. A lone buck traverses a nearby ridge, but we pass. Perry feels certain we can do better. The animal has a single drop tine on one antler, an unusual configuration for a desert whitetail. I hope my guide's decision is right.

I arrive back in camp that evening with my body tired but my optimism high. What I have come such a great distance to hunt is certainly here. Maybe I can be less obvious and more muffled next time I get a chance.

It is already well after dark when we finish supper around the campfire. Ross Johnson has a dedicated following of hunters, and after only one night I understand why. Not only is he able to find and hunt the best New Mexico has to offer, he also has a vast collection of hunting tales, which he relates with style and gusto. He is a bit out of the mold as outfitters go, but very likable and knowledgeable. Before too late, though, we all drift away to catch up on sleep. I am sleeping soundly by 7 P.M.

My early morning wake-up call is accompanied by a tent-flapping wind, seldom a good sign for hunting. But time is short and I have no choice but to try. We trek to many of the same high ridges once more, seeing precious few deer of any kind; the ones we do spot are desert mule deer, which are by nature less intimidated by the wind. As I would have thought, these desert whitetails are just as spooky as their Georgia cousins when it comes to a blustering gale and whipping vegetation.

The next day is more of the same, as is the following. In spite of the conditions, Perry keeps me alert, never allowing thoughts of defeat to enter my head. We check every pocket in the area, climbing to dizzying heights to overlook vast areas of high desert, examining every ridge and draw.

It is near the middle of the fourth day of the hunt, and I haven't seen a buck since the first day. I am tired of leg and starting to sag in spirit, but we push on. As if in answer to a prayer, the wind ceases as we eat lunch. Hope wells up. These deer have to move sometime.

Suddenly there are deer everywhere. It is the "magic hour," as Perry refers to noontime, when Coues deer eat lunch. I am amazed at so many animals suddenly all around us.

"I see a buck. No, two bucks. Man, there are more! Five bucks!" exclaims Perry as he wields his binoculars. He points to a ridge a half-mile distant, and I finally see the band feeding down the slope in dense scrub oaks. One is darn decent, so we watch with great interest for an hour or more. They are in no hurry to bed down, by all appearances, the pent-up energy of nearly three days of inactivity keeping them on the move.

We will attempt a dangerous stalk toward a moving band of Coues deer. Such a maneuver is usually unsuccessful, and their position makes approaching within shooting distance unlikely even if we could see them bed down. Perry checks me over to see if I'm noise-proof and then digs in his pack to produce a wool sweater. Grateful, I pull the garment over my shirt.

We drop off into a deep ravine and move briskly toward them. Down we go, then up again to put us on the ridge opposite. I can still see them frolicking and feeding, but they are slightly out of range and seem to be moving down and away. We hurry down to get ahead of them, spotting them again on the ridgeline at the edge of impenetrable brush. Perry estimates the range at a good 300 yards, but it seems farther as I look through my 7X scope. There is little time, as one of the smaller bucks has already pegged us and is staring intently, his ears alert and head upright.

I crawl up to a shaky snag I intend to use as a rest and place my rifle in a precarious fork. I can see the small buck now, but he is the only animal

visible. All I can do is wait and hope. Perry slides silently in beside me to offer counsel.

"There he is! He's crossing the opening left of the little guy!"

I shift the rifle slightly and immediately find the buck easing across the only available opening. Already his head and antlers have disappeared into the dense covert. It is my only chance, so I hurriedly line up on him and touch off the shot. I am kicked by the departure of the 150-grain Nosler handload. I have an uneasy feeling that I fired in too much haste.

"You missed," observes Perry a bit disgustedly.

"I thought I heard a smack," I lie. We climb the ridge, battling thick and thorny brush, simply to confirm the miss. No blood. No hair. No bone. Nothing except fresh tracks.

I always feel sheepish after a miss. I am most unreliable when I have to hurry a shot, and this debacle is a classic. I resolve to do better if I get another opportunity.

We return to camp to find that one of our party took an awesome Coues deer a few ridges over from us. I would be ecstatic to take a deer like that, but he is unimpressed because it is short of book minimums. As far as I'm concerned, who cares? It is a grand buck, and I would be more than satisfied with one like it. Lord, put me in range of a beauty like that, I plead.

Early wake-up comes for my last day of hunting. Our favorite ridge is a bedlam of scattering deer as a pair of splendid mountain lions stroll casually along a deep rocky draw to our north. The incident forces us to rethink our plans. Perhaps we should seek our buck elsewhere on this final day, since the local deer seem upset by the predators. We decide to go up and over the top and down an unfamiliar ridge, one of the few places we haven't traversed this week. We eat lunch overlooking a deep draw where Ross claims to have seen a world-record Coues deer during elk season, but the animal keeps his precious head hidden. When nothing materializes by lunchtime, we eat our sandwiches and move on. I am beginning to get that familiar feeling of defeat.

The sun is already beginning to approach the westward mountaintops as we ease along a sheer cliff overlooking excellent whitetail habitat. The purple draws across the way are ever deepening and the air carries a distinct chill. My legs are weary, and it is a long way back to camp. Tonight I must ride out to make my plane home. Hope fades as I settle into the bittersweet melancholy of disappointment in the midst of natural grandeur.

"I see one. No, I see three! Three bucks!" exclaims my companion softly. I locate his find, and we are soon peering through the spotting scope. One is a fairly good three-by-three, not a book specimen but an acceptable last-day buck.

All three of the animals bed as we move slowly toward them. We must first negotiate some of the most vertical terrain I have ever encountered while hunting. A rocky spine rises to the left of the flat where the animals are bedded, so we utilize that cover to approach much closer than I ever thought possible. From the spine we can't see the animals, even though we should be in good range. Darn the thick brush.

Perry is a bow hunter of the first order, and he has me take off my boots for the final stalk, an

Cacti are a danger when hunting desert game.

act of desperation I ordinarily would disdain in this cactus-studded country. By this method, however, I am amazed at how close we are able to approach. By the time we stop in a shallow gully, we are a mere fifty yards from where we last saw the bedding animals, and I am expecting them to burst forth in a dead run at any moment. The wind has arisen again, though, and blesses us by being firmly in our faces.

"There he is," whispers Perry, pointing a finger straight ahead. I make out a gray form under a bush, stately antlers rising into the air. I see several points, a three-by-three for certain. I can't pass up this buck on the last moment of my last day, not after such a stalk.

The shot proves utterly painless for the little buck. The animal is facing me, and the bullet breaks his neck as it traverses the length of the body, anchoring the deer on the spot. I approach my fallen prize with a muted sense of triumph. I had hoped for bigger, of course, but I have finally won.

Caping, quartering, and boning out the animal follow after a quick picture session, all in failing light. We then shoulder heavy packs for the brutal nighttime trek back to camp. Pitifully insufficient flashlights illuminate awful expanses of thin air as we are greeted at every turn by more vertical cliffs. We finally make our way down a narrow chute that runs with water during the monsoon season. By the time we reach the distant camp, everyone has left except for our horses, and it is near midnight. Oh, for someone to understand the sacrifices made by the hunter!

It has been a difficult hunt for an elusive species. But my heart glows with satisfaction. There will be other, perhaps bigger, Coues deer in the future, but for now I am thankful for this success, coming as it has at the end of a grueling hunt. The long ride out is a time of deep reflection as the rising moon illuminates the ghostly rock formations.

I am near exhaustion as I collapse into my motel bed, antlers nearby and my rifle stowed in a sturdy case. I can't wait to come back here again, despite the many trials. I quickly drift off to sleep with dreams of giant bucks amid the mountain mahogany. And I hope fervently that someday I can make those dreams a reality.

Carmen Mountains white-tailed deer. (Photo: from the author's collection)

CARMEN MOUNTAINS WHITE-TAILED DEER
(Odocoileus virginianus carminis)

"Man I am grown, a man's work must I do.
Follow the deer? Follow the Christ, the King.
Live pure, speak true, right wrong, follow the King-
Else wherefore born?"

—Alfred, Lord Tennyson (1809-1892), *Gareth and Lynette*

By the reckoning of the great poet, I perhaps have followed the deer a bit too much in my lifetime. By the time I took my Carmen Mountains whitetail, which was the very last animal of the quest detailed in this book, my obsession had begun to overshadow quite a few aspects of life that are no doubt of more importance. Retrospective analysis allows one to be a bit more rational in making such judgments. But even so, the significance of following the deer on that hunt, and the culmination of the quest, will forever be seared into my memory.

These deer are generally found above 4,500 feet but have been encountered on rare occasions as low as 3,000 feet. They strongly prefer the mountaintops, similar to their Coues deer cousins, and are denizens of the same juniper/oak/piñon habitat. When they descend below 4,500 feet in most parts of their range they begin to encounter the desert mule deer, which typically inhabits the desert floor and more arid lower country. They compete somewhat for food in the zone between 4,000 and 4,500 feet, but that does not seem to be a major survival factor for either species. Such competition has been important in establishing their distinct habitat.

Besides a basic food supply, the Carmen Mountains whitetail has two other needs: a water source and dense cover. Mule deer can survive without either in some areas, and these two factors may account for the elevational separation of the species. In most desert mountain ranges where these diminutive whitetails live, surface water and dense cover play out as the terrain becomes lower, so the whitetails have adapted to living the high life. Competition with domestic livestock in much of the deer's range in Mexico is another struggle that intensifies in lower terrain.

This may also be one of the rarer of the animals hunted as big game in North America. It seems unlikely that there are more than 3,500 Carmen Mountains whitetails in the entire extent of their range, though that is little more than a guess. Some of their best habitat is in the Big Bend National Park of Texas, where perhaps five to six hundred are present. Smaller populations exist north of the park in isolated mountain ranges of the TransPecos region of Texas, the Rosillos, the Christmas, the Chinati, and the Davis Mountains. In some cases, such as in the Christmas Mountains, the number of deer is so small as to be near minimal viability. Mexico may hold larger numbers, but how many is uncertain. Recent changes in that country to encourage stewardship of wildlife by landowners may have a positive effect, though only time will tell. All told, it seems unlikely that there are huge numbers of Carmen Mountains whitetails on the planet, and hunting this elusive bantam deer is a privilege.

The tendency of these deer to inhabit higher mountain terrain has allowed subspecies characteristics to develop. The floor of the Chihuahuan Desert intervenes in all directions, separating these deer from their nearest relatives by an inhospitable zone they dare not traverse. In times past, the terrain was doubtless wetter and allowed a contiguous whitetail population in all parts of the region, but changes in rainfall and vegetation in the lowlands have isolated the Carmen Mountains whitetail. Their current recognized range extends from the TransPecos region southward as far as Jaral in Mexico, with a major segment of the population in the namesake Carmen Mountains, which run right up into the eastern end of Big Bend National Park from south of the Mexican border. Except where they have been extirpated by subsistence hunting, competition with livestock, poaching, and perhaps to some extent predators, all the mountain ranges in the northern part of Coahuila, Mexico, have populations of Carmen Mountains whitetails.

These tiny deer are perhaps the smallest of the "big game" animals of North America by my own definition. A mature gray wolf will often weigh in at 120 pounds, as will a Coues whitetail buck. The average size of the Carmen Mountains white-tailed deer in one classic study was a mere 104 pounds for mature bucks, meaning that the animal almost failed to make this book for sheer lack of size! Nevertheless, that the creature qualifies by

carrying a scientific designation, being legally sport hunted, being resident in the United States or Canada, and weighing at least 100 pounds for a mature male is a matter of record.

It is only educated speculation on my part, but I believe that the largest Carmen deer live in the range of mountains I hunted for the subspecies—the Serranias del Burro of western Coahuila. Our party took five bucks, and they averaged around 130 pounds, considerably more than those in the Big Bend National Park. Two carried antlers that scored above 125 points, certainly large for this subspecies. Probably this eastern zone was the area of most recent intergrade with the larger lowland subspecies of whitetails in Texas and Mexico. All one needs to do now is fly over the area to see the broad line of demarcation that separates the Carmen deer of this area from their larger cousins in the brush country of Texas and Mexico. While there is much inhospitable terrain in this wide gulf of desert, it is also possible that some interbreeding with the lowland whitetails still takes place.

A great deal of scientific study was necessary to delineate this subspecies and establish exactly where it occurs. Krausman and Ables did the definitive work in the 1970s, based in great part on skull dimensions and to a lesser extent on antler characteristics. They discovered that despite the smaller average body size of the Carmen deer, the skull is consistently larger than that of the Coues in virtually all measured dimensions. The antlers were also larger on average, both in beam and tine length, than those of Coues deer. They tend to have taller racks, tending more toward the Texas whitetail type of antler than the stockier ones found on Coues deer.

For record-book purposes, the Carmen Mountains whitetail gets little respect. The animals are the only one of the Mexican white-tailed deer subspecies that crosses into the

Carmen Mountains white-tailed deer. Coahuila, December 1998.

United States, other than the lowland whitetail, *texanus,* and the Coues deer. They are distinctive in many respects from the more southerly subspecies with which Safari Club International lumps them, and are almost as small as the tropical subspecies of the Yucatan and farther south. The deer of the Mexican lowlands, many of which are much larger in both body and antler size and have other distinguishing characteristics, are classified as Texas whitetails by SCI. The Boone and Crockett Club recognizes no distinctions among any of these subspecies.

While *carminis* bucks usually average a little over one hundred pounds in most of their range, the does weigh only sixty. They are colored much more like Texas whitetails than like Coues deer, which have a distinctly grayer pelage. They also lack the reddish hair uniformly found on top of the tail of Coues deer. Despite the larger skull size they have ears smaller than those of Coues deer.

Every species has its share of amazing facts, but the Carmen deer have a couple that top the list. Minutiae buffs should enjoy knowing that these are the only deer that will inhabit caves. Also, they have a very high incidence of maxillary canine teeth. Such teeth don't ordinarily occur on North American deer, although they are not unusual on Central American white-tailed deer. The incidence of these extra teeth in Carmen Mountains whitetails is as high as 33 percent in the isolated Christmas Mountains population, and ranges from 5 percent to 25 percent in other populations. Look for these unusual teeth on your own Carmen Mountains whitetail, should you be fortunate enough to hunt them.

The food these deer eat is similar to the diet of the Coues deer, reflecting their high desert habitat. Browse accounts for 35 percent, succulents some 28 percent, forbs 14 percent, and grasses 4 percent. Succulents (such as certain cacti) probably contribute significantly to their water intake, especially during dry times. Two plants that Carmen deer utilize heavily are the lecheguilla and the prickly pear. Other significant plants include the acacia, oaks and their fruit, and euphorbia.

For most of the year the bucks and does remain apart, like all whitetails. Their home range is quite restricted, similar to that of other whitetails, and seldom do they roam more than a

couple of miles. The bucks sometimes form bachelor groups of two or three, and the does may gather in family groups of four or five, including fawns. Bucks drop their antlers around the first of April, and by the end of that month or the first of May new ones are growing. The velvet sheds by late September, and by the first of October the antlers are polished. The rut begins in late November and peaks in late December and early January. Virtually all these events occur about a month later than equivalent episodes in the lives of more northerly and easterly whitetails. Unlike typical Coues bucks, Carmen bucks frequently form true scrapes.

Gestation is assumed to be 201 days, though apparently nobody has thus far accurately measured it. Fawns are born in the impenetrable brush, most often in July. That coincides with the wettest time in the Chihuahuan Desert, when lush plant growth encourages generous lactation by the doe and rapid growth of the fawn. While twins are common in most whitetail populations, the Carmen Mountains whitetail almost never has twins.

Mountain lions are by far the most prevalent predator of these deer. Analysis of their scat shows that bobcats and coyotes also consume Carmen deer. One would expect that these latter two predators would be more likely to catch fawns than adult deer, but the small size of the adults perhaps makes them vulnerable.

Relatively few diseases and parasites afflict the Carmen Mountains whitetails. Even the common tick is not prevalent in their high alpine habitat, and few deer here have any at all. Nasal bots are generally neither numerous nor obvious. Screw worms will attack an open wound and can be deadly, but that is probably uncommon. No internal parasites such as roundworms and brainworms have been described in this deer.

Hunting Carmen Mountains whitetails is one of those high mountain experiences most closely akin to Coues deer hunting. It combines terrain as vertical as sheep country with an animal that is legendary in its wariness. I find that a most challenging and satisfying blend. I thought Coues deer were the ultimate in North America when it comes to vigilance and caution, but now I'm not so sure. One study relates that 76 percent of observed Carmen deer terminated the contact by

The beautiful and bewitching Serranias del Burro Mountains with yucca blooming in foreground.

leaving the area! I've seen a lot of Coues deer, and most of them never knew I was there. The Carmen Mountains whitetail may be a cut above even the wary Coues deer when it comes to staying alert.

Hunting these pygmy whitetails requires more than stealth and silence, though. The terrain and habitat they occupy is characterized by deep oak draws that are the ultimate in impenetrable cover. When you do spot one, the small size and the probability of a long shot blend to make a successful hit most difficult, especially if the animal has broken cover and is receding over the adjacent ridge. Add to that the heaving of your chest from intense climbing and you get the picture.

What constitutes a good trophy? This judgment can be deceptive because of the small body size. Usually there will be no nearby deer with which to compare them, so judging them like any other whitetail seems to be in order. The tines should be long relative to beam length, and the main beam should extend well outside the smaller ears. For a person accustomed to judging Coues bucks, the transition should not be too difficult, but expect less mass and more length on an

exemplary animal. Nontypical racks seem to be fairly uncommon.

I like cotton clothing for hunting Coues deer, and the same applies to the Carmen Mountains deer. I recently switched to cotton camouflage for such outings, after wearing khaki climbing pants and colorful shirts for years. My theory has always been to be quiet and stay out of sight, and thus you do not need camouflage. That approach has always worked well for sheep, though somewhat less so for Coues deer—but my pictures look great with the added color. For the spooky Carmen Mountains whitetail, however, quiet and camouflaged is the way to hunt.

It can be very cold early, so a soft wool or synthetic outer garment is useful. In case it gets brutally cold, take a down parka. Leather gloves are great for warding off sharp vegetation. I recommend taking rain gear, though you are unlikely to need it. I certainly needed mine and was glad I had it. You can leave it in camp if it looks like a bluebird day. Leather boots, standard height and with waffle soles, are best for dry mountains such as you will hunt for these animals. If you do get significant precipitation,

Cow skull and prickly pear cactus; fresh snow falling in Mexico.

the waffle soles accumulate sticky mud so that you feel like you're walking on stilts. But what the heck, the higher you are the better you can see into that thick brush.

You will not need much power to kill a Carmen Mountains whitetail if you can place your bullet well. I believe a .243 or a .223 would be the ideal rifle for these deer. As when I was after cougar, I felt a little conspicuous carrying a cannon like a .30-06 on my shoulder. Any rifle with which you are comfortable and that allows you to take fairly long shots consistently will do the trick. If you hunt in Mexico, you will need the special gun permit and undergo the intense border scrutiny that always accompanies such a trek. If that intimidates you, these deer are also available on the Texas side of the border.

These are pretty little deer with a big head, big antlers on good bucks, and relatively small ears. Seems to me like a trophy every serious hunter needs.

DWARFS OF COAHUILA

There are not many places in the world to hunt Carmen Mountains white-tailed deer. I find

myself today looking over one of the very best. The ranch through which we are cruising is typical mountainous terrain of the vast Chihuahuan Desert. The airstrip next to the ranch house registers 3,800 feet on the altimeter of the light aircraft we used to fly in. The owner of Rancho El Cedrito is Mario Fernandez, an affluent Mexican businessman whose special retreat I am privileged to sample. It is a first. Nobody except friends and family has ever before been allowed to hunt here.

Mario has several ranches, but this slice of paradise is his largest and by far the most remote. The majority of the Serranias del Burro, the mountains where the ranch is situated, are far from the madding crowd, with no discernible encroachment by civilization. Getting here requires a six-hour drive from Ciudad Acuna along some of the most challenging roads on the continent, or else a twenty-five-minute airplane ride in Mario's Cessna 210. We chose the latter, naturally, and were treated to a spectacular view off one wing of the Pico del Burro, an imposing peak that marks the eastern boundary of the ranch and the beginning of the high mountain range.

This is the easternmost habitat of the Carmen Mountains whitetail.

Actually, one hunter has already been here and left this year, though he was scheduled to be a part of our party. Ivan Flores, a friend of mine and Mario's who had a big part in opening the door to the ranch for hunters like me, connected on an awesome ten-pointer the day before we arrived. He left the antlers behind for us to see, so we already have a standard that will be difficult, if not impossible, to attain. A preliminary measurement reveals that his is the second largest Carmen Mountains whitetail ever recorded. The four of us in camp are accustomed to thinking of these unique little deer as having antlers akin to those of Coues deer, and to some degree the impression is accurate. Here in the Burros, though, are bucks that make the biggest Coues deer in the world pale by comparison. Ivan's deer green-scores over 133 and is 21 inches wide. We will have to work like dogs, and get a lot of breaks, to equal it.

Perhaps the main instigator of this hunt is me. I've been searching for a place to finish my quest for the forty-two North American species (counting the darted jaguar), and this will be it if I'm successful.

I bounced the idea of a Carmen Mountains whitetail hunt off several outfitters and a number of booking agents, and Wes Vining of the Trophy Connection was the only one who took a heartfelt interest. He worked through Ivan Flores to arrange the hunt, fully realizing that such a specialty affair has a limited market potential. Our trip is also in no small amount experimental, so Wes is here to see how everything goes and try to take a trophy himself. The other two hunters are father and son, Bob and Jason Ferche of Minnesota. Both are somewhat fanatical whitetail hunters who have signed on to get a little different brand of experience.

I could have done this hunt in Texas, but most of the Texas population resides in Big Bend National Park, where no hunting is allowed. The deer here are bigger, both in body and antler size, and the opportunity to hunt a ranch that is virtually untouched has lured me to Mexico once more. I am attempting to finish a task that has been in process for more than twenty-three years. Taking one of these unique little deer will complete it.

Mario Fernandez is possibly the most prosperous man I know. His construction company employs more than three thousand people in and

Carmen Mountains white-tailed doe in a snowy mountain meadow.

around Monterrey, Mexico. He is also the owner of a major hotel and travels much of the time in his ten-passenger jet aircraft. Today he is trekking by pickup truck and will personally guide me. Never before have I had such an unusual guide. And probably never will I again.

This ranch is indeed huge. Originally deeded by the king of Spain to a family that kept it for centuries, their descendants finally consented to sell it to Mario after intense negotiations. It seems they wanted out of the cattle business and preferred money in the pocket to land in the Burros. Rancho El Cedrito (Little Cedar Ranch) consists of some 120,000 acres of deeded land, and the elevation ranges from perhaps 3,000 feet up to almost 8,000. Vertical bluffs are common, rocky outcroppings are a prominent feature, and the beauty of the location is spellbinding. The red-roofed ranch house is nestled in a picturesque valley, surrounded by mountains of the Serranias del Burro. The valley floor is dominated by thick stands of ironwood, mesquite, *uña de gato,* and the ubiquitous prickly pear cactus. Farther up on the hillsides, the most ostentatious plant is the sotol, from which the locals make a potent alcoholic brew. Sotol looks like a palm tree of sorts, with the bottom two-thirds covered with disintegrating fronds that give them a grass skirt appearance. There are also scattered plants called *palmitas,* with longer and sharper leaves, which can mete out much punishment to the unwary.

This ecosystem is similar to that of the Sonoran Desert in many ways, but bewitchingly different. The ocotillo cactus, so prominent farther west, is rare here. The larger species of cacti, such as the saguaro and the pitaya, are also absent, but the prickly pear grows in even greater abundance. Lacking here as well are the terrible cholla and tasajillo cacti, though other species can inflict as much damage on the incautious. One flat cactus has such dreadful spines that it is called *matacaballo,* or horse killer. Lecheguilla, the favorite food of the Carmen Mountains whitetail, is practically everywhere on the higher terrain.

We are heading down a bumpy road that parallels the airstrip and then breaks around a ridge and ascends to higher terrain. Several nice bucks have been spotted around the airstrip, but we see nothing except a lone roadrunner. An alarmed flock of meadowlarks bursts from the grass as we pass. It is quite steep as we begin the ascent, and we pass through a crude wire gate into another section. We are perched atop a carpeted riding seat in typical Tex-Mex deer hunting fashion, and I can't help but wonder if these spooky whitetails won't avoid us altogether as we ride along in such a rig.

Bright blue sky dominates the top of the ridge. Evidence of centuries of ranching abound, the ancient fence posts along the way still holding quaint barbed wire that must be many decades old. Here and there deeply worn cow trails break into the brush and disappear.

A red-tailed hawk flushes from a recent kill, its plumage flashing in the warming sun. An overflowing water tank in the distance gradually comes nearer, and we park next to it and disembark for a much-needed break. The lecheguilla grows thick here, so the deer certainly lack nothing for food. While Mario and our driver, Hermann, do some glassing, I snap pictures.

"Mire! Unos venados!" comes the surprise announcement, causing me to hasten back.

The sun has climbed high, but I had been prepared to see nothing until evening. I ascend the elevated truck seat and begin studying with my Zeiss minis the place Mario is indicating, perhaps a half-mile distant. An ancient corral, the boards falling away in places, is where I spot my first Carmen Mountains whitetail. The animal is a doe, but more deer feed nearby. After glassing a few minutes, we can see that one animal has antlers.

There is little hesitation. I must look him over at closer range. Mario suggests we walk to our right and behind a hill that overlooks the site to avoid telegraphing the animals our scent on the contrary breeze.

As I start on the stalk my mind races. The old .30-06 rests comfortably on my shoulder, where it has ridden on so many stalks over the years. Will this very stalk, an approach to the last North American subspecies I have yet to take with this old rifle, terminate my journey? After being such a part of my life, I don't even know for certain I want it to end. It will certainly mark the end of an era.

I check the scope power, making certain that it is 3X. I fondle the leather sling, made in Mexico and given to me as a gift by my sister Ellen many years ago. It is impossible not to wonder if this stalk will be the swan song for the rifle, and perhaps for me. Uncertainty briefly clouds my mind, but down deep I know my decision. I want to complete the task in good fashion. If this is a good deer, I will take him. I pray that I will be a good hunter and do the right thing like a true sportsman. I really don't want to let down my quarry, my chosen avocation, my host, or anyone else.

Spines reach out to stab the imprudent, interrupting my thinking. The immediate aggressor is a prickly pear, but everything else has sharp points as well. We weave and wend our way, glassing occasionally to be certain our quarry is still there and unaware. Each stop finds the animals unsuspecting, and we continue on a crosswind track to the hill, putting us directly downwind.

Mario is an excellent hunter. He negotiates the rough vegetation with minimal noise, and I try earnestly to follow suit. Just over the brow of the hill, another group of deer bursts from their resting place and crashes away in the direction of the first. We have no idea whether they are bucks, does, or fawns, only the flash of white flags identifying them as deer. I remark in a whisper to Mario that perhaps they will spook the buck. He points a finger upward and wags it silently in my direction, a mannerism he uses often, indicating I shouldn't worry about it. We continue our stalk, weaving back and forth just behind the ridgeline from the old corral.

As we break over the top at exactly the right place, Mario whispers that I should creep downhill until I can see the buck. I immediately spot a sleek doe lying in the shade under a small tree, and another bedded out in the open. The cool breeze ripples the grass in front of them, and the sotol fronds bend in my direction as well. One doe eyes me momentarily, but after a couple of minutes of immobility on my part she decides I am benign and looks away. I ease toward a lone juniper tree where I can glass the entire area.

I slowly position myself to try to find antlers. Another doe is visible to the left, but the buck is nowhere to be seen. I shift position and catch a glint in the bright sunlight. An antler! There he is, resting in the shade near the archaic fence, looking toward the distant truck where Wes and Hermann are waiting and watching. Perhaps he has taken note of them, but he certainly has not seen me. I examine the antlers carefully; a lesser

deer is not what I am here for, if I can help it. There are four points on each side, counting the scant brow tines. Unfortunately, all the tines are short and the width is hardly what I had hoped to see. After a good scan, I decide that this buck isn't the one for me. The size of the monster Ivan took is still vivid in my mind. Surely there is another like that here somewhere.

Backing off to rejoin Mario, I explain the situation. He is disappointed but understands. I ask if I may approach and try to get some telephoto pictures of the deer, and he agrees. We angle back of the ridgetop to optimize the wind advantage, and then drop back directly toward the deer. Fully alerted by our movement and a bit of unexpected noise, the animals are quickly up and looking at us. Before I can snap a single picture, they bound away at top speed.

"*Mire! Otro venado!*" exclaims my guide, indicating another buck.

Indeed there is one, standing a hundred yards to the right of the others. He has seen us and is nervous. I quickly raise my binoculars. His head is turned now, perusing the departure of the other deer. The right antler obviously has five points, with tall back tines, but I can't tell how wide the rack is nor whether the left antler matches the right. Given that my success on this excursion seems critical, I make my choice. Ending the long quest right now seems the only thing to do.

I chamber a round, one of my few remaining handloads crafted by the late Dick Green, and drop to my knees behind a treacherous *uña de gato* bush. The spindly tops offer no support, and the distance is too long for a confident offhand shot. I attempt to steady the rifle atop the wobbly bush, but the cross hairs refuse to settle, and the stiff wind makes it even worse. I do my best to squeeze slowly. At the report, the animal is obviously hit and spins around, facing us in an open area, confused. Now he moves slightly to one side so that I can see him from a lower vantage point. I shuck in another of the precious handloads, drop to the ground, and use my bipod to get off the clincher. The animal tumbles.

I don't believe Mario grasps the significance of the moment for me. It is 7 December 1998. I killed my first of several pronghorn antelope with this same rifle, and the first big-game animal I took with it, on

Vegetation—such as this snow-covered century plant—is intriguing in the high desert.

5 October 1975. Forty-one species later has taken twenty-three years, two months, and two days.

Wes and Hermann arrive, and we admire my prize. The buck is considerably smaller than that taken earlier by Ivan, and for that I am unavoidably disappointed. He also lacks the fifth point on the left antler. On the positive, he is extremely typical of the species and is a fitting end to my quest. A smiling Wes sticks out his hand in congratulations, the meaning of this kill well known to him. We admire the prize, I give insufficient thanks to God for the victory, and pictures follow.

It has been far too easy. I expected this to take several days and for the spooky little deer to put up more resistance. Reflecting as we return to camp, I wonder how I will be able to function without my hunting quest.

Mario has made it clear from the start that we can take a second buck if we so desire. Looking at the awesome antlers on Ivan's buck, I decide to spend the remainder of the week seeking such an uncommon creature. My old rifle is certainly up to the task, and I have fifteen handloads left. I will put them away when I return home, just in case I ever get the chance to hunt a jaguar or a Manitoba elk, but I could spare a couple of them.

On the way back to the ranch house I snap some great shots of a nice buck beside the road near the airstrip. The rest of the afternoon I am on a photography mission, accompanying Jason and his guide on a tour of the desert mountains to our south. We see only a few does, and return to the ranch house tired but content. Mario has decided that tomorrow he will take this gringo hunting again. We will use horses to explore the northern portion of the ranch, where a really large buck has been recently spotted. He well understands that my standards have been raised considerably by the completion of my required hunting.

As dawn breaks, another day of the chase awaits. Nobody else has connected, so we need three more bucks. I will be highly selective, and will also be trying to find one for the others as I hunt. After coffee and a light breakfast, we are up and out with the morning star still visible. The pink desert dawn is quiet and beautiful, and we have put several miles of riding behind us by the time the sun peeks over imposing Pico del Burro.

517

There are fresh bear tracks on one of the ridges as we thread our way through the treacherous landscape. Frequent dry arroyos intervene, deep and rocky, so we retrace our steps in many places to find a crossing. The sotol plants are everywhere, as is the ever-present lecheguilla. There are countless small oak trees along the higher ridges, many of which have abundant acorns. The ground is surprisingly floral for December, being covered with tiny violet flowers and numerous varieties in yellow and white. A lone forkhorn buck stares at us from a brushy draw, but no other deer are present. It has been a beautiful and enchanting morning.

The evening hunt is a solo for me. I sit overlooking a water hole, hoping to intercept a *muy grande* buck that has been seen here. In the deepening darkness I catch a glimpse of movement far back in the brush, but discerning antlers is impossible. Mario's headlights soon are visible, and he is excited. He has seen a very nice buck, and tomorrow evening we will go there.

Despite the hopeful sighting, another new day is uneventful. A monumental effort provides no success, and we see but few deer. The wind shifts to the east toward dark, and the penetrating cold of the high desert chills me profoundly. I nestle into my comfortable bed that night under an extra blanket, but it is still an hour or more before the ice in my veins melts.

After breakfast, we take on a different job. Wes connected on a true monster yesterday, one he believes should rival the buck taken earlier by Ivan. He shot the animal so close to dark that they couldn't find him in the deep brush. We return to search for the lost deer, and finally we locate him. The antlers are so large that my first-day trophy will easily fit inside them. Determination to find a *muy grande* for my own collection now ratchets up a few notches.

This next-to-last day dawns with frigid rain and high winds buffeting the ancient ranch house. Mario takes me out for an extended drive, but the fog is so thick it is hopeless. Bob connects early on the airport buck I saw on the first day, a classy eight-pointer that is high, wide, and turns out to be better than the one I took. Mario unexpectedly decides he has had enough of guiding and turns me over to Hermann, who manages Rancho El Cedrito. My new guide takes me on a grueling walk in the wind-driven rain for much of the afternoon. We keep the ranch in view as we climb and walk a complete circle on the mountains around it. We see only a couple of small bucks and quite a few does.

By the time we return to the ranch house, my rain gear is in shreds from countless spiny plants, and my spirits are sinking as time slips away. Still, I am glad that the main aspect of the expedition is complete. The only sadness I feel is that the mission to find a bigger specimen is not going well. The passions I have felt on so many shutout hunts in the past are surfacing again, and I struggle against a creeping and inappropriate sensation of ingratitude.

The last day dawns with continuing rain and wind. Jason is the only one of five hunters who has not taken a deer, though he has seen several nice ones. The little critters live up to their billing, though, and none have given him adequate opportunity. I wish him the best as we depart on our respective quests. If I am to take one of the truly outstanding bucks, I must brave these brutal conditions. Hermann will be my guide once more. We cover more terrain by foot along an isolated range I haven't seen before, and then many more miles by pickup. The higher country now wears a mantle of snow, and the cacti and sotol are likewise adorned.

The deer are not out, though, and the day is fruitless. The numerous high mesas with their ancient Indian caves and grim vertical faces are beautiful to behold, even when garnished with clouds. By late afternoon the blue sky finally peeks through, and hopes for better visibility and movement by the deer increase. We hear by radio that Jason has at last taken a truly nice buck, and my optimism surges. To no avail, however, we walk a couple of fast miles across a flat where the brush is thick and an exceptional buck has been seen by a *vaquero.* We are unable to find him, despite our brisk effort.

On this last day we will fly out to Del Rio for the trip home. The plan is to leave around noon, so that leaves a little time. Hermann takes me up a canyon that holds great promise, but in the few short hours available we see only one young six-pointer and a half-dozen does. At the same time that I am a winner, I am also defeated, and both on

Ubiquitous sotol plant covered with snow high in the Serranias del Burro.

the same hunt. It seems a fitting ending. We return to the ranch house to prepare for departure.

As I fly out past magnificent Pico del Burro, I am highly reflective. I can hardly believe the depth of feeling one can experience in this activity we call hunting. I have taken a great trophy, and yet there is a sense of incompleteness. No matter the effort of the hunter, sometimes our highest aspiration just isn't meant to be. My vision and the reality of circumstance somehow do not integrate. My buck is the smallest of the five, and yet he is still outstanding. Powers beyond my control refused to allow me a second and better one, and the denial is resounding. Such is hunting. I have come to understand this, and I accept it without question. Despite a measure of frustration, tranquillity wins my heart.

Perhaps Hermann summed it up best with his final comment to me as we returned to the ranch house this morning. He said, "*No faltamos por lucha.*" We didn't fail for lack of effort. In that I find satisfaction.

This final hunt is somewhat of a microcosm of hunting in general, as few hunts have ever elevated me so high and brought me so low in such a short span of time. I completed my quest. I got my buck. But still something about this experience is less than perfect, and the hunter's heart endlessly yearns for the perfect ending.

In the final analysis, we must all come to grips with the highs and lows of hunting. The Carmen Mountains white-tailed deer has helped me in my own self-analysis. For that, and for the whole adventure at Rancho El Cedrito, I am grateful. A deep contentment fills me as we wing confidently toward Del Rio, Texas, and homeward. I am much the better for this hunt; better off for the success and, in an even more profound way, for the failure.

COMING CLEAN ON MISSES

I brought my rifle to my shoulder with a convulsive jerk,
pointed it at him and fired without thinking of the sights,
and of course scored an ignominious miss. . . .
I stood there, like a mile post by the roadside. . . .
If I could only get another chance such as I had on that buck,
wouldn't I down him in fine style? . . . I fired a second shot at him as he went,
but with no better result than the first.

—George Oliver Shields, *Cruising in the Cascades and*
Other Hunting Adventures, 1870

The first time I ever missed a big-game animal was on my very first big-game hunt, when one of the baying dogs chased a deer across the road perhaps fifty yards from me as this fledgling hunter paced nervously on the stand. That something was about to happen couldn't be missed, because the continuously barking hounds were coming my way. My heart pounded in my breast and tight fingers clenched the only firearm I owned capable of killing a deer, a Stevens 12-gauge double-barrel shotgun loaded with 00 buckshot. There were perhaps thirty hunters surrounding the woodlot, and I could hardly believe my luck. Fingering the shotgun's safety as the canine sounds came nearer, I vacillated wildly between the impulse to shout for joy and to run the other way.

The deer popped out in an unexpected location, as they so often do, far to the right of where it seemed the dogs might appear and well away from the heavily used deer trail I was guarding. My peripheral vision caught fleeting movement and the gun almost involuntarily jerked in that direction. Although many a squirrel and rabbit had fallen before me, never before had I thrown lead in the direction of anything larger than a raccoon. On such a large target it was natural not to lead, and the dozen lethal balls that exploded from my old shotgun cut not a hair. When we finally returned to the clubhouse, the ritual of cutting away the shirttail of the unlucky hunter who misses was not to be denied, not even for a stranger who was a guest of one of the club members.

Next trip was better. Stationed well off the main farm road with a better view of a weed-littered clear-cut, it seemed that it should be my turn to have the action go in another direction. Once more, though, the dogs miraculously came my way, but this time the deer was up against a once-humiliated hunter who had much more time to prepare. The buckshot cut four clean holes into the skull of the deer, killing him instantly. My wife and I had venison felled by my own gun for the first time in our lives, a most welcome adjunct to a medical school diet heavily weighted toward aged ground beef and cheap hot dogs.

I've tried hard to think of all the misses to which I've been victim in my big-game hunting career so that this chapter will be comprehensive. I must say from the outset that one category has been eliminated, because at least a dozen times I've missed white-tailed does in our culling operation at my river property. There are more than twenty large food plots on the property, each of which has a covered stand, and for the past several years it has been my inviolable practice to shoot the selected animals in the head. Some of the shots are as long as two hundred yards, and sometimes a miss occurs. Every time I line up one of those long shots, it is uppermost in my mind that the slightest indiscretion on my part or the smallest movement by the deer may result in a clean miss. If I hit, the deed is accomplished painlessly and quickly. In the case of a miss, the animal is still absolutely healthy almost every time, although on one occasion a bullet apparently grazed a doe. She got up quickly and ran into the underbrush, then snorted at me for a full fifteen minutes before retreating for good. Likely the long shot creased her noggin and gave her a migraine but nothing more.

This chapter is about real hunting situations during which the opportunity has presented to take an animal under actual field conditions, and a miss occurs. I think I remember every one of them, and lest my pride should swell at some of the fine animals I've been privileged to take, I've assembled those embarrassing instances here for your inspection, criticism, learning, and probably for your amusement as well.

The first "missed" animal was, in fact, killed painlessly with a single bullet. Despite that, in retrospect it is obvious that I pulled the shot badly. In that instance the errant shot was at the first big-game animal I ever took with my Remington .30-06. The event is in chapter 4, and that story is the first time I've ever fully confessed that I hadn't been aiming for the neck. I've come clean.

To my shame, less than a decade later the major hunting atrocity of my career occurred, the wounding of another of the fleet pronghorns with a long shot that was just a little too long. I watched helplessly as the injured creature limped off into the distance, crossing onto land where we didn't have permission to hunt. It had felt like a good shot, but the projectile dropped a little low and broke the shoulder below the kill zone. I took nearly a whole day, trying, hoping, praying to find that injured animal. I still hurt to think that my bullet caused days or more of pain to an animal. If there is a case against hunting, it has to be the bad shot, the wounding, the lost quarry that escapes, bleeding. The hunter who pulls the trigger carries an awesome burden, because wounding is absolutely not an option. Except for that antelope and the doe I grazed lightly, my only other such instance, as far as my memory will retrieve, is detailed below.

When I moved to my present location in the middle 1970s, there was no good place for me to hunt such as I have these days. A friend, Glenn Windham, invited me to hunt with him on his property, and in 1978 I took my first real trophy whitetail buck from his land. The following year we were hunting together regularly. One crisp morning while sitting comfortably on the stand, a marvelous warming sun rose behind my back. My eye caught a movement to the right, and shortly a

fat doe was cavorting immediately in front of the stand. I wasn't interested in her, but my hope that she would have a boyfriend was quickly fulfilled. The largest deer I have ever seen in the Georgia woods materialized in the thick brush, a massive rack blending among intertwined branches of sweetgum and sumac. Any quick movement and the animal would be off, so I slowly eased the rifle in that direction. My heart pounded as the gigantic tines and massive beams imparted a mesmerizing effect on me. I finally centered the animal, only forty yards away, in the scope—a certain kill, it seemed. The only problem was that a good-size pine tree blocked the vital zone, so I waited. He was facing a small clearing and would be in the open any second. I held my breath and waited impatiently as he eased forward ever so slowly. When the ribs behind the shoulder appeared, taut fingers squeezed the trigger.

At the report the buck leaped high in the air, did a complete cartwheel, and disappeared into the underbrush. Confident he was dead, I climbed down immediately and began a search of the area for blood. There were a few bits of hair on the ground but no sign of blood, bone, or lung tissue. My friend arrived shortly, and we searched for two hours, finding no other sign of a hit except the sparse telltale hair where the animal had stood. *He has to be dead,* I kept telling myself. Both of us had to go to work, so we finally left after scouring the area without success.

I called my good friend Eddie Smith, who has accompanied me on several big-game hunts out of state, and who mentored me extensively in Georgia deer hunting. Eddie was off that day, so he volunteered to take his Labrador retriever out to see if he could find that deer. When he telephoned me later, he had solved the mystery. There was a singularly deep gouge on the pine tree that had been shielding the buck, and most of the bullet's energy had expended itself on the dense wood. A little shrapnel had reached the animal's hide and cut off a few hairs but did no real damage. That critter probably was so smart thereafter that he never saw another hunter, eventually dying of old age, as most mature bucks apparently do.

On that same property the next year, I cleanly missed a buck that was easily in range. My climbing stand was in the same tree from which I had killed my first trophy buck, and I had spotted the animal in plenty of time to prepare. I had placed the cross hairs in the right place, thought I squeezed off the shot flawlessly, and hadn't even cut a hair, as far as we were ever able to determine. I probably pulled the shot off the animal by the trigger squeeze, but I will never know with certainty. I can say that the bullet either went over or under the buck, however, because an extensive search turned up no sign of damage by the bullet. Other than long culling shots at the head, these white-tailed deer misses are the only ones I can recall.

Animals commonly hunted are also the most common misses. The exposure is greater so the possibility of miscue is higher. But for this hunter misses haven't come only while hunting Georgia white-tailed deer. There have been mistakes on some pretty darned expensive and important shots as well.

The earliest such incident took place in 1986, the year of my first Stone sheep hunt in British Columbia. After three full days trying to get within range of the sheep my Indian guide and I had been watching, my chance finally presented. How the situation developed is a classic example of unfairness, but who says life's fair? We had worked our way above the band of rams, but they had sensed our presence and the chase was on. They were virtually running 150 yards below us and out of sight, looking to climb out of danger, and we were trying to keep up with them in some of the steepest rockfalls in the world. We had paused on a rocky seam above them when we saw a ram cross well below us, and my guide told me to prepare to shoot. The dark ram we wanted hadn't crossed the hump yet, but the animal was trailing and would shortly be up. I was out of breath and there was nothing on which to rest the rifle. As the animal topped the rise the rifle barrel heaved up and down maliciously as the command to shoot came. It took little effort to pull the shot harmlessly over the sheep's back. Then it was off to the races once more. We got that sheep, though, with a fortunate 400-yard running shot that made me proud. Proud to be blessed with such a magnificent break, I mean. An ethical hunter of experience likely wouldn't consider launching a round with such low odds. But even though I hit the animal with the second shot, that didn't erase the bad first shot.

I've missed two other sheep. In 1990 on a great Dall sheep hunt in the Alaska range, my chance finally came at dark on the last day. My first shot missed for unknown reasons. The animal tumbled on the second shot. Sometimes it seems I'm a much better and more consistent shot when there isn't time to ponder. The same thing happened on my California bighorn hunt, and that species might still be lacking in this book if the ram hadn't spooked toward us instead of away. It appears I'm fairly deadly when given a second chance.

Until 1988, misses on guided hunts included only the Stone sheep. It's perhaps debatable whether that should count as a miss, since I killed the animal within a few minutes with my lucky shot. The first time I really missed an opportunity at a trophy animal, and one that still haunts me, was on a Coues deer hunt in New Mexico that same year. We knew that bucks were feeding along a ridge and that a long shot opportunity might present. There was a convenient rest, and we could see the deer moving, but for some reason it wasn't immediately apparent which was the best buck. By the time I figured out which one my guide intended me to take, the deer was starting to disappear into thick underbrush. There was no choice but to hurry the shot, and naturally the bullet went wide. I took a much smaller buck a couple of days later, the only Coues buck ever killed by the old .30-06, though I have since taken a much bigger one with a different rifle.

I have pulled the trigger on only one elk without hitting the target, though there was an even greater embarrassment when I failed to get off a shot on a very close bugling bull, detailed in chapter 19. When we finally got our last-day chance at a tule elk, a perfect rest was available, the animals were easily within range, and there was no excuse. I missed for reasons known only to God. He was down on the second shot, and no more were needed. Once more, my follow-up skills and my indisputable tendency to blunder on the initial attempt were on public display.

I've missed only once while hunting mule deer. After one terribly long stalk, a running buck eluded my best efforts to bring him down. I shot more times at that one deer than at any other animal I've hunted, emptying my magazine of precious handloads as the deer receded across the open prairie. I killed a buck just as good later on, but the experience cemented in my mind the fact that the running shot isn't my strong suit. Going out of my way to avoid them whenever possible seems highly prudent.

Hunting barren ground muskox in 1996, there was finally a credible excuse when my first shot was a miss. That was the first symptom of my barrel dilation debacle, covered in detail in chapter 2. The front sight screw hole had apparently weakened the steel and allowed an almost imperceptible distention in that part of the barrel. An easy neck shot at a muskox bull with a good rest should be a gimme, but it sailed wide, though the same shot placement killed the animal cleanly within seconds. When I performed a check to see how the rifle was patterning, it was not a surprise that a miss had occurred. The groups were closer to a foot at a hundred yards than inches, some shots in good position and others scattered wildly. Apparently a dilation like that causes the speeding bullet to "rattle around" just before it exits the barrel, and its flight is erratic. This instance was a rare case of the rifle's being at fault instead of the shooter. Don't claim that excuse very often, though, is my advice.

My most embarrassing miss was on a grizzly hunt in 1994, when we weren't having much success. An easy black bear was feeding close to our cabin, so a consolation prize seemed to be in order. We made a terrific stalk to within a hundred yards and caught the bruin feeding in a steep avalanche slide in plain view. The bipod was on the rifle, and I plopped down on a small rise to position everything properly. There was no hurry. When the animal was perfectly still in broadside presentation, I gently squeezed off the shot. The bear did triple axles into the brush, and my guide thought we had a badly tagged bear on our hands. It turned out to be the start of a twenty-four-hour struggle to find what we deemed to be a dead bear. After all, there was no way an experienced hunter could have missed such a shot. But I did, because not only did we never find the slightest indication of a hit, but another bear, very possibly the same one, showed up on that same slope some time later. I took him easily with only one shot.

I also missed a great mountain caribou in 1989, as detailed in chapter 23. In that section I offer several excuses, none of which are adequate. I did take a fine bull later in the hunt.

My Peary caribou was a clean miss on the first shot, but he toppled on the second try. He was on the dead run both times, and that is my best excuse.

Why it was so easy to down him with the second bullet is anybody's guess. As I said, sometimes a little spontaneity seems to be good for one's shooting. When we've missed or we jump something and the animal is rapidly going away, nobody expects too much of your shooting. And we inexplicably shoot better, or at least it appears so sometimes.

I failed to make immediate kills on several other animals, including the walrus and the alligator, though certainly I hit them and did considerable initial damage. Thankfully there have been far more one-shot kills than abject misses, and to this day only three animals have escaped with bullet damage, and only the pronghorn seemed to have serious injury. That's not a perfect record, though it's a pretty good one. However, nothing short of perfection in this area should satisfy us as hunters.

After all, animals die with extreme rapidity most of the time when we make a great one-shot kill, especially when the shot hits the brain. A kill should be accomplished quickly, the more so the better. When we wound an animal and it travels some distance before we can dispatch it, we can expect that there may be a regrettable amount of discomfort. When we miss them with the first shot, we also inflict a degree of mental distress, however immeasurable, whether or not we kill them with subsequent attempts. No matter how much of a hunter's heart is within me, down deep I must admit I really don't like the actual killing of animals. That's why I've taken to shooting my meat deer in the head. They never know what hit them, and I like it that way.

Misses by the big-game hunter are inevitable but also lamentable. Sometimes they are due simply to excitement, but many other complex factors also come into play. Perhaps Clyde Ormond put it best in his book *Hunting Our Biggest Game* (1956), and some comfort can be garnered from his assessment: "Seldom is the big-game hunter at his best [when taking the] shot. He is usually leg-weary, out of breath, on uncertain footing, lungs pumping fast for oxygen in high altitudes, or with sweat streaming down his glasses from sheer exertion. The opportunity comes, not after he's had time to catch his breath, but right then. There is no time to get better footing, assume a more solid shooting position, wipe the glasses, or indeed to allow the quarry to turn into a better shooting angle. It is then or never."

So there it is, a record of all the mistakes I can remember, along with a few excuses. If a past guide of mine comes forward with a tale of some other like episode, I won't quibble about it and will likely admit it's probably true. After all, our natural tendency is to downplay our faults, magnify our few good points, and pretend to be something we aren't, something pretty nearly perfect. There may be memories of misses so deeply buried in my mind that I can't find them. And darned if I'll go to a shrink for help looking.

But I'm as clean on misses as my hidden thoughts will allow. And that's how I want it to be.

A TRIBUTE AND CRITIQUE REGARDING GUIDES AND OUTFITTERS

No, no, thou hast not felt the lapse of hours.
For what wears out the life of mortal men?
'Tis that from change to change their being rolls:
'Tis that repeated shocks, again, again,
Exhaust the energy of strongest souls,
And numb the elastic powers.
Till having used our nerves with bliss and teen,
And tired upon a thousand schemes our wit,
To the just-pausing Genius we remit
Our worn-out life, and are—what we have been.

—Matthew Arnold (1822–1888), *The Scholar-Gypsy*

Jack Atcheson Sr. has hunted all over the world and has been in the taxidermy, guiding, outfitting, and booking businesses for the better part of a half-century. He is also an author of some renown. He says that every time he thinks he's seen it all, a hunter or guide will do something utterly unexpected. Such is hunting. By his observation, the animals really have not changed over the years, despite population dynamics and the influences of development and other activities. The changes in hunting have occurred because people today are different from a generation ago.

I have been on almost sixty guided hunts in North America, and when it comes to guides and outfitters there have unquestionably been the good, the bad, and the ugly. Outfitters vary in experience, quality, proficiency, and dependability, and in the course of so many hunts I've encountered the entire spectrum. However, what impresses me more than their divergent characteristics are the consistent similarities between good outfitters. An outstanding degree of competence exists in the outfitting and guiding business in North America, and bad eggs are indeed few.

Let me distinguish the two central terms here. An outfitter is the person who organizes, books clients, coordinates the enterprise, obtains the needed government or private permission, buys the food and supplies, provides the equipment, and hires the guides—among other things. A guide is on the front line in the field with the hunter, and most often works for an outfitter, although there is some overlap at times.

Local friends guided my first big-game hunts, since this avocation began flowering while I was in medical school and had only a meager income. My parents were ill able to contribute to my support, so I lived and ate in an inexpensive fraternity house. Our diet there benefited from occasional small game such as squirrels, some of which we shot in the yard of the facility, fraternity brothers in rare instances being willing to bend local ordinances for the good of the stomach.

Many guides and outfitters follow that same philosophy, apparently. Gross infractions of the law are strictly prohibited, but many seem willing to tolerate a minor deviation from the rules for the sake of practicality. I have run into a minuscule number over the years who held an outright disregard for the law, but most have been sticklers on the major points of legal decorum. One outfitter (who was also my guide) was apparently convinced I was working for the FBI and that my main objective was to catch him in a violation. He may perhaps still believe it. Such paranoia is uncommon, but the authorities do send in ringers sometimes to see how outfitters are behaving, so the more apprehensive types may get the feeling that they are being watched. That is regrettable, because it sets up a tone of tension that is difficult to escape. For guides and outfitters, an unequivocal recommendation should be that they never mention it if they think their hunter is a clandestine agent, not even if they see a badge in the hunter's backpack. Just follow the rules and don't say anything about it, and everybody's safe.

Getting back to my original guides, a man named Steve Jordan introduced me to the joys of deer hunting. Steve is today a practicing internist in Statesboro, Georgia, which was his hometown. I took my first deer while hunting with dogs on a club to which Steve belonged. After medical school, an internship, a year in Vietnam, and a U.S. Army ophthalmology residency interrupted my big-game aspirations. While at my last duty station in Fort Lewis, Washington, my neighbor Bill Butler guided me on an elk hunt. There was also a semiguided mountain goat hunt with fellow hunter Bob (I can't remember his last name), and a pronghorn antelope hunt guided by optometrist Tom Clyde of Wyoming. My only success (except for the deer) was on the pronghorn hunt.

None of these "guides" looked upon themselves as such, but instead they were intent only on helping an insistent amateur. I shared expenses with them, but they never received reimbursement otherwise. That encounter with a professional guide/outfitter had to await my being in practice long enough to be able to afford to pay someone to take me hunting.

Eddie Smith, a general surgeon in my town of Dublin, Georgia, showed me the ropes in the local area when I arrived in my new home to open my practice. He invited me to join the Rangers Hunting Club, which is now the centerpiece of the Beaverdam Wildlife Management Area. Eddie showed me where to hunt and how to avoid getting lost in the trackless Oconee River swamp, a quick course I duplicate frequently and occasionally still flunk. Under his tutelage we scouted for white-tailed deer and wild hogs and established a deer stand where I would later take my first Laurens County deer. Eddie did a good job. Since arriving in my present location, well over twenty-five years ago, I have failed only once to kill a deer each year, and that year was one when I had little time for hunting.

After a few years in practice Eddie and I began scouting the magazine ads for a place to go hunting out West. We hit the Clyde Ranch once again and then we purchased a semiguided hunt in Wyoming for pronghorns, but our first fully guided hunt was with Moose Creek Outfitters, owned by Dick and Fran Norris. I'll never forget the five-mile trail ride through majestic virgin forest from the airstrip to camp, two novices who had hardly ever mounted horses before, riding off into the Selway-Bitterroot Wilderness in search of the elusive Rocky Mountain elk. We returned three more times to hunt with the Norrises, and finally each of us took a fine wilderness bull.

Even back then there was a battle of wits going on between the U.S. Forest Service and anyone who utilized the national forests for profitable enterprise. Moose Creek Outfitters kept the trails open and cut firewood with crosscut saws so they wouldn't disturb the wilderness with the noise of chain saws (which were, and still are, illegal in wilderness areas). The outfitter and his hired men also provided a contact point for other users to radio the outside world as needed, and they guarded their portion of the back country as if it were their own piece of paradise. They also paid the required per diem fee for utilizing government land, based on the number of hunter-days they scheduled.

For their efforts to earn a fair day's pay, it seemed to me that they were harassed unmercifully. They were required to pack out every scrap of their gear at the end of each season, simply because their area was designated wilderness. For a few years they were able to hide a couple of the heavier items, such as the cook stove, in a big woodpile at the camp. However, when the rangers discovered their clever deception Dick paid a heavy fine for failing to cart the two-hundred-pound apparatus five miles to the Ranger Station and on out of the wilderness. No wonder outfitting is a tough business. And the conflicts still go on. When it is impossible to continue on account of burdensome rules, much of today's accessible back country will become inaccessible because the trails will close.

Outfitting is hard and demanding work, and it seems a little slack could be cut. It makes one shudder to think what would be the consequences of such a rule if it were applied to Canadian outfitters. In that land of endless distances, they would be shut down or reduced to very basic tent camps only. Bureaucracy thrives in the United States, even in the most remote corners of the wilderness.

Today Moose Creek Outfitters still survives in the hands of son Darryl, who guided me to my first two elk. He has struggled to keep his area, although he was ejected for some years as a part of the seemingly mindless realignments that have afflicted many U.S. outfitters from Florida to Alaska. I recently wrote letters requesting that the U.S. Forest Service increase the number of hunter-days they were allocating him, which they had inexplicably slashed in half. Under their unrealistic proposal, he may be simply out of business, and his part of the Selway-Bitterroot Wilderness will be closed to everyone as a consequence. For reasons perhaps impossible to fathom, our government appears to be trying to kill the outfitting business, and it increasingly seems that Canada is trying to do the same.

Outfitters fight some monstrous battles, and in many cases their profit margin is as thin as tissue paper. Those who make a lot of money are a very small minority. Most stay in the business because they love the outdoors, they love hunting, and they love the animals they hunt. They are, by and large, hunters who have taken sharing the experience to the logical extreme, helping people like me to achieve success whenever possible, with the hunter supplying money for the expenses and (they hope) providing enough profit margin to make the effort worthwhile. Most of them are excellent and knowledgeable conservationists who deeply care about the wild areas.

There are two basic kinds of outfitters in North America. One is the part-timer, by far the most common. Full-time outfitters are the others, and those are virtually nonexistent in the Lower Forty-eight and Mexico. For the most part only Canada and Alaska consistently support outfitters on a vocational basis, and Alaska is becoming increasingly problematic in that regard. Capricious changes in regulations, seemingly casual shuffling of guiding areas by the government, and hostile public and private institutions make it harder every day to maintain an outfitting business of any kind in the United States.

Practically all guides, except for those full-time outfitters who also do active guiding, are seasonal. Most have "real lives" they lead apart from their guiding, and many times one marvels at their dedication. From the Arctic to the jungle, their devotion to the hunter-client, to the task at hand, to conservation, to following the rules, and to getting the hunter home safely and successfully is astounding. They brave icy winds and snow, deep rivers, unpredictable horses, mechanical breakdowns, finicky cook stoves, mosquitoes and biting flies, and unsavory skinning and meat-cutting duties, often suffering mightily to get the jobs done. I have walked and ridden for miles behind such men (and one woman, my polar bear guide), marveling at the stamina and determination on display before me. As hunters we don't give them enough recognition, and in fact we probably can't. We can offer them a sincere thanks at the end of the hunt, whether we were successful or not, and give them a decent tip for their efforts, though.

Before going further, let me go to the worst situations I have faced. On one early hunt, I discovered that my outfitter didn't want me to mention that we were hunting with him. He didn't want me to discuss with anyone the game we were seeking, where we were going or where we had been, or any of the particulars of our hunt. He camouflaged our tents, acted like the world was after him, and supplied me with one of the most unprepared guides anywhere. For us to maneuver it became necessary to lend that man fresh socks to get him back from one long day of hunting, as he was entirely out of shape and got blisters, while I experienced no such problems. I carried a heavier pack back to camp than he, because of his condition. He was concerned about neither the letter nor the spirit of the law, and urged me to be willing to break it if the opportunity arose.

My belief about that experience now is that we were hunting in a closed area, either because my outfitter didn't have privileges there or it was some kind of park or preserve closed to hunting. Much of my hunt was spent in the worried hope that we wouldn't run afoul of the law. Returning home from that hunt left a taste of disillusionment with big-game hunting in general, but thankfully I've discovered that such a scenario is rare indeed. My lesson was that one should use a booking agent for most major hunts, unless you know someone who has hunted with an outfitter and can make a recommendation.

The best outfitter I ever encountered? Several have been excellent, and it will be necessary only to describe the characteristics that make an experience special. This should begin with communication, and it should happen early in the relationship. It makes me nervous to book a hunt and hear no word from the outfitter for months, even though I usually contact them immediately after booking. The best outfitters send something in the mail right away, either a letter of acknowledgment or a brochure or both. They let you know up front what to expect, how to prepare, what equipment to bring, how the hunting went in the area last year, when to arrive, how you'll hunt, what kind of camp you'll be in, and the like. Financial arrangements are spelled out clearly so you know when to send in payments and whether it is permissible to make the final payment at the onset of the hunt. After one arrives, timely airport pickup is necessary (or precise instructions otherwise, such as the need for a rental car reservation and a decent map). There are very few legitimate excuses for a long delay that leaves you standing around the airport hoping somebody shows up. A briefing after arrival is definitely in order, laying out the plans for your hunt, along with a discussion of alternatives that may necessitate a midcourse correction. Any late news that might alter what you have been told should be covered at that time. Someone should help you pare your pack-in gear (if this applies) to what you really will need, arrange for you to sight in your rifle or bow, and show you where to sleep and stow your gear.

At some point near the outset, you will be introduced to your guide. In the case of small outfits, this may be the outfitter himself. I've met some dubious-looking guides who actually caused me to toss and turn that night wondering if we could possibly enjoy one another's company for the duration of the hunt. Others are immediately likable and leave one with no such trepidation. Initial impressions are terrible predictors of who will be a good guide, though, and some of those offering the best first impressions were not nearly as good afield as some of the "toss-and-turn" types.

The only way to screen guides ahead of time is to talk to somebody who has used the outfit before. If you want the best guide, ask that question of people on the outfitter's reference list. If you're using an outfitter based on a friend's experience, ask him about the best guide(s) in the outfit. If one of them isn't available, you can either take your

chances or ask to be postponed a year until the one you want is open. It isn't a good idea to put the outfitter on the spot about who is his best guide, though some of them may share that with you confidentially. They'll naturally tell you that all their guides can get the job done, but with a little prior planning and firm expression of your desires you have a much higher chance of getting the very best. Good guides are hard to find, though, and it takes a long time to build the experience necessary to be superb at it. Never expect the outfitter to discourage any budding young guide by openly expressing the opinion that he isn't as good as the one you requested.

The most desirable characteristic in any guide is patience. An observant hunter can often tell how the experience may go by the way the guide prepares for the initial stages of the hunt, be it saddling horses, loading a packtrain, or servicing sleds for a snowmobile trek. Patience shows up early if it's there. One guide became highly irritated at me, and even used derogatory language, because I wasn't able to assist him perfectly in loading pack boxes onto a packstring. It finally became necessary to stop what I was doing and explain, gently but firmly, that I didn't pack horses for a living and that if he wanted my help he was going to have to show me what to do and stuff his frustration. He sobered considerably and we wound up having a grand time. Had I let him abuse me at that initial juncture, the same treatment might have been in store for the whole hunt. Lay down the ground rules, and one of them is for the guide to be patient, whether or not it is a natural inclination.

Let there be no confusion about one important fact. The quality of the outfitter and guide are only peripherally related to whether you get your game. Some animals are harder to get than others. Some areas are harder to hunt successfully than others, some hunts will be ruined by terrible weather, and sometimes a key piece of equipment will break. These factors can have important bearing on whether you are successful, but a quality outfitter lets you know the variables up front so you won't be surprised. He can't predict the unpredictable, but he should have some idea what might go wrong and be able to come up with some options. What is important is the effort and care the outfitter demonstrates, the preparation, and whether he knows his area and is willing to go the extra mile to help you have the highest possible chance of success. Just keep in mind that no matter how he prepares, success cannot be guaranteed in fair-chase hunting, though he should be able to pledge a dedicated effort on the part of himself and his staff.

A little advice I always try to follow, a tidbit most useful, is never, never to ask your guide what you'll be doing tomorrow, especially after you've come in from a tiring and fruitless day afield. Probably he doesn't know until he talks to other guides in camp or to the outfitter. Perhaps he just needs a chance to think it over. Sometimes he'll have you back in exactly the same spot doing exactly the same thing, and sometimes you'll change tactics and country entirely. Trust the guide to get the job done and don't drive him nuts with questions he can't answer.

One more item is important. Far more hunts are ruined by belligerent and unreasonable clients than by incompetent or uncaring guides and outfitters. Remember, when you are feeling critical, that the deficiencies you find in the outfitter and guide are much more likely to be your own than theirs. So you be patient, understanding, cooperative, pleasant, and peaceful, too. Whether you are glassing for animals or walking the long trail back from a hard day afield, those qualities are irreplaceable. They make for a much more pleasant hunt and dramatically reduce the chances of a bad memory, whether you take the hunted animal or not.

It was the hunter-president Theodore Roosevelt who said, "The credit belongs to the man who is actually in the arena, whose face is marred by dust and sweat and blood. . . . His place shall never be with those cold and timid souls who know neither victory nor defeat." When you go to the back country for a hunting adventure, you automatically distance yourself from the feeble and impotent crowd of spectators who increasingly characterize our nation's sporting instinct. We have become a country of passive observers who fill stadiums but never boldly enter the fray. Professional athletes increasingly shed blood vicariously for us and fight our pretended battles, and are paid well for it. Our shooting wars are all on television or at the movies. Sometimes I shudder to think what might happen were a real enemy to present at our doorstep, one that required we put our own blood on the line. Would we be able to handle it?

Never forget that your outfitter and guide have been there in the heat of battle, probably many times. Let that knowledge temper your criticism and add to your relationship with them. The extra effort on your part will be worth it as they help you in your quest to be more than a detached onlooker in the serious business of life and death.

OF HUNTERS, NONHUNTERS, AND ANTIHUNTERS

Hunting is one of our strongest instincts. We were born with it.
For thousands of generations hunting was the way our oldest parents
secured their food, clothing, and most of their other necessities. . . .
Big-game hunting is the surest and least expensive way to gain strength
for success in modern business and professional life.

—Col. Harry Snyder, *Snyder's Book of Big Game Hunting*, 1950

Hurt no living thing; Ladybird, Nor butterfly,
Nor moth with dusty wing, Nor cricket chirping cheerily,
Nor grasshopper so light of leap, Nor dancing gnat, nor beetle fat,
Nor harmless worms that creep.

—Christina Rossetti (1830–94), *Hurt No Living Thing*

In the same week that Cleveland Amory died at age eighty-one, eco-terrorists protested a planned expansion by burning $12 million worth of buildings at a Vail, Colorado, ski resort. Amory had a long career as a writer and journalist, and his life was characterized by extreme prosperity and high achievement. He was a graduate of Harvard University, and he became the youngest editor of *The Saturday Evening Post.* An author of best-selling books, Armory was also a successful radio and television commentator and humorist.

In 1967, Amory founded the Fund for Animals, and in so doing he forever set himself at odds with much of the human race. His organization and his influence through the media are credited with launching much of the modern animal-rights movement. His 1974 book, *Man Kind? Our Incredible War on Wildlife*, created a great deal of the antihunting sentiment that today's hunters still face. The book also sparked the ignominious CBS antihunting documentary *The Guns of Autumn,* an unreasonable tirade against hunting that immensely augmented the harm done by Amory's written word.

The impact of Cleveland Amory's philosophy goes far beyond mere hunting. His concepts were so radical and so appealing to a certain segment of people that a new revolution has now been set in motion, and it may be impossible to stop it. If it is ever taken to the extreme and implemented fully, it appears to me that Amory's agenda would ensure that human beings could subsist only at the most basic level, if they could survive at all. Some say critically that Amory himself felt no such compulsion to be so inconvenienced, though I cannot confirm that. I watched a number of interviews with him from time to time during his later years, and I saw little sign of the humorist. He always seemed downright mean and angry and even referred to himself as a curmudgeon. In one television segment, he breathed warnings of bodily harm toward anyone who might presume to abuse one of his cats. He showed every evidence of missing some ingredient in his life, a certain consuming vacuum that the concept of animal rights seemed to fill, at least partially. But from my own observation I saw in him little evidence of compassion toward his fellow man.

His movement lives on even after his death. The success and influence of the animal-rights movement seems to grow with each passing year. When this extremist fervor becomes linked with radical environmentalism, the stage is set for catastrophic incidents such as the arson at Vail. While Cleveland Amory and his organization doubtless bear no direct responsibility, the animal-rights movement in general must be credited with creating a situation that encourages such destruction. Similar vandalism has been meted out hundreds of times all over the world in recent years, protesting virtually every form of animal utilization, be it fox hunting, stalking a new vaccine, or seeking a better strain of beef.

Figures show that almost every day some kind of animal-rights terrorism occurs, and the cost to society amounts to millions of dollars. There have been at least eighty-five violent attacks on medical research institutions, and it is estimated that the cost of doing medical research has increased 10 to 20 percent because of the prevailing climate and material losses. Virtually all researchers agree that a cure for Acquired Immune Deficiency Syndrome will never occur apart from intensive animal research, but apparently many animal-rights groups are oblivious to that fact, or else their priorities are so distorted that they simply don't care.

Since I am a practicing Christian, my entire world view and my applied philosophy are shaped by my understanding of the Holy Bible, and it is in that context that I must interpret the question of animal rights. Whether you agree with me or not, please bear with me while I attempt a dissection that is in harmony with my faith. I do not present this as the absolute answer, because my knowledge and exposition inevitably will be imperfect. This is simply an attempt to explain the issue as best I am able.

The beginning quotations of this chapter serve to dramatically illustrate the dichotomy between the opposing sides of the debate over animal rights. As with the Arab-Israeli conflict, it appears that there is no happy medium and probably no chance of a lasting negotiated settlement. One side or the other must at last triumph, and the loser must be vanquished. For those of us who are hunters by heritage and by instinct, the search for common ground and the sincerest attempts to reason with the animal-rights fringe are an exercise in self-deception. For a number of reasons their hard-liners will never compromise, so our kind should put such foolish thinking out of our minds.

Hunters routinely, and generally with little twang of moral conscience, perform the ultimately horrific deed, according to animal rightists. Taking the life of an animal is not an act the hunter should perform lightly, and most don't. But is it wrong? In the eyes of the hunter, there is honestly no other way. Our problem as hunters is that the act is sometimes visible or audible to observers, it is generations removed from the experience of many people today, and it is regrettably repugnant to some. Doubtless there is as well a hidden aspect of hunting that is dark and mysterious to nonhunters, and perhaps may even entice them like a forbidden fruit. There may be impulsive recoil from this beckoning from the primeval depths of their consciousness. I do not know this latter psychological conflict from experience, however; I have always known that I am a hunter.

Moreover, taking the life of a wild animal is easily segregated from what the general public perceives as more essential forms of animal utilization, such as raising chickens or doing medical experiments. Worse, many hunters unwisely play directly into the hands of the animal- rights movement by displaying the carcasses of recently killed animals as they motor down the highway. They behave as if the killing were a demonstration of victory over the creature, when in truth taking an animal is a mere demonstration of God's grace toward the hunter. I will have more to say in the next chapter about this seedy, objectionable aspect of our sport that some hunters seem to have raging within them like a mortal infection. It is one affliction hunters must cure or hunting may become obsolete.

On the other extreme of the debate are those who are pushing to eliminate all use of animals. In between are those who regularly eat meat of some kind (about 97 percent of the population), own pets, benefit from and support medical research using animals, enjoy a trip to the zoo to see the "prisoners," and with no pangs of moral conscience poison the innocent cockroaches and termites who want to share their homes. It is this immense number of people who will determine the fate of hunting in the near term, and animal-rights adherents appear to hold many decisive cards. We hunters can influence this vast majority, but we won't be able to eliminate the threat to our heritage with rational arguments. Prepare to fight a holding action for the rest of your days, hunters.

The most radical of the animal-rights cohort include an attorney in Massachusetts who is pushing to have animals given full legal status, with complete protection of their "personhood" through force of law. He is himself a pet owner, and how he resolves that paradox is not clear— he probably has adopted the trendy term "animal guardian." He likens the current state of animals to that of human slaves in centuries past, a condition of injustice and exploitation that he says modern society ought to reject.

In like fashion, an Australian group is pushing for a United Nations "Universal Declaration of Animal Rights" that would "give all mammals, fish, reptiles, birds, and invertebrates" full rights that much of today's human population doesn't even enjoy. The proposed declaration would mandate "due process of law" before a human being could take an animal's life. Picture that the next time you harvest a deer or duck. And understand that adding the word "invertebrates" includes every animal without a backbone—everything from jellyfish and clams to bacteria, viruses, and fungi. Since such wording doubtless extends the declaration to yeast, which are in fact simple animals, human life itself becomes impossible as a consequence. Even vegetarians must ingest yeast extract in order to survive, because the only source of essential vitamin B12 is from animals, among the smallest of which are yeast. Such a sweeping declaration would eliminate human life on planet earth, were it enforced rigorously enough.

Such people are trying to abolish much more than hunting. These revolutionaries are attempting to rid the planet of any kind of manipulation of animal populations, including livestock production, biomedical and other animal research, pet ownership, fishing, and even human observation of animals in the wild (which is the only place animals would exist under their program).

The natural question arises: Is there a suicidal bent to the animal-rights movement? Perhaps so. If it isn't suicidal, it certainly seems "life-negating and castrating. The whole notion of anorexia as an extreme form of vegetarianism is self-destruction," to quote Dr. James Swan.

To most sensible people, such a scenario is outside the realm of possibility. But don't underestimate the power of the animal-rights minority to manipulate public opinion and further their agenda. It is painfully apparent from any study of history that a small group of dedicated, unwavering people can control the population at large, the most glaring recent example being the Nazi party of Germany under Adolf Hitler. It is for that reason that I say that the large number of uncommitted people who utilize animals now will determine the future of hunting in the short term. In the long term, something far more ominous appears inevitable to me.

It is logical to conclude that hunting may be one of the first forms of animal utilization to be banned. This right may be eliminated by a public manipulated into believing that hunting is an undesirable kind of unnecessary killing. The broader questions of animal utilization may not be decided democratically at all, but rather at some point will probably be mandated by a world dictatorship that will one day emerge and champion the cause of our enemies. Under our present democratic system in the United States, neither we hunters nor the fanatical animal-rights fringe have the votes to prevail, though time, abundant money, the apparent favor of the mass media, and even some prophetic passages of the Holy Bible, seem to forecast their victory and our defeat (though for the Christian that defeat is predicted to be short-lived indeed).

About 10 percent of the U.S. population identify themselves as active hunters. Another 10 to 15 percent oppose hunting in all its forms, though a majority of those aren't certain why and cannot adequately define the issues, nor contrast their position with the incongruity of a pet sitting at their feet or meat on their table. Most surveys show that trophy hunting is criticized in fairly consistent fashion by the population in general. That is probably because the animal-rights movement and their sympathetic media allies have effectively portrayed this highly selective activity as wasteful and frivolous, rather than being the best and most conservation-oriented use of an animal. The term "wealthy trophy hunter" has become cliché as a part of animal-rights public relations releases, even though most hunters are neither wealthy nor essentially hunters of trophies.

The above figures leave between 75 percent and 80 percent of the population uncommitted on the issue. Thus, our fate even now is not in our hands nor in those of our enemies, but rather it is in the hands of the large proportion of nonhunters who populate our increasingly urban world. We can take effective steps to counter our adversaries in the short term, though, and forestall what appears to me to be inevitable.

There are really four parties in this debate, including the animal, the hunter, the antihunter, and the nonhunter. The first character is the hunted animal, creatures the Bible refers to as "unreasoning animals, to be captured and killed." This phrase demonstrates the awesome completeness of the Holy Scriptures, if one is willing to accept it, because God Himself repeatedly puts His stamp of approval on animal utilization of all types, including this activity we call hunting.

God apparently was first to take the lives of animals when He supplied Adam and Eve with skins as clothing after the account of their fall into rebellion in the third chapter of the foundational book of Genesis. He must have actually gone "hunting" for the right animals to sacrifice to provide both a physical and spiritual covering for his disobedient first couple. This event is an ancient foreshadowing of the Jewish sacrificial system, whereby ritually taking the lives of innocent animals provided a temporary covering for man's sins. The permanent covering, it is made clear in both the Old Testament and the New Testament, is the blood of Messiah, Jesus Christ. His rejection and crucifixion are foretold as early as that same book of Genesis, though the details are more completely disclosed by various Jewish prophets down through the centuries before his coming. Just one such instance is found in Chapter 53 of the prophetic book of Isaiah, where the substitutionary sacrifice of Jesus Christ on the cross is foretold in graphic detail more than six hundred years before the event.

This theological background is necessary to establish a couple of important points. First, there is no biblical reason to oppose hunting. It is a form of utilization of wild animals that the Bible nowhere condemns in any way; in fact, it portrays it in a positive light uniformly. Jesus himself ate meat (the Passover feast in the Gospels, which was always a roasted lamb, is only one example), consumed fish (chapter 21 of the Gospel of John), declared all food clean (the Gospel of Mark, chapter 7, verse 19), and distributed fish as food for 4,000 men on one occasion and 5,000 men on another. In the Book of Acts the apostle Peter visualizes supernaturally a sheetlike object in which are all manner of animals, and a voice from Heaven commands him to "kill and eat."

Second, the hunted animal is in no way terrorized by thoughts of death, as it has no ability to reason that its life may be in danger. There is no question that animals flee predators of all kinds, and that they do so to preserve their lives. But that act is entirely "unreasoning," and as soon as the danger is past they resume their lives with no overriding sense of dread. The hunted animal has strong survival instincts imparted to it by its Creator, and every outdoorsperson is acutely aware of these. But actual worry that tomorrow may bring a hunter to take its life, or that it may be going to the slaughterhouse, or that some animal predator might pounce upon it is not among its faculties.

Animals are capable of learning, and they readily avoid situations that have put them in danger before, but that is simply another instinctive survival mechanism. Oblivious is perhaps too strong a word, but preoccupied is a more precise description of their outlook. Animals are busy meeting their natural needs for food, cover, and rest, as well as the urge to reproduce. Many essential activities are instinctively programmed into animals' lives, and these may give the impression of forethought. No matter how complex these behaviors may be, they are not the product of intelligent reasoning or decision-making. Animals do not have the faculties to shrewdly plan for the future, so they are never anxious about tomorrow. It is the present that matters to them, not the future, even though they may spend the day gathering a cache of food or feeding heavily to store up fat for the winter. It is easy to forget this in our world of scheming anthropomorphic cartoon characters, talking animal toys, and fanciful television programs that impart human characteristics to domestic and wild animals.

So the first party in the equation is the prey animal, which is usually healthiest and most abundant where it is hunted in an ethical fashion by human beings. The biblical perspective is that the animals are here for the convenience, companionship, utilization, and entertainment of mankind, as well as for our observation and wonderment. If there were any frightful dread residing in the hunted animal, it would more likely be a terror of other animals rather than human beings. Nonhuman predators are ripping, slashing, and slowly killing beasts, and often they begin consuming a downed animal while it is still alive and quite aware. These meat-eating creatures have their place and we must allow room for them, although both they and society are better served if certain major predators stay remote from human habitation and agriculture.

The point is that the most compassionate animal utilization has nothing to do with "natural" nonhuman predators. Compassion is personified in the practiced human hunter using the modern firearm or bow, propelling an accurate missile of energy unequaled in the history of the world, killing quickly, efficiently, and selectively.

The next individual to consider is the hunter. It isn't necessary to review the manifold accomplishments of this group in detail, as we are the subject of many a defensive article about our chosen avocation. Hunters are the heroes of conservation in North America and throughout much of the world.

The first thing hunters point to when defending our passion is the success of conservation efforts directed toward hunted species. We can cite figures of money contributed to conservation, protection of all kinds of species, sales of licenses from which money is derived for game departments, and the special taxes we support ad infinitum. It is undeniably true that as stewards we have been exemplary. But forget these arguments unless you're in a position to tell it effectively to your congressman. With the public at large, there are far more important points we must make, and just as important, we must make them with our fellow hunters. Gone is the day when we can prevail by simply showing what works. It isn't a strong enough argument when we are faced with unconstrained emotion. Just

look at the defeats suffered by mountain lion hunting in California and Oregon, bear hunting in Colorado, and an unfortunate number of other examples. In all cases the system was working very well, but the public didn't buy it, tossing out good management in favor of no management.

Pragmatism is still no match for passion. What works is not necessarily what the third party in the debate, the general public, will endorse. The effort to save the mountain lion in California was successful, to hear the animal-rights line. But mountain lions in California are still being killed at substantially the same rate as before the current ban. Today agents of the state, paid with taxpayer money, do the killing to remove problem lions, instead of the sport hunter paying the state for the privilege. We are on the verge of other defeats, such as losing grizzly bear hunting in British Columbia, something that looks like a sure bet for the animal-rights coalition. All the facts favor sport hunting of grizzly bears, but the public may not believe logical arguments. Worse, politicians find it easier to eliminate hunting of grizzlies than to restrict access and development in and around grizzly habitat. Conflicts between grizzlies are sure to arise, and state agents will kill as many as before the ban. It doesn't make any sense from a conservation standpoint, but such could ultimately happen, one by one, to all our hunting privileges, as the effort to save this animal or that one from hunters moves forward.

The hunter can influence the future of our beloved activity, though the final outcome may not be ours to determine. It is certainly appropriate to emphasize what we have already achieved, such as our contributions to conservation and funding of practical plans to preserve animal populations, but at the same time we must realize that these accomplishments alone are insufficient to preserve our heritage. One encouraging trend is the way hunters are finally getting organized and making our collective voice heard. The Congressional Sportsmen's Caucus is the largest council in Congress and is a bipartisan voice in that important body. Numerous activist organizations of hunters are springing up and growing, and these are contributing mightily to the cause. This is all good. These developments are healthful for the hunter, and ultimately they amount to real help for the hunted animals.

To the degree that we can influence the outcome of questions surrounding sport hunting, we should. By now you cannot miss the fact that the key is to win the confidence and respect of that important segment of the population who make up the nonhunting public. General Norman Schwarzkopf hit the nail on the head when he recently challenged the hunting community to do something good for their neighborhood, some positive act that has nothing to do with hunting. We must win the uncommitted public by demonstrating that we are not simply self-serving consumers of the wildlife that our activities and money protect and enhance. We must show that we have hearts of compassion and kindness. It is harder to convince the public that hunting and hunters are bad when food for the hungry flows from them, when blind children's faces light up as they are allowed to feel mounted animals, or when someone who hunts cares enough for the disadvantaged to give time to relieve suffering in a faraway land.

I know a man who is a physician and an avid hunter who has completed a total of eighteen missionary trips to Honduras and Jamaica and has done more than 1,000 free operations in those countries. Another hunter I know has made this kind of activity his life's work. He has a fleet of hospital ships that circle the globe providing free medical care. Yet another hunter makes regular journeys to Africa to promote and supply homes for orphaned children on that impoverished continent. Another dedicated hunter, an e-mail friend, is giving his life to the service of the people of Mozambique despite his own pressing physical problems and those of his wife. The best case both for and against hunting is hunters themselves, and it is essential that we show off the positive side.

The final character we must address is the antihunter. One necessarily must distinguish between the front-line animal-rights activist and the leadership of animal-rights groups, because the two are often unintentionally at odds, both philosophically and practically. The average person who opposes hunting may join an organization, feed its machinery with contributions and dues, and even participate in acts of protest against some forms of animal utilization. This person may never consider the implications of those actions when it comes to other animal uses in which they readily participate. For example, such an individual may take part in an organized protest of a particular hunt by walking through the woods beating a drum, since the individual opposes using guns or bows to kill animals. At the same time, that person may never reflect upon the fact that the umbrella organization also officially opposes pet ownership, medical research involving animals, leather and wool clothing, keeping animals in zoos, consumption of nonvegetarian foods, and a hundred other practices that the individual member may believe to be moral and right. It obviously never crosses the mind of such an individual that the very drum he or she may be pounding is stretched tight with the skin of an animal.

The leaders of these organizations, on the other hand, are generally purists who are hostile to all forms of animal utilization. In extreme cases they may even be "antihuman" to the extent that they advocate such concepts as the voluntary extinction of the human race, their perception being that since mankind is the main problem in the world, elimination is the only solution. These leaders are reluctant to oppose their members openly when it comes to such popular practices as pet ownership, spraying homes for pesky bugs, or using antibiotics against infections. Privately they are quite likely opposed to those as well, though I haven't heard of any volunteering to be the first to go extinct. Most of them appear to all observers to practice what they preach in most areas. They wouldn't be caught dead wearing leather shoes or wool skirts. They are strict vegetarians. Their lifestyle usually reflects their doctrinal extremism. It would be unwise to accuse them of being hypocritical, and that is one of their undeniable strengths.

The reason we can never reach a negotiated settlement with the leadership of the animal-rights contingent hinges on the principle of vested interest. The Pharisees of Jesus' time rejected the Son of God because he was a threat to the system of temple worship that had made many of them wealthy. They had a vested interest in maintaining the status quo, even if God should show up in their midst with the intention to change it. They clung to their system despite explicit warnings in their own Holy Scriptures that this is exactly what they would do when their Messiah arrived. They crucified Jesus Christ despite dire predictions of the consequences of rejecting the very changes he would propose.

In similar fashion, we can tell the leaders of the various animal cults that they are wrong and prove it with facts and figures. We can explain animal stewardship in whatever terms we want to use, and we can demonstrate beyond doubt that our way works best. We can even expose their philosophy as a sham and prove it to them so irrefutably that they are speechless. In like manner, Jesus left the Scribes and Pharisees absolutely without any ability to verbally contend with him on many occasions, but still they rejected him because of this principle. Losing the debate resoundingly and applying appropriate and deserved public chastening would not change anything with the animal-rights leaders, either, because they have an ongoing vested interest in maintaining the organization and keeping the money flowing in. They are in a position where right or wrong does not matter, truth does not matter, and neither does undeniable proof. They will continue their war of deception regardless of any effort to discredit them, in order to continue bringing in the money and keeping the membership level high.

That is not to say that the determination and intransigence of the leaders of the animal-rights movement are reason for hunters to lose the debate by default. We indeed should do everything in our power to win, and to expose this self-serving aspect of animal-rights groups is one of the best ways. They have actually tried to hang this charge around the necks of hunters, whose giving and caring are often selfless and above reproach.

This brings up the matter of exactly how the animal rightists are wrong and how they might be discredited. Their weakest points are (1) this obvious fact that they are far more self-serving than the worst of hunters, (2) the fact that they are also blindly self-righteous, and (3) they use blatant lies to advance their cause. In these they are the modern equivalent of the Pharisees of Jesus' time. It appears that being good to animals is only peripheral to raising funds and building influence in most mainline animal-rights organizations. Worse, they seize on the issues most likely to raise the most money, regardless of how ill-advised, impractical,

unworkable, or even foolish they may be. The cost paid in needless loss of animal life and increased suffering among the animals they claim to represent is often staggering. Still, onward they plod, any negative conservation implications be damned.

Dr. James Swan believes that the Achilles' heel of the animal-rights movement is their unending need for crises and enemies, though how that weakness might be exploited is not entirely clear. If there is no crisis and no enemy, these groups have no reason to exist. If there is no crisis and no enemy, they will go to great lengths to create them. They spend huge amounts of money on mailings to stir up the troops against the latest adversary and to magnify the nature of the supposed emergency, and thus create more publicity and more income. That they do not spend their funds on biologically sound conservation is a matter of record. They are far more likely to oppose than to support wildlife management activities designed and endorsed by mainline scientists, unless such actions involve closure of hunting or a reduction in hunting opportunities. By contrast, the hunting community uniformly supports closures and moratoriums on hunting whenever the scientific facts dictate that such measures be instituted to protect a population of animals.

One of the most radical animal-rights groups has a budget that exceeds $20 million each year, and it enjoys the support of many prominent people, including a number of Hollywood celebrities. Starry-eyed people give piles of money to help the animals, and children collect pennies to save this creature or that. Yet this same group spends less than $10,000 per year on animal shelters and other activities of actual benefit to the animals they profess to represent. The money goes, more often than not, to create another enemy among the myriad groups of animal utilizers, and to publicize the latest crisis threatening helpless animals. The end result is that such groups raise more funds.

One final weakness of the animal-rights camp is their absolute intolerance of any difference of opinion with them. There is no room for middle ground, as evidenced by the fact that few of their organizations endorse hunting of animals even in circumstances where humane removal of some animals is sorely needed. In the same manner that they refuse to recognize biological reality, animal-rights groups ignore cultural differences, individual upbringing, family traditions, and the absence of alternatives to hunting, and tend to lump all these together as immoral killing of animals. For example, the Inuit have subsisted solely on animals for millennia, yet the extremists make no allowance for that cultural reality. The animal-rights movement has devastated the economy of these native peoples by destroying the market for fox and sealskins, denying them access to their only source of income.

How can we ever hope to beat them? Well, as I stated, I believe that as the end of time draws near we may see them completely take over. Hitler was but a frightful foreshadowing of even worse things to come. He was an avowed vegetarian, an animal-rights advocate, and was completely opposed to using animals for medical research. Of Hitler, Dr. Harold Morowitz of the George Mason University School of Medicine has stated, "It is faint consolation to find that the most horrible imaginable crimes against humans in world history were committed by persons with a strong concern for animals."

The concept of a coming one-world government under a supreme dictator is well documented as Bible prophecy. I believe that the frightening reign of this authoritarian will feature the ultimate in promotion of animal rights. He will make Hitler's atrocities seem small by comparison, yet he will do it in much the same fashion. He will rise meteorically from obscurity to power on the strength of empty promises that he will make the world better. Hitler killed Jewish physicians on trumped-up charges of vivisection, or using animals for medical experiments. He had no aversion to having his own henchmen perform far more inhumane, even lethal, experiments on innocent humans. During those trying years it was frequently speculated that Hitler, so manifestly evil and so bent on world domination, might be the antichrist foretold in the Bible. The chilling antichrist to come will outdo Hitler in every particular.

For these present times, the uncommitted center, the nonhunting public, holds the fate of hunting in its hands. By practicing the highest hunting ethics and concentrating on purging our ranks of those who don't measure up, we have a chance in the short run. It would help immensely to engage in community projects with positive identification and high hunter visibility. We must also stay politically active and try to get prohunting candidates elected. It is absolutely mandatory that we build a coalition with other animal utilizers, including all who consume meat of any kind. People who like to eat fish or chicken have as much to lose as those of us who like to harvest fresh meat with our own hands. We must clarify the blurred lines that separate various animal-user groups and employ them to link up and fight the extremists. We must hope that when people realize what is happening, they will react by uniting and fighting.

In the final analysis, the whole animal-rights scene is a product of our remarkably affluent times combined with an unprecedented spiritual darkness. Its flourishing is a harbinger of despair, not hope. Empty lives are often filled with foolishness, and millions of people are caught in an aimless existence devoid of meaning and purpose. Doing something for the so-called goddess Earth and the creatures that inhabit it seems attractive to them. It is a monstrous deception, but one for which many are falling head over heels.

Dr. James Swan describes the average animal-rights supporter as a single white female in her late twenties to early thirties who lives in a large city on either coast and has several pets. Such a person is necessarily cut off from most contact with the natural world. He believes that many of them, if not most, are in some kind of emotional pain, and the plight of the animals they champion is often unconsciously linked with this inner anguish. Since they are unable to deal with the inward trauma, they lay hold of some outside activity that offers the possibility of progress and resolution. He does not believe that individual affluence is at issue, though it has been my observation that less affluent societies consider the concept of animal rights utterly laughable. For any particular animal rightist, though, the emotional price one has paid to achieve personal affluence can certainly be an important factor in moving toward becoming an activist.

At the very least, we hunters should resolve to accept any defeats with our eyes open to what is happening. Satan rejoices at every lie the public accepts as truth. He is the father of lies, and his proven tool is the well-constructed falsehood that contains a confusing grain of truth. We must expose the true identity of the whole animal-rights movement. I believe that they are allied with demonic forces, subservient to them, and are bent on accomplishing their aims.

The legacy left by Cleveland Amory is tragic enough, and we will be forced to fight it from now on. The unfortunate part is that precious conservation money will necessarily be diverted to wage a battle that should never have occurred, and that in itself is a disastrous defeat for animal stewardship.

But the most sorrowful wake left by Amory is not the animal-rights legacy, because his movement would almost certainly have been the brainchild of someone else had he not been involved. The part of his demise I mourn is that a man of such genius never had the chance to sit in a duck blind and watch the rebirth of another day, his mind and heart filled with the burning hope of success that hunters throughout history have known so well. He never felt the tingle of his spine on seeing a magnificent buck chasing a doe, his throat dry and his palms sweating, his heart pumping in anticipation like that of a great cat about to pounce. He likely knew little about remote sheep country with its stunning vistas and abundant opportunities to observe natural processes and wonderful creatures. The electrifying predawn gobble of a tom turkey from a hardwood swamp in spring, and the excitement and expectancy inherent in the first yelp on a box call, were likely not a part of his life. He never was privileged, as hunters often are, to step out of the observer role and participate directly in the natural world as a functioning part of God's intricate web of life.

Mr. Amory lived a life of accomplishment that overflowed with talent and abilities. Unfortunately, he abdicated his genetically and anthropologically determined role as a predator, and as a consequence he never felt the thrill of the chase, a sensation that means almost everything to the hunter. Instead he set himself at odds with my essential nature, and managed to create an enmity that cannot be resolved short of my own demise. Millions of us find this to be our unavoidable relationship to today's radical animal-rights movement.

Pray, my fellow hunter, to the Creator God of this universe. I do not believe that many animal rightists know Him as I do, although I must leave open the possibility that there could be some deceived ones who share my faith. In general, the animal-rights team has abundant money, influential and prominent personalities, authoritative people in government, a gullible public, and the pervasive power of the press working for them. Prayer to the one true God may be the only effective weapon the animal-rights camp generally lacks, but it is infinitely powerful. The fate of the world is hanging in the balance, and all of us, including the animals, will be the losers when the sinister forces of the animal-rights movement prevail. We must decide emphatically to do our part to keep that from happening on our watch.

THE ETHICAL HUNTER

My advice then to the young is:
Learn the art of hunting if you desire to grow up to be good men,
good in everything which is perfect in thought, word, and deed.
The first efforts of a youth emerging from boyhood should be directed to the chase.
If you can succeed in that, all else will seem easy to you.

—Xenophon, *The Art of Hunting*, 544 B.C.

My how things have changed since 544 B.C. For every generation since man came into being, until the past few decades, this statement by the ancient soldier and historian was true beyond question. All of us are aware of the societal changes that have isolated most people from the source of their raw materials, a separation so complete that the connection between remote and dangerous locations and the production of automobile fuel, electricity, and bricks for building never occurs to many of them. All these products come from the consumption of nonrenewable natural resources, and all require mining of some type. But ask the average person on a big city street what his opinions are on mining, and you're liable to get some fairly negative responses.

Hunting is one of those ancient and vital connections that takes us back to our roots and remains a passion for at least 10 percent of the population. For those who are nurtured in the chase and learn to love it, nothing can replace it. Those of us who must hunt to experience fulfillment should think long and hard about the world we live in, and never take for granted the right to hunt. Legal hunting can be taken from us with the stroke of a pen or the tally of the ballot box. Likely many people would resort to illegal hunting if that ever occurred, because the inborn attraction of the activity cannot be turned on and off. Without hunter dollars to turn the wheels of conservation enforcement, penalties for poaching are likely to be minimal, and the chance of being caught would probably be minuscule, at least early on. With the game warden no longer employed and the state game departments underfunded and impotent, our wild animal populations could dangerously plummet in the absence of seasons, bag limits, interested conservationist hunters, and the like.

Because of man's sinful nature and his inherent imperfection, that scenario is very likely to develop if legal hunting ever is banned. I do not say this proudly or defiantly but with a measure of grief. Many hunters won't stop hunting just because it is illegal. Hunters in general want to obey legitimate rules and regulations, but a significant percentage would simply continue to hunt, without blaze orange vests and wearing full camouflage. People who just want meat would perfect snaring techniques to take animals silently, something that is frightfully easy to do. As for me, if this activity I love is indeed someday outlawed, I will submit to the authorities and desist. But the number who would not, and perhaps even could not, might surprise us all.

It is during such a time that I fear for much more than the loss of our wildlife. Such a tyranny by the majority could lead to brutal oppression, and I imagine that hunters who continue to hunt after such a ban would eventually be shot on sight for poaching. Enforcement probably wouldn't take on such a drastic face until game populations were decimated, but an alarmed and heavily antihunting public might demand extreme measures by government agencies to save what wildlife remains. In Africa today, illegal takers of wildlife have sometimes been shot, even when no alternatives were available for the poor poachers to feed their families. I believe this brutal policy remains in effect in some areas. We may not be that many years from a similar shoot-to-kill order in our own part of the world, if the animal-rights people get their way.

How does all this relate to hunting ethics? It has a great deal to do with it, because only a supportive public can save hunting, and only ethical hunters can garner that support. A recent survey of thousands of people, conducted by the U.S. Fish and Wildlife Service, revealed interesting statistics. Fully 81 percent of the population were at least moderately supportive of hunting. However, 62 percent of those surveyed believe hunters routinely break hunting laws, become intoxicated while hunting, use firearms in a reckless fashion, and otherwise pursue their activity in an unethical manner. It is self-evident that hunters are not perceived by the public the same way we perceive ourselves, as stalwart guardians of wildlife and rugged adventurers whose activities are inherently healthful and good. This public perception of the hunting community must change for the better if we are to have a reasonable chance of keeping a legal sport hunt. As Dr. James Swan, author of the brilliant book *In Defense of Hunting,* has said, "Hunting isn't the problem; hunters are."

Before we get into the reasons for this difference of perception, let us address some aspects of the ethics of society in general. My framework for ethical behavior is based on the teachings of the Holy Bible, so I need not call on some vague, nonspecific set of natural principles. Some things are right according to the Bible and some things are wrong, and I need look no further. Some truths therein must be concluded from broader principles, but the deductions are usually not hard to understand or apply. For example, when Jesus fed fish to 5,000 men and later provided it to another 4,000, was he endorsing eating fish? I believe that he unequivocally was, even though he never emphatically states, "Thus you are commanded to eat fish." Neither is one commanded to abstain from fish. Eating fish is endorsed for those who choose to do so, but to choose to eat something else is fine as well. That affirmation is put in exactly those terms by the apostle Paul in First Corinthians 8:8, where he states that whether we eat meat or not, neither the eating nor the abstinence from eating of itself commends us to God. By extension, hunting appears to be a neutral activity in the eyes of God, and the spirit, circumstances, and methods by which it is carried out must conform only to established ethical standards and the laws of the ruling authorities.

The problem today is that for many people ethics are relative, and that view has carried over into many areas of life, including the morality of the average hunter. This relativism is something I cannot abide, because to me it appears clear that man desperately needs an absolute standard of right and wrong. For me it isn't hard to find.

The teachings of the Bible are the basis for all government, law, and justice in Western society, but somewhere along the way we have lost our direction. Relativism is the ruling paradigm, and along with it comes such concepts as survival of the fittest, doing what comes naturally, looking out for oneself above all, and feeling good about oneself. If these concepts are in agreement with the Bible, that's fine. If they are at odds with the Bible, the relativistic principles are usually considered authoritative, and those of the Bible old-fashioned. When Jefferson, Adams, Franklin, and the other Founding Fathers of the United States were constructing our system of government, reference to the teachings of the Bible was common and always commanded great respect. No longer can one assume that appeal to biblical principles will carry the argument. Too many people are skeptical or outright reject those precepts.

One more factor must be thrown in at this point. The general acceptance of the doctrine of evolution has blurred the distinction between man and animals to the extent that many consider animals and man equivalent. That doesn't apply only to the animal-rights camp, though they are the only ones who take the implications to the extreme. I reject that argument entirely. Man is the only creature with an eternal soul. Man is the only physical being created to fellowship directly with the Creator God, and I believe the only one capable of doing so.

Even most people who fervently believe in the doctrine of evolution recognize some kind of separation in responsibility and worth between man and nonhuman creatures. In fact, few evolutionary thinkers are bold enough or sufficiently confident in their naturalistic faith to claim that there is no God. Many are agnostic, many are religious but attempt to mesh their faith with evolutionary theory, but precious few are avowedly atheistic. But even the most atheistic advocate of evolutionary teaching almost invariably recognizes that the only moral agent in the physical world capable of making ethical decisions is the human being. Thus, by common definition, humanity has the moral responsibility to adhere to some code of behavior. The natural outgrowth is that practically all educated people believe that only man can be held responsible for his actions, and that animals are exempt from such accountability. Without accountability there can be no responsibility. Animals are not capable of being moral agents and thus cannot be placed on the same plane as human beings, either in rights or in responsibility. The animal-rights camp is the only place such an obvious distinction is rejected outright.

Another abstraction that causes confusion is that of worth. Jesus said that a man is worth "many sparrows." In one instance he readily sacrificed 2,000 swine to deliver a couple of demon-possessed men to good health and sanity. The evolutionary system does not make such a distinction, but recognizes a difference in the value of "cognizance" or "sentience." In that case as well, there can be no doubt about the relatively high value of human beings over animals.

Of all those who provoke me when they question my right to hunt, the most vexing are those who say that they are Christians and yet are critical of hunting because hunters violate the biblical commandment "Thou shalt not kill." While this may simply be a matter of conscience for them, it often appears to be ignorance of the meaning of that command. Somehow I always get the feeling that such a criticism indicates a lack of commitment to learn what their faith is all about. That commandment is better rendered "Never kill another human being for the sake of personal revenge." That means that the killing of other people in warfare, killing of intractable human criminals by the state, and killing of attackers in self-defense are acceptable in the sight of God. "Thou shalt not kill" has nothing whatsoever to do with taking the lives of animals, an activity repeatedly and graphically portrayed in the Bible as good and necessary when accomplished according to ethical principles.

The essence of the Christian faith is about death, the victory of Jesus Christ over it, and the ultimate triumph of the believer because of it. We all die physically. All animals die. Respectfully taking the life of a mammal or a fish or a bird is God's plan and God's way. Animals have always had to die that man may live, and that principle is still operative today.

In most parts of the world, a vegetarian lifestyle is simply unattainable. Books, videos, and television programs on vegetarian cooking are not available to detail how one gets the right mix of amino acids, vitamin B12, and other nutrients. People in many places would rapidly succumb to malnutrition if their meat supply, however meager, were interrupted. God originally planned for man to be a vegetarian, and gave him "all plants with fruit having seeds" as food. Anyone eating the flesh of animals in the pre-Flood world was in direct violation of God's command. After the Great Flood of Noah, however, one of the first things God told Noah was that he could now eat meat. The world had changed drastically; many nutrients are only sparingly available in the plants that survived the flood, and a few, such as vitamin B12, are not available at all without consuming meat. It was pragmatic for God to suddenly and emphatically say that eating meat was now allowed.

I am not saying that an appreciable number of vegetarians are out to kill off the uneducated and less fortunate of the world. Very few of the most belligerent might fit that description, but not many. Just don't point fingers at me because I reject that lifestyle, and don't demonize me for my choice of meat; nor those who are unable to construct a purely vegetarian diet to sustain them. While vegetarianism is a possible lifestyle, it is nonetheless most difficult, highly inconvenient, and of no more than marginal value—and may even be harmful—to the health of the individual, even in a very modern, materially abundant society. I say this not as an uneducated layman but as a physician, and as one who has followed a daughter through a major university program in which she earned a degree in foods and nutrition.

The point of this discussion is not to create a comprehensive treatise but to establish the fact that man is responsible for his behavior when it comes to animal stewardship. Animals that prey on other animals or eat the farmer's crops or invade our houses as pests are not exercising a moral choice. They are doing what comes naturally. Only man, in taking the life of an animal, is capable of making an ethical judgment as to whether the action is right or wrong. Only man is able to make decisions about killing or not killing an animal, choosing which one to kill, and how he behaves with the carcass. Only man can decide the manner in which he deals with his emotions after the fact. It is a responsibility all human beings, especially those of us who hunt, must take seriously. It is an area in which many of us still fall far short, and in so doing we leave open a huge wound to be exploited by our enemies. If we can't act responsibly in every area of our hunting life, we don't deserve to be called hunters. We don't merit the privilege of hunting, and it is up to hunters to expel from our ranks those who fail to do their best to live up to the established and accepted standards. Some standards are already in place, and I'd like to touch on a few of them.

Several recent incidents stand out as examples of unethical conduct on the part of hunters. Driving down the interstate highway on the way to Atlanta in the fall, it is not uncommon to see deer hunters motoring along in their rigs. Often they are pulling a trailer on which an ATV rides conspicuously, and their attire, their camouflage caps, and the muddy condition of their gear make it obvious where they have been. Of course there's nothing wrong so far. The problem arises when the hunter has been successful. I remember a truck carrying a dead doe a few years ago, and the animal was positioned obnoxiously on the top of the tool box. It was high above the truck bed, so that no passing motorist could miss it. It had not even been field dressed, the belly was beginning to bloat, and the creature's tongue flapped grotesquely in the slipstream. The sight almost gave me antihunting feelings, and I literally cringed as I passed the vehicle.

In two other incidents just this year, I witnessed successful hunters who had taken bucks (rather mediocre ones at that) and had positioned the dead animals in the back of the truck with the heads propped up so the antlers would be visible to everyone on the highway. It was a gesture of pride, a way of saying, "Look what I did." A good buck is something to show your hunting buddies, and might be a trophy worth putting on your wall. But it is crass, absolutely disrespectful to the animal, and deeply harmful to hunting to show it off to the public at large. To display the animal like that demonstrates not good hunting skill but how rare it must be for them to experience success.

How many antihunters did those guys create? Could any possible good come from letting the driving public know that they had been successful? Hardly. I felt like taking a shot at them myself, so anyone neutral in the matter of hunting, or of an animal-rights bent, must have been absolutely livid. Could it be that such a person went home and joined the Fund for Animals or the Humane Society of the United States? Perhaps they hadn't previously cared if these men enjoyed their hunting, but after being subjected to such abuse of their sensibilities I frankly wouldn't really blame them for being just a little bit more antihunting in outlook.

Too many hunters are utterly atrocious in their application of ethical standards to hunting. I've seen people do things in the field that they likely would never consider doing on the job, in dealing with a neighbor, or in functioning as a member of society generally. An alarming number of hunters in my area have no hesitancy or feelings of guilt about killing forty or fifty mourning doves on a single outing, even though the legal limit is twelve. This is one of the most common transgressions in my own part of the country, and it is such an accepted crime in certain circles that they make no effort to cover up the deed and no shame attaches to it. I have heard many brag openly about how many birds they felled on opening day, often three or four times the legal limit. Ingenious methods of hiding the excess are often used to foil the game warden, should he show up. Occasionally people are caught and fined, but the deed is so common and customary that no amount of law enforcement can stamp it out.

It is not that the excess birds are wasted, which they most often aren't, but simply the matter that such wickedness is against the law. What is it that won't let such people just pick up their allotted twelve birds, unload their shotgun, and come back another day? If everybody did that there would be plenty of birds left for another dove shoot the next day or the next week. Until the community of hunters openly condemns such illegal ways, the problem will remain.

All of us must remember that hunting's future is on the line. These people are not simply building a portfolio of unprincipled transgressions for which they will have to answer to God someday. They are placing our beloved avocation at risk of being outlawed by public sentiment, through no fault of the ethical hunter.

One final incident from just yesterday comes to mind. An elderly patient I have seen many times was sitting in my examination room, and he asked about my recent hunting experiences. After my reply, he related that he had killed two wild turkeys some time back, using his .22 rifle on a flock he encountered near his home. He had no hesitation in relating this to me, and indicated that he killed them during a recent summer. Not only is the weapon he used illegal, but he took the animals out of season. He expected no reprimand from me, of course, and talked as if there were nothing unusual about the act.

Such people would never think of using a weapon to rob a bank or hold up a gas station. They would never sneak into their neighbor's garage and steal his tools. How they can steal wild game from the public, put our hunting rights at risk, take a chance on being caught in a criminal act, and yet seemingly have no remorse is beyond me. Perhaps it grows out of the leftover legacy of the distant past, when game laws were nonexistent or poorly enforced and wild creatures were simply there for the taking. Perhaps it is simple ignorance of the implications of such theft and greed. But as a hunting community, we must resolve to call it what it is and forcefully insist on stopping it. Nobody else can, in truth, except the ethical hunting fraternity. The city public isn't in the woods as we are and wouldn't know to whom to report. But we know who they are, what they've done, and how to catch them. It is a travesty if we choose not to act.

There is another matter of utmost interest to me as a trophy hunter, and I call it by a name I have heard bantered about several places. This is the infamous and despicable "record-book syndrome." I have heard of people who want to kill only record-book animals, and sometimes they want to hunt only those animals that will be tops in their category. One person I've met reputedly maintains a standing offer of $50,000 for any wild sheep that will score over minimums for the Boone and Crockett record book. If he can afford it, there's technically nothing illegal about making such an offer, but it sets an unhealthy precedent, to say the least.

Much worse are individuals so intent on getting a record-book animal that anything less they consider contemptible. They will sometimes even shoot several of a species if the first ones fall short of their expectations. The fact that they usually pay well for the extra chances isn't the point. Any trophy hard-earned is precious and valuable, but one simply bought is by definition cheapened for all of us, and so is hunting in general. Myriad animals that fall short of the record book may be wonderful specimens, far beyond the wildest dreams of many sportsmen. These super hunters simply relegate them to the status of garbage. In my book that is a disgrace.

There are some truly great hunters who will hunt forever to get the biggest and the best, and it isn't them I criticize. Many ethical hunters are more than willing to go home empty-handed if they can't get an animal that meets certain standards, and that's trophy hunting at its best. The problem is those who push legality to the very edge of criminality, and beyond if necessary, to achieve at all costs. Getting one's name in the book with the number one specimen can become so important that conservation doesn't matter, the health of the animal population being hunted doesn't matter, and anything goes in their self-centered quest. They are robbing me and you of respectability when they do this. Somehow the record books should be restructured to reflect more accurately good sportsmanship and fair chase. There also should be awards for the biggest animal passed up, the fewest animals taken per number of days hunted, the oldest specimens taken regardless of record- book score, and the like. With a bit of brainstorming, we could ethicize the record books as never before. Bigger isn't better; it's only bigger. That statement should be printed in the front of every record book in letters several inches high.

I have no problem with recognizing high achievement in hunting, but somehow we are going to have to insist that recognition be given only to fair-chase hunts, in which the hunter does something extra to add to the conservation value of the quest, and where the benefits to such conservation receive more acclaim than the score or number of the trophies taken. We can cure record-book syndrome by changing some of our own rules. We can't control the public and the laws that are passed, but we can certainly control our own record books with an iron hand. Where good conservation isn't served by the structure of awards and listings, it should be summarily changed for the better. Whether the various record-keeping organizations have the will to do so over the objections of a few vocal members is another question.

Let me make it clear that I don't believe there is anything inherently wrong with hunting behind a fence. I was recently in Mexico where a friend has a 25,000-acre enclosure in which he has red sheep, blackbuck, ibex, and other exotics. Taking one of those animals is going to require the same effort it takes to harvest any high-mountain game. This will indeed be real hunting, even though protection of the surrounding countryside from invasion by nonnative animals requires that he construct and maintain a fence. It is not this type of fenced hunting that is objectionable. But there are times when the animal and the hunting setup deserve just condemnation.

We should unequivocally condemn and boycott so-called hunters who "hunt" in small enclosures and take animals that are essentially tame. To do less is a disservice to helpless animals, and moreover it places our beloved avocation in danger of extinction so a few can gratify their lust for unusual trophies and for recognition, however unmerited. These may be hard words to some, but I have a feeling that most hunters will agree wholeheartedly. I hope so, and I fully expect that soon such practices will be universally condemned by the hunting fraternity.

I have named a number of situations and circumstances I find repugnant, but what I've covered has been by no means exhaustive. It bothers me greatly, for example, for hunters to stand out so vividly in any airport. Why must we wear camouflage hats and coats when we travel?

Can't we look a little more like Joe Citizen? At the very least we traveling hunters should try to look more ordinary, and then surprise the person in the seat next to us when we tell him we're going hunting. It will often open doors to a productive discussion if our neighbor hasn't already placed us in some pigeonhole that has cemented his mind shut.

Fellow hunters, take pride in your personal appearance, and let's stop getting called names. Be proud of who you are and where you're going. You don't have to look like Arnold Schwarzenegger, but for goodness sakes try to lose some extra weight if at all possible. Your outfitter and his horses will appreciate the effort, too.

Crass language is another problem that could use some attention. I have no hesitation in recommending that hunters never, ever use bad language in public. Maybe salespeople or doctors or lawyers can get away with it, but we can't. If you're going hunting, put on your very best behavior. We've got to portray a wholesome image. I've seen hunters clustered in airports, decked out in camouflage, making little old ladies blush because of their loud jokes, foul language, and boisterous laughter. Sometimes it's so bad I want to hide my head in shame and claim I'm going on a business trip. It's great to have a good time, but don't forget that our hunting privileges are on trial every time you're identified as a hunter amid the traveling public.

For goodness sakes, don't drink excessively while you're traveling. It's fine with me if you have a good slug of something to drink, alcoholic or otherwise, after a day's hunting, but don't get drunk, and don't drink much before you're in camp. It goes without saying that alcohol and loaded guns don't mix, so leave off the alcohol until after the day's hunt is over. Remember, you're sending a message to those who will decide the fate of hunting every time you're in public.

If we keep that in mind, we'll be on our best behavior. Maybe we can even manage to pass on good habits that our children and grandchildren will want to emulate. And just maybe we can preserve this great sport we all love, so they will be able to enjoy it, too.

FINAL THOUGHTS

I want to see every man among you . . .
a religious man, having the fear of God before his eyes
and the love of God glowing in his heart.

—Sir William Edward Parry, British admiral and Arctic explorer, spoken
in 1857 and quoted in Pierre Berton's *The Arctic Grail*

It was 5 October 1975 when I harvested my first trophy animal with my Remington 700 .30-06, a pronghorn antelope I took in Wyoming. The final animal of the forty-one was the Carmen Mountains white-tailed deer, taken twenty-three years, two months, and two days later, on 7 December 1998. In the interim there were fifty-six guided North American hunts for big game, and those took place in ten states of the United States, six Canadian provinces and territories, and four states of Mexico. The success rate, if one defines that as a hunt on which I took a trophy specimen, was a shade under 70 percent. Seventeen hunts resulted in no trophy, and four others yielded a "consolation prize," when I took an animal that was not my primary quarry.

It requires several ingredients for those wishing to complete such an undertaking. First, they must want to do it. Next, they must have the finances to do it, and those are considerable. Lastly, they must have the physical ability to do it, including good health and a body that can be buffeted into shape. It helps to have a spouse who is supportive. It also helps to have a steady shooting hand, or at least passably so. All these components are unavailable on the basis of human effort, but rather they are gifts from God. I give Him all the credit for the success of the project and for the means He granted me to attain it.

Just a short time before this writing, my medical partner of twenty-one years, Dr. Roger Smith, told me that he was going to retire in about six months. I brought Roger into my practice two years after I started in 1976, and he has wisely invested his money, developed a dynamic portfolio of stocks, lived well but with thrifty habits, and built a healthy retirement account. He can afford to retire, and he deserves to.

For me it's going to be several years, at least, before I can begin to contemplate a similar move. I've made different choices about how I spent my money, and I've used up a considerable amount on hunting, taxidermy, and travel. The biggest single expense, however, has been time away from my practice. While I was out hunting, Roger was back home working.

Since I started the systematic quest to take all the animals in this book, I've known that I'd have to hunt certain animals while I was still young enough to do so. There are a lot of mountains that seem to grow taller as we become older. The slopes get steeper, too, and the old legs just won't do what they once could.

I don't reflect upon any of these choices, nor the experiences that grew out of them, with regret. Each was special and added to a timeless set of memories that cannot be taken from me. Some of my hunts could have been made better by a more favorable set of circumstances, but most of the time that was beyond human control. To sit and listen to the chorus of nature, to walk and climb in its vastness, to be unencumbered by the cares of civilization, even when it's raining or snowing, is truly a privilege. That is not to say it is impossible for the nonhunter, or even the antihunter, to find the same solace in the wilderness. Most don't make the effort, though, and when they do they seldom venture far from the parking pullout on the scenic highway. Generally, only the hunter becomes enmeshed within the great web of life, uninsulated from its brutal cutting edge by distance or philosophy or by glass, concrete, and bricks. The hunter returns to his roots and participates in the natural processes of life and death that are irrevocably woven into the fabric of existence. Truly we hunters are a favored few.

It is hard for me to imagine a hunter who doesn't believe there is a mighty and majestic Creator whose artful handiwork is this universe and all it contains. I was sitting on a deer stand just a couple of days ago pondering these thoughts as the sun sank into a labyrinth of interlacing pink clouds, leaving a reddish glow emanating from the spot where the fiery ball finally disappeared. A doe and fawn were feeding in the meadow in front of me, and the full moon was rising ghostlike in the east. A flock of four pintails wheeled up from a slough behind me, riding whistling wings to a night of rest on some hidden body of water. To me these are intricate evidences of a God who is real.

It is my hope that virtually every chapter of this book contains some element of the spiritual. It would not be worth writing if it recorded only the pitiful musings of a single hunter and did not contain anything of the eternal. My fervent effort has been to include the aspects of life that truly matter, and in the final analysis nothing except our relationship with that very genuine Creator will be of importance. Everything else falls far short and is ultimately lost in the ocean of time. Even the greatest hunter is soon forgotten. Percy Bysshe Shelley wrote almost two hundred years ago of a decaying desert statue, half buried by shifting sands and surrounded by miles of trackless wastes, on which was engraved in fading letters: "My name is Ozymandias, King of Kings; Look on my works, ye Mighty, and despair."

My life has traversed several phases, from innocent childhood and youth to backsliding and worldly adulthood, then back to total dependence on the God of my teenage years. Only by God's grace have I overcome some of my more base tendencies, and only through my relationship with Him through his Son, Jesus Christ, has my life become truly worth living. Without end I observe a parade of people who are trying, through money, influence, power, or some other godless avenue, to find fulfillment. Now I know that were all my trophies number one in their class and all my hunts successes, that alone could not bring the true happiness that is so elusive for so many.

My friends, even if you find a measure of fulfillment in worldly pursuits, it won't last, and most certainly when you're gone your dreams will perish with you unless you've made peace with the eternal and omnipotent God. He has provided the way, and only one way, for you to have that peace. Ask Jesus Christ into your life today, and he will forgive your trespasses and imperfections, give you eternal life, and put you on the road to true fulfillment. He promises to give you the freedom and peace that only he can grant. He wants to do it, so I urge you to look into the claims of Jesus Christ, the God-man whose voluntary sacrificial death is the only adequate payment for man's sins. He paid a debt he didn't owe because we owed a debt we couldn't pay. Take advantage of the offer, because it's the best one you'll ever get. I guarantee it.

If even one person does as I suggest, my quest will take on eternal value. The sacrifices made, the money spent, the mountains climbed, the long trails traveled, the disappointments endured, the baths and meals skipped, and the long final stalks will all have been worth it.

And if you are that person, we'll talk about it forever.

INDEX